W9-AGG-803

Language A

Content and
Teaching Strateg

Family of Faith Library

Third Edition

Language A

Content and
Teaching Strategies

GAIL E. TOMPKINS
California State University, Fresno

KENNETH HOSKISSON
*Virginia Polytechnic Institute and
State University*

Merrill, an imprint of Prentice Hall
Englewood Cliffs, New Jersey / Columbus, Ohio

Library of Congress Cataloging-in-Publication Data

Tompkins, Gail E.
   Language arts : content and teaching strategies / Gail E.
Tompkins, Kenneth Hoskisson.—3rd ed.
      p.   cm.
   Includes bibliographical references and indexes.
   ISBN 0-02-420852-3
   1. Language arts (Elementary)   I. Hoskisson, Kenneth.   II. Title.
   LB1576T655 1995
   372.6—dc20

LCC#

LCCN
94-15178
CIP

Cover art: Susan Sturgill
Editor: Linda James Scharp
Developmental Editor: Carol Sykes
Production Editor: Jonathan Lawrence
Text Designer: Anne Flanagan
Cover Designer: Anne Flanagan
Production Buyer: Pamela D. Bennett
Chapter opening illustrations: Susan Sturgill
Text illustrations: Carlisle Communications, Ltd.

This book was set in Korinna by Carlisle Communications, Ltd., and was printed and bound by Von Hoffman Press, Inc. The cover was printed by Von Hoffmann Press, Inc.

© 1995 by Prentice-Hall, Inc.
A Simon & Schuster Company
Englewood Cliffs, New Jersey 07632

All rights reserved. No part of this book may be reproduced, in any form or by any means, without permission in writing from the publisher.

Earlier editions © 1991 by Macmillan Publishing Company, 1987 by Merrill Publishing Company.

Photo credits: pp. 11, 262, and 317 by Timothy J. Bernard; p. 294 by Anne Vega/Macmillan; all other photos by Gail Tompkins.

Printed in the United States of America

10 9 8 7 6 5 4 3 2

ISBN: 0-02-420852-3

Prentice-Hall International (UK) Limited, *London*
Prentice-Hall of Australia Pty. Limited, *Sydney*
Prentice-Hall Canada Inc., *Toronto*
Prentice-Hall Hispanoamericana, S. A., *Mexico*
Prentice-Hall of India Private Limited, *New Delhi*
Prentice-Hall of Japan, Inc., *Tokyo*
Simon & Schuster Asia Pte. Ltd., *Singapore*
Editora Prentice-Hall do Brasil, Ltda., *Rio de Janeiro*

To our editor, Linda James Scharp,

You're one in a million!

—G.E.T.

To my wife, Virginia, and my children,

Heather, Mark, and Tamora.

—K.H.

About the Authors

Gail E. Tompkins is a Professor at California State University, Fresno, in the Department of Literacy and Early Education, where she teaches courses in language arts, reading, and writing for preservice and inservice teachers. She co-directs the San Joaquin Valley Writing Project and works regularly with teachers, both by teaching model lessons in classrooms and by leading inservice workshops. Previously, Dr. Tompkins taught at Miami University in Ohio and at the University of Oklahoma, where she received the prestigious Regent's Award for Superior Teaching. She was also an elementary teacher in Virginia for eight years.

Dr. Tompkins is also the author of *Teaching Writing: Balancing Process and Product* (2nd ed.) (Merrill/Macmillan, 1994) and co-author, with Lea McGee, of *Teaching Reading with Literature* (Merrill/Macmillan, 1993). She has written numerous articles related to language arts that have appeared in *Language Arts, The Reading Teacher, Journal of Reading,* and other professional journals.

Dr. Kenneth Hoskisson teachers courses in reading and language arts at Virginia Tech in Blacksburg, Virginia. He has published in the *Elementary School Journal, Language Arts,* and *The Reading Teacher.* Dr. Hoskisson is well known for his conceptualization and development of assisted reading. He earned a Ph.D. in curriculum and instruction with emphasis in reading and language arts at the University of California, Berkeley. His major interests are writing and helping teachers examine the relationships between theory and practice. Dr. Hoskisson was a teacher and administrator with the Department of Defense schools in Europe for 10 years.

Preface

The third edition of *Language Arts: Content and Teaching Strategies* is a significant revision of this popular core text designed for elementary and middle-school language arts methods courses and language and literacy methods "block" courses. These revisions reflect the changes that are occurring in how language arts is taught in elementary and middle schools, most notably in the areas of emergent literacy, multicultural learning, the reader response perspective, and authentic assessment.

Both preservice and inservice teachers find this text valuable enough to keep for their professional libraries. For preservice teachers who will work with students in kindergarten through eighth grades, the text provides a consistent model of instruction that helps beginning teachers control the number of instructional decisions they have to make. For inservice teachers, the text provides a rich array of strategies and ideas that experienced teachers can adapt to suit their personal instructional style.

The philosophy of the text reflects an integrated, constructivist approach to teaching throughout. In turn, the teaching strategies are based on cognitive, psycholinguistic, and sociolinguistic theories about how children learn—how they learn language, in particular. Then, the strategies are applied through minilessons in each language mode: listening, talking, reading, and writing.

The goal of the text is to present the content of the language arts curriculum and effective strategies for teaching this content so that teachers can help students develop **communicative competence.** Demonstrating this competence requires students to develop these complementary abilities:

The ability to transmit meaning through talk and writing.

The ability to interpret meaning through listening and reading.

Not only is communicative competence developed through a discussion and understanding of language processes, it is nurtured through genuine communication activities. These activities include conducting oral interviews of community residents; participating in debates on topics of relevance to students; writing stories and sharing these stories with genuine audiences; keeping learning logs in science classes; and writing letters to state or national political figures in conjunction with social studies themes.

Helping students learn to communicate effectively using listening, talking, reading, and writing is a great challenge facing teachers today. It is the intent of the third edition to be a useful resource to teachers as they accept and meet this challenge.

New to the Third Edition

- New chapter: **Emergent Literacy** (Chapter 7). This chapter explores how children learn to read and write and how teachers can build on what emerging readers already know about environmental print.
- New chapter: **Expecting Diversity: The Multicultural Classroom** (Chapter 13). This chapter examines the needs of culturally and linguistically diverse learners and some ways to create multicultural classroom environments that meet those needs and prepare all students to interact effectively in an increasingly multicultural American society.
- New **study cards** for each chapter. These perforated study cards are located in the back of the book. The cards can be removed for reference and inserted in the appropriate chapter or in a notebook. The chapter outline appears on the front of the card. On the back is a list of key terms and concepts as well as a review of teaching strategies presented in that chapter.
- More about **reading and writing connections.** This edition presents the reading process, reader response, and reading and writing workshops in the six full chapters on reading and writing stories, informational text, and poetry.
- An increased emphasis on **authentic assessment** and **adapting instruction.** Information on how to adapt and assess each component of the language arts curriculum to meet the needs of all students is presented in each chapter.

Special Features

- Each chapter begins with an **Insight,** a question to direct readers' thinking as they begin to read. These questions are also designed for initiating discussion in cooperative groups.
- Lists of topics for **Minilessons** related to the content of the chapter are provided.
- **Teacher's Notebook** pages contain practical information and tips.
- **Adapting to Meet the Needs of Every Student** boxes list ways to modify instruction so that every student, including second-language learners and students with learning disabilities, can achieve success.
- **PRO-Files** displayed in a file folder design precede each chapter. This feature provides an opportunity to recognize 13 of the many outstanding teachers with whom the authors have had the privilege to work.
- **Key terms** are italicized and defined in the text.
- Lists of **trade books** and steps in **teaching strategies** are highlighted in figures.
- Chapter **summaries** follow each chapter.
- **Extension activities** help readers apply information, and many invite them to observe and interact with students in elementary and middle-school classrooms. Others ask them to prepare instructional materials, consult outside readings, or examine how they use language themselves.

Acknowledgments

Many people helped and encouraged us during the development of this text and during the revisions. Our heartfelt thanks goes to each of them. First, we thank our students at California State University, Fresno, the University of Oklahoma, and Virginia Tech, who taught us as we taught them. Their insightful questions challenged and broadened our thinking, and their willingness to experiment with the teaching strategies that we were developing furthered our own learning.

We want to express our appreciation to the teachers who invited us into their classrooms and shared their expertise with us. In particular we want to thank the teachers we have profiled: Pat Bishop, Heaton Elementary School, Fresno, CA; Marie Whiteside, Norseman Elementary School, Fresno, CA; Pat Daniel, South Rock Creek School, Norman, OK; Glenna Jarvis, Western Hills School, Lawton, OK; Judy Reeves, Western Hills School, Lawton, OK; Mary Yamazaki, Truckee Elementary School, Truckee, CA; Carol Ochs, Jackson Elementary School, Norman, OK; Kathy Brown, Jackson Elementary School, Selma, CA; Albena Reinig, Thomas Oleatas Elementary School, Atwater, CA; Sandy Harris, Anadarko Middle School, Anadarko, OK; Gordon Martindale, Columbia Elementary School, Fresno, CA; Paula Schiefer, Washington School, Selma, CA; and Loretta Toews, Bellevue Elementary School, Atwater, CA.

Thanks, too, to the children whose writing samples and photographs appear in the book and to the teachers and administrators who welcomed us into their schools to take photographs and collect writing samples: Max Ballard, Nicoma Park Intermediate School, Nicoma Park, OK; Helen Bauer, Hester Elementary School, Farmersville, CA; Anita Beard, Norman, OK; Marc Bell, Monroe Elementary School, Norman, OK; Kathy Bending, Highland Elementary School, Downers Grove, IL; Linda Bessett, Sulphur Elementary School, Sulphur, OK; Gracie Branch, Eisenhower Elementary School, Norman, OK; Juli Carson, Jefferson Elementary School, Norman, OK; Shirley Carson, Wayne Elementary School, Wayne, OK; Chris Edge-Christensen, Whittier Elementary School, Lawton, OK; Patty Cejda, Hubbard Elementary School, Noble, OK; Kimberly Clark, Aynesworth Elementary School, Fresno, CA; Pam Cottom, James Griffith Intermediate School, Choctaw, OK; Jean Davis, James Griffith Intermediate School, Choctaw, OK; Deanie Dillen, Putnam City Schools, Oklahoma City, OK; Whitney Donnelly, Williams Ranch School, Penn Valley, CA; Polly Dwyer, University of Oklahoma, Norman, OK; Susan Fields, Noble Junior High School, Noble, OK; Charlotte Fleetham, Pioneer Intermediate School, Noble, OK; Parthy Ford, Whittier Elementary School, Lawton, OK; Debbie Frankenberg, Purcell Elementary School, Purcell, OK; Chuckie Garner, Kennedy Elementary School, Norman, OK; Peggy Givens, Watonga Middle School, Watonga, OK; Teri Gray, James Griffith Intermediate School, Choctaw, OK; Garett Griebel, Chickasha, OK; Debbie Hamilton, Irving Middle School, Norman, OK; Lori Hardy, James Griffith Intermediate School, Choctaw, OK; Sandra Harris, Anadarko Middle School, Anadarko, OK; Paula Harrington, Southgate Elementary School, Moore, OK; Ernestine Hightower, Whittier Elementary School, Lawton, OK; Beth Hogh, Pioneer Intermediate School, Noble, OK; Linda Hopper, Wilson Elementary School, Norman, OK; Nancy Hutter, Tioga Elementary School, Bensenville, IL;

Annette Jacks, Blanchard Elementary School, Blanchard, OK; Suzie Jennings, Lindsay, OK; Alison Johns, Fremont Junior High School, Fowler, CA; Judy Kenney, Jackson Elementary School, Selma, CA; Janet Kretschmer, McGuffey Foundation School, Oxford, OH; Helen Lawson, Deer Creek School, Oklahoma City, OK; Glenda LoBaugh, Ranchwood Elementary School, Yukon, OK; Mark Mattingly, Central Junior High School, Lawton, OK; Carolyn Mays, Garfield Elementary School, Lawton, OK; Pam McCarthy, Hubbard Elementary School, Noble, OK; Tissie McClure, Nicoma Park Intermediate School, Nicoma Park, OK; John McCracken, Nevin Coppock School, Tipp City, OH; Gina McCook, Whittier Middle School, Norman, OK; Teresa Miller, Hester Elementary School, Farmersville, CA; Mary Oldham, University of Oklahoma, Norman, OK; Teresa Ossenkop, Eisenhower Elementary School, Norman, OK; Sandra Pabst, Monroe Elementary School, Norman, OK; Cindy Perez, John Adams Elementary School, Lawton, OK; JoAnne Pierce, Horace Mann Elementary School, Duncan, OK; Alice Rakitan, Highland Elementary School, Downers Grove, IL; Jelta Reneau and M'Lynn Emanuel, Lincoln Elementary School, Norman, OK; Jenny Reno, Kay Preston, Eunice Edison, Pat Blackburn, Linda Riley, Marilyn Williams, Pat Pittman, Western Hills Elementary School, Lawton, OK; Kim Schmidt, La Petite Academy, Oklahoma City, OK; Becky Selle, Bethel School, Shawnee, OK; Jo Ann Steffen, Nicoma Park Junior High School, Nicoma Park, OK; Gail Warmath, Longfellow Middle School, Norman, OK; Letty Watt, Jefferson Elementary School, Norman, OK; Jeanne Webb, Norman Christian Academy, Norman, OK; MaryBeth Webeler, Highland Elementary School, Downers Grove, IL; Linda White, University of Oklahoma, Norman, OK; Brenda Wilkins, Horace Mann Elementary School, Duncan, OK; Vera Willey, Lincoln Elementary School, Norman, OK; Jean Winters and Diane Lewis, Irving Middle School, Norman, OK; Susie Wood, Marlow, OK. And, thanks, too, to the parents who welcomed us into their homes to take photographs of their children and shared their children's writing with us: Regina Blair, Sherry Bynum, Carole and Bill Hamilton, Martha and Rob Lamm, John and Lois McCracken, Kendra Magness, and Susan Steele.

We also want to thank our colleagues who served as reviewers for this edition: Joan B. Elliot, Indiana University of Pennsylvania; Bonnie O. Ericson, California State University–Northridge; Katherine Schlick Noe, Seattle University; Barbara Perry-Sheldon, North Carolina Wesleyan College; Tonja Root, Valdosta State College; and Patrice Werner, Southwest Texas State University. We appreciate their thoughtful analyses and insights.

Finally, we express sincere appreciation to Jeff Johnston and our editors in Columbus, Ohio. We want to thank our editor, Linda James Scharp, who created the innovative design and special features for this edition and spurred us on toward impossible deadlines. We also thank Jonathan Lawrence, our steadfast production editor, who moved the book so expertly through the maze of production details. Thanks, too, go to Maggie Shaffer, our copyeditor, who wielded her blue pen so effectively to prepare the manuscript for typesetting.

Brief Contents

1   Learning and the Language Arts   1

2   Teaching Language Arts   35

3   Listening to Learn   81

4   Sustaining Talk in the Classroom   119

5   Writing in Journals   163

6   The Reading and Writing Processes   197

7   Emergent Literacy   241

8   Looking Closely at Words   281

9   Reading and Writing Stories   315

10   Reading and Writing Information   361

11   Reading and Writing Poetry   409

12   Language Tools: Spelling, Handwriting, and Grammar   459

13   Expecting Diversity: The Multicultural Classroom   513

14   Extending Language Arts Across the Curriculum   553

APPENDIX A   Award-Winning Books for Children   587
APPENDIX B   Resources About Authors and Illustrators   591
APPENDIX C   Joint Statement on Literacy Development and Pre-First Grade   597
APPENDIX D   Common Spelling Options for Phonemes   601

Contents

1 Learning and the Language Arts 1

How Children Learn 2

The Cognitive Structure 3
The Process of Learning 3
Social Contexts of Learning 4
Implications for Learning Language Arts 4

How Children Learn Language 7

The Four Language Systems 7
Stages of Language Development 9
Development in the Elementary Grades 12
Implications for Learning Language Arts 14

How Children Learn Language Arts 17

Communicative Competence 17
The Four Language Modes 17
A Paradigm for Language Arts Instruction 21
A Teaching Strategy 22
Assessing Students' Learning 25
Resources for Teachers 28

2 Teaching Language Arts 35

Language-Rich Classrooms 36

The Physical Arrangement 37
Textbooks 42
Trade Books 43
Computers 47

Instructional Approaches 50

Literature Focus Units 50
Theme Cycles 51
Reading-Writing Workshops 51
Adapting to Meet the Needs of Every Student 58

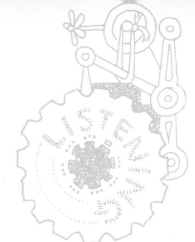

Assessing Students' Learning   61
  Monitoring Students' Progress   62
  Collecting Students' Work in Portfolios   64
  Assigning Grades   70

3 Listening to Learn   81

The Listening Process   82
  Steps in the Listening Process   83
  Purposes for Listening   84
  Teaching Listening Strategies   85
Listening to Literature   85
  Aesthetic Listening   86
  Teaching Aesthetic Listening   91
  Assessing Students' Aesthetic Listening   96
Listening Across the Curriculum   97
  Efferent Listening   97
  Teaching Efferent Listening   102
  Assessing Students' Efferent Listening   104
  Critical Listening   104
  Teaching Critical Listening   108
  Assessing Students' Critical Listening   112

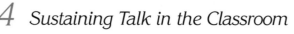

4 Sustaining Talk in the Classroom   119

Conversations   120
  Guidelines for Conducting Conversations   122
  Types of Conversations   123
  Teaching Students to Talk in Small Groups   123
  Teaching Minilessons on Talk   123
  Adapting to Meet the Needs of Every Student   124
  Assessing Students' Talk   124
Aesthetic Talk   127
  Conversations About Literature   127
  Storytelling   129
  Readers Theatre   132
Efferent Talk   134
  Conversations During Theme Cycles   134
  Show-and-Tell   136
  Oral Reports   140
  Interviews   144
  Debates   146

Dramatic Activities   147
   Role-Playing   148
   Puppets and Other Props   151
   Scriptwriting and Theatrical Productions   153

5 Writing in Journals   163

Types of Journals   164
   Personal Journals   166
   Dialogue Journals   168
   Writing Notebooks   170
   Reading Logs   171
   Learning Logs   176
   Simulated Journals   178
   Young Children's Journals   180
Teaching Students to Write in Journals   181
   Introducing Journal Writing   183
   Sustaining Journal Writing   183
   Adapting to Meet the Needs of Every Student   186
   Assessing Students' Journal Entries   188

6 The Reading and Writing Processes   197

The Reading Process   198
   Aesthetic and Efferent Reading   198
   Stage 1: Preparing to Read   200
   Stage 2: Reading   202
   Stage 3: Responding   205
   Stage 4: Exploring the Text   205
   Stage 5: Extending the Interpretation   206
   Teaching the Reading Process   206
The Writing Process   211
   Stage 1: Prewriting   211
   Stage 2: Drafting   215
   Stage 3: Revising   216
   Stage 4: Editing   219
   Stage 5: Publishing   222
   Teaching the Writing Process   226
Connections Between Reading and Writing   230
   Comparing the Two Processes   230
   Classroom Connections   233

7 Emergent Literacy 241

Concepts About Written Language   243
  Concepts About the Functions of Language   243
  Concepts About Print   244
  Concepts About Words   244
  Concepts About the Alphabet   245
Young Children Emerge Into Reading   248
  Assisted Reading   250
  Shared Reading   253
  Language Experience Approach   259
Young Children Emerge Into Writing   264
  Introducing Young Children to Writing   265
  Opportunities for Writing   268

8 Looking Closely at Words 281

History of the English Language   282
  Old English (A.D. 450–1100)   283
  Middle English (1100–1500)   284
  Modern English (1500–Present)   284
  Learning About Word Histories   285
Words and Their Meanings   286
  Root Words and Affixes   286
  Synonyms and Antonyms   290
  Homonyms   292
  Multiple Meanings   293
  Idioms   294
  Borrowed Words   295
  Other Sources of New Words   297
Teaching Students About Words   298
  Word Walls and Word Study Activities   299
  Minilessons on Words   302
  In Literature Focus Units   305
  Adapting to Meet the Needs of Every Student   307
  Assessing Students' Use of Words   307

9 Reading and Writing Stories 315

Developing Students' Concept of Story   316
  Elements of Story Structure   317
  Teaching Students About Stories   330
  Assessing Students' Concept of Stories   333

Reading Stories 334

　Aesthetic Reading 335

　In Literature Focus Units 339

　In Reading Workshop 343

　In Theme Cycles 345

　Assessing Students' Interpretation of Stories 346

Writing Stories 347

　In Literature Focus Units 347

　In Theme Cycles 351

　In Writing Workshop 352

　Assessing the Stories Students Write 354

10 Reading and Writing Information

Developing Students' Knowledge About Informational Books 362

　Types of Informational Books 362

　Expository Text Structures 366

　Teaching Students About Expository Text Structures 369

　Assessing Students' Use of Expository Text Structures 373

Reports 373

　Young Children's Reports 373

　Collaborative Reports 376

　Individual Reports 378

　Teaching Students to Write Research Reports 378

　Assessing Students' Research Reports 382

Letters 383

　Friendly Letters 383

　Business Letters 388

　Simulated Letters 389

　Teaching Students to Write Letters 389

　Assessing Students' Letters 390

Life-Stories 390

　Autobiographies 391

　Biographies 393

　Teaching Students to Write Life-Stories 396

　Assessing Students' Life-Stories 400

11 Reading and Writing Poetry　　409

Playing With Words 410

　Laughing With Language 410

　Creating Word Pictures 412

　Experimenting With Rhyme 413

　Other Poetic Devices 415

Reading Poems   418

   Types of Poems Children Read   418

   Children's Favorite Poems   418

   Teaching Students to Read Poems   421

   Assessing Students' Experiences With Poems   430

Writing Poems   432

   Formula Poems   432

   Free-Form Poems   436

   Syllable- and Word-Count Poems   437

   Rhymed Verse Forms   439

   Model Poems   440

   Teaching Students to Write Poems   442

   Assessing Poems That Students Write   450

12 Language Tools: Spelling, Handwriting, and Grammar

459

SPELLING   460

Children's Spelling Development   460

   Invented Spelling   461

   Older Students' Spelling Development   464

   Analyzing Children's Spelling Development   465

Teaching Spelling in the Elementary Grades   467

   Components of Spelling Instruction   467

   Weekly Spelling Tests   472

   Adapting to Meet the Needs of Every Student   475

   Assessing Students' Progress in Spelling   475

HANDWRITING   477

Handwriting Forms   478

   Manuscript Handwriting   478

   Cursive Handwriting   480

   D'Nealian Handwriting   480

Children's Handwriting Development   480

   Handwriting Before First Grade   480

   Handwriting in the Primary Grades   483

   Transition to Cursive Handwriting   484

   Handwriting in the Middle and Upper Grades   485

   Left-Handed Writers   485

Teaching Handwriting in the Elementary Grades   488

   The Teaching Strategy   488

Adapting to Meet the Needs of Every Student   490
Elements of Legibility   491
Diagnosing and Correcting Handwriting Problems   492

GRAMMAR   492
Types of Grammar   495
Traditional Grammar   495
Structural Grammar   495
Transformational Grammar   497
Teaching Grammar to Elementary Students   500
Grammar Minilessons   500
Learning Grammar Through Writing   504
Adapting to Meet the Needs of Every Student   505
Assessing Students' Knowledge About Grammar   505

13   Expecting Diversity: The Multicultural Classroom   513
Linguistically and Culturally Diverse Students   515
Impact of Culture on Learning Language Arts   515
Bilingual Students and Students Who Speak English as a Second Language   517
Nonstandard English Speakers   523
Teaching Linguistically and Culturally Diverse Students   525
Multicultural Education   531
Components of Multicultural Classrooms   533
Culturally Conscious Literature   534
Teaching About Cultural Diversity   543

14   Extending Language Arts Across the Curriculum   553
Learning Through Language   554
Learning Science Through Language   555
Learning Social Studies Through Language   556
Learning Literature Through Language   560
Learning Other Content Areas Through Language   562
Theme Cycles   565
Planning Theme Cycles   565
Primary-Grade Theme Cycles   570
Middle-Grade Theme Cycles   573
Upper-Grade Theme Cycles   578
Instructional Activities   582
Assessing Students' Learning   583

APPENDIX A   *Award-Winning Books for Children*   *587*
APPENDIX B   *Resources About Authors and Illustrators*   *591*
APPENDIX C   *Joint Statement on Literacy Development and Pre-First Grade*   *597*
APPENDIX D   *Common Spelling Options for Phonemes*   *601*

                Title and Author Index   *603*
                Subject Index   *611*

Special Features

PRO-FILES

Fourth Graders Become Authors   32
Kindergarteners Listen to and Retell Predictable Stories   78
Sixth-Grade Debaters   116
First Graders Write in Reading Logs   160
Writing Workshop in a Third-Grade Classroom   194
Kindergarteners Read Books at Home   238
Fourth Graders Learn About Word Families   278
Literature Groups in a Fourth-Grade Classroom   312
Kindergarteners Make "Me" Boxes   358
Seventh Graders Read and Write Poems   406
Assessing Handwriting as Part of the Writing Process   456
Becoming Literate in a Bilingual Classroom   510
Second Graders Listen, Talk, Read, and Write About Whales   550

TEACHER'S NOTEBOOK

Activities Illustrating the Seven Language Functions   15
Magazines and Journals About Language Arts   29
Seven Types of Conferences   65
Five Graphic Organizers   100
A KWL Chart   137
Types of Journals   165
Key Features of the Reading Process   201
Key Features of the Writing Process   212
Writing Forms   214
37 Rimes and Some Common Words Using Them   249
Root Words   288
Affixes   291
Ways to Encourage Interpretation   337
Activities to Explore Stories   340
Forms for Friendly and Business Letters   384
Guidelines for Reading Poems   426
Ways to Respond to a Poem   428
Guidelines for Writing Poetry   445
The 100 Most Frequently Used Words   469
Guidelines for Teaching Left-Handed Students   487
Guidelines for Teaching Language-Minority Students   530
Projects to Extend Learning in Theme Cycles   569

MINILESSONS *Language Arts 52*
Listening 95
Talking 125
Journal Writing 185
The Reading and Writing Processes 208
Emergent Literacy 269
Words 304
Reading and Writing Stories 333
Reading and Writing Information 399
Reading and Writing Poetry 447
Language Tools 473

ADAPTING . . . TO *Listening Instruction 111*
MEET THE NEEDS *Talk Activities 126*
OF EVERY STUDENT *Journal Writing 189*
The Reading Process 210
The Writing Process 229
Vocabulary Instruction 308
Reading and Writing Stories 334
Reading and Writing Information 401
Reading and Writing Poetry 451
Spelling Instruction 476

Language Arts

Content and
Teaching Strategies

1

Learning and the Language Arts

INSIGHT _____

For years people felt that children learned to read and write by mastering skills, one by one. For example, a student learned to recognize and write individual letters, combined familiar letters to form words, and later combined words into sentences. Each new skill was built on the previous one. Now we believe that children learn to read and write through immersion in a language-rich environment. The new approach is based on observations of how children learn to talk. This connection between talking, reading, and writing suggests that all three are more alike than they are different. An issue to think about is:

How does the way children learn to talk influence how they learn to read and write?

*U*nderstanding how children learn and particularly how they learn language influences how we teach language arts. The instructional program should never be construed as a smorgasbord of materials and activities; instead, teachers design instruction based on what they know about how children learn. The teacher's role in the elementary classroom is changing. Teachers are now decision makers, empowered with both the obligation and the responsibility to make curricular decisions. In the language arts program these curricular decisions have an impact on the content (information being taught) and the teaching strategies (techniques for teaching content).

Our approach in this textbook incorporates cognitive, psycholinguistic, and sociolinguistic theories of learning. This approach couples the *constructivist,* or cognitive, theories of learning proposed by Jean Piaget and Jerome Bruner with the psycholinguistic theories described by Frank Smith and Kenneth Goodman, and the sociolinguistic theories of Lev Vygotsky. *Psycholinguistics* is a discipline that combines cognitive psychology with linguistics (the study of language) to focus on the cognitive or mental aspects of language learning. *Sociolinguistics* is a similar combination of disciplines—sociology and linguistics—to emphasize the social and cultural implications of language learning.

HOW CHILDREN LEARN

Jean Piaget (1886–1980) was a Swiss psychologist who developed a new theory of learning, or cognitive development, that radically changed our conceptions of child development. Piaget's theoretical framework (1969) differs substantially from behavioral theories that had influenced education for decades. Piaget described learning as the modification of students' cognitive structures as they interact with and adapt to their environment. This definition of learning requires a reexamination of the teacher's role. Instead of dispensing knowledge, teachers engage students with experiences and environments that require them to modify their cognitive structures and construct their own knowledge.

Psycholinguists view language as an example of children's cognitive development, of their ability to learn. Young children learn to talk by being immersed in a language-rich environment and without formal instruction. In a period of only 3 or 4 years, children acquire a sizable vocabulary and internalize the grammar of language. Preschoolers' oral language development provides a model of language learning that can be used in discussing how children learn to read and write.

Sociolinguists view language learning as a social activity and as a reflection of the culture and community in which students live (Heath, 1983; Vygotsky, 1978, 1986). According to Vygotsky, language helps to organize thought, and children use language to learn as well as to communicate and share experiences with others. Understanding that children use language for social purposes allows teachers to plan instructional activities that incorporate a social component, such as having students share their writing with classmates. And, because children's language and concepts of literacy reflect their cultures and home communities, teachers must respect students' language and appreciate cultural differences in their attitudes toward learning and learning language arts in particular.

The Cognitive Structure

The *cognitive structure* is the organization of knowledge in the brain, and knowledge is organized into category systems called *schemata*. (A single category is called a *schema*.) Within the schemata are three components: categories of knowledge, the features or rules for determining what constitutes a category and what will be included in each category, and a network of interrelationships among the categories (Smith, 1975). These schemata may be compared to a conceptual filing system in which children and adults organize and store the information derived from their past experiences. Taking this analogy further, information is filed in the brain in "file folders." As children learn, they add file folders to their filing system, and as they study a topic, that file folder becomes thicker.

As children learn, they invent new categories, and while each person has many similar categories, schemata are personalized according to individual experiences and interests. Some people, for example, may have only one general category, bugs, into which they lump their knowledge of ants, butterflies, spiders, and bees, while other people distinguish between insects and spiders and develop a category for each. Those who distinguish between insects and spiders also develop a set of rules based on the distinctive characteristics of these animals for classifying them into one category or the other. In addition to bug or spider categories, a network of interrelationships connects these categories to other categories. Networks, too, are individualized, depending on each person's unique knowledge and experiences. The category of spiders might be networked as a subcategory of arachnids, and the class relationship between scorpions and spiders might be made. Other networks, such as a connection to a poisonous animals category or a webs and nests category could have been made. The networks that link categories, characteristics, and examples with other categories, characteristics, and examples are extremely complex.

As children adapt to their environment, they add new information about their experiences that requires them to enlarge existing categories or to construct new ones. According to Piaget (1969), two processes make this change possible. *Assimilation* is the cognitive process by which information from the environment is integrated into existing schemata. In contrast, *accommodation* is the cognitive process by which existing schemata are modified or new schemata are restructured to adapt to the environment. Through assimilation, children add new information to their picture of the world; through accommodation, they change their picture of the world on the basis of new information.

The Process of Learning

Learning occurs through the process of *equilibration* (Piaget, 1975). Encountering something a child does not understand or cannot assimilate causes *disequilibrium,* or cognitive conflict. Disequilibrium typically produces confusion and agitation, feelings that impel children to seek *equilibrium,* or a comfortable balance with the environment. In other words, when confronted with new or discrepant information, children (as well as adults) are intrinsically motivated to try to make sense of it. If the child's schemata can accommodate the new information, then the disequilibrium caused by the new experience will

motivate the child to learn. Equilibrium is thus regained at a higher developmental level. These are the steps of this process:

1. Equilibrium is disrupted by the introduction of new or discrepant information.
2. Disequilibrium occurs, and the dual processes of assimilation and accommodation function.
3. Equilibrium is attained at a higher developmental level.

If the new information is too difficult, however, and children cannot relate it
to what they already know, they will not learn. The important implication for
teachers is that new information must be puzzling, challenging, or, to use
Piaget's words, "moderately novel." Information that is too easy is quickly
assimilated, and information that is too difficult cannot be accommodated and
will not be learned.

Prediction occurs as children put their schemata to use in interpreting their
environment. They anticipate what will happen if they act in certain ways and
predict the results of their actions. When children enter any situation, they
organize their behavior according to what they can anticipate, using those
schemata that would be appropriate to assimilate whatever in the environment
interests them. If their schemata can assimilate all the stimuli in the situation,
they relax, because they are in a comfortable state of equilibrium. If there are
stimuli in the environment for which they cannot predict the results, however,
they will proceed more cautiously, trying to discover the meanings of the
stimuli they cannot anticipate. Children seek equilibrium, but they are always
undergoing disequilibrium because they cannot assimilate discrepant stimuli
without some accommodation.

Social Contexts of Learning

Vygotsky (1978) asserted that children learn through social interaction, and
language is an important facilitator of learning. Children's experiences are
organized and shaped by society, but rather than merely absorbing these
experiences, children negotiate and transform them as a dynamic part of
culture. They learn to talk through social interactions with other people and to
read and write through interactions with literate children and adults.

Vygotsky's (1978) concept of "zone of proximal development" explains
how social contexts affect learning. Through interactions with adults and
collaboration with other children, children learn things they could not learn on
their own. Adults guide and support children as they move from their current
level of knowledge toward a more advanced level. Bruner (1978) used the
term *scaffold* as a metaphor to describe adults' contributions to children's
learning. Scaffolds are temporary launching platforms that support children's
development to more complex levels.

Implications for Learning Language Arts

Students interact with their environment and actively construct knowledge
using the processes of assimilation and accommodation. Learning takes place
when existing schemata must be enlarged because of assimilated information
and when the schemata must be restructured to account for new experiences
being acted on and accommodated.

When students work in cooperative groups, they use language to facilitate their learning.

As students engage in learning activities, they are faced with learning and discovering some new element in an otherwise known or familiar system of information. Students recognize or seek out the information embedded in a situation that makes sense and is moderately novel. When students are forced to contend with the novel part of the information, their schemata are disrupted, or put in a state of disequilibrium. Accommodation of the novel information causes a reorganization of the schemata, resulting in students having more complex schemata and being able to operate on more complex information than was previously possible.

Students learn by relating the known to the unknown as they try to make sense of what they encounter in their environment. Teachers need to tailor instruction to help students relate what they know to what they do not know. The amount of new information in a lesson should be within students' capacity to assimilate and accommodate without experiencing long periods of disequilibrium.

Vygotsky's (1978) concept of a zone of proximal development can be used to explain how children learn through social interactions with adults. Adults use scaffolds to help children move from their current stage of development toward their potential, and teachers provide a similar type of assistance as they support students in learning language arts (Applebee & Langer, 1983).

In the lessons they prepare for their students, teachers can create optimal conditions for learning. When students do not have the schemata for predicting and interpreting the new information, teachers must help students relate what they know to what they do not know. Therefore, the new information must appear in a situation that makes sense and must be moderately novel; it must not be too difficult for students to accommodate to it.

Students learn using one of the three modes: experience, observation, and language (Smith, 1975). Imagine, for example, that a boy has just received a new two-wheel bicycle for his fifth birthday. How will he learn to ride it? Will his parents read him a book about bicycles? Will his father demonstrate how to ride the new bicycle while the boy observes? Will the boy get on his new bicycle and learn to ride it by trial and error? Of course, he will get on the new bicycle and learn to ride it by riding. Later, the father might demonstrate a tricky maneuver his son is having trouble mastering, or the boy may become so interested in bicycling that he will be motivated to read a book to learn more about it. Yet the learning process begins with experience for both in-school and out-of-school learning.

Experience is the most basic, concrete way of learning. According to Piaget (1969), elementary students are concrete thinkers and learn best through active involvement. The second and third learning modes, observation and language, are progressively more abstract and further removed from experience. Activities involving observation and language can be made more meaningful when used in conjunction with direct experience and real-life materials. A list of school experiences using each mode is presented in Figure 1–1.

How children learn has important implications for how children learn language arts in school and how teachers teach language arts. These implications delineate the socio-psycholinguistic orientation presented in this chapter:

• Students learn using the processes of assimilation and accommodation.
• Students learn best when the information and experiences being presented to them are moderately novel or in a "zone of proximal development."

Figure 1–1   Activities Using the Three Learning Modes

Experience	Observation	Language
Interviewing	Creating filmstrips	Brainstorming
Manipulating objects	Drawing and painting	Choral reading
Participating in dramatic	pictures	Debating
play	Making diagrams, clus-	Dictating stories
Participating in field	ters, and story maps	Discussing
trips	"Reading" wordless pic-	Listening to audiotapes
Participating in role-play	ture books	Listening to stories read
activities	Viewing films, filmstrips,	aloud
Using puppets	and videotapes	Participating in grand
Using the five senses	Viewing charts, maps,	conversations
Wordplay activities	and models	Participating in readers
Writing simulated jour-	Viewing plays and pup-	theatre
nals and newspapers	pet shows	Reading
	Viewing and writing con-	Taking notes
	crete poetry	Talking
	Watching demonstra-	Writing
	tions	
	Writing class collabora-	
	tion stories	

- Students learn by relating the known to the unknown.
- Students learn through social interactions with their classmates and their teacher.
- Students learn using three modes: experience, observation, and language.

HOW CHILDREN LEARN LANGUAGE

Language is a complex system for creating meaning through socially shared conventions (Halliday, 1978). Before children enter elementary school, they learn the language of their community. They understand what community members say to them, and they share their ideas with others through that language. In an amazingly short period of 3 or 4 years, children master the exceedingly complex system of their native language, allowing them to understand sentences they have never heard before and to create sentences they have never said before. Young children are not "taught" how to talk; this knowledge about language develops tacitly or unconsciously. Children move through a series of developmental stages as they learn the language of their community. These stages are similar across English-speaking children and children who speak other languages.

The Four Language Systems

As children learn to talk, they implicitly develop an understanding of the four language (or cueing) systems. These four systems are:

- The phonological or sound system of language
- The syntactic or structural system of language
- The semantic or meaning system of language
- The pragmatic or social and cultural use system of language

Together these four systems make communication possible, and children use all four systems simultaneously as they listen, talk, read, and write.

The Phonological System.   Children develop an awareness of the *phonological,* or sound, system as they learn to pronounce each of the approximately 44 English speech sounds. These sounds, or *phonemes,* are represented in print with diagonal lines to differentiate them from *graphemes* (letter or letter combinations). Thus, the first letter in *mother* is written *m,* while the phoneme is written /m/, and the phoneme in *soap,* represented by the grapheme *oa,* is written /o/.

The phonological system is important in both oral and written language. Regional and cultural differences exist in the way people pronounce phonemes. For example, Jimmy Carter's speech was characteristic of the southeastern United States, and John F. Kennedy's of New England. Similarly, the English spoken in Australia is different from American English. Children use their knowledge of phoneme-grapheme relationships (also known as phonics) as they learn to read and spell during the primary grades. Students in the primary grades use invented spelling based on their understanding of the phonological system of language to create temporary spellings. Second graders might, for example, spell *school* as *skule,* based on their knowledge of phoneme-grapheme relationships and the English spelling patterns.

The Syntactic System.   The second system is the *syntactic,* or structural, system of language. This system is the grammar that regulates the way words are combined into sentences in English. The word *grammar* here means the rules governing how words are combined in sentences, not the grammar of English textbooks or the conventional etiquette of language.

Children use the syntactic system as they combine words to form sentences. Word order is important in English, and English speakers must arrange words into a sequence that makes sense. Young Spanish-speaking children who are learning English as a second language, for example, learn to say, "This is my red sweater," not "This is my sweater red," which is the literal translation from Spanish. Children also learn to comprehend and produce statements, questions, and other types of sentences during the preschool years.

Many of the capitalization and punctuation rules that elementary students learn reflect the syntactic system of language. Similarly, when students learn about simple, compound, and complex sentences, they are learning about the syntactic system.

Another component of syntax is word forms. Words such as *dog* and *play* are *morphemes,* the smallest meaningful units in language. Words parts that change the meaning of a word are also morphemes. When the plural marker *-s* is added to *dog* to make *dogs,* for instance, or the past-tense marker *-ed* is added to *play* to make *played,* these words now have two morphemes because the inflectional endings changed the meaning of the words. The words *dog* and *play* are *free morphemes* because they convey meaning while standing alone. The endings *-s* and *-ed* are *bound morphemes* because they must be attached to a free morpheme to convey meaning.

As they learn to talk, children quickly learn to combine words and word parts, such as adding *-s* to *cookie* to create a plural and adding *-er* to *big* to indicate a comparison. They also learn to combine two or more free morphemes to form compound words. *Birthday* is an example of a compound word created by combining two free morphemes.

During the elementary grades students learn to add affixes to words. Affixes that are added at the beginning of a word are *prefixes,* and affixes added at the end are *suffixes.* Both kinds of affixes are bound morphemes. The prefix *un-* in *unhappy* is a bound morpheme, whereas *happy* is a free morpheme because it can stand alone as a word.

The Semantic System.   The third language system is the *semantic,* or meaning, system. Vocabulary is the key component of this system. As children learn to talk, they acquire a vocabulary that is continually increasing through the preschool years and the elementary grades. Researchers estimate that children have a vocabulary of 5,000 words by the time they enter school, and they continue to acquire 3,000 words each year during the elementary grades. Not only do children acquire new words, but they also learn that many English words have more than one meaning. They also learn about shades of meaning, synonyms, and antonyms.

The Pragmatic System.   The fourth language system is *pragmatics,* which deals with the social and cultural aspects of language use. People use language for many different purposes, and how they talk or write varies according to purpose and audience. Language use also varies among social classes, cultural and ethnic groups, and geographic regions. These varieties are known as *dialects*. School is one cultural community, and the language of school is *standard English*. This register is formal, the one used in textbooks, in newspapers and magazines, and by television newscasters. Other forms, including those spoken in urban ghettos, in Appalachia, and by Mexican Americans in the Southwest, are generally classified as *nonstandard English*. These nonstandard forms of English are alternatives, in which the phonology, syntax, and semantics differ from those of standard English. These forms are neither inferior nor substandard. They reflect the communities of the speakers, and the speakers communicate as effectively as others who use standard English in their communities.

In this book we will refer to the four language systems again and again using the terminology introduced in this section. Because the terminology can be confusing, the words and their definitions are reviewed in Figure 1–2.

Stages of Language Development

Young children acquire oral language in a fairly regular and systematic way (Lindfors, 1987; Morrow, 1989). Children begin by using one or two words to represent a whole sentence of meaning. Then as children learn more about syntax and semantics, their speech grows longer, and they construct and express meaning in more conventional ways. All children pass through the same stages, but, because of developmental differences as well as differences in social and cultural communities, they do so at widely different ages (Jaggar, 1985). The ages mentioned in this section are estimates, for reference only.

Birth to Age One. The first real evidence that children are developing language occurs when they speak their first words. Before that time, they experiment with sounds. Typically, during the first year of life, babies vocalize a wide variety of speechlike sounds. The sounds they produce are repeated strings of consonant plus vowel syllables. Amazingly, babies' vocalizations include English sounds as well as sounds heard in German, Russian, Japanese, and other languages. The sounds not common to English gradually drop out, probably as a result of both listening to sounds in the environment and parents' reinforcement of familiar sounds, such as the eagerly awaited *ma-ma* and *da-da*. By 9 months, children use a few familiar words such as *milk, doggie,* and *Mommy* to express whole ideas. These first words are most often nouns and invented words, and it is difficult to understand meaning without observing children's accompanying actions or gestures. For example, *ball* may mean "Look, I see a ball," "I want that ball," or "Oops, I dropped my ball, and I can't reach it."

One to Two Years of Age. Children's vocabularies expand rapidly in this stage, and children begin putting two words together. For example, they may say *bye-bye car* and *allgone cookie.* This language is also known as *telegraphic speech* because nonessential words are omitted as they are in telegrams. Children use nouns, verbs, and adjectives—all high-information words; they usually omit low-information words—prepositions, articles, and conjunctions. Children's speech in this stage is rule-governed, but it is very different from adult speech, thus offering evidence for the psycholinguists' belief that children create their own ways to represent meaning rather than simply imitate adult language.

Figure 1–2   Overview of the Four Language Systems

System	Description	Terms	Uses in the Elementary Grades
Phonological System	The sound system of English with approximately 44 sounds	• Phoneme (the smallest unit of sound) • Grapheme (the written representation of a phoneme using one or more letters)	• Pronouncing words • Detecting regional and other dialects • Decoding words when reading • Using invented spelling • Reading and writing alliterations and onomatopoeia
Syntactic System	The structural system of English that governs how words are combined into sentences	• Syntax (the structure or grammar of a sentence) • Morpheme (the smallest meaningful unit of language) • Free morpheme (a morpheme that can stand alone as a word) • Bound morpheme (a morpheme that must be attached to a free morpheme)	• Adding inflectional endings to words • Combining words to form compound words • Adding prefixes and suffixes to root words • Using capitalization and punctuation to indicate beginnings and ends of sentences • Writing simple, compound, and complex sentences • Combining sentences
Semantic System	The meaning system of English that focuses on vocabulary	• Semantics (meaning)	• Learning the meanings of words • Discovering that some words have multiple meanings • Studying synonyms, antonyms, and homonyms • Using a dictionary and thesaurus • Reading and writing comparisons (metaphors and similes)
Pragmatic System	The system of English that varies language according to social and cultural uses	• Function (the purpose for which a person uses language) • Standard English (the form of English used in textbooks and by television newscasters) • Nonstandard English (other forms of English)	• Varying language to fit specific purposes • Reading and writing dialogue in dialects • Comparing standard and nonstandard forms of English

Two to Three Years of Age.   Telegraphic speech begins to evolve into longer utterances and to sound more like adult forms of talk. Word order becomes important when children begin to use utterances of three and four words. At this point grammatical relations such as subject, verb, and object begin to appear in overt syntactic structures. Children's development continues to come closer and closer to the adult form of the language used in their speech communities, and their vocabularies reach about 1,000 words by the end of their third year.

Three to Four Years of Age.   Children now use more complex sentences that include pronouns, adjectives, adverbs, possessives, and plurals. They generalize knowledge about language and then learn about exceptions, such as irregular past-tense markers. At first children use the unmarked form of irregular verbs such as *ate,* as in "I ate my cereal," which they hear in the speech of those around them. Then they perceive that past tense is marked with the *-ed* morpheme and begin to use it with practically all past-tense verbs, so that they now say, "I eated my cereal." Finally children realize that some verbs are regular, with the past tense marked by *-ed* (as in *talk-talked),* whereas other verbs have different past-tense forms. Then they again say, "I ate my cereal." This tendency to overgeneralize the *-ed* past-tense marker of regular verbs continues in some children's speech until age 5. Children's vocabularies reach about 1,500 words by the end of this year.

Four to Five Years of Age.   During this period children's sentences grow in length and complexity. They develop the auxiliary systems (e.g., using forms

Language is a means of both classifying experiences into categories and communicating experiences to other people.

of *do* and *is*) and transformations (e.g., changing statements into questions), and they learn to change the word order of their sentences to express desired meanings. Their sentences are grammatical by adult standards, and children use language for a wider range of purposes. The initial physical and emotional context of speech with objects, people, events, and locations continues to play an important role in language development. Children's vocabularies grow to 3,000 words, and they have acquired most of the elements of adult language by the end of this year.

Five to Six Years of Age.   By age 5 children's language is similar to adult language. Most grammatical rules have been mastered, and language patterns and sentence forms are complex. Children use language for a variety of purposes, including to entertain. They are beginning to use language in humorous ways, and their interest in jokes and riddles usually develops at this age.

During the preschool years, parents make an important contribution to language development by expanding and extending children's talk. To the child's utterance, "Dog bark," for example, a parent might respond, "Yes, the dog is barking at the kitty," and provide information about why the dog is barking (Cazden, 1972). This social interaction helps the child interpret what is happening in the environment and adds grammatical information. It is a model to learn from, not a sample to copy, and it is another example of scaffolding (Cazden, 1983).

Development in the Elementary Grades

Although the most important period in oral language acquisition is the preschool years, children's phonological, syntactic, semantic, and pragmatic development continues in the elementary grades and beyond. They continue to acquire additional sentence patterns; their vocabularies expand tremendously; and they master the remaining sounds of English. They also learn how to vary their language according to social use.

Phonological Development.   Children have mastered most of the phonemes of English by the time they come to school. A few sounds, especially in medial and final positions, however, are not acquired until after age 5 or 6. These sounds include /v/, /th/, /ch/, /sh/, and /zh/. Even at age 7 or 8, some students still make sound substitutions, especially in consonant clusters. They may, for example, substitute /w/ for /r/ or /l/, as in *cwack* for *crack* (DeStefano, 1978). When students are learning to read and write, they read words aloud the same way they say them, and they spell words phonetically, the same way they say them.

Syntactic Development.   Students acquire a variety of sentence patterns during the elementary grades. They begin to construct complex sentences and use embedding techniques to combine ideas. Whereas primary-grade students use the connector *and* to string together a series of ideas, middle- and upper-grade students learn to use dependent clauses and other connectors. A young child might say, "I have a hamster *and* he is brown *and* his name is Pumpkin *and* he likes to run on his wheel," but an older student can embed these ideas: "My brown hamster named Pumpkin likes to run on his wheel." Older students learn to use connectors such as *because, if, unless, meanwhile, in spite of,* and *nevertheless* (Loban, 1976). The constructions students learn to use in their talk also appear in their writing. Ingram (1975) found that fifth- and seventh-grade students used more complex, embedded structures in writing than in talking. This finding makes sense because when students write, they must organize their thoughts and, for efficiency, embed as much information as possible.

Students also learn more about word order in English sentences. Consider these two sentences:

Ann told Tom to leave.

Ann promised Tom to leave.

Who is going to leave? According to the Minimal Distance Principle, the noun closest to the complement verb (i.e., *to leave*) is the subject of that verb. In the first sentence *Tom* is the person who will leave. Substitute these other verbs for *told: asked, wanted, tried, urged, commanded, implored.* In each case *Tom* is the person to leave. *Promise* is an exception, however, so in the second sentence, it is *Ann* who will leave, not *Tom.* Chomsky (1969) found that primary-grade students overgeneralize this principle and equate *promise* sentences with *tell* sentences. During the middle grades, however, students learn to distinguish the exceptions to the rule.

As students learn to read, they are introduced to the more complex syntactic forms and other conventions found in written language. One form unique to writing is the passive voice. The active voice is almost always used in talk (e.g., "Bobby broke the vase"), rather than the passive voice (e.g., "The vase was broken by Bobby").

Semantic Development.   Of the language systems, Lindfors (1987) says, semantic growth is the most vigorous in the elementary grades. Children's vocabulary increases rapidly, by perhaps as much as 3,000 words per year. At the same time that children are learning new words, they are also learning that many words have more than one meaning. Meaning is usually based on context, or the surrounding words. The common word *run,* for instance, has more than 30 meanings listed in *The Random House Dictionary of the English Language* (Flexner, 1987), and the meaning is tied to the context in which it is used:

Will the mayor *run* for reelection?

The bus *runs* between Dallas and Houston.

The advertisement will *run* for three days.

The plan made a bombing *run.*

Will you *run* to the store and get a loaf of bread for me?

The dogs are out in the *run.*

Oh, no! I got a *run* in my new pair of pantyhose!

Primary-grade students do not have the full, adult meaning of many words; rather, they learn meanings through a process of refinement (Clark, 1971). They add "features," or layers of meaning. In the elementary grades, students use this refinement process to distinguish between pairs of words such as *ask* and *tell* to expand their range of meanings for many common words.

Pragmatic Development.   When children come to school, they speak the language of their family and community, and at school they are introduced to standard English, which may be quite similar to or different from their own language dialect. They learn about appropriateness and to vary the language they speak or write according to form, purpose, and audience. M. A. K. Halliday (1973, 1975) has identified seven functions or purposes of language that apply to oral and written language and even to the nonlanguage forms of communication such as gestures and pantomime. These are Halliday's seven categories:

1. Instrumental language—language to satisfy needs
2. Regulatory language—language to control the behavior of others
3. Interactional language—language to establish and maintain social relationships
4. Personal language—language to express personal opinions
5. Imaginative language—language to express imagination and creativity
6. Heuristic language—language to seek information and to find out about things
7. Informative language—language to convey information

During the elementary grades, students learn to use oral language for a wider range of functions, and they learn written language alternatives for the oral language functions. The Teacher's Notebook on page 15 lists some oral and written language alternatives for the seven language functions.

Frank Smith (1977) explains that these language functions are learned through genuine communication experiences, rather than through practice activities, and that the ability to use one language function does not generalize to skill in other functions. He also notes that language is rarely used for just one function at a time; typically, two or more language functions are involved in talking or writing.

Implications for Learning Language Arts

Imagine how different life would be in homes with young children if adults tried to teach children to talk as they have been traditionally taught to read and write. Parents would bring workbooks and charts listing talk skills home from the hospital with the baby. Children would be kept in a quiet room, and parents would first speak to the babies only in single, one-syllable words, then in two-syllable words, and finally in short sentences. Parents would introduce consonant sounds in a particular order, and at some point they would try to use all short vowel words in silly nonsense sentences. Ridiculous, right?

Language learning is both natural and social. Children learn to talk in the short period of 3 or 4 years using a natural, immersion approach and interaction with family and community members. It seems unreasonable that teachers should use an entirely different method to help children learn to read and write only a year or two later. Educators now recognize that the strategies parents use to help children learn to talk can be adapted for teaching language arts in the elementary school.

Teacher's Notebook
Activities Illustrating the Seven Language Functions

Function	Oral Language Activity	Written Language Activity
1. Instrumental Language	Conversations Commercials	Notes Business letters Letters to the editor Advertisements
2. Regulatory Language	Directions Gestures Dramatic play	Directions Classroom rules
3. Interactional Language	Conversations Sharing Discussions	Friendly letters Pen pal letters Courtesy letters Dialogue journals
4. Personal Language	Discussions Debates Show-and-tell Sharing Commercials	Personal journals Dialogue journals Response to literature activities Advertisements
5. Imaginative Language	Storytelling Readers theatre Dramatic play Role-playing	Reading and writing stories and poems Writing scripts Simulated journals
6. Heuristic Language	Interviews Role-playing Discussions	Learning logs Clustering Researching and report writing
7. Informative Language	Oral reports Discussions	Researching and report writing Reading and writing newspapers Reading and writing timelines, charts, and maps

Language is both predictable and aesthetic (Edelsky, Altwerger, & Flores, 1991). The four language systems working together make language predictable. Each language system contributes to this predictability. For example, the phonological system provides consistency in pronunciation and some spelling patterns, and the syntactic system regulates sentence structures and word-order options within sentences. Children use this predictability in learning to talk as well as in learning to read and write. Many kindergartners, for example, can read books like Bill Martin, Jr.'s, *Brown Bear, Brown Bear, What Do You See?* (1983) because of the predictable sentence patterns.

Language also has aesthetic qualities, including rhythm and rhyme, imagery, comparisons, and alliteration. Edelsky and her colleagues (1991) explain that language is a plaything and children are "inveterate players" (p. 13). Creating word plays, riddles, and raps is a natural part of childhood, not something that only creative or gifted students do.

Children learn to use oral and written language for all seven language functions through actual use, and the teacher's role is to foster a wide range of language activities in the classroom, and to find ways to extend children's language in real-life situations. Because children's ability to use one language function does not generalize to ability in other functions, it is essential that students have opportunities to use each of the seven language functions. In her study of the functions of talk in a primary-grade classroom, Pinnell (1975) found that first graders most commonly used interactional language (for social purposes) and rarely used heuristic language (to seek information) when they talked and worked in small groups. Camp (1987) studied seventh graders' language functions during science class and found that students used the same language functions—interactional and heuristic—most commonly and least commonly. These two researchers concluded that students need to experiment with all seven language functions to learn what they can accomplish with language. Some of the language functions may not occur spontaneously in students' talking and writing, and teachers need to plan genuine communication experiences that incorporate all the language functions.

How children learn to talk has important implications for how children learn language arts in school and how teachers teach language arts. Seven implications are:

- Children learn to talk by being immersed in the language of their community, not by being taught talking skills in a prescribed sequential order.
- Children use the four language systems simultaneously as they listen, talk, read, and write.
- Children construct their own knowledge as they make and test hypotheses, leading to progressive refinements of their talk.
- Children learn and use language for meaningful, functional, and genuine communication purposes.
- Children learn to use the seven language functions through talking and writing.
- Adults provide models and scaffolds to support children's learning.
- Parents and other care givers expect that children will be successful in learning to talk.

HOW CHILDREN LEARN LANGUAGE ARTS

> It seems to me that the most important general goal for education in the language arts is to enable each child to communicate, as effectively as he or she can, what he or she intends and to understand, as well as he or she can, what others have communicated, intentionally or not. (Brown, 1979, p. 483)

Roger Brown's statement succinctly states the goal for language arts instruction at all grade levels. The teacher's goal, then, is to help students learn to communicate effectively with others through oral and written language.

Communicative Competence

The ability to communicate effectively is known as *communicative competence* (Hymes, 1974), and it involves two components. The first component is the ability to transmit meaning through talking and writing, and the second is the ability to interpret meaning through listening and reading. Communicative competence also involves pragmatics—students' fluency in the different registers of language as well as knowing when it is socially appropriate to use language in each register. For example, we use informal language with family members and close friends and more formal language with people we know less well or when giving a speech. Similarly, in writing we use different *registers,* or levels of formality. We write letters to close friends in a less formal register than we would use in writing a letter to the editor of the local newspaper.

We will discuss a variety of language activities for helping students develop communicative competence, such as:

- Conducting oral interviews of community resources with special knowledge, interests, or talents in connection with literature focus units and social studies and science theme cycles
- Writing simulated journal entries assuming the role of a character while reading a story or assuming the role of a historical or contemporary personality while reading a biography
- Writing stories using the writing process and then sharing the stories with classmates and other genuine audiences
- Analyzing word play or poetic devices in the poems students read and write

These activities exhibit the three characteristics of all worthwhile experiences with language. They use language in meaningful rather than contrived situations. They are functional, or real-life, activities. They are genuine rather than artificial activities, such as those typical of worksheets, because they communicate.

The Four Language Modes

Traditionally, language arts educators have defined *language arts* as the study of the four modes of language: listening, talking, reading, and writing. Thinking is sometimes referred to as the fifth language mode, but, more accurately, it permeates all the language modes.

Listening.   Beginning at birth, listening is children's first contact with language. Listening instruction is often neglected in elementary classrooms

This teacher incorporates all four language modes: She reads a story aloud, her students listen to her read, they talk about the story, and they write reactions in their reading logs.

because teachers feel that students have already learned to listen and that instructional time should be devoted to reading and writing. We present an alternative view of listening and listening instruction in Chapter 3, focusing on the following key concepts:

- Listening is a process of which hearing is only one part.
- Students listen for many purposes.
- Students listen differently according to their purpose.
- Students listen to literature and as part of across-the-curriculum studies.

Talking.   As with listening, teachers often neglect instruction in talk during the elementary grades because they feel students already know how to talk. Students use talk to respond to literature and as they learn during social studies and science theme cycles. In Chapter 4 we will discuss these key concepts about talk:

- Talk is an essential part of the language arts curriculum.
- Students use talk as part of literature focus units and across-the-curriculum theme cycles.
- Talk ranges from discussions about literature to more formal presentations, including oral reports and debates.
- Drama, including storytelling and role-playing, provides a valuable method of learning and a powerful way of communicating.

Reading.   We present an integrated approach to reading and writing instruction in this book. We discuss the reading and writing processes in Chapter 6 and focus on how young children learn to read in Chapter 7. We also make connections between reading and writing stories, reports, biographies, and poems in later chapters. We will present the following key concepts about reading:

- Reading and writing are interrelated and strategic processes.
- Students read differently for different purposes.
- Reading includes reading aloud to students, shared reading, and independent reading.
- Proofreading is a unique type of reading that writers use when they edit their compositions.

Writing.   Elementary students learn to do two types of writing. One is informal writing, such as writing in journals and learning logs and writing clusters and quickwrites. The second type is the writing process in which students use the process approach to draft, revise, edit, and publish stories, reports, poems, and other writing forms. We discuss journal writing in Chapter 5 and introduce the writing process in Chapter 6. In Chapter 12 spelling and handwriting are described as tools that writers use to communicate effectively with their readers. The key concepts about writing are:

- Informal writing is used to develop writing fluency and as a learning tool.
- Writing is a process in which students cycle recursively through prewriting, drafting, revising, editing, and publishing stages.
- Elementary students experiment with many different written language forms.
- Students learn to write stories, poems, and other forms as part of literature focus units, writing workshop, and theme cycles.
- Spelling and handwriting are tools for writers.

The four language modes can be compared and contrasted in a variety of ways. First, oral versus written: listening and talking are oral, while reading and writing are written. Second, primary versus secondary: the oral language modes are learned informally at home before children come to school, whereas the written language modes are typically considered the school's responsibility and are taught more formally. Listening and talking are called *primary language modes;* reading and writing are called *secondary language modes.* The third way to compare the modes is receptive versus productive: two language modes, listening and reading, are receptive; talking and writing are productive. In the receptive language modes, students receive or comprehend a message orally through listening or in writing as they read. In the productive language modes, students produce a message, orally or in writing. These three sets of relationships are shown graphically in Figure 1–3.

Even though we will devote chapters to specific language modes, the grouping of the four language modes is both arbitrary and artificial. This arrangement wrongly suggests that there are separate stages of development for each language mode and that children use different mental processes for listening, talking, reading, and writing (Smith, 1979). It has generally been

*Figure 1–3   Relationships
Among the Four Language Modes*

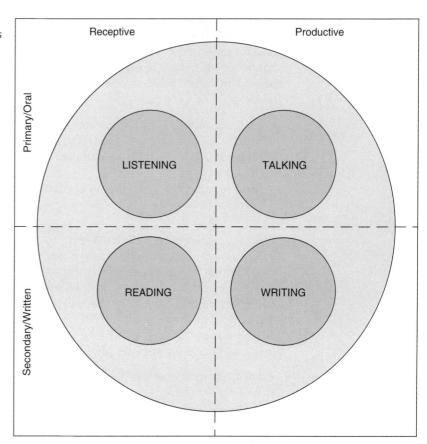

assumed that the four language modes develop in sequence from listening to talking to reading to writing. Although listening is the first form of language to develop, with talking beginning soon thereafter, parents and preschool teachers have recently documented children's early interest in both reading and writing (Baghban, 1984; Bissex, 1980). Also, Carol Chomsky (1971) and other researchers have observed young children experimenting with writing earlier than with reading. On the basis of reports from parents, teachers, and researchers, we can no longer assume that there is a definite sequence in learning and using the four language modes.

This grouping also suggests a division among the language modes, as though they could be used separately. In reality, they are used simultaneously and reciprocally. Almost any language arts activity involves more than one language mode. For instance, in learning about stories, students use all four language modes. They begin by listening when parents and teachers read aloud to them and later by reading stories themselves. Next, they retell familiar as well as original stories. They make puppets to dramatize and role-play favorite stories. From telling stories, they move to writing stories and sharing them with classmates or other genuine audiences. The cluster in Figure 1–4 lists these and other activities for learning about stories that involve all four language modes.

Over a 13-year period, researcher Walter Loban (1976) documented the language growth and development of a group of 338 students from kindergar-

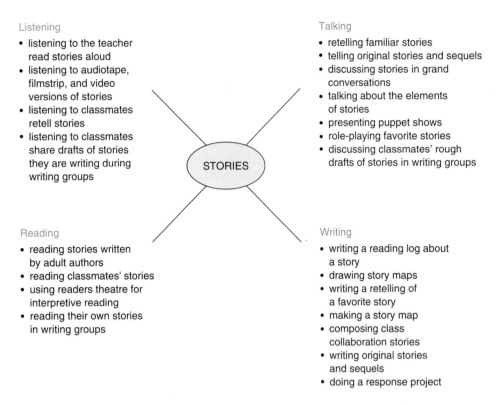

Listening
- listening to the teacher read stories aloud
- listening to audiotape, filmstrip, and video versions of stories
- listening to classmates retell stories
- listening to classmates share drafts of stories they are writing during writing groups

Talking
- retelling familiar stories
- telling original stories and sequels
- discussing stories in grand conversations
- talking about the elements of stories
- presenting puppet shows
- role-playing favorite stories
- discussing classmates' rough drafts of stories in writing groups

STORIES

Reading
- reading stories written by adult authors
- reading classmates' stories
- using readers theatre for interpretive reading
- reading their own stories in writing groups

Writing
- writing a reading log about a story
- drawing story maps
- writing a retelling of a favorite story
- making a story map
- composing class collaboration stories
- writing original stories and sequels
- doing a response project

Figure 1–4   How the Language Modes Are Used in Learning About Stories

ten through 12th grade (ages 5–18). Two purposes of his longitudinal study were to examine differences between students who used language effectively and those who did not and to identify predictable stages of language development. Three of Loban's conclusions are especially noteworthy to our discussion of the relationship among the language modes. First, Loban reported positive correlations among the four language modes. Second, he found that students with less effective oral language (listening and talking) abilities tended to have less effective written language (reading and writing) abilities. And, third, he found a strong relationship between students' oral language ability and their overall academic ability. Loban's seminal study demonstrates clear relationships among the language modes and emphasizes the need to teach oral language in the elementary school language arts curriculum.

A Paradigm for Language Arts Instruction

Instruction in language arts should be based on how children learn and how they learn language. A paradigm for learning and teaching language arts in the elementary grades includes these components:

- *Immersion.* Students learn through immersion in listening, talking, reading, and writing activities.
- *Employment.* Students need opportunities to participate in language arts activities that are meaningful, functional, and genuine.
- *Demonstration.* Students learn through demonstrations—with modeling and scaffolding—that teachers provide.

- *Responsibility.* Students become more self-reliant when they make choices about the language arts activities in which they are involved.
- *Approximation.* Students learn more confidently when they understand that teachers do not expect correctness but improvement by trial and error.
- *Expectation.* Students are more likely to be successful when teachers expect them to be successful. (Adapted from Cambourne, cited in Butler & Turbill, 1984)

Students develop communicative competence as they actively participate in listening, talking, reading, and writing activities that are meaningful, functional, and genuine. Walter Loban (1979) says, "The path to power over language is to use it in genuinely meaningful situations, whether we are reading, listening, writing, or speaking" (p. 485). Vygotsky (1978) concurs: "Reading and writing must be something the child needs" (p. 117); the activities should be "relevant to life" (p. 118). Instead of worksheets that provide drills on isolated skills, language arts activities should provide opportunities for children to use the various language functions for real-life purposes. Edelsky, Altwerger, and Flores (1991) say that when an activity has no intrinsic meaning for students, it is only an exercise, and "doing exercises is an extremely difficult way to learn language" (p. 8).

Two ways to make language arts instruction meaningful is to connect it with literature focus units and across-the-curriculum theme studies. Students use all four language modes as they read and respond to literature in focus units. For example, as fifth graders read and respond to *Number the Stars* (Lowry, 1989), a story about friendship between a Christian girl and a Jewish girl set in Denmark during World War II, they use listening, talking, reading, and writing in some of the ways shown in Figure 1–5. Across-the-curriculum connections are also possible given the historical setting of the story. Similarly, students use the four language modes as they learn and share their learning in social studies and science theme cycles. As second graders learn about the desert in a theme cycle, they use the four language modes to explore the concepts they are learning as well as to share what they have learned. Some of these across-the-curriculum connections for a theme on the desert are shown in Figure 1–6.

Classrooms are social environments in which students learn language arts through interactions with teachers and classmates. Teachers facilitate students' learning through scaffolding as well as by providing instruction, and classmates support each other's learning through collaboration. Examples of teachers' scaffolding include teaching capitalization and punctuation skills through proofreading conferences, taking young children's dictation for language experience stories, and expanding students' use of theme-related vocabulary through word walls (or charts). Examples of students' collaboration include discussing books they have read in grand conversations, responding to each other's rough drafts in writing groups, and participating together in dramatizations to learn about a story or a historical event.

A Teaching Strategy

Theories of how children learn can be applied in designing a teaching strategy. Piaget's concepts of assimilation and accommodation are important because they describe how children learn concepts and add information to their

Figure 1–5 *Ways Fifth Graders Use the Four Language Modes in a Literature Focus Unit on* Number the Stars

1. Listening

Students listen to *Number the Stars* as it is read aloud, and they listen to classmates' comments during literature discussions. They listen and watch as classmates dramatize events from the story and as classmates share reports of information or projects.

2. Talking

Students talk as they make predictions about what will happen in upcoming chapters and as they share their responses to the story during literature discussions. They may share the results of their research into World War II or report on the geography of Denmark and trace the trip the girls took from Copenhagen to the seacoast. Students also use talk as they dramatize story events and share projects they create after reading the story.

3. Reading

Students read *Number the Stars* aloud, with a buddy, or independently. They may reread brief excerpts from the story during discussions or read-arounds and read other books by the author Lois Lowry or other books about World War II and the Jewish Holocaust. Students read aloud their journal entries and quickwrites to share them with classmates. During writing groups students read aloud sequels, poems, reports, or other projects they are writing.

4. Writing

Students write their predictions about and reactions to each chapter in reading logs or keep simulated journals written from the viewpoint of one of the characters. Students write quickwrites and make charts and diagrams on topics related to the story. They also make notes after viewing films and during presentations by the teacher about World War II and the Jewish Holocaust. Students also use the writing process as they write sequels, poems, reports, and other compositions after reading *Number the Stars.*

cognitive structures, and Vygotsky's zone of proximal development is useful because it explains that teachers can support students and assist them in learning things that they cannot learn by themselves. This six-step teaching strategy establishes a sequence of instruction, and it can be adapted for teaching almost any language arts procedure, concept, strategy, or skill. The six steps in the teaching strategy are:

Step by Step

1. *Initiating.*   Teachers introduce the procedure, concept, and strategy or skill. The initiating step includes questions, statements, examples, and activities for stimulating interest in the lesson and engaging students' participation.

2. *Structuring.*   Teachers present information and relate it to what students already know so that students can begin to overcome the cognitive conflict they experienced in the first step. To overcome cognitive conflict, students begin to enlarge or restructure an existing schema to fit the information, or they begin to develop a new schema to organize the information.

3. *Conceptualizing.*   Students experiment with and analyze the information pre-sented in the second step in order to understand and make connections to related information. This step furthers the process of accommodation begun ear-lier. When the accommodation process is completed, the existing schemata have been enlarged or a new schema has been developed that fits the new informa-tion.

4. *Summarizing.*   Teachers review the major points of the lesson. The information and examples presented in the structuring step and the relationships established during the conceptualizing step are organized and summarized. This step allows students to make any necessary adjustments in the schema and in the new in-terrelationships established within their cognitive structures. For students who have not understood the information being presented, summarizing presents an-other opportunity to accommodate the information.

5. *Generalizing.*   Teachers present new examples or variations of the information introduced in the first step. This step is a check on students' understanding, and students demonstrate their understanding by generalizing from the first ex-ample to this new example.

6. *Applying.*   Students incorporate the information in an activity that allows them to demonstrate their knowledge by using the concept in a novel or unique way.

Students do not, of course, learn in such neat little steps. Rather, learning is a process of ebb and flow in which the assimilating and accommodating processes move back and forth as the student grasps pieces of information. Students may grasp a new concept in any of the steps of the teaching strategy; some students may not learn it at all. Teachers will plan additional lessons for the students who do not learn. Whether or not they learn depends on the closeness of the fit between their schemata and the information being pre-sented. Information that does not in some way relate to an existing schema is almost impossible to learn. Information must be moderately novel to fit students' existing cognitive structures.

This teaching strategy will be adapted for lessons in just about every chapter of this book. Some lessons may not lend themselves readily to this six-step sequence of instruction; for certain concepts, one or more of the steps may not be appropriate, and some adjustments may be necessary.

Two applications to illustrate how the teaching strategy can be used with almost any language arts topic are presented in Figure 1–7. The first is a lesson on fables, brief stories that teach a lesson. Our best-known fables were compiled by Aesop, a Greek slave who lived in the sixth century B.C., but many other civilizations have contributed fables as well. A number of fables have been retold for children, and, recently, children's authors such as Arnold Lobel (1980) have written their own books of fables. The goal of this lesson is for students to read fables, examine how authors construct the stories, and then tell and write their own fables. The lesson is organized around the six steps of the teaching strategy we have discussed. For the sake of clarity, other activities that would be part of this two-week unit for a fourth-grade class are not included in this plan.

Figure 1–6   Ways Second Graders Use the Four Language Modes in a Theme Cycle on the Desert

---

1. Listening

Students listen to the teacher read books about the desert. They listen to *Mojave* (Siebert, 1988), a book-length poem about one special desert, and picture books by Byrd Baylor that depict life in the desert, including *Desert Voices* (1981). Students also listen as the teacher presents information about the desert and as they watch films and videos about the desert.

2. Talking

Students talk about the desert and what they are learning in the theme cycle. After reading or listening to the teacher read a book, they participate in grand conversations in which they share their responses to the book. They also create their own riddles after listening to the teacher read the riddles in *Desert* (Hirschi, 1992). Later, students will write their riddles and add them to a desert mural they are creating.

3. Reading

Students read *Cactus Hotel* (Guiberson, 1991) in small groups and then diagram the life cycle of the cactus in their learning logs. Students read storyboards the teacher has made by cutting apart two copies of *Desert Life* (Taylor, 1992) and backing the pages with cardboard and laminating them. Each page in the book presents a close-up look at a desert animal or plant, including tortoises, cacti, locusts, and scorpions. Students read and examine three of the pages and record facts in their learning logs. Also, using books from the classroom library, students read and reread other stories, information books, and poems about deserts and desert life.

4. Writing

Students write in learning logs and make clusters, diagrams, and other charts in the logs, too. After reading *Cactus Hotel,* students make a large papier-mâché saguaro cactus and desert animals mentioned in the book. Then they use the writing process to research and write reports about the cactus and animals. They post their finished reports next to their cactus hotel. Students work together to write an ABC book about deserts. Each student chooses a letter and writes one page, and then the pages are compiled and bound into a book.

The second application presented in Figure 1–7 focuses on quotation marks. The goal of this lesson is for students to understand what quotation marks mean when they are reading and to be able to use them in their writing. This plan is also organized around the six steps of the teaching strategy. Other activities that would be part of this one-week unit for a second-grade class are omitted to show more clearly the sequence of activities.

Assessing Students' Learning

Parents expect that their children will be successful in learning to talk, and they judge their children's accomplishments by observing how they use language in meaningful, functional, and genuine ways. Some parents use videotapes of their children using language, and others repeat the unique words and sen-

Figure 1–7   Using the Teaching Strategy

Step	Fables Lesson	Quotation Marks Lesson
Initiating	The teacher reads several fables such as "The Hare and the Tortoise" and "The Lion and the Mouse" from Hague's *Aesop's Fables* (1985) and explains that these short stories that teach a moral are called *fables*.	The teacher presents a chart with sentences containing direct quotes from *Mice Twice* (Low, 1980), a book the students particularly enjoyed reading (and rereading several times) the previous week. Students and the teacher discuss the quotes, and the teacher asks what all the sentences have in common. Students notice that all the sentences include someone talking and are marked with quotation marks.
Structuring	Students and the teacher develop a chart listing the characteristics of fables. The list may include these characteristics: • Fables are short. • The characters are usually animals. • The setting is usually rural and not important to the story. • Fables involve only one event. • The moral is usually stated at the end of the story. The teacher then reads one or two other fables, and the students check that their lists of the characteristics of fables are complete.	The teacher presents information about quotation marks, explaining when to use them and that they were invented thousands of years ago to represent two talking lips. The teacher presents a second chart with sentences she has overheard students say during the day. The students work together to add quotation marks.
Conceptualizing	Students read other fables and then relate a favorite fable by telling it aloud, by drawing a series of pictures, or by writing the fable in their own words.	Students read *Pinkerton, Behave* (Kellogg, 1979), and each student chooses a page in the story to rewrite using quotation marks; for example: The little girl cried, "Pinkerton! Fetch!" Then students add illustrations and share their pages. After the pages have been edited to be sure that quotation marks were used correctly, the pages are collated to make a class collaboration version of the story.

tences their children utter. Parents' focus is on celebrating what children can do, not on identifying what they cannot do yet.

In elementary classrooms, assessment methods are changing to reflect research and theories of how children learn (Anthony, Johnson, Mickelson, & Preece, 1991; Goodman, Goodman, & Hood, 1989). Teachers observe students and conference with them as they are involved in language arts activities, and students document their language learning using portfolios (Graves & Sun-

Figure 1–7   continued

Step	Fables Lesson	Quotation Marks Lesson
Summarizing	The teacher and students review the fables they have read and the list of characteristics they have developed. Then the teacher asks students to write a paragraph explaining what a fable is. Students share their explanations and compare them to the list of characteristics.	After reviewing the rules for using quotation marks, students choose a page from a favorite story to use in making a quotation marks chart. First, they draw a picture similar to the one in their chosen stories and use talking balloons to present the dialogue. Next, they rewrite the talk in script form. Finally, they use the narrative form.
Generalizing	Students read other fables, such as Lobel's *Fables* (1980) or Lionni's *Frederick's Fables* (1985). It is important to include some fables that state the moral implicitly rather than explicitly. Students explain why these stories are or are not fables. The teacher also points out that although these fables are based on many of the same morals that Aesop used, they were created—not retold—by Arnold Lobel and Leo Lionni.	Students reread their journals and find four examples of dialogue. They copy the examples and use quotation marks correctly.
Applying	Students write their own fables based on a moral that may be explicitly stated at the end of the story or implied in the story. Students use the writing process to draft, revise, edit, and publish their work. Later they share their fables with classmates or with students in another class who are also reading and writing fables.	Students make a book of quotations from stories they have read or from remarks of classmates or family members. For each quotation, students use quotation marks and other punctuation marks correctly; for example, from *Where the Wild Things Are* (Sendak, 1963), one quotation might be, "I am a wild thing," said Max.

stein, 1992). Students collect samples of their language arts activities and place them in a folder or notebook portfolio. Sometimes snapshots are used to document art projects and displays, and videotapes are used for dramatic productions.

Tests can also be used to assess students' language learning. However, they are not as effective as other types of assessment because they don't show how students use the language modes for meaningful, functional, and genuine activities. If tests are used, they should be accompanied by other assessment approaches.

Resources for Teachers

Teachers are always interested in learning more about how to teach and assess students' learning. As you begin teaching, you will want to learn as much as possible about how to teach language arts. Most schools provide in-service or staff development programs, some of which will be devoted to language arts instruction. Two organizations dedicated to improving the quality of instruction in reading and the other language arts are the National Council of Teachers of English (NCTE) and the International Reading Association (IRA). As an undergraduate student majoring in elementary education or as an elementary language arts teacher, you will find that these organizations can help you keep in touch with new ideas in the field. Both organizations publish journals of interest to preservice and classroom teachers, with articles suggesting innovative teaching practices, reports of significant research studies, reviews of recently published books of children's literature, techniques for using computers in the classroom, and reviews of professional books and classroom materials. Journals for elementary teachers are *Language Arts,* published by NCTE, and *The Reading Teacher,* published by IRA. The two organizations also publish other journals for high school language arts and reading teachers, college faculty, and researchers. The Teacher's Notebook on page 29 lists these and other periodicals of interest to language arts teachers.

NCTE and IRA also organize yearly national conferences, which are held in major cities around the United States on a rotating basis. At these conferences teachers can listen to presentations by well-known authorities in language arts and by children's authors and illustrators, as well as by other classroom teachers who have developed innovative programs in their classrooms. Teachers can also meet in special interest groups to share ideas and concerns. Commercial publishers display textbooks and other instructional materials at the conferences. In addition, these two organizations have state and local affiliate groups that teachers can join. The affiliates also publish journals and organize conferences. The local groups enable teachers to meet other teachers with similar interests and concerns.

Elementary teachers can learn more about teaching writing by participation in workshops sponsored by affiliate groups of the National Writing Project (NWP). The NWP began as the Bay Area Writing Project at the University of California at Berkeley in 1974. It was conceived by James Gray and a group of English teachers who wanted to improve the quality of writing instruction in elementary and secondary schools. The NWP has spread to more than 150 affiliate groups located in almost every state and in Canada, Europe, and Asia; for example, the Gateway Writing Project serves the St. Louis area, the Capital Writing Project serves the Washington, DC, area, and the Oklahoma Writing Project serves the state of Oklahoma. In-service workshops are scheduled in school districts near each affiliate group. One principle on which the NWP is based is that the best teacher of other teachers is a teacher, and teachers who have been trained by the affiliate groups give presentations at the in-service workshops.

Teacher's Notebook

Magazines and Journals About Language Arts

Book Links
P.O. Box 1347
Elmhurst, IL 60126

CBC Features
Children's Book Council, Inc.
350 Scotland Rd.
Orange, NJ 07050

Childhood Education
Association for Childhood
  Education International
11141 Georgia Avenue, Suite
  200
Wheaton, MD 20902

The Elementary School Journal
University of Chicago Press
P.O. Box 37005
Chicago, IL 60637

The Good Apple Newspaper
P.O. Box 299
Carthage, IL 62321

The Horn Book
Park Square Building
31 Saint James Avenue
Boston, MA 02116

Language Arts
National Council of Teachers of
  English
1111 Kenyon Road
Urbana, IL 61801

Learning
530 University Avenue
Palo Alto, CA 94301

The Middle School Journal
National Middle School
  Association
P.O. Box 14882
Columbus, OH 43214

The New Advocate
480 Washington Street
Norwood, MA 02062

Primary Voices K–6
National Council of Teachers of
  English
1111 Kenyon Road
Urbana, IL 61801

The Reading Teacher
International Reading
  Association
800 Barksdale Road
P.O. Box 8139
Newark, DE 19711

Teaching K–8
P.O. Box 912
Farmingdale, NY 11737

*The WEB: Wonderfully Exciting
  Books*
The Ohio State University
200 Ramseyer Hall
Columbus, OH 43210

*The Whole Language Umbrella
  Newsletter*
P.O. Box 721326
Berkley, MI 48072

Writing Teacher
P.O. Box 791437
San Antonio, TX 78279

Each NWP affiliate group recruits experienced elementary teachers who have a special interest and/or expertise in teaching writing to participate in special summer training institutes. These teachers then serve as teacher/ consultants and make presentations at the in-service workshops. Many NWP affiliate groups also sponsor other workshops and study tours, young author conferences and workshops for student writers, and teacher-as-researcher projects that have direct classroom applications. For additional information about the National Writing Project or for the location of the NWP affiliate group nearest you, contact the National Writing Project, School of Education, University of California, Berkeley, CA 94720.

Review

Language arts instruction and assessment should be based on theories and research about how children learn and how they learn language in particular. This chapter has presented cognitive, psycholinguistic, and sociolinguistic theories of learning and related research to develop a paradigm for learning language arts in the elementary grades. The goal of language arts instruction is for students to develop communicative competence in the four language modes: listening, talking, reading, and writing. These four language modes are the substance of language arts instruction, and students use them in connection with literature focus units and across-the-curriculum theme studies in activities that are meaningful, functional, and genuine.

Extensions

1. Observe a language arts lesson being taught in an elementary classroom. Try to determine if the components of the language learning paradigm presented in this chapter are operational in the classroom. What conclusions can you draw about students' learning?
2. Observe and tape-record several students' talk. Analyze the development of their phonological, syntactic, semantic, and pragmatic language systems. If possible, compare primary-grade students' language with middle- and upper-grade students' language.
3. Observe in an elementary classroom and listen to students' oral language. Try to identify students'

use of each of the seven language functions discussed in this chapter. Also, examine the writing in their portfolios to determine which of the language functions they have used.
4. Interview an elementary teacher and ask how this teacher teaches the four language arts—listening, talking, reading, and writing. Or, ask how the teacher assesses students' learning. Compare the teacher's comments with the information in this chapter.
5. Sample several issues of three of the language arts magazines and journals listed in the Teacher's Notebook on page 29, and summarize your review in a brief paper.

References

Anthony, R. J., Johnson, T. D., Michelson, N. I., & Preece, A. (1991). *Evaluating literacy: A perspective for change.* Portsmouth, NH: Heinemann.

Applebee, A. N., & Langer, J. A. (1983). Instructional scaffolding: Reading and writing and natural language activities. *Language Arts, 60,* 168–175.

Baghban, M. (1984). *Our daughter learns to read and write: A case study from birth to three.* Newark, DE: International Reading Association.

Bissex, G. L. (1980). *Gnys at wrk: A child learns to write and read.* Cambridge, MA: Harvard University Press.

Brown, R. (1979). Some priorities in language arts education. *Language Arts, 56,* 483–484.

Bruner, J. S. (1978). The role of dialogue in language acquisition. In A. Sinclair, R. J. Jarvella, & W. M. Levelt (Eds.), *The child's conception of language* (pp. 241–256). New York: Springer-Verlag.

Butler, A., & Turbill, J. (1984). *Towards a reading-writing classroom.* Portsmouth, NH: Heinemann.

Camp, D. J. (1987). *Language functions used by four middle grade students.* Unpublished doctoral dissertation, Norman, University of Oklahoma.

Cazden, C. B. (1972). *Child language and education.* New York: Holt, Rinehart & Winston.

Cazden, C. B. (1983). Adult assistance to language development: Scaffolds, models, and direct instruction. In R. P. Parker & F. A. Davis (Eds.), *Developing literacy: Young children's use of language* (pp. 3–18). Newark, DE: International Reading Association.

Chomsky, C. (1969). *The acquisition of syntax in children from 5 to 10.* Cambridge, MA: MIT Press.

Chomsky, C. (1971). Write now, read later. *Childhood Education, 47,* 296–299.

Clark, E. V. (1971). On the acquisition of the meaning of *before* and *after*. *Journal of Verbal Learning and Verbal Behavior, 10,* 266–275.

DeStefano, J. S. (1978). *Language, the learner and the school.* New York: Wiley.

Edelsky, C., Altwerger, B., & Flores, B. (1991). *Whole language: What's the difference?* Portsmouth, NH: Heinemann.

Flexner, S. B. (1987). *The Random House dictionary of the English language* (2nd ed.). New York: Random House.

Goodman, K. S., Goodman, Y. M., & Hood, W. J. (1989). *The whole language evaluation book.* Portsmouth, NH: Heinemann.

Graves, D. H., & Sunstein, B. S. (Eds.). (1992). *Portfolio portraits.* Portsmouth, NH: Heinemann.

Halliday, M. A. K. (1973). *Explorations in the functions of language.* London: Edward Arnold.

Halliday, M. A. K. (1975). *Learning how to mean: Explorations in the development of language.* London: Edward Arnold.

Halliday, M. A. K. (1978). *Language as social semiotic: The social interpretation of language and meaning.* Baltimore: University Park Press.

Heath, S. B. (1983). *Ways with words: Language, life, and work in communities and classrooms.* Cambridge: Cambridge University Press.

Hymes, D. (1974). *Foundations in sociolinguistics: An ethnographic approach.* Philadelphia: University of Pennsylvania Press.

Ingram, D. (1975). If and when transformations are acquired by children. In D. P. Dato (Ed.), *Developmental psycholinguistics: Theory and applications* (pp. 99–127). Washington, DC: Georgetown University Press.

Jaggar, A. (1985). Allowing for language differences. In G. S. Pinnell (Ed.), *Discovering language with children* (pp. 25–28). Urbana, IL: National Council of Teachers of English.

Lindfors, J. W. (1987). *Children's language and learning* (2nd ed.). Englewood Cliffs, NJ: Prentice-Hall.

Loban, W. (1976). *Language development: Kindergarten through grade twelve* (Research Report No. 18). Urbana, IL: National Council of Teachers of English.

Loban, W. (1979). Relationships between language and literacy. *Language Arts, 56,* 485–486.

Morrow, L. M. (1989). *Literacy development in the early years: Helping children read and write.* Englewood Cliffs, NJ: Prentice-Hall.

Piaget, J. (1969). *The psychology of intelligence.* Paterson, NJ: Littlefield, Adams.

Piaget, J. (1975). *The development of thought: Equilibration of cognitive structures.* New York: Viking Press.

Pinnell, G. S. (1975). Language in primary classrooms. *Theory into Practice, 14,* 318–327.

Smith, F. (1975). *Comprehension and learning.* New York: Holt, Rinehart & Winston.

Smith, F. (1977). The uses of language. *Language Arts, 54,* 638–644.

Smith, F. (1979). The language arts and the learner's mind. *Language Arts, 56,* 118–125.

Vygotsky, L. S. (1978). *Mind in society.* Cambridge, MA: Harvard University Press.

Vygotsky, L. S. (1986). *Thought and language.* Cambridge, MA: MIT Press.

Children's Book References

Baylor, B. (1981). *Desert voices.* New York: Scribner.

Guiberson, B. Z. (1991). *Cactus hotel.* New York: Henry Holt.

Hague, M. (1985). *Aesop's fables.* New York: Holt, Rinehart & Winston.

Hirschi, R. (1992). *Desert.* New York: Bantam.

Kellogg, S. (1979). *Pinkerton, behave!* New York: Dial.

Lionni, L. (1985). *Frederick's fables.* New York: Pantheon.

Lobel, A. (1980). *Fables.* New York: Harper & Row.

Low, J. (1980). *Mice twice.* New York: Atheneum.

Lowry, L. (1989). *Number the stars.* Boston: Houghton Mifflin.

Martin, Bill, Jr. (1983). *Brown bear, brown bear, what do you see?* New York: Holt, Rinehart & Winston.

Sendak, M. (1963). *Where the wild things are.* New York: Harper & Row.

Siebert, D. (1988). *Mojave.* New York: HarperCollins.

Taylor, B. (1992). *Desert life.* New York: Dorling Kindersley.

PRO-File
Fourth Graders Become Authors

> *I have an author's corner in my classroom because it changes my students' attitudes about reading and writing. I want them to see a real purpose for becoming literate. Getting good grades is not reason enough for many children to learn.*

Pat Bishop
Fourth-Grade Teacher
Heaton Elementary School

PROCEDURE

I have set up an author's corner—you might call it a center—in our classroom with the materials and supplies for making books, a rack to display the students' hand-made books, and information about authors we study during the year. The information about authors includes brochures, posters, autobiographies, and videotapes and other audiovisual materials. Each month I also highlight an author with a bulletin board display, and I set out a text set of the author's books. I choose authors that my students have already read at least one book by, because I want them to be able to read the books independently. I choose authors who write stories, informational books, and poems, and I also try to choose living authors so that interested students can write to them. A list of our featured authors for this year is shown in the accompanying figure.

On the first day of school, I begin talking about making books and show three or four sample books that my students have made in previous years. Later during the first week, the first book we make is a class collaboration, one of those writing activities in which every student contributes a page. I demonstrate how to make a hardcover book and the care and pride that go along with it. Students often do their work quickly and hand it in to the teacher without any pride of ownership; that's something that making books changes.

Then, whenever we are doing a writing project, I'll just mention that if students have a particularly good piece, they may want to make it into a book. Not every student makes a hardcover book from the same writing project; instead, two or three students are always making a book.

We use the writing process to make books. Students begin by prewriting about personal experiences, about a book we have read, or as part of a social studies or science theme cycle. They write rough drafts and meet in writing groups to share their writing. A classmate will comment that this writing is so good that it should be made into a book, and that's usually when students first decide to turn their writing into books. Then students carefully revise and edit their writing and recopy it into the book they have made. Our books aren't elaborate—we use cardboard for the covers and colored tape for the binding. Students draw a picture or decorate the covers with contact paper. Then they use press-on letters for the title and author.

ASSESSMENT

My goal is for every student to make 10 books during fourth grade. When they make their first book, students add their name to our Author's Chart. Around the outside of the chart I've made a collage of pictures of authors my students love—such as Steven Kellogg and Byrd Baylor—and after students have read their book aloud to the class, they each add their name by signing the list. I've made it sort of a ritual—a rite of passage—from student to author. Then students read their books to their family, to students in another class, to the principal, to other groups of children—to whoever will listen. We keep the book in our classroom library all year, but the author can check it out whenever he or she wants to.

After a month or two, I check the list to see which students haven't written a book yet (usually five or six children) and work with them as a group to select something they have already written or a topic for a new piece. Then these students work as a writing group to support and encourage each other to make their books. I talk with the students to get to know them better as readers and writers. I also gauge their language arts skills and their confidence. It's often a lack of confidence that keeps them from publishing a book sooner.

ADAPTATIONS

I believe that every student in my class is capable of making a book, even my immigrant students who are learning English and the students who have difficulty reading and writing. This is possible because my students make so many different kinds of books. My more capable students often write stories, autobiographical events, and reports that are 8 to 10 pages long. Some of my other students write 4- and 5-page books with a picture on each page. Ricardo, for example, made an animal book with a drawing of an animal on each page and a one-word label with the animal's name. He wrote another drawing-and-label book about Plains Indians when we were studying Native Americans. Other books that my less capable writers are successful making include:

- "I Like _____ " and other sentence stem books
- Color books
- Joke and riddle books
- Number and alphabet books
- Pattern books, such as *Purple Is Part of a Rainbow* (Kowalczyk, 1985) and *A House Is a House for Me* (Hoberman, 1978)

REFLECTIONS

I want my students to think of themselves as authors, not students. When they are authors, they look at reading and writing differently. They are members of the "literacy club"; that's what Frank Smith (1988) calls it. I want all my students to become part of this club, and learning about authors and publishing their own books does it. Becoming authors literally changes their lives.

Featured Authors	
September	Steven Kellogg
October	Byrd Baylor
November	Patricia Polacco
December	Marvin Terban
January	Jack Prelutsky
February	William Steig
March	Ruth Heller
April	Aliki
May	Jane Yolen

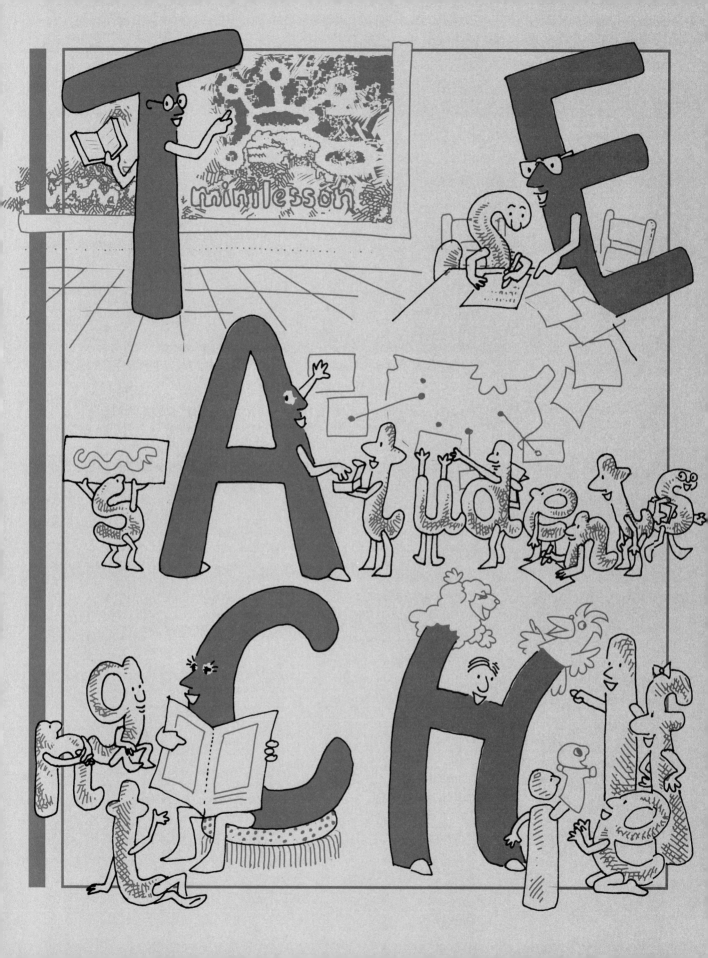

2

Teaching Language Arts

There are three ways to organize for language arts instruction. One approach is literature focus units. Teachers divide the school day into blocks and use literature as the basis of their units in the language arts block. A second approach is theme cycles. Teachers teach thematically and incorporate all content areas, including language arts, under an umbrella theme such as "changes." Or, third, teachers use a workshop approach for language arts instruction in which students read self-selected books and write on self-selected topics. Some teachers use one approach most of the time, and others alternate or adapt the approaches to meet their needs. As you think about organizing for instruction, one question is:

What are the benefits and drawbacks of each of the three approaches for organizing for instruction?

anguage arts instruction should be based on how children learn and how they learn language. More than 20 years ago, Carl Lefevre (1970) advised that language learning in school should "parallel [children's] early childhood method of learning to speak [their] native tongue—playfully, through delighted experiences of discovery—through repeated exposure to language forms and patterns, by creating imitation and manipulation, and by personal trial and error, with kindly (and not too much) correction from adults" (p. 75). Lefevre's vision is finally becoming a reality as teachers are basing instruction on cognitive, psycholinguistic, and sociolinguistic theories of learning.

Two fundamental responsibilities of elementary teachers, according to Lindfors (1989), are to provide a language-rich learning environment in the classroom and to support students in their use of it. Donald Graves (1991) admonishes teachers to build a literate environment that facilitates the development of lifelong readers and writers. The classroom environment reflects teachers' goals for their students. Classrooms with publishing centers and library centers filled with books and reading response projects reflect teachers' expectations for their students.

The teacher's role is to involve students in meaningful, functional, and genuine language learning activities. One way to create a language arts program is through theme cycles (Goodman, 1986). Units may focus on literature, social studies, or science. The second way is through reading and writing workshops (Atwell, 1987; Harwayne, 1992). In the workshop approach students read self-selected books, and they read and write about topics that interest them. We recommend that teachers incorporate a combination of both approaches in their instructional programs. Assessment, too, reflects theories about how children learn and documents how students use listening, talking, reading, and writing in language arts activities and across the curriculum.

LANGUAGE-RICH CLASSROOMS

Elementary classrooms should be authentic language environments that encourage students to listen, talk, read, and write; that is, they should be language-rich (Lindfors, 1989). As Susan Hepler (1991) explains, "The real challenge to teachers . . . is to set up the kind of classroom community where children pick their own ways to literacy" (p. 179). The physical arrangement and materials provided in the classroom play an important role in setting the stage for listening, talking, reading, and writing.

In the past, textbooks were the primary instructional material, and students sat in desks arranged in rows facing the teacher. Now a wide variety of instructional materials are available in addition to textbooks, including trade books, newspapers, and audiovisual materials. Students' desks are more often arranged in small groups, and classrooms are visually stimulating with signs, posters, charts, and other teacher-made and student-made displays related to the units and theme cycles.

These are components of a language-rich classroom:

- Desks arranged in groups to facilitate cooperative learning
- Classroom libraries stocked with many different kinds of reading materials
- Posted messages about the current day

Language-rich classrooms facilitate children's learning.

- Displays of student work and projects
- A chair designated as the author's chair
- Displayed signs, labels for items, and quotations
- Posted directions for activities or use of equipment
- Materials for recording language, including pencils, pens, paper, journals, books, typewriters, and computers
- Special places for reading and writing activities
- Reference materials related to literature focus units and social studies and science theme cycles
- A listening center and other audiovisual materials
- A puppet stage or an area for presenting plays and storytelling
- Charts on which students record information (e.g., sign-in charts for attendance or writing group charts)
- World-related print (e.g., newspapers, maps, and calendars)
- Reading and writing materials in primary students' play centers (Adapted from Hall, 1987)

Figure 2–1 elaborates on these components of a language-rich classroom.

The Physical Arrangement

No one physical arrangement best represents a language-rich classroom, but the configuration of any classroom can be modified to include many of the desirable characteristics. Student desks or tables should be grouped to encourage students to talk, share, and work cooperatively. Separate areas are needed for reading and writing, a classroom library, a listening center, centers for materials related to content area theme studies, and a center for dramatic activities. Kindergarten classrooms also need play centers. Some variations

Figure 2–1   Characteristics of a Language-Rich Classroom

1. **Classroom Organization**

   * Desks are arranged in groups.
   * The arrangement facilitates group interaction.
   * Other parts of the classroom are organized into centers such as the library center, writing center, and theme center.

2. **Classroom Library Center**

   * There are at least four times as many books as there are students in the classroom.
   * Stories, informational books, and poetry are included.
   * Multicultural books and other reading materials are included.
   * Information about authors and illustrators is displayed.
   * Some of the books were written by students.
   * Books related to literature focus units and theme cycles are highlighted.
   * Students monitor the center.

3. **Message Center**

   * Schedules and announcements about the current day are posted.
   * Some of the announcements are student-initiated.
   * There are mailboxes and/or a message board for students to use.
   * Students are encouraged to write notes to classmates.

4. **Display of Student Work and Projects**

   * All students have work displayed in the classroom.
   * Student work reflects a variety of curricular areas.
   * Students' projects and other student-made displays are exhibited in the classroom.
   * There is an area where students can display their own work.
   * Other student work is stored in portfolios.

5. **Author's Chair**

   * One chair in the classroom has been designated as the author's chair for students to use when sharing their writing.
   * The author's chair is labeled.

6. **Signs, Labels, and Quotations**

   * Equipment and other classroom items are labeled.
   * Words, phrases, and sentences are posted in the classroom.
   * Some signs, labels, and quotes are written by students.

obviously occur at various grade levels, kindergarten through eighth grade. Older students, for example, use reference centers with materials related to the units and themes they are studying. The three diagrams in Figure 2–2 suggest ways to make the classroom design language-rich.

Three important centers in language-rich classrooms are library centers, listening centers, and writing centers. Library centers are stocked with trade books that are attractively displayed and available for students to peruse. These books might be from the teacher's own collection or borrowed from the school or public library. Many of the books should relate to units of study, and

Figure 2–1 continued

---

7. Directions

- Directions are provided in the classroom so that students can work independently.
- Some of the directions are written by students.

8. Materials for Writing

- Pencils, pens, paper, journals, books, computers, and other materials are available for recording language.
- Students have access to these materials.

9. Places for Reading and Writing

- There are special places in the classroom for reading and writing activities.
- These areas are quiet and separated from other areas.

10. Reference Materials

- Word walls list important words related to literature focus units and theme cycles.
- Lists, clusters, pictures, charts, books, models, and other reference materials are available for content area study.
- Artifacts and other items related to theme cycles are labeled and displayed.
- Students use these materials as they work on projects related to theme cycles.

11. Audiovisual Materials

- A listening center is available for students to use.
- Audiovisual materials—such as CD-ROM, filmstrips, videotapes, and films—related to literature focus units and theme cycles are available.
- The equipment needed to use these audiovisual materials is available in the classroom.

12. Dramatic Center

- A puppet stage is set up in the classroom.
- Art materials are available for making puppets and other props.
- An area in the classroom is accessible for presenting plays and telling stories.
- Props are available in the classroom.
- Primary-grade classrooms have dramatic play centers, including reading and writing materials.

---

these should be changed periodically. Other books for students to read independently are also included in the library center. After studying library centers in classrooms, Leslie Morrow (1989) makes the following 10 recommendations:

1. The library center should be inviting and afford privacy.
2. The library center should have a physical definition, with shelves, carpets, benches, sofas, or other partitions.
3. Five or six students should fit comfortably in the center at one time.

KINDERGARTEN CLASSROOM

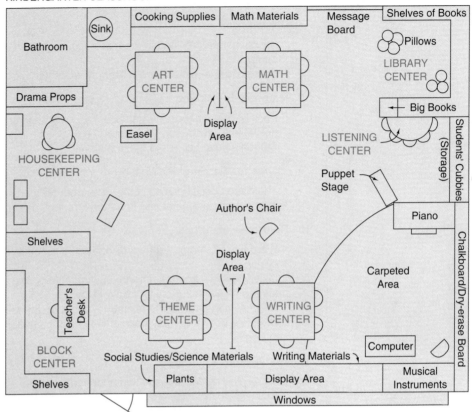

Figure 2–2 Diagrams of Language-Rich Classrooms

4. Two kinds of bookshelves are needed. Most of the collection should be shelved with the spines facing outward, but some books should be set so that the front covers are displayed.
5. Books should be shelved by category and color coded by type.
6. Books written by one author or related to a theme being studied should be displayed prominently, and the displays should be changed regularly.
7. The floor should be covered with a rug and the area furnished with pillows, beanbag chairs, or comfortable furniture.
8. The center should be stocked with at least four times as many books as students in the classroom.
9. A variety of types of reading materials, including books, newspapers, magazines, posters, and charts, should be included in the center.
10. Attractive posters that encourage reading, especially if they relate to books in the library center, should be added.

These recommendations were based on research in primary-grade classrooms, but they are equally appropriate for middle- and upper-grade students.

Listening centers equipped with tape players and headphones are another essential part of language-rich classrooms. Students listen to cassette tapes of stories and sometimes follow along in accompanying books, if they are available. Many commercially prepared tape recordings of children's books

THIRD-GRADE CLASSROOM

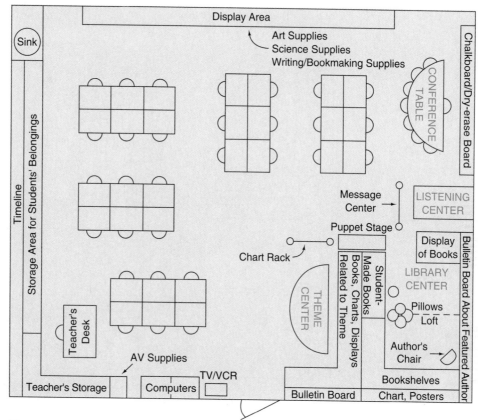

Figure 2–2 *continued*

are available, and teachers can tape-record their own reading of books so that students can reread books and listen again and again to their favorite stories. Too often teachers think of listening centers as equipment for primary-grade classrooms and do not realize their potential usefulness with older students.

Supplies of writing and art materials for students to use as they write books and respond to books they read are stored in writing centers. These materials include:

- A variety of pens, pencils, crayons, markers, and other writing and drawing instruments
- Lined and unlined paper of varied sizes and colors
- Materials for making and binding books
- One or more computers with word-processing systems and printers
- A camera and film for taking illustration photos and photos of students for their "All About the Author" pages
- Scrap art materials for illustrations

In primary-grade classrooms, there is usually a table in the center where students gather to write and share their writing. In middle- and upper-grade classrooms, however, writing materials are stored on shelves or in cabinets, and students usually write at their own desks. They meet with the teacher at a

SIXTH-GRADE CLASSROOM

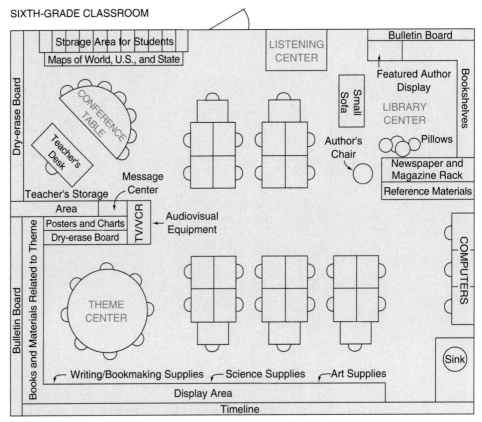

Figure 2–2   *continued*

conference table or with small groups of classmates to revise their writing wherever there is space in the classroom.

Textbooks

Textbooks are one tool for teaching language arts procedures, concepts, and strategies and skills. They are the most accessible resource that teachers have, and they have some benefits. Information about language arts topics and a sequence of topics for each grade level are provided. Textbooks present models, examples, and practice activities. These tools provide security for beginning teachers. There are drawbacks, however. The textbook's format is probably its greatest drawback because it is inappropriate for many language activities. Listening, talking, reading, and writing activities involve much more than can be contained in a single textbook. Other weaknesses are:

- Little attention to listening and talking
- Excessive emphasis on grammar and usage skills
- Emphasis on rote memorization of strategies and skills rather than on effective communication
- Focus on correctness rather than on experimentation with language
- Few opportunities to individualize instruction
- Difficulty in connecting textbook activities to literature focus units and across-the-curriculum theme cycles

Graves (1977) has admonished that textbooks cannot be the only instructional material for teaching language arts. Collections of trade books, tape recordings, puppets, concrete materials, notebooks, paper, and pencils are other necessary materials. Teachers cannot assume that textbooks are equivalent to the total language arts program. To start on the first page of the language arts textbook on the first day of school and to continue page by page through the textbook fails to consider the students' language learning needs. Instead, we recommend that textbooks serve as only one resource for the language arts program.

Trade Books

Trade books are books written for children that are not textbooks, and thousands of excellent trade books are currently available for elementary students. Trade books can be categorized in several ways. The format of the book is one consideration. Trade books are formatted as either picture books or chapter books. *Genre* is another consideration. Stories, informational books, and poems are three general categories of genre.

Picture Books. Picture books have brief texts, usually spread over 32 pages in which text and illustrations combine to tell a story or present information. The text is minimal, and the illustrations are often used to supplement the sparse text. The illustrations in many picture books are striking. Many picture books, such as Maurice Sendak's *Where the Wild Things Are* (1963), are appropriate for young children, but others, such as Chris Van Allsburg's *Jumanji* (1981), were written with middle-grade students in mind. Fairy tales, myths, and legends have also been retold beautifully as picture books. One example is Trina Schart Hyman's *The Sleeping Beauty* (1977).

Many informational books, such as *Frogs, Toads, Lizards, and Salamanders* (Parker & Wright, 1990), are published in picture book format. Single poems and collections of poems are also published as picture books. Longfellow's poem "Paul Revere's Ride" was recently published as a picture book with Ted Rand's (1990) brilliant illustrations on each page, and Larrick's collection of cat poems, *Cats Are Cats* (1988), is sensitively illustrated by Ed Young. The coveted Caldecott Medal, given annually for the best illustrations in a children's book published during the preceding year, has honored many picture books. A list of books that have won this prestigious award is included in Appendix A.

Wordless picture books are a special type of picture book. They are similar to picture books but contain no text. The story is told or the information is provided entirely through the pictures, which makes this type of book particularly useful for children who are learning English as a second language or are novice readers. Books such as the hilarious *Frog Goes to Dinner* (Mayer, 1974) and Goodall's wordless retelling of *Little Red Riding Hood* (1988) are popular with primary- and middle-grade students. Other books, such as *Anno's U.S.A.* (Anno, 1983) and *The Story of a Castle* (Goodall, 1986), appeal to middle- and upper-grade students because they can be connected to social studies and science themes.

Chapter Books. Chapter books are longer story and informational books written for elementary students in chapter format. Most are written for middle-

and upper-grade students, but Patricia Reilly Giff (1984) has written a series of stories about the kids at the Polk Street School for students reading at the second-grade level. Chapter books for middle-grade students include *Ramona Quimby, Age 8* (Cleary, 1981) and *Bunnicula* (Howe & Howe, 1979). Chapter books have only a few illustrations, if any, and the illustrations, usually small black-and-white sketches, do not play an integral role in the book.

Informational books are also written in this chapter format. *The Riddle of the Rosetta Stone* (Giblin, 1990) and *Buffalo Hunt* (Freedman, 1988a) are two examples. In informational books, illustrations (often photographs and diagrams) are used to support the text, but they are not as integral as in picture books. They also often include a table of contents, a glossary, and an index. A number of chapter books, such as *Sarah, Plain and Tall* (MacLachlan, 1985), *The Whipping Boy* (Fleischman, 1986), and *Lincoln: A Photobiography* (Freedman, 1988b), have received the Newbery Medal for distinguished children's literature. In contrast to the Caldecott Medal, awarded for outstanding illustrations, the Newbery is given for distinguished prose. Appendix A also lists the books that have received this award.

Stories.   Most stories for younger children, such as *Sylvester and the Magic Pebble* (Steig, 1969), are picture books, and stories for older children, including Natalie Babbitt's *Tuck Everlasting* (1975) and C. S. Lewis's *The Lion, the Witch and the Wardrobe* (1950), are chapter books. One exception is Arnold Lobel's series of Frog and Toad stories (1970, 1972, 1976, 1979) which have been published in a chapter book format for primary-grade students.

Three types of stories are traditional literature, fantasies, and realistic stories. Stories that began hundreds and hundreds of years ago and were passed from generation to generation by storytellers before being written down are traditional literature. Fantasies are stories that could not really take place, set in worlds that the author creates. Many stories have talking animals, such as *Charlotte's Web* (White, 1952). Realistic stories are lifelike and believable, without magic or supernatural powers. Some stories are set in the past and others in the present. Figure 2–3 presents information about the three types of stories, including some examples of each.

Informational Books.   Informational books provide information on social studies, science, math, art, music, and other topics. Some are written in a story format, such as *Octopus* (Carrick, 1978), *Castle* (Macaulay, 1977), and *Sugaring Time* (Lasky, 1983), while others are written in a more traditional informational style, with a table of contents, an index, and a glossary. Examples of traditional informational books are *Money* (Elkin, 1983) and *The Human Body* (Caselli, 1987). Some informational books are written for young children, with a phrase or sentence of text presented on each page along with a large photograph or illustration. Gibbons's *The Post Office Book: Mail and How It Moves* (1982) is an informative description of what happens to a letter after it is mailed, and cartoonlike drawings supplement the sparse text. *My Puppy Is Born* (Cole, 1991) uses photographs to illustrate a puppy's birth and first 8 weeks of life.

Another type of informational book presents language arts concepts, including opposites, homonyms, and comparisons. One example is Burningham's *Opposites* (1985), which presents pairs of opposites (e.g., *hard* and

Figure 2–3   Three Types of Stories

Type	Characteristics	Examples
Traditional Literature	These stories began hundreds and hundreds of years ago and were passed from generation to generation by storytellers before being written down. Traditional literature includes: • *Fables.* Fables are brief narratives designed to teach a moral. The first fables are attributed to the Greek slave Aesop. • *Folktales and fairy tales.* In these short stories, the problem usually revolves around a journey from home to perform some task, a journey that involves a confrontation with a monster, a miraculous change from a harsh home to a secure home, or a wise beast–foolish beast confrontation. Characters are portrayed in one dimension—good or bad, stupid or clever, or industrious or lazy. Stories often begin with "Once upon a time . . . ," and the end is happy with the good characters living ". . . happily ever after." Many versions of these stories are available, and variants are found in many cultures. • *Myths.* People around the world have created myths to explain the creation of natural phenomena. The characters are often heroes with supernatural powers, or magical powers are used. • *Legends.* Legends are old stories that are thought to have some basis in history but are not verifiable, such as stories about Johnny Appleseed or Paul Bunyan. They exemplify many of the same elements as myths, and the hero does something important enough to be remembered in story.	Aardema, V. (1975). *Why mosquitoes buzz in people's ears.* New York: Dial. (P–M) Carrick, C. (1989). *Aladdin and the wonderful lamp.* New York: Scholastic. (M) D'Aulaire, I., & D'Aulaire, E. P. (1962). *D'Aulaires' book of Greek myths.* Garden City, NY: Doubleday. (M–U) Galdone, P. (1975). *The gingerbread boy.* New York: Seabury. (P) Hague, M. (1985). *Aesop's fables.* New York: Holt, Rinehart & Winston. (P–M) Hamilton, V. (1985). *The people could fly: American black folktales.* New York: Knopf. (M–U) Hyman, T. S. (1977). *The sleeping beauty.* Boston: Little, Brown. (P–M) Kellogg, S. (1984). *Paul Bunyan.* New York: Morrow. (M) Steptoe, J. (1984). *The story of jumping mouse.* New York: Mulberry. (M) Stevens, J. (1987). *The three billy goats Gruff.* San Diego: Harcourt Brace Jovanovich. (P)
Fantasies	Fantasies are stories that could not really take place. Authors create new worlds for their characters, but these worlds must be based in reality so that readers will believe that they exist. Fantasy includes: • *Modern literary tales.* These stories are related to folktales and fairy tales because they include many characteristics of traditional literature, but they have been written recently and have identifiable authors. The best-known author is Hans Christian Andersen.	Howe, D., & Howe, J. (1979). *Bunnicula: A rabbit-tale of mystery.* New York: Atheneum. (M–U) Lewis, C. S. (1950). *The lion, the witch and the wardrobe.* New York: Macmillan. (U) Norton, M. (1980). *The borrowers.* New York: Harcourt Brace Jovanovich. (M–U) Scieszka, J. (1989). *The true story of the three little pigs.* New York: Viking. (P–M) Sendak, M. (1983). *Where the wild things are.* New York: Harper & Row. (P) Sleator, W. (1984). *Interstellar pig.* New York: Dutton. (U)

Figure 2–3   *continued*

Type	Characteristics	Examples
	• *Fantastic stories.* Fantastic stories are realistic in most details, but some events require readers to suspend disbelief. Main characters may be personified animals or toys, eccentric people, or extraordinary beings. • *Science fiction.* In science fiction stories, authors create a world in which science interacts with every area of society. Stories are set in the future, there is detailed description of scientific facts, and characters believe in advanced technology. • *High fantasy.* Heroes confront evil for the good of humanity in these long, complex stories. Often the time expands and constricts so that the story moves back and forth in time.	Steig, W. (1969). *Sylvester and the magic pebble.* New York: Simon & Schuster. (M) Van Allsburg, C. (1981). *Jumanji.* Boston: Houghton Mifflin. (M) White, E. B. (1952). *Charlotte's web.* New York: Harper & Row. (M–U)
Realistic Stories	Realistic stories are lifelike and believable, without magic or supernatural powers. The outcome is reasonable, and the story seems truthful. Two types are: • *Contemporary fiction.* In these stories readers identify with characters their own age who have similar interests and problems. Stories often deal with everyday occurrences or "relevant subjects." • *Historical fiction.* These stories are set in the past, and the setting influences the plot. The themes of these stories are universal, both within the historical period of the book and for today.	Blume, J. (1972). *Tales of a fourth grade nothing.* New York: Dutton. (M) Cleary, B. (1983). *Dear Mr. Henshaw.* New York: Morrow. (M–U) Coerr, B. (1977). *Sadako and the thousand paper cranes.* New York: Putnam. (M) Lowry, L. (1989). *Number the stars.* Boston: Houghton Mifflin. (M–U) MacLachlan, P. (1985). *Sarah, plain and tall.* New York: Harper & Row. (M) Mathis, S. B. (1975). *The hundred penny box.* New York: Viking. (M) Naylor, P. R. (1991). *Shiloh.* New York: Atheneum. (M–U) Speare, E. G. (1983). *The sign of the beaver.* Boston: Houghton Mifflin. (M–U) Viorst, J. (1972). *Alexander and the terrible, horrible, no good, very bad day.* New York: Atheneum. (M–U) Waber, B. (1972). *Ira sleeps over.* Boston: Houghton Mifflin. (P)

P = primary grades (K–2); M = middle grades (3–5); U = upper grades (6–8).

soft) illustrated on each two-page spread. ABC books are informational books, too. Although many ABC books are designed for very young children, others are appropriate for elementary students, such as *The National Air and Space Museum ABC* (Mayers, 1986). Donald Crews's books are among the most beautiful; in *Carousel* (1982), for example, Crews combines paintings and photographs to create the sounds and sights of a carousel ride.

Biographies are another type of informational book. Most biographies are chapter books, such as Hamilton's *Paul Robeson: The Life and Times of a Free Black Man* (1974), but several authors have written shorter biographies that resemble picture books. Perhaps the best-known biographer for younger children is David Adler, who has written *A Picture Book of Helen Keller* (1990) and *A Picture Book of Abraham Lincoln* (1989). Jean Fritz has written a very popular series of biographies of Revolutionary War figures such as *Will You Sign Here, John Hancock?* (1976). A few autobiographies have also been written for children, and one that is popular with upper-grade students is Roald Dahl's *Boy* (1984).

Poems. Many delightful books of poetry for children are available today. Some are collections of poems on a single topic written by one poet, such as *Tyrannosaurus Was a Beast* (Prelutsky, 1988) about dinosaurs, and Fleischman's *Joyful Noise: Poems for Two Voices* (1988) about insects. Other collections of poetry on a single topic selected by a compiler are Hopkins's *Good Morning to You, Valentine* (1976) and Carle's *Animals, Animals* (1989). Two excellent anthologies (collections of poems written by different poets on a variety of topics) are *The Random House Book of Poetry for Children* (Prelutsky, 1983) for younger children and *Knock at a Star: A Child's Introduction to Poetry* (Kennedy & Kennedy, 1982) for older children.

These types of books can be used to teach language arts or any other content area. As an illustration, Figure 2–4 presents a text set (or collection) of books on the American Revolution. Students will read stories, poems, biographies, and other informational books to learn much more about the Revolutionary War and life in those times than could ever be presented in a social studies textbook. The main drawback to using trade books is that they are not sequenced and prepackaged as textbooks are. Instead, teachers must make choices and design activities to accompany the books. Similar text sets of trade books can be collected for almost any topic.

Computers

Computers are becoming more and more a part of elementary classrooms. At first they were used primarily in mathematics, but they have great potential for all areas of the curriculum, including language arts. Several instructional uses are possible with computers. Robert Taylor (1980) suggests that computers have three educational applications: They serve as tool, tutor, and tutee.

Perhaps the most valuable application of the computer in the language arts classroom is as a tool. Students can use computers with word-processing programs to create stories, poems, and other kinds of writing (Dickinson, 1986; DeGroff, 1990; Genishi, 1988). The computer simplifies revising and editing and eliminates the tedium of recopying compositions. Several word-processing programs, such as *Bank Street Writer III, Writing Workshop,*

Figure 2–4   A Text Set of Books on the American Revolution

Stories

Avi. (1984). *The fighting ground.* New York: HarperCollins. (U)

Benchley, N. (1969). *Sam the minuteman.* New York: Harper & Row. (P)

Benchley, N. (1977). *George the drummer boy.* New York: HarperCollins. (P)

Berleth, R. (1990). *Samuel's choice.* New York: Whitman. (M–U)

Brady, E. W. (1988). *Toliver's secret.* New York: Crown. (U)

Collier, J. L., & Collier, C. (1983). *War comes to Willy Freeman.* New York: Delacorte. (U)

Forbes, E. (1970). *Johnny Tremain: A story of Boston in revolt.* Boston: Houghton Mifflin. (M–U)

Haugaard, E. C. (1983). *Adventures of John Paul Jones.* Boston: Houghton Mifflin. (M–U)

Jensen, D. (1989). *The riddle of Penncroft Farm.* San Diego: Harcourt Brace Jovanovich. (U)

Lawson, R. (1953). *Mr. Revere and I.* Boston: Little, Brown. (M–U)

Rappaport, D. (1988). *The Boston coffee party.* New York: HarperCollins. (P–M)

Roop, P., & Roop, C. (1986). *Buttons for General Washington.* Minneapolis: Carolrhoda. (P–M)

Informational Books

Carter, A. (1992). *The American Revolution: War for independence.* New York: Watts. (U)

D'Amato, A., & D'Amato, J. (1975). *Colonial crafts for you to make.* New York: Messner. (M)

Foster, G. (1970). *Year of independence, 1776.* New York: Scribner. (U)

Fradin, D. B. (1988). *The Declaration of Independence.* Chicago: Childrens Press. (M)

Johnson, N. (1992). *The battle of Lexington and Concord.* New York: Four Winds Press. (M–U)

Leckie, R. (1973). *The world turned upside down: The story of the American Revolution.* New York: Putnam. (M–U)

Loeper, J. J. (1973). *Going to school in 1776.* New York: Atheneum. (M)

McDowell, B. (1980). *Revolutionary War: America's fight for freedom* (4th ed.). Washington, DC: National Geographic Society. (M–U)

Meltzer, M. (1987). *The American revolutionaries: A history in their own words, 1750–1800.* New York: HarperCollins. (U)

Swanson, J. (1991). *David Bushnell and his turtle: The story of America's first submarine.* New York: Atheneum. (M–U)

Biographies

Adler, D. A. (1990). *A picture book of Benjamin Franklin.* New York: Holiday House. (P)

Aliki. (1988). *The many lives of Benjamin Franklin.* New York: Simon & Schuster. (M)

Evans, E. (1975). *Weathering the storm: Women of the revolution.* New York: Scribner. (M–U)

Fritz, J. (1977). *Can't you make them behave, King George?* New York: Putnam. (M–U)

Fritz, J. (1973). *And then what happened, Paul Revere?* New York: Coward-McCann. (M–U)

Fritz, J. (1975). *Where was Patrick Henry on the 29th of May?* New York: Coward-McCann. (M–U)

Fritz, J. (1976). *Will you sign here, John Hancock?* New York: Coward-McCann. (M–U)

Fritz, J. (1981). *Traitor: The case of Benedict Arnold.* New York: Viking. (U)

Giblin, J. C. (1992). *George Washington: A picture biography.* New York: Scholastic. (M)

Meltzer, M. (1986). *George Washington and the birth of our nation.* New York: Watts. (U)

Meltzer, M. (1991). *Thomas Jefferson: The revolutionary aristocrat.* New York: Watts. (U)

Stevenson, A. (1983). *Molly Pitcher: Young patriot.* New York: Aladdin Books. (M–U)

Poems

Bangs, E. (1984). *Yankee Doodle.* New York: Four Winds Press. (P–M)

Benet, R., & Benet, S. V. (1961). *A book of Americans.* New York: Henry Holt. (U)

Fisher, L. E. (1976). *Liberty book.* New York: Doubleday. (M–U)

Hopkins, L. B. (1977). *Beat the drum: Independence day has come.* San Diego: Harcourt Brace Jovanovich. (P–M)

Longfellow, H. W. (1990). *Paul Revere's ride.* New York: Dutton. (M–U)

FirstWriter, Magic Slate, and *Quill,* have been developed especially for elementary students and are easy to learn to use.

Computers with word-processing programs can be used effectively to record young children's language experience stories (Barber, 1982; Smith, 1985). Teachers take children's dictation as they do in traditional language experience activities, but using a computer rather than paper and pencil. After entering the child's dictation, the child and the teacher read the text and make revisions. Next the text is printed out, and the child can add a drawing. If the child has already drawn a picture, the printout can be cut and taped onto the drawing. The computer simplifies the process of taking children's dictation because teachers can record dictation more quickly than they can write, the dictation can be revised easily, and a clean copy of the revised text can be printed out.

Whereas teachers can use computers to record language experience stories for children, first- and second-grade students can write their own compositions on the word processor. For an interesting report of first graders writing on a computer, check Phenix and Hannan's article "Word Processing in the Grade One Classroom" (1984). Their first graders wrote and revised a variety of compositions on computers and "learned that writing does not have to come out right the first time, that it can be manipulated by the author, that a writer has to take risks, that revising is a normal way writing is done" (p. 812).

Students can also use the word processor to write notes and letters to classmates and pen pals. They write these letters on the computer, revise and edit them, and then transmit them using a modem hooked up to the computer. The *Quill* word-processing program, for instance, includes a Mailbag for exchanging messages.

A second application is as tutor—a use known as *computer-assisted instruction.* Instructional software programs are available for drill and practice, educational games, simulations, and tutorials. Programmed instruction in language skills such as letter sounds, parts of speech, and affixes is currently available. Many programs resemble textbook exercises except that they are presented on a monitor screen rather than in a book. Even though students enjoy using computers, it is important to remember that some activities are little more than electronic workbooks and are subject to the same criticisms as language arts textbooks. High-quality software programs can be useful, however, in providing individualized practice on a particular topic.

The number of software programs has grown tremendously in the past few years; some are effective, but others are inferior. Chomsky (1984) says the primary criterion in identifying high-quality software programs is whether they stimulate students to think about language in new and creative ways. Because of both quality and cost considerations, it is important to preview software carefully before purchasing it. Students should also help preview software programs and offer opinions and recommendations.

A third computer application is as tutee. Students can learn computer languages, such as Logo, and how to program computers. Students who are gifted can especially benefit from learning computer languages as a way of extending their repertoire of communication modes.

In summarizing the promises and pitfalls of computers in the classroom, Zaharias (1983) concludes that the small number of computers available in elementary classrooms restricts their usefulness. More than 10 years later this conclusion is, unfortunately, still valid. Because few computers are available, few students have the opportunity to use them regularly. Educators continue to strive to find ways to make computers more available to elementary students. As computers increasingly become an integral part of daily life, it seems inevitable that they will become more available in the classroom.

INSTRUCTIONAL APPROACHES

Three approaches for teaching language arts are literature focus units, theme cycles, and reading-writing workshops. All three approaches embody the characteristics of learning described in Chapter 1, and they provide opportunities for students to be involved in meaningful, functional, and genuine activities. We recommend that students have opportunities to participate in all three approaches.

Literature Focus Units

In literature focus units students read books and respond to them together as a class or in small groups. Because students are reading together, they share their interpretations about the story and become a community of readers. Sometimes students read a single book, and at other times they may read a collection of books by the same author, in the same genre, or on a theme or other topic. Four components of literature focus units are:

1. *Reading books.* Students read books together as a class or in small groups. Students may read independently or together with a partner, or they may read along as the teacher (or a capable reader) reads the book aloud.
2. *Responding.* Students respond to the book to record their initial impressions of it and to develop their interpretations. Students write in reading logs and participate in discussions called *grand conversations.*
3. *Teaching minilessons.* Teachers teach minilessons on language arts procedures, concepts, and strategies and skills and connect the lesson to books students are reading or compositions they are writing (Atwell, 1987). These lessons are brief explanations, discussions, and demonstrations usually completed in 15 minutes or less. The steps in teaching a minilesson are based on the teaching strategy presented in Chapter 1. The steps are:
   • Introduce the language arts procedure, concept, or strategy or skill.
   • Share examples of the topic using children's writing or trade books written for children.
   • Provide information about the topic and make connections to trade books or to children's writing.
   • Have students make notes about the topic on a poster to be displayed in the classroom or in their writer's notebooks. Or, practice the procedure, concept, or strategy or skill being taught.
   • Ask students to reflect or speculate on how they can use this information in their reading and writing.
       The purpose of minilessons is to highlight the topic, not to isolate it or provide drill-and-practice (Crafton, 1991). Worksheets are not used in minilessons; instead, students apply the lesson to their own language arts

activities. Minilessons can be conducted with the whole class, small groups of students who have indicated that they need to learn more about a particular topic, and individual students. Teachers can also plan minilessons on a regular basis to introduce or review topics. A list of possible topics for minilessons is shown on page 52.

4. *Creating projects.* Students create projects to extend their reading. A list of projects is presented in Figure 2–5. Students usually choose the projects they create based on their interests and the opportunities the book presents to them. For example, after reading *Jumanji* (Van Allsburg, 1981), students often choose to write sequels; and after reading *Sylvester and the Magic Pebble* (Steig, 1969), students may work together as a small group to dramatize the story, or they may choose to read other books written by William Steig.

Theme Cycles

Theme cycles are a new type of interdisciplinary unit that integrate language arts with social studies, science, math, and other curricular areas (Altwerger & Flores, 1994; Gamberg, Kwak, Hutchings, Altheim, & Edwards, 1988). They often extend across most or all of the school day, and students are involved in planning the direction for the theme. Topics for theme cycles are broad and encompass many possible directions for exploration. Possible topics include inventions, why we have laws, wild animals, houses and homes, natural disasters, and cultures.

Students use listening, talking, reading, and writing as they investigate, solve problems, and learn during theme cycles. They also use language arts to demonstrate their new learning at the end of the theme. Three types of language arts activities during theme cycles are:

1. *Keeping learning logs.* Students keep learning logs and write entries about new concepts they are learning, record new and interesting words, make charts and diagrams, and make reflections about their learning.

2. *Reading books.* Students read informational books and magazines as well as other types of books related to the theme.

3. *Creating projects.* Students create projects to extend their learning and demonstrate their new knowledge. During theme cycles students do the same types of projects that were presented in Figure 2–5.

Reading-Writing Workshops

Two types of workshops are reading workshop and writing workshop. Reading workshop fosters real reading of self-selected stories, poems, and informational books, and writing workshop fosters real writing (and the use of the writing process) for genuine purposes and authentic audiences. Teachers often use the two workshops, or if their schedule does not allow, they may alternate the two. Schedules for reading and writing workshop at second-grade, fifth-grade, and eighth-grade levels are presented in Figure 2–6 (p. 55).

Reading Workshop. In reading workshop students read books that they choose themselves and respond to books by writing in reading logs and by creating response projects (Atwell, 1987; Hornsby, Sukarna, & Parry, 1986).

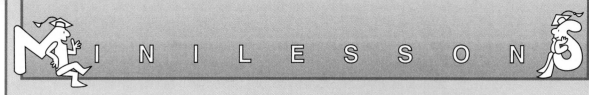

Language Arts

Procedures	Concepts	Strategies and Skills
Share books from the author's chair	Aesthetic listening	Brainstorm
Bind books	Aesthetic reading	Capitalize first words in sentences
Use buddy reading	Alliteration	Capitalize proper nouns
Choose books	Author information	Choose titles
Choose writing topics	Comparisons (metaphors and similes)	Cluster ideas
Do choral reading	Critical listening	Connect to background information
Conference	Efferent reading	Connect to life
Decode words	Expository text structures (compare-contrast, cause-effect, etc.)	Connect to literature
Do projects		Elaborate ideas
Do writing groups	Genres (folktales, historical fiction, etc.)	Empathize with characters
Do independent reading		Use handwriting skills
Keep a portfolio	Illustrator information	Identify with characters
Make a table of contents	Literary elements (plot, characters, etc.)	Use invented spelling
Make "All About the Author" pages		Monitor
	Notable language	Predict and confirm
Make clusters/diagrams	Personification	Preview
Participate in grand conversations	Persuasion	Proofread
	Poetic devices	Punctuate ends of sentences
Reflect on work	Poetic forms	Punctuate abbreviations, dates, etc.
Do role-playing	Propaganda	
Take notes	Symbolism	Punctuate dialogue
Use word-processing programs	Types of illustrations	Ask questions
	Types of texts (stories, poems, informational books)	Retell
Write in reading logs		Revise
Write journal entries	Wordplay	Combine sentences
Write rough drafts	Writing forms (personal, narrative, expository, persuasive)	Use conventional spelling
		Use study skills
		Summarize
		Take a position
		Use dialogue
		Visualize
		Use word identification skills

The components of reading workshop are:

1. *Teaching minilessons.* The teacher spends 10 to 20 minutes teaching brief lessons on reading workshop procedures, literary concepts, and reading strategies and skills.

2. *Reading and responding.* Students spend 30 to 60 minutes independently reading books and other reading materials. They also keep reading logs to

Figure 2–5   Projects

Art Projects

1. Experiment with the illustration techniques (e.g., collage, watercolor, line drawing) used in a favorite book. Examine other books illustrated with the same technique.
2. Make a diagram or model using information from a book.
3. Create a collage to represent the theme of a book.
4. Design a book jacket for a book, laminate it, and place it on the book.
5. Decorate a coffee can or a potato chip can using scenes from a book. Fill the can with quotes from characters in the story. Other students can guess the identity of the characters. Or fill the can with quotes from a poem with words missing. Other students guess the missing words.
6. Construct a shoebox or other miniature scene of an episode for a favorite book (or use a larger box to construct a diorama).
7. Make illustrations for each important event in a book.
8. Make a map or relief map of a book's setting or something related to the book.
9. Construct the setting of the book in the block center, or use other construction toys such as Lego's or Lincoln Logs.
10. Construct a mobile illustrating a book.
11. Make a roll-movie of a book by drawing a series of pictures on a long strip of paper. Attach ends to rollers and place in a cardboard box cut like a television set.
12. Make a comic strip to illustrate the sequence of events in a book.
13. Make a clay or soap model of a character.
14. Prepare bookmarks for a book and distribute them to classmates.
15. Prepare flannel board pictures to use in retelling the story.
16. Use or prepare illustrations of characters for pocket props to use in retelling the story.
17. Use or prepare illustrations of the events in the story for clothesline props to use in retelling the story.
18. Experiment with art techniques related to the mood of a poem.
19. Make a mural of the book.
20. Illustrate the box with scenes from a book. Place objects, poems, and illustrations that represent characters, events, or images from the book.

Writing Projects

21. Write a review of a favorite book for a class review file.
22. Write a letter about a book to a classmate, friend, or pen pal.
23. Dictate or write another episode or sequel for a book.
24. Create a newspaper with news stories and advertisements based on characters and episodes from a book.
25. Make a five-senses cluster about the book.
26. Write a letter to a favorite character (or participate in a class collaboration letter).
27. Write a simulated letter from one book character to another.
28. Copy five "quotable quotes" from a book and list them on a poster.
29. Make a scrapbook about the book. Label all items in the scrapbook and write a short description of the most interesting ones.
30. Write a poem related to the book. Some types of poems to choose from are acrostic, concrete poem, color poem, "I wish" poem, "If I were" poem, haiku, or limerick.
31. Write a lifeline related to the book, the era, the character, or the author.
32. Write a business letter to a company or organization requesting information on a topic related to the book.

Figure 2–5   continued

33. Keep a simulated journal from the perspective of one character from the book.
34. Write a dictionary defining specialized vocabulary in a book.
35. Write the story from another point of view (e.g., write the story of *The Little Red Hen* from the perspective of the lazy characters).
36. Make a class collaboration book. Each child dictates or writes one page.
37. Write a letter to a famous person from a character in a book.
38. Make a ladder to accomplishment listing the steps taken to achieve some goal.

Reading Projects

39. Read another book by the same author.
40. Read another book by the same illustrator.
41. Read another book on the same theme.
42. Read another book in the same genre.
43. Read another book about the same character.
44. Read and compare another version of the same story.
45. Listen to and compare a tape, filmstrip, film, or video version of the same story.
46. Tape-record a book or an excerpt from it to place in the listening center.
47. Read a poem that complements the book aloud to the class. Place a copy of the poem in the book.
48. Tape-record a book using background music and sound effects.

Drama and Talk Projects

49. Give a readers theatre presentation of a book.
50. Improvise the events in a book.
51. Write a script and present a play about a book.
52. Make puppets and use them in retelling a book.
53. Dress as a character from the book and answer questions from classmates about the character.
54. Have a grand conversation with a small group or the whole class about a book.
55. Write and present a rap about the book.
56. Videotape a commercial for a book.
57. Interview someone in the community who is knowledgeable about a topic related to the book.

Literary Analysis Projects

58. Make a chart to compare the story with another version or with the film version of the story.
59. Make a character cluster.
60. Make a character sociogram.
61. Make a plot diagram of the book.
62. Make a plot profile of the book.

Research Projects

63. Research the author of the book and compile information in a chart or summary. Place the chart or summary in the book.
64. Research a topic related to the book. Present the information in a report.

Other Projects

65. Cook and eat a food described in or related to a book.
66. Collect or make objects related to the book.

Figure 2–6   Schedules for Reading and Writing Workshop

Second-Grade Schedule

15 minutes	Reading aloud to students
15 minutes	Teaching a minilesson (on a reading or writing topic)
30 minutes	Reading and responding
15 minutes	Sharing

—Later—

30 minutes	Writing
15 minutes	Sharing

This 2-hour schedule is broken into two parts. The first 75 minutes, scheduled in the morning, focuses on reading, and the second 45 minutes, scheduled after lunch, is devoted to writing.

Fifth-Grade Schedule

40 minutes	Reading and responding
20 minutes	Teaching a minilesson (on a reading or writing topic)
40 minutes	Writing
20 minutes	Sharing

This schedule is also planned for 2 hours. The minilesson separates the two independent work sessions, and during the sharing session students share books they have read, response projects they have created, and compositions they have published.

Eighth-Grade Schedule

40 minutes	Reading and responding or writing
15 minutes	Teaching a minilesson (on Mondays–Thursdays)
	Sharing (on Fridays)

The eighth-grade schedule is for 55 minutes. Because of time limitations, students alternate reading and writing workshop, minilessons are scheduled for 4 days each week, and sharing is held on Fridays.

---

write their initial responses to their reading and create response projects to extend their understanding of favorite books.

3. *Sharing.* For the last 15 minutes of reading workshop, the class gathers together to share books and response projects.

Writing Workshop.   Writing workshop is a new way of implementing the writing process (Atwell, 1987; Calkins, 1986; Graves, 1983; Parry & Hornsby, 1985). Students usually write on topics that they choose themselves, and they assume ownership of their learning. At the same time, the teacher's role changes from being a provider of knowledge to serving as a facilitator and guide. The classroom becomes a community of writers who write and share their writing.

In a writing workshop classroom, students have writing folders in which they keep all papers related to the writing project they are working on. They also keep writing notebooks in which they jot down images, impressions, dialogue, and experiences that they can build upon for writing projects (Calkins, 1991). Students have access to different kinds of paper, some lined and some unlined, and writing instruments, including pencils and red and blue pens. They also have access to the classroom library and many other items.

Students' writing grows out of favorite books. They may write a sequel to a favorite book or retell a story from a different viewpoint. Primary-grade students often use patterns from a book they have read to structure a book they are writing.

Students sit at desks or tables arranged in small groups as they write. The teacher circulates around the classroom, conferencing briefly with students, and the classroom atmosphere is free enough that students converse quietly with classmates and move around the classroom to assist classmates or share ideas. There is space for students to meet together for writing groups, and often a sign-up sheet for writing groups is posted in the classroom. A table is available for the teacher to meet with individual students or small groups for conferences, writing groups, proofreading, and minilessons.

Writing workshop is a 1-hour to 1½-hour period scheduled each day. During this time the teacher and the students are involved in three activities:

1. *Teaching minilessons.* During this 5- to 15-minute period, teachers provide brief lessons on writing workshop procedures, literary concepts, and writing strategies and skills.
2. *Writing.* Students spend 30 to 45 minutes working independently on writing projects. They move through all five stages of the writing process—prewriting, drafting, revising, editing, and publishing—at their own pace. Many times students compile their final copies to make books during writing workshop, but sometimes they attach their writing to artwork, make

The teacher teaches a minilesson to a small group during writing workshop.

posters, write letters that are mailed, or perform scripts as skits or puppet shows.

3. *Sharing.* For the last 10 to 15 minutes of writing workshop, the class gathers together to share their new publications and make other related announcements. A student who has just finished writing a puppet show script and making puppets may ask for volunteers to help perform the puppet show, which could be presented several days later during sharing time. Younger students often sit in a circle or gather together on a rug for sharing time. If an author's chair is available, each student sits in the special chair to read his or her composition. After the reading, classmates clap and offer compliments. They may also make other comments and suggestions, but the focus in on celebrating completed writing projects, not on revising the composition to make it better.

Sometimes teachers add a fourth component to writing workshop in which they talk about authors of children's literature and read literature aloud to share examples of good writing with students. This activity also helps students to feel part of the community of writers. Teachers can also connect reading workshop with writing workshop.

In these two approaches teachers play many roles. They instruct, guide, model, assess, support, encourage, respond, insist upon, and explain, to name only a few of the roles. Cazden (1983) categorizes these roles as *scaffolds, models,* and *instruction.*

Just as parents provide support for their children as they learn to talk, teachers also provide temporary supports as students are listening, talking, reading, and writing. For example, teachers serve as coaches as they encourage students who are preparing a puppet show or writing reports. They respond to and reflect on students' writing as any interested audience would. Through these roles, teachers provide a "scaffold" or framework to support students when they tackle complex learning tasks (Applebee & Langer, 1983; Bruner, 1978; Cazden, 1980). As students learn, the need for this scaffolding diminishes, but when they tackle a new concept, the need for support returns. Teachers must continue to be responsive to students' growing competencies to provide this assistance. It is important, too, that teachers appreciate the power of their interactions with students and how they can support students' learning.

In everything they do, teachers are models for students. If you watch children play school at home, you will appreciate just how well children internalize what the teacher models. Teachers model language learning and ways to use language; for instance, they model ways of talking, and how students interact with classmates often reflects what the teacher has modeled. Teachers model a love of reading when they share favorite books. When they check the dictionary for the spelling or meaning of a word they are unsure of, they model its use more powerfully than any assignment could.

Almost everything a teacher does might be called "teaching," and certainly teachers are teaching as they informally support and nurture students' learning and as they model language and literacy behaviors. Another type of teaching is more direct: when teachers plan and teach lessons and minilessons using the teaching strategy presented in Chapter 1. This strategy can be adapted to teach the whole class, small groups, and individual students, and it can be used to teach procedures, concepts, and strategies and skills related to the four language modes.

Adapting to Meet the Needs of Every Student

In every classroom some students do not learn as well as their classmates or as well as the teacher believes they can. Others do not seem to be challenged by the activities they are engaged in, or they have limited proficiency in English because they are learning English as a second language. Every year classroom teachers encounter students with a variety of strengths and needs. It is important for teachers to be aware of students with special needs in their classrooms and to find ways to adapt the instructional program so that every student can be successful (Wood, 1993).

Seven types of students with special needs are:

- Students with specific learning disabilities
- Students with mental retardation
- Students with behavior disorders
- Students with language disorders
- Students with attention deficit disorder
- Students who are learning English as a second language
- Students who are gifted

Each type of student is discussed in the following sections, and suggestions are made in the text and in Figure 2–7 about how to adapt the instructional program to meet these students' needs.

Students With Specific Learning Disabilities.   Students with specific learning disabilities have significant difficulties in learning and using one or more of the following abilities: listening, speaking, reading, writing, and math. Even though these students can have severe learning difficulties, they have average or above-average intelligence. Students with specific learning disabilities may not express themselves well, may not read fluently, and may have trouble spelling words correctly and using other written language skills. They may exhibit poor coordination and have difficulty with handwriting. In addition, they may have low self-images, exhibit socially inappropriate behaviors, and have difficulty relating to their classmates.

Students with specific learning disabilities are capable of learning the academic content in their weak areas. They learn to compensate for their learning problems. These students are usually mainstreamed into regular education classrooms for much of the school day and are "pulled out" to a resource room for special instruction. Perhaps the most important consideration in working with these students is that the classroom and the instruction be structured. Other suggestions for teaching language arts to students with specific learning disabilities are listed in Figure 2–7.

Students With Mental Retardation.   Students with mental retardation have significantly subaverage intellectual functioning, along with limitations in two or more of the following areas: communicating, self-care, home living, social skills, self-direction, health and safety, functional academics, leisure, and work. Their academic performance lags 3 or 4 years behind those of other students, but they can learn to read and write. The focus of instruction should be to help students develop the functional skills considered essential to living independently. The most valuable activities for these students are concrete,

Figure 2–7   Adapting to Meet the Needs of Every Student

Students With Specific Learning Disabilities

Use multisensory approaches.
Allow students to work at their own level.
Keep assignments short.
Use peer-tutors and cross-age tutors.
Connect listening and reading experiences.
Allow students to use talking rather than writing whenever possible (e.g., dictate stories and give oral reports instead of written reports).
Try word processing for students with handwriting problems.

Students With Mental Retardation

Focus on functional skills for independent living.
Connect activities to students' personal experiences.
Use concrete examples.
Provide many opportunities to practice skills.
Use peer-tutors to reread familiar books.
Have students tell and dictate stories using wordless picture books.
Teach students to read and spell very high frequency words.

Students With Behavior Disorders

Closely monitor students' frustration levels and help them find ways to communicate their frustration.
Involve students in talk and drama activities to develop oral language fluency.
Have students work with a buddy or two to develop socialization skills.
Structure learning experiences.
Have students write their feelings and frustrations in personal journals.
Have students who have trouble expressing themselves use art as an alternative form of communication.

Students With Language Disorders

Encourage students to participate in conversations.
Share books with predictable language patterns.
Use dramatic play, role-playing, and puppetry.
Have students retell familiar stories.
Have students listen to stories at the listening center.
Have students work with a buddy or two to develop socialization skills.

Students With Attention Deficit Disorders

Allow students to move around the classroom.
Structure learning experiences.
Monitor students closely as they work.
Encourage students to participate in talk and drama activities.
Use a checklist to organize steps in completing an activity or project.
Provide choices for students.
Use graphic organizers for students to complete while reading or listening.

Figure 2–7   continued

Students Who Are Learning English as a Second Language

Foster understanding and appreciation of the student's native language and culture.

Have English-speaking students serve as peer-tutors and buddies for LEP students.

Teach survival words and phrases.

Have students draw and write in journals.

Show films, filmstrips, and videotapes to provide background before teaching concepts or reading books.

Teach literal and figurative meanings of idioms.

Encourage students to retell familiar stories.

Students Who Are Gifted

Encourage risk-taking and experimentation.

Provide students with tools for learning, including research skills and problem-solving skills.

Create a noncompetitive and individualized classroom environment.

Invite community persons with particular areas of expertise to serve as mentors.

Encourage students to use all language functions.

Provide opportunities for gifted students to publish their writing in a variety of formats (e.g., anthologies, scripts, and newspapers).

---

meaningful, and based on personal experience. When the pace of classroom activities is too fast, individualized instruction with peer-tutors can be provided. This individualized instruction should involve more repetition and practice than is necessary for other students. A list of suggestions for helping students with mental retardation is provided in Figure 2–7.

Students With Behavior Disorders.   Students whose behavior interferes with learning are characterized as having behavior disorders. They often exhibit inappropriate behavior and feelings under normal circumstances; they may be either aggressive and disruptive or anxious and withdrawn. These students have difficulty in developing satisfactory relationships with classmates and the teacher. Often, they are unhappy or depressed, and they may develop physical symptoms or fears associated with personal or school problems. Although any student can exhibit one of these behaviors for a brief period, students with behavior disorders exhibit more than one of these behaviors to a marked degree and consistently over time. Students with behavior disorders need a structured and positive classroom environment in order to be successful. Students need to learn to control their disruptive and socially inappropriate behavior and develop interpersonal skills. Some suggestions for adapting the language arts instruction to meet these students' needs are provided in Figure 2–7.

Students With Language Disorders.   Students who have grown up in an English-speaking community but have difficulty understanding or expressing language are classified as having a language disorder. Often these children talk very little, speak in childlike phrases, and lack the language to understand basic concepts. This is a very serious problem because a student's limited ability to communicate has a negative impact on learning as well as social interaction with classmates and the teacher. Some suggestions for helping these students are provided in Figure 2–7. It is important to note that students who speak their native language fluently and are learning English as a second language do not have a language disorder.

Students With Attention Deficit Disorder. Students with attention deficit disorder (ADD) have great difficulty attending to tasks and activities. There is no universally accepted definition, but these students display distractibility, impulsiveness, inattention, and mood fluctuations. It is crucial that students with ADD be able to be successful in the classroom, and that teachers structure their environment to minimize the effects of their distractibility. Some suggestions are provided in Figure 2–7.

Students Who Are Learning English as a Second Language. Many children living in the United States come from Mexican American, Asian American, Native American, and other language and cultural communities. These students acquire their native language before they come to school, and at school they learn English. These children are described as Limited English Proficient (LEP) until they become fluent in English; then they are bilingual. Research suggests that students learn a second language similar to the way they learned to speak their native language, and that it takes 5 to 7 years for students to become fluent in a second language. Teachers provide a supportive environment and use classmates as buddies for LEP students. Other suggestions are listed in Figure 2–7.

Students Who Are Gifted. Gifted students are academically advanced, but giftedness is more than a high IQ score. Gifted students also grasp relationships quickly, are curious, have unusually good memories, express themselves well, enjoy working independently, have a well-developed sense of humor, and are perfectionistic. However, not all gifted students are high achievers. Some are underachievers who do not work up to their potential because of a lack of motivation, peer pressure, or fear of success. Gifted students require special adaptations to meet their needs. Some suggestions for enriching learning opportunities for gifted students are also presented in Figure 2–7.

Our position is that students with special learning needs benefit from the same language arts content and teaching strategies that other students do. The material in this book capitalizes on the natural ways children learn, and it can be used effectively with almost all learners, given some adaptations. Glass, Christiansen, and Christiansen (1982) point out that no one way exists to teach students with special needs that is significantly different from how nonhandicapped students are taught. Moreover, educators recommend a holistic, integrated approach as especially valuable for learning disabled and remedial learners (Rhodes & Dudley-Marling, 1988) and for students learning English as a second language (Heald-Taylor, 1986).

ASSESSING STUDENTS' LEARNING

Assessing students' learning in the language arts is a difficult task. Although it may seem fairly easy to develop and administer a criterion-referenced test, tests measure language skills rather than language use. Tests do not measure listening and talking very well, and a test on punctuation marks, for example, does not indicate students' ability to use punctuation marks correctly in their own writing. Instead, tests typically evaluate students' ability to add punctuation marks to a set of sentences created by someone else, or to proofread and spot punctuation errors in someone else's writing. An alternative and far better approach is to examine how students use punctuation marks in their own writing.

Assessment is more than testing; it is an integral part of teaching and learning (Goodman, Goodman, & Hood, 1989). Through assessment, teachers learn about their students, about themselves as teachers, and about the impact of the instructional program. Similarly, students learn about themselves as learners and about their learning. We suggest three assessment procedures:

- Monitoring students' progress
- Collecting students' work in portfolios
- Assigning grades

Information from these procedures together provides a more complete and more personal assessment picture. And, these procedures are more authentic forms of assessment.

Monitoring Students' Progress

Teachers monitor students' progress as they are involved in language arts and across-the-curriculum activities using either the unit approach or the workshop approach. Four ways to monitor students' progress are classroom observations, anecdotal notes, conferences, and checklists (Baskwill & Whitman, 1988).

Classroom Observations. We suggest that teachers become *kid watchers,* a term that Goodman (1978) coined and defined as "direct and informal observation of students." To be effective kid watchers, teachers must understand how children develop language and must understand the role of errors in language learning. In Chapter 1 we described language development as a natural, hypothesis-testing process. Children often make miscues, or "errors," as they learn to talk (Goodman & Burke, 1972). They may, for instance, say "keeped" or "goodest" when they are learning rules for forming past tense or superlatives. Instead of errors, however, these words are clues to language development. Children's sentence structure, spelling, and other "errors" provide equally valuable clues to their written language development.

Teachers use kid watching spontaneously when they interact with children and are attentive to their behavior and comments. Other observation times should be planned, however, during which the teacher focuses on particular children and makes anecdotal notes about a child's use of language. Students' behavior during testing situations often does not reflect their actual ability to communicate using the language modes.

Anecdotal Notes. While teachers kid-watch, they make anecdotal notes about students' performance in listening, talking, reading, and writing activities, as well as questions students ask and concepts and skills they indicate confusion about. These records document students' growth and pinpoint problem areas that need direct instruction from the teacher. A year-long collection of records provides a comprehensive picture of a student's language development. Instead of recording random samples, teachers should choose events that are characteristic of each student. An excerpt from a fifth-grade teacher's anecdotal notes about one student's progress during a unit on the American Revolution appears in Figure 2–8.

Several organizational schemes are possible, and teachers should use the format that is most comfortable for them. Some teachers make a card file with dividers for each child and write anecdotes on notecards. They feel comfortable jotting notes on these small cards or even carrying around a set of cards in their pockets. Other teachers divide a spiral-bound notebook into sections

Figure 2–8　Anecdotal Notes About One Student's Learning During a Theme Cycle on the American Revolution

Notes About Matthew	
March 5	Matthew selected Ben Franklin as historical figure for American Revolution projects.
March 11	Matthew fascinated with information he has found about B. F. Brought several sources from home. Is completing B. F.'s lifeline with many details.
March 18	Simulated journal. Four entries in four days! Interesting how he picked up language style of the period in his journal. Volunteers to share daily. I think he enjoys the oral sharing more than the writing.
March 25	Nine simulated journal entries, all illustrated. High level of enthusiasm.
March 29	Conferenced about cluster for B. F. biography. Well-developed with five rays, many details. Matthew will work on "contributions" ray. He recognized it as the least-developed one.
April 2	Three chapters of biography drafted. Talked about "working titles" for chapters and choosing more interesting titles after writing that reflect the content of the chapters.
April 7	Drafting conference. Matthew has completed all five chapters. He and Dustin are competitive, both writing on B. F. They are reading each other's chapters and checking the accuracy of information.
April 12	Writing group. Matthew confused Declaration of Independence with the Constitution. Chapters longer and more complete since drafting conference. Compared with autobiography project, writing is more sophisticated. Longer, too. Reading is influencing writing style—e.g., "Luckily for Ben." He is still somewhat defensive about accepting suggestions except from me. He will make 3 revisions—agreed in writing group.
April 15	Revisions: (1) eliminated "he" (substitute), (2) re-sequenced Chapter 3 (move), and (3) added sentences in Chapter 5 (add).
April 19	Proofread with Dustin. Working hard.
April 23	Editing conference—no major problems. Discussed use of commas within sentences, capitalizing proper nouns. Matthew and Dustin more task-oriented on this project; I see more motivation and commitment.
April 29	Final copy of biography completed and shared with class.

for each child and write anecdotes in the notebook, which they keep on their desks. A third technique is to write anecdotes on small sheets of paper and clip the sheets into students' assessment folders.

Conferences.   Teachers often hold short, informal conferences to talk with students about their work or to help them solve a problem related to what they are studying. Often these conferences concern students' reading or writing activities, but they could be held with the actors in a play or the students working in a small group to create an advertisement or commercial. Conferences can be held at students' desks while the teacher moves around the classroom, at the teacher's desk, or at a special conference table. Seven types of conferences are described in the Teacher's Notebook on page 65.

The teacher's role is to be listener and guide. Teachers can learn a great deal about students and their learning if they listen as students talk about their reading, writing, or other activities. When students explain a problem they are having, the teacher is often able to decide on a way to work through it. Graves (1983) suggests that teachers balance the amount of their talk with the student's talk during the conference and, at the end, reflect on what the student has taught them, what responsibilities the student can take, and whether the student understands what to do next.

Checklists.   Teachers can use checklists as they observe students or track their progress using particular procedures, strategies, or skills. For example, when students participate in writing conferences in which they read their compositions to small groups of classmates and ask for suggestions for improving their writing, teachers can note whether students participate fully in the group, share their writing with classmates, gracefully accept suggestions about improving their writing, and make substantive changes in their writing based on some of their classmates' suggestions. Students can even help develop the checklists so that they understand what types of behavior are expected of them.

Three checklists appear in Figure 2–9. The first is a "Weekly Reading-Writing Workshop Activity Sheet" that middle-grade students might complete each week to monitor their work during reading and writing workshop. Notice that students are directed to write a letter to the teacher on the back of the sheet, reflecting on their work during that week. Next is a "Projects Checklist" that either the teacher or the student might use to keep track of the projects the student chooses to participate in after reading. The third checklist is an "Independent Reading Record" that students keep as they read. Students list the title and author of each book they read, the dates on which they read the book, the date of their conference with the teacher, the project they do to extend their reading, and the date on which the student shared the project with the class.

Collecting Students' Work in Portfolios

Portfolios are systematic and meaningful collections of students' writings and other works that show students' progress over a period of time (De Fina, 1992). These collections are dynamic and reflect students' day-to-day learning activities in language arts and across the curriculum. Students not only

Teacher's Notebook
Seven Types of Conferences

1. On-the-Spot Conferences

Teachers visit briefly with students at their desks to monitor some aspect of the students' work or to check on progress. These conferences are brief; the teacher may spend less than a minute at each student's desk.

2. Prereading or Prewriting Conferences

The teacher and student make plans for reading or writing at the conference. At a prereading conference, they may talk about information related to the book, difficult concepts or vocabulary words related to the reading, or the reading log the student will keep. At a prewriting conference, they may discuss possible writing topics or how to narrow a broad topic.

3. Revising Conferences

A small group of students and the teacher meet to get specific suggestions about revising their compositions. These conferences offer student writers an audience to provide feedback on how well they have communicated.

4. Book Discussion Conferences

Students and the teacher meet to discuss the book they have read. They may share reading log entries, discuss plot or characters, compare the story to others they have read, or make plans to extend their reading.

5. Editing Conferences

The teacher reviews students' proofread compositions and helps them correct spelling, punctuation, capitalization, and other mechanical errors.

6. Minilesson Conferences

The teacher meets with students to explain a procedure, strategy, or skill (e.g., writing a table of contents, using the visualization strategy when reading, or capitalizing proper nouns).

7. Assessment Conferences

The teacher meets with students after they have completed an assignment or project to talk about their growth as readers or writers. Students reflect on their competencies and set goals.

Figure 2–9   Three Assessment Checklists

Weekly Reading-Writing Workshop Activity Sheet			
Name _____		Week _____	
Read independently	M T W Th F	Made a cluster	M T W Th F
Wrote in a reading log	M T W Th F	Wrote a rough draft	M T W Th F
Listened to the teacher read aloud	M T W Th F	Went to a writing group	M T W Th F
Did a response project	M T W Th F	Made revisions	M T W Th F
Read with a class-mate	M T W Th F	Proofread my own writing	M T W Th F
Read at the listening center	M T W Th F	Proofread for a classmate	M T W Th F
Had a reading con-ference	M T W Th F	Had a writing con-ference	M T W Th F
Shared a book with classmates	M T W Th F	Shared my writing with classmates	M T W Th F
Other		Other	
Interesting words read this week		Spelling words needed this week	
Titles of books read		Titles of writings	
Write a letter on the back, thinking about the week and your reading and writing.			

select pieces to be placed in their portfolios but learn to establish criteria for their selections. Because of students' involvement in selecting pieces for their portfolios and reflecting on them, portfolio assessment respects students and their abilities.

Students usually choose the items to place in their portfolios within the guidelines provided by the teacher. Some students submit the original piece of work; others want to keep the original, so they place a copy in the portfolio instead. In addition to the writing and art samples that can go directly into portfolios, students also record oral language and drama samples on audio-tapes and videotapes to place in their portfolios. Large-size art and writing

Figure 2–9 continued

Projects Checklist	
Name _____	Grading Period 1 2 3 4
book jacket	plot diagram
book mark	poem
cartoons	point of view retelling
character cluster	portrait of character
commercial or ad	poster
crossword puzzle	puppets
diorama	quotable quotes
dramatization	read other books
dress as character	research
exhibit	script
filmstrip	sequel
interview	simulated journal
letter to author	simulated letter
map or diagram	story boards
mobile	story box
movie roll	story map
mural	travel brochure
newspaper article	Venn diagram
oral reading	Win, Lose, or Draw

projects can be photographed, and the photographs placed in the portfolio. The following types of student work might be placed in a portfolio:

ABC books

"All About Me" books

autobiographies

biographies

books

choral readings (on audiotape)

clusters

drawings, diagrams, and charts

learning log entries

Figure 2–9   *continued*

Independent Reading Record				
Name _____ Grading Period 1 2 3 4				
Title/Author	Dates Read	Conference	Project	Sharing

letters to pen pals, businesses, and authors (copies because the originals have been sent)

lists of books read

newspaper articles

oral reading (on audiotape)

oral reports (on audiotape or videotape)

poems

puppet shows (on videotape)

puppets (on photographs)

quickwrites

readers theatre presentations (on audiotape or videotape)

reading log entries

reports

response projects (on photographs)

simulated journal entries

stories

timelines and lifelines

Students conference with the teacher during writing workshop.

This variety of work samples takes into account all four language modes. Also, samples from workshops, literature focus units, and across-the-curriculum theme cycles should be included.

Portfolios are not just a collection of carefully chosen work samples in a manila folder or notebook. They provide a way of learning about students and how they use language; they give evidence of both the products that students create and the processes they use. The difference between a folder and a portfolio is reflection (D'Aoust, 1992). Reflection requires students to pause and become aware of themselves as language users.

Not all work that is placed in a student's portfolio needs to be graded for quality. Teachers will, of course, be familiar with most pieces, but it is not necessary to correct them with a red pen. Many times, students' work is simply graded as "done" or "not done." When a piece of work is to be graded, students should choose it from the items being placed in their portfolios.

The third grader's letter to Peter Rabbit from Mr. McGregor shown in Figure 2–10 is an interesting example. The student wrote the letter to Peter as a response project after the class read *The Tale of Peter Rabbit* (Potter, 1902). At about the same time, the teacher taught a minilesson on persuasive writing, and this student incorporated what he learned in this letter. He placed it in his portfolio because it looked good and because his classmates had really liked it when he had shared it with them. His prewriting drawing and rough draft were tacked to the final copy shown in the figure.

The third grader then chose his letter to be graded. His teacher liked it, too, but not just because it looked good. First, the papers attached to the final copy indicated that he had used the writing process to gather ideas and to draft and revise his letter. Second, he had applied what he had learned about persuasion in the letter, as well as content from the story. He suggested a deal to Peter and

Figure 2–10 A Third Grader's Letter to Peter Rabbit from Mr. McGregor

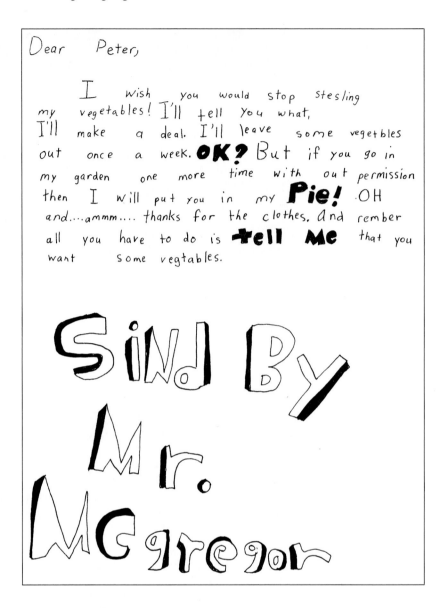

made a threat about what would happen if the rabbit came back into the garden. Third, his writing style was lively, and he highlighted important words in his letter. Of course, his teacher noticed five misspelled words (*stesling-stealing, vegetbles-vegetables, rember-remember, vegtables-vegetables,* and *sind-signed*), but they were minor and did not interfere with reading the letter. This student's grade was an A.

Assigning Grades

Assigning grades is one of the most difficult responsibilities placed on teachers. "Grading is a fact of life," according to Donald Graves (1983, p. 93), but he adds that teachers should use grades to encourage students, not to hinder their achievement. The assessment procedures described earlier in this section encourage students because they document how students are using listening, talking, reading, and writing in authentic ways. Reviewing and translating this documentation into grades is the difficult part. Two other ways to collect information for assigning grades are unit checklists and tests.

Unit Checklists. Unit checklists are the grading sheets that students use to keep track of their progress during the unit and that the teacher uses to assign grades for the unit. Teachers create the unit checklist as the literature focus unit or theme cycle is planned. Students receive a copy of the checklist at the beginning of the unit and keep it in their unit folder. Then, as they complete the assignments, they check them off, and it is easy for the teacher to make periodic checks. At the end of the unit, the teacher collects the unit folders and grades the work.

A checklist for a second-grade theme on hermit crabs is presented in Figure 2–11. Eight assignments are included on the checklist, and they include both science and language arts activities. Students put a check in the boxes in the "Student's Check" column when they complete each assignment, and the teacher adds the grade in the right-hand column. Some assignments will be graded as "done" or "not done," and others will be graded for quality.

Teachers of middle- and upper-grade students often assign points to each activity in the unit checklist so that the total point value for the unit is 100 points. Activities that involve more time and effort earn more points. The second checklist in Figure 2–11 is for a fifth-grade literature focus unit on *Number the Stars* (Lowry, 1989). The point value for each activity is listed in parentheses. Students make check marks on the lines on the left side of the grading sheet, and the teacher marks the numerical grades on the right side.

Tests. Students can create their own tests. Teachers identify a concept, such as the skeleton, the Oregon trail, the water cycle, or pyramids, from a unit or theme cycle, and students draw and write information about the concept. Students divide a piece of a paper into two parts. On one part they draw pictures, diagrams, maps, or charts to describe the concept, and they label the drawings with key words and phrases. On the other part of the paper they describe the concept with words. Then teachers grade the test by identifying which of the important components of the concept students included in either their drawings or their writings.

A third grader's test on the skeletal system is presented in Figure 2–12. Students could choose to draw and write about the skeletal, circulatory, or digestive systems, and they were to draw three pictures and write three things about the system. This student drew three pictures of the skeletal system, illustrating different kinds of bones, and he wrote about two functions of the skeleton—to give the body shape and to protect organs. He also points out that the bones, joints, and muscles work together to help a person move. Two other things that the class studied about the skeletal system that this child did not mention are that bone marrow helps keep blood healthy and that there are 206 bones in the body. In the middle of the written part, the child included unrelated information about the functions of the heart, lungs, and brain. Out of a possible score of 6, the child received a 5. There are a few misspelled words and missing punctuation marks, but they do not affect the grade since they do not interfere with the information presented.

Figure 2–11   Two Unit Checklists

Checklist for Theme Cycle on Hermit Crabs

Name _____   Begin _____
End _____

	Student's Check	Teacher's Check

1. Keep an observation log on the hermit crab on your table for 10 days. ☐ ☐
2. Make a chart of a hermit crab and label the parts. ☐ ☐
3. Make a map of the hermit crab's habitat. ☐ ☐
4. Read three books about hermit crabs and do quickwrites about them. ☐ ☐
   ____ *Hermit Crabs*
   ____ *A House for Hermit Crab*
   ____ *Is This a House for Hermit Crab?*
5. Do two science experiments and write lab reports. ☐ ☐
   ____ Wet-Dry Experiment
   ____ Light-Dark Experiment
6. Write about hermit crabs. Do one: ☐ ☐
   ____ *All About Hermit Crabs* book
   ____ A poem about hermit crabs
   ____ A story about hermit crabs
7. Do a project about hermit crabs. Share it. ☐ ☐
8. Keep everything neatly in your hermit crab folder. ☐ ☐

***Number the Stars* Grading Sheet**

Name _____   Date _____

____ 1. Read *Number the Stars*.   _____
____ 2. Write 5 entries in a reading log or simulated journal.   (25) _____
____ 3. Talk about your reading in 5 grand conversations.   (25) _____
____ 4. Make a Venn diagram to compare characters. Summarize what you learned from the diagram in an essay.   (10) _____
____ 5. Make a cluster about one word on the word wall.   (5) _____
____ 6. Make a square with a favorite quote for the story quilt.   (10) _____
____ 7. Do a response project.   (25) _____
Total   (100) _____

These tests are an example of writing across the curriculum. Students use writing to demonstrate their knowledge in a content area. Using both drawing and writing allows students who are weaker in written language to express their knowledge. Teachers might also allow students with serious motor problems to talk out or dramatize their response rather than to write it.

To assess students' learning systematically, teachers should use at least three evaluation approaches. Approaching an evaluation through at least three

Figure 2–12 *A Third Grader's Test on the Skeletal System*

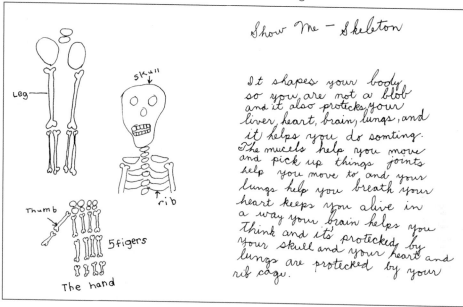

different viewpoints is called *triangulation*. In addition to tests, teachers can use kid watching, anecdotal records, conferences, checklists, portfolios, and unit checklists. Using a variety of techniques enables teachers to be much more accurate in charting and assessing students' language growth.

Review

This chapter focuses on how teachers teach language arts. As Lefevre (1970) suggests, teachers need to provide opportunities for discovery. Creating a language-rich classroom is important. Through application of the characteristics of a literate environment and arrangement of the classroom, teachers can promote this language-rich setting.

Three instructional approaches presented in this chapter are literature focus units, theme cycles, and reading-writing workshops. Teachers facilitate students' learning in three ways: They provide scaffolds, models, and instruction. One type of instruction is minilessons, and teachers teach these brief lessons on procedures, concepts, and strategies and skills related to language arts. Tests are only one way to assess students' learning; other ways are classroom observations, anecdotal records, conferences, checklists, interviews, language samples, and across-the-curriculum applications.

Extensions

1. Visit an elementary classroom and note which characteristics of a language-rich classroom it exemplifies. What might the teacher change in the classroom to incorporate other characteristics?

2. Choose one of the following categories of children's literature that were discussed in this chapter:
   • Picture books
   • Chapter books

- Stories
- Informational books
- Poems

Read at least 10 books in the category and write a brief report describing the types of books within the category and annotating the books you read.

3. Create a text set of at least 10 books on a social studies or science topic taught in the elementary school similar to the text set on the American Revolution presented in Figure 2–4. Include stories, informational books, biographies, and poems, if possible.

4. Reflect on the advantages and disadvantages of the three ways to organize for language arts instruction—literature focus units, theme cycles, and reading and writing workshops—and how you plan to organize your classroom. Write a brief paper about your reflections and your plans.
5. Interview an elementary teacher and ask about the kinds of assessment he or she uses.
6. Read Kitagawa's article (1989) about classroom observations of individual students; then make your own day-long observation of an elementary student.

References

Altswerger, B., & Flores, B. (1994). Theme cycles: Creating communities of learners. *Primary Voices K–6, 2,* 2–6.

Applebee, A. N., & Langer, J. A. (1983). Instructional scaffolding: Reading and writing and natural language activities. *Language Arts, 60,* 168–175.

Atwell, N. (1987). *In the middle: Writing, reading, and learning with adolescents.* Portsmouth, NH: Heinemann.

Barber, B. (1982). Creating BYTES of language. *Language Arts, 59,* 472–475.

Baskwill, J., & Whitman, P. (1988). *Evaluation: Whole language, whole child.* New York: Scholastic.

Bruner, J. (1978). The role of dialogue in language acquisition. In A. Sinclair, R. J. Jarvelle, & W. J. M. Levelt (Eds.), *The child's concept of language.* New York: Springer-Verlag.

Calkins, L. M. (1986). *The art of teaching writing.* Portsmouth, NH: Heinemann.

Calkins, L. M. (1991). *Living between the lines.* Portsmouth, NH: Heinemann.

Cazden, C. B. (1980). Peekaboo as an instructional model: Discourse development at home and at school. *Papers and Reports of Child Language Development, 17,* 1–29.

Cazden, C. B. (1983). Adult assistance to language development: Scaffolds, models, and direct instruction. In R. P. Parker & F. A. Davis (Eds.), *Developing literacy: Young children's use of language* (pp. 3–18). Newark, DE: International Reading Association.

Chomsky, C. (1984). Finding the best language arts software. *Classroom Computer Learning, 4,* 61–63.

Crafton, L. K. (1991). *Whole language: Getting started . . . moving forward.* Katonah, NY: Richard C. Owen.

D'Aoust, C. (1992). Portfolios: Process for students and teachers. In K. B. Yancy (Ed.), *Portfolios in the writing classroom* (pp. 39–48). Urbana, IL: National Council of Teachers of English.

De Fina, A. A. (1992). *Portfolio assessment: Getting started.* New York: Scholastic.

DeGroff, L. (1990). Is there a place for computers in whole language classrooms? *The Reading Teacher, 43,* 568–572.

Dickinson, D. K. (1986). Cooperation, collaboration, and a computer: Integrating a computer into a first–second grade writing program. *Research in the Teaching of English, 20,* 357–378.

Gamberg, R., Kwak, W., Hutchings, M., Altheim, J., & Edwards, G. (1988). *Learning and loving it: Theme studies in the classroom.* Portsmouth, NH: Heinemann.

Genishi, C. (1988). Kindergartners and computers: A case study of six children. *The Elementary School Journal, 89,* 185–201.

Glass, R. M., Christiansen, J., & Christiansen, J. L. (1982). *Teaching exceptional students in the regular classroom.* Boston: Little, Brown.

Goodman, K. (1986). *What's whole in whole language?* Portsmouth, NH: Heinemann.

Goodman, K. S., Goodman, Y. M., & Hood, W. J. (Eds.). (1989). *The whole language evaluation book.* Portsmouth, NH: Heinemann.

Goodman, Y. M. (1978). Kid watching: An alternative to testing. *National Elementary Principals Journal, 57,* 41–45.

Goodman, Y. M., & Burke, C. L. (1972). *The reading miscue inventory manual.* New York: Richard C. Owen.

Graves, D. H. (1977). Research update: Language arts textbooks: A writing process evaluation. *Language Arts, 54,* 817–823.

Graves, D. H. (1983). *Writing: Teachers and children at work.* Portsmouth, NH: Heinemann.

Graves, D. H. (1991). *Build a literate classroom.* Portsmouth, NH: Heinemann.

Hall, N. (1987). *The emergence of literacy*. Portsmouth, NH: Heinemann.

Harwayne, S. (1992). *Lasting impressions: Weaving literature into the writing workshop*. Portsmouth, NH: Heinemann.

Heald-Taylor, G. (1986). *Whole language strategies for ESL primary students*. Toronto: The Ontario Institute for Studies in Education Press.

Hepler, S. (1991). Talking our way to literacy in the classroom community. *The New Advocate, 4*, 179–191.

Hornsby, D., Sukarna, D., & Parry, J. (1986). *Read on: A conference approach to reading*. Portsmouth, NH: Heinemann.

Kitagawa, M. M. (1989). Observing Carlos: One day of language use in school. In G. S. Pinnell & M. L. Matlin (Eds.), *Teachers and research: Language learning in the classroom* (pp. 3–7). Newark, DE: International Reading Association.

Lefevre, C. A. (1970). *Linguistics, English, and the language arts*. Boston: Allyn and Bacon.

Lindfors, J. W. (1989). The classroom: A good environment for language learning. In P. Rigg & V. G. Allen (Eds.), *When they don't all speak English: Integrating the ESL student into the regular classroom* (pp. 39–54). Urbana, IL: National Council of Teachers of English.

Morrow, L. M. (1989). Designing the classroom to promote literacy development. In D. S. Strickland & L. M. Morrow (Eds.), *Emerging literacy: Young children learn to read and write*. Newark, DE: International Reading Association.

Parry, J., & Hornsby, D. (1985). *Write on: A conference approach to writing*. Portsmouth, NH: Heinemann.

Phenix, J., & Hannan, E. (1984). Word processing in the grade one classroom. *Language Arts, 61*, 804–812.

Rhodes, L. K., & Dudley-Marling, C. (1988). *Readers and writers with a difference: A holistic approach to teaching learning disabled and remedial students*. Portsmouth, NH: Heinemann.

Smith, F. (1988). *Joining the literacy club: Further essays into education*. Portsmouth, NH: Heinemann.

Smith, N. J. (1985). The word processing approach to language experience. *The Reading Teacher, 38*, 556–559.

Taylor, R. (1980). *Computers in the schools: Tool, tutor, and tutee*. New York: Teachers College Press.

Wood, J. W. (1993). *Mainstreaming: A practical approach for teachers* (2nd ed.) New York: Merrill/Macmillan.

Zaharias, J. A. (1983). Microcomputers in the language arts classroom: Promises and pitfalls. *Language Arts, 60*, 990–996.

Children's Book References

Adler, D. A. (1989). *A picture book of Abraham Lincoln*. New York: Holiday House.

Adler, D. A. (1990). *A picture book of Helen Keller*. New York: Holiday House.

Anno, M. (1983). *Anno's U.S.A.* New York: Philomel.

Babbitt, N. (1975). *Tuck everlasting*. New York: Farrar, Straus & Giroux.

Burningham, J. (1985). *Opposites*. New York: Crown Books.

Carle, E. (1989). *Animals, animals*. New York: Philomel.

Carrick, C. (1978). *Octopus*. New York: Clarion.

Caselli, G. (1987). *The human body*. New York: Grosset & Dunlap.

Cleary, B. (1981). *Ramona Quimby, age 8*. New York: Morrow.

Cole, J. (1991). *My puppy is born*. New York: Morrow.

Crews, D. (1982). *Carousel*. New York: Greenwillow.

Dahl, R. (1984). *Boy*. New York: Farrar, Straus & Giroux.

Elkin, B. (1983). *Money*. Chicago: Childrens Press.

Fleischman, P. (1988). *Joyful noise: Poems for two voices*. New York: Harper & Row.

Fleischman, S. (1986). *The whipping boy*. New York: Greenwillow.

Freedman, R. (1988a). *Buffalo hunt*. New York: Holiday House.

Freedman, R. (1988b). *Lincoln: A photobiography*. New York: Clarion.

Fritz, J. (1976). *Will you sign here, John Hancock?* New York: Coward-McCann.

Gibbons, G. (1982). *The post office book: Mail and how it moves*. New York: Harper & Row.

Giblin, J. C. (1990). *The riddle of the rosetta stone: Key to ancient Egypt*. New York: Crowell.

Giff, P. R. (1984). *The beast in Ms. Rooney's room*. New York: Bantam.

Goodall, J. S. (1986). *The story of a castle*. New York: Macmillan.

Goodall, J. S. (1988). *Little Red Riding Hood*. New York: Macmillan.

Hamilton, V. (1974). *Paul Robeson: The life and times of a free black man*. New York: Harper & Row.

Hoberman, M. A. (1978). *A house is a house for me.* New York: Viking.

Hopkins, L. B. (1976). *Good morning to you, valentine.* New York: Harcourt Brace Jovanovich.

Howe, D., & Howe, J. (1979). *Bunnicula.* New York: Atheneum.

Hyman, T. S. (1977). *The sleeping beauty.* Boston: Little, Brown.

Kennedy, X. J., & Kennedy, D. M. (1982). *Knock at a star: A child's introduction to poetry.* Boston: Little, Brown.

Kowalczyk, C. (1985). *Purple is part of a rainbow.* Chicago: Childrens Press.

Larrick, N. (1988). *Cats are cats.* New York: Philomel.

Lasky, K. (1983). *Sugaring time.* New York: Macmillan.

Lewis, C. S. (1950). *The lion, the witch and the wardrobe.* New York: Macmillan.

Lobel, A. (1970). *Frog and Toad are friends.* New York: Harper & Row.

Lobel, A. (1972). *Frog and Toad together.* New York: Harper & Row.

Lobel, A. (1976). *Frog and Toad all year.* New York: Harper & Row.

Lobel, A. (1979). *Days with Frog and Toad.* New York: Harper & Row.

Longfellow, H. W. (1990). *Paul Revere's ride.* New York: Dutton.

Lowry, L. (1989). *Number the stars.* Boston: Houghton Mifflin.

Macaulay, D. (1977). *Castle.* Boston: Houghton Mifflin.

MacLachlan, P. (1985). *Sarah, plain and tall.* New York: Harper & Row.

Mayer, M. (1974). *Frog goes to dinner.* New York: Dial.

Mayers, F. C. (1986). *The National Air and Space Museum ABC.* New York: Abrams.

Parker, N. W., & Wright, J. R. (1990). *Frogs, toads, lizards, and salamanders.* New York: Greenwillow.

Potter, B. (1902). *The tale of Peter Rabbit.* New York: Warne.

Prelutsky, J. (1983). *The Random House book of poetry for children.* New York: Random House.

Prelutsky, J. (1988). *Tyrannosaurus was a beast.* New York: Greenwillow.

Sendak, M. (1963). *Where the wild things are.* New York: Harper & Row.

Steig, W. (1969). *Sylvester and the magic pebble.* New York: Simon & Schuster.

Van Allsburg, C. (1981). *Jumanji.* Boston: Houghton Mifflin.

White, E. B. (1952). *Charlotte's web.* New York: Harper & Row.

" I integrate listening, talking, reading, and writing in my kindergarten classroom, but listening is the most basic. That's where I start. Then I integrate the others. **"**

Marie Whiteside
Kindergarten Teacher
Norseman Elementary School

PROCEDURE

We're doing a theme cycle contrasting life in the city and life in the country, and as part of the theme I read aloud *Who Took the Farmer's Hat?* (Nodset, 1963) to the class. It's a repetitive story about how some animals use the farmer's hat. First, we read the story for pleasure, but if my children really like it, that's just the beginning. And did they ever like it! It is so predictable that after a second reading, they were reading along with me. Next, the children dictate sentences about the events of the story, and we put them in sequence and place them in a pocket chart. We add pictures to illustrate each line, and the children are ready to read the chart. Two pictures and the corresponding sentences are shown in the accompanying figure.

At first I read each sentence aloud and they recite it, like an echo. After they are familiar with the words, we vary the way we read the chart. Sometimes we read it in unison; sometimes the boys and the girls alternate reading sentences; and sometimes individual children read the sentences. Then students assume the roles of each character and read the sentences. Before long children are picking out words from the sentences and writing words and sentences from the chart or the book in their journals and reciting the entire story to anyone who will listen.

That's where we are now. The children know the story well and want to make books with the sentences to take home and read to their moms and dads. This will be their 23rd book this school year! I write each sentence on a sheet of paper and duplicate the sheets. Then the children collect the sheets, illustrate them, compile the books, and add cardboard covers. Next they practice reading their books (sometimes it is really reciting or telling about the picture on each page) in class for several days before taking them home to share with their families.

ASSESSMENT

I'm a "kid-watcher"—I watch my children throughout the theme cycle and make mental notes about who asks me to reread the story, who volunteers sentences for the pocket chart, and who reads aloud the sentences on the chart. I also try to note which children are holding back, and I plan opportunities for the children who aren't actively participating to reread the book, act it out, and read the sentences on the chart in a small group setting. Once or twice a week, I transfer these mental notes to a checklist. I keep a list of the children's names on a clipboard in the classroom and add check marks and other comments next to each child's name to indicate how everyone is doing. The great thing about kindergarten is that everyone can be successful, and I watch my children and use checklists to make sure everyone is learning.

ADAPTATIONS

I use a variety of repetitive books in the same way I used *Who Took the Farmer's Hat?* Ten of my kindergartners' favorite repetitive books are:

Jan Brett's (1989) version of *The Mitten*

Ruth Brown's (1981) *A Dark Dark Tale* and *The Big Sneeze*

Eric Carle's (n.d.) *The Very Hungry Caterpillar*

Mem Fox's (1989) *Night Noises*

Paul Galdone's (1975) version of *The Gingerbread Boy*

Debra Guarino's (1989) *Is Your Mama a Llama?*

Bill Martin, Jr.'s (1983) *Brown Bear, Brown Bear, What Do You See?*

Pierr Morgan's (1990) retelling of *The Turnip*

Audrey Wood's (1984) *The Napping House*

Because these books have repeated events and predictable language, my kindergartners are able to read and recite the stories after listening to me read them aloud several times.

REFLECTIONS

Kindergarten used to be the "readiness" class, but now my children are using literature as the basis for listening, talking, reading, and writing. I'm excited about this new integrated approach because it works! They are quickly learning to use language to communicate. A number of the children in my class have been in the United States less than a year or come from homes in which parents speak little or no English. Even so, these children learn English rapidly through our listening, talking, reading, and writing activities.

Mouse said,
"I saw a big brown mousehole."

Fly said,
"I saw a flat brown hill."

3

Listening to Learn

INSIGHT _____

Listening has been called the "neglected language art" for almost 50 years because it is rarely taught in elementary classrooms. Students are admonished to listen, but few teachers teach students how to improve their listening strategies and skills. It has been assumed that children come to school already knowing how to listen. Also, some teachers feel that it is more important to spend the limited instructional time available on reading and writing instruction. Despite these concerns about teaching listening in the elementary grades, most teachers agree that students need to know how to listen because it is the most used language art. One question to reflect on as you read this chapter is:

What does a good listener do?

*L*istening is the first language mode that children acquire, and it provides the basis for the other language arts (Lundsteen, 1979). Infants use listening to begin the process of learning to comprehend and produce language. From the beginning of their lives, children listen to sounds in their immediate environment, attend to speech sounds, and construct their knowledge of oral language. Listening is also important in learning to read. Children are introduced to written language by listening to stories that parents and other care givers read to them. When children are read to, they begin to see the connection between what they hear and what they see on the printed page. The processes of reading and listening and the strategies and skills used during reading and listening are similar in many ways (Sticht & James, 1984).

Listening also influences writing. As Hansen (1987) explains, "A writing/reading program begins with listening, and listening holds the program together" (p. 69). Writing begins as talk written down, and the stories that students read become models for their writing. Listening is essential for students sharing their writing in conferences and receiving feedback on how to improve it. Inner listening, or "dialoguing" with oneself, also occurs as students write and revise their writing. Listening is "the most used and perhaps the most important of the language (and learning) arts" (Devine, 1982, p. 1).

Researchers have found that more of children's and adults' time is spent in listening than in the total time spent reading, writing, and talking (Rankin, 1926; Wilt, 1950; Werner, 1975). Figure 3–1 illustrates the amount of time we communicate in each language mode. Both children and adults spend approximately 50% of their communication time listening. Language researcher Walter Loban compared the four language modes this way: "We listen a book a day, we speak a book a week, we read a book a month, and we write a book a year" (cited in Erickson, 1985).

Despite the importance of listening in our lives, listening has been called the "neglected" or "orphan" language art for almost 50 years (Anderson, 1949). Little time has been devoted to listening instruction in most classrooms, and teachers often complain that they do not know how to teach listening (Devine, 1978; Landry, 1969; Wolvin & Coakley, 1985).

We begin this chapter with a description of the listening process and an overview of students' purposes for listening. We discuss three types of listening: aesthetic listening for enjoyment, efferent listening to take away information, and critical listening to evaluate a message. We show how students use these three types of listening as tools for learning about literature and learning across the curriculum. Finally, we present teaching strategies for each of the three types of listening and suggest ways to assess students' listening capabilities.

THE LISTENING PROCESS

Listening is elusive because it occurs internally. Lundsteen (1979) described listening as the "most mysterious" language process. In fact, teachers often do not know whether listening has occurred until they ask students to apply what they have listened to through discussions, projects, and other assignments. Even then, there is no guarantee that the students' responses indicate that they have listened, because they may have known the material before listening or may have learned it from someone else at about the same time.

Figure 3–1   Percentage of Communication Time in Each Language Mode

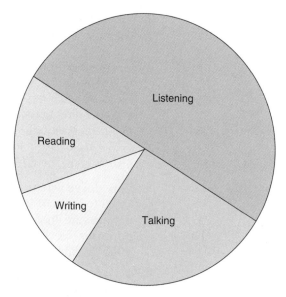

Data from Rankin, 1926; Werner, 1975; Wilt, 1950.

Listening is a complex, multistep process "by which spoken language is converted to meaning in the mind" (Lundsteen, 1979, p. 1). As this definition suggests, listening is more than just hearing, even though children and adults often use the two terms *hearing* and *listening* synonymously. Rather, hearing is an integral component, but only one component, of the listening process. The crucial part is thinking or converting to meaning what one has heard.

Steps in the Listening Process

The three steps in the listening process are receiving, attending, and assigning meaning (Wolvin & Coakley, 1985). In the first step listeners receive the aural stimuli or the combined aural and visual stimuli presented by the speaker. Next, listeners focus on or attend to selected stimuli while ignoring other distracting stimuli. Because so many stimuli surround students in the classroom, they must attend to the speaker's message, focusing on the most important information in that message. In the third step listeners assign meaning to, or understand, the speaker's message. Listeners assign meaning using assimilation and accommodation to fit the message into their existing cognitive structures or to create new structures if necessary. Responding or reacting to the message is not considered part of the listening process; the response occurs afterward, and it sets another communication process into action in which the listener becomes the message sender.

The second step of Wolvin and Coakley's listening process model may be called the "paying attention" component. Elementary teachers spend a great deal of instructional time reminding students to pay attention; unfortunately, however, children often do not understand the admonition. When asked to explain what "paying attention" means, some children equate it with physical behaviors such as not kicking their feet or cleaning off their desks. Learning to attend to the speaker's message is especially important because researchers have learned that students can listen to 250 words per minute, two to three times the normal rate of talking (Foulke, 1968). This differential allows listeners time to tune in and out as well as to become distracted during listening.

Furthermore, the intensity of students' need to attend to the speaker's message varies with the purpose for listening. Some types of listening require more attentiveness than others. Effective listeners, for example, listen differently to directions on how to reach a friend's home than to a poem or story being read aloud.

Purposes for Listening

Why do we listen? Students often answer that question by explaining that they listen to learn or to avoid punishment (Tompkins, Friend, & Smith, 1984). It is unfortunate that some students have such a vague and limited view of the purposes for listening. Communication experts (Wolvin & Coakley, 1979, 1985) delineate five more specific purposes:

- Discriminative listening
- Aesthetic listening
- Efferent listening
- Critical listening
- Therapeutic listening

The terms *aesthetic,* meaning "for pleasure," and *efferent,* meaning "to carry away information," come from reader response theories (Rosenblatt, 1985, 1991).

Discriminative Listening.   People listen to distinguish sounds and to develop a sensitivity to nonverbal communication. Teaching discriminative listening involves one sort of activity in the primary grades and a different activity for older students. Having kindergarten and first-grade students listen to tape-recorded animal sounds and common household noises is one discriminative listening activity. Most children are able to discriminate among sounds by the time they reach age 5 or 6. In contrast, developing a sensitivity to the messages that people communicate nonverbally is a lifelong learning task.

Aesthetic Listening.   People listen aesthetically to a speaker or reader when they listen for enjoyment. Listening to someone read stories aloud or recite poems is a pleasurable activity. Teachers encourage children's aesthetic listening by reading aloud and teaching students how to visualize characters and episodes and notice interesting language. Listening to classmates converse or talk about literature they have read or listened to someone else read aloud is another kind of aesthetic listening.

Efferent Listening.   People listen efferently to understand a message, and this is the type of listening required in many instructional activities, particularly in theme cycles. Students determine the speaker's purpose and then organize the information they are listening to in order to remember it. Elementary students usually receive little instruction in efferent listening; rather, teachers assume that students simply know how to listen. Note-taking is typically the one efferent listening strategy taught in the elementary grades, although there are other strategies elementary students can learn and use.

Critical Listening.   People listen to get information and then to evaluate a message. Critical listening is an extension of efferent listening. As in efferent listening, listeners seek to understand a message, but they must filter the message to detect propaganda devices and persuasive language. Critical listening is used when people listen to debates, commercials, political speeches, and other arguments.

Therapeutic Listening.   People listen to allow a speaker to talk through a problem. Children, as well as adults, serve as sympathetic listeners for friends and family members. Although this type of listening is important, it is less appropriate for elementary students, so we will not discuss it in this chapter.

Our focus will be on the three listening purposes that are most appropriate for elementary students: aesthetic listening, or listening for pleasure; efferent listening, or listening for information; and critical listening, or listening to evaluate a message.

Teaching Listening Strategies

Activities involving listening go on in every elementary classroom. Students listen to the teacher give directions and instruction, to tape-recorded stories at listening centers, to classmates during discussions, and to someone reading stories and poetry aloud. Since listening plays a significant role in these and other classroom activities, listening is not neglected. However, while these activities provide opportunities for students to practice listening strategies and skills they already possess, they do *not* teach students how to become more effective listeners.

Language arts educators have repeatedly cited the need to teach listening strategies (Brent & Anderson, 1993; Devine, 1978; Lundsteen, 1979; Pearson & Fielding, 1982; Wolvin & Coakley, 1985). Most of what has traditionally been called "listening instruction" has been merely practice. When students listen to a story at a listening center and then answer questions about it, for example, teachers assume that the students know *how* to listen and that they will be able to answer the questions. However, a listening center activity is practice, not instruction!

In contrast to practice activities, students need to learn how to vary how they listen to fit the purpose for listening, and they need to develop specific strategies to use when listening (Brent & Anderson, 1993; Jalongo, 1991). Many students have only one approach to listening, no matter what the purpose. They say they listen as hard as they can and try to remember everything. This strategy seems destined to fail for at least two reasons: First, trying to remember everything places an impossible demand on short-term memory; and second, many items in a message are not important enough to remember. Other students equate listening with intelligence, assuming that they are poor listeners because they "just aren't smart enough."

LISTENING TO LITERATURE

Many children come to school with a rich experience of listening to oral presentations of literature at home and in their communities. Parents and other care givers typically read stories aloud to preschoolers on a daily basis, and grandparents and siblings share family stories with young children. Children may listen to Bible stories told at church and watch television shows, video-taped stories, and films at home. Through these experiences students learn that listening can be a pleasurable activity.

Teachers expand these aesthetic listening experiences. They read aloud daily and provide opportunities for students to talk about the stories they have listened to. They also arrange for students to listen to readers theater productions, view puppet shows and plays that classmates stage, listen to storytellers and classmates read books they have written, and view productions at community theaters. Through these activities students develop aesthetic listening strategies and refine their concept of a story. Stories are the most common type of literature that children listen to aesthetically, but they also listen aesthetically to poetry and sometimes to informational books, if their purpose for listening is enjoyment.

Aesthetic Listening

Louise Rosenblatt (1938, 1978) coined the term *aesthetic reading* to describe one stance readers take. During aesthetic reading, readers are concerned with the experience they are living through and with their relationship with the literature they are reading. The focus is on the during-reading experience, not on the information they will carry away from the experience. The term *aesthetic listening* can be applied to describe the type of listening children and adults do as they listen to storytellers tell stories, poets recite poems, actors perform a play, singers sing songs, or readers read stories aloud. The focus of this type of listening is on the lived-through experience and the connections the listeners are making to the literature they are listening to. More traditional names for aesthetic listening are appreciative listening or listening for pleasure.

Teachers often take aesthetic listening for granted, assuming that students are experienced listeners and know how to listen to literature. Teachers should not take this for granted; it is important to explain to students that they listen differently for various purposes. For aesthetic listening, students focus on the experience of the literature, forming mental images, predicting what will happen next, appreciating the beauty of the language, and making connections to other experiences or other literature. Students do not concentrate on remembering specific information; instead, they listen for the emotional impact.

Strategies for Aesthetic Listening.   Students use specific strategies as they listen aesthetically, and these strategies are different from those they use for other types of listening. Six strategies that elementary students can learn to use when listening aesthetically are:

1. *Predicting.* As students listen to a story read aloud or view a puppet show, they are predicting or making guesses about what will happen next in the story. Then they revise their predictions as they continue listening to and/or viewing the story. When they read aloud, teachers help students develop the predicting strategy by asking them what they think will happen next.
2. *Creating a mental image.* Students create an image or picture in their minds while listening to a story that has strong visual images, details, or descrip-

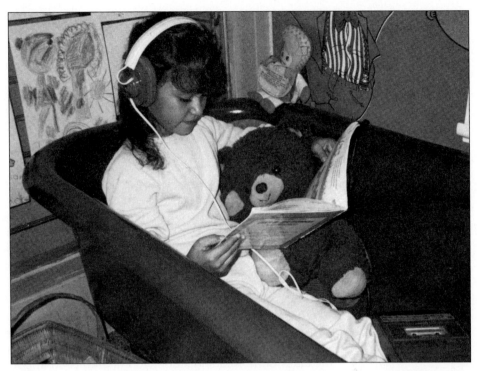

This student uses aesthetic listening as she listens to a favorite story and follows along in the trade book.

tive words. Students practice this strategy by closing their eyes and trying to draw mental pictures while they listen to a story and then reproducing these pictures on paper after reading.

3. *Connecting to personal experiences.* Students make personal connections between the story they are listening to and experiences in their own lives. Students might share these connections in reading log entries and in literature conversations after reading.

4. *Connecting to literature.* Students make connections between the story they are listening to and other stories they have listened to read aloud, stories they have read themselves, or films they have viewed. Students make connections between the story they are listening to and another story with the same theme, or a character or episode in this story and a character or episode in another story. Teachers help students use this strategy by asking them to talk about any connections they are making as the story is discussed or by having them make entries in their reading logs.

5. *Noticing the power and beauty of language.* As they are listening, students should be sensitive to the author's choice of language, to the way sentences are phrased, and to the author's use of comparisons or wordplay. Children take over the language they hear and make it part of their own (Cullinan, 1987). Teachers comment on examples of powerful and beautiful language as they are reading or after reading, and students can collect examples in their reading logs, on charts, or in story quilts.

6. *Applying knowledge of story structure.* As they listen to stories read aloud, students apply their knowledge of plot, characters, setting, theme, and

point of view in order to anticipate what will happen next and how the problem introduced in the beginning of the story will be resolved at the end. They also apply their knowledge of various genres (e.g., fantasy, historical fiction, contemporary realistic fiction) in order to understand stories they are listening to.

Students also use these strategies as they listen aesthetically to poems or informational books read aloud. They create mental images and make connections between what they are listening to and their own lives and other literature they know. Instead of using story structure to help them organize what they are listening to, they use their knowledge about how poetry or informational books are organized. Similarly, as they think about the powerful and beautiful language of poems, they consider the impact that rhyme, alliteration, or repetition has on readers and listeners. When listening to informational books, they think about how the author's use of factual information, examples, diagrams, and photographs helps students to create mental images. It is also important to point out that readers use these same strategies when they read aesthetically.

Reading Aloud to Students.   Sharing stories, poems, and informational books orally with students is a wonderful way to develop an appreciation of literature, encourage interest in reading, and create a community of learners in the classroom. Reading stories to children is an important component in most kindergarten and first-grade classrooms. Unfortunately, teachers often think they need to read to children only until they learn to read for themselves; however, reading aloud and sharing the excitement of books, language, and reading should remain an important part of the language arts program at all grade levels.

A common complaint is that there is not enough time in the school day to read to children, but reading a story or a chapter of a longer story aloud can take as little as 10 or 15 minutes a day. Many educators (Kimmel & Segel, 1983; Sims, 1977; Trelease, 1989) point out the necessity of finding time to read aloud so as to take advantage of the many benefits:

- Stimulating children's interest in books and in reading
- Broadening children's reading interests and developing their taste for quality literature
- Introducing children to the sounds of written language and expanding their vocabulary and sentence patterns
- Sharing with children books that are "too good to miss"
- Allowing children to listen to books that would be too difficult for them to read on their own or books that are "hard to get into"
- Expanding children's background of experiences
- Introducing children to concepts about written language, different genres of literature, poetry, and elements of story structure
- Providing a pleasurable, shared experience
- Modeling to children that adults read and enjoy reading, to increase the likelihood that children will become lifelong readers

Guidelines for choosing literature to read aloud are simple: Choose books that you like and that you think will appeal to your students. Trelease (1989) suggests four additional criteria of good read-aloud books: They should be fast-paced to hook children's interest as quickly as possible; contain well-developed characters; include easy-to-read dialogue; and keep long descriptive passages to a minimum. There are a number of annotated guidebooks to help teachers select books for reading aloud as well as for independent reading. Figure 3–2 lists these guides.

Books that have received awards or other acclaim from teachers, librarians, and children make good choices. Two of the most prestigious awards are the Caldecott Medal and the Newbery Medal, listed in Appendix A. Other lists of outstanding books are prepared annually by professional groups such as the National Council of Teachers of English and the National Council of Teachers of Social Studies. In many states children read and vote on books to receive recognition, such as the Buckeye Book Award in Ohio and the Sequoia Book Award in Oklahoma. The International Reading Association sponsors a Children's Choices competition in which children read and select their favorite books; a list is published annually.

Teachers in many primary-grade classrooms read one story aloud as part of a literature focus unit and later during the day read informational books aloud as part of social studies or science theme cycles. Poems, too, are read aloud in connection with content area themes. It is not unusual for primary-grade

---

Figure 3–2   *Guides for Choosing Literature to Read Aloud to Students*

Books

Carroll, F. L., & Mecham, M. (Eds.). (1984). *Exciting, funny, scary, short, different, and sad books kids like about animals, science, sports, families, songs, and other things.* Chicago: American Library Association.

Freeman, J. (1984). *Books kids will sit still for.* Hagerstown, MD: Alleyside Press.

Jensen, J. M., & Roser, N. L. (1993). *Adventuring with books: A booklist for pre-K–grade 6* (10th ed.). Urbana, IL: National Council of Teachers of English.

Jett-Simpson, M. (Ed.) (1989). *Adventuring with books: A booklist for pre-K–grade 6* (9th ed.). Urbana, IL: National Council of Teachers of English.

Kids' favorite books. (1992). Newark, DE: International Reading Association.

Lipson, E. R. (1988). *The New York Times parents' guide to the best books for children.* New York: Random House.

McMullan, K. H. (1984). *How to choose good books for kids.* Reading, MA: Addison-Wesley.

Nilsen, A. P. (Ed.). (1991). *Your reading: A booklist for junior high and middle school students* (8th ed.). Urbana, IL: National Council of Teachers of English.

Recommended readings in literature: Kindergarten through grade eight. (1988). Sacramento: California State Department of Education.

Teens' favorite books. (1992). Newark, DE: International Reading Association.

Trelease, J. (1989). *The new read-aloud handbook.* New York: Penguin.

Webb, C. A. (Ed.). (1989). *Your reading: A booklist for junior high and middle school students* (9th ed.). Urbana, IL: National Council of Teachers of English.

Journals and Newsletters

Book Links. American Library Association, 50 E. Huron Street, Chicago, IL 60611–2795.

CBC Features. The Children's Book Council, 67 Irving Place, New York, NY 10003.

The Horn Book. Park Square Building, 31 St. James Avenue, Boston, MA 02116.

Language Arts. National Council of Teachers of English, 1111 Kenyon Road, Urbana, IL 61801.

The New Advocate. Christopher-Gordon Publishers, P.O. Box 809, Needham Heights, MA 02194.

The Reading Teacher. International Reading Association, P.O. Box 8139, Newark, DE 19711.

students to listen to their teacher read aloud three or more stories and other books during the school day. If children are read to only once a day, they will listen to fewer than 200 books during the school year, and this is not enough! More than 40,000 books are available for children, and reading stories and other books aloud is an important way to share more of this literature with children. Students in middle and upper grades should also read and listen to chapter books and poems read aloud as part of literature or author units and informational books, magazines, and newspaper articles in content area units.

Children, especially preschoolers and kindergartners, often beg to have a familiar book reread. Although it is important to share a wide variety of books with children, researchers have found that children benefit in specific ways from repeated readings (Yaden, 1988). Through repetition, students gain control over the parts of a story and are better able to synthesize the story parts into a whole. The quality of children's responses to a repeated story changes (Beaver, 1982), and children become more independent users of the classroom library center (Martinez & Teale, 1988).

Martinez and Roser (1985) examined young children's responses to stories and found that as stories become increasingly familiar, students' responses indicate a greater depth of understanding. They found that children talked almost twice as much about familiar books that had been reread many times as about unfamiliar books that had been read only once or twice. The form and focus of children's talk changed, too. While children tended to ask questions about unfamiliar stories, they made comments about familiar stories. Children's talk about unfamiliar stories focused on characters; the focus changed to details and word meanings when they talked about familiar stories. The researchers also found that children's comments after repeated readings were more probing and more specific, suggesting that they had greater insight into the story. Researchers investigating the value of repeated readings have focused mainly on preschool and primary-grade students, but rereading favorite stories may have similar benefits for older students as well.

Other Oral Presentation Modes.   Stories can be shared with students through storytelling, readers theatre, and plays; these oral presentation modes will be discussed in Chapter 4. Students can also benefit from other forms of oral presentations, such as tape recordings of stories and filmstrip and film versions of stories. Audiovisual story presentations are available from:

American School Publishers
P.O. Box 408
Hightstown, NJ 08520–9377

Listening Library, Inc.
One Park Avenue
Old Greenwich, CT 06870–1727

Pied Piper
P.O. Box 320
Verdugo City, CA 91046

Weston Woods
Weston, CT 06883

Spoken Arts, Inc.
10100 SBF Drive
Pinellas Park, FL 34666

Teaching Aesthetic Listening

As teachers read aloud, they need to provide opportunities for students to listen aesthetically and know the lived-through experience of aesthetic listening. They also learn how to use the aesthetic listening strategies.

Steps in Reading Literature Aloud.   As teachers read literature aloud, they structure the experience to enhance students' opportunities for aesthetic listening. The four steps in reading aloud are:

*Step
by
Step*

1. *Preparing to Share the Story.*   The teacher provides necessary background information or experiences so that students can successfully listen to the story. The teacher may also set the purpose for reading.

2. *Reading Aloud to Students.*   The teacher reads the story aloud to students or plays an audiotape of the story. One procedure teachers can use to read the story aloud is the Directed Listening-Thinking Approach (DLTA), in which the teacher asks students to make predictions about the story and then listen to confirm or reject their predictions. The DLTA procedure is described in Figure 3–3.

3. *Capturing an Initial Response.*   Immediately after reading, students reflect on the story (or a chapter of a longer book) by talking about the story or writing in a reading log. In these initial responses, students focus on personal feelings, connections to their own lives, questions and confusions, and identifying favorite characters, events, and quotations.

Students need an opportunity to talk about a story after reading. They may talk about the book with a partner, in small groups, or with the entire class. In these conversations or discussions, students share their reactions and listen to classmates' responses. The focus is on interpreting the story, not answering the teacher's questions about the story.

Hickman (1980) cites the example of a kindergartner named Ben who talked about *Pezzetino* (Lionni, 1975), a story his teacher had just read aloud to the class:

> Ben says, "I like *Pezzetino* because of all the colors 'n stuff, and the way it repeats. He keeps saying it. And there's marbleizing—see here? And this very last page . . . " Then Ben turns to the end of the book and holds up a picture for the group to see. "He cut paper. How many think he's good cutter?" Ben conducts a vote, counting the raised hands that show a majority of the group believes Leo Lionni to be "a good cutter." (p. 525)

Ben's knowledge and enjoyment of the text and illustrations are obvious. Through his comments and the class vote, Ben is involving his classmates in the story, and it seems likely that *Pezzetino* will be passed from student to student in the class. Spontaneous responses to literature, like Ben's, occur at all grade levels in supportive classrooms where students are invited to share their ideas and feelings.

Students also capture initial responses to a story by writing entries in a reading log. Primary-grade students keep a reading log by writing the title and author

Figure 3–3   The Directed Listening-Thinking Approach

The Directed Listening-Thinking Approach (DLTA) is based on the *Directed Reading-Thinking Activity,* a procedure developed by Russell Stauffer (1975). In DLTA the teacher reads the story or other piece of literature aloud to students, who are actively listening by making predictions and listening to confirm their predictions. After reading, students discuss their predictions and give reasons to support them. The three steps are:

1. Preparing to Read

Teachers provide necessary information related to the story or the author, thereby stimulating student's interest in the story. Teachers might discuss the topic or theme, show pictures, or share objects related to the story to draw on prior knowledge or to create new experiences. For example, teachers might talk about students' favorite games before reading Van Allsburg's jungle adventure game, *Jumanji* (1981). Then the teacher shows students the cover of the book and reads the title and asks them to make a prediction about the story using questions like these:

What do you think a story with a title like this might be about?

What do you think might happen in this story?

Does this picture give you any ideas about what might happen in this story?

If necessary, the teacher reads the first paragraph or two to provide more information for students to use in making their predictions. After a brief discussion in which all students commit themselves to one or another of the alternatives presented, the teacher asks these questions:

Which of these ideas do you think would be the likely one?

Why do you think that idea is a good one?

2. Reading Aloud to Students

After students set their purposes for listening, the teacher reads part of the story aloud and then asks students to confirm or reject their predictions by answering questions such as the following:

What do you think now?

What do you think will happen next?

What would happen if . . . ?

Why do you think that idea is a good one?

The teacher continues reading the story aloud, stopping at several key points to repeat this step.

3. Reflecting on Students' Predictions

Students talk about the story, expressing their feelings and making connections to their own lives and experiences with literature. Then students reflect on the predictions they made as they listened to the story being read aloud, and they provide reasons to support their predictions. Teachers ask these questions to help students think about their predictions:

What predictions did you make?

What in the story made you think of that prediction?

What in the story supports that idea?

DLTA is useful only when students are reading or listening to an unfamilar story so that the prediction actively involves them in the story. This strategy can be used both when students are listening to the teacher read literature aloud and when they are doing the reading themselves.

of the story and drawing a picture related to the story. They can also add a few words or a sentence. During an author unit on Tomie de Paola, for instance, second graders, after listening to each de Paola story, record the title on a page in their reading logs, draw a picture related to the story, and write a sentence or two telling what they liked about the story, describing what it made them think of, or summarizing it. Older students write an entry after each chapter. After drawing and writing, students often share their reading logs with classmates, and this sharing provides another opportunity for classmates to listen aesthetically.

4. *Extending the Response.*   Students extend or expand their responses through reading, writing, talk, drama, research, and other response-to-literature projects. Students choose response projects they are interested in pursuing to extend their enjoyment and interpretation of a book. These projects include making puppets to use in retelling a favorite story, writing letters to authors, creating a mobile for a favorite story, and reading other books by the same author or on a similar theme, to name only a few possibilities.

Teaching Minilessons About Aesthetic Listening.   The following teaching strategy, developed from the instructional model presented in Chapter 1, can be used to teach minilessons on the six aesthetic listening strategies:

Step by Step

1. *Introducing the Strategy.*   Explain the listening strategy, the way it is used, and the types of listening activities for which it is most effective. Develop a chart with the students to list the characteristics or steps of the strategy. For example, after introducing imagery, you can list the following steps in creating a mental image on a chart:

   • Close your eyes.
   • Draw a picture of the story in your mind.
   • Listen for details and add them to your picture.
   • Add colors to your mind picture.

2. *Demonstrating the Strategy.*   Demonstrate the strategy as you read a story aloud or as students listen to an audiotape of a story. Stop the presentation periodically to talk aloud about what you are doing or how you are using the strategy. After completing the activity, discuss your use of the strategy with students. For example, you might demonstrate how to create mental images of the characters and story events while reading aloud the first four or five chapters of Judy Blume's *Tales of a Fourth Grade Nothing* (1972).

3. *Practicing the Strategy.*   Provide students with opportunities to practice the strategy as you read aloud several other stories. Stop reading periodically to ask students to describe how they are using the strategy to listen aesthetically. For example, you might provide opportunities for students to practice creating mental images as they continue listening to the last five or six chapters of *Tales of a Fourth Grade Nothing.* Children especially enjoy creating mental images about

the last chapter when Peter finds out that his little brother Fudge ate his turtle, Dribble.

4. *Reviewing the Strategy.* After using an aesthetic listening strategy, have a student summarize the strategy and explain how he or she used it. Students can also write in their reading logs about how they used what they have learned, or they can draw pictures. For example, after reading the last chapter of *Tales of a Fourth Grade Nothing,* one fourth grader explained his mental images:

> *I made a picture in my mind of how upset Peter was that Fudge ate his turtle. He was crazy for wanting to find his turtle and mad at his brother and because no one cared about his turtle, only about his brother. He's been running and looking all over for his turtle. His face was red because he was crazy mad and he was yelling at Fudge and at his mom. He was crying, too, and wiping at his eyes because his turtle was eaten. Then I had a new picture in my mind when Peter got the big box—but with no wrapping paper or a bow—with a puppy in it from his dad at the end. He was calm but not really happy. He was still sad about his turtle being dead. He had a smart look on his face because he knew it had to be a puppy and he thought to name him Turtle so he wouldn't forget. I see him holding the black and white dog and that dog is licking him all over his face. Now he's going to start giggling and giggling and he's happy.*

5. *Teaching Minilessons About Other Strategies.* Teachers use the preceding four steps to teach other aesthetic listening strategies.

6. *Applying the Strategies.* After students develop a repertoire of the aesthetic listening strategies, they practice the strategies as they listen to stories and other types of literature read aloud.

Teachers also teach minilessons to introduce, practice, and review procedures, concepts, and skills related to aesthetic listening. See page 95 for a list of topics for minilessons on aesthetic listening and the other types of listening. The teaching strategy discussed in the previous section can be taught as a series of minilessons, or minilessons can be taught when teachers are reading stories aloud or as part of literature focus units.

For example, during a literature focus unit on *The Sign of the Beaver* (Speare, 1983), a historical fiction set in the Maine wilderness in 1768, teachers might review the imagery strategy and ask fifth graders to create a mental image of the cabin Matt and his father built in the wilderness. Then students might recall their mental images as they design and construct a tabletop diorama of the cabin. Another possibility is that teachers use a series of minilessons to teach students about literature discussions and how to listen to and build on their classmates' reactions. Or, through a discussion or in reading log entries, students might practice the connecting-to-personal-experience strategy by thinking about what they would do in Matt's position of having to stay behind at the cabin while his father walks back to Massachusetts to bring the rest of the family to the new homestead. As another alternative, a teacher might introduce the connecting-to-literature strategy and ask students to compare *The Sign of the Beaver* to another survival story such as *Robinson*

MINI LESSONS

Listening

	Procedures	Concepts	Strategies and Skills
Aesthetic Listening	Listen to a story read aloud Respond to classmates' comments Listen to a poem read aloud Write a response in a reading log Choose favorite quotations from a story Work on projects	Aesthetic listening Difference between aesthetic and efferent listening Concept of story	Predict Confirm Create a mental image Connect to personal experiences Connect to other stories Notice the power and beauty of language Apply knowledge of text structure
Efferent Listening	Take notes Do note-taking/note-making Use graphic organizers	The listening process Efferent listening Organizational patterns of informational texts	Categorize information Monitor Ask questions of the speaker Ask self questions Discover the plan Note cue words Choose key points for note-taking Get clues from the speaker
Critical Listening	Write advertisements Make storyboards Film commercials	Critical listening Persuasion Three types of persuasion Propaganda Persuasion compared to propaganda Deceptive language Propaganda devices	Identify propaganda devices Recognize deceptive language

Crusoe (Defoe, 1983). After listening to both stories read aloud, students might work in small groups to draw Venn diagrams to compare and contrast the stories.

Assessing Students' Aesthetic Listening

Students need to learn how to listen aesthetically so that they can engage more fully in the lived-through experience of literature. Teachers can assess whether or not students are listening aesthetically in several ways. First of all, they can listen to the comments students make during literature conversations and discussions, and they can read entries in students' reading logs to see if they are

- Making predictions
- Creating mental images
- Connecting to personal experience
- Connecting to literature
- Noticing the power and beauty of language
- Applying knowledge of story structure

Teachers can also convert the list of aesthetic listening procedures, concepts, and strategies and skills presented in the list of minilessons on page 95 into a checklist and keep track of each topic as it is introduced, practiced, and reviewed.

Two students present their film-strip retelling a favorite story for an audience of their classmates.

LISTENING ACROSS THE CURRICULUM

As students participate in social studies and science theme cycles, they use all three types of listening, but efferent and critical listening are especially important. Students use efferent listening as they listen to their teachers and classmates present information about the themes, as they view films and videotapes on science and social studies topics, and as they listen to teachers read informational books. Students use critical listening during theme cycles when they evaluate the information they are listening to and consider different viewpoints.

Efferent Listening

Efferent listening is practical listening to understand a message. The term *efferent,* coined by Louise Rosenblatt (1938, 1978), means "to carry away information." It is the most common type of listening students do in school. For example, a fifth-grade teacher who discusses the causes of the American Revolution, a first-grade teacher who explains how to dial 911 in an emergency, and an eighth-grade teacher who discusses the greenhouse effect are all providing information for students to relate to what they already know and remember. Students use efferent listening to identify the important pieces of information and remember them.

Whether or not students comprehend and remember the message is determined by many factors. Some factors are operative before listening, others during and after. First, students need a background of prior knowledge about the content they are listening to. They must be able to relate what they are about to hear to what they already know, and speakers can help provide some of these links. Second, as they listen, students use a strategy to help them remember. They need to organize and "chunk" the information they receive, and they may want to take notes to help them remember. Then, after listening, students should somehow apply what they have heard so that there is a reason to remember the information.

Strategies for Efferent Listening.   Students use specific strategies as they listen efferently, and the purpose of each strategy is to help students organize and remember the information they are listening to. Six strategies elementary students use for efferent listening are:

   1.   Categorizing Information.   Students categorize or organize information in groups when the speaker's message or the book the teacher is reading aloud contains many pieces of information, comparisons, or contrasts. Students use this strategy, for example, as they listen to a comparison of reptiles and amphibians. The teacher can make a two-column chart on the chalkboard, labeling one column *reptiles* and the other *amphibians*. Then, together, teacher and students make notes in the columns while they listen or immediately thereafter. Students can also divide a sheet of paper into two columns and make notes themselves.

When students are listening to a presentation or an informational book that contains information on more than two or three categories, they can make a cluster diagram, write each category on a ray, and then add details. For example, when students are listening to a presentation on the five basic food groups, the teacher might make a cluster diagram on the chalkboard to help students classify what they are listening to as shown in Figure 3–4. After the presentation students add notes about each of the food groups. Students can also draw a cluster diagram on a sheet of paper and take notes about each food group by drawing lines from each food group and adding details.

2. Monitoring. Students monitor their listening to make sure they are understanding. Monitoring is important so that students know when they are not listening successfully, when a listening strategy is not working, or when they need to ask a question. Students can use these self-questions to monitor their understanding while they are listening:

Why am I listening to this message?

Do I know what _____ means?

Does this information make sense to me?

3. Asking Questions to Clarify Information. As they are listening, students sometimes need to ask the speaker questions to clarify information, eliminate confusion, or increase their understanding of the message. While asking questions can disturb other students' and the speaker's train of thought, students should usually be allowed to ask questions because confusion inhibits their listening and learning.

4. Discovering the Plan. Informational speakers and authors of informational books use several types of organization to structure a message. Five common organizational patterns are *description, sequence, comparison, cause and effect,* and *problem and solution.* Students learn to recognize these patterns and use them to understand and remember a speaker's message more easily. They can develop graphic organizers for each of the five organizational patterns (Smith & Tompkins, 1988); sample organizers are shown in

Figure 3–4 A Cluster Diagram on the Food Groups

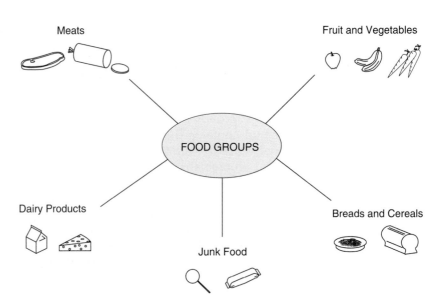

the Teacher's Notebook on page 100. Graphic organizers help students visualize the organization of a message.

Speakers often use certain words to signal the organizational patterns they are following. Signal words include *first, second, third, next, in contrast,* and *in summary.* Students can learn to attend to these signals to identify the organizational pattern the speaker is using as well as to better understand the message.

5. Note-taking. Note-taking helps students become more active listeners. Devine (1981) describes note-taking as "responding-with-pen-in-hand" (p. 156). Students' interest in note-taking begins with the realization that they cannot store unlimited amounts of information in their minds; they need some kind of external storage system. Many listening strategies require listeners to make written notes about what they are hearing. Note-taking is often thought of as a listing or an outline, but notes can also be written in clusters and other diagrams.

Teachers introduce note-taking by taking notes with the class on the chalkboard. During an oral presentation the teacher stops periodically, asks students to identify what important information was presented, and lists their responses on the chalkboard. Teachers often begin by writing notes in a list format, but the notes can also be written in outline or cluster formats. Similarly, the teacher can use key words, phrases, or sentences in recording notes. After an introduction to various note-taking strategies, students develop personal note-taking systems in which they write notes in their own words and use a consistent format.

Upper-grade students might try a special kind of note-taking in which they divide their papers into two columns. They label the left column "note-taking" and the right column "note-making." They take notes in the left column, but more importantly, they think about the notes, make connections, and personalize the notes in the right column, "note-making" (Berthoff, 1981). Students can use this strategy when listening to oral presentations as well as when reading a content area textbook or an informational book. Students need to stop periodically and reflect on the notes they have taken. The "note-making" column should be more extensive than the other column. A sample note-taking and note-making sheet is presented in Figure 3–5. In this figure a sixth grader is taking notes as she reads about illegal drugs.

Children's awareness of note-taking as a strategy "to help you remember what you are listening to" begins in the primary grades. Teachers begin demonstrating the usefulness of note-taking on the chalkboard or on charts with kindergartners and first graders. Second and third graders then begin taking notes in their learning logs as a part of social studies and science classes.

Outlining is a useful note-taking strategy, but it has gained a bad reputation from misuse in secondary and college English classes (Devine, 1981). It may be preferable to use print materials to introduce outlining, because oral presentations are often less structured than print materials, and students must discover the speaker's plan in order to outline. Teachers who want to teach outlining through oral presentations, however, should begin with a simple organization of perhaps three main ideas with two subordinate ideas for each main idea. Teachers can also give students a partial outline to complete while they give an oral presentation.

Teacher's Notebook

Five Graphic Organizers

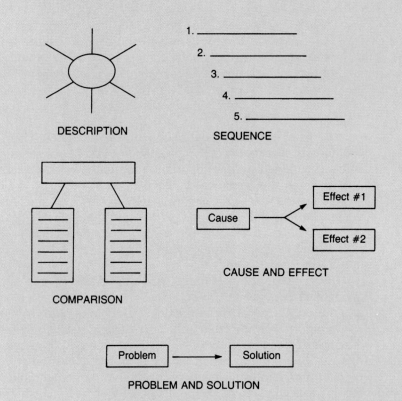

DESCRIPTION

1. _____
2. _____
3. _____
4. _____
5. _____

SEQUENCE

COMPARISON

Cause → Effect #1 / Effect #2

CAUSE AND EFFECT

Problem → Solution

PROBLEM AND SOLUTION

100

Figure 3–5 A Fifth Grader's Note-Taking and Note-Making Sheet

DRUGS

Take notes	Make Notes
pot affects your brain mariquania is a ilegal drug and does things to your lungs makes you forget things. Affects your brain	How long does it take to affect your brain? how long does it last? Could it make you forget how to drive?
Crack and coacain is illegal a small pipeful can cause death. It can cause heart atachs. is very dangerous It doesent make you cool. It makes you a dummy. you and your friends might think so but others think your a dummy. people are stupid if they attemp to take drugs. The ansew is no, no, no, no.	Like basketball players? Why do people use drugs? How do people get the seeds to grow drugs?

The information that students should include in the notes they take depends on their purpose for listening. Thus, it is essential that students understand the purpose for listening before they begin to take notes. Some listening tasks require noting main ideas or details; other tasks require noting sequence, cause and effect, or comparisons.

Students can take notes from informational books they are reading and from reference materials; however, taking notes from a speaker is an equally important strategy. When they are taking notes from a speaker, students cannot control the speed at which information is presented. They usually cannot relisten to a speaker to complete notes, and the structure of oral presentations is often not as formal as that of printed materials. Students need to become aware of these differences so that they can adapt their note-taking system to the presentation mode.

6.   *Getting Clues From the Speaker.* Speakers use both visual and verbal cues to convey their messages and direct their listeners' attention. Visual cues include gesturing, writing or underlining important information on the chalkboard, and changing facial expressions. Verbal cues include pausing, raising or lowering the voice, slowing down speech to stress key points, and repeating important information. Surprisingly, many students are not aware of these attention-directing behaviors, so teachers must point them out. Once students are aware of these cues, they can use them to increase their understanding of a message.

Teaching Efferent Listening

Learning to listen efferently is an important school task, and students use efferent listening as they listen to presentations as part of theme cycles. Using the efferent listening strategies helps students to more efficiently remember information and better understand the message they are listening to. Teachers need to explain the differences between aesthetic and efferent listening and teach students to use the efferent listening strategies. Teachers also teach minilessons about procedures, concepts, and strategies and skills related to efferent listening. Then students use what they have learned about efferent listening as part of theme cycles and other across-the-curriculum learning.

Teaching Minilessons About Efferent Listening.   Teachers teach minilessons to introduce, practice, and review procedures, concepts, and strategies related to efferent listening. The list of topics for minilessons presented on page 95 includes topics related to efferent listening. The teaching strategy discussed in the previous section on aesthetic listening can be used to teach minilessons on efferent listening, or minilessons can be taught as part of theme cycles.

After students have developed a repertoire of the six efferent listening strategies, they need to learn to select an appropriate strategy for specific listening purposes. The choice depends on both the listener's and the speaker's purpose. Although students must decide which strategy to use before they begin to listen, they need to continue to monitor their selection during and after listening. Students can generate a list of questions to guide their selection of a strategy and monitor its effectiveness. Asking themselves questions like these before listening will help them select a listening strategy:

What is the speaker's purpose?

What is my purpose for listening?

What am I going to do with what I listen to?

Will I need to take notes?

Which strategies could I use?

Which strategy will I select?

These are possible questions to use during listening:

Is my strategy still working?

Am I putting information into groups?

Is the speaker giving me cues about the organization of the message?

Is the speaker giving me nonverbal cues, such as gestures and facial expressions?

Is the speaker's voice giving me other cues?

These questions are appropriate after listening:

Do I have questions for the speaker?

Is any part of the message unclear?

Are my notes complete?

Did I make a good choice of strategies? Why or why not? (Tompkins, Friend, & Smith, 1987, p. 39)

Presenting Information as Part of Theme Cycles. During theme cycles, students use efferent listening in order to remember the important information that teachers present. Students need to understand the differences between aesthetic and efferent listening and know how to use the efferent listening strategies to help them identify and remember the important information. The way teachers present information often determines whether or not students understand the presentation. The three steps in giving a presentation of information are:

Step by Step

1. **Building Students' Backgrounds.** Before beginning the presentation, teachers make sure that students have the necessary background information; then, when teachers present the new information, they link it to the background information. Teachers explain the purposes of the listening activity and review a strategy or several strategies students can use to facilitate their understanding.

2. **Presenting the Information.** While the students listen, teachers can draw graphic organizers on the chalkboard and add key words to help students organize the information being presented. This information can also be the basis for the notes students take either as they are listening or immediately after they have listened. Teachers can also pass out sheets with skeleton notes that students complete while they are listening or after they have listened.

   Teachers use both visual and verbal cues—writing notes on the chalkboard, repeating key concepts, raising their voices to highlight conclusions—to direct students' attention to the important information being presented. As teachers draw the presentation to a close, they summarize the important points or draw conclusions.

3. Providing Application Opportunities.   After students listen to the presentation, teachers provide opportunities to apply the new information in a meaningful way. For example, as part of a theme cycle on rivers, a sixth-grade teacher might give a presentation on the Mississippi River. First, the teacher builds background knowledge by locating the river on a large map of the United States and then asking students to trace the river from its source in Minnesota to its mouth in the Gulf of Mexico on their smaller, individual maps. Then the teacher explains that he will talk about four topics related to the Mississippi: uses, boats, floods, and plant and animal life. Students divide a sheet of paper into four sections to take notes as each topic is discussed.

Then the teacher gives the first part of the presentation, talking briefly about how the river is used as an inland waterway. He writes *corn, coal, steel,* and *oil* on the chalkboard as he describes the northbound and southbound commercial traffic on the Mississippi. Then he stops for students to take notes using the key words he has written. He also asks students to monitor their listening, think about what he has said, and ask themselves if they have understood. Then the teacher repeats this process as he talks briefly about the other three topics.

After this presentation, students review their notes with a classmate and add any important information they have not included. Later during the theme cycle, students will divide into small groups to teach their classmates about other rivers of the world using the same procedure.

Assessing Students' Efferent Listening

Teachers often use objective tests to measure students' efferent listening. For example, if teachers have provided information about the causes of the American Revolution, how to dial 911 for an emergency, or the greenhouse effect, they can check the students' understanding of the information and infer whether or not students listened. Teachers should also assess students' listening more directly. Specifically, they should check how well students understand efferent listening procedures, strategies, and skills and how they apply them in listening activities. Asking students to reflect on and talk about the strategies they use and what they do before, during, and after listening provides insights into children's thinking in a way that objective tests cannot. Teachers can also take the list of efferent listening minilesson topics presented on page 95, turn it into a checklist, and keep track of each topic as it is introduced, practiced, and reviewed.

Critical Listening

Students, even those in the primary grades, need to develop critical listening skills because they are exposed to many types of persuasion and propaganda. Peer pressure to dress, behave, and talk like their classmates exerts a strong pull on students. Interpreting books and films requires critical thinking and listening. And social studies and science lessons on topics such as pollution, political candidates, and drugs demand that students listen and think critically.

Television commercials are another form of persuasion and source of propaganda, and because many commercials are directed at children, it is essential that they listen critically and learn to judge the advertising claims. For example, do the jogging shoes actually help you to run faster? Will the breakfast cereal make you a better football player? Will a particular toy make you a more popular child?

Persuasion.   There are three basic ways to persuade people. The first is by reason. People seek logical conclusions, whether from absolute facts or from strong possibilities; for example, people can be persuaded to practice more healthful living as the result of medical research. It is necessary, of course, to distinguish between reasonable arguments and unreasonable appeals. To suggest that diet pills will bring about exaggerated weight loss is an unreasonable appeal.

A second means of persuasion is an appeal to character. We can be persuaded by what another person recommends if we trust that person. Trust comes from personal knowledge or the reputation of the person who is trying to persuade. We must always question whether we can believe the persuader. We can believe what scientists say about the dangers of nuclear waste, but can we believe what a sports personality says about the effectiveness of a particular sports shoe?

The third way to persuade people is by appealing to their emotions. Emotional appeals can be as strong as intellectual appeals. We have strong feelings and concern for ourselves and other people and animals. Fear, a need for peer acceptance, and a desire for freedom of expression are all strong feelings that influence our opinions and beliefs.

Any of the three types of appeals can be used to try to persuade someone. For example, when a child tries to persuade her parents that her bedtime should be delayed by 30 minutes, she might argue that neighbors allow their children to stay up later—an appeal to character. It is an appeal to reason when the argument focuses on the amount of sleep a 10-year-old needs. And when the child announces that she has the earliest bedtime of anyone in her class and it makes her feel like a baby, the appeal is to emotion. The same three appeals apply to in-school persuasion. To persuade classmates to read a particular book in a book report "commercial," a student might argue that they should read the book because it is short and interesting (reason); because it is hilarious and they'll laugh (emotion); or because it is the most popular book in the second grade and everyone else is reading it (character).

Propaganda.   Children need to learn to become critical consumers of advertisements (Rudasill, 1986; Tutolo, 1981). Advertisers use appeals to reason, character, and emotion just as other persuaders do to promote products, ideas, and services; however, advertisers may also use *propaganda* to influence our beliefs and actions. Propaganda suggests something shady or underhanded. Like persuasion, propaganda is designed to influence people's beliefs and actions, but propagandists may use certain techniques to distort, conceal, and exaggerate. Two of these techniques are deceptive language and propaganda devices.

People seeking to influence us often use words that evoke a variety of responses. They claim that something is *improved, more natural,* or *50% better—loaded words* that are deceptive because they are suggestive. When a product is advertised as 50% better, for example, consumers need to ask, "50% better than what?" Advertisements rarely answer that question.

Doublespeak is another type of deceptive language characterized as evasive, euphemistic, confusing, and self-contradictory. Janitors may be called *maintenance engineers,* and repeats of television shows are termed *encore telecasts.* Lutz (1984) cited a number of kinds of doublespeak. Elementary students can easily understand two kinds: euphemisms and inflated language. Other kinds of doublespeak—such as jargon specific to particular groups, overwhelming an audience with words, and language that pretends to communicate but does not—are more appropriate examples for older students.

Euphemisms are words or phrases (e.g., *passed away*) that are used to avoid a harsh or distasteful reality, often out of concern for someone's feelings rather than to deceive. *Inflated language* includes words intended to make the ordinary seem extraordinary. Thus, car mechanics become *automotive internists,* and used cars become *pre-owned* or *experienced* cars. Examples of deceptive language are listed in Figure 3–6.

Children need to learn that people sometimes use words that only pretend to communicate; sometimes they use words to intentionally misrepresent, as when someone advertises a vinyl wallet as "genuine imitation leather" or a ring with a glass stone as a "faux diamond." Children need to be able to interpret deceptive language and to avoid using it themselves.

Advertisers use propaganda devices such as testimonials, the bandwagon effect, and rewards to sell products. Nine devices that elementary students can learn to identify are listed in Figure 3–7. Students can listen to commercials to

Figure 3–6   Examples of Deceptive Language

Loaded Words	Doublespeak
best buy	bathroom tissue (toilet paper)
better than	civil disorder (riot)
carefree	correctional facility (jail, prison)
discount	dentures (false teeth)
easier	disadvantaged (poor)
extra strong	encore telecast (rerun)
fortified	funeral director (undertaker)
fresh	genuine imitation leather (vinyl)
guaranteed	inner city (slum, ghetto)
improved	inoperative statement or misspeak (lie)
longer lasting	memorial park (cemetery)
lowest	mobile home (house trailer)
maximum	nervous wetness (sweat)
more natural	occasional irregularity (constipation)
more powerful	passed away (died)
new/newer	people expressways (sidewalks)
plus	personal preservation flotation device (life preserver)
stronger	pre-owned or experienced (used)
ultra	pupil station (student's desk)
virtually	senior citizen (old person)
	terminal living (dying)
	urban transportation specialist (cab driver, bus driver)

Source: Lutz, n.d.

Figure 3-7   Propaganda Devices

1. Glittering Generality

Generalities such as "motherhood," "justice," and "The American Way" are used to enhance the quality of a product or the character of a political figure. Propagandists select a generality so attractive that listeners do not challenge the speaker's real point. If a candidate for public office happens to be a mother, for example, the speaker may say, "Our civilization could not survive without mothers." The generalization is true, of course, and listeners may—if they are not careful—accept the candidate without asking these questions: Is she a mother? Is she a good mother? Does being a mother have anything to do with being a good candidate?

2. Testimonial

To convince people to purchase a product, an advertiser associates it with a popular personality such as an athlete or film star. For example, "Bozo Cereal must be good because Joe Footballstar eats it every morning." Similarly, film stars endorse candidates for political office and telethons to raise money for medical research and other causes. Consider these questions: Is the person familiar with the product being advertised? Does the person offering the testimonial have the expertise necessary to judge the quality of the product, event, or candidate?

3. Transfer

In this device, which is similar to the testimonial technique, the persuader tries to transfer the authority and prestige of some person or object to another person or object that will then be accepted. Good examples are found regularly in advertising: A film star is shown using Super Soap, and viewers are supposed to believe that they too may have healthy, youthful skin if they use the same soap. Likewise, politicians like to be seen with famous athletes or entertainers in hopes that the luster of the stars will rub off on them. This technique is also known as guilt or glory by association. Questions to determine the effect of this device are the same as for the testimonial technique.

4. Name-calling

Here advertisers try to pin a bad label on something they want listeners to dislike so that it will automatically be rejected or condemned. In a discussion of health insurance, for example, an opponent may call the sponsor of a bill a socialist. Whether or not the sponsor is a socialist does not matter to the name-caller; the purpose is to have any unpleasant associations of the term rub off on the victim. Listeners should ask themselves whether or not the label has any effect on the product.

5. Plain Folks

Assuming that most listeners favor common, ordinary people (rather than elitish, stuffed shirts), many politicians like to assume the appearance of common folk. One candidate, who really went to Harvard and wore $400 suits, campaigned in clothes from J.C. Penney's and spoke backcountry dialect: "Look at me, folks," the candidate wanted to say. "I'm just a regular country boy like you; I wouldn't sell you a bill of goods!" To determine the effect of this device, listeners should ask these questions: Is the person really the type of person he or she is portraying? Does the person really share the ideas of the people with whom he or she professes to identify?

6. Card Stacking

In presenting complex issues, the unscrupulous persuader often chooses only those items that favor one side of an issue. Any unfavorable facts are suppressed. To consider the argument objectively, listeners must seek additional information about other viewpoints.

7. Bandwagon

This technique appeals to many people's need to be a part of a group. Advertisers claim that everyone is using this product and you should, too. For example, "more physicians recommend this pill than any other." (Notice that the advertisement doesn't specify what "any other" is.) Questions to consider include the following: Does everyone really use this product? What is it better than? Why should I jump on the bandwagon?

8. Snob Appeal

In contrast to the plain folks device, persuaders use snob appeal to try to appeal to the people who want to become part of an elite or exclusive group. Advertisements for expensive clothes, cosmetics, and gourmet foods often use this technique. Listeners should consider these questions in evaluating the commercials and advertisements using this device: Is the product of high quality or does it have an expensive nametag? Is the product of higher quality than other non-snobbish brands?

9. Rewards

Increasingly, advertisers offer rewards for buying their products. For many years, snack food and cereal products offered toys and other gimmicks in their product packages. More often, adults are being lured by this device, too. Free gifts, rebates from manufacturers, low-cost financing, and other rewards are being offered for the purchase of expensive items such as appliances and automobiles. Listeners should consider the value of these rewards and whether they increase the cost of the product.

Techniques 1–6 adapted from Devine, 1982, pp. 39–40.

find examples of each propaganda device and discuss the effect the device has on them. They can also investigate to see how the same devices vary in commercials directed toward youngsters, teenagers, and adults. For instance, a snack food commercial with a sticker or toy in the package will appeal to a youngster, and a videotape recorder advertisement offering a factory rebate will appeal to an adult. The propaganda device for both ads is the same: a reward! Propaganda devices can be used to sell ideas as well as products. Public service announcements about smoking or wearing seat belts, as well as political advertisements, endorsements, and speeches, use these devices.

When students locate advertisements and commercials they believe are misleading or deceptive, they can write letters of complaint to the following watchdog agencies:

Action for Children's Television
46 Austin St.
Newton, MA 02160

Federal Trade Commission
Pennsylvania Ave. at Sixth St. NW
Washington, DC 20580

Children's Advertising Review Unit
Council of Better Business Bureaus
845 Third Ave.
New York, NY 10022

Zillions Ad Complaints
256 Washington St.
Mt. Vernon, NY 10553

In their letters, students should carefully describe the advertisement and explain what bothers them about it. They should also tell where and when they saw or heard the advertisement or commercial.

Teaching Critical Listening

The steps in teaching students to be critical listeners are similar to the steps in teaching aesthetic and efferent listening strategies. In this teaching strategy students view commercials to examine propaganda devices and persuasive language. Later they can create their own commercials and advertisements. The steps are:

*Step
by
Step*

1. **Introducing Commercials.** Talk about commercials and ask students about familiar commercials. Videotape some commercials and view them with students. Discuss the purpose of each commercial. Use these questions about commercials to probe students' thinking about persuasion and propaganda:

   What is the speaker's purpose?
   What are the speaker's credentials?
   Is there evidence of bias?
   Does the speaker use deceptive language?
   Does the speaker make sweeping generalizations or unsupported inferences?
   Do opinions predominate the talk?
   Does the speaker use any propaganda devices?
   Do you accept the message? (Devine, 1982, pp. 41–42)

2. **Explaining Deceptive Language.** Present the terms *persuasion* and *propaganda*. Introduce the propaganda devices and view the commercials again to look for examples of each device. Introduce loaded words and doublespeak, and view the commercials a third time to look for examples of deceptive language.

Students listen critically while classmates present puppet show "commercials" for their favorite Beverly Cleary books.

3. **Analyzing Deceptive Language.** Have students work in small groups to critique a commercial as to the types of persuasion, propaganda devices, and deceptive language. Students might also want to test the claims made in the commercial.

4. **Reviewing Concepts.** Review the concepts about persuasion, propaganda devices, and deceptive language introduced in the first three steps. It may be helpful for students to make charts about these concepts.

5. **Providing Practice.** Present a new set of videotaped commercials for students to critique. Ask them to identify persuasion, propaganda devices, and deceptive language in the commercials.

6. **Creating Commercials.** Have students apply what they have learned about persuasion, propaganda devices, and deceptive language by creating their own products and writing and producing their own commercials to advertise them. Possible products include breakfast cereals, toys, beauty and diet products, and sports equipment. Students might also create homework and house-sitting services to advertise, or they can choose community or environmental issues to campaign for or against. The storyboard for a commercial created by a group of fifth graders appears in Figure 3–8. As the students present the commercials, classmates act as critical listeners to detect persuasion, propaganda devices, loaded words, and doublespeak.

Figure 3–8 Fifth Graders' Storyboard for Their "Dream Date" Commercial

Adapting . . .
Listening Instruction
To Meet the Needs of Every Student

1. Identifying a Purpose for Listening

Whenever students listen to an oral presentation, they need a specific purpose for listening. By identifying the purpose for listening, students understand why they are listening and know what they will be expected to do after listening.

2. Using the Directed Listening-Thinking Approach

The Directed Listening-Thinking Approach is a good way to introduce the aesthetic listening strategies. Many teachers use DLTA whenever they read aloud to actively involve their students in listening.

3. Teaching Students to Take Notes

Many students have difficulty identifying the key concepts in order to take useful notes. Teachers demonstrate note-taking by writing notes on chart paper as they give oral presentations, and afterwards they talk about why some points were more important than others.

4. Teaching Students to Monitor Their Listening

Too often students view listening as something that happens automatically, and they don't realize that listeners are actively involved in the listening process. It is important for students to learn to monitor themselves as they listen and to ask themselves if they are understanding what they are listening to and whether or not the listening strategies they are using are working.

5. Making the Listening Process Visible

Listening is an invisible process, but students can make it more visible by talking, drawing, and writing about what they do when they listen. Encourage students to think about how they vary the way they listen for different purposes and to think about the strategies they use.

Using Advertisements.   Students can use the same procedures and activities with advertisements they collect from magazines and product packages. Have children collect advertisements and display them on a bulletin board. Written advertisements also use deceptive language and propaganda devices. Students examine advertisements and then decide how the writer is trying to persuade them to purchase the product. They can also compare the amount of text to the amount of pictures. Fox and Allen (1983) reported that children who examined advertisements found that, in contrast to advertisements for toys, cosmetics, and appliances, ads for cigarettes had comparatively little text and used pictures prominently. The students quickly speculated on the reasons for this approach.

Teaching Minilessons About Critical Listening.   Teachers also teach mini-lessons to introduce, practice, and review procedures, concepts, and strategies and skills related to critical listening. See page 95 for a list of topics for minilessons on critical listening. These topics can be taught when students are studying commercials or writing advertisements as part of a social studies or science theme cycle, or they can be taught as minilessons during reading and writing workshops.

Adapting to Meet the Needs of Every Student.   Because listening is the most often used language mode, it is especially important that all students be effective listeners. Too often teachers simply admonish students to listen or assume that students are listening because they are sitting quietly. To become effective listeners, students need to learn how to vary the way they listen for different purposes and how to use the listening strategies presented in this chapter. See page 111 for a list of ways to adapt listening instruction to meet the needs of all students.

Assessing Students' Critical Listening

After teaching about persuasion and propaganda, teachers can assess students' knowledge of critical listening by having them view and critique commercials, advertisements, and other oral presentations. They can note the critical listening procedures, strategies, and skills their students use. A second way to assess students' understanding of critical listening is to have them develop their own commercials and advertisements. Critical listening goes beyond one unit, however, and is something that teachers should return to again and again during the school year.

Review

Listening is the most basic and most used of the language modes. Despite its importance, listening instruction has been neglected in elementary class-rooms. Three purposes for listening are aesthetic listening, efferent listening, and critical listening. In aesthetic listening students listen for enjoyment, and students listen aesthetically to stories and dramatic productions. Efferent listening is listening to carry away information, and students use this type for learning information during theme cycles. Critical listening is listening to evaluate the message, and students use this type when they listen to commercials and speeches. Students use different procedures, strategies, and skills for each type of listening.

Extensions

1. Visit a classroom and observe how listening is taught or practiced. Consider how practice activities might be changed into instructional activities.

2. Interview primary-, middle-, and upper-grade students about strategies they use while listening; ask questions such as these:

What is listening?

Why do people listen? Why else?

What do you do while you are listening?

What do you do to help you remember what you are listening to?

Do you always listen in the same way, or do you listen differently to stories read aloud and to information your teacher is telling you?

How do you know what is important in the message you are listening to?

What is the hardest thing about listening?

Are you a good listener? Why? Why not?

Compare students' responses across grade levels. Are older students more aware of the listening process than younger students are? Can older students identify a greater variety of listening strategies than younger students can?

3. Plan and teach a minilesson on one of the aesthetic listening strategies and on one of the efferent listening strategies discussed in this chapter. Reflect on the lessons and on the differences between aesthetic and efferent listening.
4. Using the Directed Listening-Thinking Approach presented in Figure 3–3, read a story with a group of students. Notice the students' interest in the story and the types of predictions they make.
5. Become a pen pal with several students and correspond about the books their teacher is reading aloud to them. As you write to the students, ask them about their listening process and invite them to share their reactions to the story with you. You might want to read "Sixth Graders Write About Reading Literature" (Smith, 1982) for a description of a pen pal program.
6. Using the teaching strategy presented in the section on critical listening, teach a unit about commercials or advertisements.

References

Anderson, H. (1949). Teaching the art of listening. *School Review, 57,* 63–67.

Beaver, J. M. (1982). *Say it!* over and over. *Language Arts, 59,* 143–148.

Berthoff, A. E. (1981). *The making of meaning.* Montclair, NJ: Boynton/Cook.

Brent, R., & Anderson, P. (1993). Developing children's classroom listening strategies. *The Reading Teacher, 47,* 122–126.

Cullinan, B. E. (1987). Inviting readers to literature. In B. E. Cullinan (Ed.), *Children's literature in the reading program* (pp. 2–14). Newark, DE: International Reading Association.

Devine, T. G. (1978). Listening: What do we know after fifty years of theorizing? *Journal of Reading, 21,* 296–304.

Devine, T. G. (1981). *Teaching study skills: A guide for teachers.* Boston: Allyn and Bacon.

Devine, T. G. (1982). *Listening skills schoolwide: Activities and programs.* Urbana, IL: ERIC Clearinghouse on Reading and Communication Skills and the National Council of Teachers of English.

Erickson, A. (1985). Listening leads to reading. *Reading Today, 2,* 13.

Foulke, E. (1968). Listening comprehension as a function of word rate. *Journal of Communication, 18,* 198–206.

Fox, S. E., & Allen, V. G. (1983). *The language arts: An integrated approach.* New York: Holt, Rinehart & Winston.

Hansen, J. (1987). *When writers read.* Portsmouth, NH: Heinemann.

Hickman, J. (1980). Children's response to literature: What happens in the classroom. *Language Arts, 57,* 524–529.

Jalongo, M. R. (1991). *Strategies for developing children's listening skills* (Phi Delta Kappan Fastback Series # 314). Bloomington, IN: Phi Delta Kappa Educational Foundation.

Kimmel, M. M., & Segel, E. (1983). *For reading aloud! A guide for sharing books with children.* New York: Delacorte.

Landry, D. (1969). The neglect of listening. *Elementary English, 46,* 599–605.

Lundsteen, S. W. (1979). *Listening: Its impact on reading and the other language arts* (rev. ed.). Urbana, IL: National Council of Teachers of English.

Lutz, W. (1984). Notes toward a description of double-speak. *Quarterly Review of Doublespeak, 10,* 1–2.

Lutz, W. (n.d.). *Some examples of doublespeak.* Unpublished manuscript, National Council of Teachers of English.

Martinez, M., & Roser, N. (1985). Read it again: The value of repeated readings during storytime. *The Reading Teacher, 38,* 782–786.

Martinez, M., & Teale, W. H. (1988). Reading in a kindergarten classroom library. *The Reading Teacher, 41,* 568–572.

Pearson, P. D., & Fielding, L. (1982). Research update: Listening comprehension. *Language Arts, 59,* 617–629.

Rankin, P. R. (1926). The importance of listening ability. *English Journal, 17,* 623–640.

Rosenblatt, L. (1935). Viewpoints: Transaction versus interaction—A terminological rescue operation. *Research in the Teaching of English, 19,* 98–107.

Rosenblatt, L. (1991). Literature-S.O.S! *Language Arts, 68,* 444–448.

Rosenblatt, L. M. (1928). *Literature as exploration.* New York: Appleton-Century-Crofts.

Rosenblatt, L. M. (1978). *The reader, the text, the poem: The transactional theory of the literary work.* Carbondale: Southern Illinois University Press.

Rudasill, L. (1986). Advertising gimmicks: Teaching critical thinking. In J. Golub (Ed.), *Activities to promote critical thinking* (Classroom practices in teaching English, pp. 127–129). Urbana, IL: National Council of Teachers of English.

Sims, R. (1977). Reading literature aloud. In B. E. Cullinan & C. W. Carmichael (Eds.), *Literature and young children* (pp. 108–119). Urbana, IL: National Council of Teachers of English.

Smith, L. B. (1982). Sixth graders write about reading literature. *Language Arts, 59,* 357–363.

Smith, P. L., & Tompkins, G. E. (1988). Structured notetaking: A strategy for content area readers. *Journal of Reading, 32,* 46–53.

Stauffer, R. G. (1975). *Directing the reading-thinking process.* New York: Harper & Row.

Sticht, T. G., & James, J. H. (1984). Listening and reading. In P. D. Pearson (Ed.), *Handbook of reading research* (pp. 293–318). New York: Longman.

Tompkins, G. E., Friend, M., & Smith, P. L. (1984). Children's metacognitive knowledge about listening. Presentation at the American Educational Research Association Convention, New Orleans, LA.

Tompkins, G. E., Friend, M., & Smith, P. L. (1987). Strategies for more effective listening. In C. R. Personke & D. D. Johnson (Eds.), *Language arts and the beginning teacher* (Chapter 3). Englewood Cliffs, NJ: Prentice-Hall.

Trelease, J. (1989). *The new read-aloud handbook.* New York: Penguin.

Tutolo, D. (1981). Critical listening/reading of advertisements. *Language Arts, 58,* 679–683.

Werner, E. K. (1975). *A study of communication time.* Unpublished master's thesis, University of Maryland, College Park.

Wilt, M. E. (1950). A study of teacher awareness of listening as a factor in elementary education. *Journal of Educational Research, 43,* 626–636.

Wolvin, A. D., & Coakley, C. G. (1979). *Listening instruction* (TRIP Booklet). Urbana, IL: ERIC Clearinghouse on Reading and Communication Skills and the Speech Communication Association.

Wolvin, A. D., & Coakley, C. G. (1985). *Listening* (2nd ed.). Dubuque, IA: William C. Brown.

Yaden, D. (1988). Understanding stories through repeated read-alouds: How many does it take? *The Reading Teacher, 41,* 556–560.

Children's Book References

Blume, J. (1972). *Tales of a fourth grade nothing.* New York: Dutton.

Brett, J. (1989). *The mitten.* New York: Putnam.

Brown, R. (1981). *A dark dark tale.* New York: Dial.

Brown, R. (1985). *The big sneeze.* New York: Lothrop, Lee & Shepard.

Carle, E. (n.d.). *The very hungry caterpillar.* New York: Philomel.

Defoe, D. (1983). *Robinson Crusoe.* New York: Scribner.

Fox, M. (1989). *Night noises.* San Diego: Harcourt Brace Jovanovich.

Galdone, P. (1975). *The gingerbread boy.* New York: Seabury.

Guarino, D. (1989). *Is your mama a llama?* New York: Scholastic.

Lionni, L. (1975). *Pezzetino.* New York: Pantheon.

Martin, B., Jr. (1983). *Brown bear, brown bear, what do you see?* New York: Holt, Rinehart & Winston.

Morgan, P. (1990). *The turnip.* New York: Philomel.

Nodset, J. L. (1963). *Who took the farmer's hat?* New York: Harper & Row.

Speare, E. G. (1983). *The sign of the beaver.* Boston: Houghton Mifflin.

Van Allsburg, C. (1981). *Jumanji.* Boston: Houghton Mifflin.

Wood, A. (1984). *The napping house.* San Diego: Harcourt Brace Jovanovich.

PROCEDURE

We brainstorm possible debate topics, and the class votes to narrow our list: more sports for students, the Loch Ness Monster, soft drink machines for students, and women for president. My students enjoy defending answers, presenting logical reasons, or sharing their creative thought processes. I capitalize on the fact that they are entering a developmental stage ripe for questioning authority. Debates provide a supportive, appropriate environment for testing their ideas. Careful preparation allows students to build sound arguments and build confidence in expressing their opinions.

Students select the topic they want to debate. They divide into "pro" and "con" teams of three or four members each. Some groups have to choose numbers to form the teams; consequently, some students debate against the way they believe. The groups prepare for the debate by interviewing students, administrators, parents, and teachers; researching information in the library; and developing charts to present the data they collect. I provide in-class time for the students to prepare. We talk about how to present information and how to be persuasive.

One debate is held each day. Each debate takes about 20 minutes, so all debates can be held within a week's time. Students arrange a podium in the front of the classroom; the podium divides the pro and con teams. Students hang their charts and other visuals on the wall behind the podium for easy reference. Another student is chosen as moderator, who opens and closes the debate. The moderator states the question in debate format, for example, "Should there be more sports for students at South Rock Creek School?" The first member of the pro team presents a prepared statement, referring to notecards. These remarks are followed by a response from the con team. Students alternate until each student has spoken once. Then comes the rebuttal—a time that students really need to think on their feet. The rebuttal is more freewheeling. I allow it to continue as long as someone has something to say—usually about 10 minutes. Students have learned that comments such as "out of the ball

> **Debates are one way I encourage my students to become independent thinkers and to see another point of view.**
>
> Pat Daniel
> Sixth-Grade Teacher
> South Rock Creek School

park" or "you're wrong" are not polite. They quickly learn to substitute facts for emotional responses. The moderator closes with a statement such as "That concludes our debate."

ASSESSMENT

The students develop a list of criteria that the judges—three community members—use in assessing each student's performance in the debate and deciding the "winning" team. The winning team is the one that earns more overall points. The checklist for assessing one debate is shown in the accompanying figure.

ADAPTATIONS

My students have participated in debates on topics of special interest to them—issues in their lives and questions related to our theme cycles. A number of my students have suggested that we plan a debate on a topic related to a book we have read. For example, after reading *Tuck Everlasting* (Babbitt, 1975), we could debate whether people should live forever. Three other books that many of my students read that lend themselves to debates are *The Midnight Fox* (Byars, 1968), *Shiloh* (Naylor, 1991), and *Nothing But the Truth* (Avi, 1991).

My students have strong feelings about the issues raised in these books, and now they understand that a debate provides a forum for thinking about important issues.

REFLECTIONS

I believe in using talk in my classroom. My students regularly work in small groups and give book talks, but debates are something special. My students learn to take a stand and to marshall facts to support their position. They also learn about the power of language to solve real problems in their lives.

DEBATE

Resolved: there should be more sports for students at South Rock Creek School.

Rating Code:
1–5; 5 = highest, 1 = lowest

Pro	Appearance	Delivery	Factual information	Keeping to the point	Persuasiveness	Teamwork	Participation in rebuttal	Total
Sundee Aday	___	___	___	___	___	___	___	___
James Zientek	___	___	___	___	___	___	___	___
Jeremy Bailey	___	___	___	___	___	___	___	___
Kim Vassaur	___	___	___	___	___	___	___	___
							Total	___
Con								
Melody Brooks	___	___	___	___	___	___	___	___
Whitney Lawson	___	___	___	___	___	___	___	___
Darth Taylor	___	___	___	___	___	___	___	___
							Total	___

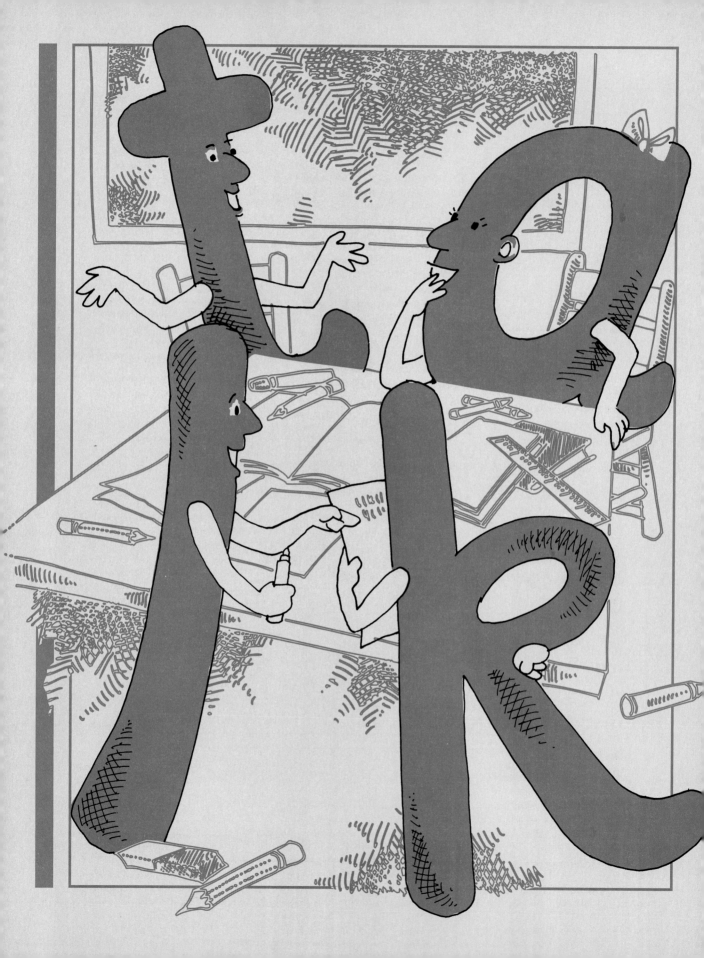

4

Sustaining Talk in the Classroom

INSIGHT _____

Quiet classrooms have traditionally been considered good learning environments, and teachers, administrators, and parents have assumed that students learn best when they work quietly and individually. This notion that a quiet environment facilitates learning has been challenged in recent years with the introduction of new instructional strategies that encourage talk. In literature discussion groups, for example, students develop interpretations of stories they have read as they ask questions and share responses with classmates. Similarly, in writing groups, students read rough drafts of compositions they are writing and talk with group members about how to revise their papers in order to communicate more effectively. As you read this chapter about talk, one issue to consider is:

What are the uses of talk in the classroom?

*T*alk is the primary expressive language mode. Both children and adults use it more frequently than writing, and children learn to talk before they learn to read and write. Talk is also the communication mode that all peoples around the world develop. Stewig (1983a) reports that of the 2,796 languages spoken today, only a fraction of them—approximately 153—have developed written forms.

When they come to school, most children are fluent oral language users. They have had 4 or 5 years of extensive practice talking and listening. Because students have acquired basic oral language competencies, teachers often assume that they do not need to emphasize talk in the elementary school curriculum. Research shows, however, that students benefit from participating in talk activities throughout the school day and that talk is a necessary ingredient for learning (Cazden, 1986, 1988; Golub, 1988; Heath, 1983).

Heath (1983) questioned the value of talk in elementary classrooms and concluded that children's talk is an essential part of language arts and is necessary for academic success in all content areas. Quiet classrooms have been considered the most conducive to learning, but research now suggests that talk is a necessary ingredient for learning. Shuy (1987) says talk is often thwarted in elementary classrooms because of large class size and the mistaken assumption that silence facilitates learning. Teachers must make an extra effort to provide opportunities for socialization and talk.

CONVERSATIONS

Brief, informal conversations are common occurrences in the social environment of school. Students converse with classmates as they work on a mural as part of a theme cycle, as they sort books in the class library center, and after they listen to a story at the listening center. In these brief conversations, students use talk for different purposes (Wilkinson, 1984). They try to control the behavior of classmates, maintain social relationships, convey information, and share personal experiences and opinions. Teachers use spare minutes before class begins or while conferencing with students for similar conversations with students. The purpose of these conversations is socialization, and they are essential to creating a climate of trust in the classroom.

Other conversations serve instructional purposes. Students meet in small groups to react to literature they have read, to respond to each other's writing, to work on projects, and to explore concepts they are learning in literature focus units and theme cycles. Students use talk for both aesthetic and efferent purposes, and the most important feature of small group conversations is that they promote thinking. Teachers take students' ideas seriously, and Nystrand and his colleagues (1993) point out that students are validated as thinkers, not just "rememberers," in these conversations. As students work in groups, they become engaged in the learning process as well as feel ownership of the knowledge they produce.

Researchers have compared the effectiveness of small group conversations with other instructional approaches, and they have found that students' learning is enhanced when students relate what they are learning to their own experiences, and especially when they do so in their own words (Wittrock &

Alesandrini, 1990). Similarly, Pressley (1992) reported that students' learning was promoted when they had opportunities to elaborate on ideas through talk.

Students use talk to work out problems, accomplish a goal, or generate an interpretation or new knowledge in small group conversations. These conversations can be used at all grade levels, kindergarten through eighth grade. Kindergartners might work together in a small group to experiment with objects and sort them according to whether or not they float. Middle-grade students might work in a small group to plan a dramatization of a story they have read.

Students' talk is spontaneous and reflects their thinking. Group members extend and expand each other's comments as the conversation grows. They disagree, ask questions, and seek clarification for comments they do not understand. In the conversation, students' talk determines the direction of the activity because students are not hunting for predetermined correct answers. For example, in a small group conversation during a theme cycle on weather, students might brainstorm a list of ways weather impacts on their lives, but they would not talk about weather in order to recall the four types of clouds that they had studied. Characteristics of small group conversations are listed in Figure 4–1.

Teachers play an important role in planning activities for small group conversations. The activities and projects should be interesting to students, and teachers should ask authentic questions—questions without obvious answers—that require students to interpret or think critically. As students work in small groups, teachers assist groups and make suggestions as they are needed, but they do not impose their ideas on students. Teachers are confident

Figure 4–1   Characteristics of Small Group Conversations

1. Each group has three to six members. These groups may be permanent, or they may be established for specific activities. It is important that group members be a cohesive group and be courteous to and supportive of each other. Students in established groups often choose names for their groups.
2. The purpose of the small group conversation or work session is to develop interpretations and create knowledge.
3. Students' talk is meaningful, functional, and genuine. They use talk to solve problems and discover answers to authentic questions—questions that require interpretation and critical thinking.
4. The teacher clearly defines the goal of the group work and outlines the activities to be completed. Activities should require cooperation and collaboration and could not be done as effectively through independent work.
5. Group members have assigned jobs. Sometimes students keep the same jobs over a period of time, and at other times specific jobs are identified for a particular purpose.
6. Students use strategies to begin the conversation, keep it moving forward and on task, and end it.
7. Students feel ownership of and responsibility for the activities they are involved in and the projects they create.

Adapted from Cintorino, 1993; Nystrand, Gamoran, & Heck, 1993; Shafer, 1993.

of students' ability to create knowledge, are respectful of their ideas, and take their comments and questions seriously.

Guidelines for Conducting Conversations

Students learn and refine their strategies and skills for socializing and conversing with classmates as they participate in small group conversations (Cintorino, 1993). Students learn how to begin the conversation, take turns, keep the conversation moving forward, support comments and questions that group members make, deal with conflicts, and bring the conversation to a close. And, they learn how powerful talk is in making meaning and creating knowledge.

Beginning the Conversation.   To begin the conversation, a student volunteers or someone is appointed. Sometimes teachers provide an authentic question to be discussed. Then the teacher or a student begins the conversation by repeating or reading the question, and a group member offers a response or subdivides the question into manageable parts. If students have written quickwrites or journal entries, one student might begin by reading his or her writing aloud to the group.

Keeping the Conversation Going.   Students take turns making comments and asking questions, and they support the other group members and elaborate on and expand their comments. The tone is exploratory, and throughout the conversation the group is progressing toward a common goal (Cintorino, 1993). The goal may be creating a project, developing an interpretation to a book the group has read, or responding to a question the teacher has asked. From time to time the conversation slows down and there may be a few minutes of silence (Sorenson, 1993). Then a group member asks a question or makes a comment that sends the conversation in a new direction.

Students are courteous, and they receive comments made by group members attentively and respectfully. Students support one another in groups. Perhaps the most important way is by calling each other by name. They also cultivate a climate of trust in the group by expressing agreement, sharing feelings, voicing approval, and referring to comments that group members made earlier.

Conflict in small group conversations is inevitable, but students need to learn how to deal with it so that it does not get out of control. Students need to accept that they will have differing viewpoints and interpretations and learn to respect each other's ideas and make compromises. Cintorino (1993) reported that her eighth graders used humor to defuse disagreements in small group conversations.

Ending the Conversation.   At the end of a conversation, students reach consensus, conclude that they have explored all dimensions of a question, or complete a project. Sometimes students have a product from the conversation. It may be a brainstormed list or a collection of notes. At other times it may be a product or project students have created. Group members may be responsible for collecting and storing materials they have used or reporting on the group's work.

Types of Conversations

Students participate in many types of small group conversations, and they use talk for both aesthetic and efferent purposes. Ten examples are to:

- Analyze propaganda in commercials and advertisements
- Compare characters in two stories
- Brainstorm questions for an interview
- Design a mural or bulletin board display
- Assess the effectiveness of a cross-age tutoring program
- Share writing in writing groups and get feedback from classmates about how to revise rough drafts
- Write a script for a puppet show, design puppets, and plan for the puppet show performance
- Discuss reactions and develop interpretations as students read a chapter book
- Make a cluster (weblike diagram) about information presented in a film
- Plan a storytelling project

These examples create situations where students have opportunities to talk with classmates and to listen, to argue, and to agree. The activities and projects are authentic and integrate talking with listening, reading, and writing. Students do not hunt for correct answers; they talk to develop interpretations and create knowledge.

Teaching Students to Talk in Small Groups

For small group conversations to be successful, teachers need to create a climate of trust in their classrooms. Teachers do this by demonstrating to students that they trust them and their ability to learn. Similarly, students learn to socialize with classmates and to trust each other as they work together in small groups. For primary- and middle-grade students, reading Diane Stanley's *The Conversation Club* (1983) is a good way to introduce the climate of trust and to explain the roles of speakers and listeners during conversations.

Sorenson (1993) begins the school year by telling her eighth-grade students that they will participate in a different type of discussion in her classroom. She hangs a sign in the classroom that says "Teach Each Other," and she tells them that it is a quote from one of her students about why this different kind of discussion works. The students learn that what they say is just as important as what the teacher says and that through conversations, students are teaching each other.

The teacher models working in small groups and discusses how students can begin conversations, sustain them, and bring them to a close. Together the teacher and students summarize what they have learned and develop guidelines for small group conversations. The teacher observes students as they work in small groups and teaches minilessons on needed procedures, concepts, and strategies and skills.

Teaching Minilessons on Talk

Even though children come to school speaking fluently, they need to learn new ways to use talk. Small group conversations provide one of these new ways.

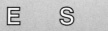

Talking

	Procedures	Concepts	Strategies and Skills
Conversations	Begin a conversation Take turns Expand or extend a classmate's comment Sustain a conversation Deal with conflicts End a conversation	Small group conversations Climate of trust Roles of speakers and listeners	Share ideas and feelings Refer to previous comments Call group members by name Look at classmates Ask questions Extend and expand classmates' comments Seek clarification
Aesthetic Talk	Participate in literature conversations Choose a story to tell Prepare and tell a story Make props Select a script for readers theatre	Aesthetic talk Literature conversations Storytelling Readers theatre Parts of a script	Include the beginning, middle, and end Incorporate interesting or repeated phrases Use dialogue Use props Use facial expressions or gestures
Efferent Talk	Participate in theme cycle conversations Do a show-and-tell presentation Prepare and present an oral report Do a book talk and/or a book review Conduct an interview Participate in a debate	Efferent talk Theme cycle conversations Facts and opinions Guidelines for speakers and listeners Persuasion	Present information Vary points of view Support opinions Ask clarifying questions Choose a topic Gather information Organize information Use visuals Rehearse Speak loudly Use notecards Look at the audience
Dramatic Activities	Role-play Participate in a dramatic production Participate in a puppet show Make puppets Write scripts Make a storyboard	Narrator Types of puppets Scripts Dramatic conventions Storyboards	Assume the role of a character Create dialogue for a character Interpret a character Sequence events Explore themes and issues

Teachers are wrong to assume that because students know how to talk, they know how to work in small groups, tell stories, participate in debates, and use talk in other ways. Teachers need to explain and demonstrate various ways of talk and teach minilessons on procedures, concepts, and strategies and skills for different types of talk. A list of minilesson topics is presented on page 124. Teachers use the procedure developed in Chapter 1 for these minilessons so that students are introduced to the topic and have opportunities to use talk in meaningful ways.

Adapting to Meet the Needs of Every Student

Talk is a useful learning tool, and it is important that activities be adapted so that every student can use talk. Small group conversations and the other talk activities discussed in this chapter can be adapted in many ways to meet students' needs. Perhaps the most basic way to meet the needs of students who are uncomfortable speaking in a large group or who are hesitant to speak because they are learning English as a second language or have other language disabilities is to have them work in a small, comfortable group and to keep the language use informal. It is much easier to work in a small group to accomplish a project than to give an oral report in front of the class or participate in a debate.

Drama is a powerful way of knowing, and many students benefit from dramatizing stories they have read and events they are learning about in theme cycles to understand them better. Also, many students are more comfortable talking in front of a group when they have a puppet on their hand than when they are standing in front of a group by themselves. These and other ways to adapt talk activities to meet the needs of every student are presented in the Adapting suggestions on page 126.

Assessing Students' Talk

Students' talk can be assessed, although it rarely is in elementary classrooms. However, because students and their parents often value what can be assessed, it is important to assess talk, and all of the types of talk discussed in this chapter can be assessed. In small group conversations, teachers can simply note whether or not students are contributing members of their groups, or they can observe students' behavior and assess in which ways students contribute to their groups. Wilkinson (1984) recommends that teachers "listen in" on students' conversations to learn about their language competencies and their abilities to work in small groups. Teachers of primary-grade students might assess whether students:

- Contribute to the conversation
- Share ideas and feelings
- Are courteous
- Listen carefully to classmates' comments
- Call group members by name
- Look at classmates when talking to them

Middle- and upper-grade students learn more sophisticated procedures, strategies, and skills, and in addition to the six behaviors listed above, teachers of older students might assess whether students:

Adapting . . .
Talk Activities
To Meet the Needs of Every Student

1. *Including All Students in Conversations*

Conversations have social as well as instructional purposes. As students learn ways to talk with classmates—how to ask questions, share information, and keep the conversation moving—they build a sense of community and a climate of trust.

2. *Using Smaller Groups*

Some students may feel more comfortable working in small groups of class-mates they know well or in the same cultural group. These students might be more successful in small group conversations, or they might be more articu-late in giving book talks to a small group than to the whole class.

3. *Giving Group Presentations*

Instead of preparing oral presentations individually, students can work in pairs or small groups to interview, tell stories, and give oral reports and book talks. When students work with a partner or in a small group, they share the re-sponsibility and the talking. Students also learn important socialization skills and develop friendships.

4. *Using Manipulatives*

Many students find it easier to talk in front of a group when they are talking about an object they are holding. Young children bring objects for show-and-tell, and students can make charts and posters to use in oral reports.

5. *Creating Drama Projects*

Drama is a powerful mode for students who have difficulty using written lan-guage. Students can use dramatic activities, such as role-playing and puppet shows, as projects for literature focus units and in theme cycles.

- Volunteer to begin the conversation
- Perform their assigned jobs in the group
- Extend and expand classmates' comments
- Ask questions and seek clarifications
- Invite other group members to contribute
- Stay on task
- Take turns
- Deal with conflict within the group
- Help to end the conversation
- Assume a leadership role in the group

Teachers can use these items to create a self-assessment checklist so that students can assess their own contributions to small group conversations. It is important that students know what is expected of them during conversations and that they reflect on their behavior and contributions.

AESTHETIC TALK

Aesthetic talk, like aesthetic listening, deals with the lived-through experience of literature and creating interpretations. Students use aesthetic talk in discussing literature, telling stories, and participating in readers theatre.

Conversations About Literature

Students talk about literature they are reading, listening to the teacher read aloud in small groups, or reading together as a class to dig deeper into the story and develop their interpretations. Students voice their opinions and support their views with examples from the literature. Through these conversations, students take responsibility for learning. They talk about what puzzles them, what they find interesting, personal connections to the story, and connections between this story and others they have read. They also encourage classmates to contribute to the discussion.

Teachers can sit in on conversations about literature as a participant or an observer, but not as a judge; the talk is primarily among the students. In the past, conversations about literature have been "gentle inquisitions" during which students located answers to questions teachers asked in books they were reading. Instead, the type of literature conversations that we advocate are "grand conversations" (Eeds & Wells, 1989). Students use the procedures, strategies, and skills from small group conversations to talk about literature. They make comments, ask questions, and build on each other's comments. They call classmates by name and look at the person they are talking to. Students also use the same strategies to begin a conversation, keep it moving, and bring it to a conclusion.

Literature conversations can be held with the whole class or in small groups. Young children usually meet together as a class, while older students often talk in small groups. When students meet together as a class, there is a shared feeling of community, and the teacher can be a part of the group. Young children usually meet together as a class, and older students meet together when they are learning literature conversation procedures and when they are listening to the teacher read a book aloud to the class. Students meet in small groups when they are reading different books and when they want to have more opportunities to talk. When the entire class meets together, students have only a few opportunities to talk, but when they meet in small groups, they have many, many more opportunities to share their interpretations.

Steps in Literature Conversations. Literature conversations often have two parts. The first part is open-ended; students talk about their reactions to the book, and the direction of the conversation is determined by students' comments. In the second part the teacher focuses students' attention on one aspect of the book that they did not talk about in the first part of the conversation. The steps are:

Step by Step

1. **Meeting in Groups.**   Students meet together as a class or in small groups to talk about a book or a section of the book. When students meet together as a class, they sit in a circle in order to see each other, and when they meet in a small group, they sit close together so that they can talk without disturbing their classmates.

2. **Sharing Responses.**   Students share their reactions to the book. To begin the conversation, a student or the teacher asks, "Who would like to begin? What did you think? Who would like to share a reaction?" As students share their responses, they comment on the events in the story, on the literary elements, or on the author's language, and they might make connections to their own lives and to other literature they have read. Each student participates and may build on classmates' comments and ask for clarifications. In order that everyone may participate, teachers often ask students to make no more than three comments until everyone has spoken at least once. Students may refer to the book or read a short piece to make a point, but there is no round-robin reading. Students do not raise their hands and are not called on by the teacher or a group leader. Instead, students take turns and speak when no else is speaking, much like adults do when they talk with friends. Pauses and brief silences may occur, and when students indicate that they have run out of things to say, the discussion may end or continue on to the second part.

3. **Asking Questions.**   Teachers ask open-ended questions to focus students' attention on one or two aspects of the book that have been missed. Four possible directions are:

   - *Focus on illustrations.* After reading *El Chino* (Say, 1990), teachers might ask, "Did you like the illustrations in *El Chino?* How did the illustrations change during the book? Why do you think Allen Say did that?"

   - *Focus on authors.* During a literature focus unit on Chris Van Allsburg, teachers might say, "This is the third book we've read by Chris Van Allsburg. What is so special about his books? Why do we like his books so much? Is there something they all share?"

   - *Focus on comparison.* Teachers ask students to make a comparison: "How did this book compare with _____ ? Did you like the book or the film version better? Why? Which of Beverly Cleary's characters is your favorite?"

   - *Focus on literary elements/stylistic devices/genre.* After reading *Johnny Appleseed* (Kellogg, 1988), teachers might ask, "Is *Johnny Appleseed* a legend? What are the characteristics of legends? Which of these characteristics did you notice in the book? What was the theme of the book? How did the author tell us the theme?"

After the literature conversation, students often write (or draw) in their reading logs or write again if they wrote before the literature conversation. Then they continue reading the book if they have read only part of it. Both participating in literature conversations and writing entries in reading logs help students to think about and respond to what they have read.

It is not necessary to have questions for conversations about literature, but teachers or students can develop questions. The most useful questions cannot be answered with yes or no, and they require students to give personal opinions. Reardon (1988) reports that her third graders write their own questions, and the literature conversation group spends the first few minutes of group time considering the questions and deciding which ones to actually use. A fifth grader developed these questions for a conversation about *Do Bananas Chew Gum?* (Gilson, 1980):

> I wonder if Sam ever learned how to read. How could he learn?
>
> I wonder why Sam had a reading problem. What do you think? Why did people hate Alicia?
>
> I wonder why they called the book *Do Bananas Chew Gum?*
>
> What would you have called the book? Why?
>
> Do you think Alicia gets braces? Would you want braces?
>
> Do you think Sam has other friends besides Alicia and Wally? Who?
>
> I wonder if Sam ever gets fired from baby-sitting. Do you?
>
> Would you fire him? Why or why not? (Fiderer, 1988, pp. 60–61)

Benefits of Conversations About Literature. From their observational study of fifth and sixth graders conducting conversations about literature, Eeds and Wells (1989) found that, through talk, students extend their individual interpretations of their reading and even create a better understanding of it. They talk about their understanding of the story and can change their opinions after listening to classmates' alternative views. Students share personal stories related to their reading in poignant ways that trigger other students to identify with them. They are active readers who use prediction as they read. Students also gain insights about how authors use the elements of story structure to develop their message.

An additional benefit is that when students talk in depth about literature, their writing shows the same kind of critical thinking and interpretations (Sorenson, 1993). Students seem to be more successful in literature conversations if they have written in journals first and more successful in writing journal entries if they have participated in literature conversations first.

Storytelling

Storytelling is an ancient art that is a valuable instructional tool. Teachers share literature with their students using storytelling techniques, and students tell stories, too. Storytelling is entertaining and stimulates children's imaginations. It expands their language abilities, and it helps them internalize the characteristics of stories and develop interpretations of stories (Morrow, 1985).

Steps in Telling Stories. Storytelling involves four steps:

Step by Step

1. **Choosing a Story.** Traditional stories, such as folktales, are often chosen for storytelling activities; however, any type of literature can be used. The most important considerations in choosing a story are to select a story you like, know well, and want to tell. Morrow (1979) lists other considerations:

The story has a simple, well-rounded plot.

The story has a clear beginning, middle, and end.

The story has an underlying theme.

The story has a small number of well-defined characters.

The story contains dialogue.

The story uses repetition.

The story uses colorful language or "catch phrases."

Figure 4–2 lists stories that contain many of these characteristics. Children can also create and tell stories to accompany wordless picture books. For example, Tomie de Paola's *Pancakes for Breakfast* (1978) is the charming story of a little old woman who tries to cook pancakes for breakfast but runs into a series of

Figure 4–2   *Stories for Storytelling Activities*

Aardema, V. (1975). *Why mosquitoes buzz in people's ears.* New York: Dial. (M–U)

Andersen, H. C. (1965). *The nightingale.* New York: Harper & Row. (U)

Brett, J. (1989). *The mitten.* New York: Putnam. (P–M)

Brown, M. (1972). *The runaway bunny.* New York: Harper & Row. (P)

Brown, R. (1985). *The big sneeze.* New York: Lothrop, Lee & Shepard. (P)

Carle, E. (1970). *The very hungry caterpillar.* Cleveland: Collins-World. (P)

de Paola, T. (1975). *Strega nona.* Englewood Cliffs, NJ: Prentice-Hall. (P–M)

Flack, M. (1932). *Ask Mr. Bear.* New York: Macmillan. (P)

Fox, M. (1986). *Hattie and the fox.* New York: Bradbury Press. (P–M)

Gag, W. (1956). *Millions of cats.* New York: Coward McCann. (P)

Galdone, P. (1973). *The three billy goats Gruff.* Boston: Houghton Mifflin. (P)

Gipson, M. (1975). *Rip Van Winkle.* New York: Doubleday. (M–U)

Hague, K., & Hague, M. (1980). *East of the sun and west of the moon.* New York: Harcourt Brace Jovanovich. (U)

Hastings, S. (1985). *Sir Gawain and the loathly lady.* New York: Mulberry. (U)

Hyman, T. S. (1983). *Little Red Riding Hood.* New York: Holiday House. (P–M–U)

Kasza, K. (1987). *The wolf's chicken stew.* New York: Putnam. (P–M)

Kellogg, S. (1973). *The island of the skog.* New York: Dial. (M)

Lester, H. (1988). *Tacky the penguin.* Boston: Houghton Mifflin. (P–M)

Lionni, L. (1969). *Alexander and the wind-up mouse.* New York: Pantheon. (M)

Lobel, A. (1977). *How the rooster saved the day.* New York: Greenwillow. (M)

Mahy, M. (1990). *The seven Chinese brothers.* New York: Scholastic. (M)

Martin, B., Jr., & Archambault, J. (1985). *The ghost-eye tree.* New York: Holt, Rinehart & Winston. (M–U)

Mayer, M. (1978). *Beauty and the beast.* New York: Macmillan. (U)

Mayer, M. (1987). *There's an alligator under my bed.* New York: Dial. (P–M)

Morgan, P. (1990). *The turnip.* New York: Philomel. (P)

Numeroff, L. J. (1985). *If you give a mouse a cookie.* New York: Harper & Row. (P–M–U)

Polacco, P. (1988). *Rechenka's eggs.* New York: Philomel. (M)

Polacco, P. (1990). *Thunder cake.* New York: Philomel. (M)

Slobodkina, E. (1947). *Caps for sale.* New York: Scott. (P)

Steig, W. (1982). *Doctor DeSoto.* New York: Farrar, Straus & Giroux. (M)

Thurber, J. (1974). *Many moons.* New York: Harcourt Brace Jovanovich. (P–M–U)

Wood, A. (1984). *The napping house.* San Diego: Harcourt Brace Jovanovich. (P)

Xiong, B. (1989). *Nine-in-one Grr! Grr!* San Francisco: Children's Book Press. (M)

Zelinsky, P. O. (1986). *Rumpelstiltskin.* New York: Dutton. (M–U)

Zemach, M. (1976). *It could always be worse.* New York: Farrar, Straus & Giroux. (P–M–U)

P = primary grades (K–2); M = middle grades (3–5); U = upper grades (6–8).

problems as she tries to assemble the ingredients. In the end, her neighbors invite her to their home for pancakes. The repetition of events in this story makes it easy for primary-grade children to tell.

2. *Preparing to Tell a Story.* Students plan and rehearse a familiar story before telling it. It is not necessary to memorize a story to tell it effectively. Kingore recommends that students choose a familiar story that they really like, and that they reread the story once or twice to review details about characters and to place major events in proper sequence. Then students choose interesting or repeated phrases from the story to enliven the language of their retelling and consider how to vary their speaking voice to make the story more interesting for listeners. Students also plan simple props or gestures to accompany the story. Then they prepare a brief introduction that relates the story to the audience's experiences. Students rehearse the story several times, incorporating phrases to enliven the story, varying their speaking voices, and using props or gestures. This process can be abbreviated when very young children tell stories. They choose a story they already know well and make props to guide the telling. (Try a set of puppets representing the main characters or a series of drawings.) They are then ready to tell their stories.

3. *Adding Props.* Students can use several techniques to make the story come alive as it is told. Three types of props that add variety and interest to stories are:

- *Flannel board pictures.* Students place drawings or pictures cut from books and backed with flannel on the flannel board as the story is told.
- *Puppets.* Students use puppets they have made or commercially available puppets representing the main characters to tell a story with dialogue.
- *Objects.* Students use stuffed animals to represent animal characters or other small objects to represent important things in the story being told. For instance, students can use a pile of caps in telling Slobodkina's *Caps for Sale* (1947) or a small gold ball for Thurber's *Many Moons* (1974).

4. *Telling the Story.* Students tell the stories they have prepared to small groups of classmates or to younger children. Teachers may want to divide the audience into small groups so that more students can tell stories at one time.

Assessing Students' Storytelling Activities. Teachers can assess both the process students use to tell stories and the quality of the products they produce, but the process of developing interpretations is far more important than the quality of the product. Teachers check that students move through the steps of planning and rehearsing the story before telling it, and that they:

- Introduce the story to the audience
- Include the beginning, middle, and end of the story
- Incorporate interesting or repeated phrases in their story
- Add dialogue
- Vary their voices for more interest
- Use props or gestures

As students gain experience telling stories, they become more comfortable in front of an audience and learn ways to "play" to their audience.

Readers Theatre

Readers theatre is "a formalized dramatic presentation of a script by a group of readers" (Busching, 1981, p. 330). Each student assumes a role and reads the character's lines in the script. The reader's responsibility is to interpret a story without using much action. Students may stand or sit, but they must carry the whole communication of the plot, characterization, mood, and theme by using their voices, gestures, and facial expressions.

Steps in Readers Theatre Presentations.   Readers theatre avoids many of the restrictions inherent in theatrical productions. Students do not memorize their parts, and elaborate props, costumes, and backdrops are not needed. Neither do students spend long, tedious hours rehearsing the presentation. Three steps in developing readers theatre presentations are:

Step by Step

1. *Selecting a Script.*   Quality play scripts exhibit the same characteristics as do other types of fine literature. Five essential characteristics are an interesting story, a well-paced plot, recognizable and believable characters, plausible language, and a distinct style (Manna, 1984). The arrangement of the text on the page is also an important consideration when selecting a script. There should be a clear distinction between stage directions and dialogue through adequate spacing and variation in the print types and colors. This distinction is especially important for students who are not familiar with script format.

   Readers theatre is a relatively new idea, and the number of quality scripts available is limited, although more are being published each year. Some of the scripts currently available are Gackenback's *Hattie, Tom and the Chicken Witch* (1980), Dahl's *Charlie and the Chocolate Factory* (George, 1976), *Plays from African Folktales* (Korty, 1975), and Laurie's *Children's Plays from Beatrix Potter* (1980).

   Students can also prepare their own scripts for readers theatre from books of children's literature. Laughlin and Latrobe (1989) suggest that students begin by reading the book and thinking about its theme, characters, and plot. Next students choose a scene or scenes to script, and they make copies of the scene and use felt-tip pens to highlight the dialogue. They then adapt the scene by adding narrators' lines to bridge gaps, set the scene, and summarize. Students assume roles and read the script aloud, revising and experimenting with new text until they are satisfied with the script. The final version is typed, duplicated, and stapled into pamphlets. Some recommended stories are presented in Figure 4–3.

2. *Rehearsing the Presentation.*   To begin, students choose the parts they will read. One student is needed for each character and one for a narrator, if the script calls for one. Students read through the presentation once or twice, then stop to discuss the story. Busching (1981) recommends using questions to probe students' understanding. Through this discussion, students gain a clearer understanding of the story and decide how to interpret their characters.

Figure 4–3   Stories That Can Be Scripted for Readers Theatre

Atwater, R., & Atwater, F. (1938). *Mr. Popper's penguins.* Boston: Little, Brown. (M)

Babbitt, N. (1975). *Tuck everlasting.* New York: Farrar, Straus & Giroux. (U)

Blume, J. (1972). *Tales of a fourth grade nothing.* New York: Dutton. (M)

Brittain, B. (1983). *The wish giver.* New York: Harper & Row. (M–U)

Burch, R. (1980). *Ida Early comes over the mountain.* New York: Viking. (M)

Byars, B. (1968). *The midnight fox.* New York: Viking. (M–U)

Cleary, B. (1973). *Ramona and her father.* New York: Morrow. (M)

Coerr, E. (1977). *Sadako and the thousand paper cranes.* New York: Putnam. (M)

Cohen, B. (1974). *Thank you, Jackie Robinson.* New York: Lothrop. (M–U)

Dahl, R. (1970). *Fantastic Mr. Fox.* New York: Knopf. (M)

Erickson, R. (1974). *A toad for Tuesday.* New York: Lothrop, Lee & Shepard. (M)

Fleischman, S. (1986). *The whipping boy.* New York: Greenwillow. (M–U)

Gilson, J. (1983). *Thirteen ways to sink a sub.* New York: Lothrop, Lee & Shepard. (U)

Howe, D., & Howe, J. (1979). *Bunnicula: A rabbit-tale of mystery.* New York: Atheneum. (M–U)

King-Smith, D. (1988). *Martin's mice.* New York: Crown. (M–U)

Lewis, C. S. (1950). *The lion, the witch and the wardrobe.* New York: Macmillan. (M–U)

Lobel, A. (1970). *Frog and Toad are friends.* New York: Harper & Row. (P)

Lowry, L. (1989). *Number the stars.* Boston: Houghton Mifflin. (M–U)

MacLachlan, P. (1985). *Sarah, plain and tall.* New York: Harper & Row. (M)

Mathis, S. B. (1975). *The hundred penny box.* New York: Viking. (M)

Milne, A. A. (1974). *Winnie-the-Pooh.* New York: Dutton. (P–M)

Naylor, P. R. (1991). *Shiloh.* New York: Atheneum. (M–U)

Rockwell, T. (1973). *How to eat fried worms.* New York: Watts. (M–U)

Sebestyen, O. (1979). *Words by heart.* Boston: Little, Brown. (U)

Stolz, M. (1960). *A dog on Barkham Street.* New York: Harper & Row. (M)

Wallace, B. (1980). *A dog called Kitty.* New York: Holiday House. (M)

After students decide how to use their voice, gestures, and facial expressions to interpret the characters, they should read the script one or two more times, striving for accurate pronunciation, strong voice projection, and appropriate inflections. Obviously, less rehearsal is needed for an informal, in-class presentation than for a more formal production; nevertheless, interpretations should always be developed as fully as possible.

3. *Staging the Presentation.* Readers theatre can be presented on a stage or in a corner of the classroom. Students stand or sit in a row and read their lines in the script. They must stay in position throughout the presentation or enter and leave according to the characters' appearances "on stage." If readers are sitting, they may stand to read their lines; if they are standing, they may step forward to read. The emphasis is not on production quality; rather, it is on the interpretive quality of the readers' voices and expressions. Costumes and props are unnecessary; however, adding a few enhances interest and enjoyment, as long as they do not interfere with the interpretive quality of the reading.

Assessing Students' Presentations. Students work in small groups to plan and rehearse their readers theatre presentation. Teachers can assess students' work in small groups as well as their interpretation of the story during the presentation. The focus is on students' interpretation of the text, and teachers need to assess students' understanding of the story and the characters they performed. Teachers may want to ask students to explain how they interpreted their character and how this interpretation influenced the way they read their part.

EFFERENT TALK

Students use efferent talk to inform and persuade. They use efferent talk in conversations during theme studies. In addition, they use four other types of efferent talk: show-and-tell, oral reports, interviews, and debates. These activities are more formal, and students prepare and rehearse their talks before giving them in front of an audience.

Conversations During Theme Cycles

Conversations are an important part of theme cycles. Students talk about concepts they are learning and issues such as pollution, nuclear weapons, and apartheid. These conversations can take place in small groups or together as a class. In contrast to literature conversations in which students use primarily aesthetic talk to create and deepen their interpretations, students use primarily efferent talk to create knowledge and understand relationships among concepts they are learning. Students gather information for the conversation through giving or listening to oral presentations, reading informational books and newspapers, and watching television news reports and films. As they participate in conversations—offering information, considering other points of view, searching for additional information to support opinions, and listening to alternative viewpoints—students learn social skills as well as content area information.

Questioning Strategies.   Teachers often use questions to initiate conversations during theme cycles, and the questions that teachers ask go beyond knowledge-level thinking with single correct answers to authentic questions in which students analyze and synthesize information and make connections to their own lives. For example, during a theme cycle on pioneers, teachers might ask these questions:

- As part of a conversation on the concept of *pioneers,* teachers ask if there are pioneers today. After students conclude that there are, teachers ask where modern-day pioneers go, what they do, and why they are pioneers.
- After making a list of the reasons why people moved west, teachers ask students which reason seems most important to them.
- After sharing a map of the westward trails that pioneers traveled, teachers ask students to choose a destination and plan their travel along one of the trails.
- Together as a class, students brainstorm a list of the possessions pioneers carried with them, and then students work in small groups to choose the five most important possessions for pioneers traveling to and settling in particular areas.

Wilen (1986) reviewed the research about questioning strategies and offers these suggestions:

Ask carefully planned questions to organize and direct the lesson.

Ask clearly phrased questions rather than vaguely worded or multiple questions.

Sequence questions to move from factual-level questions to higher-level questions that require critical thinking.

Ask questions to follow up on students' responses.

Teachers need to allow students sufficient time to think about questions and plan their responses. Sometimes the most effective way to do this is to have students talk about the question in small groups and then report back to the class. It is important to encourage wide participation and interaction among students and draw in students who do not volunteer contributions. Seating students in a circle is one technique, and having students work in small groups is another. Other ways to promote student involvement include having students create questions, lead the conversation, and follow up on ideas developed during the conversation. The emphasis in these conversations is on creating knowledge and making connections about information students are learning. Students also use persuasive language as they argue their viewpoints and try to persuade classmates as to the importance of the points they make and the issues they discuss.

KWL Charts.   KWL charts are a good way to help students take an active role in talking about what they are learning in theme cycles (Ogle, 1986, 1989). The letters *K-W-L* stand for *Know, Want to learn,* and *Learned.* Teachers use these charts at the beginning of theme cycles to help students think about what

Third graders write what they know and what they want to learn on a KWL chart at the beginning of a theme cycle on geology.

they will study and to encourage them to ask questions to direct their learning during the theme.

To begin, the teacher asks students to brainstorm what they know about a topic. Then the teacher records the information in the "K" or "What we know" column on a class chart, as shown in the Teacher's Notebook on page 137. As students suggest information and as confusion arises, the teacher adds questions in the "W" or "What we want to learn" column. Students also suggest questions they would like to explore during the theme. Brainstorming information in the "K" column helps students activate prior knowledge, and developing questions in the "W" column provides students with specific purposes for learning. Next, students look for ways to "chunk" or categorize the information they brainstormed and for information they expect to find in the text they will read. For example, second graders making a KWL chart on penguins might identify these categories: what they look like, where they live, how they move, and what their families are like. Older students might use categories such as appearance, habitat, enemies, and classification.

Next, students participate in activities related to the theme, looking for new information and for answers to questions in the "W" column. Later, students reflect on what they have learned and complete the "L" or "What we learned" column. The KWL chart helps prepare students to learn, and it helps them organize their learning, clarify their misconceptions, and appreciate their learning.

Teachers can make class KWL charts on a bulletin board. Students can also work in small groups to make smaller charts on chart paper, or they can make individual KWL charts in their learning logs. Class charts are best for primary-grade students or for older students who have not made KWL charts before.

Show-and-Tell

Daily sharing time is a familiar ritual in many kindergarten and primary-grade classrooms. Children bring favorite objects to school and talk about them. This is a nice bridge between home and school, and show-and-tell is a good introduction to speaking in front of a group.

Guidelines for Speakers and Listeners.   Sharing time can become repetitive and children can lose interest, so teachers must play an active role to make sharing a worthwhile activity. Teachers can discuss the roles and responsibilities of both speakers and listeners. A second-grade class developed the list of responsibilities for speakers and listeners shown in Figure 4–4. This list, with minor variations, has been used with students in upper grades as well.

Some children need prompting even if they have been advised to plan in advance two or three things to say about the object they have brought to school. It is tempting for teachers to speed things up by asking questions and, without realizing it, to answer their own questions, especially for a very quiet child. Show-and-tell could go like this:

Teacher:	Jerry, what did you bring today?
Jerry:	(Holds up a stuffed bear.)
Teacher:	Is that a teddy bear?
Jerry:	Yeah.

Teacher's Notebook

A KWL Chart

K What we know	W What we want to learn	L What we learned

Categories of information we expect to use

A.

B.

C.

D.

Ogle, 1986, p. 565.

Figure 4–4   *A Second-Grade Class List of Responsibilities of Talkers and Listeners*

Our Rules for Show-and-Tell

What a Speaker Does

Brings something interesting to talk about.

Brings the same thing *only* one time.

Thinks of three things to say about it.

Speaks loudly so everyone can hear.

Passes what he/she brought around so everyone can see it.

What Listeners Do

Be interested.

Pay attention.

Listen.

Ask a question.

Say something nice.

Teacher:	Is it new?
Jerry:	(Shakes head yes.)
Teacher:	Can you tell us about your bear?
Jerry:	(Silence.)
Teacher:	Jerry, why don't you walk around and show your bear to everyone?

Jerry needed prompting, but the teacher in this example dominated the conversation, and Jerry said only one word—"yeah." Two strategies may help. First, talk with children like Jerry and help them plan something to say. Second, invite listeners to ask the speakers questions using the question words *what, who, when, where, why,* and *how.*

Classmates are the audience for show-and-tell activities, but often teachers become the focus (Cazden, 1988). To avoid this, teachers join the audience rather than direct the activity. They also limit their comments and allow the student who is sharing to assume responsibility for the activity and the discussion that follows. Students can ask three or four classmates for comments before choosing which student will share next. It is difficult for teachers to share control of their classrooms, but young students are capable of handling the activity themselves.

Show-and-Tell for Older Students. Show-and-tell or sharing activities should continue throughout the elementary grades, because informal talk is a necessary part of classroom life (Camp & Tompkins, 1990). Many middle-grade teachers find the first few minutes of the day an appropriate time for sharing; often, the class becomes a more cohesive and caring group through sharing. Teachers of upper-grade students who change classes every 50 minutes must plan more carefully for sharing activities because of time constraints. Nonetheless, spending 2 or 3 minutes at the beginning of each class period in informal sharing, or planning a 50-minute, more formal sharing time every other week, will provide these needed opportunities.

Middle- and upper-grade students participate in sharing activities in much the same way as primary students do. Together students and teachers need to establish guidelines for sharing and discuss how to prepare and present their show-and-tell presentations. The steps are planning, presenting, and critiquing (Camp & Tompkins, 1990). Teachers should model a show-and-tell presentation for students by sharing a hobby or another interest.

Students choose an object, experience, or current events topic to share and plan what information to include in their presentation. To encourage students to choose a meaningful topic for sharing, teachers might read *The Show-and-Tell War* (Smith, 1988). Students plan their presentation by deciding what they want to say and then clustering an effective planning strategy. In clustering, students draw a schematic diagram on a sheet of paper and list main ideas and details. They begin by writing the name of the topic in the center of the paper and drawing a circle around the word. Next, they draw lines or rays out from the circle and list three, four, or five main ideas about the topic. They circle these words, then draw more lines from the circles and add details related to the main ideas. An upper-grade student's cluster on porcelain dolls is presented in Figure 4–5. The main ideas and details are drawn out from the center. These clusters are used for gathering and organizing ideas during planning and as notes to refer to during the presentations.

Students' presentations are brief, usually lasting only a minute or two. Students share their objects and experiences using the ideas gathered and organized during planning. They concentrate on speaking clearly and standing

Figure 4–5   An Upper-Grade Student's Cluster for a Sharing Presentation

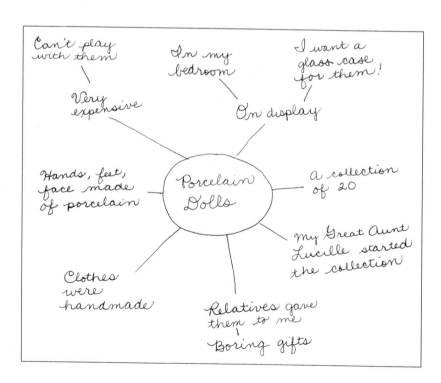

appropriately so as to not distract listeners. Older students who have not participated in sharing activities often find talking in front of their classmates intimidating. The planning step is crucial to a successful presentation. Other students should listen effectively by paying attention, asking pertinent questions, and responding to the speaker nonverbally. After the talk, listeners may ask questions to clarify and expand the speaker's comments.

Assessing Show-and-Tell Presentations.   Students can discuss the effectiveness of their presentations using the guidelines in Figure 4–4. These guidelines can be converted into a checklist that both speakers and listeners can complete for each presentation. Through the checklists and discussion, students learn to give interesting presentations and gain confidence in speaking in front of a group.

Show-and-tell can evolve into an informal type of oral report for middle-grade students. When this method is used effectively, older students gain valuable practice talking in an informal and nonthreatening situation. For example, to begin a sharing activity, students can talk about a collection of sharks' teeth, a program from an Ice Capades show, a recently found snakeskin, or snapshots of a vacation at Yellowstone National Park. Such show-and-tell presentations can lead to informal dramatics, reading, and writing activities. One student may act out dances recalled from the Ice Capades show; another student may point out the location of Yellowstone National Park on a map or check an almanac for more information about the park. A third student may write about the prized collection of sharks' teeth and how they were collected. Experience plus oral rehearsal helps students gear up for other language activities.

Oral Reports

Learning how to prepare and present an oral report is an important efferent talk activity for middle- and upper-grade students. But students are often simply assigned to give an oral report without any guidance about how to prepare and give one. Too many students simply copy the report verbatim from an encyclopedia and then read it aloud. The result is that students learn to fear speaking in front of a group instead of building confidence in their oral language abilities.

We will focus on the steps in teaching students how to prepare and present two types of oral reports. The first type includes reports on social studies or science topics, such as Native Americans, the solar system, or Canada. The second type includes book talks and reviews of television shows and films. Oral reports have genuine language functions—to inform or to persuade—and they are often done as projects during theme cycles.

Reports of Information.   Students prepare and give reports about topics they are studying in social studies and science. Giving a report orally helps students to learn about topics in specific content areas as well as to develop their speaking abilities. Students need more than just an assignment to prepare a report for presentation on a particular date; they need to learn how to prepare and present research reports. The four steps in preparing reports are: choosing a topic, gathering information, organizing information, and making the presentation.

This student is presenting an oral report on the lungs to his classmates, using a skeleton as a prop.

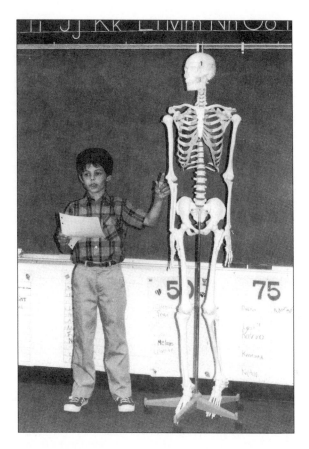

Step by Step

1. ***Choosing a Topic.*** The class begins by choosing a topic for the reports. For example, if a second-grade class is studying the human body, each student might select a different part of the body for a report. After students have chosen their topics, they need to inventory, or think over, what they know about the topic and decide what they need to learn about it. They can learn to focus on the key points for their reports in several ways. One strategy is to create a cluster with the topic written and circled in the center of a piece of paper; the key points are drawn out from the topic like rays from the sun. Then students write the details on rays drawn from each main idea.

    Another strategy is a data chart, wherein the teacher provides a chart listing three or more key points to guide students as they gather information for their reports (McKenzie, 1979). Figure 4–6 shows a cluster and a data chart for a report on a part of the human body.

    A third strategy is brainstorming ideas for possible key points by asking questions about the topic prefaced with the "5 Ws plus one" words: *who, what, when, where, why,* and *how.* The number and complexity of the key points depend on the students' ages or levels of experience.

2. ***Gathering and Organizing Information.*** Students gather information using a variety of reference materials, including, but not limited to, informational books, magazines, newspapers, encyclopedias, almanacs, and atlases. Encyclopedias are a valuable resource, but they are only one possible source, and other

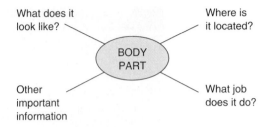

HUMAN BODY REPORT DATA CHART				
Source of information	What does it look like?	Where is it located?	What job does it do?	Other important information

Figure 4–6   A Cluster and a Data Chart for a Report on the Human Body

reference materials must be available. In addition to print sources, students can view filmstrips, films, and videotapes and can interview people in the community who have special expertise on the topic. For students who have had limited experience locating information in a library, a class trip to the school library and a public library to collect reference materials is useful.

The preliminary organization—deciding on the key points—completed in the first step gives direction for gathering the information. Now students review the information they have gathered and decide how best to present it so that the report will be both interesting and well organized. Students can transfer the "notes" they want to use for their reports from the cluster or data chart onto notecards. Only key words—not sentences or paragraphs—should be written on the cards.

3. **Creating Visuals.**   Students may also develop visuals such as charts, diagrams, maps, pictures, models, and timelines. For example, the second graders who gave reports on parts of the body made drawings and clay models of the parts and used a large skeleton hanging in the classroom to show the location of the organ in the body. Visuals provide a "crutch" for the speaker and add an element of interest for the listeners.

4. **Giving the Presentation.**   The final step is to rehearse and then give the presentation. Students can rehearse several times by reviewing key points and reading over their notecards. They should not, however, read the report verbatim from the notecards. Students might want to choose a particularly interesting fact to begin the presentation.

Before the presentations begin, teachers teach minilessons on the characteristics of successful presentations. For instance, speakers should talk loudly enough for all to hear, look at the audience, keep to the key points, refer to notecards for important facts, and use the visuals they have prepared.

Students are usually the audience for the oral reports, and members of the audience have responsibilities. They should be attentive, listen to the speaker, ask questions, and applaud the speaker. Usually students give presentations to the whole class, but it is possible to divide the class into groups so that students can present reports in each group simultaneously.

Teachers can assess students' oral reports according to the steps students move through in developing their reports as well as the presentations of their reports in front of the class. Students can also assess their own presentations, considering each of the four steps involved in developing the oral report. These points might be used in developing an assessment checklist:

Did you choose a narrow topic?

Did you collect and organize information on a cluster or a data chart?

Did you prepare a chart or other visual to use in the presentation?

Did you rehearse the presentation?

Students can also reflect on the presentation itself and can respond to questions such as:

Did you present the report as you planned?

Did you speak loudly enough to be heard?

Did you look at the audience?

Did you use your visuals?

Did you make your key points?

How did the audience respond to your presentation?

What are you most pleased with about your presentation?

What will you change or do differently when you give another report?

Book Talks and Other Reviews.   Students give oral reports to review books they have read or television shows and films they have viewed. These book talks and reviews are one type of project students create in literature focus units, reading workshop, and theme cycles. The steps in preparing and presenting reviews are similar to those for reports of information:

*Step
by
Step*

1. *Gathering Information.*   Students select information for the report, including a brief summary of the selection and bibliographic information; comparisons to other selections (e.g., with similar themes, written by the same author, starring the same actor); strengths and weaknesses; and opinions and conclusions. They also choose a brief excerpt from the book to read or an excerpt from a videotape to show.

2. *Organizing Information.*   Students record and organize the information on a cluster and then copy key words onto notecards.

3. *Creating Visuals.*   Students locate or create a prop to show during the review. Students may show the book in a book talk or an advertisement for the film. Or, they may bring an object from home to share or create a prop out of clay or other art materials.

4. *Giving the Presentation.* Students briefly rehearse the review, and then they give the presentation, referring to the notecards but not reading them, and sharing the prop.

Interviews

Almost all children see interviews on television news programs and are familiar with the interviewing techniques reporters use. Interviewing is an exciting, real-life communication activity that helps students refine questioning skills and practice all four language modes—listening, talking, reading, and writing (Haley-James & Hobson, 1980).

Interviewing is an important language tool that can be integrated effectively in theme cycles. Primary-grade students, for instance, can interview community helpers as part of a theme on the community, and older students can interview long-time area residents about local history. Students can also interview people who life far away, such as a favorite author, legislator, or Olympic athlete, using a long-distance telephone conference call.

One way to introduce interviewing is to watch interviews conducted on a television newscast and discuss what the purpose of the interview is, what a reporter does before and after an interview, and what types of questions are asked. Interviewers use a variety of questions, some to elicit facts and others to probe for feelings and opinions, but all questions are open-ended. Rarely do interviewers ask questions that require only a yes or no answer.

Steps in Conducting Interviews. Interviewing involves far more than simply conducting the actual interview. There are three steps in the interview process: planning the interview, conducting it, and sharing the results.

Step by Step

1. *Planning the Interview.* In the planning step, students arrange for the interview and brainstorm questions to ask the person being interviewed. Students choose which questions from the brainstormed list they will ask, making sure to avoid questions that require only yes or no answers. Students often write the questions on notecards. Then they sequence the cards in a reasonable order.

2. *Conducting the Interview.* The second step is conducting the actual interview. Students greet the person being interviewed and conduct the interview by asking questions they have prepared in advance. They take notes or tape-record the answers. They ask follow-up questions about points that are not clear, and if the answer to one question brings up another question that has not been written down, students ask it anyway. Students are polite and respectful of the answers and opinions of the person being interviewed. At the end of the interview, students thank the person for participating in the interview.

3. *Sharing the Results.* Students share the results of the interview in one of several ways. They may present an oral report, write a report or newspaper article, or make a poster.

Topics for Interviews. Students can conduct interviews with family members and other members of the community on a variety of topics. Cooper's *Who Put the Cannon in the Courthouse Square? A Guide to Uncovering the Past* (1985) and Weitzman's *My Backyard History Book* (1975) are excellent books to use with students in planning a community history project. Students work individually or in small groups to interview long-time residents about the community's history, growth and changes, modes of dress, transportation, communication, types of work, and ways to have fun. After gathering information through interviews, they write reports that are published in a class or community newspaper or in a book.

As part of a theme cycle on school, for example, a class of first graders invited the local high school principal to visit their class to be interviewed. The principal, who had been blinded several years earlier, brought his guide dog with him. The children asked him questions about how visually impaired people manage everyday tasks as well as how he performed his job as a principal. They also asked questions about his guide dog. After the interview students drew pictures and wrote summaries of the interview. One first grader's report is shown in Figure 4–7.

Figure 4–7   A First Grader's Interview Report

Mr. Kirtley came down. We asked him questions. He answered them. He is blind. His dog's name is Milo.

After reading excerpts from Studs Terkel's book *Working* (1974), a class of eighth graders interviewed people in the community to learn about their jobs. To begin, students brainstormed a list of 25 questions they might ask people about their jobs; they interviewed people they had selected; and then they shared the answers with the class. Afterwards, students wrote reports of their interviews, either in first person as Terkel did or in third person (Bowser, 1993). Students worked in small groups several times during this project. They brainstormed questions before the interviews in small groups, and they met again in small groups to revise and edit their compositions. The papers were both informative and insightful, as this excerpt from one student's report about being a real estate agent shows:

> Long and unpredictable hours are what she hates most about her job. You never know how much time you'll be spending with a customer. . . . She does not have close friends at work because the business is so competitive. (Bowser, 1993, p. 40)

Assessing Students' Interviews.   Teachers assess students' interviews by checking that they followed the three steps of the interview process and by examining the quality of their final products. Similarly, students can assess their own use of the interview process and their reports, much like they assess other types of efferent talk projects.

Debates

Debates are useful when the whole class is excited about an issue and most or all of the students have taken supporting or opposing positions. As they participate in debates, students learn to use language to persuade their classmates and to articulate their viewpoints. Two types of debates are impromptu debates and formal debates.

Impromptu Debates.   The class decides on an issue, clarifies it, and identifies positions that support or oppose the issue. Then students who wish to speak in favor of the issue move to one side of the room designated for supporters, and students who wish to speak against the issue move to the other side. Class members who have not formulated a position sit in the middle of the room.

A podium is set up in the front of the classroom, and students take turns going to the podium and speaking in support of or in opposition to the issue. When students wish to participate, they go to the side of the room for the position they support and wait in line for their opportunity to speak. After hearing arguments, students may change their minds and move to the opposite side of the room; if they are no longer certain what side they are on, they take a seat in the middle.

The teacher initiates the debate by asking a student from the supporting side to state that position on the issue. After the opening statement the opposing side makes a statement. From then on, each side takes turns making statements. Students who have just made a statement are often asked a question before a student for the other side makes a return statement. Sixth graders who used this informal debate procedure in their social studies class enjoyed the experience and furthered their abilities to express themselves effectively.

Formal Debates.   A more formal type of debate is appropriate for students in the upper-elementary grades. Debates take the form of arguments between opposing sides of a proposition. A proposition is a debate subject that can be discussed from opposing points of view; for example:

Resolved, that students should have a role in setting standards of behavior in classes and in disciplining those students who disrupt classes.

After the proposition has been determined, teams of three or four students are designated to support the proposition (the affirmative team) or oppose it (the negative team).

Depending on the number of members on each team, the debate proceeds in this order:

1. The first and third statements support the proposition.
2. The second and fourth statements reject the proposition.
3. The first and third rebuttal statements are made by the affirmative team.
4. The second and fourth rebuttal statements are made by the negative team.

Each member makes both a statement about the proposition and a rebuttal statement to the opposite team. Normally there are as many rebuttal statements as there are statements about the proposition. Teachers may vary the procedure to fit the class and their purposes. Students can also choose judges to determine the winning team.

If judges evaluate the debates, let students decide the criteria for judging. Have them brainstorm questions that will form the basis for their criteria. Questions similar to the following might initiate the brainstorming sessions:

Did the speakers communicate their ideas to the listeners?

Was a mastery of information evident in the presentations and rebuttals?

Was there evidence that the speakers knew the topic well?

Was the team courteous?

Did the team work cooperatively?

Did the second speaker on each team pick up and extend the statement of the first team member?

Students may want to interview the high school debating team for ideas on judging and presenting their topics. They might also enjoy attending a high school debate.

DRAMATIC ACTIVITIES

Drama provides a medium for students to use language, both verbal and nonverbal, in a meaningful context. Drama is not only a powerful form of communication but also a valuable way of knowing. When children participate in dramatic activities, they interact with classmates, share experiences, and explore their own understanding. According to Dorothy Heathcote, a highly acclaimed British drama teacher, drama "cracks the code" so that the message can be understood (Wagner, 1976). Drama has this power because it involves both logical, left-brain thinking and creative, right-brain thinking;

it requires active experience (the basic, and the first, way of learning); and it integrates the four language modes. Recent research confirms that drama has a positive effect on both students' oral language development and their literacy learning (Kardash & Wright, 1987; Wagner, 1988). Drama is often neglected, however, because some consider it a nonessential part of the language arts curriculum.

Dramatic activities range from role-playing to scripted plays that students produce. When students role-play an experience or present a puppet show, the focus is on interpretation and lived-through dramatic experience. Students create imaginary worlds through their drama, and they increase their understanding of themselves and the world in which they live (Booth, 1985; Kukla, 1987).

Many dramatic activities that elementary students participate in are informal and spontaneous. Others involve some rehearsal and are presented for an audience. The most formal dramatic activities are theatrical productions which are polished performances of a play produced on a stage and before a large audience. They require extensive rehearsal and are quite formal. Because the purpose of theatrical productions is a polished presentation, they are audience-centered rather than child-centered. Rather than encourage students to be spontaneous and improvisational, they require that students memorize lines. They are not recommended for students in elementary grades unless students write the scripts themselves.

Again and again educators caution that drama activities should be informal during the elementary years (Stewig, 1983b; Wagner, 1976). The one exception is the case when students write their own play and puppet show scripts and want to perform them.

Role-Playing

Students assume the role of another person as they act out stories or re-enact historical events. Through role-playing, students step into someone else's shoes and view the world from another perspective. Role-playing activities are usually informal. Students assume roles and then act out the drama as the teacher narrates or guides the dramatization.

In Literature Focus Units. Students role-play stories during literature focus units. These activities can be done as students are reading, after reading, or as projects. Teachers often use role-playing as they are reading a story with students to emphasize key points in the story or to clarify misunderstandings. For example, a key point in *Johnny Tremain* (Forbes, 1970) for a role-playing activity occurs when Johnny tragically burns his hand. This moment is important because of the ramifications of the event on the rest of the story. Another key point for role-playing occurs when Johnny has given up hope and lies among the graves on Copp's Hill. Because students enjoy the role-playing activity, they often ask to role-play the part about the Boston Tea Party— because it is fun, not because they do not understand.

After reading, students often act out folktales and other stories told in picture books using both dialogue and body movements. Teachers use role-playing to review and sequence the events in the story and to develop students' concept of story. Folktales such as *The Three Little Pigs* (Galdone, 1970) and *The Gingerbread Boy* (Galdone, 1975) are good for younger

These kindergartners role-play the beginning, middle, and end of a favorite story for an audience of their classmates.

children to dramatize because they are repetitive (and predictable) in sequence, plot, and dialogue. Middle- and upper-grade students act out favorite scenes from longer stories such as *The Wind in the Willows* (Grahame, 1961) and *Mrs. Frisby and the Rats of NIMH* (O'Brien, 1971). Students can also read biographies and dramatize events from these people's lives.

David Booth (Kukla, 1987) recommends that students explore the issues, themes, and deeper meanings of a story through drama. For example, after reading *The King's Fountain* (Alexander, 1971), the story of a king who takes away the water from the villagers so that he can build a grand fountain, students think about how people can survive without water, how the villagers would react to having their water taken away, and how kings can use their power and grandeur. Working in small groups, students create the drama by dramatizing a problem from the story (e.g., the villagers' pleading with the king not to redirect the water). As they role-play, children participate in the story and explore situations different from their own lives. After role-playing, the groups come together to share their experiences. Teachers can also assume a role, and the role they choose should not be the most important role, but one that serves as a catalyst for the events in the story. After the activity, students reflect on the story, made richer and more memorable through drama.

Students also use role-playing to create dramatic productions of a favorite story as a project. Students follow approximately the same steps they do in storytelling. They choose roles in the story, reread the story, identify key parts to include in the dramatization, collect simple props, and rehearse the story several times. Then they present the story to their classmates.

In Theme Cycles. Role-playing in theme cycles is designed to help students gain insights about how to handle real-life problems and understand historical and current events (Nelson, 1988). Students assume the role of another person—not roles in a story, but rather the roles people play in society—and re-enact events they are studying.

Heathcote has developed an innovative approach to role-playing to help students experience and better understand historical events (Wagner, 1976). Through a process she calls *funneling,* Heathcote chooses a dramatic focus from a general topic (e.g., Ancient Rome, the Civil War, the Pilgrims). She begins by thinking of all the aspects of the general topic and then decides on a dramatic focus—a particular critical moment. For example, using the topic of the Pilgrims, one possible focus is the night of December 20, 1620, eleven weeks after the Pilgrims set sail from England on the *Mayflower* and the night before the ship reached Plymouth.

The improvisation begins when students assume roles; the teacher becomes a character, too. As they begin to role-play the event, questions draw students' attention to certain features and probe their understanding. Questions about the Pilgrims might include:

Where are you?

After 11 weeks sailing the Atlantic Ocean, what do you think will happen?

How are you feeling?

Why did you leave England?

What kind of life do you dream of in the new land?

Can you survive in this cold winter weather?

These questions also provide information by reminding students of the time of year, the problems they are having, and the length of the voyage.

Sometimes Heathcote stops students in the middle of role-playing and asks them to write what they are thinking and feeling. As part of the Pilgrim improvisation, students might be asked to write an entry in their simulated journals for December 20, 1620. An example of a simulated journal entry written by a fourth-grade "Pilgrim" is shown in Figure 4–8. After the writing activity, students continue role-playing. (For more information on journals, see Chapter 5.)

Heathcote uses drama to begin study on a topic rather than as a culminating activity in which students apply all they have learned, because she believes role-playing experiences stimulate children's curiosity and make them want to read books and learn more about a historical or current event. Whether you use role-playing as an introduction or as a conclusion, it is a valuable activity

Figure 4–8   A Fourth-Grade Pilgrim's Simulated Journal Entry

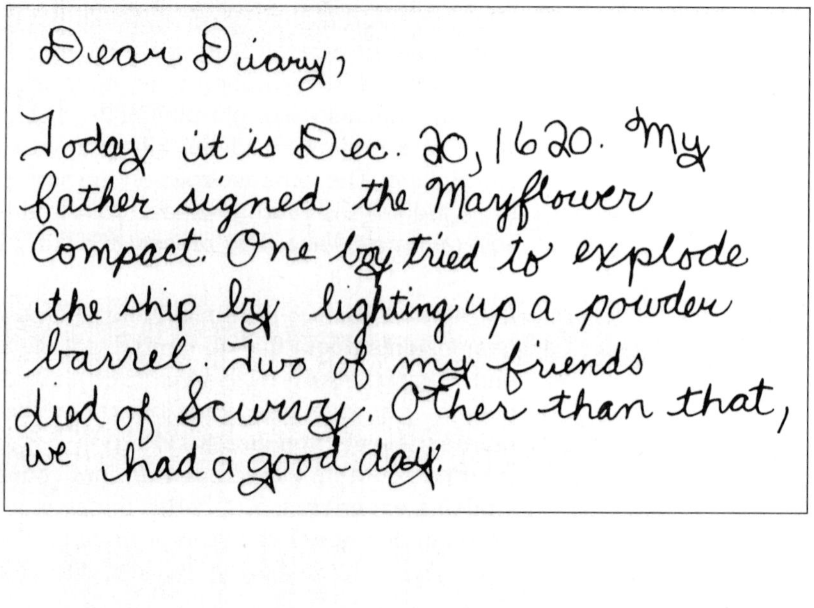

Dear Diary,

Today it is Dec. 20, 1620. My father signed the Mayflower Compact. One boy tried to explode the ship by lighting up a powder barrel. Two of my friends died of Scurvy. Other than that, we had a good day.

because students become immersed in the event. By reliving it, they are learning far more than mere facts.

Puppets and Other Props

Students create characters with puppets. A second grader pulls a green sock on one hand and a brown sock on the other hand, and with these socks that simply have buttons sewed on for eyes, the characters of Frog and Toad from Arnold Lobel's award-winning books *Frog and Toad Are Friends* (1970) and *Frog and Toad Together* (1972) come to life. The student talks in the voices of the two characters and involves the characters in events from the stories. While adults often feel self-conscious with puppets, children do not.

Children can create puppet shows with commercially manufactured puppets, or they can construct their own. When children create their own puppets, the only limitations are their imaginations, their ability to construct things, and the materials at hand. Puppets can be especially useful with shy students. Puppets can be used not only in all types of drama activities but also as a novel way to introduce a language skill, such as quotation marks. Teachers can use puppets to improvise a dialogue and then record it using quotation marks.

Simple puppets provide children with the opportunity to develop both creative and dramatic ability. The simpler the puppet, the more is left to the imagination of the audience and the puppeteer. Constructing elaborate puppets is beyond the resources of both teachers and students. The type of puppets the students make, however, depends on how they will be used. Students can construct puppets using all sorts of scrap materials. We will describe how to make eight types of hand and finger puppets; the puppets are illustrated in Figure 4–9.

Stick Puppets. Stick puppets are versatile and perhaps the easiest to make. Sticks, tongue depressors, dowels, and straws can be used. The rest of the puppet that is attached to the stick can be constructed from papier-mâché, Styrofoam balls, pictures students have drawn, or pictures cut from magazines and mounted on cardboard. Students draw or paint the features on the materials they have selected for the head and body. Some puppets may need only a head; others may also need a body. Making stick puppets provides an opportunity to combine art and drama.

Paper Bag Puppets. This is another simple puppet to make. The paper bags should be the right size to fit students' hands. Paper lunch bags are a convenient size, although smaller bags are better for kindergartners. What characters they portray and what emphasis the students give the size of the character are the determining factors, however. Students can place the puppet's mouth at the fold of the paper bag. Then they can paint on faces and clothes, add yarn for hair, and attach arms and legs. Students should choose ways to decorate their bag puppets to match the characters they develop.

Cylinder Puppets. Cylinder puppets are made from cardboard tubes from bathroom tissue, paper towels, and aluminum foil. The diameter and length of the cylinder determine the size of the puppet. The cylinders can be painted, and various appendages and clothing can be attached. Again, the character's

Figure 4-9   Types of Puppets Students Can Make

Stick Puppet   Paper Bag Puppet   Cylinder Puppet

Sock Puppet   Styrofoam Puppet   Paper Plate Puppet

Finger Puppet
(with tabs)

Finger puppet
(from glove finger)

Cloth Puppet

role should determine how the puppet is costumed. Students insert their fingers in the bottom of the cylinder to manipulate the puppet.

Sock Puppets.   Sock puppets are quite versatile. A sock can be used as is, with button eyes, yarn hair, pipe-cleaner antennae, and other features added. The sock can also be cut at the toe to create a mouth, and whatever else is needed to give the impression of the character can be added.

Cup Puppets.   Even primary-grade students can make puppets from Styrofoam cups. They glue facial features, hair, wings, and other decorations on the cup. Pipe cleaners, toothpicks, and Q-tips tipped with glitter can easily be attached to Styrofoam cups. Then sticks or heavy-duty straws are attached to the inside of the cup as the handle.

Paper Plate Puppets.   Paper plates can be used for face puppets as well as for masks. Students add junk materials to decorate the puppets, then tape sticks or rulers to the back of the plates as handles.

Finger Puppets.   Students can make several different types of finger puppets. For one type, students can draw, color, and cut out small figures, then add tabs to either side of the figure and tape the tabs together to fit around the finger. Larger puppets can be taped to fit around the hand. For a second type of finger puppet, students can cut the finger section from a glove and add decoration. The pointed part that separates the compartments of an egg carton can also be used for a finger puppet.

Cloth Puppets.   If parents are available to assist with the sewing, students can make cloth puppets. Two pieces of cloth are sewn together on all sides except the bottom; then students personalize the puppets using scraps of fabric, lace, yarn, and other materials.

After students have created their puppets, they can perform the puppet show almost any place. They can make a stage from an empty appliance packing crate or an empty television cabinet. They can also drape blankets or cloths in front of classroom tables and desks. They might also turn a table on its side. There may be other classroom objects your students can use as makeshift stages.

Scriptwriting and Theatrical Productions

Scripts are a unique written language form that elementary students need opportunities to explore. Scriptwriting often grows out of role-playing and storytelling. Soon students recognize the need to write notes when they prepare for plays, puppet shows, readers theatre, and other dramatic productions. This need provides the impetus for introducing students to the unique dramatic conventions and for encouraging them to write scripts to present as theatrical productions.

Play Scripts.   Once students want to write scripts, they will recognize the need to add the structures unique to dramatic writing to their repertoire of written language conventions. Students begin by examining scripts. It is especially effective to have students compare narrative and script versions of the same story; for example, Richard George has adapted two of Roald Dahl's fantastic stories, *Charlie and the Chocolate Factory* (1976) and *James and the Giant Peach* (1982), into scripts.

Then students discuss their observations and compile a list of the unique characteristics of scripts. An upper-grade class compiled this list of unique dramatic conventions:

1. Scripts are divided into acts and scenes.
2. Scripts have these parts:
    a. a list of characters (or cast)
    b. the setting at the beginning of each act or scene
    c. stage directions written in parentheses
    d. dialogue

3. The dialogue carries the action.
4. Descriptions and other information are set apart in the setting or in stage directions.
5. Stage directions give actors important information about how to act and how to feel.
6. The dialogue is written in a special way:
   Character's Name: Dialogue.
7. Sometimes a narrator is used to quickly fill in parts of the story.

The next step is to have students apply what they have learned about scripts by writing a class collaboration or group script. With the whole class, develop a script by adapting a familiar story. As the script is being written, refer to the chart of dramatic conventions and ask students to check that they are using these conventions. Collaborative writing affords unique teaching opportunities and needed practice for students before they must write individually. After the script is completed, have students read it using readers theatre procedures, or produce it as a puppet show or play.

Once students are aware of the dramatic conventions and have participated in writing a class collaboration script, they can write scripts individually or in small groups. Students often adapt familiar stories for their first scripts; later, they will want to create original scripts. "The Lonely Troll," a script written by a team of five upper-grade students, appears in Figure 4–10 as an example of the type of scripts older students can compose. Although most of the scripts they write are narrative, students can also create scripts about famous people or historical events.

Film and Video Scripts.   Students use a similar approach in writing scripts that will be filmed or videotaped, but they must now consider the visual component of the film as well as the written script. They often compose their scripts on storyboards, which focus their attention on how the story they are creating will be filmed (Cox, 1983, 1985). *Storyboards,* or sheets of paper divided into three sections, are used to sketch in scenes. Students place a series of three or four large squares in a row down the center of the paper, with space for dialogue and narration on the left and shooting directions on the right. Cox compares storyboards to road maps because they provide directions for filming the script. The scene renderings and the shooting directions help students tie the dialogue to the visual images that will appear on the film or videotape. Figure 4–11 shows a sample storyboard form with an excerpt from a fourth-grade class collaboration script.

The script can be produced several different ways—as a live-action play, as a puppet show, or through animation. After writing the script on the storyboards or transferring a previously written script to storyboards, students collect or construct the properties they will need to produce the script. As with other types of drama, the properties do not need to be extensive or elaborate—a simple backdrop and costumes will suffice. Students should also print the title and credits on large posters to appear at the beginning of the film. After several rehearsals, the students film the script using a movie or video camera.

As video cameras and VCR playback systems become common equipment in elementary schools, we anticipate that they will be chosen more often than movie cameras for filming student scripts. Video cameras and tapes are

Figure 4–10   A Script Written by a Group of Upper-Grade Students

The Lonely Troll

NARRATOR: Once upon a time, in a far, far away land, there was a troll named Pippin who lived all alone in his little corner of the woods. The troll hated all the creatures of the woods and was very lonely because he didn't have anyone to talk to since he scared everyone away. One day, a dwarf named Sam wandered into Pippin's yard and . . .

PIPPIN: Grrr. What are you doing here?

SAM: Ahhhhh! A troll! Please don't eat me!

PIPPIN: Why shouldn't I?

SAM: (Begging) Look, I'm all skin and bones. I won't make a good meal.

PIPPIN: You look fat enough for me. (Turns to audience) Do you think I should eat him? (Sam jumps off stage and hides in the audience.)

PIPPIN: Where did he go? (Pippin jumps off stage and looks for Sam. When he finds Sam, he takes him back on stage, laughing; then he ties Sam up.) Ha, ha, ha. Boy, that sure did tire me out. (Yawn) I'll take a nap. Then I'll eat him later. (Pippin falls asleep. Lights dim. Sam escapes and runs behind a tree. Lights return, and Pippin wakens.)

PIPPIN: (To audience) Where's my breakfast? (Sam peeps out from behind a tree and cautions the audience to be quiet.) Huh? Did someone say he was behind that tree? (Points to tree. Pippin walks around. Sam kicks him in the rear. Pippin falls and is knocked out.)

SAM: I must get out of here, and warn the queen about this short, small, mean, ugly troll. (Sam leaves. Curtains close.)

NARRATOR: So Sam went to tell Queen Muffy about the troll. Meanwhile, in the forest, Pippin awakens, and decides to set a trap for Sam. (Open curtains to forest scene, showing Pippin making a box trap.)

PIPPIN: Ha, ha, ha! That stupid dwarf will come back here looking for me. When he sees this ring, he'll take it. Then, I'll trap him! Ha, ha, ha, ha. (Pippin hides.)

NARRATOR: The dwarf finally reaches Queen Muffy's castle and hurries to tell her his story.

SAM: (Open curtains to Queen Muffy sitting on a throne, eating. Sam rushes in, out of breath.) I have some very important news for you. There's . . .

QUEEN: I don't have time for you.

SAM: But, I . . .

QUEEN: Come, come. Don't bother me with small things.

SAM: There's an ugly old . . .

QUEEN: You're wasting my time.

SAM: I just wanted to warn you, there's a big, ugly, mean . . .

Figure 4–10   *continued*

QUEEN:	Hurry up.
SAM:	. . . man-eating . . .
QUEEN:	This had better be important.
SAM:	(Angry, he yells) THERE'S A TROLL IN THE FOREST!!!
QUEEN:	Who cares if there's a . . . a . . . (Screams) A TROLL!!!
SAM:	That's what I've been saying. A troll—in the forest.
QUEEN:	Then I must send out my faithful knight . . . Sir Skippy . . . to kill him. I shall offer a reward. (Queen exits.)
SAM:	A reward, huh? Hmmmm. I think I'll go out and get that troll myself—and collect that reward! (Close curtains.)
NARRATOR:	So Sam sets out to capture the troll, not knowing that Pippin set a trap out for him. (Open curtains to trap scene.)
SAM:	(Carries a huge net) Ohhh Mr. Troll. (He spots the ring and reaches for it.) Wow! A ring! (Pippin sneezes.) What was that? Aha! (Sam sees Pippin, and swings the net. Pippin dives for Sam and gets trapped in his own trap.)
SAM:	He's trapped! I did it! Oh boy, now I can get that reward. I get a hundred dollars . . . or maybe a thousand dollars . . . possibly a million.
SKIPPY:	(Comes in smiling) I am here to rid the forest of this mean, awful, ugly troll. I also want the reward. (Said in an evil way)
SAM:	The reward is mine. I caught him. It's all mine.
SKIPPY:	I want that reward, and I shall get it. (Takes sword) I will carve your throat if you don't hand him over. I'll kill him and take him to the queen, so she will see what a great warrior I am.
SAM:	You're going to kill him? I won't let you!
SKIPPY:	Do you think I'm stupid? I won't take a live troll to Queen Muffy.
SAM:	If you are going to kill him, I will release him. (Throws off box) Hey, Pippin, he's going to kill you. Run away, run for your life, and I shall protect you.
PIPPIN:	(Confused) You are trying to save me, after I tried to kill you?
SAM:	I don't want to see you hurt.
PIPPIN:	Then I will stay here and help you defeat Skippy.
SAM AND PIPPIN:	Friends, forever! (Skippy steps forward and swings at Pippin. Pippin ducks. Pippin and Sam give Skippy the Three Stooges treatment. Skippy is defeated.)
PIPPIN:	Leave my forest, now, Sir Skippy, before we kill you. (Skippy leaves.)
SAM:	Thank you, my friend. We will stay together always, and you will never be lonely again. (Close curtains.)
NARRATOR:	Pippin and Sam became best friends, and the queen never bothered them. They lived happily ever after.

Figure 4–11   An Excerpt from a Class Collaboration Storyboard Script

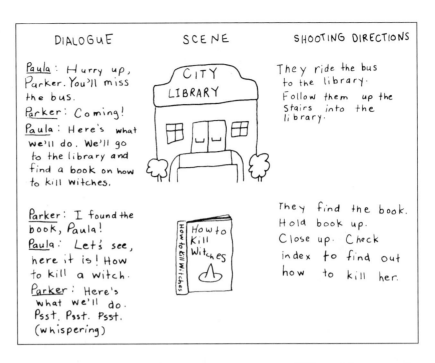

easier and less expensive to use than movie cameras and film; videotapes do not need to be developed as film does and can be reused; and the audio component can be recorded at the same time as the video. Many teachers prefer videotapes to films because they can tape rehearsals, which allows students to review their performances and make necessary changes before the final taping.

Review

Teachers sustain talk in the elementary classroom because talk has definite benefits for elementary students. Too often teachers assume that students already know how to talk, and so they concentrate on reading and writing. The four types of talk activities—conversations, aesthetic talk, efferent talk, and dramatic activities—are important to develop children's talk, and they also complement students' written language development. In conversations, students learn to converse with classmates, and they use talk to develop interpretations, create knowledge, and complete projects. Aesthetic talk, such as storytelling and readers theatre, gives students ways to deepen their interpretations of stories. Efferent talk includes show-and-tell, oral reports, interviews, and debates, and these more formal talk activities are presented before audiences. Drama includes role-playing and theatrical productions. Through drama, students explore another medium of expression and tap into a powerful way of knowing.

Extensions

1. Read Stanley's *The Conversation Club* (1983) to a group of primary-grade students to introduce conversation activities. Then organize a conver-sation club with the students and plan several activities with the group.

2. In an elementary classroom observe what types of oral language activities students participate in and what language functions they use.
3. Teach students how to participate in conversations about literature. Then, as you read a collection of picture books or a chapter book with a group of students, have the students participate in a series of literature conversations. Observe students as they talk about the book, and notice how they interact with their classmates as well as how they develop their interpretations.
4. Plan and conduct a debate with a group of upper-grade students. Help them choose a topic from current events, school and community issues, or a theme cycle.
5. Plan and direct a role-playing activity with a group of students in conjunction with a theme cycle. Following the guidelines in this chapter, integrate a writing activity with the role-playing (e.g., by having students keep a journal or write a letter).
6. Assist a small group of middle- or upper-grade students as they prepare to tell stories to a class of primary-grade students. Help students use the procedure discussed in this chapter.
7. Introduce scriptwriting to a group of middle- or upper-grade students by having them compile a list of the unique dramatic conventions used in scriptwriting. Then write a class collaboration script by adapting a familiar folktale.

References

Booth, D. (1985). "Imaginary gardens with real toads?": Reading and drama in education. *Theory into Practice, 24,* 193–198.

Bowser, J. (1993). Structuring the middle-school classroom for spoken language. *English Journal, 82,* 38–41.

Busching, B. A. (1981). Readers theatre: An education for language and life. *Language Arts, 58,* 330–338.

Camp, D. J., & Tompkins, G. E. (1990). Show-and-tell in middle school? *Middle School Journal, 21,* 18–20.

Cazden, C. B. (1986). Classroom discourse. In M. C. Wittrock (Ed.), *Handbook of research on teaching* (3rd ed.) (pp. 432–463). New York: Macmillan.

Cazden, C. B. (1988). *Classroom discourse: The language of teaching and learning.* Portsmouth, NH: Heinemann.

Cintorino, M. A. (1993). Getting together, getting along, getting to the business of teaching and learning. *English Journal, 82,* 23–32.

Cox, C. (1983). Young filmmakers speak the language of film. *Language Arts, 60,* 296–304, 372.

Cox, C. (1985). Filmmaking as a composing process. *Language Arts, 62,* 60–69.

Eeds, M., & Wells, D. (1989). Grand conversations: An exploration of meaning construction in literature study groups. *Research in the Teaching of English, 23,* 4–29.

Fiderer, A. (1988). Talking about books: Readers need readers. In J. Golub (Ed.), *Focus on collaborative learning* (Classroom Practices in Teaching English, 1988) (pp. 59–65). Urbana, IL: National Council of Teachers of English.

Golub, J. (1988). Introduction. In J. Golub (Ed.), *Focus on collaborative learning* (Classroom Practices in Teaching English, 1988) (pp. 1–2). Urbana, IL: National Council of Teachers of English.

Haley-James, S. M., & Hobson, C. D. (1980). Interviewing: A means of encouraging the drive to communicate. *Language Arts, 57,* 497–502.

Heath, S. B. (1983). Research currents: A lot of talk about nothing. *Language Arts, 60,* 999–1007.

Kardash, C. A. M., & Wright, L. (1987, Winter). Does creative drama benefit elementary school students: A meta-analysis. *Youth Theater Journal, 11*–18.

Kingore, B. W. (1982). Storytelling: A bridge from the university to the elementary school to the home. *Language Arts, 59,* 28–32.

Kukla, K. (1987). David Booth: Drama as a way of knowing. *Language Arts, 64,* 73–78.

Laughlin, M. K., & Latrobe, K. H. (1989). *Readers theatre for children: Scripts and script development.* Englewood, CO: Libraries Unlimited.

Manna, A. L. (1984). Making language come alive through reading plays. *The Reading Teacher, 37,* 712–717.

McKenzie, G. R. (1979). Data charts: A crutch for helping pupils organize reports. *Language Arts, 56,* 784–788.

Morrow, L. M. (1979). Exciting children about literature through creative storytelling techniques. *Language Arts, 56,* 236–243.

Morrow, L. M. (1985). Reading and retelling stories: Strategies for emergent readers. *The Reading Teacher, 38,* 870–875.

Nelson, P. A. (1988). Drama, doorway to the past. *Language Arts, 65,* 20–25.

Nystrand, M., Gamoran, A., & Heck, M. J. (1993). Using small groups for response to and thinking about literature. *English Journal, 82,* 14–22.

Ogle, D. M. (1986). K-W-L: A teaching model that develops active reading of expository text. *The Reading Teacher, 39,* 564–570.

Ogle, D. M. (1989). The know, want to know, learn strategy. In K. D. Muth (Ed.), *Children's comprehension of text: Research into practice* (pp. 205–223). Newark, DE: International Reading Association.

Pressley, M. (1992). Encouraging mindful use of prior knowledge: Attempting to construct explanatory answers facilitates learning. *Educational Psychologist, 27,* 91–109.

Reardon, S. J. (1988). The development of critical readers: A look into the classroom. *The New Advocate, 1,* 52–61.

Shafer, K. (1993). Talk in the middle: Two conversational skills for friendship. *English Journal, 82,* 53–55.

Shuy, R. W. (1987). Research currents: Dialogue as the heart of learning. *Language Arts, 64,* 890–897.

Sorenson, M. (1993). Teach each other: Connecting talking and writing. *English Journal, 82,* 42–47.

Stewig, J. W. (1983a). *Exploring language arts in the elementary classroom.* New York: Holt, Rinehart & Winston.

Stewig, J. W. (1983b). *Informal drama in the elementary language arts program.* New York: Teachers College Press.

Wagner, B. J. (1976). *Dorothy Heathcote: Drama as a learning medium.* Washington, DC: National Education Association.

Wagner, B. J. (1988). Research currents: Does classroom drama affect the arts of language? *Language Arts, 65,* 46–55.

Wilen, W. W. (1986). *Questioning skills for teachers* (2nd ed.). Washington, DC: National Education Association.

Wilkinson, L. C. (1984). Research currents: Peer group talk in elementary school. *Language Arts, 61,* 164–169.

Wittrock, M. C., & Alesandrini, K. (1990). Generation of summaries and analogies and analytic and holistic abilities. *American Research Journal, 27,* 489–502.

Children's Book References

Alexander, L. (1971). *The king's fountain.* New York: Dutton.

Avi. (1991). *Nothing but the truth.* New York: Orchard.

Babbitt, N. (1975). *Tuck everlasting.* New York: Farrar, Straus & Giroux.

Byars, B. (1968). *The midnight fox.* New York: Viking.

Cooper, K. (1985). *Who put the cannon in the courthouse square? A guide to uncovering the past.* New York: Walker.

Dahl, R. (1961). *James and the giant peach.* New York: Knopf.

Dahl, R. (1964). *Charlie and the chocolate factory.* New York: Knopf.

de Paola, T. (1978). *Pancakes for breakfast.* New York: Harcourt Brace Jovanovich.

Forbes, E. (1970). *Johnny Tremain: A story of Boston in revolt.* Boston: Houghton Mifflin.

Gackenback, D. (1980). *Hattie, Tom and the chicken witch.* New York: Harper & Row.

Galdone, P. (1970). *The three little pigs.* New York: Seabury.

Galdone, P. (1975). *The gingerbread boy.* New York: Seabury.

George, R. E. (1976). *Roald Dahl's Charlie and the chocolate factory.* New York: Knopf.

George, R. E. (1982). *Roald Dahl's James and the giant peach.* New York: Knopf.

Gilson, J. (1980) *Do bananas chew gum?* New York: Lothrop, Lee & Shepard.

Grahame, K. (1961). *The wind in the willows.* New York: Scribner.

Kellogg, S. (1988). *Johnny Appleseed.* New York: Morrow.

Korty, C. (1975). *Plays from African folktales.* New York: Scribner.

Laurie, R. (1980). *Children's plays from Beatrix Potter.* New York: Warne.

Lobel, A. (1970). *Frog and Toad are friends.* New York: Harper & Row.

Lobel, A. (1972). *Frog and Toad together.* New York: Harper & Row.

Naylor, P. R. (1991). *Shiloh.* New York: Atheneum.

O'Brien, R. C. (1971). *Mrs. Frisby and the rats of NIMH.* New York: Atheneum.

Say, A. (1990). *El chino.* Boston: Houghton Mifflin.

Slobodkina, E. (1947). *Caps for sale.* New York: Scott.

Smith, J. (1988). *The show-and-tell war.* New York: Harper & Row.

Stanley, D. (1983). *The conversation club.* New York: Macmillan.

Terkel, S. (1974). *Working.* New York: Pantheon.

Thurber, J. (1974). *Many moons.* New York: Harcourt.

Weitzman, D. (1975). *My backyard history book.* Boston: Little, Brown.

> 66 We write every day and then the boys and girls share their journals in our circle. Sharing is the most important part of writing in my classroom. 99

Glenna Jarvis
First-Grade Teacher
Western Hills Elementary School

PROCEDURE

My 6-year-old children write in journals—one kind or another—every day. Sometimes they write about anything they want to. I usually start with these free-choice or personal journals at the beginning of the school year. Later, they write in reading logs about the stories we are reading and in learning logs about what they are learning about in social studies or science.

This week the boys and girls are writing in bear-shaped booklets that I made to go along with our literature focus unit on *Corduroy* (Freeman, 1968) and its sequel, *A Pocket for Corduroy* (Freeman, 1972). Yesterday I read *A Pocket for Corduroy,* and we made a chart of things my students would keep in their pockets. After we read a story, my children write in their reading logs. I see the ideas from the books about Corduroy and other bear books I've read to them appear again and again in the children's writing. The cover and one page from Melissa's

reading log are presented in the accompanying figure. Melissa writes:

✏ *I love Corduroy. I would choose him to be my very own bear.*

Each morning as the children finish writing in their journals, they leave their desks and come to sit on the carpet in our circle area. The first child to finish usually sits in our author's chair and gets to be the first one to share. As they share, boys and girls read or tell about their journal entries and then show them to the audience. Children in the audience raise their hands to offer comments and compliments. I always let the child who is sharing choose the children to offer comments and compliments. After three or four children have given compliments, the child who is sitting in the author's chair chooses the next boy or girl to share.

Sharing moves really quickly; the entire class can share in about 20 minutes, so I usually encourage everyone to share. If I'm pressed for time, I sometimes have half the children share in the morning and postpone the rest of sharing until afternoon. I've also tried having only five or six children share each day, but I prefer to have everyone be a part of the sharing every day so that I know what every child is doing and what is happening in his or her life.

ASSESSMENT

Observing the boys and girls as they share is probably the most important thing I do. I notice what topics they choose to write about, how they use drawing and writing to convey their message, and the confidence they have as they share their journals. I also look to see how they act when they are in the audience, the types of comments and compliments they offer, and how they respond to their classmates' journals. I participate in sharing every day, and I watch and listen. I try to take a few minutes each day to write anecdotal notes on index cards

that I keep for each student in the class.

ADAPTATIONS

I encourage my children to communicate in their journals, whether they draw or write or use a combination of the two. I think that by making time to share each day, I am emphasizing the communicative function of writing. My children do different things in their journals. Some only draw pictures and others use a combination of drawing and writing. At the beginning of the school year, only a few children are writing, but I model "kid writing" and show them how to use a letter or two to represent an entire word. I also teach mini-lessons about sound-symbol cor-

respondences, handwriting skills, using capital letters and periods, and writing sentences. Their writing matures as they learn more about written language. I realize that writing is a developmental process, and I value my children's journal entries as evidence of their development.

REFLECTIONS

My students are first graders, and I try hard to tailor my program to meet their needs. Journal writing is the perfect activity for these students, because they are applying what they are learning about reading and literature, letters of the alphabet, and writing within a socialized and cooperative group setting.

5

Writing in Journals

Writing in personal journals has become a common occurrence in elementary classrooms, and students gain valuable writing experience through this activity. Students become more fluent writers as they learn how to choose a promising topic and develop an idea. They move through the stages of invented spelling and learn many of the conventions of written language, including how to use capital letters and punctuation marks appropriately. However, in time, some students grow bored writing journal entries about themselves, their families, and accounts of their daily activities and want to do other types of writing. Because teachers recognize the value of journals as a tool for learning, they wonder how they might adapt journal writing for other instructional purposes. One issue about journal writing is:

What are some ways journals can be used in elementary classrooms?

All kinds of people—artists, scientists, dancers, politicians, writers, assassins, and children—keep journals (Mallon, 1984). People usually record in their journals the everyday events of their lives and the issues that concern them. These journals, typically written in notebook form, are personal records, not intended for public display. Other journals might be termed "working" journals, in which writers record observations and other information to use for another purpose; for example, farmers might record weather or crop data, or gardeners the blooming cycle of their plants.*

The journals of some public figures have survived for hundreds of years and provide a fascinating glimpse of their authors and the times in which they lived. For example, the Renaissance genius Leonardo da Vinci recorded his daily activities, dreams, and plans for his painting and engineering projects in more than 40 notebooks. In the 1700s Puritan theologian Jonathan Edwards documented his spiritual life in his journal. In the late 1700s American explorers Meriwether Lewis and George Rogers Clark kept a journal of their travels across the North American continent, more for geographical than personal use. In the nineteenth century the American writer Henry David Thoreau filled 39 notebooks with his essays. French author Victor Hugo carried a small pocket notebook to record ideas as they came to him—even at inopportune moments such as while talking with friends. American author F. Scott Fitzgerald filled his notebooks with snippets of overheard conversations, many of which he later used in *The Great Gatsby* and other novels. Anne Frank, who wrote while in hiding from the Nazis during World War II, is the best-known child diarist.

TYPES OF JOURNALS

Elementary students use journals for a variety of purposes, just as adults do. Six types of journals are described in the Teacher's Notebook on page 165. In each type of journal the focus is on the writer, and the writing is personal and private. Students' writing is spontaneous and loosely organized, and it often contains mechanical errors because students are focusing on thinking, not on spelling, capitalization, and punctuation. James Britton and his colleagues (1975) compare this type of writing to a written conversation, and that conversation may be with oneself or with trusted readers who are interested in the writer. Some of the purposes for journal writing are to:

Record experiences

Stimulate interest in a topic

Explore thinking

Personalize learning

Develop interpretations

Wonder, predict, and hypothesize

Engage the imagination

---

*The terms *diary* and *journal* are often used synonymously; diaries are sometimes considered the more personal and private of the two. Whether the records that children write are called diaries or journals is unimportant; for convenience, we use the term *journal* to refer to this type of writing.

Teacher's Notebook
Types of Journals

Personal Journals

Students write about events in their own lives and about other topics of special interest in personal journals. These journals are the most private type; sometimes students share them and sometimes they don't. If teachers read these journals, they do not correct spelling or other errors. Instead, they respond as interested readers, often asking questions and offering comments about their own lives.

Dialogue Journals

Dialogue journals are similar to personal journals except that they are written to be shared with the teacher or a classmate. The person who receives the journal reads the entry and responds to it. These journals are like a written conversation.

Writing Notebooks

Students make notes and write lists of useful information about writing and the other language arts in writing notebooks. Then students refer to the information—such as poetic formulas and lists of homonyms—as needed. These journals are rarely read or graded.

Reading Logs

Students respond to stories, poems, and informational books they are reading in reading logs. They write and draw entries after reading, record key vocabulary words, make charts and other diagrams, and write memorable quotes. Students often share entries with classmates, and teachers check to see that students have completed assignments.

Learning Logs

Students write in learning logs as part of social studies and science theme cycles and math units. They write quickwrites, draw diagrams, take notes, and write vocabulary words.

Simulated Journals

In simulated journals students assume the role of a book character or a historical personality and write journal entries from that person's viewpoint. Students take care to include details from the story or historical period in their entries. Students often share these entries with classmates.

Ask questions

Activate prior knowledge

Assume the role of another person

Share experiences with trusted readers

Fulwiler (1985) shared excerpts from his daughter Megan's third-grade journal in *Language Arts,* demonstrating how she used writing for many of these functions. Later when she was a teenager, Megan Fulwiler (1986) reflected on her journal writing experiences and her reasons for writing. Most importantly, Megan described her journal as an extension of her mind that she used to work out her feelings, ask questions and find answers, and write down and organize her thoughts. She noted that as time passed, her entries grew more personal and became a record of her growing up.

As with Megan, journal writing gives students valuable writing practice. They gain fluency and confidence that they can write. They can also experiment with writing conventions that must be considered in more public writing. If they decide to make an entry ''public,'' students can later revise and edit their writing.

Personal Journals

Students often keep *personal journals* in which they recount events in their lives and write about topics of their choosing. An excerpt from a third grader's personal journal is presented in Figure 5–1. This excerpt shows the variety of topics students may choose to write about, as well as the depth of elementary students' feelings. It is normal for students to misspell a few words in their entries, as this third grader did; when students write in personal journals, the emphasis is on what they say, not how correctly they write.

It is often helpful to develop a list of possible journal writing topics on a chart in the classroom or on sheets of paper for students to clip inside their journal notebooks. Figure 5–2 shows a list of possible journal writing topics developed by a class of fourth and fifth graders. Students can add topics to their lists throughout the year, which may include more than 100 topics by the end of the school year. Students choose their own topics for personal journals. Although they can write about almost anything, some students will complain that they don't know what to write about, so a list of topics gives them a crutch. Referring students to the list or asking them to brainstorm a list of topics encourages them to become more independent writers and discourages them from becoming too dependent on teachers for writing topics.

Privacy becomes an important issue as students grow older. Most young children are willing to share what they have written, but by third or fourth grade, students grow less willing to read their journal entries aloud to the class, although they are usually willing to share the entries with a trusted teacher. Teachers must be scrupulous about respecting students' privacy and not insist that they share their writing when they are unwilling to do so. It is also important to talk with students about respecting each other's privacy and not reading each other's journals. To protect students' privacy, many teachers keep personal journals on an out-of-the-way shelf when they are not in use.

When students share personal information with teachers through their journals, a second issue arises. Sometimes teachers learn details about students' problems and family life that they do not know how to deal with.

Figure 5–1   *Entries from a*
Third Grader's Personal Journal

> **Monday Oct. 19.**
>
> About a month ago I went to Pennsylvania to see my grandfather but I call him Papap I don't know why. He was in the hospital for kemothereipee treatment. Once we were there he cheered up. But now he dosn't feel good. He is still in the haspital. I think of him all the time.
>
> **Tuesday Oct. 20**
>
> I am having a terrible day! First I had to go to G.T. lab. We have to do work there and we have homework Then I still have to do the same work in school that everybody does there and were gone all morning. Now I am stuck writing in this journal. I am sick of it, every Tuesday it is like this cause on tuesday mornings is when we go to G.T. lab. I am still not finished with my work.
>
> **Wednesday Oct. 21**
>
> You know I had a terrible day on Tuesday Well today I am having a good day. I have all my work finished.
>
> **Friday Oct. 23**
>
> My mom is in Pennsylvania today because of that today is a desaster. First I have to get up at six thirty then I forget my lunchpail at home and at this rate I will never finish my work. I havn't seen or talked to my mom sinsed Wednesday and I hate it.

Entries about child abuse, suicide, or drug use may be the child's way of asking for help. While teachers are not counselors, they do have a legal obligation to protect their students and report possible problems to appropriate school personnel. Occasionally a student invents a personal problem in a journal entry as an attention-getting tactic; however, asking the student about

Figure 5–2   *Fourth and Fifth Graders' List of Possible Writing Topics*

Things to Write About in Personal Journals

my favorite place in town	if I had three wishes
boyfriends/girlfriends	my teacher
things that make me happy or sad	TV shows I watch
music	my favorite holiday
an imaginary planet	if I were stranded on an island
cars	what I want to be when I grow up
magazines I like to read	private thoughts
what if snow were hot	how to be a superhero
dreams I have	dinosaurs
cartoons	my mom/my dad
places I've been	my friends
favorite movies	my next vacation
rock stars	love
if I were a movie/rock star	if I were an animal or something else
poems	books I've read
pets	favorite things to do
football	my hobbies
astronauts	if I were a skydiver
the president	when I get a car
jokes	if I had a lot of money
motorcycles	dolls
things that happen in my school	if I were rich
current events	wrestling and other sports
things I do on weekends	favorite colors
a soap opera with daily episodes	questions answered with "never"

or ANYTHING else I want to write about

the entry or having a school counselor do so will help to ensure that the student's safety is fully considered.

Dialogue Journals

Another approach to journal writing is the *dialogue journal*. In this approach students and teachers converse with each other through writing (Bode, 1989; Gambrell, 1985; Staton, 1980, 1987). These journals are interactive, are conversational in tone, and provide the opportunity for real student-teacher communication—something that is often missing in elementary classrooms. Each day students write informally to the teacher about something of interest or concern, and the teacher responds. Students choose their own topics and usually control the direction the writing takes. Staton (1987) offers these suggestions for responding to students' writing and continuing the dialogue:

1. Acknowledge students' ideas and encourage them to continue to write about their interests.
2. Support students by complimenting them about behavior and school work.
3. Provide new information about topics, so that students will want to read your responses.
4. Write less than the students do.

5. Avoid unspecific comments like "good idea" or "very interesting."
6. Ask few questions; instead, encourage students to ask you questions.

Teachers' responses do not need to be lengthy; a sentence or two is often enough. Even so, it is time-consuming to respond to 25, 30, or more journal entries every day. As an alternative, many teachers read and respond to students' journal entries on a rotating basis. They might respond to one group of students one week and another group the next week.

In this fifth grader's dialogue journal, Daniel shares the events and problems in his life with his teacher, and she responds sympathetically. Daniel writes:

Over spring break I went down to my grandma's house and played basketball in their backyard and while we were there we went to see some of my uncles who are all Indians. Out of my whole family down there they are all Indians except Grandpa Russell.

And Daniel's teacher responds:

What a fun spring break! That is so interesting to have Indians in your family. I think I might have some Indian ancestors too. Do you still plan to go to Padre Island for the summer?

The next day Daniel writes:

My family and I plan to go to Padre Island in June and I imagine we will stay there for quite a while. I think the funnest part will probably be swimming or camping or something like that. When we get there my mom says we will probably stay in a nice motel.

Daniel's teacher responds:

That really sounds like a fun vacation. I think swimming is the most fun, too. Who will go with you?

Daniel continues to talk about his family, now focusing on the problems he and his family are facing:

Well, my mom and dad are divorced so that is why I am going to court to testify on Tuesday but my mom, me, and my sister and brother are all going and that kind of makes me sad because a couple of years ago when my mom and dad were together we used to go a lot of places like camping and hiking but now after what happened we hardly go anywhere.

His teacher responds:

I am so sorry your family is having problems. It sounds as if your mom and dad are having problems with each other, but they both love you and want to be with you. Be sure to keep talking to them about how you feel.

Daniel replies:

I wish my mom and dad did not have problems because I would have a lot more fun and get to go and do a lot more things together, but since my mom and dad are divorced I have to take turns spending time with both of them.

His teacher offers a suggestion:

I'm sure that is hard. Trevor and Carla have parents who are divorced, too. Maybe you could talk to them. It might help.

This journal is not a series of teacher questions and student answers; instead, the student and teacher are having a dialogue, or conversation, and the interchange is built on mutual trust and respect.

Dialogue journals can be effective in dealing with students who have behavior problems or other types of problems in school (Staton, 1980). The teacher and student write back and forth about the problem and identify ways to solve it. In later entries the student reflects on his or her progress toward solving the problem. The teacher responds to the student's message, asks clarifying questions, or offers sympathy and praise.

Kreeft (1984) believes that the greatest value of dialogue journals is that they bridge the gap between talking and writing; they are written conversations. As the journal excerpts between Daniel and his teacher show, a second value is the strong bond that develops between student and teacher through writing back and forth to each other.

Dialogue journals are especially effective in promoting the writing development of children who are learning English as a second language. Researchers have found that these students who are limited English proficient are more successful writers when they choose their own topics for writing and their teachers contribute to the dialogue with requests for a reply, statements, and other comments (Peyton & Seyoum, 1989; Reyes, 1991). Not surprisingly, they found that students wrote more when teachers requested a reply than when teachers made comments that did not require a response. Also, when a student was particularly interested in a topic, it was less important what the teacher did, and when the teacher and the student were both interested in a topic, the topic seemed to take over as they shared and built on each other's writing. Reyes also found that bilingual students were much more successful in writing dialogue journal entries than in writing in response to books they had read.

Writing Notebooks

Writing notebooks are a specialized type of journal in which students record a variety of information about writing. Often students use these notebooks to take notes during minilessons. Entries include ideas for writing, other content information, rules about using commas, and other mechanical information about punctuation, capitalization, and writing conventions that writers need to know to write well. Other information students keep in writing notebooks include these examples:

- Lists of ideas for future compositions, interesting settings, or character descriptions
- Snippets of dialogue (overheard or invented)
- Notes about the elements of story structure, including characteristics of beginnings, middles, and ends of stories
- Charts describing poetic formulas
- Lists of comparisons that they locate in books they are reading
- Synonyms for overused words, such as *said* or *pretty* or *nice*
- Capitalization and punctuation rules
- Lists of commonly misspelled words
- Lists of homonyms (e.g., *their-there-they're*)

By recording this information about writing in a journal notebook, students create a permanent reference book.

Two sample pages from a fifth grader's writing notebook are shown in Figure 5–3. On the first page the student lists synonyms for the overused word *said* collected over several months from books she was reading and from a thesaurus. On the second page she organizes the words into five categories (ranging from *loud* to *soft*) that she developed to locate the synonyms more easily.

Writing notebooks also function much like writing folders in which students write drafts of stories, poems, and other pieces of writing. Some students write long stories in chapters or episodes, which they work on during writing workshop, daily journal writing, or free activity periods.

Reading Logs

Students write in *reading logs* about the stories and other books they are reading or listening to the teacher read aloud during literature focus units and reading workshop. Rather than simply summarize their reading, students relate

Figure 5–3 *Entries from a Fifth Grader's Writing Notebook*

Words for *Said*

screamed	called	talked
remarked	screeched	giggled
insisted	hollered	warned
sighed	yelled	bellowed
answered	barked	ordered
cried	quoted	shrieked
pleaded	replied	whined
sobbed	wondered	mumbled
whimpered	moaned	responded
whispered	shouted	hissed
exclaimed	commanded	reminded
directed	raved	muttered
grumbled	questioned	murmured
bawled	argued	snapped
proclaimed	repeated	explained
bragged	laughed	

Words for *Said* Arranged According to Loudness

Loudest ————————————————————————————➤ *Softest*

yelled	snapped	questioned	whined	moaned
shouted	reminded	laughed	giggled	whispered
raved	called	answered	grumbled	muttered
bellowed	exclaimed	insisted	sighed	murmured
cried	commanded	wondered	sobbed	mumbled
hollered		pleaded		whimpered
screamed		replied		
screeched				
shrieked				

their reading to their own lives or to other literature they have read. Students may also list interesting or unfamiliar words, jot down quotable quotes, and take notes about characters, plot, or other story elements; but the primary purpose of these journals is for students to think about the book, connect literature to their lives, and develop their own interpretations. These journals go by a variety of names, including story journals (Farris, 1989), literature response journals (Hancock, 1992), literature journals (Five, 1986), and reading journals (Wollman-Bonilla, 1989); but no matter what they are called, their purpose remains the same.

Teachers and researchers (Barone, 1990; Dekker, 1991; Hancock, 1992) have examined students' reading log entries and have identified these categories of response:

- Questions related to understanding the text
- Interaction with characters
- Empathy with characters
- Prediction and validation
- Personal experiences
- Personal feelings and opinions
- Simple and elaborate evaluations
- Philosophical reflections
- Retellings and summaries

Two reading log entries about *Bunnicula: A Rabbit-Tale of Mystery* (Howe & Howe, 1979) are shown in Figure 5–4. The picture entry was made by a second grader, and the handwritten entry by a fourth grader. Both students

This second grader writes and draws her reactions to a story in a reading log.

were listening to their teachers reading the chapter book aloud. The second grader's entry is a summary of the chapter, and the fourth grader's entry includes personal feelings and a prediction about what will happen in the next chapter.

When students begin writing entries in reading logs, their first entries are often retellings and plot summaries, as the second grader's entry was, but as students gain experience reading and responding to literature, their entries become more interpretive and personal. Teachers can model writing "I think" reactions, share student entries that are interpretive, and respond to students' entries by asking questions.

Dialoguing About Literature.   Students can use dialogue journals to write to classmates or the teacher about books they are reading (Atwell, 1987; Barone, 1990; Dekker, 1991). In these journal entries, students write about the books they are reading, compare the books to others by the same author or others they have read, and offer opinions about the book and whether a classmate or the teacher might enjoy reading it.

This approach is especially effective in reading workshop classrooms when students are reading different books. Students are often paired and write back-and-forth to their reading buddies. This activity provides the socialization that independent reading does not. Depending on whether students are reading

Figure 5–4   *Entries From Two Students' Reading Logs About* Bunnicula: A Rabbit-Tale of Mystery

When Bunicula bites a vegteble it turns white.

Chapter 1
"The Arrival"

I thought the part where Toby sat on Bunnicula at the movies and then popped out of his seat and shouted "I set on something!" was funny and sad. It was funny when Toby popped out of his seat but it was sad that Bunnicula got squished. And I already like it even though I've only heard one chapter and I think you would to! Oh ya, I forgot to tell about the note around Bunnicula's neck. But none of them could read because it was in a diffrent language, but Herald their dog could and it said "Take care of my baby." Next I think Chester the cat and Herald will get jellous and run away. Oh ya, Bunnicula is a rabbit.

relatively short picture books or longer chapter books, they can write dialogue journal entries every other day or once a week, and then classmates write back.

Fourth graders wrote these entries to classmates and their teacher about informational books they were reading during reading workshop:

Dear Adam,
I'm reading the coolest book. It's about snakes and it's called A Snake's Body *[Cole, 1981]. Look at the pictures on pages 34, 35, 36, 37, 38, 39, 40, 41, and 42 to see how a python strangles and eats a chick. It's awesome.*

Your Friend, Todd

Dear Elizabeth,
Do you like maps? If you do, you will want to read As the Crow Flies *[Hartman, 1991]. I'm reading it now and you can have it next. I like to make maps and that's what this book is all about.*

From Missy

Dear Mrs. Parker,
I just finished reading The Magic School Bus Inside the Human Body *[Cole, 1989]. I think you would like it, too, because it's about a teacher named Ms. Frizzle and she's sort of magic. She takes her kids on a field trip and Ms. Frizzle drives the school bus inside a human body. The book takes a long time to read because it has lots of cartoons and extra things to read and look at. I'd say it was one of the best books I've ever read. I think everyone in our class should read it. What do you think?*

Love, Ali

Trevor,
The book I'm reading is A Wall of Names *[Donnelly, 1991]. It's ok, if you want to know about the Vietnam wall memorial. I picked this book because my Gramps was in that war and last summer we went to Washington, D.C. on vacation and I got to see the wall. It's shiny and black and all the names of the soldiers that died fighting in it are written on the wall. Have you ever heard of it?*

From your friend, David

Before the students began writing dialogue journal entries, the teacher taught a minilesson about how to format their entries, about how to capitalize and underline book titles, and about the importance of asking questions in their entries so that respondents could answer them in their replies. In their entries most students incorporated what they had learned in the minilesson.

Double-Entry Journals.   A special type of reading log is the double-entry journal (Barone, 1990; Berthoff, 1981). Students divide their journal pages into two columns; in the left column they write quotes from the story or other book they are reading, and in the right column they relate each quote to their own life and to literature they have read. Through this type of reading log, students become more engaged in what they are reading, note sentences that have personal connections, and become more sensitive to the author's language.

Students in a fifth-grade class kept a double-entry journal as they read C. S. Lewis's classic *The Lion, the Witch and the Wardrobe* (1950). After they read each chapter, they reviewed the chapter and selected one, two, or three brief quotes. They wrote these excerpts in the left columns of their journals, and they wrote reactions beside each quote in the right column. An excerpt from a fifth grader's journal is presented in Figure 5–5. This student's responses indicate that she is engaged in the story and is connecting the story to her own life as well as to another story she has read.

Double-entry journals can be used in several other ways. Instead of recording quotes from the book, students can write "Reading Notes" in the left column and then add "Reactions" in the right column. In the left column students write about the events they read about in the chapter. Then in the right column they make personal connections to the events.

As an alternative, students can use the heading "Reading Notes" for one column and "Discussion Notes" for the second column. Students write reading notes as they read or immediately after reading. Later, after discussing the story or chapter of a longer book, students add discussion notes. As with other types of double-entry journals, it is the second column in which students make more interpretive comments.

Younger students can use the double-entry format for a prediction journal (Macon, Bewell, & Vogt, 1991). They label the left column "Predictions" and the right column "What Happened." In the left column they write or draw a picture of what they predict will happen in the story or chapter before reading

Figure 5–5   *Excerpts from a Fifth Grader's Double-Entry Journal about* The Lion, the Witch and the Wardrobe

In the Text	My Response
Chapter 1	
I tell you this is the sort of house where no one is going to mind what we do.	I remember the time that I went to Beaumont, Texas to stay with my aunt. My aunt's house was very large. She had a piano and she let us play it. She told us what we could do whatever we wanted to.
Chapter 5	
"How do you know?" he asked, "that your sister's story is not true?"	It reminds me of when I was little and I had an imaginary place. I would go there in my mind. I made up all kinds of make-believe stories about myself in this imaginary place. One time I told my big brother about my imaginary place. He laughed at me and told me I was silly. But it didn't bother me because nobody can stop me from thinking what I want.
Chapter 15	
Still they could see the shape of the great lion lying dead in his bonds.	When Aslan died I thought about when my Uncle Carl died.
They're nibbling at the cords.	This reminds me of the story where the lion lets the mouse go and the mouse helps the lion.

it. Then after reading, in the right column they draw or write what actually happened.

Learning Logs

Students write entries in *learning logs* to record or react to what they are learning in math, science, social studies, or other content areas. Fulwiler (1987) explains: "When people write about something they learn it better" (p. 9). As students write in these journals, they reflect on their learning, discover gaps in their knowledge, and explore relationships between what they are learning and their past experiences.

In Math.   Students use learning logs to write about what they are learning in math (Salem, 1982). They record explanations and examples of concepts presented in class, and they react to the mathematical concepts they are learning and any problems they may be having. Some upper-grade teachers allow students the last 5 minutes of math class to summarize the day's lesson and react to it in their learning logs (Schubert, 1987). Through these activities, students practice taking notes, writing descriptions and directions, and using other writing skills. They also learn how to reflect on and evaluate their own learning (Stanford, 1988).

Figure 5–6 presents an entry from a sixth grader's learning log in which she describes how to change improper fractions. Notice that after she describes the steps in sequence, she includes a review of the six steps.

In addition to the benefits to students, teachers use learning logs to informally assess students' learning. Through students' math entries, teachers can assess what students already know about a topic before teaching, discover what students are learning, and check on confusions and misconceptions. Teachers can also use the entries to monitor students' attitudes toward math and assess their learning of a concept after teaching (McGonegal, 1987). Sometimes teachers simply read these entries, and at other times the learning logs become dialogue journals as teachers respond to students by clarifying misconceptions and offering encouragement.

In Science.   Science-related learning logs can take several different forms. One type is an observation log in which students make daily entries to track the growth of plants or animals. For instance, a second-grade class observed caterpillars as they changed from caterpillars to chrysalides to butterflies over a period of 4 to 6 weeks. Students each kept a log with daily entries, in which they were to describe the changes they observed using shape, color, size, and other property words. Two pages from a second grader's log documenting the caterpillars' growth and change are presented in Figure 5–7.

A second type of learning log is one in which students make entries during a theme cycle. Students may take notes during presentations by the teacher or after reading, after viewing films, or at the end of each class period. Sometimes students make entries in list form, sometimes in clusters, charts, or maps, and at other times in paragraphs.

Lab reports are a third type of learning log. In these logs, students list the materials and procedures used in the experiment, present data on an observation chart, and then discuss the results. A fourth grader's lab report for an

Figure 5–6   A Sixth Grader's Math Learning Log Entry

Changing to Improper Fractions

To Change a mixed number Such as $5\frac{2}{3}$, you must must multiply the denominator, which is the bottom number, times the whole number which is 5, So now we have : 3×5=15, Next you add the numerator to the problem like this! 15+2=17, Put the same denominater, the bottom number, and it should look like this! $\frac{17}{3}$. To check your answer, find out how many times 3 ,the bottom number, goes into the top number, 17. It goes in 5 times. There are two left over, So the answer is $5\frac{2}{3}$. It is correct.

6 Steps!

1. $5\frac{2}{3}$
2. 3×5=15
3. 15+2=17
4. $\frac{17}{3}$
5. $3\overline{)17}^{\,5\,2}=5\frac{2}{3}$
6. $5\frac{2}{3}$ – Correct

experiment with hermit crabs is presented in Figure 5–8. When students write in science logs, they are assuming the role of scientists, learning to make careful observations and to record them accurately.

In Social Studies.   Students often keep learning logs as part of theme cycles in social studies. In their logs, students write in response to stories and informational books, note interesting words related to the theme, create

Figure 5–7   Two Entries From a Second Grader's Science Log on Caterpillars

> Day 3
>
> The Caterpillars are 3 cm. They are Black and brown. they have littel Spikes on their Bodies. They have 9 legs. They have un tanas on their heads.

> Day 25
>
> They are turning white. They are turning into Chrysalis and they are hanging from the roof.

timelines, and draw diagrams, charts, and maps. For example, as part of a theme cycle on the Civil War for eighth graders, students might include the following in their learning logs:

- Informal quickwrites about the causes of the war and other topics related to the war
- A list of words related to the theme
- A chart of major battles in the war
- A Venn diagram comparing the northern and southern viewpoints
- A timeline showing events related to the war
- A map of the United States at the time of the war with battle locations marked
- Notes after viewing several films about the Civil War era
- A list of favorite quotes from Lincoln's "Gettysburg Address"
- Their response to a chapter book such as *Charley Skedaddle* (Beatty, 1987), *Brady,* (Fritz, 1987), *Across Five Aprils* (Hunt, 1987), or *The 290* (O'Dell, 1976)

Through these learning log activities, students explore concepts they are learning and record information they want to remember about the Civil War.

Simulated Journals

In *simulated journals* students assume the role of another person and write from that person's viewpoint. They can assume the role of a historical figure when they read biographies or as part of social studies theme cycles. As they read stories, students can assume the role of a character in the story. In this

Figure 5–8   *A Fourth Grader's Lab Report on Hermit Crabs*

Lab Repot

Do hermit crabs prefer a wet or dry habitat?

Materials
trough
trough cover
2 paper towels
water sprinkler

Procedures
1. Put one wet and one dry paper towel in the trough.
2. Place the hermit crab in the center of the trough and put on the cover.
3. Wait 60 seconds.
4. Open the cover and observe the location of the hermit crab.
5. Mark the location on the observation chart.
6. Do the experiment 6 times.

Observation Chart

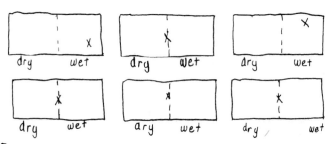

Results
Wet: 2
Dry: 0
Center 4

Our hermit crab liked the center part best. 4 out of 6 times it stayed in the center. Then it liked the wet part next best. It didn't like the dry part at all.

way students gain insight into other people's lives and into historical events. A look at a series of diary entries written by a fifth grader who has assumed the role of Betsy Ross shows how she carefully chose the dates for each entry and wove in factual information:

May 15, 1773
Dear Diary,
This morning at 5:00 I had to wake up my husband John to get up for work but he wouldn't wake up. I immediately called the doc. He came over as fast as he could. He asked me to leave the room so I did. An hour later he came out and told me he had passed away. I am so sad. I don't know what to do.

June 16, 1776
Dear Diary,
Today General Washington visited me about making a flag. I was so surprised. Me making a flag! I have made flags for the navy, but this is too much. But I said yes. He showed me a pattern of the flag he wanted. He also wanted six-pointed stars but I talked him into having five-pointed stars.

July 8, 1776
Dear Diary,
Today in front of Carpenter Hall the Declaration of Independence was read by Tom Jefferson. Well, I will tell you the whole story. I heard some yelling and shouting about liberty and everyone was gathering around Carpenter Hall. So I went to my next door neighbors to ask what was happening but Mistress Peters didn't know either so we both went down to Carpenter Hall. We saw firecrackers and heard a bell and the Declaration of Independence was being read aloud. When I heard this I knew a new country was born.

June 14, 1777
Dear Diary,
Today was a happy but scary day. Today the flag I made was adopted by Congress. I thought for sure that if England found out that a new flag was taking the old one's place something bad would happen. But I'm happy because I am the maker of the first American flag and I'm only 25 years old!

Ira Progoff (1975) uses a similar approach, called "dialoguing," in which students converse with a historical figure or other character in a journal by writing both sides of the conversation. He suggests focusing on a milestone in the person's life and starting the journal at an important point. A dialogue with Martin Luther King, Jr., for instance, might take place the day he gave his "I Have a Dream" speech in Washington, DC.

Young Children's Journals

Young children can write in journals by drawing, or they can use a combination of drawing and writing (Elliott, Nowosad, & Samuels, 1981; Hipple, 1985; Nathan, 1987). Children may write scribbles, random letters and numbers, simple captions, or extended texts using invented spelling. Their invented spellings often seem bizarre by adult standards, but they are reasonable in terms of children's knowledge of phoneme-grapheme correspondences and spelling patterns. Other children want parents and teachers to take their dictation and write the text. After the text has been written, children can usually read it immediately, and they retain recognition of the words several days later.

Young children usually begin writing in personal or dialogue journals and then expand their repertoire of journal forms to include reading logs and

This kindergartner uses letters and letterlike forms as she writes in her journal.

learning logs. Four kindergartners' journal entries are presented in Figure 5–9. The top two entries are from personal journals, and the bottom two entries are from reading logs. In the top left entry this 5-year-old focuses on the illustration, drawing a detailed picture of a football game (note that the player in the middle right position has the ball); he adds five letters for the text so that his entry will have some writing. In the top right entry the kindergartner writes, "I spent the night at my dad's house." The child wrote the entry on the bottom left after listening to his teacher read *The Three Billy Goats Gruff* (Stevens, 1987) and then acting out the story. As he shared his entry with classmates, he read the text this way: "You are a mean bad troll." The kindergartner wrote the entry on the bottom right after listening to the teacher read *The Jolly Postman or Other People's Letters* (Ahlberg & Ahlberg, 1986). This child drew a picture of the three bears receiving a letter from Goldilocks. She labeled the mom, dad, and baby bear in the picture and wrote, "I [am] sorry I ate your porridge."

Despite the variety of forms and purposes, journal writing helps elementary students discover the power of writing to record information and explore ideas. Students usually cherish their journals and are amazed by the amount of writing they contain.

TEACHING STUDENTS TO WRITE IN JOURNALS

Journals are typically written in notebooks. Spiral-bound notebooks are useful for long-term personal and dialogue journals and writing notebooks; small booklets of paper stapled together are more often used for reading logs, learning logs, and simulated journals. Most teachers prefer to keep the journals

Figure 5–9   *Entries From Young Children's Personal Journals*

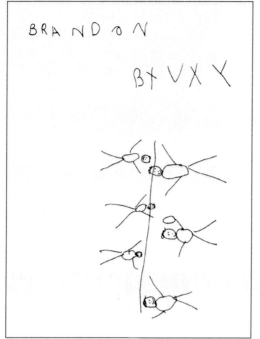

in the classroom so that they will be available for students to write in each day, but students might write in journals at home as well.

Students usually write at a particular time each day. Many teachers have students make personal or dialogue journal entries while they take attendance or immediately after recess. Writing notebooks are often used during minilessons to record information about topics such as poetic forms or quotation marks. Entries are made in reading logs during literature focus units and reading workshop. Learning logs and simulated journals can be written in as part of math class or social studies or science theme cycles.

Introducing Students to Journal Writing

Teachers introduce students to journal writing using minilessons in which they explain the purpose of the journal writing activity and the procedures for gathering ideas, writing the entry, and sharing it with classmates. Teachers often model the procedure by writing a sample entry on the chalkboard or on chart paper as students observe. This sample demonstrates that the writing is to be informal, with ideas emphasized over correctness. Then students make their own first entries, and several read their entries aloud. Through this sharing, students who are still unclear about the activity have additional models on which to base their own writing.

Similar procedural minilessons are used to introduce each type of journal. Whereas all journals are informal writing activities, the purpose of the journal, the information included in the entries, and the viewpoint of the writer vary according to the type of journal.

Journal writing can also be introduced with examples from literature. Characters in children's literature, such as Harriet in *Harriet the Spy* (Fitzhugh, 1964), Leigh in *Dear Mr. Henshaw* (Cleary, 1983), and Catherine Hall in *A Gathering of Days* (Blos, 1979), keep journals in which they record events in their lives, their ideas, and their dreams. A list of books in which characters and historical personalities keep journals is presented in Figure 5–10. In these books the characters demonstrate the process of journal writing and illustrate both the pleasures and the difficulties of keeping a journal (Tway, 1981).

Sustaining Journal Writing

Students write in journals on a regular schedule, usually daily. After they know how to write the appropriate type of entry, they can write independently. While some children prefer to write private journals, others will volunteer to read their journal entries aloud each day no matter what type of journal they are writing. Young children share their picture journal entries and talk about them. If the sharing becomes too time-consuming, students can share in small groups or with partners. Then, after everyone has had a chance to share, several students can be selected to share with the entire class. Teachers and classmates may offer compliments about the topic, word choice, humor, and so on.

Students may write in personal journals throughout the school year, or they may alternate other types of journals, starting and stopping with particular literature focus units and social studies and science theme cycles. Sometimes students seem to lose interest in personal journals. If this happens, many teachers find it useful to put the personal journals away and try another type of journal.

Figure 5–10   Books in Which Characters and Historical Personalities Keep Journals

Anderson, J. (1987). *Joshua's westward journey.* New York: Morrow. (M)

Avi. (1991). *Nothing but the truth.* New York: Orchard. (M–U)

Banks, L. R. (1993). *The mystery of the cupboard.* New York: Morrow. (M–U)

Blos, J. (1979). *A gathering of days: A New England girl's journal, 1830–1832.* New York: Scribner. (U)

Bourne, M. A. (1975). *Nabby Adams's diary.* New York: Coward. (U)

Cleary, B. (1983). *Dear Mr. Henshaw.* New York: Morrow. (M)

Cleary, B. (1991). *Strider.* New York: Morrow. (M)

Conrad, P. (1991). *Pedro's journal: A voyage with Christopher Columbus (August 3, 1492–February 14, 1493).* Honedale, PA: Boyds Mills Press. (M–U)

Fisher, L. E. (1972). *The death of evening star: Diary of a young New England whaler.* New York: Doubleday. (M–U)

Fitzhugh, L. (1964). *Harriet the spy.* New York: Harper & Row. (M)

Frank, A. (1952). *Anne Frank: The diary of a young girl.* New York: Doubleday. (U)

George, J. C. (1959). *My side of the mountain.* New York: Dutton. (M–U)

Glaser, D. (1976). *The diary of Trilby Frost.* New York: Holiday House. (U)

Harvey, B. (1986). *My prairie year: Based on the diary of Elenore Plaisted.* New York: Holiday House. (M)

Harvey, B. (1988). *Cassie's journey: Going west in the 1860s.* New York: Holiday House. (M)

Leslie, C. W. (1991). *Nature all year long.* New York: Greenwillow. (M)

Lowry, L. (1986). *Anastasia has the answers.* Boston: Houghton Mifflin. (M)

Mazer, N. F. (1971). *I, Trissy.* New York: Delacorte. (U)

Oakley, G. (1987). *The diary of a church mouse.* New York: Atheneum. (M)

Orgel, D. B. (1978). *The devil in Vienna.* New York: Dial (U)

Reig, J. (1978). *Diary of the boy king Tut-Ankh-Amen.* New York: Scribner. (M)

Roop, P., & Roop, C. (Eds.). (1990). *I Columbus: My journal 1492–1493.* New York: Avon Books. (M–U)

Roop, P., & Roop, C. (1993). *Off the map: The journals of Lewis and Clark.* New York: Walker. (M–U)

Roth, S. L. (1990). *Marco Polo: His notebook.* New York: Doubleday. (U)

Sachs, M. (1975). *Dorrie's book.* New York: Doubleday. (M)

Smith, R. K. (1987). *Mostly Michael.* New York: Delacorte Press. (M)

Thaxter, C. (1992). *Celia's island journal.* Boston: Little, Brown. (P–M)

Thesman, J. (1993). *Molly Donnelly.* Boston: Houghton Mifflin. (U)

Van Allsburg, C. (1991). *The wretched stone.* Boston: Houghton Mifflin. (M–U)

Wilder, L. E. (1962). *On the way home.* New York: Harper & Row. (M)

Williams, V. B. (1981). *Three days on a river in a red canoe.* New York: Greenwillow. (P–M)

P = primary grades (K–2); M = middle grades (3–5); U = upper grades (6–8).

Minilessons.   Teachers teach minilessons on procedures, concepts, and strategies and skills about writing in journals. A list of minilesson topics is presented on page 185. Minilessons are especially important when students are learning a new type of journal or when they are having difficulty with a particular procedure or strategy, such as changing point of view for simulated journals or writing in two columns in double-entry journals. Two strategies that students often use when writing in journals are quickwriting and clustering, described in the following sections.

Quickwriting.   *Quickwriting* is a strategy that students use as they write in journals or do other types of impromptu writing. Students reflect on what they know about a topic, ramble on paper, generate words and ideas, and make connections among the ideas. Students write about a topic for 5 to 10 minutes and let their thoughts flow from their minds to their pens without focusing on

M I N I L E S S O N S

Journal Writing

Procedures	Concepts	Strategies and Skills
Write a journal entry	Kinds of journals	Choose a topic
Share entries	Uses of journals	Generate ideas
Give feedback about	Values of writing in journals	Organize ideas
classmates' entries	Informal versus polished	Focus on ideas
Respond in dialogue journals	writing	Interpret
Write in writers' notebooks	Personal journals	Predict
Write reading log entries	Dialogue journals	Describe
Write double-entry journals	Writers' notebooks	Analyze
Use logs in math	Reading logs	Report
Write science observation logs	Double-entry journals	Value
Write science lab reports	Learning logs	Incorporate key vocabulary
Use logs in theme cycles	Simulated journals	Assume another viewpoint
Write simulated journals	Qualities of a good entry	
Quickwrite or quickdraw	Respecting classmates'	
Cluster	privacy	
Make charts and diagrams		

mechanics or revisions. This strategy, originally called *freewriting* and popularized by Peter Elbow (1973), is a way to help students focus on content rather than mechanics. Even by second or third grade, students have learned that many teachers emphasize correct spelling and careful handwriting more than the content of a composition. Elbow explains that focusing on mechanics makes writing "dead" because it does not allow students' natural voices to come through.

During a theme cycle on the solar system, fourth graders each chose a word from the word wall (a list of vocabulary words hanging in the classroom) to quickwrite about. This is one student's quickwrite on Mars:

✐ *Mars is known as the red planet. Mars is Earth's neighbor. Mars is a lot like Earth. On Mars one day lasts 24 hours. It is the fourth planet in the solar system. Mars may have life forms. Two Viking ships landed on Mars. Mars has a dusty and rocky surface. The Viking ships found no life forms. Mars' surface shows signs of water long ago. Mars has no water now. Mars has no rings.*

Another student wrote about the sun:

✐ *The sun is an important star. It gives the planets light. The sun is a hot ball of gas. Even though it appears large, it really isn't. It's pretty small. The sun's light takes time to travel to the planets so when you see light it's really from a different time. The closer the planet is to the sun the quicker the light reaches it. The sun has spots where gas has cooled. These are called sun spots. Sun spots look like black dots. The sun is the center of the universe.*

These quickwrites, which took 10 minutes for students to draft, provide both a good way of checking on what students are learning and an opportunity to clarify misconceptions. After students write, they usually share their quick-writes in small groups, and then one student in each group shares with the class. Sharing also takes about 10 minutes, and the entire activity can be completed in approximately 20 minutes.

Before starting a new unit of study, teachers might ask students to quickwrite on the new topic to check their knowledge about the topic, to relate personal experiences about it, and to stimulate interest. For example, students can participate in the following quickwrites in connection with current events, literature, social studies, and science themes:

- Before discussing a current events topic, quickwrite on freedom or a geographic location.
- Before reading *Bridge to Terabithia* (Paterson, 1977), quickwrite on the theme of friendship.
- Before studying the Oregon Trail, quickwrite on a trip students have taken.
- Before studying reptiles, quickwrite on snakes.
- Before studying nutrition, quickwrite on junk food.

After completing the theme, students quickwrite again on the topic, applying what they have learned. Then they compare the two quickwrites as one measure of what they have learned.

Clustering.   *Clustering* is a strategy that students use as they gather and organize information they are learning in a learning log or on a chart or poster (Rico, 1983). Students also use clustering to organize ideas before beginning to write a composition. Clusters are weblike diagrams with the topic or nuclear word written in a circle centered on a sheet of paper. Main ideas are written on rays drawn out from the circle, and branches with details and examples are added to complete each main idea.

Two clusters are presented in Figure 5–11. The top cluster on birds was developed by a sixth-grade teacher during a theme cycle on birds. The purpose of the cluster was to assist students in categorizing birds such as cardinals, penguins, vultures, chickens, and ducks. As the class talked about the categories, students wrote the names of examples beside each category to complete the cluster. Later in the theme study students each chose one bird to research, and then they presented the results of their research in cluster form. The bottom cluster on bald eagles presents the results of one student's research. The information in the cluster is divided into four categories: life, hunters, symbol, and body; other, more general, information is listed at the top of the figure.

Adapting to Meet the Needs of Every Student

Journals can easily be adapted to meet the needs of every student. Students who have not had a lot of experience with journals may be more successful in writing personal or dialogue journals in which they focus on experiences from their own lives rather than on literature they are reading or on across-the-curriculum theme studies. Research suggests that students learning English as a second language are more successful using dialogue journals than other types.

Figure 5–11   *Two Clusters About Birds*

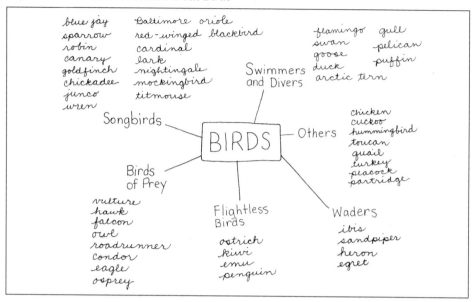

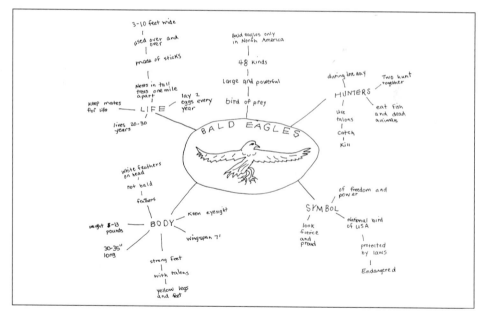

For students who have difficulty writing, spelling, or expressing themselves in English, two alternatives are drawing illustrations or dictating entries to the teacher or a cross-age tutor. Some students may benefit from talking about their reactions to stories before writing in reading logs or from talking about topics for quickwrites before writing in learning logs. No matter what type of journals students are writing, it is important to help them focus on their ideas and the interpretations they are expressing, not on mechanical correctness. A list of suggestions for adapting journal writing activities to meet the needs of every student is presented on page 189.

This student draws a cluster to gather and organize the information she is learning during a theme cycle on whales.

Assessing Students' Journal Entries

Students can write in journals independently with little or no sharing with the teacher, or they can make daily entries that the teacher monitors or reads regularly (Tway, 1984). Typically, students are accustomed to having teachers read all or most of their writing, but the quantity of writing students produce in journals is often too great for teachers to keep up with. Some teachers try to read all entries; others read selected entries and monitor remaining entries; still others rarely check students' journals. The three management approaches can be termed *private journals, monitored journals,* and *shared journals.* When students write private journals, they write primarily for themselves, and sharing with classmates or the teacher is voluntary—the teacher does not read the journals unless invited to. When students write monitored journals, they write primarily for themselves, but the teacher monitors the writing to ensure that entries are being made regularly. The teacher simply checks that entries have been made and does not read the entries unless they are specially marked "Read me." Students write "shared" journals primarily for the teacher; the teacher regularly reads all entries, except those marked "private," and offers encouragement and suggestions.

How to grade journal entries is a concern. Because the writing is usually not revised and edited, teachers should not grade the quality of the entries. One option is to give points for each entry made, especially in personal journals. However, some teachers grade the content in learning logs and simulated journals because they can check to see if the entries include particular pieces of information. For example, if students were writing simulated

Adapting . . .
Journal Writing
To Meet the Needs of Every Student

1. *Drawing Journal Entries*

Students can draw their thoughts and ideas in journal entries instead of writing them, or they can draw pictures before writing. What is important is that students explore their thoughts and feelings or record important information they are learning.

2. *Talking Before Writing*

Students can talk about topics to generate and narrow ideas before beginning to write. As they talk, students find the words and sentences to express their ideas, and they use these words and expand them as they write.

3. *Dictating Entries*

Teachers or cross-age tutors can take students' dictation and write the entries for students. Then students reread their dictation with the teacher's or cross-age tutor's assistance. They can also pick key words and phrases from the dictated text and use the words to label drawings.

4. *Sharing in Small Groups*

Sharing is an important part of writing, but some students may not feel comfortable sharing with the whole class. These students may prefer sharing their journal entries with a partner or in small groups, which are less threatening than large groups.

5. *Focusing on Ideas*

Students focus on ideas, not mechanical correctness, as they write journal entries because they use journal writing to develop writing fluency and explore the ideas they are learning. Similarly, when teachers assess students' entries, they should consider whether or not students have developed their ideas and not correct their mechanical errors.

journals about the Crusades, they could be asked to include five pieces of historically accurate information in their entries. (It is helpful to ask students to identify the five pieces of information by underlining and numbering them.) Rough-draft journal entries should not be graded for mechanical correctness. Students need to complete the writing process and revise and edit their entries if they are to be graded for mechanical correctness.

Figure 5–12 presents two first graders' reading log entries written after they listened to *Sam, Bangs, and Moonshine* (Ness, 1966) read aloud. The Caldecott medal story is about a girl named Sam who has a cat named Bangs. Sam tells "moonshine" about a make-believe baby kangaroo to her friend Thomas. The results are almost disastrous. The two reading logs illustrate the

Figure 5–12   *Two First Graders' Reading Log Entries About* Sam, Bangs, and Moonshine

problems in grading students' journal entries. In her entry Andi draws a picture of Bangs and the baby kangaroo and writes, "If you lie you will get in big trouble and you will hurt your friends." She has thoughtfully and accurately described the theme of the story. In his entry Julio writes from the point of view of Thomas. His picture is of the make-believe kangaroo, and the text originally read, "He is lying to me. He don't have a kangaroo." After he shared his entry with classmates and they mentioned that Sam was a girl, not a boy, Julio changed the *he* to *she* and added the picture of Sam. Julio writes two sentences and spells all words correctly; Andi, on the other hand, uses invented spelling and punctuates her text as one sentence.

Which reading log entry is better? Which deserves a higher grade? It is very difficult to make these types of decisions, and such decisions are probably unnecessary. In both entries students have explored the story through illustrations and text, and both entries are remarkable in one way or another: We particularly like Andi's articulation of the theme and Julio's viewpoint and his ability to make revisions that reflect the feedback he received from classmates. Andi and Julio's teacher marked the two entries the same way. They each received a check in the gradebook for a reading log entry that was completed and met these two requirements: (1) the entry contains both an illustration and some writing and (2) the entry contains information about the story.

Review

Six types of journals are personal journals, dialogue journals, writing notebooks, reading logs, learning logs, and simulated journals. Students use journal writing to share events in their lives and record what they are learning in literature focus units and theme cycles. Students write responses to stories they are reading in reading logs, and they assume the roles of story characters and historical personalities in simulated journals. Young children can keep personal journals and reading logs, and in these journals students combine drawing with writing. The focus in journal writing is to develop writing fluency and use writing as a tool for learning.

Extensions

1. Have elementary students keep reading logs as they read and respond to a chapter book. Or, experiment with one of the other types of journals with elementary students.
2. Using dialogue journals, write back and forth with three students who are having difficulty in your classroom. Continue for several weeks. Use this opportunity to get to know these students better and make the activity a positive experience for students. What changes do you see in students' entries and your own over the period?
3. Keep a personal journal in which you record experiences and feelings, or keep a double-entry journal in which you reflect on the material in this book as well as your teaching experiences for the remainder of the school term.
4. Have a small group of students write a quickwrite and a cluster as part of a social studies or science theme cycle. Then examine these writings to determine which concepts students are learning, as well as any misconceptions they may have.
5. Read two of the books listed in Figure 5–10 in which characters or historical personalities keep journals, and share the books with classmates.
6. Plan and teach a minilesson on a topic related to journal writing to a small group or a class of elementary students. Be sure to have students apply the topic as they write in journals.

References

Atwell, N. (1987). *In the middle: Reading, writing, and learning with adolescents.* Portsmouth, NH: Heinemann.

Barone, D. (1990). The written responses of young children: Beyond comprehension to story understanding. *The New Advocate, 3,* 49–56.

Berthoff, A. E. (1981). *The making of meaning.* Montclair, NJ: Boynton/Cook.

Bode, B. A. (1989). Dialogue journal writing. *The Reading Teacher, 42,* 568–571.

Britton, J., Burgess, T., Martin, N., McLeod, A., & Rosen, H. (1975). *The development of writing abilities* (pp. 11–18). London: Macmillan.

Dekker, M. M. (1991). Books, reading, and response: A teacher-researcher tells a story. *The New Advocate, 4,* 37–46.

Elbow, P. (1973). *Writing without teachers.* London: Oxford University Press.

Elliott, S., Nowosad, J., & Samuels, P. (1981). "Me at home," "me at school": Using journals with preschoolers. *Language Arts, 58,* 688–691.

Farris, P. J. (1989). Story time and story journals: Linking literature and writing. *The New Advocate, 2,* 179–185.

Five, C. L. (1986). Fifth graders respond to a changed reading program. *Harvard Educational Review, 56,* 395–405.

Fulwiler, M. (1986). Still writing and learning, grade 10. *Language Arts, 63,* 809–812.

Fulwiler, T. (1985). Writing and learning, grade 3. *Language Arts, 62,* 55–59.

Fulwiler, T. (1987). *The journal book.* Portsmouth, NH: Boynton/Cook.

Gambrell, L. B. (1985). Dialogue journals: Reading-writing interaction. *The Reading Teacher, 38,* 512–515.

Hancock, M. R. (1992). Literature response journals: Insights beyond the printed page. *Language Arts, 61,* 141–150.

Hipple, M. L. (1985). Journal writing in kindergarten. *Language Arts, 62,* 255–261.

Kreeft, J. (1984). Dialogue writing—Bridge from talk to essay writing. *Language Arts, 61,* 141–150.

Macon, J. M., Bewell, D., & Vogt, M. E. (1991). *Responses to literature: Grades K–8.* Newark, DE: International Reading Association.

McGonegal, P. (1987). Fifth-grade journals: Results and surprises. In T. Fulwiler (Ed.), *The journal book* (pp. 201–209). Portsmouth, NH: Boynton/ Cook.

Mallon, T. (1984). *A book of one's own: People and their diaries.* New York: Ticknor & Fields.

Nathan, R. (1987). I have a loose tooth and other unphotographic events: Tales from a first grade journal. In T. Fulwiler (Ed.), *The journal book* (pp. 187–192). Portsmouth, NH: Boynton/Cook.

Peyton, J. K., & Seyoum, M. (1989). The effect of teacher strategies on students' interactive writing: The case of dialogue journals. *Research in the Teaching of English, 23,* 310–334.

Progoff, I. (1975). *At a journal workshop: The basic text and guide for using the intensive journal process.* New York: Dialogue House.

Reyes, M. de la Luz. (1991). A process approach to literacy using dialogue journals and literature logs with second language learners. *Research in the Teaching of English, 25,* 291–313.

Rico, G. L. (1983). *Writing the natural way.* Los Angeles: Tarcher.

Salem, J. (1982). Using writing in teaching mathematics. In M. Barr, P. D'Arcy, & M. K. Healy (Eds.), *What's going on? Language/learning episodes in British and American classrooms, grades 4–13* (pp. 123–134). Montclair, NJ: Boynton/Cook.

Schubert, B. (1987). Mathematics journals: Fourth grade. In T. Fulwiler (Ed.), *The journal book* (pp. 348–358). Portsmouth, NJ: Boynton/Cook.

Stanford, B. (1988). Writing reflectively. *Language Arts, 65,* 652–658.

Staton, J. (1980). Writing and counseling: Using a dialogue journal. *Language Arts, 57,* 514–518.

Staton, J. (1987). The power of responding in dialogue journals. In T. Fulwiler (Ed.), *The journal book* (pp. 47–63). Portsmouth, NH: Boynton/Cook.

Tway, E. (1981). Come, write with me. *Language Arts, 58,* 805–810.

Tway, E. (1984). *Time for writing in the elementary school.* Urbana, IL: ERIC Clearinghouse on Reading and Communication Skills and the National Council of Teachers of English.

Wollman-Bonilla, J. E. (1989). Reading journals: Invitations to participate in literature. *The Reading Teacher, 43,* 112–120.

Children's Book References

Ahlberg, J., & Ahlberg, A. (1986). *The jolly postman or other people's letters.* Boston: Little, Brown.

Beatty, P. (1987). *Charley Skedaddle.* New York: Morrow.

Blos, J. (1979). *A gathering of days: A New England girl's journal, 1830–1832.* New York: Scribner.

Cleary, B. (1983). *Dear Mr. Henshaw.* New York: Morrow.

Cole, J. (1981). *A snake's body.* New York: Morrow.

Cole, J. (1989). *The magic school bus inside the human body.* New York: Scholastic.

Donnelly, J. (1991). *A wall of names: The story of the Vietnam Veterans Memorial.* New York: Random House.

Fitzhugh, L. (1964). *Harriet the spy.* New York: Harper & Row.

Freeman, D. (1968). *Corduroy.* New York: Viking.

Freeman, D. (1972). *A pocket for Corduroy.* New York: Viking.

Fritz, J. (1987). *Brady.* New York: Penguin.

Hartman, G. (1991). *As the crow flies: A first book of maps.* New York: Bradbury Press.

Howe, D., & Howe, J. (1979). *Bunnicula: A rabbit-tale of mystery.* New York: Atheneum.

Hunt, I. (1987). *Across five Aprils.* New York: Berkley.

Lewis, C. S. (1950). *The lion, the witch and the wardrobe.* New York: Macmillan.

Ness, E. (1966). *Sam, Bangs, and moonshine.* New York: Holt, Rinehart & Winston.

O'Dell, S. (1976). *The 290.* Boston: Houghton Mifflin.

Paterson, K. (1977). *Bridge to Terabithia.* New York: Crowell.

Stevens, J. (1987). *The three billy goats Gruff.* San Diego: Harcourt Brace Jovanovich.

> " My students are comfortable working in groups. They learn just as much from each other as they learn from me. That really surprised me, but it's true! "
>
> **Judy Reeves**
> *Third-Grade Teacher*
> *Western Hills Elementary School*

PROCEDURE

Six third graders are meeting with me in a small group during our Writing Workshop. My purpose today is to touch base with these students about their new writing projects. Students are choosing their own topics and writing forms for this project. Jason eagerly tells us that he is making a joke book, and he has already begun writing and illustrating his collection of favorite jokes. He's pleased with this opportunity to pursue a hobby. Trina wants to write a fairy tale, and she shows us a cluster she has made with ideas about the story. Lance is thinking about writing a Nintendo adventure story, but he says he isn't sure how to start. Group members encourage him to begin with one of his fantastic drawings. Nikki has just read a biography about Benjamin Franklin that she shares with us. She can't decide whether she should write a retelling of this biography or write her own autobiography. The students give her suggestions, but she hasn't decided yet. Eliza wants to write a letter to Beverly Cleary, her favorite author, and as her prewriting, she has made a list of the things she wants to include in her letter. Derek doesn't seem to have an idea yet, but Lance and Jason offer several suggestions.

Throughout this 20-minute meeting, my students are active group members. They take turns sharing ideas for their projects and talk about how they have developed their ideas, using writing process terminology such as "rough draft" and "clustering" ideas. They are also supportive of their classmates. They listen thoughtfully and offer compliments and encouragement.

The group comes to an end with students each briefly explaining what they will do next. Those who are ready to prewrite or draft move back to their desks while I talk with Derek and Nikki, who are not sure what they want to write about. Nikki decides to try her hand at writing her autobiography, and she begins to draw a lifeline of her life. Derek decides to brainstorm a list of three possible topics and share them with me later today.

ASSESSMENT

My students use the writing process, and I confer with them during almost every stage. I want to see that they are on task. It is too easy for third graders to get sidetracked or bogged down with a problem that I or their classmates can solve.

I give my students contracts for each writing project. A copy of the contract is shown in the accompanying figure. The contract lists the steps of the writing process and the activities students will complete in each step. My students staple the contracts inside the front cover of their writing folders and check off each activity as they complete it. This is how I keep track of each student and how they keep track of themselves. I ask them to confer with me several times during the writing process, and I schedule time for the conferences three mornings a week. I think touching base is important.

ADAPTATIONS

My students spend 70 minutes each afternoon in Writing Workshop. For the first 15 minutes, I teach a minilesson, and then students work on writing projects for the next 45 minutes. During the last 15 minutes, we get together as a class to share our published books and other completed writings.

I use a similar approach for Reading Workshop during the morning. I begin by reading a book aloud to the class. Sometimes I read a picture book and sometimes I read a chapter book, a chapter or two each day. After I read, we take a few minutes to share our reactions to the book. Then my students read books they have chosen themselves. They have Reading Workshop folders and keep track of their reading by listing book titles on their reading lists and by writing entries in their reading logs. I move around the classroom, conferencing with students about their reading on a regular basis. Once or twice a month, my students create a project to extend their interpretation of a favorite book. On most days, I teach a reading-related minilesson, and students who have finished reading a book or have created a project share their books and projects during the last 15 minutes of Reading Workshop.

REFLECTIONS

I have been very pleased—maybe even amazed—at how well my third graders work in small groups and how responsible they have become. They are learning from each other and supporting each other as they learn. Cooperative learning really works! Besides conferences to touch base with students, we use conferences in this classroom when students want feedback on their writing, to teach language skills in minilessons, and to discuss authors we are studying.

Writing Workshop Contract

Name _____   Title _____

1. Prewriting
   Make a cluster.   _____
   Conference with Mrs. Reeves.   _____
2. Drafting
   Mark it ROUGH DRAFT.   _____
   Skip lines.   _____
3. Revising
   Read your draft in writing group.   _____
   Make at least 2 changes.   _____
   Conference with Mrs. Reeves.   _____
4. Editing
   Proofread carefully.   _____
   Proofread with a partner.   _____
   Conference with Mrs. Reeves.   _____
5. Publishing
   Make the final copy.   _____
   Share in the author's chair.   _____

6

The Reading and Writing Processes

INSIGHT _____

Reading and writing have been assumed to be very different processes. When people read, they decode or decipher the message that the author has written, and when they write, they produce their own ideas for others to read. Educators have suggested that reading and writing are the flip sides of the literacy coin because readers decode meaning and writers encode meaning. Newer theories of literacy suggest that reading and writing are both processes of constructing meaning, and readers and writers use similar problem-solving strategies. Both readers and writers, for example, generate ideas, draw on personal experience, monitor the meaning they are creating, and revise when the meaning has broken down. One issue to think about as you read this chapter is:

How are reading and writing alike and how are they different?

*I*n the past 20 years there has been a significant shift in thinking about what people do as they read and write. Reading and writing are now viewed as transactive processes in which readers and writers create meaning through the lived-through experience of reading or writing (Harste, Woodward, & Burke, 1984; Rosenblatt, 1978).

According to socio-psycholinguistic theories, meaning is created through the negotiation of either readers and the texts they are reading or writers and the texts they are writing. Readers use their life and literature experiences and knowledge of written language as they read, and writers bring similar knowledge and experiences to writing. It is quite common for two people to read the same story and come away with different interpretations, and for two writers to write different compositions about the same event. Meaning does not exist on the pages of the book that a reader is reading or in the words of the composition that a writer is writing; instead, meaning is created through the transaction between readers and what they are reading or writers and what they are writing.

The reading process involves a series of stages during which readers construct interpretations as they read and then respond to the text they have read. The term *text* includes all reading materials—stories, maps, newspapers, cereal boxes, textbooks, and so on; it is not limited to basal reader textbooks. The writing process is a similar recursive process involving a variety of activities as students gather and organize their ideas, draft their compositions, revise and edit the drafts, and, finally, publish their writings.

Reading and writing have been thought of as the flip sides of a coin—they were opposites; readers decoded or deciphered written language, and writers encoded or produced written language. Then researchers began to note similarities between reading and writing and talked of both of them as processes. Now reading and writing are viewed as parallel processes of meaning construction, and readers and writers use similar strategies for making meaning with text.

THE READING PROCESS

Reading is a transactive process in which readers negotiate meaning or interpretation. During reading, the meaning does not go from the page to the reader; instead, it is a complex negotiation between the text and the reader that is shaped by the immediate situational context and broader sociolinguistic contexts (Weaver, 1988). The immediate situational context includes the reader's knowledge about the topic, the reader's purpose for reading, and other factors related to the situation. Broader sociolinguistic contexts include the language community that the reader belongs to and how closely it matches the language used in the text, the reader's culturally based expectations about reading, and the reader's expectations about reading based on his or her previous experiences. This description of reading is presented schematically in Figure 6–1.

Aesthetic and Efferent Reading

Readers read for different purposes, and the way they approach the reading process varies according to their purpose. Often they read for enjoyment, but

Figure 6–1   The Reading Process

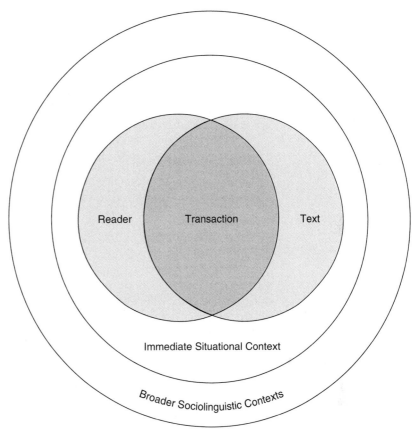

Reader   Transaction   Text

Immediate Situational Context

Broader Sociolinguistic Contexts

Weaver, 1988, p. 30.

at other times they read to carry away information. When reading for enjoyment or to be entertained, readers assume an aesthetic stance and focus on the lived-through experience of reading. They concentrate on the thoughts, images, feelings, and associations evoked during reading. Readers also respond to these thoughts, images, feelings, and associations. For example, as children read Cynthia Rylant's story *The Relatives Came* (1985), they may relate the events in the book to a time when their relatives visited; or as they read Diane Siebert's *Sierra* (1991), they may respond to the language of the text.

When reading to carry away information, readers assume an efferent stance. They concentrate on the public, common referents of the words and symbols in the text. For example, as children read Patricia Lauber's *Seeing Earth From Space* (1990), with its breathtaking photographs of the earth taken by satellites, their focus is on the information in the text and illustrations, not on the experience of reading.

Almost every reading experience calls for a balance between aesthetic and efferent reading (Rosenblatt, 1978). Readers do not simply read stories and poems aesthetically and informational books efferently. As they read a story, poem, or informational book, readers move back and forth between the aesthetic and efferent stances. Literature, however, should be read primarily from the aesthetic stance.

During both aesthetic and efferent reading, readers move through the five stages of the reading process. The stages are preparing to read, reading, responding, exploring the text, and extending the interpretation. The key features of each stage are reviewed in the Teacher's Notebook on page 201. Many of the features are characteristic of both aesthetic and efferent reading, but a few features exemplify one stance or the other.

Stage 1: Preparing to Read

The reading process does not begin as readers open a book and begin reading. The first stage is preparing to read. As readers prepare to read, they:

- Choose books
- Make connections
- Plan for reading

Choosing Books.   Readers begin the reading process by choosing the book or other text they will read. Choosing an appropriate book is not easy. First of all students need to know about themselves as readers: What types of books do they like? Who are their favorite authors? As they become readers, students learn the answers to these questions. They can also point to books they have read and can tell about them and explain why they enjoyed reading them.

Students need to learn to choose books that they can read. Ohlhausen and Jepsen (1992) developed a strategy for choosing books called the "Goldilocks Strategy." These teachers developed three categories of books—Too Easy, Too Hard, and Just Right—using "The Three Bears" folktale as their model. The books in the Too Easy category were books they had read before or could read fluently. Too Hard books were unfamiliar and confusing, and books in the Just Right category were interesting with just a few unfamiliar words. The books in each category vary according to the students' reading levels. This approach was developed with a second-grade class, but the categorization scheme can work at any grade level. Figure 6–2 presents a chart about choosing books using the Goldilocks principle developed by a fifth-grade class. Sometimes teachers choose the book for students, but it is important that readers have many opportunities to choose books they are interested in reading.

Making Connections.   Readers activate their prior knowledge or schemata about the book or other text they plan to read. They make connections to personal experiences, to literary experiences, or to theme studies in the classroom. This activation may be triggered by the topic of the book, the title, the author, the genre, an illustration, a comment someone makes about the text, or something else; but for readers to make meaning from the text, schema must be activated. For instance, readers who love horses and are very knowledgeable about them often choose horse books such as *Misty of Chincoteague* (Henry, 1963) to read. Others who like books written by Beverly Cleary or Dr. Seuss choose books by these favorite authors.

Planning for Reading.   Readers make predictions as they begin to read. Their predictions about stories focus on characters and events that will take

Teacher's Notebook
Key Features of the Reading Process

Stage 1: Preparing to Read

- Choose a book.
- Connect to prior personal and literary experiences.
- Connect to theme studies or special interests.
- Make predictions.
- Preview the text.
- Consult the index to locate information.

Stage 2: Reading

- Use the predict-confirm cycle.
- Use word identification and meaning-making skills and strategies.
- Read independently, with a partner, or using shared reading or guided reading; or listen to the text read aloud.
- Read the illustrations, charts, and diagrams.
- Read the entire text from beginning to end.
- Read one or more sections of the text to learn specific information.

Stage 3: Responding

- Write in a reading log.
- Take notes.
- Participate in a grand conversation.

Stage 4: Exploring the Text

- Reread and think more deeply about the text.
- Make connections with personal experiences.
- Make connections with other literary experiences.
- Examine the author's craft.
- Identify memorable quotes.
- Learn new vocabulary words.
- Participate in minilessons.

Stage 5: Extending the Interpretation

- Construct projects.
- Use information in theme cycles.
- Connect with related books.
- Reflect on their interpretations.
- Value the reading experience.

Figure 6–2   A Fifth-Grade Class
Chart on Choosing Books

The Goldilocks Strategy

Too Easy Books

1. You have read this book before.
2. This book has lots of illustrations.
3. You know almost every word in the book.
4. You are an expert on this topic.

Just Right Books

1. The book looks interesting.
2. The topic is something you know about.
3. You can read most of the words in the book.
4. You have read other books by this author.
5. You have seen a film or video on the book.
6. Your teacher has read the book aloud before.

Too Hard Books

1. The print in the book is very small.
2. There are very few illustrations in the book.
3. There are a lot of words you don't know.
4. The book is long.
5. You don't know very much about this topic.

place in the story, and predictions about informational books deal with the kinds of information they might learn in the book. In the classroom, teachers often ask students to verbalize these predictions and then read to confirm them, but as students read independently, they make predictions on their own, perhaps even at an unconscious level.

When students are preparing to read informational books, they often consult the index to locate the specific information they want to read, or they may preview the text before beginning to read. When students preview a book, they read the table of contents or flip through the pages, noting major headings, illustrations, diagrams, and other charts. They may also notice unfamiliar terminology and other words that they can check in the glossary, ask a classmate or the teacher about, or look up in a dictionary. Previewing is a useful strategy because informational books are organized in various ways, and when readers preview a text, they are better able to organize their reading and anticipate the flow of the text.

Stage 2: Reading

In the second stage students read the book or other text. Students use the prediction cycle and read to confirm their predictions. They sample the text and recognize some words. They use word identification strategies to identify unfamiliar words. It is not necessary for readers to recognize every word or to look at every letter in a word to decode it. Students also use meaning-making strategies such as visualizing, elaborating, and monitoring. From this sampling readers construct personal meaning using the text as a blueprint.

As readers construct meaning, they continue reading, and as long as what they are reading fits the meaning that they are constructing, the transaction continues. When something doesn't make sense, readers slow down, back up, and reread until they are making meaning again.

Outside of school, readers usually read silently and independently. Sometimes, however, people listen as someone else reads. Young children often sit in a parent's lap and look at the illustrations as the parent reads a picture book aloud. Adults also listen to books read aloud on cassette tapes. In the classroom, teachers use five types of reading:

- Reading aloud
- Shared reading
- Buddy reading
- Guided reading
- Independent reading

Reading Aloud. Students listen to the teacher read the text, or they may listen to the text read aloud at a listening center. The listening center is especially useful when students want to listen to the book a second time.

Shared Reading. Students follow along in the text as the teacher reads it or as the class reads it together. Shared reading is possible if there are multiple copies of the text, if the text is displayed on a chart, with an enlarged copy of a book, or using sentence strips.

Buddy Reading. Two students read the text together. Sometimes they take turns reading aloud, sometimes they both read silently, and at other times the classmates read aloud together. This approach is similar to shared reading, and it is especially useful for rereading familiar texts or for providing successful reading experiences for students who are not fluent readers.

Guided Reading. Students read the text with the teacher's guidance. Teachers invite students to make predictions before reading, and then students read silently to confirm or reject their predictions. Teachers repeat the prediction cycle several times during reading and may also stop students to discuss parts of the text. Guided reading can be used with small groups or with the entire class when multiple copies of the same text are available. This approach is used when students are reading unfamiliar texts and when they need scaffolding in order to be able to interpret the text.

Independent Reading. Students read independently. All students may read the same text, or they may choose different texts. Independent reading is the most authentic type of reading, and it allows students to be responsible in choosing reading materials, read texts they want to read, and learn the pleasures of reading. The advantages and drawbacks of each type of reading are outlined in Figure 6–3.

Students may read the entire text, or they may read only sections of it. When students are reading aesthetically, they usually read the entire text, but when they are reading efferently, they may be searching for specific information and read only until they locate that information. Also, students may decide to put a book down if it does not capture their interest, if it is too difficult to read, or if it does not have the information they are searching for. It is

Figure 6–3   *Types of Reading*

Type	Advantages	Drawbacks
Reading Aloud Teacher reads aloud to students.	Access to books students could not read themselves. Teacher models fluent reading. Opportunities to model reading strategies. Develops a community of readers. Use when only one copy of text is available.	No opportunity for students themselves to read. Text may not be appropriate for all students. Students may not be interested in the text.
Shared Reading Teacher reads aloud while students follow along using individual copies of book, a class chart, or a big book.	Access to books students could not read themselves. Teacher models fluent reading. Opportunities to model reading strategies. Students practice fluent reading. Develops a community of readers.	Multiple copies, a class chart, or a big book needed. Text may not be appropriate for all students. Students may not be interested in the text.
Buddy Reading Two students read a text together.	Collaboration between students. Students assist each other. Use to reread familiar texts. Students talk and share interpretations.	Less teacher involvement and control.
Guided Reading Teachers use the prediction cycle to guide students as they read a text.	Practice the prediction cycle. Teacher provides scaffolding. Opportunities to model reading strategies. Use with unfamiliar texts.	Multiple copies of text needed. Teacher controls the reading experience. Some students may not be interested in the text.
Independent Reading Students read a text independently and often choose the text themselves.	Develops responsibility and ownership. Self-selection of texts. Experience is more authentic.	Students may need assistance to read the text. Little teacher involvement and control.

unrealistic to assume that students will always read entire texts or finish reading every book they begin.

Stage 3: Responding

During the third stage readers respond to their reading and continue to negotiate meaning. Two ways that students make tentative and exploratory comments immediately after reading are:

- Writing in reading logs
- Participating in grand conversations

Writing in Reading Logs. Students write and draw thoughts and feelings about what they have read in reading logs. Rosenblatt (1978) explains that as students write about what they have read, they unravel their thinking and, at the same time, elaborate on and clarify their responses. When students read informational books, they sometimes write in reading logs as they do after reading stories and poems, but at other times they make notes of important information or draw charts and diagrams to use in theme cycles.

Participating in Grand Conversations. Students also talk about the text with classmates in grand conversations or other literature discussions. Peterson and Eeds (1990) explain that students share their personal responses and tell what they liked about the text. After sharing personal reactions, they shift the focus to "puzzle over what the author has written and . . . share what it is they find revealed" (p. 61). Often students make connections between the text and their own lives or other literature they have read. If they are reading a chapter book, they also make predictions about what will happen in the next chapter.

Stage 4: Exploring the Text

Students go back into the text to explore it more analytically. They participate in some of these activities:

- Rereading the text
- Examining the author's craft
- Learning new vocabulary words
- Participating in minilessons

As students reread the text and think again about what they have read, they deepen their interpretations and make connections between the book and their own lives and other literature they have read. They examine the author's craft and focus on the author's use of characters in a story or metaphor in a poem. Students also identify memorable quotes and learn interesting words selected from the text.

In the classroom, teachers often provide exploring activities to focus students' attention on the structure of the text, literary language, and vocabulary. Also, during this stage teachers often teach minilessons on procedures, concepts, and strategies and skills related to the reading process.

Stage 5: Extending the Interpretation

During the extending stage readers deepen their interpretations, reflect on their understanding, and value the reading experience. Students build on the initial and exploratory responses they made immediately after reading. They also create projects which can involve reading, writing, talk and drama, art, or research and which may take many forms, including murals, readers theatre scripts, oral reports, or reading other books by the same author. A list of projects was presented in Chapter 2. The purpose of these activities is for students to expand the ideas they read about, create a personal interpretation, and value the reading experience.

Teaching the Reading Process

Teachers apply the five-stage reading process in the reading lessons they teach, no matter whether they organize instruction into literature focus units, theme cycles, or reading workshop. Teachers also teach minilessons about reading procedures, concepts, and strategies and skills as part of any of the three approaches.

These fifth graders used the reading process to read, respond to, explore, and extend their interpretations of Bridge to Terabithia.

Minilessons on the Reading Process. Students need to learn about the process approach to reading—aesthetic and efferent—and about ways to develop interpretations. They learn reading process procedures, concepts, and strategies and skills through minilessons and then apply what they are learning through active involvement in literature focus units, theme cycles, and reading workshop. A list of topics for minilessons about the reading process is presented on page 208. Minilessons on these topics can be taught as part of the exploring stage of the reading process in literature focus units and theme cycles, or as regularly scheduled minilessons during reading workshop.

In Literature Focus Units. In literature focus units students might read a single book, such as *Bunnicula: A Rabbit-Tale of Mystery* (Howe & Howe, 1979), and as they read, they will move through the five stages of the reading process. Or, they might read a collection of books on the same theme, about dogs, for instance; in the same genre, such as folktales; or by the same author, such as books by Dr. Seuss. When students read several books together, they move back and forth among the second, third, and fourth stages as they read, respond to, and explore each book before moving on to the extending-the-interpretation stage.

Figure 6–4 shows one way to organize a literature focus unit on *Bunnicula: A Rabbit-Tale of Mystery*. In this unit students work through all five stages of the reading process. They use shared reading to read the chapter book; then they respond to their reading and participate in exploration activities. Students also construct projects to extend their interpretation of the book.

In Theme Cycles. Teachers often coordinate the books that students are reading with what they are studying during theme cycles. For example, during a theme cycle on insects in a second-grade classroom, students read *It's a Good Thing There Are Insects* (Fowler, 1990) at the beginning of the theme. Students moved through all five stages of the reading process. First they read the easy-to-read informational book using shared reading; then they read it a second time with reading buddies; and the third time they read it independently. During the grand conversation held after students read the book the first time, they brainstormed a list of reasons why it's a good thing there are insects. Later they wrote their own books about insects. The teacher also used this book to teach several minilessons about informational books and the differences between stories and informational books. *It's a Good Thing There Are Insects* is a good example of an informational book because photos are used as illustrations and a glossary and an index are included in the book.

Later in the theme cycle the teacher paired two books about ladybugs for the students to read: *The Grouchy Ladybug* by Eric Carle (1986), a repetitive story about an unfriendly ladybug who is looking for a fight, and *Ladybug* (Watts, 1987), an informational book with one line of large-size type on each page for students to read and additional information in smaller-size type that students or the teacher can read. The teacher had enough copies of each book for half the class, so the students divided into two groups. One group read one book and the other group read the other book; then the two groups traded books. As the students were reading these two books, the teacher had many opportunities to continue comparing stories and informational books. After

The Reading and Writing Processes

	Procedures	Concepts	Strategies and Skills
The Reading Process	Choose books to read Use the Goldilocks Strategy Listen to books read aloud Do shared reading Do buddy reading Do guided reading Do independent reading Respond in reading logs Participate in grand conversations Reread a book Create projects Participate in reading workshop	The reading process Aesthetic reading Efferent reading Interpretation	Decode words Predict Confirm Visualize Retell Connect to literature Connect to life Empathize Identify with characters Monitor
The Writing Process	Choose a topic Cluster Quickwrite Participate in writing groups Proofread Make hardcover books Write "All About the Author" pages Share published writing	The writing process Functions of writing Writing forms Audience Focus on content Focus on mechanics Proofreaders' marks Publish writing	Gather ideas Organize ideas Draft Revise Edit Identify and correct spelling errors Use capital letters correctly Use punctuation marks correctly Value the composition

reading, students talked about which book they liked best, and they worked on projects to extend their understanding of ladybugs and other insects.

In Reading Workshop. In Chapter 2 we described the workshop approach and outlined the three components of reading workshop: reading and responding, sharing, and minilessons. Students move through the five stages of the reading process as they participate in reading workshop activities. Students choose books and make connections with the book as they begin to read (stage 1). Next they read the book independently (stage 2). After reading, they write in reading logs and conference with the teacher. At these conferences

Figure 6–4 *A Plan for Teaching a Literature Focus Unit on* Bunnicula: A Rabbit-Tale of Mystery

---

Stage 1: Preparing to Read

Students and the teacher talk about pets and their antics. The teacher invites students to share pictures of their pets with the class and to tell stories about their pets.

Stage 2: Reading

The teacher uses the shared reading approach to read the chapter book. Each student has a copy of the book and follows along as the teacher reads the book aloud. One or two chapters are read aloud each day.

Stage 3: Responding

After reading a chapter or two, students write responses in reading logs and share these logs with classmates. Students also participate in grand conversations and make connections between the story and their own lives and other experiences with literature.

Stage 4: Exploring the Text

Students write interesting and important words from the book on a word wall (chart paper hanging on the wall).

The teacher teaches several minilessons on characterization and the meaning-making strategy of identifying with a character. The teacher asks students to choose the character they identify with the most (Harold the dog, Chester the cat, or Bunnicula the rabbit) and explain why they chose that character.

Stage 5: Extending the Interpretation

Students each choose a project from a list of choices posted in the classroom. A number of students choose to read one of the sequels and other stories about Bunnicula: *Howliday Inn* (1982), *The Celery Stalks at Midnight* (1983), *Nighty-Nightmare* (1987), *Return to Howliday Inn* (1992), *Scared Silly* (1989), *The Fright Before Christmas* (1989), and *Hot Fudge* (1990). Other students choose these projects:

- Write a letter to author James Howe.
- Perform a play about an episode of the book.
- Make a box about the book and place five items related to the book with explanations in the box.
- Write a sequel to the book.
- Make a tabletop display of the Monroes' house.
- Research Dracula and vampires.

---

students talk about the books they are reading (stage 3). Sometimes students create a project after every book they read, and sometimes they read three or four books and choose one book for a response project (stage 5). Students also talk about the books they read during sharing time and share their completed response projects with classmates (stages 3 and 5). In reading workshop, teachers also teach minilessons to small groups of students or the whole class, and during these lessons students learn about the reading process (stage 4).

Adapting . . .
The Reading Process
To Meet the Needs of Every Student

Stage 1: Preparing to Read

- Spend more time activating prior knowledge and building background.
- Use concrete experiences, audiovisual presentations, and photos.
- Introduce important vocabulary related to the topic, but not necessarily the vocabulary in the text.

Stage 2: Reading

- Read books aloud.
- Use shared reading or buddy reading.
- Have students listen to the book at the listening center.
- Use easy-to-read or predictable books on the same topic.
- Break the reading time into smaller chunks.
- Provide more challenging alternative texts.

Stage 3: Responding

- Have students draw responses in reading logs.
- Take time in grand conversations to clarify misconceptions.

Stage 4: Exploring the Text

- Role-play important events in the book.
- Reread the text with a buddy.
- Teach minilessons to individual students and small groups of students.

Stage 5: Extending the Interpretation

- Encourage students to create art projects.
- Encourage students to produce dramatic productions.
- Set out clear expectations about the projects students develop.
- Encourage students to pursue projects that they are interested in and that challenge them.

Adapting to Meet the Needs of Every Student. Activities during each stage of the reading process can be adapted to help every student become a more successful reader. For students with limited experiences or for those who are learning English as a second language, more time can be spent preparing them to read. In the reading stage teachers can read books aloud or use shared reading for students who are not yet fluent readers. Many easy-to-read stories and information books that are well written and enticing to students are currently available, so it is possible to have several books at different reading levels on almost any topic. During the responding stage students can draw instead of write their responses in reading logs, and grand conversations take on an even greater importance for students who need to clarify misconceptions about their reading. Students can reread the text with a buddy during the exploring stage. Extending the interpretation in the fifth stage is important for all students, and many students who find reading difficult are very successful in creating art projects and dramatic productions. These and other suggestions for adapting the reading process to meet the needs of every student are presented on page 210.

THE WRITING PROCESS

The focus in the writing process is on what students think and do as they write. The five stages are prewriting, drafting, revising, editing, and publishing, and the key features of each stage are shown in the Teacher's Notebook on page 212. The labeling and numbering of the stages does not mean that the writing process is a linear series of neatly packaged categories. Research has shown that the process is cyclical, involving recurring cycles, and labeling is only an aid to identifying and discussing writing activities. In the classroom the stages merge and recur as students write.

Stage 1: Prewriting

Prewriting is the getting-ready-to-write stage. The traditional notion that writers have a topic completely thought out and ready to flow onto the page is ridiculous. If writers wait for ideas to fully develop, they may wait forever. Instead, writers begin tentatively—talking, reading, writing—to see what they know and what direction they want to go. Prewriting has probably been the most neglected stage in the writing process; however, it is as crucial to writers as a warm-up is to athletes. Murray (1982) believes that at least 70% of writing time should be spent in prewriting. During the prewriting stage students:

- Choose a topic
- Consider function, form, and audience
- Generate and organize ideas for writing

Choosing a Topic.   Choosing a topic for writing can be a stumbling block for students who have become dependent on teachers to supply topics. For years teachers have supplied topics by suggesting gimmicky story starters and relieving students of the "burden" of topic selection. Often, these "creative" topics stymied students, who were forced to write on topics they knew little about or were not interested in. Graves (1976) calls this "writing welfare." Instead, students need to choose their own writing topics.

Some students complain that they do not know what to write about, but teachers can help them brainstorm a list of three, four, or five topics and then identify the one topic they are most interested in and know the most about. Students who feel they cannot generate any writing topics are often surprised that they have so many options available. Then, through prewriting activities, students talk, draw, read, and even write to develop information about their topics.

Teacher's Notebook
Key Features of the Writing Process

Stage 1: Prewriting

- Students write on topics based on their own experiences.
- Students engage in rehearsal activities before writing.
- Students identify the audience to whom they will write.
- Students identify the function of the writing activity.
- Students choose an appropriate form for their compositions based on audience and function.

Stage 2: Drafting

- Students write a rough draft.
- Students emphasize content rather than mechanics.

Stage 3: Revising

- Students reread their own writing.
- Students share their writing in writing groups.
- Students participate constructively in discussions about classmates' writing.
- Students make changes in their compositions to reflect the reactions and comments of both teacher and classmates.
- Between the first and final drafts, students make substantive rather than only minor changes.

Stage 4: Editing

- Students proofread their own compositions.
- Students help proofread classmates' compositions.
- Students increasingly identify and correct their own mechanical errors.
- Students meet with the teacher for a final editing.

Stage 5: Publishing

- Students publish their writing in an appropriate form.
- Students share their finished writing with an appropriate audience.

Asking students to choose their own topics for writing does not mean that teachers never give writing assignments; teachers do provide general guidelines. Sometimes they may specify the writing form, and at other times they may establish the function, but students should choose their own specific content.

Considering Function. As students prepare to write, they need to think about their function or purpose for writing. Are they writing to entertain? To inform? To persuade? Understanding the function of a piece of writing is important because function influences other decisions students make about audience and form. Students learn to use all seven of Halliday's (1973, 1975) language functions (delineated in Chapter 1) during the elementary grades.

Considering Audience. Students may write primarily for themselves—to express and clarify their ideas and feelings—or they may write for others. Possible audiences include classmates, younger children, parents, foster grandparents, children's authors, and pen pals. Other audiences are more distant and less well known. For example, students write letters to businesses to request information, articles for the local newspaper, or stories and poems for publication in literary magazines.

Children's writing is influenced by their sense of audience. Britton and his colleagues (1975) define *sense of audience* as "the manner in which the writer expresses a relationship with the reader in respect to the writer's understanding" (pp. 65–66). Students adapt their writing to fit their audience just as they vary their speech to meet the needs of the people who are listening to them.

Considering Form. One of the most important considerations is the form the writing will take: A story? A letter? A poem? A journal entry? A writing activity could be handled in any one of these ways. As part of a science theme cycle on hermit crabs, for instance, students could write a story about a hermit crab, draw a picture and label body parts, explain how hermit crabs obtain shells to live in, or keep a log of observations about the pet hermit crabs in the classroom. There is an almost endless variety of forms that children's writing may take. A list of these forms is presented in the Teacher's Notebook on page 214. Students need to experiment with a wide variety of writing forms and explore the potential of these functions and formats.

Through reading and writing, students develop a strong sense of these forms and how they are structured. Langer (1985) found that by third grade, students responded in distinctly different ways to story and report writing assignments; they organized the writing differently and included varied kinds of information and elaboration. Similarly, Hidi and Hildyard (1983) found that elementary students could differentiate between stories and persuasive essays. Because children are clarifying the distinctions between various writing forms during the elementary grades, it is important that teachers use the correct terminology and not label all children's writing "stories."

Decisions about function, audience, and form influence each other. For example, if the function is to entertain, an appropriate form might be a story, poem, or script—and these three forms look very different on a piece of paper. Whereas a story is written in the traditional block format, scripts and poems have unique page arrangements. Scripts are written with the character's name

Teacher's Notebook

Writing Forms

ABC books
advertisements
"All About the Author"
announcements
anthologies
apologies
applications
autobiographies
awards
ballots
bibliographies
biographies
book jackets
book reports
books
brochures
bumper stickers
campaign speeches
captions
cartoons
catalogues
certificates
character sketches
charts
clusters
comics
comparisons
complaints
computer programs
coupons
crossword puzzles
definitions
descriptions
dialogue

diagrams
dictionaries
directions
editorials
essays
evaluations
explanations
fables
fairy tales
folktales
freewrites
greeting cards
hink-pinks
instructions
interviews
invitations
jokes
journals
lab reports
labels
learning logs
letters
letters to the editor
lists
lyrics
maps
menus
mysteries
myths
newspapers
notes
obituaries
oral histories
paragraphs

personal narratives
persuasive letters
poems
postcards
posters
proverbs
puzzles
questionnaires
questions
quickwrites
quizzes
recipes
research reports
reviews
riddles
schedules
scripts
sentences
signs
slogans
stories
study guides
tall tales
telegrams
telephone directories
thank-you notes
thesauruses
thumbnail sketches
tongue twisters
valentines
Venn diagrams
word-finds
wordless picture books
words

and a colon, and the dialogue is set off. Action and dialogue, rather than description, carry the story line in a script. In contrast, poems have unique formatting considerations, and words are used judiciously. Each word and phrase is chosen to convey a maximum amount of information.

Gathering and Organizing Ideas.   Students engage in activities to gather and organize ideas for writing. Graves (1983) calls what writers do to prepare for writing "rehearsal" activities. Rehearsal activities take many forms, including:

1. *Drawing.* Drawing is the way young children gather and organize ideas for writing. Primary-grade teachers notice that students often draw before they write, and, thinking that the children are eating dessert before the meat and vegetables, the teachers insist that they write first. But many young children cannot because they don't know what to write until they see what they draw (Dyson, 1982, 1983, 1986).
2. *Clustering.* Students make clusters—weblike diagrams—in which they write the topic in a center circle and draw out rays for each main idea. Then they add details and other information on rays drawn out from each main idea. Through clustering, students organize their ideas for writing. Clustering is a better prewriting strategy than outlining because it is nonlinear.
3. *Talking.* Students talk with their classmates to share ideas about possible writing topics, try out ways to express an idea, and ask questions.
4. *Reading.* Students gather ideas for writing and investigate the structure of various written forms through reading. They may retell a favorite story in writing, write new adventures for favorite story characters, or experiment with repetition, onomatopoeia, or another poetic device used in a poem they have read. Informational books also provide raw material for writing. For example, if students are studying polar bears, they read to gather information about the animal, its habitat, and its predators, which they may use in writing a report.
5. *Role-playing.* Children discover and shape ideas they will use in their writing through role-playing. During theme cycles and after reading stories, students can re-enact events to bring an experience to life. Heathcote (Wagner, 1976, 1983) suggests that teachers choose a dramatic focus or a particular critical moment for students to re-enact. For example, after reading *Sarah, Plain and Tall* (MacLachlan, 1985), children might re-enact the day Sarah took the wagon to town. This is a critical moment: Does Sarah like them and their prairie home well enough to stay?
6. *Quickwriting.* Students can expand a quickwrite (or a journal entry) that they wrote during a literature focus unit or a theme cycle into a polished composition.

Stage 2: Drafting

Students write and refine their compositions through a series of drafts. During the drafting stage students focus on getting their ideas down on paper. Because writers do not begin writing with their compositions already composed in their minds, students begin with tentative ideas developed through prewriting activities. The drafting stage is the time to pour out ideas, with little concern about spelling, punctuation, and other mechanical errors.

When students write their rough drafts, they skip every other line to leave space for revisions. They use arrows to move sections of text, cross-outs to delete sections, and scissors and tape to cut apart and rearrange text just as adult writers do. They write on only one side of a sheet of paper so that it can be cut apart or rearranged. As word processors become more available in elementary classrooms, revising, with all its shifting and deleting text, will be much easier. However, for students who handwrite their compositions, the wide spacing is crucial. Teachers might make small x's on every other line of students' papers as a reminder to skip lines as they draft their compositions.

Students label their drafts by writing "Rough Draft" in ink at the top of the paper or by stamping them with a ROUGH DRAFT stamp. This label indicates to the writer, other students, parents, and administrators that the composition is a draft in which the emphasis is on content, not mechanics. It also explains why the teacher has not graded the paper or marked mechanical errors.

During drafting, students may need to modify their earlier decisions about function, audience, and, especially, the form their writing will take. For example, a composition that began as a story may be transformed into a report, a letter, or a poem. The new format allows the student to communicate more effectively. The process of modifying earlier decisions continues into the revising stage.

As students write rough drafts, it is important not to emphasize correct spelling and neatness. In fact, pointing out mechanical errors during the drafting stage sends students a false message that mechanical correctness is more important than content (Sommers, 1982). Later, during editing, students can clean up mechanical errors and put their composition into a neat, final form.

Stage 3: Revising

During the revising stage writers refine ideas in their compositions. Students often break the writing process cycle as soon as they complete a rough draft, believing that once they have jotted down their ideas, the writing task is complete. Experienced writers, however, know that they must turn to others for reactions and revise on the basis of these comments. Revision is not just polishing; it is meeting the needs of readers by adding, substituting, deleting, and rearranging material. The word *revision* means "seeing again," and in this stage writers see their compositions again with the help of classmates and teacher. Activities in the revising stage are:

- Rereading the rough draft
- Sharing the rough draft in a writing group
- Revising on the basis of feedback

Rereading the Rough Draft.   After finishing the rough draft, writers need to distance themselves from the draft for a day or two, then reread the draft from a fresh perspective, as a reader might. As they reread, students make changes—adding, substituting, deleting, and moving—and they place question marks by sections that need work. It is these trouble spots that students ask for help with in their writing groups.

Two students share their rough drafts, ask questions, and suggest ways to revise.

Writing Groups. *   Students meet in writing groups to share their compositions with classmates. Because writing must meet the needs of readers, feedback is crucial. Mohr (1984) identifies four general functions of writing groups: to offer the writer choices; to give the writer's responses, feelings, and thoughts; to show different possibilities in revising; and to speed up revising. Writing groups provide a scaffold in which teachers and classmates talk about plans and strategies for writing and revising (Applebee & Langer, 1983; Calkins, 1983).

Writing groups can form spontaneously when several students have completed drafts and are ready to share their compositions, or they can be formal groupings with identified leaders. In some classrooms writing groups form when four or five students finish writing their rough drafts. Students gather together around a conference table or in a corner of the classroom. They take turns reading their rough drafts aloud, and classmates in the group listen and respond, offering compliments and suggestions for revision. Sometimes the teacher joins the writing group, but if the teacher is involved in something else, students work independently.

In other classrooms the writing groups are established. Students get together when all students in the group have completed their rough drafts and are ready to share their writing. Sometimes, the teacher participates in these groups, providing feedback along with the students. Or, the writing groups can function independently. Four or five students are assigned to each group, and a list of groups and their members is posted in the classroom. The teacher puts a star by one student's name, and that student serves as group leader. The leader changes every quarter.

---

*Adapted from Tompkins & Friend, 1988, pp. 4–9.

In writing groups students share their writing through these activities:

Step by Step ▼

1. **The Writer Reads.** Students take turns reading their compositions aloud to the group. All the students listen politely, thinking about compliments and suggestions they will make after the writer finishes reading. Only the writer looks at the composition, because when classmates and teacher look at it, they quickly notice and comment on mechanical errors, even though the emphasis during revising is on content. Listening to the writing read aloud keeps the focus on content.

2. **Listeners Offer Compliments.** Next, writing group members say what they liked about the writing. These positive comments should be specific, focusing on strengths, rather than the often heard "I liked it" or "It was good." Even though these are positive comments, they do not provide effective feedback. When teachers introduce revision, they should model appropriate responses because students may not know how to offer specific and meaningful comments. Teachers and students can brainstorm a list of appropriate comments and post it in the classroom for students to refer to. Comments may focus on organization, leads, word choice, voice, sequence, dialogue, theme, and so on. Possible comments are:

I like the part where . . .

I'd like to know more about . . .

I like the way you described . . .

Your writing made me feel . . .

I like the order you used in your writing because . . .

3. **The Writer Asks Questions.** After a round of positive comments, writers ask for assistance with trouble spots they identified earlier when rereading their writing, or they may ask questions that reflect more general concerns about how well they are communicating. Admitting that they need help from their classmates is a major step in learning to revise. Possible questions to classmates are:

What do you want to know more about?

Is there a part that I should throw away?

What details can I add?

What do you think the best part of my writing is?

Are there some words I need to change?

4. **Listeners Offer Suggestions.** Members of the writing group ask questions about things that were unclear to them, and they make suggestions about how to revise the composition. Almost any writer resists constructive criticism, and it is especially difficult for elementary students to appreciate suggestions. It is important to teach students what kinds of comments and suggestions are acceptable so that they will word what they say in helpful rather than hurtful ways. Possible comments and suggestions that students can offer are:

I got confused in the part about . . .

Do you need a closing?

Could you add more about . . .?

I wonder if your paragraphs are in the right order . . .

Could you combine some sentences?

5. *The Process Is Repeated.*   The first four steps are repeated for each student's composition. This is the appropriate time for teachers to provide input as well. They should react to the piece of writing as any other listener would—not error-hunting with red pen in hand (Sommers, 1982). In fact, most teachers listen to students read their compositions aloud rather than read them themselves and become frustrated by the numerous misspelled words and nearly illegible hand-writing common in rough drafts.

6. *Writers Plan for Revision.*   At the end of the writing group session, students each make a commitment to revise their writing based on the comments and suggestions of the group members. The final decisions on what to revise always rest with the writers themselves, but with the understanding that their rough drafts are not perfect comes the realization that some revision will be necessary. When students verbalize their planned revisions, they are more likely to complete the revision stage. Some students also make notes for themselves about their revision plans. After the group disbands, students make the revisions.

Making Revisions.   Students make four types of changes: additions, substitutions, deletions, and moves (Faigley & Witte, 1981). As they revise, students might add words, substitute sentences, delete paragraphs, and move phrases. Students often use a blue or red pen to cross out, draw arrows, and write in the space left between the double-spaced lines of their rough drafts so that revisions will show clearly. That way teachers can examine the types of revisions students make by examining their revised rough drafts. Revisions are another gauge of students' growth as writers.

Stage 4: Editing

Editing is putting the piece of writing into its final form. Until this stage the focus has been primarily on the content of students' writing. Once the focus changes to mechanics, students polish their writing by correcting spelling and other mechanical errors. The goal here is to make the writing "optimally readable" (Smith, 1982). Writers who write for readers understand that if their compositions are not readable, they have written in vain because their ideas will never be read.

Mechanics are the commonly accepted conventions of written standard English. They include capitalization, punctuation, spelling, sentence structure, usage, and formatting considerations specific to poems, scripts, letters, and other writing forms. The use of these commonly accepted conventions is a courtesy to those who will read the composition.

The best time to teach mechanical skills is during the editing stage, not through workbook exercises. When editing a composition that will be shared with a genuine audience, students are more interested in using mechanical skills correctly so that they can communicate effectively. In a study of two third-grade classes, Calkins (1980) found that the students in the class who learned punctuation marks as a part of editing could define or explain more marks than the students in the other class who were taught punctuation skills in a traditional manner, with instruction and practice exercises on each punctuation mark. In other words, the results of this research, as well as other studies (Bissex, 1980; Elley, Barham, Lamb, & Wyllie, 1976; Graves, 1983), suggest that teaching mechanical skills as part of the writing process is more effective than practice exercises.

Students move through three activities in the editing stage:

- Getting distance from the composition
- Proofreading to locate errors
- Correcting errors

Getting Distance.   Students are more efficient editors if they set the composition aside for a few days before beginning to edit. After working so closely with a piece of writing during drafting and revising, they are too familiar with it to be able to locate many mechanical errors. With the distance gained by waiting a few days, children are better able to approach editing with a fresh perspective and gather the enthusiasm necessary to finish the writing process by making the paper optimally readable.

Proofreading.   Students proofread their compositions to locate and mark possible errors. Proofreading is a unique type of reading in which students read slowly, word by word, hunting for errors rather than reading quickly for meaning (King, 1985). Concentrating on mechanics is difficult because of our natural inclination to read for meaning. Even experienced proofreaders often find themselves reading for meaning and thus overlooking errors that do not inhibit meaning. It is important, therefore, to take time to explain proofreading and demonstrate how it differs from regular reading.

To demonstrate proofreading, teachers take a piece of student writing and copy it on the chalkboard or display it on an overhead projector. The teacher reads it several times, each time hunting for a particular type of error. During each reading, the teacher reads the composition slowly, softly pronouncing each word and touching the word with a pencil or pen to focus attention on it. The teacher marks possible errors as they are located.

Errors are marked or corrected with special proofreaders' marks. Students enjoy using these marks, the same ones that adult authors and editors use. Proofreaders' marks that elementary students can learn to use in editing their writing are presented in Figure 6–5.

Editing checklists help students focus on particular types of error. Teachers can develop checklists with two to six items appropriate for the grade level. A first-grade checklist, for example, might include only two items—perhaps one about capital letters at the beginning of sentences and a second about periods at the end of sentences. In contrast, a middle-grade checklist might include items such as using commas in a series, indenting paragraphs, capitalizing proper nouns and adjectives, and spelling homonyms correctly. Teachers can revise the checklist during the school year to focus attention on skills that have recently been taught.

A sample third-grade editing checklist is presented in Figure 6–6. The writer and a classmate work together as partners to edit their compositions.

Figure 6–5 *Proofreaders' Marks*

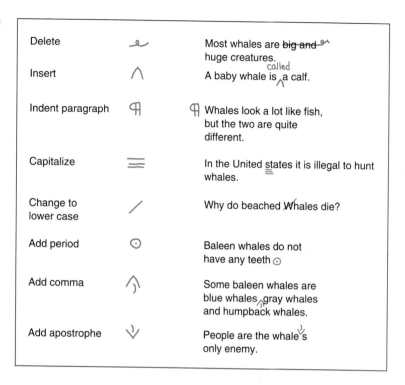

Delete	ℒ	Most whales are big and ~~huge creatures.~~
Insert	∧	A baby whale is ^{called} a calf.
Indent paragraph	¶	¶ Whales look a lot like fish, but the two are quite different.
Capitalize	≡	In the United <u>s</u>tates it is illegal to hunt whales.
Change to lower case	/	Why do beached Whales die?
Add period	⊙	Baleen whales do not have any teeth ⊙
Add comma	⌢	Some baleen whales are blue whales gray whales and humpback whales.
Add apostrophe	⌄	People are the whales only enemy.

Figure 6–6 *A Third-Grade Editing Checklist*

EDITING CHECKLIST

Author   Editor

☐ ☐ 1. I have circled the words that might be misspelled.

☐ ☐ 2. I have checked that all sentences begin with capital letters.

☐ ☐ 3. I have checked that all sentences end with punctuation marks.

☐ ☐ 4. I have checked that all proper nouns begin with a capital letter.

Signatures:

Author: _____ Editor: _____

First, students proofread their own compositions, searching for errors in each category on the checklist; after proofreading, they check off each item. Then, after completing the checklist, students sign their names and trade checklists and compositions. Now they become editors and complete each other's checklist. Having both writer and editor sign the checklist helps them to take the activity seriously.

Correcting Errors.   After students proofread their compositions and locate as many errors as possible, they correct the errors individually or with an editor's assistance. Some errors are easy to correct, some require use of a dictionary, and others involve instruction from the teacher. It is unrealistic to expect students to locate and correct every mechanical error in their compositions. Not even published books are error-free! Once in a while students may change a correct spelling or punctuation mark and make it incorrect, but they correct far more errors than they create.

Editing can end after students and their editors correct as many mechanical errors as possible, or after students meet with the teacher in a conference for a final editing. When mechanical correctness is crucial, this conference is important. Teachers proofread the composition with the student, and they identify and make the remaining corrections together, or the teacher makes check marks in the margin to note errors for the student to correct independently.

Stage 5: Publishing

In this stage students bring their compositions to life by publishing them or sharing them orally with an appropriate audience. When they share their writing with real audiences of classmates, other students, parents, and the community, students come to think of themselves as authors. In this stage students:

- Make books
- Share their writing

Making Books.   One of the most popular ways for children to publish their writing is by making books. Simple booklets can be made by folding a sheet of paper into quarters, like a greeting card. Students write the title on the front and use the three remaining sides for their compositions. They can also construct booklets by stapling sheets of writing paper together and adding construction paper covers. Sheets of wallpaper cut from old sample books also make sturdy covers. These stapled booklets can be cut into various shapes, too. Students can make more sophisticated books by covering cardboard covers with contact paper, wallpaper samples, or cloth. Pages are sewn or stapled together, and the first and last pages (endpapers) are glued to the cardboard covers to hold the book together. Directions for making one type of hardcover book are shown in Figure 6–7.

In addition, students can add an "All About the Author" page with a photograph at the end of their books, just as information about the author is often included on the jackets of published books. A fifth grader's "All About the Author" page from a collection of poetry he wrote is presented in Figure 6–8.

Figure 6–7 *Directions for Making Hardcover Books*

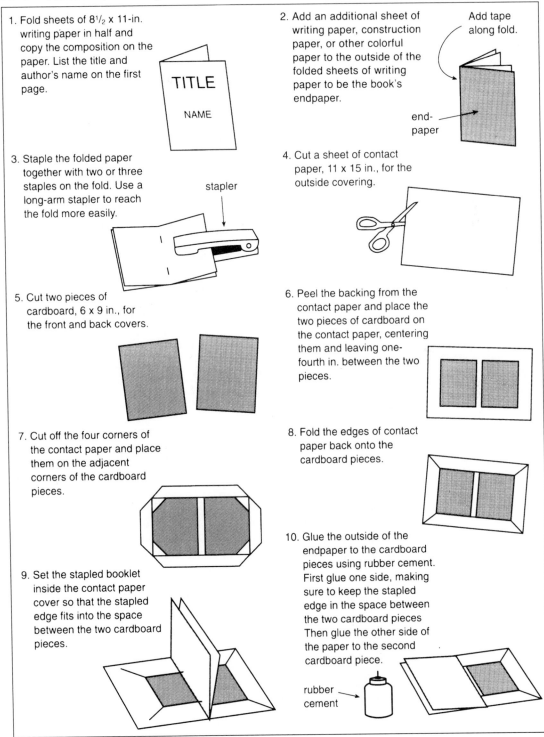

1. Fold sheets of 8½ x 11-in. writing paper in half and copy the composition on the paper. List the title and author's name on the first page.

TITLE

NAME

2. Add an additional sheet of writing paper, construction paper, or other colorful paper to the outside of the folded sheets of writing paper to be the book's endpaper.

Add tape along fold.

endpaper

3. Staple the folded paper together with two or three staples on the fold. Use a long-arm stapler to reach the fold more easily.

stapler

4. Cut a sheet of contact paper, 11 x 15 in., for the outside covering.

5. Cut two pieces of cardboard, 6 x 9 in., for the front and back covers.

6. Peel the backing from the contact paper and place the two pieces of cardboard on the contact paper, centering them and leaving one-fourth in. between the two pieces.

7. Cut off the four corners of the contact paper and place them on the adjacent corners of the cardboard pieces.

8. Fold the edges of contact paper back onto the cardboard pieces.

9. Set the stapled booklet inside the contact paper cover so that the stapled edge fits into the space between the two cardboard pieces.

10. Glue the outside of the endpaper to the cardboard pieces using rubber cement. First glue one side, making sure to keep the stapled edge in the space between the two cardboard pieces Then glue the other side of the paper to the second cardboard piece.

rubber cement

Figure 6–8   A Fifth Grader's
"All About the Author" Page

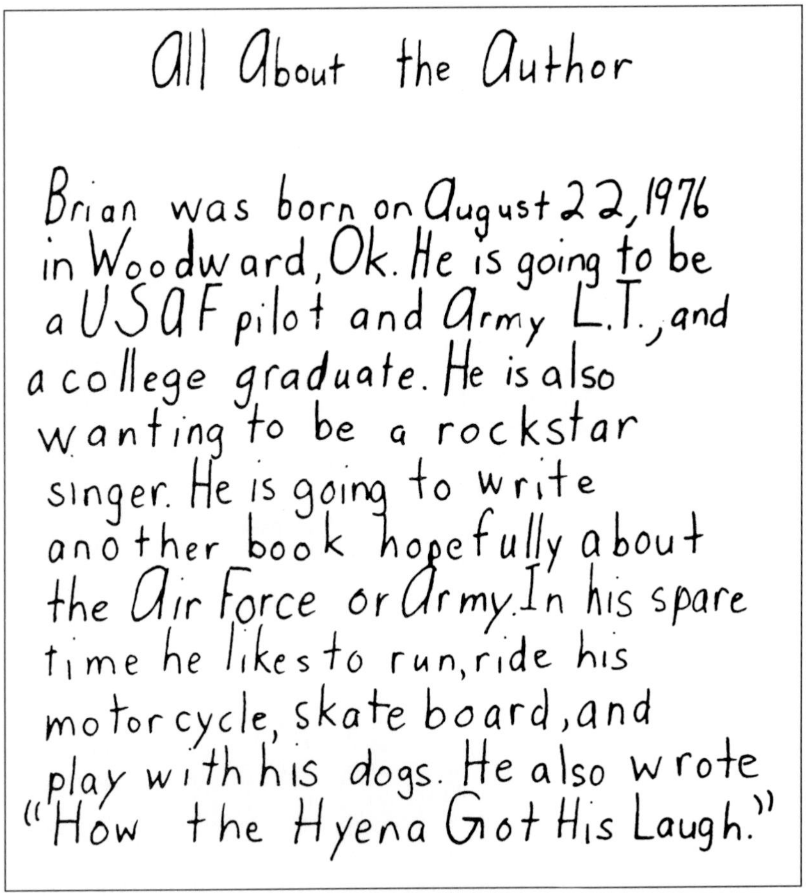

> # All About the Author
>
> Brian was born on August 22, 1976 in Woodward, Ok. He is going to be a USAF pilot and Army L.T., and a college graduate. He is also wanting to be a rockstar singer. He is going to write another book hopefully about the Air Force or Army. In his spare time he likes to run, ride his motorcycle, skateboard, and play with his dogs. He also wrote "How the Hyena Got His Laugh."

Notice that the student wrote about himself in the third person, as in adult biographical sketches.

Sharing Writing.   Students read their writing to classmates or share it with larger audiences through hardcover books placed in the class or school library, class anthologies, letters, newspaper articles, plays, filmstrips and videotapes, or puppet shows. Other ways to share children's writing are to:

Read the writing aloud in class
Submit the piece to writing contests
Display the writing as a mobile
Contribute to a class anthology
Contribute to the local newspaper
Make a shape book
Record the writing on a cassette tape
Submit it to a literary magazine
Read it at a school assembly
Share at a read-aloud party
Share with parents and siblings

Produce a videotape of it

Display poetry on a "poet-tree"

Send it to a pen pal

Make a hardbound book

Produce it as a roller movie

Display it on a bulletin board

Make a filmstrip of it

Make a big book

Design a poster about the writing

Read it to foster grandparents

Share it as a puppet show

Display it at a public event

Read it to children in other classes

Through this sharing, students communicate with genuine audiences who respond to their writing in meaningful ways.

Sharing writing is a social activity that helps children develop sensitivity to audiences and confidence in themselves as authors. Dyson (1985) advises that teachers consider the social interpretations of sharing—students' behavior, teacher's behavior, and interaction between students and teacher—within the classroom context. Individual students interpret sharing differently. More than just providing the opportunity for students to share writing, teachers need to teach students how to respond to their classmates. Teachers themselves

Students sit in the author's chair to share writing with classmates.

serve as a model for responding to students' writing without dominating the sharing.

Teaching the Writing Process

Students learn to use the writing process as they write compositions in literature focus units and theme cycles and as they participate in writing workshop. Learning to use the writing process is more important than any particular writing projects students might be involved in, because the writing process is a tool. Students need many opportunities to learn to use the writing process. Teachers model the writing process by writing class collaborations, and they teach minilessons on the procedures, concepts, and strategies and skills that writers use.

Writing Class Collaborations.   One way to introduce the writing process is to write a collaborative or group composition. The teacher models the writing process and provides an opportunity for students to practice the process approach to writing in a supportive environment. As students and the teacher write a composition together, they move through the five stages of the writing process just as writers do when they work independently. The teacher demonstrates the strategies that writers use and clarifies misconceptions during the group composition, and students offer ideas for writing as well as suggestions for tackling common writing problems.

The teacher begins by introducing the idea of writing a group composition and by reviewing the project. Students compose the class collaboration composition with the teacher's assistance, moving through the drafting, revising, editing, and publishing stages of the writing process. The teacher records students' dictation, noting any misunderstandings about the writing assignment or process. When necessary, the teacher reviews concepts and offers suggestions. Students first dictate a rough draft, which the teacher records on the chalkboard or on chart paper. Then teacher and students read the composition and identify ways to revise it. Some parts of the composition will need reworking, and other parts may be deleted or moved. More specific words will be substituted for less specific ones, and redundant words and sentences will be deleted. Students may also want to add new parts to the composition. After making the necessary content changes, students proofread the composition, checking for mechanical errors, for paragraph breaks, and for sentences to combine. They correct errors and make changes. Then the teacher or a student copies the completed composition on chart paper or on a sheet of notebook paper. Copies can be duplicated and given to each student.

Fine (1987) explains how her middle-grade class of students with behavior disorders wrote a novel collaboratively. All of the students contributed to the writing and, through the experience, learned that they could write and that they had valuable contributions to make. Fine sums up the experience this way: "Collaboration is learning to learn and to work together. . . . Collaboration is a great solution" (p. 487).

Collaborative compositions are an essential part of many writing experiences, especially when students are learning to use the writing process or a new writing form. Group compositions serve as a "dry run," during which students' questions and misconceptions can be clarified.

Minilessons on the Writing Process.   Students need to learn how to move through the five stages of the writing process, how to gather and organize ideas for writing, how to participate in writing groups, how to proofread, and how to share their writing. Teachers teach these procedures, concepts, and strategies and skills during minilessons. Minilessons can be taught as part of class collaborations, during literature focus units and theme cycles, and in writing workshop. Topics for minilessons on the writing process are listed on page 208.

Many teachers use the editing stage as a time to informally assess students' spelling, capitalization, punctuation, and other mechanical skills and to give minilessons on a skill that a student or several students are having trouble with. The teacher notes which students are having difficulty with a particular skill—paragraphing, capitalizing proper nouns, or using the apostrophe in possessives—and conducts an impromptu minilesson using the students' writing as the basis of the lesson. In this brief, 5-minute lesson, the teacher reviews the particular skill, and students practice the skill as they correct their own writing and help to correct their classmates' writing. This procedure individualizes instruction and teaches the skill when learning it matters and is relevant to students.

In Literature Focus Units.   Students use the writing process as they create projects during the extending-the-interpretation stage of the reading process. Sometimes the class works together to write a class collaboration; sometimes students work in small groups on the same writing project; and at other times students work on a variety of writing projects. Here are three examples:

- After reading Freeman's teddy bear story *Corduroy* (1968), a class of first graders worked together to write a retelling of the story which they published as a big book.
- During an author unit on Chris Van Allsburg, fifth graders each chose an illustration from *The Mysteries of Harris Burdick* (1984) and wrote a description or story about it.
- As part of a unit on point of view, seventh-grade students rewrote familiar folktales from the viewpoint of one character after reading *The True Story of the Three Little Pigs!* (Scieszka, 1989) which is told from the wolf's viewpoint.

In each of these projects, students used the writing process and moved through all five stages as they drafted, revised, edited, and published their compositions.

In Theme Cycles.   Teachers often plan writing projects in connection with theme cycles. Sometimes all students in the classroom work together on a single project, such as making an ABC book about the ocean as part of a theme on the oceans; or they write a collection of animal poems to put with the animal sculptures they made in art. When teachers do this, they review the writing form in a minilesson, and students work through the stages of the writing process together.

At other times, however, students choose projects and work independently. For example, during a theme cycle on pioneers, students might choose different types of projects, including:

- Write a simulated journal from the viewpoint of a pioneer.
- Write a story about a pioneer family.
- Write an informational book about covered wagons.
- Write poems about life on the Oregon Trail.
- Write an explanation to accompany a relief map of the pioneer trails across the United States.
- Make a timeline for the westward expansion, with notes about important dates and events.
- Write an essay comparing pioneers in the 1800s with immigrants coming to America today.
- Make posters about pioneer legends (e.g., Johnny Appleseed, Pecos Bill, and Paul Bunyan).

For each of these projects, students use the writing process to develop their compositions. They meet in writing groups to share their rough drafts and revise their pieces on the basis of feedback from classmates. They also edit their compositions to identify and correct as many mechanical errors as possible. Then they make final copies of their compositions and share them with classmates or other audiences.

In Writing Workshop. In Chapter 2 we described the three components of writing workshop: writing, sharing, and minilessons. Students move through the stages of the writing process during the writing time. It would be convenient if the writing process equated to prewriting on Monday, drafting on Tuesday, revising on Wednesday, editing on Thursday, and publishing on Friday, but it does not. Writers move back and forth through the stages to develop, refine, and polish their compositions, and they participate in some activities, such as revising, throughout the writing process (Hayes & Flower, 1980). A special sharing time is set aside for students to share their published writing projects with classmates. Sharing is a social experience, and when students share their writing with real audiences, they feel the satisfaction of a job well done.

Adapting to Meet the Needs of Every Student. Teachers can adapt the activities involved in each stage of the writing process to make writing a successful experience for all students. Teachers often shorten the writing process to three stages—prewriting, drafting, and publishing—for young children and for students with few successful writing experiences. Then, as students become more fluent writers and develop audience awareness, teachers add the revising and editing stages.

Teachers can develop checklists with activities for each stage of the writing process listed so that students with short attention spans or students who have trouble completing an assignment can stay on task. Other suggestions for adapting each stage are listed on page 229.

Responding to Student Writing. The teacher's role should not be restricted to that of evaluator. Again and again researchers report that although teachers are the most common audience for student writing, they are also one of the worst audiences, because they read with a red pen in their hands. Teachers should instead read their students' writing for information, for enjoyment, and for all the other purposes that other readers do. Much of students' writing does

Adapting . . .
The Writing Process
To Meet the Needs of Every Student

Stage 1: Prewriting

- Use drawing as a rehearsal activity.
- Have students "talk out" their compositions before beginning to write.
- Draw a cluster for students, using the ideas and words they suggest.

Stage 2: Drafting

- Have students dictate their rough drafts.
- Mark students' papers so that they write on every other line.
- Reassure students that spelling and other mechanical skills are not important in this stage.

Stage 3: Revising

- Participate in writing groups with students.
- Focus on compliments rather than on suggestions for revisions when students begin writing groups.
- Expect students to make only one or two revisions at first.

Stage 4: Editing

- Teach students how to proofread.
- Have students mark possible errors; then correct errors with them.
- Have students identify and correct errors on the first page of their compositions; then correct remaining errors for students.

Stage 5: Publishing

- Use a word processor for final copies.
- Handwrite the final copy for students.
- Provide opportunities for students to share their writing with a trusted group of classmates.
- Do not correct any remaining errors on the final copy.

not need to be assessed; it should simply be shared with the teacher as a "trusted adult" (Martin, D'Arcy, Newton, & Parker, 1976).

When children use a process approach to writing, there is less chance they will plagiarize because they will have developed their compositions step by step—from prewriting and drafting to revising and editing. Nonetheless, at some time or other, most teachers fear that a composition they are reading is not the student's own work. Jackson, Tway, and Frager (1987) cite several reasons that children might plagiarize. First, some students may simply internalize a piece of writing through repeated readings so that, months or years later, they do not realize that it is not their own work. Second, some students may plagiarize because of competition to succeed. Third, some students plagiarize by accident, not realizing the consequences of their actions. A final reason some students plagiarize is that they have not been taught to write by means of a process approach, so they may not know how to synthesize information for a report from published sources. The two best ways to avoid having students copy work from another source and pass it off as their own are to teach the writing process and have students write at school rather than at home. Students who work at school and move through the various writing process activities know how to complete the writing project.

Assessing Students' Use of the Writing Process.   To measure students' growth in writing, it is not always necessary to assess finished products (Tway, 1980). Teachers make judgments about students' progress in other ways. One of the best ways is to observe students while they write and note whether they engage in prewriting activities, whether they focus on content rather than mechanics in their rough drafts, and whether they participate in writing groups.

When it is necessary to assess students' writing, teachers can judge whether students have completed all components of the writing project as well as the quality of the final product.

By observing students while they are writing, teachers can note how they move through the writing process stages, from gathering and organizing ideas during prewriting, to pouring out and shaping ideas during drafting, to meeting in writing groups to get feedback, to making substantive changes during revising, to proofreading and correcting mechanical errors in editing, and finally, to publishing and sharing their writing in the last stage (McKenzie & Tompkins, 1984). Figure 6–9 lists several characteristic activities in each stage of the writing process. Teachers can observe students while they write and participate in other writing process–related activities, and they can place check marks and add comments as necessary for each observed activity. Students can also use the checklist for self-assessment to help make them aware of the activities in the writing process.

The writing process checklist can also be adapted for various types of writing projects. If students are writing autobiographies, for example, the checklist can include items in the prewriting stage about developing a lifeline and clustering ideas for each chapter topic. The sharing stage can include items such as adding a table of contents or an illustration for each chapter and sharing the complete autobiography with at least two other people.

CONNECTIONS BETWEEN READING AND WRITING

Reading and writing are both meaning-making processes, and readers and writers are involved in many similar activities. It is important that teachers plan literacy activities so that students can connect reading and writing.

Comparing the Two Processes

The reading and writing processes have comparable activities at each stage (Butler & Turbill, 1984). As shown in Figure 6–10, reading and writing activities at each stage are similar, and in both reading and writing the goal is to construct meaning. Notice the activities listed for responding and revising

Figure 6–9   The Writing Process Checklist

	Dates					
Student: _____						
Prewriting Can the student identify the specific audience to whom he/she will write?						
Does this awareness affect the choices the student makes as he/she writes?						
Can the student identify the purpose of the writing activity?						
Does the student write on a topic that grows out of his/her own experience?						
Does the student engage in rehearsal activities before writing?						
Drafting Does the student write rough drafts?						
Does the student place a greater emphasis on content than on mechanics in the rough drafts?						
Revising Does the student share his/her writing in conferences?						
Does the student participate in discussions about classmates' writing?						
In revising, does the student make changes to reflect the reactions and comments of both teacher and classmates?						
Between first and final drafts, does the student make substantive or only minor changes?						
Editing Does the student proofread his/her own papers?						
Does the student help proofread classmates' papers?						
Does the student increasingly identify his/her mechanical errors?						
Publishing Does the student publish his/her writing in an appropriate form?						
Does the student share this finished writing with an appropriate audience?						

Figure 6-10   A Comparison of the Reading and Writing Processes

	What Readers Do	**What Writers Do**
Stage 1	*Preparing to Read*	*Prewriting*
	Readers use knowledge about	Writers use knowledge about
	• the topic • reading • literature • language systems	• the topic • writing • literature • language systems
	Readers' expectations are cued by	Writers' expectations are cued by
	• previous reading/writing experiences • format of the text • purpose for reading • audience for reading	• previous reading/writing experiences • format of the text • purpose for writing • audience for writing
	Readers make predictions.	Writers gather and organize ideas.
Stage 2	*Reading*	*Drafting*
	Readers	Writers
	• use word identification strategies • use meaning-making strategies • monitor reading • create meaning	• use transcription strategies • use meaning-making strategies • monitor writing • create meaning
Stage 3	*Responding*	*Revising*
	Readers	Writers
	• respond to the text • interpret meaning • clarify misunderstandings • expand ideas	• respond to the text • interpret meaning • clarify misunderstandings • expand ideas
Stage 4	*Exploring the Text*	*Editing*
	Readers	Writers
	• examine the impact of words and literary language • explore structural elements • compare the text to others	• identify and correct mechanical errors • review paragraph and sentence structure
Stage 5	*Extending the Interpretation*	*Publishing*
	Readers	Writers
	• go beyond the text to extend their interpretations • share projects with classmates • reflect on the reading process • make connections to life and literature • value the piece of literature • feel success • want to read again	• produce the finished copy of their compositions • share their compositions with genuine audiences • reflect on the writing process • value the composition • feel success • want to write again

Adapted from Butler & Turbill, 1984.

during the third stage, for example. Fitzgerald (1989) analyzed these two activities and concluded that they draw on similar processes of author-reader-text interactions. Similar analyses can be made for other activities, as well.

Tierney (1983) explains that reading and writing are multidimensional and involve concurrent, complex transactions between writers, between writers as readers, between readers, and between readers as writers. Writers participate in several types of reading activities. They read other authors' works to obtain ideas and to learn about the structure of stories, but they also read and reread their own work—to problem-solve, discover, monitor, and clarify. The quality of these reading experiences seems closely tied to success in writing. "Readers as writers" is a newer idea, but readers are involved in many of the same activities that writers use. They generate ideas, organize, monitor, problem-solve, and revise. Smith (1982) believes that reading influences writing skills because readers unconsciously "read like writers":

> To read like a writer we engage with the author in what the author is writing. We can anticipate what the author will say, so that the author is in effect writing on our behalf, not showing how something is done but doing it with us. . . . Bit by bit, one thing at a time, but enormous numbers of things over the passage of time, the learner learns through reading like a writer to write like a writer. (pp. 563–564)

Also, both reading and writing are recursive, cycling back through various parts of the process, and, just as writers compose text, readers compose their meaning.

Classroom Connections

Teachers can help students appreciate the similarities between reading and writing in many ways. Tierney (1983) explains: "What we need are reading teachers who act as if their students were developing writers and writing teachers who act as if their students were readers" (p. 151). These are some ways to point out the relationships between reading and writing:

- Help writers assume alternative points of view as potential readers.
- Help readers consider the writer's purpose and viewpoint.
- Point out that reading is much like composing, so that students will view reading as a process, much like the writing process.
- Talk with students about the reading and writing processes.
- Talk with students about reading and writing strategies.

Readers and writers use a number of strategies for constructing meaning as they interact with print. As readers, we use a variety of problem-solving strategies to make decisions about an author's meaning and to construct meaning for ourselves. As writers, we also use problem-solving strategies to decide what our readers need as we construct meaning for them and for ourselves. Comparing reading to writing, Tierney and Pearson (1983) described reading as a composing process because readers compose and refine meaning through reading much as writers do.

Langer (1985) followed this line of thinking in identifying four strategies that both readers and writers use to interact with text. The first strategy is generating ideas: Both readers and writers generate ideas as they get started, as they become aware of important ideas and experiences, and as they begin to plan and organize the information. Formulating meaning is the second strategy—the essence of both reading and writing. Readers and writers formulate meaning by developing the message, considering the audience, drawing on personal experience, choosing language, linking concepts, summarizing, and paraphrasing. Assessing is the next strategy. In both reading and writing, students review, react to, and monitor their understanding of the message and the text itself. The fourth strategy is revising, wherein both readers and writers reconsider and restructure the message, recognize when meaning has broken down, and take appropriate action to change the text to improve understanding.

There are practical benefits of connecting reading and writing. Reading contributes to students' writing development, and writing contributes to students' reading development. Shanahan (1988) has outlined seven instructional principles for relating reading and writing so that students develop a clear concept of literacy:

1. Involve students in reading and writing experiences every day.
2. Introduce reading and writing processes in kindergarten.
3. Plan instruction that reflects the developmental nature of the reading-writing relationship.
4. Make the reading-writing connection explicit to students.
5. Emphasize both the processes and the products of reading and writing.
6. Emphasize the functions for which students use reading and writing.
7. Teach reading and writing through meaningful, functional, and genuine literacy experiences.

Review

Students use the five stages in the reading process for both aesthetic and efferent reading. The stages are preparing to read, reading, responding, exploring the text, and extending the interpretation. Teachers use a variety of approaches for reading, including reading aloud to students, shared reading, buddy reading, guided reading, and independent reading. The writing process involves five stages: prewriting, drafting, revising, editing, and publishing. Students learn to use the reading and writing processes through literature focus units, theme cycles, and reading and writing workshop.

Extensions

1. Observe students using the reading process in an elementary classroom. In what types of preparing-to-read, reading, responding, exploring, and extending-the-interpretation activities are they involved?
2. Observe students using the writing process in an elementary classroom. In what types of prewriting, drafting, revising, editing, and publishing activities are they involved?
3. Plan a literature focus unit or theme cycle and include a variety of reading and writing process activities.

4. Sit in on a writing group meeting in which students share their writing and ask classmates for feedback in revising their compositions. Make a list of the students' questions and comments. What conclusions can you draw about their interactions with each other? You might want to compare your findings with those reported in the article "Talking About Writing: The Language of Writing Groups" (Gere & Abbott, 1985).
5. Reflect on your own reading process. What stages do you use? How do you vary your reading when you read aesthetically and efferently? Write a two-

to three-page paper comparing your reading process to the process described in this chapter.

6. Reflect on your own writing process. Do you write single-draft papers, or do you write a series of drafts and refine them? Do you ask friends to read and react to your writing or to help you proofread your writing? Write a two- to three-page paper comparing your writing process to the process described in this chapter. How might you modify your own writing process in light of the information in this chapter?

7. Read Shanahan's (1988) article, "The Reading-Writing Relationship: Seven Instructional Principles." Think about how you will implement these principles in your classroom, and share your thinking in a brief paper.

References

Applebee, A. L., & Langer, J. A. (1983). Instructional scaffolding: Reading and writing and natural language activities. *Language Arts, 60,* 168–175.

Bissex, G. L. (1980). *Gyns at wrk: A child learns to write and read.* Cambridge, MA: Harvard University Press.

Britton, J., Burgess, T., Martin, N., McLeod, A., & Rosen, H. (1975). *The development of writing abilities* (pp. 11–18). London: Schools Council Publications.

Butler, A., & Turbill, J. (1984). *Towards a reading-writing classroom.* Portsmouth, NH: Heinemann.

Calkins, L. M. (1980). When children want to punctuate: Basic skills belong in context. *Language Arts, 57,* 567–573.

Calkins, L. M. (1983). *Lessons from a child: On the teaching and learning of writing.* Portsmouth, NH: Heinemann.

Dyson, A. H. (1982). The emergence of visible language: Interrelationships between drawing and early writing. *Visible Language, 6,* 360–381.

Dyson, A. H. (1983). *Early writing as drawing: The developmental gap between speaking and writing.* Presentation at the Annual Meeting of the American Educational Research Association, Montreal, Canada.

Dyson, A. H. (1985). Second graders sharing writing: The multiple social realities of a literacy event. *Written Communication, 2,* 189–215.

Dyson, A. H. (1986). The imaginary worlds of childhood: A multimedia presentation. *Language Arts, 63,* 799–808.

Elley, W. B., Barham, I. H., Lamb, H., & Wyllie, M. (1976). The role of grammar in a secondary school English curriculum. *Research in the Teaching of English, 10,* 5–21.

Faigley, L., & Witte, S. (1981). Analyzing revision. *College Composition and Communication, 32,* 400–410.

Fine, E. S. (1987). Marbles lost, marbles found. Collaborative production of text. *Language Arts, 64,* 474–487.

Fitzgerald, J. (1989). Enhancing two related thought processes: Revision in writing and critical thinking. *The Reading Teacher, 43,* 42–48.

Gere, A. R., & Abbott, R. D. (1985). Talking about writing: The language of writing groups. *Research in the Teaching of English, 19,* 362–381.

Graves, D. H. (1976). Let's get rid of the welfare mess in the teaching of writing. *Language Arts, 53,* 645–651.

Graves, D. H. (1983). *Writing: Teachers and children at work.* Exeter, NH: Heinemann.

Halliday, M. A. K. (1973). *Explorations in the functions of language.* London: Edward Arnold.

Halliday, M. A. K. (1975). *Learning how to mean: Explorations in the development of language.* London: Edward Arnold.

Harste, J. C., Woodward, V.A., & Burke, C. L. (1984). Examining our assumptions: A transactional view of literacy and learning. *Research in the Teaching of English, 18,* 84–108.

Hayes, J. R., & Flower, L. S. (1980). Identifying the organization of writing processes. In L. W. Gregg & E. R. Steinberg (Eds.), *Cognitive processes in writing* (pp. 3–30). Hillsdale, NJ: Erlbaum.

Hidi, S., & Hildyard, A. (1983). The comparison of oral and written productions in two discourse modes. *Discourse Processes, 6,* 91–105.

Jackson, L. A., Tway, E., & Frager, A. (1987). Dear teacher, Johnny copied. *The Reading Teacher, 41,* 22–25.

King, M. (1985). Proofreading is not reading. *Teaching English in the two-year college, 12,* 108–112.

Langer, J. A. (1985). Children's sense of genre. *Written Communication, 2,* 157–187.

Martin, N., D'Arcy, P., Newton, B., & Parker, R. (1976). *Writing and learning across the curriculum* (pp. 11–16). London: Schools Council Publications.

McKenzie, L., & Tompkins, G. E. (1984). Evaluating students' writing: A process approach. *Journal of Teaching Writing, 3,* 201–212.

Mohr, M. M. (1984). *Revision: The rhythm of meaning.* Upper Montclair, NJ: Boynton/Cook.

Murray, D. H. (1982). *Learning by teaching.* Montclair, NJ: Boynton/Cook.

Ohlhausen, M. M., & Jepsen, M. (1992). Lessons from Goldilocks: "Somebody's been choosing my books but I can make my own choices now!" *The New Advocate, 5,* 31–46.

Peterson, R., & Eeds, M. (1990). *Grand conversations: Literature groups in action.* New York: Scholastic.

Rosenblatt, L. (1978). *The reader, the text, the poem: The transactional theory of the literary work.* Carbondale: Southern Illinois University Press.

Shanahan, T. (1988). The reading-writing relationship: Seven instructional principles. *The Reading Teacher, 41,* 636–647.

Smith, F. (1982). *Writing and the writer.* New York: Holt, Rinehart & Winston.

Sommers, N. (1982). Responding to student writing. *College Composition and Communication, 33,* 148–156.

Tierney, R. J. (1983). Writer-reader transactions: Defining the dimensions of negotiation. In P. L. Stock (Ed.), *Forum: Essays on theory and practice in the teaching of writing* (pp. 147–151). Upper Montclair, NJ: Boynton/Cook.

Tierney, R. J., & Pearson, P. D. (1983). Toward a composing model of reading. *Language Arts, 60,* 568–580.

Tompkins, G. E., & Friend, M. (1988). After your students write: What's next? *Teaching Exceptional Children, 20,* 4–9.

Tway, E. (1980). Teacher responses to children's writing. *Language Arts, 57,* 763–772.

Wagner, B. J. (1976). *Dorothy Heathcote: Drama as a learning medium.* Washington, DC: National Education Association.

Wagner, B. J. (1983). The expanding circle of informal classroom drama. In B. A. Busching and J. I. Schwartz (Eds.), *Integrating the language arts in the elementary school* (pp. 155–163). Urbana, IL: National Council of Teachers of English.

Weaver, C. (1988). *Reading process and practice: From socio-psycholinguistics to whole language.* Portsmouth, NH: Heinemann.

Children's Book References

Carle, E. (1986). *The grouchy ladybug.* New York: Harper & Row.

Fowler, A. (1990). *It's a good thing there are insects.* Chicago: Childrens Press.

Freeman, D. (1968). *Corduroy.* New York: Viking.

Henry, M. (1963). *Misty of Chincoteague.* Chicago: Rand McNally.

Howe, D., & Howe, J. (1979). *Bunnicula: A rabbit-tale of mystery.* New York: Atheneum.

Howe, J. (1990). *Hot fudge.* New York: Atheneum.

Howe, J. (1989). *The fright before Christmas.* New York: Atheneum.

Howe, J. (1982). *Howliday Inn.* New York: Atheneum.

Howe, J. (1983). *The celery stalks at midnight.* New York: Atheneum.

Howe, J. (1987). *Nighty-nightmare.* New York: Atheneum.

Howe, J. (1989). *Scared silly.* New York: Atheneum.

Howe, J. (1992). *Return to Howliday Inn.* New York: Atheneum.

Lauber, P. (1990). *Seeing earth from space.* New York: Orchard Books.

MacLachlan, P. (1985). *Sarah, plain and tall.* New York: Harper & Row.

Rylant, C. (1985). *The relatives came.* New York: Bradbury Press.

Scieszka, J. (1989). *The true story of the three little pigs!* New York: Viking.

Siebert, D. (1991). *Sierra.* New York: HarperCollins.

Van Allsburg, C. (1984). *The mysteries of Harris Burdick.* Boston: Houghton Mifflin.

Watts, B. (1987). *Ladybug.* Morristown, NJ: Silver Burdett.

> 66 I want every child in my class to be a reader, but some of them haven't had many experiences with books. To compensate, I have my children take books home every week to read with their parents. 99
>
> Mary Yamazaki
> Bilingual Kindergarten Teacher
> Truckee Elementary School

PROCEDURE

I began a book bag project in my classroom several years ago. My aide and I bought the cloth, and together we sewed 40 book bags with handles. Next we collected two or three related books to put into each bag. We have book bags about dinosaurs, trucks, dogs, "The Three Bears," colors, and other topics. The three books in the book bag about colors, for example, are *Mary Wore Her Red Dress* (Peek, 1985), Dr. Seuss's *Green Eggs and Ham* (1988), and *Color Zoo* (Ehlert, 1989). Some of the bags have books written in English, and others have books written in Spanish. It's taken us a while to collect enough books, and most of them are paperbacks that I've bought inexpensively through book clubs. The PTA gave us some money for books, too. I also put a reading log notebook—20 sheets of paper stapled together with a construction paper cover that has been laminated—in each bag and a pencil. Children write their names and the date in the reading log after their parents have read the books in the book bag to them. The children are also invited to add a picture or write comments. Parents, too, are encouraged to draw pictures and write comments in the log.

I introduce the book bag project at our Back-to-School Night program and explain how parents should read the books with their children. I emphasize that parents are not expected to teach their children to read and that they should not expect their children to read the books independently. I demonstrate how to read with a child so that it is a pleasurable experience and how to talk with the child about the book after reading without asking a long series of comprehension questions. I also demonstrate how to write in a reading log with a child. My aide translates my comments for the Spanish-speaking parents. I also include a one-page list of guidelines in each book bag. The guidelines are printed in English on one side and in Spanish on the other. The English version of this list is shown in the accompanying figure.

Then my kindergartners begin taking book bags home once a week. On Friday the children select the book bag they want to take home with them. They check out the bag using a cardfile system. An index card is in each bag, and children take the card out of the bag and sign it. Then they place the card on our checkout chart. The chart has a pocket for each child, and the child puts the card in the pocket with his or her name on it. The children keep the book bags at home over the weekend and the first part of the next week. I have them bring the bags back to school on Wednesday. The children take the checkout card out of the chart and put it back in the book bag. Then on Thursday my aide and I check the bags and get them ready to go home again on Friday.

ASSESSMENT

I use a checkout system to keep track of the book bags, and I talk informally with the children about the books and the reading activities that go on at home. I try to take a look at the reading logs and read the entries the children have made, but I do it very informally. I don't assign grades or anything like that. What is important to me is that my children are being read to on a regular basis at home and that it is a positive experience for both the children and their parents.

ADAPTATIONS

Book bags wouldn't work without the parents' cooperation and assistance. I've found that my parents are very enthusiastic and want to read with their children. I've wondered what I would do if parents weren't interested in or capable of reading with their children. I've thought about using wordless books such as *Pancakes for Breakfast* (de Paola, 1978) and *Picnic* (McCully, 1984). I've also wondered about using small, battery-operated audiotape players so that my children and their parents could listen to the book read aloud together. So far I haven't had to adapt my program, but I would if it were necessary.

REFLECTIONS

Teaching and learning go on at school and at home. I couldn't possibly do the job alone. I need parents to work with me, and I think that my children's parents appreciate the opportunity. They take good care of the book bags at home and almost always remember to return them to school on Wednesdays. Many of my children's families come from cultures where school and home were kept separate, but when you show them how you want them to work with their children, they are very responsible.

Guidelines for Reading Book Bag Books

1. Plan a special, 10-minute period several times a week for reading with your child.
2. Read one of the books in the book bag. Ask your child to choose which book to read.
3. Have your child sit in your lap or next to you, and invite him or her to hold the book and turn the pages as you read.
4. Make this reading experience a pleasant one. It is not a reading lesson, and your child should not be quizzed on reading skills.
5. Begin by reading aloud the title and the name of the author. Then read to your child or encourage your child to read along with you if the book is a familiar one. Do not expect your child to read the book independently!
6. After reading, talk to your child about the book. You might ask one of these questions:

   What part of the book did you like best?
   Did you like the book? Why?
   What did the book make you think of?

7. Choose another book from the book bag the next day and repeat steps 1–6.
8. After reading the books, help your child write his or her name in the Reading Log that is in the book bag. Your child may also draw a picture or write a message, if he or she is interested in doing so.
9. Return the book bag on Wednesday.

7

Emergent
Literacy

INSIGHT _____

Is there a magic age when a child becomes a reader? Researchers used to think that at the age of 6½ most children were ready to read. We now know that children begin the process of becoming literate gradually during the preschool years. Very young children notice signs, logos, and other environmental print. Who hasn't observed children making scribbles on paper as they try to "write"? As children are read to, they learn how to hold a book and turn pages, and they observe how the text is read. Children come to kindergarten and first grade with knowledge about written language and experiences with reading and writing. As you read this chapter, think about this question:

How can teachers extend and support young children as they emerge into literacy?

*L*iteracy is a process that begins well before the elementary grades and continues into adulthood, if not throughout life. It used to be that 5-year-old children came to kindergarten to be "readied" for reading and writing instruction, which would formally begin in first grade. The implication was that there was a point in children's development when it was time to begin teaching them to read and write. For those not ready, a variety of "readiness" activities would prepare them for reading and writing. Since the 1970s this view has been discredited by teachers' and researchers' observations (Clay, 1989). The children themselves demonstrated that they could recognize signs and other environmental print, retell stories, scribble letters, invent printlike writing, and listen to stories read aloud to them. Some children even taught themselves to read.

This new perspective on how children become literate—that is, how they learn to read and write—is known as *emergent literacy.* New Zealand educator Marie Clay is credited with coining the term. Studies from 1966 on have shaped the current outlook (Clay, 1967; Durkin, 1966; Holdaway, 1979; Taylor, 1983; Teale, 1982; Teale & Sulzby, 1989). Now, researchers are looking at literacy learning from the child's point of view. The age range has been extended to include children as young as 12 or 14 months of age who listen to stories being read aloud, notice labels and signs in their environment, and experiment with pencils. The concept of literacy has been broadened to include the cultural and social aspects of language learning, and children's experiences with and understanding about written language—both reading and writing—are included as part of emergent literacy.

Teale and Sulzby (1989) paint a portrait of young children as literacy learners with these characteristics:

- Children begin to learn to read and write very early in life.
- Young children learn the functions of literacy through observing and participating in real-life settings in which reading and writing are used.
- Young children's reading and writing abilities develop concurrently and interrelatedly through experiences in reading and writing.
- Young children learn through active involvement with literacy materials, by constructing their understanding of reading and writing.

Teale and Sulzby describe young children as active learners who construct their own knowledge about reading and writing with the assistance of parents and other literate persons. These care givers help by demonstrating literacy as they read and write, by supplying materials, and by structuring opportunities for children to be involved in reading and writing. The environment is positive, with children experiencing reading and writing in many facets of their everyday lives and observing others who are engaged in literacy activities.

The way children learn about written language is remarkably similar to the way they learn to talk. Children are immersed in written language as they are first in oral language. They have many opportunities to see reading and writing taking place for real purposes and to experiment with written language. Through these experiences children actively construct their knowledge about literacy. As parents and other adults model the processes of reading and writing, they provide a scaffold for children's learning. The "Joint Statement on Literacy Development and Pre-first Grade" presented in Appendix C reinforces these conclusions.

CONCEPTS ABOUT WRITTEN LANGUAGE

Children's introduction to written language begins before they come to school. Parents and other care givers read to young children, and the children observe adults reading. They learn to read signs and other environmental print in their community. Children experiment with writing and have parents write for them. They also observe adults writing. When young children come to kindergarten, their knowledge about written language expands quickly as they participate in meaningful, functional, and genuine experiences with reading and writing.

Students also grow in their ability to stand back and reflect on language. The ability to talk about concepts of language is called *metalinguistics* (Yaden & Templeton, 1986), and children's ability to think metalinguistically is developed by their experiences with reading and writing (Templeton & Spivey, 1980).

Concepts About the Functions of Language

Through experiences in their homes and communities, young children learn that print carries meaning and that reading and writing are used for a variety of functions or purposes. They read menus in restaurants to know what foods are being served, write and receive letters to communicate with friends and relatives, and read (and listen to) stories for enjoyment. Children also learn about language functions as they observe parents and teachers using written language for all these purposes.

Children's understanding about the functions of reading and writing reflects how written language is used in their community. While reading and writing are part of daily life for almost every family, families use written language for different purposes in different communities (Heath, 1983). It is important to make clear that children have a wide range of literacy experiences in both middle-class and working-class families, even though they might be different (Taylor, 1983; Taylor & Dorsey-Gaines, 1987). In some communities written language is used mainly as a tool for practical purposes such as paying bills, and in some communities reading and writing are also used for leisure time activities. In other communities written language serves even wider functions, such as debating social and political issues.

Teachers demonstrate the functions of written language and provide opportunities for students to experiment with reading and writing in these ways:

- Posting signs in the classroom
- Making a list of classroom rules
- Using literacy materials in dramatic play centers
- Writing notes to students in the class
- Exchanging messages with classmates
- Reading and writing stories
- Making posters about favorite books
- Labeling classroom items
- Drawing and writing in journals
- Writing morning messages
- Recording questions and information on charts
- Writing notes to parents

- Reading and writing letters to pen pals
- Reading and writing charts and maps

Concepts About Print

Through their early experiences with reading and writing, children learn that talk can be written down and read; they also learn how text is arranged in books, letters, charts, and other reading materials. They acquire three types of concepts about print:

1. *Book orientation concepts.* Students learn how to hold books and turn pages, and they learn that the text, not the illustrations, carries the message.
2. *Direction concepts.* Students learn that print is written and read from left to right and from top to bottom on a page, and they match voice to print, pointing word by word to text, as it is read aloud. Students also notice punctuation marks and learn their names and purposes.
3. *Letter and word concepts.* Students learn to identify letter names and match upper- and lowercase letters. They also learn that words are composed of letters; that sentences are composed of words, and capital letters highlight the first word in a sentence; and that spaces mark boundaries between words and between sentences (Clay, 1972, 1979).

Children acquire these concepts about print as they are read to and read books themselves, as they view demonstrations of writing, and as they engage in writing activities. These concepts are not prerequisites for learning to read or write; rather, children learn these concepts about print through literacy experiences.

Concepts About Words

Children's understanding of the concept of "a word" is an important part of becoming literate. Young children have only vague notions of language terms, such as *word, letter, sound, sentence,* that teachers use in talking about reading and writing (Downing, 1970, 1971–1972). Researchers have found that young children move through several levels of awareness and understanding about this terminology during the primary grades (Downing & Oliver, 1973–1974).

Preschoolers equate words and the objects the words represent. As they are introduced to reading and writing experiences, children begin to differentiate between objects and words, and finally they come to appreciate that words have meanings of their own. Templeton (1980) explains children's development with these two examples:

> When asked if "dog" were a word, a four-year-old acquaintance of mine jumped up from the floor, began barking ferociously, and charged through the house, alternatively panting and woofing. Confronted with the same question, an eight-year-old friend responded "of course 'dog' is a word," and went on to explain how the spelling represented spoken sounds and how the word *dog* stood for a particular type of animal. (p. 454)

Several researchers have investigated children's understanding of a word as a unit of language. Papandropoulou and Sinclair (1974) identified four stages of word consciousness. At the first level young children do not differen-tiate between words and things. At the next level children describe words as labels for things. They consider words that stand for objects as words, but do not classify articles and prepositions as words because words such as *the* and *with* cannot be represented with objects. At the third level children understand that words carry meaning and stories are built from words. At the fourth level more fluent readers and writers describe words as autonomous elements having meanings of their own with definite semantic and syntactic relation-ships. Children might say, "You make words with letters." Also, at this level children understand that words have different appearances: They can be spoken, listened to, read, and written.

In reading, children move from recognizing environmental print to reading decontextualized words in books. Young children begin reading by recognizing logos on fast food restaurants, department stores, grocery stores, and com-monly used household items within familiar contexts (Harste, Woodward, & Burke, 1984). They recognize the golden arches of McDonald's and say "McDonald's," but when they are shown the word *McDonald's* written on a sheet of paper without the familiar sign and restaurant setting, they cannot read the word. Researchers have found that young emergent readers depend on context to read familiar words and memorized texts (Dyson, 1984; Sulzby, 1985). Slowly, children develop relationships linking form and meaning as they learn concepts about written language and gain more experience reading and writing.

When children begin writing, they use scribbles or single letters to repre-sent complex ideas (Clay, 1975; Schickedanz, 1990). As they learn about letter names and phoneme-grapheme correspondences, they use one letter or two or three to stand for words. At first they run their writing together, but they slowly learn to segment words and leave spaces between words. They sometimes add dots or lines as markers between words, or they draw circles around words. They also move from capitalizing words randomly to using capital letters at the beginning of sentences and to mark proper nouns and adjectives. Similarly, children move from using periods at the end of each line of writing to marking the ends of sentences with periods. Then they learn about other end-of-sentence markers and finally punctuation marks that are embed-ded in sentences.

Concepts About the Alphabet

The fourth concept that children develop is about the alphabet and how letters are used to represent phonemes. Children use this phonics knowledge to decode unfamiliar words as they read and to create spellings for words as they write. Too often it is assumed that phonics instruction is the most important component of the reading program for young children, but phonics is only one of the four language systems. Emerging readers and writers use all four language systems as well as their knowledge about written language concepts as they read and write.

The Alphabetic Principle. The *alphabetic principle* suggests a one-to-one correspondence between the phonemes (or sounds) and graphemes (or letters) such that each letter consistently represents one sound. English, however, is not a purely phonetic language. The 26 letters represent approximately 44 phonemes, and three letters—*c, q,* and *x*—are superfluous because they do not represent unique phonemes. The letter *c,* for example, can represent either /k/ as in *cat* or /s/ as in *city,* and it can be joined with *h* for the digraph /ch/. To further complicate the situation, there are more than 500 spellings to represent the 44 phonemes. Consonants are more consistent and predictable than vowels. Long *e,* for instance, is spelled 14 different ways in common words (Horn, 1957).

Researchers estimate that words are spelled phonetically approximately half the time (Hanna, Hanna, Hodges, & Rudorf, 1966), and the nonphonetic spellings of many words reflect morphological information. The word *sign,* for instance, is a shortened form of *signature,* and the spelling shows this relationship. Spelling the word phonetically (e.g., *sine*) might seem simpler, but the phonetic spelling lacks semantic information (Venezky, 1970).

Other reasons for this mismatch between phonemes, graphemes, and spellings can be found by examining events in the history of the English language (Tompkins & Yaden, 1986). The introduction of the printing press in England in 1476 helped to stabilize spelling. The word *said,* for example, continues to be spelled as it was pronounced in Shakespeare's time. Our pronunciation today does not reflect the word's meaning as the past tense of *say* because pronunciations have continued to evolve in the last 500 years, but only a few spellings have been "modernized." In addition, approximately 75% of English words have been borrowed from languages around the world, and many of the words, especially the more recently acquired words, have retained their native spellings. For example, *souvenir* was borrowed from French in the middle 1700s and retains its French spelling. It literally means "to remember."

Richard Hodges (1981) concludes that English spelling cannot be explained by the alphabetic principle alone. It is not merely a reflection of phoneme-grapheme correspondences; rather, our spelling system includes morphological, semantic, and syntactic elements, and it has been influenced by historical events.

Letter Names.   The most basic information that children learn about the alphabet is how to identify and form the letters in handwriting. They notice letters in environmental print and they often learn to sing the ABC song. By the time children enter kindergarten, they can usually recognize some letters, especially those in their own names, names of family members and pets, and common words in their homes and communities. Children can also write some of these familiar letters.

Young children associate letters with meaningful contexts—names, signs, tee-shirts, and cereal boxes. Baghban (1984) notes that the letter *M* was the first letter her daughter noticed. She pointed to *M* in the word *K Mart* and called it *McDonald's.* Even though the child confused a store and a restaurant, this account demonstrates how young children make associations with letters. Research suggests that children do not learn alphabet letter names in any particular order or by isolating letters from meaningful written language. McGee and Richgels (1990) conclude that learning letters of the alphabet depends on many, many experiences with meaningful written language.

Children become aware that words are composed of letters by reading environmental print (e.g., signs on restaurants and stores, labels on food packages) and also seeing their own name and the names of family members written. Even when children know the names of several letters and use mock letters as well as real letters in their writing, they have different concepts about letters. For example, Anne Haas Dyson (1984) reports that 5-year-old Dexter said, "N spell my grandmama" when his grandmother's name was Hele*n* (p. 262). This child's comments about letters show that emergent readers do not have the same concepts about letters that more accomplished readers have.

Being able to name the letters of the alphabet is the best predictor of beginning reading achievement, even though knowing the names of the letters does not directly impact on a child's ability to read (Adams, 1990). A more likely explanation for this relationship between letter knowledge and reading is that children who have been actively involved in reading and writing activities before entering first grade know the names of the letters, and they are more likely to emerge quickly into reading. Simply teaching children to name the letters without the accompanying reading and writing experiences does not have this effect.

Phoneme-Grapheme Correspondences.   Many letter names provide information about phonemes. For example, when children pronounce the letter *B* or *M,* the letter name helps them predict the phonemes /b/ and /m/. Letter names are especially useful for identifying consonant and long vowel sounds. Children deduce the phonemes for many letters, and teachers teach other phoneme-grapheme correspondences through demonstrations, minilessons, and reading and writing experiences.

Teachers demonstrate how to sound out words as they write messages with children, showing children how to draw out the pronunciation of a word in order to hear several sounds. They conduct minilessons on phoneme-grapheme correspondences using words taken from literature that children have read or listened to read aloud. In kindergarten a teacher might focus on /m/ using Max's name after reading *Where the Wild Things Are* (Sendak, 1962), and a second-grade teacher might teach the hard sound (/k/) and the soft sound (/s/) of the letter *c* after reading *The City Mouse and the Country Mouse* (Cauley, 1984).

Children apply what they are learning about phoneme-grapheme correspondences as they read and write, but without meaningful reading and writing activities, children see little reason to learn about the alphabetic principle (Freppon & Dahl, 1991). Teachers sit with children as they read and write, supporting them as they sound out words. As they read, children use the beginning sound of the word together with other syntactic and semantic information to guess the unknown word. As they write, children pronounce the word slowly and write the letters they hear. For example, children often use MI to spell *my* and use BK for *book.* At first children use one or two letters to stand for an entire word, but as they learn more about written language, they include letters to represent all sound features in their spellings.

Children develop the ability to break apart a word such as *bell* into its three component sounds (/b/, /e/, and /l/) and manipulate them by changing *bell* to *well* or *bell* to *best* (Adams, 1990). This understanding that words are composed of a series of individual sounds, called *phonemic awareness,* develops as a consequence of learning to read and write, or it may be a prerequisite for fluent reading and writing (Yopp, 1992). Researchers are not sure how phonemic awareness develops, but they recognize its importance in becoming literate.

Onsets and Rimes.   Syllables can be divided into two parts: onsets and rimes. The *onset* is the consonant sound, if any, that precedes the vowel, and the *rime* is the vowel and any consonant sounds that follow it (Treiman, 1985). For example, in *show*, *sh* is the onset and *ow* is the rime, and in *ball*, *b* is the onset and *all* is the rime. For *at* and *up*, there is no onset; the entire word is the rime. Research has shown that children make more errors decoding and spelling final consonants than initial consonants, and they make more errors on vowels than on consonants (Treiman, 1985). These problem areas correspond to rimes, and educators now speculate that onsets and rimes could provide the key to unlocking phonemic awareness.

Children can separate the onsets and rimes in words and focus their attention on a rime, such as *ake*, and its related words: *bake, cake lake, make rake, take, wake*. These words can be read and spelled by analogy because the vowel sounds are consistent in rimes. Wylie and Durrell (1970) identified 37 rimes that can be used to produce nearly 500 words that primary-grade students read and write. These rimes and some common words using them are presented in the Teacher's Notebook on page 249. Educators speculate that this approach to decoding and spelling words holds more promise than the traditional approach to long and short vowel rules, and research is under way to assess the usefulness of onsets and rimes.

YOUNG CHILDREN EMERGE INTO READING

Children move through three stages as they learn to read during the primary grades: emergent, early, and fluent (Cutting, n.d.). The first stage is emergent reading, and children enter this stage expecting to learn to read. Children learn to behave like a reader and read books. They reread familiar books and examine new books. Children often memorize the story and use picture cues to guide their "readings." Children come to realize that the text, not the pictures, carries the story, and they begin pointing at familiar words and searching for other words. As children try to match the story in their heads with the words on each page of the text, they begin to move into the second stage.

The second stage is early reading. Children read orally, but their reading is slow and deliberate as they match each word they say with a word on the page. Often they point at each word as they say it aloud. They continue to depend on their memory of the text, and picture clues are still important, but children increasingly use phonological, semantic, syntactic, and pragmatic cues in the text. They feel success in their growing ability as readers, and they increasingly make self-corrections as they read.

The third stage is fluent reading, and children at this stage have learned how to read. Children usually read silently, and their reading is automatic except when they meet difficult words. Then they use phonological, semantic, syntactic, and pragmatic cues to identify these words so that they can continue reading. Students read widely and, if they enjoy reading, develop a lifelong interest in reading.

Teacher's Notebook

37 Rimes and Some Common Words Using Them

-ack	black, pack, quack, stack
-ail	mail, nail, sail, tail
-ain	brain, chain, plain, rain
-ake	cake, shake, take, wake
-ale	male, sale, tale, whale
-ame	came, flame, game, name
-an	can, man, pan, than
-ank	bank, drank, sank, thank
-ap	cap, clap, map, slap
-ash	cash, dash, flash, trash
-at	bat, cat, rat, that
-ate	gate, hate, late, plate
-aw	claw, draw, jaw, saw
-ay	day, play, say, way
-eat	beat, heat, meat, wheat
-ell	bell, sell, shell, well
-est	best, chest, nest, west
-ice	ice, mice, nice, rice
-ick	brick, pick, sick, thick
-ide	bride, hide, ride, side
-ight	bright, fight, light, might
-ill	fill, hill, kill, will
-in	chin, grin, pin, win
-ine	fine, line, mine, nine
-ing	king, sing, thing, wing
-ink	pink, sink, think, wink
-ip	drip, hip, lip, ship
-ir	fir, sir, stir
-ock	block, clock, knock, sock
-oke	choke, joke, poke, woke
-op	chop, drop, hop, shop
-ore	chore, more, shore, store
-or	for, or
-uck	duck, luck, suck, truck
-ug	bug, drug, hug, rug
-ump	bump, dump, hump, lump
-unk	bunk, dunk, junk, sunk

Kindergartners match pictures and sentence strips as they retell a familiar story.

Assisted Reading

Assisted reading is one approach to help young children emerge into reading. It extends the familiar routine of parents reading to their children (Hoskisson, 1974, 1975a, 1975b, 1977; Hoskisson & Krohm, 1974; Hoskisson, Sherman, & Smith, 1974). In this approach a child and a teacher (or another fluent reader) sit together to read a book. As the teacher reads aloud, the child listens and looks at the illustrations in the book. Gradually the child assumes more and more of the reading until the child is doing most of the reading and the teacher fills in the difficult words. The three stages in assisted reading are:

    1. Reading to Children. Teachers read to children and have them repeat each phrase or sentence. At first most children's attention will not be on the lines of print as they repeat the words. They may be looking around the room or at the pictures in the book. To direct their attention to the lines of print, the teacher points to the words on each line as they are read. This allows children to see that lines of print are read from left to right, not randomly. Many different books are read and reread during this stage. Rereading is important because the visual images of the words must be seen and read many times to ensure their recognition in other books. Later, one repetition of a word may be sufficient for subsequent recognition of the word in context.

    2. Shared Reading. When children begin to notice that some words occur repeatedly, from book to book, they enter the second stage of assisted reading. In this stage the teacher reads and children repeat or echo the words; however, the teacher does not read the words the children seem to recognize. The teacher omits those words, and children fill them in. The fluency, or flow, of the reading should not be interrupted. If fluency is not maintained during this stage, children will not grasp the meaning of the passage, because the syntactic and semantic cues that come from a smooth flow of language will not be evident to them.

3. Becoming Independent Readers. The transition to stage 3 occurs when children begin to ask the teacher to let them read the words themselves. Stage 3 may be initiated in this manner by the child, or it may be introduced by the teacher. When children know enough words to do the initial reading themselves, they read and the teacher willingly supplies any unknown words. It is important to assist children so that the fluency of the reading is not disrupted. In stage 3, children do the major portion of the reading, but they tire more easily because they are struggling to use all the information they have acquired about written language. Children at this stage need constant encouragement; they must not feel a sense of frustration, because moving to independent reading is a gradual process.

A list of easy-to-read books that are written at approximately the second-grade level is presented in Figure 7–1. These books include humorous stories such as Peggy Parish's *Amelia Bedelia* (1963), *The Josefina Story Quilt* (Coerr, 1986) and other historical stories, and informational books such as *It Could Still Be Water* (Fowler, 1992). These books are a transition between picture books and chapter books, and they have more text on each page even though they are sized more like a chapter book than a picture book and most pages include a picture. Young children who are developing confidence as readers enjoy reading these books, as do older students who are less successful readers.

Teachers use assisted reading whenever they read with individual children during reading workshop and literature focus units. They sense the child's familiarity with the book and his or her comfort level, and then they support the child by doing most of the reading or supplying only the words the child does not seem to know. Parents, aides, and cross-age reading buddies also need to understand the three stages of assisted reading and how to use assisted reading to support young children as they emerge into reading.

Cross-Age Reading Buddies. One way to use assisted reading in a kindergarten or first-grade classroom is with cross-age reading buddies. A class of upper-grade students can be paired with a class of primary-grade children, and the students become reading buddies. Older students read books aloud to younger children, and they also read with the children using assisted reading. Cross-age tutoring is supported by research (Cohen, Kulik, & Kulik, 1982), and teachers report that students' reading fluency increases and their attitudes toward school and learning become more positive (Labbo & Teale, 1990; Morrice & Simmons, 1991).

Teachers arranging a buddy reading program decide when to get together, how long each session will last, and what the reading schedule will be. Primary-grade teachers explain the program to their students and talk about activities the buddies will be doing together. Primary-grade students may want to draw pictures in advance to give to their buddies. Upper-grade teachers

Figure 7–1   Easy-to-Read Books

Stories

Benchley, N. (1979). *Running owl the hunter.* New York: Harper & Row.

Blume, J. (1971). *Freckle juice.* New York: Dell.

Blume, J. (1981). *The one in the middle is the green kangaroo.* New York: Dell.

Brown, M. (1984). *There's no place like home.* New York: Parents Magazine Press.

Cohen, M. (1977). *When will I read?* New York: Dell.

Delton, J. (1992). *Lights, action, land-ho!* New York: Dell. (And other books in the series)

Eastman, P. D. (1960). *Are you my mother?* New York: Random House.

Giff, P. R. (1984). *The beast in Ms. Rooney's room.* NY: Dell. (And other books in the series)

Giff, P. R. (1993). *The great shamrock disaster.* New York: Dell. (And other books in the series)

Hoban, L. (1976). *Arthur's pen pal.* New York: Harper & Row.

Lewison, W. C. (1992). *Buzz said the bee.* New York: Scholastic.

Lobel, A. (1970). *Frog and Toad are friends.* New York: Harper & Row. (And other books in the Frog and Toad series)

Lobel, A. (1972). *Mouse tales.* New York: Harper & Row.

Lobel, A. (1978). *The pancake.* New York: Greenwillow.

Marzollo, J., & Marzollo, C. (1987). *Jed and the space bandits.* New York: Dial.

Parish, P. (1963). *Amelia Bedelia.* New York: Harper & Row. (And other books in the series)

Schwartz, A. (1982). *There is a carrot in my ear and other noodle tales.* New York: Harper & Row.

Schwartz, A. (1984). *In a dark, dark room.* New York: Scholastic.

Sharmat, M. W. (1974). *Nate the great goes undercover.* New York: Dell. (And other books in the Nate the Great series)

Smith, J. (1991). *But no elephants.* New York: Parents Magazine Press.

Yolen, J. (1980). *Commander Toad in space.* New York: Coward-McCann. (And other books in the Commander Toad series)

Ziefert, H. (1983). *Small potatoes club.* New York: Dell. (And other books in the series)

Poetry

Hopkins, L. B. (1984). *Surprises.* New York: Harper & Row.

Hopkins, L. B. (1985). *More surprises.* New York: Harper & Row.

Biographies

Adler, D. A. (1989). *A picture book of Abraham Lincoln.* New York: Holiday House. (And other biographies by the author)

Krensky, S. (1991). *Christopher Columbus.* New York: Random House.

History

Benchley, N. (1969). *Sam the minuteman.* New York: Harper & Row.

Benchley, N. (1977). *George the drummer boy.* New York: Harper & Row.

Brenner, B. (1978). *Wagon wheels.* New York: Harper & Row.

Byars, B. (1985). *The Golly sisters go west.* New York: Harper & Row.

Coerr, E. (1988). *Chang's paper pony.* New York: Harper & Row.

Coerr, E. (1986). *The Josefina story quilt.* New York: Harper & Row.

Greeson, J. (1991). *An American army of two.* Minneapolis: Carolrhoda.

Monjo, F. N. (1970). *The drinking gourd.* New York: Harper & Row.

Roop, P., & Roop, C. (1985). *Keep the lights burning, Abbie.* Minneapolis: Carolrhoda.

Roop, P., & Roop, C. (1986). *Buttons for General Washington.* Minneapolis: Carolrhoda.

Sandin, J. (1981). *The long way to a new land.* New York: Harper & Row.

Schulz, W. A. (1991). *Wil and Ory.* Minneapolis: Carolrhoda.

Wetterer, M. K. (1990). *Kate Shelley and the midnight express.* Minneapolis: Carolrhoda.

Science

Brown, M. (1984). *There's no place like home.* New York: Parents Magazine Press.

Cole, J. (1986). *Hungry, hungry sharks.* Chicago: Random House.

Fowler, A. (1990). *It could still be a bird.* Chicago: Childrens Press. (And other books in the series)

Fowler, A. (1990). *It's a good thing there are insects.* Chicago: Childrens Press.

Parish, P. (1974). *Dinosaur time.* New York: Harper & Row.

Smith, M. (1991). *A snake mistake.* New York: HarperCollins.

Ziefert, H. (1991). *Bob and Shirley: A tale of two lobsters.* New York: HarperCollins.

teach a series of minilessons about how to work with young children, how to read aloud and encourage children to make predictions, how to use assisted reading, how to select books to appeal to younger children, and how to help them respond to books. Then older students choose books to read aloud and practice reading them until they can read the books fluently.

At the first meeting, the students pair off, get acquainted, and read together. They also talk about the books they have read and perhaps write in special reading logs. Buddies also may want to go to the library and choose the books they will read at the next session.

There are significant social benefits to cross-age tutoring programs, too. Children get acquainted with other children that they might otherwise not meet, and they learn how to work with older or younger children. As they talk about books they have read, they share personal experiences and interpretations. They also talk about reading strategies, how to choose books, and their favorite authors or illustration styles. Sometimes reading buddies write notes back and forth, or the two classrooms plan holiday celebrations together, and these activities strengthen the social connections between the children.

Traveling Bags of Books.   Teachers can collect text sets of three, four, or five books on various topics for children to take home and read with their parents (Reutzel & Fawson, 1990). For example, teachers might collect copies of *Hattie and the Fox* (Fox, 1986), *The Gingerbread Boy* (Galdone, 1975), *Flossie and the Fox* (McKissack, 1986), and *Rosie's Walk* (Hutchins, 1968) for a traveling bag of fox stories. Then children and their parents read one or more of the books and draw or write a response to the books they have read in the reading log that accompanies the books in the traveling bag. Children keep the bag at home for several days and then return it to school so that another child can borrow it. Text sets for 10 traveling bags are listed in Figure 7–2. Many of these text sets include combinations of stories, informational books, and poems. Teachers can also add small toys, stuffed animals, audiotapes of one of the books, or other related objects to the bags.

Teachers often introduce traveling bags at a special parents' meeting or an open house get-together and explain how parents use assisted reading to read with their children. It is important that parents understand that their children may not be familiar with the books and that it is not expected that children will be able to read them independently. Teachers also talk about the responses children and parents write in the reading log and show sample entries done the previous year.

Shared Reading

Teachers often share stories and other books with children by reading the book aloud as they follow along in individual books or enlarged texts called *big books* which everyone can see. This approach is called *shared reading,* and teachers use it to share the enjoyment of good books with students when the students cannot read the books independently (Holdaway, 1979). Through shared reading, teachers also demonstrate how print works, provide opportunities for students to use the prediction strategy, and increase children's confidence in their ability to read. Shared reading is often used with emergent readers. However, teachers also use shared reading with older students who

Figure 7–2   *Text Sets for Traveling Bags of Books*

Books About Airplanes

Barton, R. (1982). *Airport*. New York: Harper & Row.
McPhail, D. (1987). *First flight*. Boston: Little, Brown.
Petersen, D. (1981). *Airplanes* (A new true book). Chicago: Childrens Press.
Ziegler, S. (1988). *A visit to the airport*. Chicago: Childrens Press.

Books About Dogs

Barracca, D., & Barracca, S. (1990). *The adventures of taxi dog*. New York: Dial.
Bridwell, N. (1963). *Clifford the big red dog*. New York: Greenwillow.
Cole, J. (1991). *My puppy is born*. New York: Morrow.
Reiser, L. (1992). *Any kind of dog*. New York: Greenwillow.

Books by Ezra Jack Keats

Keats, E. J. (1962). *The snowy day*. New York: Viking.
Keats, E. J. (1964). *Whistle for Willie*. New York: Viking.
Keats, E. J. (1967). *Peter's chair*. New York: Harper & Row.
Keats, E. J. (1969). *Goggles*. New York: Macmillan.
Keats, E. J. (1970). *Hi cat!* New York: Macmillan.

Books About Frogs and Toads

Lobel, A. (1970). *Frog and Toad are friends*. New York: Harper & Row.
Mayer, M. (1974). *Frog goes to dinner*. New York: Dial.
Pallotta, J. (1990). *The frog alphabet book: And other awesome amphibians*. Watertown, MA: Charlesbridge.
Watts, B. (1991). *Frog*. New York: Lodestar.
Yolen, J. (1980). *Commander Toad in space*. New York: Coward-McCann.

Books About Mice

Cauley, L. B. (1984). *The city mouse and the country mouse*. New York: Putnam.
Henkes, K. (1991). *Chrysanthemum*. New York: Greenwillow.
Lionni, L. (1969). *Alexander and the wind-up mouse*. New York: Pantheon.
Lobel, A. (1977). *Mouse soup*. New York: Harper & Row.
Numeroff, L. J. (1985). *If you give a mouse a cookie*. New York: Harper & Row.

Books About Numbers

Aker, S. (1990). *What comes in 2's, 3's, & 4's?* New York: Simon & Schuster.
Bang, M. (1983). *Ten, nine, eight*. New York: Greenwillow.
Giganti, P., Jr. (1992). *Each orange had 8 slices: A counting book*. New York: Greenwillow.
Tafuri, N. (1986). *Who's counting?* New York: Greenwillow.

Books About Plants

Ehlert, L. (1987). *Growing vegetable soup*. San Diego: Harcourt Brace Jovanovich.
Ehlert, L. (1991). *Red leaf, yellow leaf*. San Diego: Harcourt Brace Jovanovich.
Fowler, A. (1990). *It could still be a tree*. Chicago: Childrens Press.
Gibbons, G. (1984). *The seasons of Arnold's apple tree*. San Diego: Harcourt Brace Jovanovich.
King, E. (1990). *The pumpkin patch*. New York: Dutton.
Lobel, A. (1990). *Alison's zinnia*. New York: Greenwillow.

Books About Rain

Branley, F. M. (1985). *Flash, crash, rumble, and roll*. New York: Harper & Row.
Polacco, P. (1990). *Thunder cake*. New York: Philomel.
Shulevitz, U. (1969). *Rain rain rivers*. New York: Farrar, Straus & Giroux.
Spier, P. (1982). *Rain*. New York: Doubleday.

Books About the Three Bears

Cauley, L. B. (1981). *Goldilocks and the three bears*. New York: Putnam.
Galdone, P. (1972). *The three bears*. New York: Clarion Books.
Tolhurst, M. (1990). *Somebody and the three Blairs*. New York: Orchard Books.
Turkle, B. (1976). *Deep in the forest*. New York: Dutton.

Books About Trucks

Crews, D. (1980). *Truck*. New York: Greenwillow.
Rockwell, A. (1984). *Trucks*. New York: Dutton.
Siebert, D. (1984). *Truck song*. New York: Harper & Row.

cannot read the shared book independently. Multiple copies must be available for students to follow along in.

Step by Step

1. *Introducing the Book.* Teachers introduce the book by activating children's knowledge about the topic or by presenting new information on a topic related to the book, and then by showing the cover of the book and reading the title and author. Then children make predictions about the book. The purpose of these introductory activities is to involve children in the reading activity and to build their anticipation.

2. *Reading the Book.* The teacher reads the book aloud while children follow along in individual copies of the book or on a big book positioned on a chart rack beside the teacher. The teacher models fluent reading and uses a dramatic style to keep the children's attention. Teachers encourage children to chime in on words they can predict and phrases, sentences, and refrains that are repeated. Periodically, teachers stop to ask students to make predictions about the story or to redirect their attention to the text.

3. *Responding to the Book.* Children respond to the book by drawing and writing in reading logs and sharing their responses in a grand conversation. Whenever children read books, enjoyment is the first and foremost goal. Afterwards, they use the book to learn more about written language.

4. *Doing Repeated Readings.* Children and the teacher read the book again together in a group, and children reread the book independently or with partners. Children need to read the book several times in order to become comfortable with the text. They may also reread the book using a listening center.

5. *Exploring the Text.* Teachers use the book as the basis for minilessons to explore letters, words, and sentences in the text. Minilessons may also focus on rhyme, word identification strategies, and reading procedures, strategies, and skills.

6. *Extending the Interpretation.* Students extend their interpretations of the book through other reading activities and through talk, drama, and writing projects.

Figure 7–3 presents a plan for using these six steps for a shared reading of *A House Is a House for Me* (Hoberman, 1978), a rhyming list of the dwellings of various animals and other things. This lesson is appropriate for second and third graders.

Predictable Books. The stories and other books that teachers use for shared reading with young children often have repeated words and sentences, rhyme, or other patterns. Books that use these patterns are known as *predictable books*. They are a valuable tool for emergent readers because the repeated words and sentences, patterns, and sequence enable children to predict the next sentence or episode in the story or other book (Bridge, 1979; Heald-Taylor, 1987; Rhodes, 1981; Tompkins & Webeler, 1983). Four types of predictable books are:

Figure 7–3   *A Plan for Shared Reading Using* A House Is a House for Me

1. Introduce the Book

The teacher introduces *A House Is a House for Me* (Hoberman, 1978) through a discussion about houses. Children talk about the houses they live in—apartments, mobile homes, and single family dwellings—and hotels and motels, tents, and other temporary houses. Next the teacher shows children objects and pictures of a fish, a bird, a cloud, and a car, and they think of houses for these things. Then the teacher shows the cover of a big book version of *A House Is a House for Me* and explains that this book is about houses. Before beginning to read, the teacher asks students to name some houses that might be included in the book.

2. Read the Book

The teacher reads the book aloud while children follow along in a big book positioned on a chart rack. The children sit on a rug on the floor immediately in front of the teacher so that all children can see the text in the big book. The teacher points to each word as it is read and encourages the children to join in on predictable and rhyming words. The teacher reads the book expressively, highlighting the catchy rhythm and rhyme of the book.

3. Respond to the Book

Immediately after reading, the children move into a circle for a grand conversation to share their reactions to the book. One child might begin by reciting a "house is a house" verse he has invented:

> *A nest is a home for a bird,*
> *The ground is the house for a worm*
> *And a house is a home for me!*

Other children take turns talking about the book and inventing their own verses. Children draw pictures of their favorite parts of the book, and the teacher helps them write the verses. These pictures are added to a bulletin board display about the book.

4. Do Repeated Readings

Children and the teacher read the book again together in a group, and children reread the book independently or with partners. Children need to read the book several times in order to become comfortable with the text. They may also reread the book using a listening center.

5. Explore the Text

The teacher uses the book for minilessons about the sentence pattern "A _____ is a house for a _____" and about rhyming words. Children also identify important words and phrases from the book and write them on a word wall.

6. Extend the Interpretation

The teacher reads aloud two other books about houses, *The House on Maple Street* (Pryor, 1987) and *A House for a Hermit Crab* (Carle, 1987), and sets out a set of Marc Brown's *There's No Place Like Home* (1984), an easy-to-read book that is similar to Hoberman's, for children to read and respond to in small groups. Students also work on projects to extend their interpretation of *A House Is a House for Me*. One group might construct a variety of houses for a display, a second group might write its own version of the book, and a third group might decide to learn more about a special kind of house—Indian teepees. Other children write books about their own homes, make charts of rhyming words, or pursue other projects.

Repetition. In some books, phrases and sentences are repeated over and over. Sometimes each episode or section of the text ends with the same words or a refrain, and in other books the same statement or question is repeated. For example, in *The Little Red Hen* (Galdone, 1973), the animals repeat "Not I" when the little red hen asks them to help her plant the seeds, harvest the wheat, and bake the bread. After their refusals to help, the hen each time says, "Then I will."

Cumulative sequence. The cumulative sequence category includes books in which phrases or sentences are repeated and expanded in each episode. In *The Gingerbread Boy* (Galdone, 1975), for instance, the gingerbread boy repeats and expands his boast as he meets each character on his run away from the little old man and the little old woman.

Rhyme and rhythm. Rhyme and rhythm are important devices in these books. The sentences have a strong beat, and rhyme is used at the end of each line or in another poetic scheme. Also, some books have an internal rhyme within lines rather than at the end of lines. One example of a book in this category is Dr. Seuss's *Hop on Pop* (1963).

Sequential patterns. Books in this category use a familiar sequence—such as months of the year, days of the week, numbers 1 to 10, or letters of the alphabet—to structure the text. For example, *The Very Hungry Caterpillar* (Carle, 1969) combines number and day of the week sequences as the caterpillar eats through an amazing array of foods during the week.

A list of predictable books illustrating each of these patterns is presented in Figure 7–4.

Big Books. *Big books* are greatly enlarged picture books that teachers use in shared reading, most commonly with primary-grade students. According to this technique, developed in New Zealand, teachers use an enlarged picture book placed on an easel or chart rack where all children can see it; the teacher reads the big book with small groups of children or with the whole class (Holdaway, 1979). Trachtenburg and Ferruggia (1989) used big books with their class of transitional first graders and found that making and reading big books dramatically improved children's reading scores on standardized achievement tests. The teachers reported that children's self-concepts as readers were decidedly improved as well.

Many picture books can be purchased in big book format, and teachers can make big books themselves by printing the text of a picture book on large sheets of posterboard and adding illustrations. The steps in making a big book are listed in Figure 7–5. Almost any type of picture book may be turned into a big book, but predictable books, nursery rhymes, songs, and poems are most popular. Heald-Taylor (1987) lists these types of big books that teachers can make:

Replica book—an exact copy of a picture book

Newly illustrated book—familiar book with new illustrations

Adapted book—a new version of a familiar picture book

Original book—an original book composed by students or the teacher

Figure 7–4   Books With Predictable Patterns

Repetitive Sentences

Asch, F. (1981). *Just like Daddy.* New York: Simon & Schuster.

Bennett, J. (1985). *Teeny tiny.* New York: Putnam.

Brown, M. W. (1947). *Goodnight moon.* New York: Harper & Row.

Brown, R. (1981). *A dark, dark tale.* New York: Dial.

Carle, E. (1973). *Have you seen my cat?* New York: Philomel.

Carle, E. (1984). *The very busy spider.* New York: Philomel.

Carle, E. (1990). *The very quiet cricket.* New York: Philomel.

Cauley, L. B. (1982). *The cock, the mouse, and the little red hen.* New York: Putnam.

Charlip, R. (1969). *What good luck! What bad luck!* New York: Scholastic.

Gag, W. (1956). *Millions of cats.* New York: Coward-McCann.

Galdone, P. (1973). *The little red hen.* New York: Seabury.

Galdone, P. (1973). *The three billy goats Gruff.* Boston: Houghton Mifflin.

Ginsburg, M. (1972). *The chick and the duckling.* New York: Macmillan.

Guarino, D. (1989). *Is your mama a llama?* New York: Scholastic.

Hill, E. (1980). *Where's Spot?* New York: Putnam.

Hutchins, P. (1968). *Rosie's walk.* New York: Macmillan.

Hutchins, P. (1972). *Good-night, owl!* New York: Macmillan.

Hutchins, P. (1986). *The doorbell rang.* New York: Morrow.

Martin, B., Jr. (1983). *Brown bear, brown bear, what do you see?* New York: Holt, Rinehart & Winston.

Martin, B., Jr. (1992). *Polar bear, polar bear, what do you hear?* New York: Holt, Rinehart & Winston.

Nelson, J. (1989). *There's a dragon in my wagon.* Cleveland: Modern Curriculum Press.

Peek, M. (1981). *Roll over!* Boston: Houghton Mifflin.

Peek, M. (1985). *Mary wore her red dress.* New York: Clarion.

Rosen, M. (1989). *We're going on a bear hunt.* New York: Macmillan.

Tafuri, N. (1984). *Have you seen my duckling?* New York: Greenwillow.

Viorst, J. (1972). *Alexander and the terrible, horrible, no good, very bad day.* New York: Atheneum.

Weiss, N. (1987). *If you're happy and you know it.* New York: Greenwillow.

Weiss, N. (1989). *Where does the brown bear go?* New York: Viking.

Westcott, N. B. (1988). *The lady with the alligator purse.* Boston: Little, Brown.

Wickstrom, S. K. (1988). *Wheels on the bus.* New York: Crown.

Williams, S. (1989). *I went walking.* San Diego: Harcourt Brace Jovanovich.

Repetitive Sentences in a Cumulative Structure

Bolton, F. (1986). *The greedy goat.* New York: Scholastic.

Brett, J. (1989). *The mitten.* New York: Putnam.

Carle, E. (1971). *Do you want to be my friend?* New York: Crowell.

Ets, M. H. (1972). *Elephant in a well.* New York: Viking.

With the big book on a chart stand or an easel, the teacher reads it aloud, pointing to every word. Before long, students join in the reading. Then the teacher rereads the book, inviting students to help with the reading. The next time the book is read, the teacher reads to the point that the text becomes predictable, such as the last word of a sentence or the beginning of a refrain, and the students supply the missing text. Having students supply missing text is important because it leads to independent reading. When students have become familiar with the text, they are invited to read the big book independently (Slaughter, 1983).

Student-Made Big Books. Students can also make big books of favorite stories. First, students choose a familiar story and write or dictate a retelling of it. Next they divide the text page by page and prepare illustrations. They write

Figure 7–4   *continued*

Flack, M. (1932). *Ask Mr. Bear.* New York: Macmillan.

Fox, H. (1986). *Hattie and the fox.* New York: Bradbury.

Galdone, P. (1975). *The gingerbread boy.* New York: Seabury.

Hutchins, P. (1968). *Rosie's walk.* New York: Macmillan.

Kellogg, S. (1974). *There was an old woman.* New York: Parents.

Kraus, R. (1970). *Whose mouse are you?* New York: Macmillan.

Peppe, R. (1970). *The house that Jack built.* New York: Delacorte.

Tolstoi, A. (1968). *The great big enormous turnip.* New York: Watts.

Westcott, N. B. (1980). *I know an old lady who swallowed a fly.* Boston: Little, Brown.

Zemach, H. (1969). *The judge.* New York: Farrar, Straus & Giroux.

Zemach, H., & Zemach, M. (1966). *Mommy, buy me a china doll.* Chicago: Follett.

Zemach, M. (1983). *The little red hen.* New York: Farrar, Straus & Giroux.

Rhyme and Rhythm

Brown, M. (1987). *Play rhymes.* New York: Dutton.

De Paola, T. (1985). *Hey diddle diddle and other Mother Goose rhymes.* New York: Putnam.

Messenger, J. (1986). *Twinkle, twinkle, little star.* New York: Macmillan.

Sendak, M. (1962). *Chicken soup with rice.* New York: Harper & Row.

Seuss, Dr. (1963). *Hop on Pop.* New York: Random House.

Seuss, Dr. (1988). *Green eggs and ham.* New York: Random House.

Sequential Patterns

Alain. (1964). *One, two, three, going to sea.* New York: Scholastic.

Carle, E. (1969). *The very hungry caterpillar.* Cleveland: Collins-World.

Carle, E. (1977). *The grouchy ladybug.* New York: Crowell.

Carle, E. (1987). *A house for a hermit crab.* Saxonville, MA: Picture Book Studio.

Domanska, J. (1985). *Busy Monday morning.* New York: Greenwillow.

Keats, E. J. (1973). *Over in the meadow.* New York: Scholastic.

Mack, S. (1974). *10 bears in my bed.* New York: Pantheon.

Martin, B., Jr. (1970). *Monday, Monday, I like Monday.* New York: Holt, Rinehart & Winston.

Numeroff, L. J. (1985). *If you give a mouse a cookie.* New York: HarperCollins.

Numeroff, L. J. (1991). *If you give a moose a muffin.* New York: HarperCollins.

Schulevitz, U. (1967). *One Monday morning.* New York: Scribner.

Sendak, M. (1975). *Seven little monsters.* New York: Harper & Row.

Wood, A. (1984). *The napping house.* San Diego: Harcourt Brace Jovanovich.

---

the text on large sheets of posterboard and add the illustrations. They make the title page and cover, and then they compile the pages. Teachers can use the book with young children just as they would use commercially produced big books and big books they made themselves.

Language Experience Approach

The *language experience approach* (LEA) is based on children's language and experiences (Ashton-Warner, 1965; Lee & Allen, 1963; Stauffer, 1970). In this approach children dictate words and sentences about their experiences, and the teacher writes the dictation for the children. The text they develop becomes the reading material. Because the language comes from the children themselves, and because the content is based on their experiences, they are usually able to read the text easily. Reading and writing are connected as students are actively involved in reading what they have written.

Figure 7–5   Steps in Constructing a Big Book

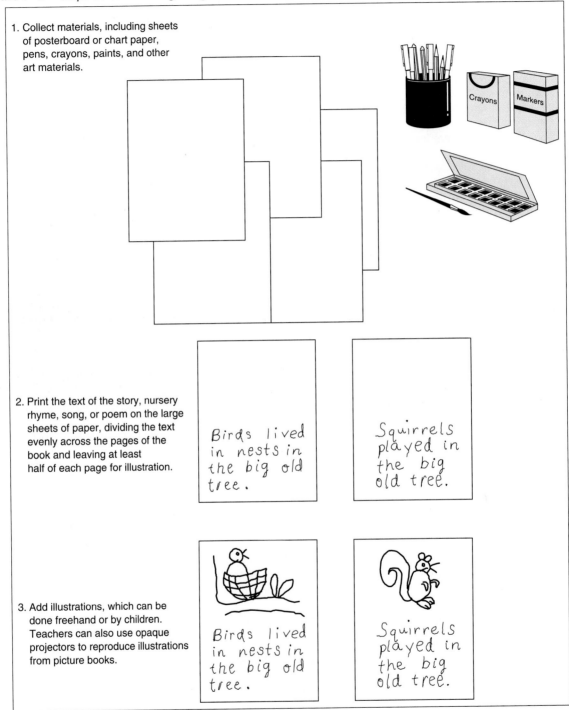

1. Collect materials, including sheets of posterboard or chart paper, pens, crayons, paints, and other art materials.

2. Print the text of the story, nursery rhyme, song, or poem on the large sheets of paper, dividing the text evenly across the pages of the book and leaving at least half of each page for illustration.

    Birds lived in nests in the big old tree.

    Squirrels played in the big old tree.

3. Add illustrations, which can be done freehand or by children. Teachers can also use opaque projectors to reproduce illustrations from picture books.

    Birds lived in nests in the big old tree.

    Squirrels played in the big old tree.

Figure 7–5   *continued*

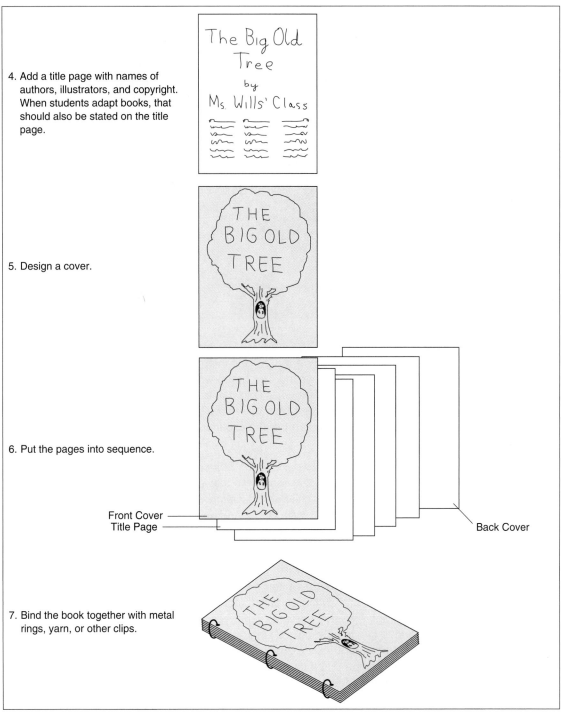

4. Add a title page with names of authors, illustrators, and copyright. When students adapt books, that should also be stated on the title page.

5. Design a cover.

6. Put the pages into sequence.

Front Cover
Title Page

Back Cover

7. Bind the book together with metal rings, yarn, or other clips.

A first-grade class made a big book with their retelling of Corduroy.

Step by Step

1. ***Providing the Experience.***   A meaningful experience is identified to serve as the stimulus for the writing. For group writing, it can be an experience shared in school, a book read aloud, a field trip, or some other experience—such as having a pet or playing in the snow—that all children are familiar with. For individual writing, the stimulus can be any experience that is important for the particular child.

2. ***Talking About the Experience.***   Students and teacher discuss the experience prior to writing. The purpose of the talk is to generate words and review the experience so that the children's dictation will be more interesting and complete. Teachers often begin with an open-ended question, such as, "What are you going to write about?" As children talk about their experiences, they clarify and organize ideas, use more specific vocabulary, and extend their understanding.

3. ***Recording the Dictation.***   Teachers write down the child's dictation. Texts for individual children are written on sheets of writing paper or in small booklets, and group texts are written on chart paper. Teachers print neatly, spell words correctly, and preserve students' language as much as possible. It is a great temptation to change the child's language to the teacher's own, in either word choice or grammar, but editing should be kept to a minimum so that children do not get the impression that their language is inferior or inadequate.

   For individual texts, teachers continue to take the child's dictation and write until the child finishes or hesitates. If the child hesitates, the teacher rereads what has been written and encourages the child to continue. For group texts, children take turns dictating sentences, and after writing each sentence, the teacher rereads it.

   It is interesting that as children become familiar with dictating to the teacher, they learn to pace their dictation to the teacher's writing speed. At first, children dictate as they think of ideas, but with experience, they watch as the teacher writes and supply the text word by word.

4. *Reading the Text.*   After the text has been dictated, the teacher reads it aloud, pointing to each word. This reading reminds children of the content of the text and demonstrates how to read it aloud with appropriate intonation. Then children join in the reading. After reading group texts together, individual children can take turns rereading. Group texts can also be copied so that each child has a copy to read independently.

5. *Extending the Text.*   After dictating, reading, and rereading their texts, children can extend the experience in several ways; for example, they can:

> Add illustrations to their writing
>
> Read their texts to classmates from the author's chair
>
> Take their texts home to share with family members
>
> Add this text to a collection of their writings
>
> Pick out words from their texts that they would like to learn to read

The language experience approach is an effective way to help children emerge into reading. Even students who have not been successful with other types of reading activities can read what they have dictated. There is a drawback, however: Teachers provide a "perfect" model when they take children's dictation—they write neatly and spell all words correctly. After language experience activities, some young children are not eager to do their own writing, because they prefer their teacher's "perfect" writing to their own childlike writing. To avoid this problem, teachers should have young children do their own writing in personal journals and writing and drawing in response-to-literature activities at the same time they are participating in language experience activities. In this way, children learn that sometimes they do their own writing and at other times the teacher takes their dictation.

Despite the differences, the language experience approach and process writing are compatible and can be used together to help kindergartners experiment with print. Karnowski (1989) points out that the two approaches are alike in several ways. Students are actively involved in creating their own text in both LEA and process writing. Reading and writing are presented as meaningful, functional, and genuine in both, and the two approaches stress the meaning-making nature of communication. Karnowski suggests that LEA can be modified to make it more like process writing:

1. *Prewriting.* Children gather ideas for writing through experiences, talk, and art.
2. *Drafting.* Children dictate the LEA text, which the teacher records. This writing is a first draft.
3. *Revising.* Children and the teacher read and reread the LEA text. They talk about the writing and make one or more changes.
4. *Editing.* Children and the teacher reread the revised text and check that spelling, punctuation, capital letters, and other mechanical considerations are correct. Then children recopy the text in a book format.

5. *Publishing.* Children share the text with classmates from the author's chair. In addition, the text can be used for other reading activities.

With these modifications, students can learn that reading and writing are whole processes.

The Morning Message.   Teachers demonstrate writing by composing morning messages for their classes to read (Kawakami-Arakaki, Oshiro, & Farnan, 1989). The teacher writes the morning message on chart paper or on the chalkboard as students watch. The message includes classroom news and should be interesting to students. An example of a morning message is:

Today is Wednesday, February 14. Happy Valentine's Day! Be sure to mail your valentines this morning. Our party is at 1:30. We will open valentines and have delicious snacks and drinks. Mrs. Gonzales and Mrs. Jenkins are coming to help with the party. We will have a good time!

As the message is written, the teacher demonstrates that writing is done from left to right and top to bottom. Then the teacher reads the message aloud, pointing to each word as it is read. The class talks about the meaning of the message, and the teacher uses the message to point out spelling, capitalization, or punctuation skills. Afterwards, children are encouraged to reread the message and pick out familiar words. Students may want to write their own messages using drawings, scribbles, and invented spellings, but they should never be asked to copy the morning message from the chalkboard. As the school year progresses, the morning message grows longer, and students assume a greater role in reading and writing the message.

Through the routine of writing and reading morning messages, young children learn a variety of things about written language. Reading and writing are demonstrated as integrated processes, and children learn that written language can be used to convey information. They learn about the direction of print, concepts about the alphabet, spelling, and other conventions used in writing. Children also learn about appropriate topics for messages and how to organize ideas into sentences.

Teachers can also take children's dictation to write messages about what the class is learning about literature or in their social studies or science theme cycles. As part of a theme cycle on bears, for instance, a kindergarten class dictated this message about bears which the teacher recorded on chart paper:

Bears are big and dangerous animals. You can see bears at the zoo or at the circus. Some bears live wild in the mountains, too. There are white polar bears and brown and black bears. Bears eat meat and fish. They really love to eat honey. Bears hibernate in the winter. Baby bears are called cubs. They stay with their moms until they are grown up.

YOUNG CHILDREN EMERGE INTO WRITING

Many young children become writers before entering kindergarten; others are introduced to writing during their first year of school (Harste, Woodward, & Burke, 1984; Temple, Nathan, Burris, & Temple, 1988). Opportunities for writing begin on the first day of kindergarten and continue on a daily basis throughout the primary grades regardless of whether children have already learned to read or write letters and words. Children often begin using a combination of art and scribbles or letterlike forms to express themselves. Their writing moves toward conventional forms as they apply concepts they are learning about written language.

Young children participate in many of the same types of writing activities that older students do. They use letters or words to label pictures they have drawn, describe experiences in journals, write letters to family members, and make books to share information. In their writing, children use a combination of adult spelling and invented spelling, or an idiosyncratic approach of using letters and other marks to represent words. Three samples of 5-year-old John's writing are presented in Figure 7–6. In the first sample, John drew a picture of a creature from outer space and labeled it "A Martian." The second sample is a menu listing the food John ate for lunch. It reads, "Peanut butter and jelly sandwich, applesauce." The third sample is a letter John wrote to his mother: "Dear Mom, I hope you are having a very Merry Christmas. Me."

Introducing Young Children to Writing

Children are introduced to writing as they watch their parents and teachers write and as they experiment with drawing and writing. Teachers help children emerge into writing as they show them how to use kid writing, teach minilessons about written language, and involve them in writing activities.

Kid Writing. Teachers demonstrate to children through morning messages and other language experience activities that people use written language to represent their thoughts. However, adult models can be very intimidating to young children, who feel at a loss to produce adult writing that is neatly written and uses conventional spelling. Teachers can contrast their writing—adult writing—with kid writing that children do. Kid writing takes many different forms. It can be scribbles or a collection of random marks on paper. Sometimes children are imitating adults' cursive writing as they scribble. Children can string together letters that have no phoneme-grapheme correspondences, or they can use one or two letters to represent entire words. Children with more experience with written language can invent spellings that represent more sound features of words, and they can apply spelling rules. A child's progressive spellings of "Abbie is my good dog. I love her very much" over a period of a year-and-a-half are presented in Figure 7–7. The child moves from using scribbles to single letters to represent words (top two entries), to spelling phonetically and misapplying a few spelling rules (third and fourth entries). Note that in the fourth example, the child is experimenting with using periods to mark spaces between words.

Kid writing is an important concept for young children because it gives them permission to experiment with written language when they draw and write. Too often children assume that they should write and spell like adults do, and they cannot. Without this confidence children do not want to write, or they ask teachers to spell every word or copy text out of books or from charts. Kid writing teaches students several strategies for writing and gives them permission to invent spellings that reflect their knowledge of written language.

Young children's writing grows out of talking and drawing. As they begin to write, their writing is literally their talk written down, and children can usually express in writing the ideas they talk about. At the same time, children's

Figure 7–6   *Three Samples of a 5-Year-Old's Writing*

Figure 7–7   A 5-Year-Old's Kid Writing

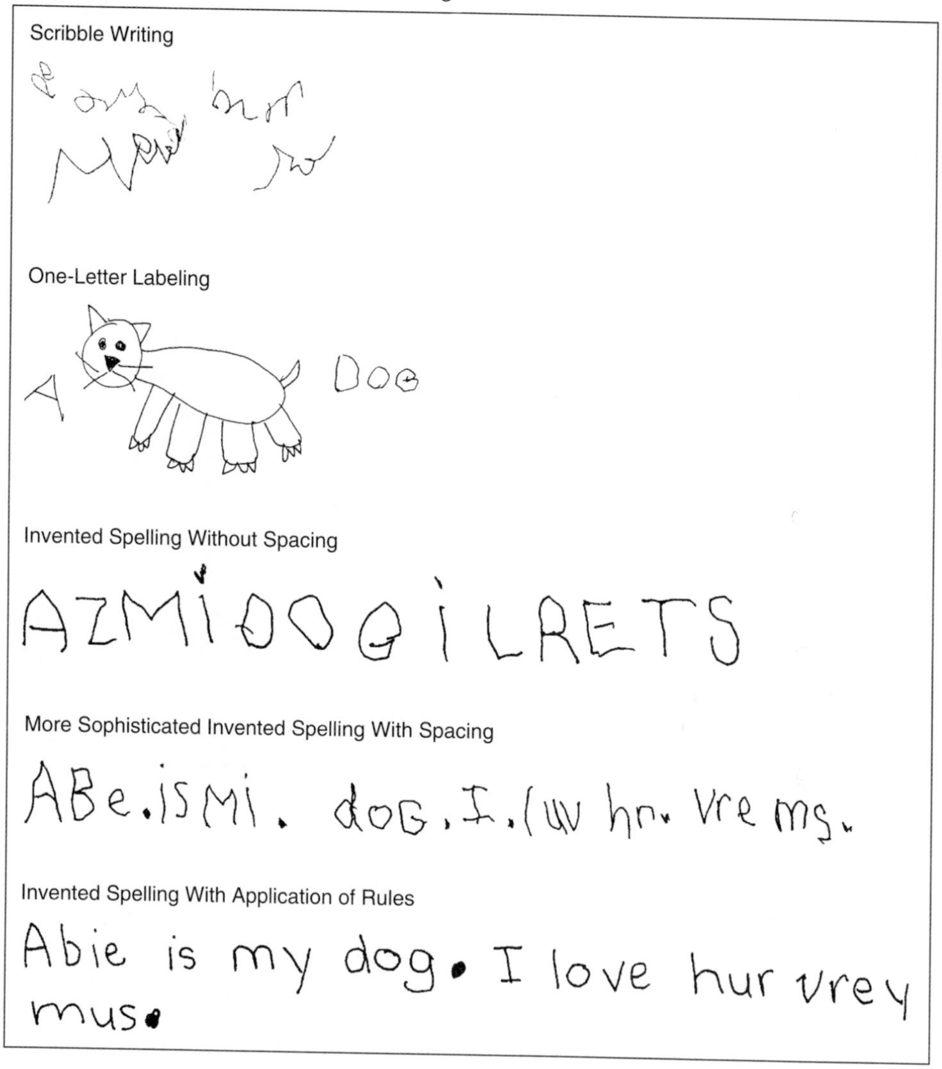

Scribble Writing

One-Letter Labeling

A   DOG

Invented Spelling Without Spacing

AZMIDOGiLRETS

More Sophisticated Invented Spelling With Spacing

ABe.isMi. doG.I.(w hn. vre ms.

Invented Spelling With Application of Rules

Abie is my dog. I love hur vrey mus.

letterlike marks develop from their drawing. With experience, children differentiate drawing and writing. Some kindergarten teachers explain to children that they should use crayons when they draw and use pencils when they write. Teachers can also differentiate where on a page children write and draw. The writing might go at the top or bottom of a page, or children can use paper with space for drawing at the top and lines for writing at the bottom.

Minilessons About Reading and Writing.   Teachers teach minilessons about written language concepts and other reading and writing topics to young children in kindergarten and the primary grades. Children learn about how reading and writing are used to convey messages and how children behave as readers and writers. A list of these topics is presented on page 269; these minilessons can be taught during reading workshop and literature focus units and through other activities.

This first grader used a combination of drawing and writing in her book about penguins.

Using the Writing Process With Young Children.   Teachers often simplify the writing process for young children by abbreviating the revising and editing stages of the writing process. At first children's revising is limited to reading the text to themselves or to the teacher to check that they have written all that they want to say. Revising becomes more formal as children learn about audience and want to "add more" or "fix" their writing to make it appeal to their classmates. Some emergent writers ignore editing altogether, and as soon as they have dashed off their drafts, they are ready to publish or share their writing. However, others change a spelling, fix a poorly written letter, or add a period to the end of the text as they read over their writings. When children begin writing, teachers accept their writing as it is written and focus on the message. As children gain experience with writing, teachers encourage them to "fix" one or two errors. Guidelines for using the writing process with emergent writers are presented in Figure 7–8.

Opportunities for Writing

Primary-grade teachers arrange the classroom, create an environment for reading and writing, and plan activities to provide opportunities for writing. Through activities such as signing in when they arrive in the classroom and exchanging mail with classmates, children use writing for authentic purposes and genuine audiences.

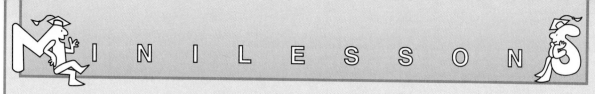

Emergent Literacy

Procedures	Concepts	Strategies and Skills
Hold a book correctly	Purposes for reading	Locate familiar words and signs
Turn pages correctly	Purposes for writing	Sing ABC song to identify a
Separate words into onsets and	Direction of print	letter
rimes	A word	Identify letter names
Behave like a reader	Uppercase letters	Match upper- and lowercase
Point at words as they are read	Lowercase letters	letters
Match each word as it is read	Alphabetic principle	Notice letters in words
aloud with the word on the	Rhyming words	Identify phoneme-grapheme
page	Repetition of words, phrases,	correspondences
Do assisted reading	and sentences	Read environmental print
Do buddy reading	Big books	Look at words as text is read
Do shared reading	Audience awareness	aloud
Dictate language experience	The author's chair	Match printed words with words
stories	Kid writing	read aloud
Behave like a writer	Adult spelling	Make predictions
Write name on sign-in sheets	Invented spelling	Notice repetition
Use writing in play activities		Notice rhyme patterns
Exchange messages with		Notice sequential patterns
classmates		Identify familiar words
Share writing in the author's		Use scribbles and random
chair		letters for writing
		Write own name
		Copy familiar words and
		environmental print
		Space between words
		Use capital letters to begin
		sentences
		Use punctuation marks to end
		sentences
		Use invented spelling
		Use sentence patterns for
		writing

Sign-In Sheets. Teachers use sign-in sheets to provide opportunities for children to practice writing their names for genuine purposes. To take attendance, they can set out a piece of paper each day with writing instruments, and children write their names as they arrive in the classroom (Harste, Woodward, & Burke, 1984). These sign-in sheets document children's learning to print their names and other concepts about written language.

Bobbi Fisher (1991), a kindergarten teacher, uses other sign-in procedures. She makes a T chart with a question written at the top of the chart and

Figure 7–8   Guidelines for Using the Writing Process With Emergent Writers

Prewriting

Prewriting is as important to young children as it is to other writers. Children write about topics they know well and have the vocabulary to express ideas about. Topics include personal experiences, classroom activities, stories students have listened to read aloud or have read independently, and theme cycle topics. Children use drawing to gather and organize ideas before writing. Children often talk about the topic or dramatize it before beginning to write.

Drafting

Young children usually write single-draft compositions. They add words to accompany drawings they have already made. The emphasis is on expressing ideas, not on handwriting skills or conventional spelling. Often children write in small booklets of paper, and they write equally well on lined or unlined paper.

Revising

Teachers play down this stage until children have learned the importance of revising to meet the needs of their readers. At first children reread their writings to see that they have included everything they wanted to say, and they make very few changes. As they gain experience, they begin to make changes to make their writing clearer and add more information to make their writing more complete.

Editing

Like revising, this stage is de-emphasized until children have learned conventional spellings for some words and have gained control over rules for capitalizing words and adding punctuation marks. To introduce editing, teachers help children make one or two corrections by erasing the error and writing the correction in pencil on the child's writing. Teachers do not circle errors on a child's paper with a red pen. As children become more fluent writers, teachers help them make more corrections.

Publishing

Children read their writings to their classmates and share their drawings. Through sharing, children develop a concept of audience and learn new ways of writing from their classmates. Kindergartners and first graders usually do not recopy their writings, but sometimes the teacher or an assistant types the final copy, changing the child's writing into conventional form. When adults recopy children's writing, however, they send a strong message that the children's writing is inadequate, unless there is a good reason for converting the kid writing to adult writing.

two answer columns, and the children write their names in the answer columns in response to the question. For example, after she brought a green pumpkin to class, she wrote, "Will this pumpkin turn orange?" Students answered the question by writing their names in the Yes column or the No column.

Teachers can develop other types of sign-in charts that ask students to make choices or offer opinions. For example, students can choose favorite books during an author study, or they can report information during a theme cycle on nutrition, such as what they eat for breakfast. Other first- and second-grade teachers have sign-up sheets for students to make books, work at a computer, or air a problem during a class meeting.

Dramatic Play Centers.   Young children learn about the functions of reading and writing as they use written language in their play. As they construct block buildings, children write signs and tape them on the buildings. As they play doctor, they write prescriptions on slips of paper, and as they play teacher, they read stories aloud to friends who are pretending to be students or to doll and stuffed-animal "students." Young children use these activities to re-enact familiar, everyday activities and to pretend to be someone or something else. Through these dramatic play activities, children use reading and writing for a variety of functions.

Housekeeping centers are probably the most common play centers in primary classrooms, but these centers can be transformed into a grocery store, a post office, or a medical center by changing the props. Materials for reading and writing are included in each of these play centers. Food packages, price stickers, and money are props in grocery store centers; letters, stamps, and mailboxes in post office centers; and appointment books, prescription pads, and folders for patient records in medical centers. A variety of dramatic play centers can be set up in classrooms to coordinate with units and theme cycles. Ideas for 10 dramatic play centers are offered in Figure 7–9. Each center includes authentic literacy materials that children can experiment with and use to learn more about the functions of written language.

Writing Centers.   A writing center can be set up in kindergarten classrooms so that children have a special place to come and write. The center should be located at a table with chairs, and a box of supplies—including pencils, crayons, a date stamp, different kinds of paper, journal notebooks, a stapler, blank books, note paper, and envelopes—should be stored nearby. The alphabet printed in upper- and lowercase letters should be available on the table for children to refer to as they write. In addition, there should be a crate for children to file their work in. They can also share their completed writings by sending them to classmates or sharing them in the author's chair.

When children come to the writing center, they draw and write in journals, compile books, and write messages to classmates. Teachers should be available to encourage and assist children at the center. They can observe children as they invent spellings and can provide information about letters, words, and sentences as needed. If the teacher cannot be at the writing center, perhaps an aide, a parent volunteer, or an upper-grade student can assist.

Mailboxes: Exchanging Messages With Classmates.   Children draw and write messages to classmates and exchange them with classmates at a message center. Either mailboxes or a small bulletin board can be used as the message center. Students write to classmates to say hello, offer a compliment, share news, trade telephone numbers, offer birthday wishes, and develop friendships. They practice writing their names and their classmates' names and a few words. They also gain practice reading the messages they receive. Teachers write brief messages to classmates, too, for many of the same purposes. Examples of one kindergarten teacher's messages to her students are presented in Figure 7–10. The messages are brief, but they convey the

Figure 7–9   Props for Dramatic Play Centers

Post Office Center

mailboxes	wrapping paper	package seals
envelopes	tape	address labels
stamps (stickers)	packages	cash register
pens	scale	money

Hairdresser Center

hair rollers	towel	curling iron (cordless)
brush and comb	posters of hair styles	ribbons, barrets, clips
mirror	wig and wig stand	appointment book
empty shampoo bottle	hairdryer (cordless)	open/closed sign

Office Center

typewriter/computer	hole punch	stamps
calculator	file folders	telephone
paper	in/out boxes	message pad
notepads	pens and pencils	rubber stamps
transparent tape	envelopes	stamp pad
stapler		

Medical Center

appointment books	thermometer	prescription bottles
white shirt/jacket	tweezers	and labels
medical bag	bandages	walkie-talkie (for
stethoscope	prescription pad	paramedics)
hypodermic syringe	folders (for patient	
(play)	records)	

Grocery Store Center

grocery cart	price stickers	marking pen
food packages	cash register	cents-off coupons
plastic fruit and	money	advertisements
artificial foods	grocery bags	

teacher's interest in and caring for her students. As children write and receive messages, they discover new social purposes for written language.

The Author's Chair.   In primary-grade classrooms a special chair should be designated as the author's chair (Graves & Hansen, 1983). This chair might be a rocking chair, a lawn chair with a padded seat, a wooden stool, or a director's chair, and it should be labeled "Author's Chair." Children and the teacher sit in the chair to share books they have read and other books they have written, and this is the only time anyone sits in the chair.

When teachers sit in the chair to read books aloud to children, they name the author of the book and tell a little something about the author, if they can. In this way, children gain an awareness of authors, the people who write books. Children also sit in the author's chair to share books and other compositions they have written. Sitting in the special author's chair helps children gradually

Figure 7–9 continued

Restaurant Center

tablecloth	napkins	apron for waitress
dishes	menus	vest for waiter
glasses	tray	hat and apron for chef
silverware	order pad and pencil	

Travel Agency Center

travel posters	airplane, train tickets	cash register
travel brochures	wallet with money and	suitcases
maps	credit cards	

Veterinarian Center

white shirt/jacket	medical bag	bandages
stuffed animals	stethoscope	popsicle stick splints
cages (cardboard	medicine bottles	hypodermic syringe
boxes)	prescription labels	(play)

Library Center

children's books and	date stamp and stamp	book return box
magazines (with card	pad	posters about books
pockets and date due	library cards	
slips)		

Bank Center

teller window	play money	money bags
passbooks	roll papers for coins	signs
checks	deposit slips	receipts

---

realize that they are authors. Graves and Hansen describe children's growing awareness of authors and themselves as authors in three steps:

1. *Authors write books.* After hearing many books read to them and reading books themselves, children develop the concept that authors are the people who write books.
2. *I am an author.* Sharing the books they have written with classmates from the author's chair helps children view themselves as authors.
3. *If I wrote this published book now, I wouldn't write it this way.* Children learn that they have options when they write, and this awareness grows after they have experimented with various writing functions, forms, and audiences.

When children share their writings, one child sits in the author's chair, and a group of children sit on the floor or in chairs in front of the author's chair. The child sitting in the author's chair reads the book or other piece of writing aloud

Figure 7–10   A Kindergarten Teacher's Messages to Her Students

Juan,
Happy Birthday to you!
How old are you?
           Love,
           Ms. R.

Dear Lee,
I like the big building
you made in the Blocks
Center.
                Love,
                Ms. R.

Dear Aleta,
Would you like to read
with me today?
           Love,
           Ms. R.

Natasha,
Thank you for cleaning
Snowball's cage. You are
a good helper.
                Love,
                Ms. R.

and shows the accompanying illustrations. Then children who want to make a comment raise their hands, and the author chooses several children to ask questions, give compliments, and make comments. Then the author chooses another child to share and takes a seat in the audience.

Review

Emergent literacy is the new perspective on how children learn to read and write. They learn about written language in much the same way they learned to talk—by being immersed in language. Young children learn about written language—language functions, concepts about print and words, and the alphabetic principle. They move through three stages—emergent, early, and fluent—as they become readers. Assisted reading, shared reading, and language experience are three approaches for reading with young children. Children emerge into writing as they learn to use graphic symbols to represent their thoughts, and they refine their kid writing as they learn about phoneme-grapheme correspondences. Opportunities for writing in kindergarten and first-grade classrooms include sign-in sheets, dramatic play centers, writing centers, mailboxes, and an author's chair.

Extensions

1. Observe in a kindergarten or first-grade classroom to see how children are learning concepts about written language. Examine reading materials available in the classroom, including predictable books and big books, and opportunities for writing, such as sign-in sheets, dramatic play and writing centers, mailboxes, and an author's chair.
2. Establish and monitor a buddy reading program between a primary-grade class and an upper-grade class.
3. Collect books and other materials for two traveling bags of books, and share them with first and second graders.
4. Plan a literature focus unit using a big book, and share the book with a group of emergent readers.
5. Prepare a big book for a predictable book, or create a big book for a favorite story with a group of young children.
6. Create a dramatic play center that incorporates authentic reading and writing materials, and observe as children use the materials over the course of a week or two.
7. Set up a writing center in a kindergarten classroom, and work with children for several weeks. Keep track of the types of writing that children do and their growth as writers.

References

Adams, M. J. (1990). *Beginning to read: Thinking and learning about print.* Cambridge, MA: MIT Press.

Ashton-Warner, S. (1965). *Teacher.* New York: Simon & Schuster.

Baghban, M. J. M. (1984). Our daughter learns to read and write: A case study from birth to three. Newark, DE: International Reading Association.

Bridge, C. A. (1979). Predictable materials for beginning readers. *Language Arts, 56,* 503–507.

Clay, M. (1967). The reading behavior of five-year-old children: A research report. *New Zealand Journal of Education Studies,* 11–31.

Clay, M. (1989). Foreword. In D. S. Strickland & L. M. Morrow (Eds.), *Emerging literacy: Young children learn to read and write.* Newark, DE: International Reading Association.

Clay, M. M. (1972). *Reading: The patterning of complex behavior.* Portsmouth, NH: Heinemann.

Clay, M. M. (1975). *What did I write? Beginning writing behavior.* Portsmouth, NH: Heinemann.

Clay, M. M. (1979). *The early detection of reading difficulties.* Portsmouth, NH: Heinemann.

Cohen, P., Kulik, J. A., & Kulik, C. (1982). Educational outcomes of tutoring: A meta-analysis of findings. *American Educational Research Journal, 19,* 237–248.

Cutting, B. (n.d.). *Getting started in whole language: The complete guide for every teacher.* San Diego: The Wright Group.

Downing, J. (1970). The development of linguistic concepts in children's thinking. *Research in the Teaching of English, 4,* 5–19.

Downing, J. (1971–1972). Children's developing concepts of spoken and written language. *Journal of Reading Behavior, 4,* 1–19.

Downing, J., & Oliver, P. (1973–1974). The child's conception of "a word." *Reading Research Quarterly, 9,* 568–582.

Durkin, D. (1966). *Children who read early.* New York: Teachers College Press.

Dyson, A. H. (1984). "N spells my grandmama": Fostering early thinking about print. *The Reading Teacher, 38,* 262–271.

Fisher, B. (1991). *Joyful learning: A whole language kindergarten.* Portsmouth, NH: Heinemann.

Freppon, P. A., & Dahl, K. L. (1991). Learning about phonics in a whole language classroom. *Language Arts, 68,* 190–197.

Graves, D. H., & Hansen, J. (1983). The author's chair. *Language Arts, 60,* 176–183.

Hanna, P. R., Hanna, J. S., Hodges, R. E., & Rudorf, E. H. (1966). *Phoneme-grapheme correspondences as cues to spelling improvement.* Washington, DC: US Office of Education.

Harste, J., Woodward, V., & Burke, C. (1984). *Language stories and literacy lessons.* Portsmouth, NH: Heinemann.

Heald-Taylor, G. (1987). How to use predictable books for K–2 language arts instruction. *The Reading Teacher, 40,* 656–661.

Heath, S. B. (1983). *Ways with words.* New York: Oxford University Press.

Hodges, R. E. (1981). *Learning to spell.* Urbana, IL: ERIC Clearinghouse on Reading and Communication Skills and the National Council of Teachers of English.

Holdaway, D. (1979). *The foundations of literacy.* Portsmouth, NH: Heinemann.

Horn, E. (1957). Phonetics and spelling. *Elementary School Journal, 57,* 425–432.

Hoskisson, K. (1974). Should parents teach their children to read? *Elementary English, 51,* 295–299.

Hoskisson, K. (1975a). The many facets of assisted reading. *Elementary English, 52,* 312–315.

Hoskisson, K. (1975b). Successive approximation and beginning reading. *Elementary School Journal, 75,* 442–451.

Hoskisson, K. (1977). Reading readiness: Three viewpoints. *Elementary School Journal, 78,* 44–52.

Hoskisson, K., & Krohm, B. (1974). Reading by immersion: Assisted reading. *Elementary English, 51,* 832–836.

Hoskisson, K., Sherman, T., & Smith, L. (1974). Assisted reading and parent involvement. *The Reading Teacher, 27,* 710–714.

Karnowski, L. (1989). Using LEA with process writing. *The Reading Teacher, 42,* 462–465.

Kawakami-Arakaki, A., Oshiro, M., & Farnan, S. (1989). Research to practice: Integrating reading and writing in a kindergarten curriculum. In J. Mason (Ed.), *Reading and writing connections* (pp. 199–218). Boston: Allyn and Bacon.

Labbo, L. D., & Teale, W. H. (1990). Cross-age reading: A strategy for helping poor readers. *The Reading Teacher, 43,* 362–369.

Lee, D. M., & Allen, R. V. (1963). *Learning to read through experience* (2nd ed.). New York: Meredith.

McGee, L. M., & Richgels, D. J. (1990). *Literacy's beginnings: Supporting young readers and writers.* Boston: Allyn and Bacon.

Morrice, C., & Simmons, M. (1991). Beyond reading buddies: A whole language cross-age program. *The Reading Teacher, 44,* 572–577.

Papandropoulou, I., & Sinclair, H. (1974). What is a word? Experimental study of children's ideas on grammar. *Human Development, 17,* 241–258.

Reutzel, D. R., & Fawson, P. C. (1990). Traveling tales: Connecting parents and children in writing. *The Reading Teacher, 44,* 222–227.

Rhodes, L. K. (1981). I can read! Predictable books as resources for reading and writing instruction. *The Reading Teacher, 34,* 511–518.

Schickedanz, J. A. (1990). *Adam's righting revolutions: One child's literacy development from infancy through grade one.* Portsmouth, NH: Heinemann.

Slaughter, J. P. (1983). Big books for little kids: Another fad or a new approach for teaching beginning reading? *The Reading Teacher, 36,* 758–762.

Stauffer, R. G. (1970). *The language experience approach to the teaching of reading.* New York: Harper & Row.

Sulzby, E. (1985). Kindergartners as readers and writers. In M. Farr (Ed.), *Advances in writing research,* vol. 1: *Children's early writing development* (pp. 127–199). Norwood, NJ: Ablex.

Taylor, D. (1983). *Family literacy: Young children learning to read and write.* Exeter, NH: Heinemann.

Taylor, D., & Dorsey-Gaines, C. (1987). *Growing up literate: Learning from inner-city families.* Portsmouth, NH: Heinemann.

Teale, W. H. (1982). Toward a theory of how children learn to read and write. *Language Arts, 59,* 555–570.

Teale, W. H., & Sulzby, E. (1989). Emerging literacy: New perspectives. In D. S. Strickland & L. M. Morrow (Eds.), *Emerging literacy: Young children learn to read and write* (pp. 1–15). Newark, DE: International Reading Association.

Temple, C., Nathan, R., Burris, N., & Temple, F. (1988). *The beginnings of writing.* Boston: Allyn and Bacon.

Templeton, S. (1980). Young children invent words: Developing concepts of "word-ness." *The Reading Teacher, 33,* 454–459.

Templeton, S., & Spivey, E. (1980). The concept of word in young children as a function of level of cognitive development. *Research in the Teaching of English, 14,* 265–278.

Tompkins, G. E., & Webeler, M. B. (1983). What will happen next? Using predictable books with young children. *The Reading Teacher, 36,* 498–502.

Tompkins, G. E., & Yaden, D. B., Jr. (1986). *Answering students' questions about words.* Urbana, IL: ERIC Clearinghouse on Communication Skills and the National Council of Teachers of English.

Trachtenburg, R., & Ferruggia, A. (1989). Big books from little voices: Reaching high risk beginning readers. *The Reading Teacher, 42,* 284–289.

Treiman, R. (1985). Phonemic analysis, spelling, and reading. In T. H. Carr (Ed.), *The development of reading skills* (pp. 5–18). San Francisco: Jossey-Bass.

Venezky, R. L. (1970). *The structure of English orthography.* The Hague: Mouton.

Wylie, R. E., & Durrell, D. D. (1970). Teaching vowels through phonograms. *Elementary English, 47,* 787–791.

Yaden, D. B., Jr., & Templeton, S. (Eds.). (1986). *Metalinguistic awareness and beginning literacy: Conceptualizing what it means to read and write.* Portsmouth, NH: Heinemann.

Yopp, H. K. (1992). Developing phonemic awareness in young children. *The Reading Teacher, 45,* 696–703.

Children's Book References

Brown, M. (1984). *There's no place like home.* New York: Parents.

Carle, E. (1969). *The very hungry caterpillar.* Cleveland: Collins-World.

Carle, E. (1987). *A house for a hermit crab.* Saxonville, MA: Picture Book Studio.

Cauley, L. B. (1984). *The city mouse and the country mouse.* New York: Putnam.

Coerr, E. (1986). *The Josefina story quilt.* New York: Harper & Row.

de Paola, T. (1978). *Pancakes for breakfast.* New York: Harcourt Brace Jovanovich.

Ehlert, L. (1989). *Color zoo.* New York: Lippincott.

Fowler, A. (1992). *It could still be water.* Chicago: Childrens Press.

Fox, M. (1986). *Hattie and the fox.* New York: Bradbury Press.

Galdone, P. (1973). *The little red hen.* New York: Seabury.

Galdone, P. (1975). *The gingerbread boy.* New York: Seabury.

Hoberman, M. A. (1978). *A house is a house for me.* New York: Viking.

Hutchins, P. (1968). *Rosie's walk.* New York: Macmillan.

McCully, E. A. (1984). *Picnic.* New York: Harper & Row.

McKissack, P. C. (1986). *Flossie and the fox.* New York: Dial.

Parish, P. (1963). *Amelia Bedelia.* New York: Harper & Row.

Peek, M. (1985). *Mary wore her red dress.* New York: Clarion.

Pryor, B. (1987). *The house on Maple Street.* New York: Morrow.

Sendak, M. (1962). *Where the wild things are.* New York: Harper & Row.

Seuss, Dr. (1963). *Hop on Pop.* New York: Random House.

Seuss, Dr. (1988). *Green eggs and ham.* New York: Random House.

PROCEDURE

Before I start a new literature focus unit, I read the books and highlight words that my students may need help with or that I might want to use in vocabulary lessons. This gets me ready to teach. Then I hang a long sheet of butcher paper in the classroom—often from the ceiling to the floor. I call it a "word wall." As we read, I point out some important words, my students spot others, and we write these words on the word wall. I usually ask students to write the words themselves because I want them to be involved in the activity. I also have them keep a reading log—a notebook with about 20 pages in it. They keep a list of words on one page in the log. Many of the words come from our word wall, but students also choose other words as they read.

Right now we're into a unit on children's author Chris Van Allsburg. In *The Garden of Abdul Gasazi* (1979), I highlighted these words: *sinking (teeth into . . .), bolted, shadowed, bruised, detest, blurted, awesome,* and *incredible.* I explain most of the words informally as we come to them, and we add them to our word wall. The one word that I've decided to teach more formally is *incredible.* To prepare, I look the word up in an unabridged dictionary, check its meaning and etymology, and make a list of related words. Then I decide how to present the lesson. For *incredible,* I start with the words *credit* and *credit card* because they are familiar. Then I make a cluster with the root word *cred-* in the middle as shown in the accompanying figure. I draw out *credit, credit card,* and then add *incredible* from the story and a few other related words. My students are amazed because they don't see a relationship among the words until we start talking about them. Then a light comes on! For the students who need to be challenged, I add the words *credulity* and *credulous* and talk about their meanings.

ASSESSMENT

I want my students to "own" these words. I use the words when I talk to students and notice when they use the words. I do give tests to check their

> ❝ I don't teach vocabulary — at least not in the traditional way. Instead, my students are immersed in words through the books we read and the themes we are studying. I know it sounds corny, but my students learn words because they are living them. ❞
>
> Carol Ochs
> Fifth-Grade Teacher
> Jackson Elementary School

knowledge of some words, but, more importantly, I check to see if students apply the words in their writing. Sometimes I ask students to highlight vocabulary words in their reading log entries or in their stories and reports. That's when I know my students "own" the words.

ADAPTATIONS

I love using literature as the basis of my language arts program, but I feel an added responsibility to make the books we read accessible to my less able readers. I use a variety of strategies to ensure that every student in my classroom is successful. Four of my strategies are:

1. *Previewing the book.* Sometimes I preview the book with my less able readers the day before I introduce it to the class. I introduce the title of the book and allow these students to look through the book to get the gist of the story. If the story is available on tape, I encourage these students to listen to it at the listening center. I also preteach any essential vocabulary, such as the names of the characters.

2. *Rereading the book.* I encourage my less able readers to reread the story with a buddy or at the listening center. This added practice allows these students to read more fluently and to better understand the story.

3. *Exploring the book with storyboards.* I prepare a set of storyboards by cutting apart two extra copies of the book, backing each page with cardboard, and laminating them. Then I pass out the storyboards, one to each student. We do a variety of activities using the storyboards: We read the cards, sequence them, and examine the important vocabulary. I pass out little sticky-backed notes and ask students to choose one or two words from the word wall that relate to the picture or text on a storyboard and write the word or words on the sticky-backed notes. Then students share their storyboards and the word or words they have selected.

4. *Writing in reading logs.* During a vocabulary minilesson, I ask my less able readers to choose a word from the word wall and write it in their reading logs. Then they draw a picture of the word and use it in a sentence to describe their picture or in a question about their picture. As a change-of-pace activity, sometimes we write riddles about the words.

REFLECTIONS

I don't have my students look up vocabulary words in the dictionary and copy the definitions into their reading logs. I tried it and it doesn't work. I have also tried having students use the words in sentences, and that doesn't work either. Instead, we use the words every day—several times a day—but we use them as we talk and write about the story and go beyond the story.

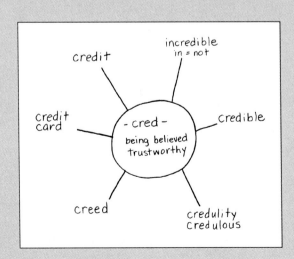

8

Looking Closely at Words

INSIGHT

While assigning students to look up the definitions of a list of words in a dictionary or to use vocabulary words in sentences may keep them busy, it does little to capture their interest in learning about words. Recent research has shown that students learn words best through meaningful, hands-on activities. As they write responses in journals, talk about books they have read, and build clusters and other charts during literature focus units and theme cycles, students learn to care about what words mean and how to choose the best words to express an idea. As you read this chapter, think about how you add new words to your vocabulary and respond to this issue:

How do teachers teach new words in a meaningful way to elementary students?

*M*ark Twain said, "The difference between the right word and the almost right word is the difference between *lightning* and the *lightning bug.*" Learning about words and how to choose the right one to express the meaning you intend is what vocabulary is all about. Vocabulary is not decoding or word identification; rather, the focus is on meaning. Choosing the best word to express meaning is important to all language users. When we listen and read, we must understand the meaning that someone else intends, and when we talk and write, we must choose exactly the right word so that our audience will understand our message.

Words are the meaning-bearing units of language. Of the three-quarters of a million words in English, most people use only about 20,000, and most of the words we commonly use come from a body of approximately 5,000 to 7,000 words (Klein, 1988). Our personal ownership of words is quite limited. We have overlapping but separate listening, talking, reading, and writing vocabularies. We may, for example, recognize a word such as *obfuscate* when listening or reading, but fewer of us would use the word in talking or writing. Our reading and listening vocabularies are more extensive than our talking and writing vocabularies, for many reasons. We may fear mispronouncing or misspelling a word, or we may fear what our friends will think if we use the word in conversation. The words we use mark us in a number of ways: by our word choice, by our pronunciation, and by the way we string the words together into sentences.

Words in our personal vocabularies reflect varying degrees of word knowledge. Klein (1988) divides our personal vocabularies, which he calls "dictionaries," into three levels: (1) the ownership dictionary of words we know and use competently; (2) the mid-level dictionary, which is accessible with contextual assistance; and (3) the low-level dictionary, composed of words we know marginally and which we use at the risk of making an error. We have each of the three dictionary levels in our heads, and when we learn a new word, it usually enters either the low- or the mid-level dictionary. After additional experiences or instruction, it is transferred into the ownership dictionary. Even though the number of words in the three dictionary categories grows, the number of categories does not.

HISTORY OF THE ENGLISH LANGUAGE*

Understanding the history of English and how words entered the language contributes greatly to understanding words and their meanings. English is a historic language, and this fact accounts for word meanings and some spelling inconsistencies. English has a variety of words for a single concept, and the history of English in general and the etymology of the words in particular explains apparent duplications. Consider these words related to *water*: *aquatic, hydrant, aquamarine, waterfall, hydroelectric, watercress, watery, aquarium, waterproof, hydraulic, aqualung,* and *hydrogen,* to name a few. These words have one of three root words that each mean water: *water* is English, of course, while *aqua* is Latin and *hydro* is Greek. The root word that

---

*This section is adapted from Tompkins & Yaden, 1986.

is used depends on the people who created the word, the purpose of the word, and when the word entered English.

The development of the English language is divided into three periods: Old English, Middle English, and Modern English. The beginning and end of each period is marked by a significant event, such as an invasion or an invention.

Old English (A.D. 450–1100)

The recorded history of the English language begins in A.D. 449, when Germanic tribes, including the Angles and Saxons, invaded Britain. The invaders pushed the original inhabitants, the Celts, to the northern and western corners of the island. This annexation is romanticized in the King Arthur legends. Arthur is believed to have been a Celtic military leader who fought bravely against the German invaders.

The English language began as an intermingling of the dialects spoken by the Angles, Saxons, and other Germanic tribes in Britain. Many people assume that English is based on Latin, but it has Germanic roots and was brought to Britain by these invaders. Although 85% of Old English words are no longer used, many everyday words remain (e.g., *child, foot, hand, house, man, mother, old,* and *sun.* In contrast to Modern English, Old English had few loan words (words borrowed from other languages and incorporated into English) and had a highly developed inflectional system for indicating number, gender, and verb tense. The Anglo-Saxons added affixes to existing words, including *be-, for-, -ly, -dom,* and *-hood.* They also invented vividly descriptive compound words. The Old English word for *music,* for example, was "ear-sport," *world* was "age of man," and *folly* was "wanwit." The folk epic *Beowulf,* the great literary work of the period, illustrates the poetic use of words; for instance, the sea is described as a "whale-path" and a "swan's road."

Through contact with other cultures, foreign words began to make their way into the predominantly Germanic word stock. The borrowed words came from two main sources: Romans and Vikings. A number of words were borrowed from Latin and incorporated into English. Contact between the Roman soldiers and traders and the Germanic tribes on the continent, before they had invaded England, contributed some words, including *cheese, copper, mile, street,* and *wine.* The missionaries who re-introduced Christianity to Britain in 597 also brought with them a number of religious words (e.g., *angel, candle, hymn).*

In 787, the Vikings from Denmark and other areas of Scandinavia began a series of raids against English villages, and for the next three centuries they attacked, conquered, and occupied much of England. Their influence was so great that the Danish king Canute ruled England during the first part of the 11th century. The Vikings' contributions to the English language were significant: They provided the pronouns *they, their, them;* introduced the /g/ and /k/ sounds (e.g., *kid, get*); contributed most of our *sc-* and *sk-* words (e.g., *skin, sky*); and enriched our vocabulary with more than 500 everyday words, including *husband* and *window.*

In Old English some consonant combinations were pronounced that are not heard today, including the /k/ in words like *knee.* The letter *f* represented both /f/ and /v/, resulting in the Modern English spelling pattern of *wolf* and *wolves.* The pronunciation of the vowel sounds was very different, too; for example, the Old English *stan* (*a* = *a* in *father*) has become our word *stone.*

The structure, spelling, and pronunciation of Old English were significantly different from those of Modern English—so much so that we would not be able to read an Old English text or understand someone speaking Old English. It was a highly inflected language with many different word endings, and the arrangement of words in sentences was different, too, with verbs often placed at the end of sentences. In many ways, Old English was more like Modern German than Modern English.

Middle English (1100–1500)

An event occurred in 1066 that changed the course of the English language and ushered in the Middle English period: the Norman Conquest. In that year William the Conqueror crossed the English Channel from the French province of Normandy and defeated the English king, Harold, at the Battle of Hastings. William claimed the English throne and established a French court in London. This event had far-reaching consequences. For nearly 300 years French was the official language in England, spoken by the nobility and upper classes, although the lower classes continued to speak English. By 1300, the use of French had declined, and before the end of the 14th century, English was restored as the official language. Chaucer's *Canterbury Tales,* written in the late 1300s, provides evidence that English was also replacing French as the preferred written language. Political, social, and economic changes contributed to this reversal.

The Middle English period was one of tremendous change. A large portion of the Old English vocabulary was lost as 10,000 French words were added to the language, reflecting the Norman impact on English life and society (Baugh & Cable, 1978). They included military words *(soldier, victory)*, political words *(government, princess),* medical words *(physician, surgeon),* and words related to the arts *(comedy, music, poet).* Many of the new loan words duplicated Old English words. Typically, one word was eventually lost; if both words remained in the language, they developed slightly different meanings. Often it was the Old English word that disappeared. For example, the words *hardy* (Old English) and *cordial* (French) were originally synonyms, both meaning "from the heart." In time they differentiated and now express different meanings.

Most of the French loan words were derived from Latin. In addition, a few Latin words (e.g., *individual, polite*) passed directly into English during this period. In contrast to the French loan words, Latin borrowings were more sophisticated words, used more often in writing than in speech. Also, several words (e.g., *dock, freight*) were borrowed from the Dutch during the Middle English period as a result of trade with the Low Countries.

During this period there was a significant reduction in the use of inflections or word endings. Many irregular verbs were lost, and others developed regular past and past-participle forms (e.g., *climb, talk*), although Modern English still retains some irregular verbs (e.g., *sing, fly*) that contribute to our usage problems. By 1000, *-s* had become the accepted plural marker, although the Old English plural form *-en* was used in some words; this artifact remains in a few plurals, such as *children.*

Modern English (1500–Present)

The Modern English period is characterized not by invasions or other significant political events, but by the development of the printing press and the tremendous upswing in exploration, colonization, and trade with countries around the world. The introduction of the printing press in England by William Caxton in 1476 marks the dividing point between the Middle and Modern English periods. The printing press was a powerful force in standardizing English spelling, as well as a practical means for providing increasing numbers of people with books. Until the invention of the printing press, English spelling kept pace with pronunciation, but the printing press served to standardize and fix spelling, and the lag between pronunciation and spelling began to widen. The tremendous increase in exploration, colonization, and trade with many different parts of the world resulted in a wide borrowing of words from more than 50 languages. Borrowings include *alcohol* (Arabic), *chocolate* (French), *cookie* (Dutch), *czar* (Russian), *hallelujah* (Hebrew), *hurricane* (Spanish), *kindergarten* (German), *smorgasbord* (Swedish), *tycoon* (Chinese), and *violin* (Italian).

Many Latin and Greek words were added to English during the Renaissance to increase the language's prestige; for example, *congratulate, democracy,* and *education* came from Latin, and *catastrophe, encyclopedia,* and *thermometer* came from Greek. Many modern Greek and Latin borrowings are scientific words (e.g., *aspirin, vaccinate*), and some of the very recently borrowed forms (e.g., *criterion, focus*) have retained their native plural forms, adding confusion about how to spell these forms in English. Also, some recent loan words from French have retained their native spellings and pronunciations, such as *hors d'oeuvre* and *cul-de-sac.*

Although vocabulary expansion has been great during the Modern English period, there have also been extensive sound changes. The short vowels have remained relatively stable, but there was a striking change in the pronunciation of long vowels. This change, known as the Great Vowel Shift, has been characterized as "the most revolutionary and far-reaching sound change during the history of the language" (Alexander, 1962, p. 114). The change was gradual, occurring during the first century of this period. Because spelling had become fixed before the shift, the vowel letter symbols no longer corresponded to the sounds. To illustrate the change, the word *name* rhymed with *comma* during the Middle English period, but during the Great Vowel Shift, the Modern English pronunciation of *name* shifted to rhyme with *game* (Hook, 1975).

The Modern English period brought changes in syntax, particularly the disappearance of double negatives and double comparatives and superlatives. Eliminations came about slowly; for instance, Shakespeare still wrote, "the most unkindest cut of all." Also, the practice of using *-er* or *-est* to form comparatives and superlatives in shorter words and *more* or *most* with longer words was not standardized until after Shakespeare's time.

Learning About Word Histories

The best source of information about word histories is an unabridged dictionary, which provides basic etymological information about words: the language the word was borrowed from, the form of the word in that language or the representation of the word in our alphabet, and the original meaning of the word. Etymologies are enclosed in square brackets and may appear at the beginning or the end of an entry. They are written in an abbreviated form to save space, and they use abbreviations for language names such as *Ar* for

Arabic and *L* for *Latin.* We will look at three etymologies for words derived from very different sources: *king, kimono,* and *thermometer.* Each etymology is from *The Random House Dictionary of the English Language* (Flexner, 1987); we will translate and elaborate each etymology using a process we call *extrapolation.* First, let's look at *king:*

> *king*   [bef. 900; ME, OE *cyng*]

Extrapolation: The word *king* is an Old English word originally spelled *cyng.* It was used in English before the year 900. In the Middle English period the spelling changed to its current form. Next let's consider *kimono:*

> *kimono*   [1885–1890; < Japn: clothing, garb,
> equiv. to *ki* wear + *mono* thing]

Extrapolation: Our word *kimono* comes from Japanese, and it entered English between 1885 and 1890. *Kimono* means "clothing" or "garb," and it is equivalent to the Japanese words *ki,* meaning "wear" and *mono,* meaning "thing." Finally, we will examine *thermometer:*

> *thermometer*   [1615–1625; thermo < Gr
> *thermos,* hot + meter < *metron,* measure]

Extrapolation: The first recorded use of the word *thermometer* in English was between 1615 and 1625. Our word was created from two Greek words meaning "hot" and "measure."

Figure 8–1 lists books about the history of English that are appropriate for elementary students. The books include fascinating stories about how words grew and changed because of historical events and linguistic accidents.

WORDS AND THEIR MEANINGS

Students' vocabularies grow at a rate of about 3,000 words a year (Nagy & Herman, 1985). Through literature focus units and theme cycles, students experiment with words and concepts, and their knowledge of words and meanings grows. Young children assume that every word has only one meaning, and words that sound alike, such as *son* and *sun,* are confusing to them. Through continuing experiences with language, students become more sophisticated about words and their literal and figurative meanings. During the elementary grades, students learn about words and word parts, words that mean the same and the opposite of other words, words that sound alike, words with multiple meanings, the figurative language of idioms, and how words have been borrowed from languages around the world. They also learn about how words are created and have fun playing with words (Tompkins, 1994).

Root Words and Affixes

A *root word* is a morpheme, the basic part of a word to which affixes are added. Many words are developed from a single root word; for example, the Latin word *portare* ("to carry") is the source of at least nine Modern English words: *deport, export, import, port, portable, porter, report, support,* and *transportation.* Latin is one source of English root words, and Greek and Old English are two other sources.

Figure 8–1   *Books About the History of English for Elementary Students*

Adelson, L. (1972). *Dandelions don't bite: The story of words.* New York: Pantheon. (M–U)

Arnold, O. (1979). *What's in a name: Famous brand names.* New York: Messner. (U)

Asimov, I. (1961). *Words from myths.* Boston: Houghton Mifflin. (U)

Asimov, I. (1968). *Words from History.* Boston: Houghton Mifflin. (U)

Collis, H. (1987). *101 American English idioms.* Lincolnwood, IL: Passport. (M–U)

Davidson, J. (1972). *Is that mother in the bottle? Where language came from and where it is going.* New York: Franklin Watts. (M–U)

Epstein, S., & Epstein, B. (1964). *What's behind the word?* New York: Scholastic. (M–U)

Fletcher, C. (1973). *One hundred keys: Names across the land.* Nashville, TN: Abingdon Press. (M–U)

Funk, C. E. (1948). *A hog on ice and other curious expressions.* New York: Harper & Row. (M–U)

Greenfeld, H. (1978). *Sumer is icumen in: Our ever-changing language.* New York: Crown Books. (U)

Hazen, B. S. (1979). *Last, first, middle and nick: All about names.* Englewood Cliffs, NJ: Prentice-Hall. (M–U)

Kaye, C. B. (1985). *Word works: Why the alphabet is a kid's best friend.* Boston: Little, Brown. (M–U)

Kraske, R. (1975). *The story of the dictionary.* New York: Harcourt Brace Jovanovich. (P–M)

Lambert, E. (1955). *Our language: The story of the words we use.* New York: Lothrop. (M–U)

Lambert, E., & Pei, M. (1959). *The book of place-names.* New York: Lothrop. (M–U)

McCrum, R., Cran, I., & MacNeil, R. (1986). *The story of English.* New York: Viking Press. (U)

Meltzer, M. (1984). *A book about names.* New York: Crowell. (M–U)

Pickles, C., & Meynell, L. (1971). *The beginning of words: How English grew.* New York: Putnam. (M–U)

Pizer, V. (1976). *Ink., Ark., and all that: How American places got their names.* New York: Putnam. (M–U)

Pizer, V. (1981). *Take my word for it.* New York: Dodd, Mead. (M–U)

Sacon, G. R. (1964). *Secrets in animal names.* Englewood Cliffs, NJ: Prentice-Hall. (M–U)

Sarnoff, J., & Ruffins, R. (1981). *Words: A book about the origins of everyday words and phrases.* New York: Scribner. (M–U)

Sorel, N. (1970). *Word people.* New York: American Heritage. (M–U)

Sparke, W. (1966). *Story of the English language.* New York: Abelard-Schuman. (M–U)

Sperling, S. (1979). *Poplollies and bellibones: A celebration of lost words.* New York: Penguin. (U)

Steckler, A. (1979). *101 words and how they began.* Garden City, NY: Doubleday. (P–M–U)

Steckler, A. (1981). *101 more words and how they began.* Garden City, NY: Doubleday. (P–M–U)

Terban, M. (1983). *In a pickle and other funny idioms.* Boston: Houghton Mifflin. (M–U)

Weiss, A. E. (1980). *What's that you said: How words change.* New York: Harcourt Brace Jovanovich. (U)

Wolk, A. (1980). *Everyday words from names of people and places.* New York: Elsevier/Nelson. (M–U)

P = primary grades (K–2); M = middle grades (3–5); U = upper grades (6–8).

Some root words are whole words, and others are parts of words. Some root words have become free morphemes and can be used as separate words, but others cannot. For instance, the word *act* comes from the Latin word *actus,* meaning "doing." English uses part of the word and treats it as a root word that can be used independently or in combination with affixes, as in *actor, activate, react,* and *enact.* In the words *alias, alien, unalienable,* and *alienate,* the root word *ali* comes from the Latin word *alius,* meaning "other"; it is not used as an independent root word in English. A list of root words appears in the Teacher's Notebook on page 288.

Students can compile lists of words developed from the root words listed on page 288, and they can draw root word clusters to illustrate the relationship of the root word to the words developed from it. Figure 8–2 shows a root word cluster for the Greek root *graph,* meaning "to write." Recognizing basic

Teacher's Notebook

Root Words

ann/enn (year): anniversary, annual, biennial, centennial, perennial
ast (star): aster, asterisk, astrology, astronaut, astronomy
auto (self): autobiography, automatic, automobile
bio (life): biography, biology, autobiography, biodegradable
cent (hundred): cent, centennial, centigrade, centipede, century
circ (around): circle, circular, circus, circumspect
corp (body): corporal, corporation, corps
cycl (wheel): bicycle, cycle, cyclist, cyclone, tricycle
dict (speak): contradict, dictate, dictator, predict, verdict
geo (earth): geography, geology, geometry
graph (write): biography, graphic, paragraph, phonograph, stenographer
gram (letter): diagram, grammar, monogram, telegram
grat (pleasing, thankful): congratulate, grateful, gratitude
jus/jud/jur (law, right): injury, judge, justice
man (hand): manacle, manual, manufacture, manuscript
mand (order): command, demand, mandate, remand
mar (sea): aquamarine, marine, maritime, submarine
meter (measure): barometer, centimeter, diameter, speedometer, thermometer
min (small): miniature, minimize, minor, minute
mort (death): immortal, mortal, mortality, mortician, post-mortem
ped/pod (foot): pedal, pedestrian, podiatry, tripod
phon (sound): earphone, microphone, phonics, phonograph, saxophone, symphony
photo (light): photograph, photographer, photosensitive, photosynthesis
quer/ques/quis (seek): query, question, inquisitive
rupt (break): abrupt, bankrupt, interrupt, rupture
scope (see): horoscope, kaleidoscope, microscope, periscope, telescope
struct (build): construction, indestructible, instruct
tele (far): telecast, telegram, telegraph, telephone, telescope, telethon, television
terr (land): terrace, terrain, terrarium, territory
tract (pull, drag): attraction, subtract, tractor
vict/vinc (conquer): convince, convict, evict, victor, victory
vis (see): television, visa, vision, visual
viv/vit (live): survive vitamin, vivid
volv (roll): involve, revolutionary, revolver

GRAPHic
(*ic* = characteristic of)

stenoGRAPHer
(*er* = one who)

GRAPHite
(*ite* = mineral)

GRAPH

stenoGRAPHy
(*steno* = short
y = full of)

cryptoGRAPH
(*crypto* = hidden)

seismoGRAPH
(*seismo* = shake)

GRAPH
(write)

teleGRAPH
(*tele* = far)

phonoGRAPH
(*phono* = sound)

biblioGRAPHy
(*biblio* = book
y = full of)

bioGRAPHy
(*bio* = life
y = full of)

choreoGRAPHy
(*choreo* = dance
y = full of)

bioGRAPHer
(*er* = one who)

autobioGRAPHy
(*auto* = self
y = full of)

choreoGRAPHer
(*er* = one who)

Figure 8–2   A Cluster for the Root Word Graph

elements from word to word helps students cut down on the amount of memorizing necessary to learn meanings and spellings.

Affixes are bound morphemes that are added to words and root words. Prefixes are added to the beginning of words, such as *reread,* and suffixes are added to the ends of words, such as *singing* and *player.* Like root words, affixes come from Old English, Latin, and Greek. They often change a word's meaning, such as adding *un-* to *happy* to form *unhappy.* Sometimes they change the part of speech, too. For example, when *-ion* is added to *attract* to form *attraction,* the verb *attract* becomes a noun.

When an affix is "peeled off" or removed from a word, the remaining word is usually a real word. For example, when the prefix *pre-* is removed from *preview,* the word *view* can stand alone; and when the suffix *-able* is removed from *lovable,* the word *love* can stand alone (when the final *e* is added, anyway). Some words include letter sequences that might be affixes, but because the remaining word cannot stand alone, they are not affixes. For example, the *-in* at the beginning of *include* is not a prefix because *clude* is not a word, and the *-ic* at the end of *magic* is not a suffix because *mag* cannot stand alone as a word. Sometimes, however, the root word cannot stand alone. One example is *legible.* The *-ible* is a suffix and *leg-* is the root word even though it cannot stand alone.

Some affixes have more than one form. For example, the prefixes *il-*, *im-*, and *ir-* are forms of the prefix *in-*, with the meanings of "in," "into," and "on"; these prefixes are used with verbs and nouns. The prefixes *il-*, *im-*, *ir-*, and *ig-* are also forms of another prefix *in-*, with the meaning "not"; these prefixes are used with adjectives. Both *in-* prefixes are borrowed from Latin. The prefix *a-* and its alternate form *an-* are borrowed from Greek and also mean "not." The alternate form is used when the word it is being added to begins with a vowel. Similarly, some suffixes have alternate forms; for example, the suffix *-ible* is an alternate form of *-able*. The alternate form is used with words such as *legible* whose root words cannot stand alone.

A list of prefixes and suffixes is presented in the Teacher's Notebook on page 291. White, Sowell, and Yanagihara (1989) researched affixes and identified those that are most commonly used in English words; these commonly used affixes are marked with an asterisk in the Teacher's Notebook. White and his colleagues recommend that the commonly used affixes be taught to middle- and upper-grade students because of their usefulness. Some of the most commonly used prefixes can be confusing because they have more than one meaning. The prefix *-in,* for instance, can mean either *not* or *again,* and *-un* can mean *not* or it can reverse the meaning of the word (e.g., *tie-untie*).

Students learn the meanings of affixes and how they are added to words so that they can unlock the meaning of unfamiliar words. Students often "peel off" the prefix or suffix of an unfamiliar word to find a familiar base word. Also, students use their knowledge about affixes in spelling words.

Students can experiment with adding affixes to the root words in the Teacher's Notebook to create both real and invented words. Examples of words that students have invented include *phonomatic* (makes sounds by itself), *monoscript* (written once), *jector* (hurler), *astrometer* (measures stars), and *solarscope* (sunviewer) (Dale & O'Rourke, 1971, p. 12).

Synonyms and Antonyms

Synonyms are words that have the same or nearly the same meanings as other words. English has so many synonyms because so many words have been borrowed from other languages. Synonyms are useful because they provide options, allowing us to express ourselves with more exactness. Think of all the different synonyms for the word *cold: cool, chilly, frigid, icy, frosty, freezing,* and so on. Each word has a different shade of meaning: *Cool* means moderately cold; *chilly* is uncomfortably cold; *frigid* is intensely cold; *icy* means very cold; *frosty* means covered with frost; and *freezing* is so cold that water changes into ice. Our language would be limited if we could only say that we were cold.

The largest number of synonyms entered English during the Norman occupation of Britain. Compare these pairs of synonyms: *end–finish, clothing–garments, forgive–pardon, buy–purchase, deadly–mortal.* The first word in each pair comes from Old English; the second was borrowed from the Normans. The Old English words are more basic words, and the French loan words more sophisticated. Perhaps that is why both words in each pair have survived: They express slightly different meanings. Other pairs of synonyms come from different languages. For example, in the pair *comfortable* and *cozy, comfortable* is a Latin loan word, whereas *cozy* is probably of Scandinavian origin.

Teacher's Notebook

Affixes

Prefixes	Suffixes

Prefixes

a/an- (not): atheist, anaerobic
amphi- (both): amphibian
anti- (against): antiseptic
bi- (two, twice): bifocal, biannual
contra- (against): contradict
de- (away): detract
di- (two): dioxide
*dis- (not): disapprove
*dis- (reversal): disinfect
ex- (out): export
hemi- (half): hemisphere
*il-/im-/in-/ir- (not): illegible, impolite, inexpensive, irrational
*in- (in, into): indoor
inter- (between): intermission
kilo/milli- (one thousand): kilometer, milligram
micro- (small): microfilm
*mis- (wrong): mistake
mono- (one): monarch
multi- (many): multimillionaire
omni- (all): omnivorous
*over- (too much): overflow
poly- (many): polygon
post- (after): postwar
pre-/pro- (before): precede, prologue
quad-/quart- (four): quadruple, quarter
re- (again): repay
*re-/retro- (back): replace, retroactive
*sub- (under): submarine
super- (above): supermarket
trans- (across): transport
tri- (three): triangle
*un- (not): unhappy
*un- (reversal): untie

---
* = most commonly used affixes (White, Sowell, & Yanagihara, 1989).

Suffixes

-able/-ible (worthy of, can be): lovable, audible
*-al/-ial (action, process): arrival, denial
-ance/-ence (state or quality): annoyance, absence
-ant (one who): servant
-ard (one who is): coward
-ary/-ory (person, place): secretary, laboratory
-dom (state or quality): freedom
-ed (past tense): played
-ee (one who is): trustee
*-er/-or/-ar (one who): teacher, actor, liar
-er/-or (action): robber
-ern (direction): northern
-et/-ette (small): booklet, dinette
-ful (full of): hopeful
-hood (state or quality): childhood
-ic (characterized by): angelic
-icle/-ucle (small): particle, molecule
-ify (to make): simplify
-ing (participle): eating, building
-ish (like): reddish
-ism (doctrine of): communism
-less (without): hopeless
-ling (young): duckling
-logy (the study of): zoology
*-ly (in the manner of): slowly
-ment (state or quality): enjoyment
*-ness (state or quality): kindness
-s/-es (plural): cats, boxes
-ship (state, or art or skill): friendship, seamanship
*-sion/-tion (state or quality): tension, attraction
-ster (one who): gangster
-ure (state or quality): failure
-ward (direction): homeward
*-y (full of): sleepy

Antonyms are words that express opposite meanings. Antonyms for *loud* include *soft, subdued, quiet, silent, inaudible, sedate, somber, dull,* and *colorless.* These words express shades of meaning just as synonyms do, and some opposites are more appropriate for one meaning of *loud* than for another. When *loud* means *gaudy,* for instance, appropriate opposites might be *somber, dull,* or *colorless.*

Dictionaries and thesauruses list synonyms and antonyms. A good thesaurus for students is *A First Thesaurus* (Wittels & Greisman, 1985), which includes more than 2,000 entry words. Synonyms are printed in black ink for each entry word, and the antonyms follow in red ink.

Homonyms

Homonyms, words that have sound and spelling similarities, are divided into three categories: homophones, homographs, and homographic homophones. *Homophones* are words that sound alike but are spelled differently. Most homophones developed from entirely different root words, and it is only by accident that they have come to sound alike; for example, the homophones *right* and *write* entered English before the year 900 and were pronounced differently. *Right* was spelled *reht* or *riht* in Old English; during the Middle English period the spelling was changed by French scribes to the current spelling. The verb *write* was spelled *writan* in Old English and *writen* in Middle English. *Write* is an irregular verb, suggesting its Old English heritage, and the silent *w* was pronounced hundreds of years ago. In contrast, a few words were derived from the same root words, such as *flea–flee, flower–flour, stationary–stationery,* and *metal–medal,* and the similar spellings have been retained to demonstrate the semantic relationships.

Homographs are words that are spelled the same but pronounced differently. Examples of homographs are *bow, close, lead, minute, record, read,* and *wind. Bow* is a homograph that has three unrelated meanings. The verb form, meaning "to bend in respect," was spelled *bugan* in Old English; the noun form, meaning "a gathering of ribbon" or "a weapon for propelling an arrow," is of Old English origin and was spelled *boga.* The other noun form of *bow,* meaning "forward end of a ship," did not enter English until the 1600s from German.

Homographic homophones are words that are both spelled and pronounced alike, such as *bark, bat, bill, box, fair, fly, hide, jet, mine, pen, ring, row, spell, toast,* and *yard.* Some are related words; others are linguistic accidents. The different meanings of *toast,* for example, came from the same Latin source word, *torrere,* meaning "to parch or bake." The derivation of the noun *toast* as heated and browned slices of bread is obvious; however, the relationship between the source word and *toast* as a verb, drinking to someone's honor or health, is not immediately apparent. The connection is that toasted, spiced bread flavored the drinks used in making toasts. In contrast, *bat* is a linguistic accident: Bat as a *cudgel* comes from the Old English word *batt;* the verb *to bat* is derived from the Old French word *batre;* and the nocturnal *bat* derives its name from an unknown Viking word and was spelled *bakke* in Middle English. Not only do the three forms of *bat* have unrelated etymologies, but they were borrowed from three different languages!

There are many books of homonyms for children, including Gwynne's *The King Who Rained* (1970), *A Chocolate Moose for Dinner* (1976), *The Sixteen*

Hand Horse (1980), and A Little Pigeon Toad (1988); Maestro's What's a Frank Frank? (1984); Homographic Homophones (Hanson, 1973); and Eight Ate: A Feast of Homonym Riddles (Terban, 1982). Elementary students enjoy reading these books and making their own word books. Figure 8–3 shows a page from a second grader's homonym book.

Multiple Meanings

Many words have more than one meaning. The word bank, for example, may refer to a piled-up mass of snow or clouds, the slope of land beside a lake or river, the slope of a road on a turn, the lateral tilting of an airplane in a turn, to cover a fire with ashes for slow burning, a business establishment that receives and lends money, a container in which money is saved, a supply for use in emergencies (e.g., blood bank), a place for storage (e.g., computer's memory bank), to count on, similar things arranged in a row (e.g., a bank of elevators), or to arrange things in a row. You may be surprised that there are at least 12 meanings for the common word bank. Why does this happen? The meanings of bank just listed come from three different sources. The first five meanings come from a Viking word, and they are related because they all deal with something slanted or making a slanted motion. The next five meanings come from the Italian word banca, a money changer's table. These meanings deal with financial banking except the 10th meaning, to count on, which requires a bit more thought. We use the saying "to bank on" figuratively to mean "to depend on," but it began more literally from the actual counting of money on a table. The last two meanings come from the Old French word banc, meaning "bench." Words acquired multiple meanings as society became more complex and finer shades of meaning were necessary; for example, the meanings of bank as an emergency supply and a storage place are fairly new. As with many words with multiple meanings, it is a linguistic accident that three original words from three languages, with related meanings, came to be spelled the same way.

Words assume additional meanings when an affix is added or when they are combined with another word, or compounded. Consider the word fire and the variety of words and phrases that incorporate fire: fire hydrant, firebomb, fireproof, fireplace, firearm, fire drill, under fire, set the world on fire, fire away,

Figure 8–3 A Page From a Second Grader's Homonym Book

Students apply what they are learning about words and their meanings as they read books during a literature focus unit.

and *open fire.* Students can compile a list of words or make a booklet illustrating the words; Figure 8–4 lists more than 100 *down* words that a sixth-grade class compiled.

Idioms

Idioms are groups of words, such as "spilled the beans," that have a special meaning. Idioms can be confusing to students because they must be interpreted figuratively rather than literally. "Spilling the beans" is an old expression, dating back to ancient Greece. Cox (1980) explains that at that time many Greek men belonged to secret clubs, and when someone wanted to join the club, the members took a vote to decide whether or not to admit him. They wanted the vote to remain secret, so they voted by each placing a white or brown bean in a special jar. A white bean indicated a yes vote, and a brown bean was a no vote. The club leader would then count the beans, and if all the beans were white, the person was admitted to the club. The vote was kept secret to avoid hurting the person's feelings in case the members voted not to admit him to the club. Sometimes during the voting one member would accidentally (or not so accidentally) knock the jar over, spilling the beans, and the vote would no longer be a secret. The Greeks turned this real happening into a saying that we still use today. Another idiom with a different history but a similar meaning is "let the cat out of the bag."

There are hundreds of idioms in English, and we use them every day to create word pictures that make language more colorful. Some examples are "out in left field," "a skeleton in the closet," "stick your neck out," "a chip off

Figure 8–4   Sixth Graders'
Class Collaboration List of 100
Down *Words*

downtown	climb down	reach down	downward
touchdown	down payment	write down	hunt down
get down	sit down	settle down	knock down
chow down	throw down	down it	breakdown
shake down	cut down	goose down	sundown
squat down	downhill	hop down	fall down
showdown	low down	hands down	tear down
lie down	slow down	downfall	turn down
quiet down	down right	close down	push down
shut down	beam down	run down	downstairs
shot down	downy	pin down	look down
cool down	downer	come down	inside down
crackdown	downslope	slam down	zip down
countdown	kickdown	slap down	pour down
pass down	stare down	hoe down	down pour
pass me down	boogy down	lock down	tape down
burn down	put down	water down	downgrade
downbeat	wrestle down	downturn	downstream
down to earth	flop down	stuff down	mow down
shimmey down	hung down	downcast	downhearted
downtrodden	chase down	hurl down	beat down

the old block," and "cry over spilled milk." Some of these idioms are new, and others are hundreds or thousands of years old; some are American in origin, and others come from around the world.

Four excellent books of idioms for students are *Put Your Foot in Your Mouth and Other Silly Sayings* (Cox, 1980), *From the Horse's Mouth* (Nevin & Nevin, 1977), *Chin Music: Tall Talk and Other Talk* (Schwartz, 1979), and *In a Pickle and Other Funny Idioms* (Terban, 1983). Because idioms are figurative sayings, many children have difficulty learning them. It is crucial that children move beyond the literal meanings, thus learning flexibility in using language. One way for students to learn flexibility is to create idiom posters, as illustrated in Figure 8–5.

Borrowed Words

The most common way of expanding vocabulary is to borrow words from other languages. This practice, which dates from Old English times, continues to the present day. Perhaps as many as 75% of our words have been borrowed from other languages and incorporated into English. Word borrowing has occurred during every period of language development, beginning when the Angles and Saxons borrowed over 400 words from the Romans. During the eighth and ninth centuries, the Vikings contributed approximately 900 words. The Norman conquerors introduced thousands of French words into English, reflecting every aspect of life: *adventure, fork, juggler,* and *quilt.* Later, during the Renaissance, when scholars translated Greek and Latin classics into English, they borrowed many words from Latin and Greek to enrich the language, including *chaos, encyclopedia, pneumonia,* and *skeleton.* More recently, words from at least 50 languages have been added to English through exploration,

*Figure 8–5   A Fourth Grader's
Idiom Poster*

colonization, and trade. These are some of the loan words from other languages (Tompkins & Yaden, 1986, p. 31):

African (many languages): banjo, cola, gumbo, safari, zombie
Arabic: alcohol, apricot, assassin, magazine
Australian/New Zealand (aboriginal): kangaroo, kiwi
Celtic: walnut
Chinese: chop suey, kowtow, tea, wok
Czech: pistol, robot
Dutch: caboose, easel, pickle, waffle
Eskimo: igloo, parka
Finnish: sauna
French: ballet, beige, chauffeur
German: kindergarten, poodle, pretzel, waltz
Greek: atom, cyclone, hydrogen
Hawaiian: aloha, hula, lei, luau
Hebrew: cherub, kosher, rabbi
Hindi: dungaree, juggernaut, jungle, shampoo
Hungarian: goulash, paprika

Icelandic: geyser
Irish: bog, leprechaun, shamrock, slogan
Italian: broccoli, carnival, macaroni, opera, pizza
Japanese: honcho, judo, kimono, origami
Persian: bazaar, divan, khaki, shawl
Polish: mazurka, polka
Portuguese: cobra, coconut, molasses
Russian: czar, sputnik, steppe, troika, vodka
Scandinavian (Swedish, Norwegian, Danish): egg, fiord, husband, ski, sky
Scottish: clan, golf, slogan
Spanish: alligator, guitar, mosquito, potato
Turkish: caviar, horde, khan, kiosk, yogurt
Yiddish: bagel, chutzpah, pastrami

Native Americans have also contributed a number of words to English. The early American colonists encountered many unfamiliar animals, plants, foods, and aspects of Indian life in America. They borrowed the Native American terms for these objects or events and tried to spell them phonetically. Native American loan words include *chipmunk, hickory, moccasin, moose, muskrat, opossum, papoose, pow-wow, raccoon, skunk, succotash, toboggan, tomahawk,* and *tepee.*

Other Sources of New Words

New words continually appear in English, many of which are created to describe new inventions and scientific projects. Some of the newest words come from computer science and the space program. They are created in a variety of ways, including compounding, coining, and clipping.

Compounding means combining two existing words to create a new word. *Friendship* and *childhood* are two words that the Anglo-Saxons compounded more than a thousand years ago. Recent compoundings include *latchkey kids* and *software.* Compound words usually progress through three stages: They begin as separate words (e.g., *ice cream*), then are hyphenated (e.g., *baby-sit*), and finally are written as one word (e.g., *splashdown*). There are many exceptions to this rule, such as the compound words *post office* and *high school,* which have remained separate words. Other compound words use Greek and Latin elements, such as *stethoscope* and *television.*

Creative people have always coined new words. Lewis Carroll, author of *Alice in Wonderland* and *Through the Looking Glass,* is perhaps the best-known inventor of words. He called his new words *portmanteau words* (borrowing from the British word for a suitcase that opens into two halves) because they were created by blending two words into one. His most famous example, *chortle,* a blend of *snort* and *chuckle,* is from the poem "Jabberwocky," and Zalben's beautifully illustrated picture book version of *Jabberwocky* (1977) is popular with elementary students. Other examples of blended words include:

> *brunch (breakfast* and *lunch)*
>
> *electrocute (electric* and *execute)*
>
> *guesstimate (guess* and *estimate)*
>
> *smog (smoke* and *fog)*

Two other types of coined words are *trademarks* and *acronyms.* Examples of well-known trademarks and brand names include Kleenex, Coca-Cola, Xerox, and nylon. *Nylon,* for instance, was invented by scientists working in New York and London; they named their product by combining *ny,* the abbreviation for *New York,* with *lon,* the first three letters of *London.* Acronyms, words formed by combining the initial letters of several words, include *radar, laser,* and *scuba. Scuba,* for example, was formed by combining the initial letters of *self-contained underwater breathing apparatus.*

Clipping is a process of shortening existing words. For example, *bomb* is the shortened form of *bombard,* and *zoo* comes from *zoological park.* Most clipped words are only one syllable and are used in informal conversation. Although it is unlikely that your students will create new words that will eventually appear in the dictionary, students do create words to add pizzazz to their writing, and some terms created to fill a particular need become part of the everyday jargon in a classroom. For example, a group of third graders created the word *crocket* (*cro*codile + *rocket*) to describe the crocodile who became a rocket at the end of Dahl's *The Enormous Crocodile* (1978).

Authors also create new words in their stories, and students should be alert to the possibility of finding a created word when they read or listen to stories. Adams used *woggle* in *A Woggle of Witches* (1971), the Howes (1979) created *Bunnicula* to name their spooky young rabbit (*bunny* + dra*cula*), and Horwitz describes the night as *bimulous* in *When the Sky Is Like Lace* (1975).

Sniglets are words that aren't in the dictionary, but, according to Rich Hall (1985), their creator, should be. One of his sniglets is *beavo,* a pencil covered with teeth marks. Several books of sniglets have been published, including one especially for children, *Sniglets for Kids* (Hall, 1985). Elementary students enjoy reading these books and creating their own words. To create a sniglet, they use affixes, compounding, coining, and clipping. A fifth grader's sniglet, *tappee,* is shown in Figure 8–6; the student used the Latin suffix *-ee,* meaning "one who."

TEACHING STUDENTS ABOUT WORDS

Students learn many, many words incidentally, through reading or theme cycles. In fact, reading is probably the most important way teachers promote vocabulary growth (Nagy, 1988). Writing is also important, because after students meet words in reading, they interact with the words a second time by writing them in reading logs or in projects. Repeated exposure to words is crucial because students need to see and use a new word many times before it becomes a part of their ownership dictionaries—words they understand and use competently.

Figure 8–6   A Fifth Grader's Sniglet

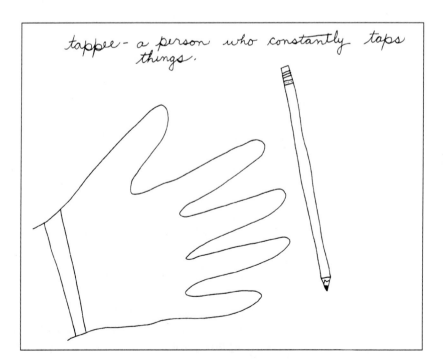

Teachers supplement incidental learning through direct instruction. All the words students learn are not equally hard or easy to learn; the degree of difficulty depends on what the student already knows about the word. Graves (1985) identifies four possible situations:

1. *Sight words*—words that are in students' talking and listening vocabularies but that they don't know how to read.
2. *New words*—words for which students have concepts but which are not in their vocabularies.
3. *New concepts*—words for which students have neither concepts nor vocabularies.
4. *New meanings*—words that are already in students' vocabularies with one or more meanings but for which additional meanings need to be learned.

Probably the most difficult category of words for students to learn is the new concept words, because they must first learn the concepts and then attach word labels. Students may benefit from direct instruction on these words.

When planning a literature focus unit or theme cycle, teachers need to give attention to the words students will learn. For example, during a theme on bears, kindergartners might learn these words: *shaggy, fur, dangerous, tame, meat-eating, polar bear, grizzly bear, brown bear, claws, hind legs, hibernate, den,* and *cubs.* Or, a study of Martin Luther King, Jr., for upper-grade students might include these words: *segregation, protest, sit-in, Nobel Peace Prize, Jim Crow laws, civil rights, boycott, Negro, prejudice, nonviolence, activist, assassinated,* and *martyr.* Which words will be sight words? Which words represent new concepts? Words that are critical to understanding a concept or reading a selection independently should be taught; however, not all words can or should be taught because of time constraints and because students can and will infer the meanings of many words on their own. Students are introduced to the words through the various activities they are involved in: They meet the words in books they read, in films they view, and during oral presentations by the teacher. As students interact with the words again and again, the words jockey for position, moving toward the ownership dictionary. According to Vygotsky's notion of "a zone of proximal development," teachers need to be alert to individual students and what words they are learning so that they can provide instruction when students are most interested in learning more about one word.

Word Walls and Word Study Activities

Words for study are chosen from books students are reading during literature focus units or from theme cycles. Teachers post *word walls,* made from large sheets of butcher paper, in the classroom. Students and the teacher write interesting, confusing, and important words on the word wall. Usually students choose the words to write on the word wall and may even do the writing themselves. Teachers add important words that students have not chosen. Words are added to the word wall as they come up in books students are reading or during a theme cycle—not in advance. Students use the word wall to locate a word they want to use during a grand conversation or to check the spelling of a word they are writing, and teachers use the words listed on the word wall for word study activities.

During a theme cycle on whales, a class of fourth graders created this word wall.

Word study activities should help students explore the meaning of the word and make associations with literature focus units and theme cycles. Students should not be asked to write words and their definitions or to use the words in sentences or a story. Here are six types of activities:

1. **Word Posters.**   Student choose a word from the word wall and write it on a small poster. Then they draw and color a picture to illustrate the word. They may also want to use the word in a sentence.

2. **Word Clusters.**   Students make a cluster and choose a word from the word wall to write in the center circle. Then they draw out rays, write important information about the word, and make connections between the word and the literature focus unit or theme cycle. Figure 8–7 shows three types of word clusters. First graders made the first cluster on *taxi* after reading *The Adventures of Taxi Dog* (Barracca & Barracca, 1990). The second is a cluster for *maple sugar* that third graders made after reading *Sugaring Time* by Kathryn Lasky (1983). The third cluster on *reminiscent* is the most structured. A small group of seventh graders developed this cluster, considering the definition of the word; its history or etymology; its part of speech; other related forms; its word parts; and antonyms, synonyms, or homonyms.

3. **Dramatizing Words.**   Students choose a word from the word wall and dramatize it for classmates to guess. Teachers might also want to choose a word from the word wall for a "word of the day."

4. **Word Sorts.**   Students sort a collection of words taken from the word wall into two or more categories. Usually students choose what categories they will use for the sort, but sometimes the teacher chooses the categories. For

Figure 8–7   Three Word
Clusters

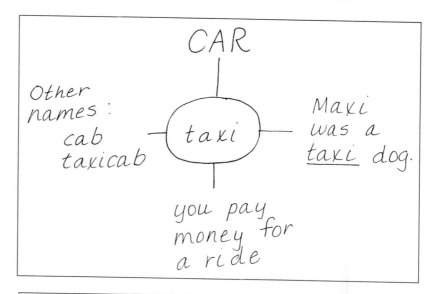

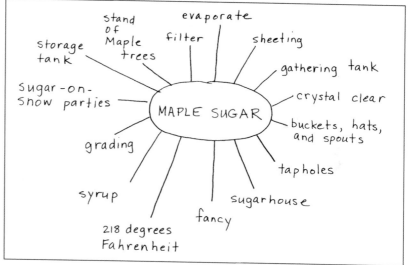

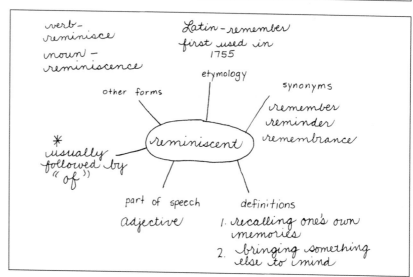

example, words from a story might be sorted by character, or words from a theme on machines might be sorted according to type of machine. The words can be written on cards, and then students sort a pack of word cards into piles. Or, students can cut apart a list of words, sort them into categories, and then paste each group on a sheet of paper.

5.   Word Chains.   Students choose a word from the word wall and then identify three or four words to sequence before or after the word to make a chain. For example, the word *tadpole* can be chained this way: *egg, tadpole, frog;* and the word *aggravate* can be chained like this: *irritate, bother, aggravate, annoy.* Students can draw and write their chains on a sheet of paper, or they can make a construction paper chain and write the words on each link.

6.   Semantic Feature Analysis.   Students select a group of related words, such as different kinds of birds, and then make a chart to classify them according to distinguishing characteristics. A semantic feature analysis on birds is presented in Figure 8–8.

Minilessons on Words

Students use four strategies to learn the meanings of words as they read or listen to information presented orally. These four strategies are:

1. *Phonics.* Students use their knowledge of phoneme-grapheme relationships to pronounce an unknown word when reading, and they often recognize the word's meaning when they hear it pronounced.
2. *Structural analysis.* Students peel the affixes off the word and then use their knowledge of root words, prefixes, and suffixes to figure out the meaning of the word.
3. *Context clues.* Students use the surrounding information in the sentence to guess the meaning of the unknown word. Context clues take a variety of forms. Sometimes the word is defined in the sentence, and at other times synonyms or antonyms are used, or examples give students an idea of the meaning of the word.
4. *Reference books.* Students locate the unknown word in a dictionary or thesaurus and read the definition or synonyms and antonyms to determine the meaning.

Students learn about these four strategies through minilessons. Through minilessons, they also learn about the history of English; root words and affixes; homonyms, synonyms, and antonyms; and figurative meanings of words, such as idioms. A list of topics for minilessons on words is presented on page 304.

The goal of vocabulary instruction is for students to learn how to learn new words, but traditional approaches, such as assigning students to look up the definitions of a list of words in a dictionary, often fail to produce in-depth understanding (Nagy, 1988). Carr and Wixon (1986) list four guidelines for effective instruction:

- Instruction should help students relate new words to their background knowledge.

Figure 8–8 A Semantic Feature Analysis

	hatches from eggs	has feathers	has wings	can fly	can swim	migrates	is a bird of prey	is extinct
bluejay	✓	✓	✓	✓	○	○	○	○
owl	✓	✓	✓	✓	○	○	✓	○
roadrunner								
eagle								
pelican								
hummingbird								
quail								
ostrich								
dodo								
robin								
penguin								
chicken								
duck								
seagull								
peacock								
flamingo								

Code: ✓ = yes

○ = no

? = don't know

303

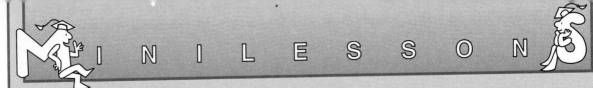

Words

Procedures	Concepts	Strategies and Skills
Choose words for word walls	History of English	Use phonics to pronounce a word
Extrapolate the etymology	Root words	Use structural analysis to identify a word
"Peel off" affixes	Affixes	Use context clues to identify a word
Make a word poster	Prefixes	Consider shades of meaning in selecting a word
Make a word cluster	Suffixes	Use a thesaurus to choose a better word
Do a word sort	Synonyms	Use a dictionary to identify a word
Make a word chain	Antonyms	Avoid trite language
Do a semantic feature analysis	Homophones	Consider multiple meanings of words
Locate a word in a dictionary	Homographs	
Locate a word in a thesaurus	Homographic homophones	
Assess use of words in a literature focus unit	Multiple meanings of words	
Assess use of words in a theme cycle	Idioms	
	Literal meanings	
	Figurative meanings	
	Borrowed words	
	Compound words	
	Coined words	
	Clipped words	
	Invented words	
	Sniglets	

- Instruction should help students develop ownership-level word knowledge.
- Instruction should provide for students' active involvement in learning new words.
- Instruction should develop students' strategies for learning new words independently.

This teaching strategy can be used to teach minilessons on a specific word or a group of related words. It is based on the strategy we discussed in Chapter 1, and it embodies Carr and Wixon's characteristics of effective vocabulary instruction:

Step by Step

1. **Introducing the Word.** Teachers present the word and explain the meaning, tying the word to students' background knowledge. Words for minilessons should be chosen from books students are reading or should be related to theme cycles in which students are involved.

2. **Using the Word in Context.** Teachers use the word in the context of the literature focus unit or theme cycle. Also, teachers identify the root word, talk about the etymology of the word, and consider related words or easily confused words, if appropriate.

3. *Applying Word Knowledge.* Teachers involve students in an activity to bring together all the information—semantic, structural, and contextual—presented earlier.

4. *Reviewing the Word.* Students and the teacher review the word and the strategies used in identifying it. Students can add the word to vocabulary notebooks or make a poster to review the information they have learned.

5. *Providing Meaningful Opportunities to Use the Word.* Students use the word in meaningful ways. They need to read the word; write the word in informal and formal writings; use the word in discussions, debates, and oral reports; and use the word in class, small group, and individual projects.

Students need to know about the English language, words and their meanings, and strategies to use to figure out the meanings of words independently. Students in the elementary grades learn about multiple meanings as well as about root words and affixes; homonyms, synonyms, and antonyms; and figurative meanings of words, such as idioms. An example of a minilesson on context clues is presented in Figure 8–9.

In Literature Focus Units

As students read books during literature focus units, they learn many new words; some they learn incidentally, and others through minilessons and word study activities. As teachers prepare to read books with students, they think about which words they will teach and how they will teach them. Some word study activities take place during the responding stage of the reading process. Immediately after reading a picture book, a short story, or a chapter or two of a longer book, students and the teacher add words to the word wall. Then students use the words as they respond to their reading in grand conversations and in reading logs. Later, during the exploring stage, students focus on specific words through activities and minilessons.

A second-grade class participated in these word study activities during a week-long literature focus unit on *Tacky the Penguin* (Lester, 1988), a story about a penguin that does not fit in with his sleek and graceful companions, but his odd behavior comes in handy when hunters come. On Monday, after reading the book using shared reading, students and the teacher wrote these words on a word wall:

Tacky	graceful divers
penguin	splashy cannonballs
icy	pretty songs
companions	"Sunrise on the Iceberg"
an odd bird	"How Many Toes Does a Fish Have?"
Goodly	distance
Lovely	hunters
Angel	maps and traps
Neatly	rocks and locks
Perfect	rough and tough
quietly	growly voices
politely	fright
hearty slap on the back	get rich
loud	"What's happening?"

Figure 8–9   A Minilesson on Context Clues

This minilesson is planned for a small group of students in a middle-grade class-room who have shown a need to learn this strategy. The teacher and students meet together at a conference table and spend approximately 15 minutes in the minilesson. The steps are as follows:

1. Introduce the Strategy

Explain to students that they often use context clues to identify a new word when they read. Context clues are the pieces of information in the sentences and illus-trations surrounding the unknown word that often supply the meaning of the word.

2. Practice the Strategy

The teacher presents copies of a paragraph with a nonsense word substituting for an important word (Klein, 1988), and asks, "What does the word *matto* mean in this paragraph?"

> Mattos are made up of many bones. Your matto is made up of 206 bones. These bones give you your shape. Nothing can change your shape because you have a matto inside you. Some of the bones in your matto protect impor-tant parts inside you. Rib bones cover your heart and lungs and the skull pro-tects your brain from injury.

Students read the paragraph and use the information in the surrounding sentences to determine that the nonsense word stands for *skeleton.*

3. Discuss Students' Use of the Strategy

Students and the teacher reread the paragraph, noting which pieces of information were most useful in determining that *matto* stood for *skeleton.*

4. Review the Strategy

The teacher and students review the steps and make a chart to hang in the class-room about the context clues strategy. They include these steps:

• When you come to a new word, keep reading and don't panic.
• You can probably figure out what the word means from the other words around it.
• Look to see if any pictures might help.
• Ask yourself if what you are reading is making sense.
• Try to guess the word.
• Write the word down in your reading log so that you can check it later.

5. Provide Practice Opportunities

The teacher asks students to practice using the context clues strategy as they read during the next two days. Then they will meet again to review this minilesson and share examples of how they used the context clues strategy in books they are reading. The teacher asks students to bring examples to share.

Students referred to the words on the word wall as they wrote entries in their reading logs and talked about the story. During the grand conversation, the teacher focused on the word *odd* and asked why Tacky was called an odd bird.

On Tuesday, the students reviewed the words on the word wall before rereading the story using buddy reading. The next day the teacher taught a minilesson on how to do a word sort, and students used word cards to sort words from the story into three categories: words about Tacky, words about the other penguins, and words about the hunters. On Thursday, students worked in small groups to cut apart a list of the words from the story, sort them into the three categories, and paste the words in each group on a sheet of paper. Many students also used these words in the projects they were involved in.

Adapting to Meet the Needs of Every Student

Learning about words is an important part of language arts, and it is crucial that teachers find ways to help every student use the words they are learning. Having a word wall in every literature focus unit and across-the-curriculum theme cycle is probably the most important way to focus students' attention on words. Teachers also need to provide a variety of word study activities to meet the needs of every student. A list of suggestions for adapting vocabulary instruction is presented on page 308. These suggestions focus on using vocabulary in meaningful, functional, and genuine ways.

Assessing Students' Use of Words

Teachers assess students' use of literature focus unit and theme-related words in a variety of ways. They listen while students talk during the theme, examine students' writing and projects, and ask students to talk or write about the theme and what they have learned. Here are some specific strategies to determine whether students have learned and are applying new words:

One way teachers can assess students' use of theme-related words is by examining their learning logs and other compositions.

Adapting . . .
Vocabulary Instruction
To Meet the Needs of Every Student

1. *Highlighting Key Words on Word Walls*

   Teachers might highlight words on word walls by writing them with colored pens. Also, they can add pictures to illustrate the words.

2. *Sorting Words*

   The word-sorting activity is very useful for students who need additional opportunities to categorize words or learn relationships among words. After reading a story, students can sort words according to characters, or during a theme cycle they can sort words according to key concepts.

3. *Teaching Idioms*

   Students who are learning English as a second language may need to learn about idioms and separate their literal and figurative meanings. Students can dramatize or draw pictures of the two meanings of idioms.

4. *Learning Multiple Meanings of Words*

   Students can draw diagrams to show multiple meanings of words. For example, students can draw a diagram to chart two meanings of *watch:*

   watch ⟨ to look at something
   a small clock on your wrist

   Students can add drawings to the diagram or use the word in sentences.

5. *Introducing New Concepts*

   Some students may need assistance in developing a concept before learning related words. Teachers need to anticipate how difficult a word might be for students and provide opportunities involving hands-on experiences, dramatic activities, or pictures.

- Check reading logs, learning logs, or simulated journals for theme-related words.
- Use words in a conference and note the student's response.
- Listen for vocabulary when students give an oral report.
- Ask students to make a cluster or do a quickwrite about the theme or about specific words.
- Ask students to brainstorm a list of words and phrases about the unit or theme.
- Check students' reports, biographies, stories, or other writings for theme-related words.
- Check students' projects for theme-related words, or ask them to label the project with five words.

- Ask students to write a letter to you, telling what they have learned in the literature focus unit or theme cycle.

Teachers can also give a test on the vocabulary words, but this is probably the least effective approach because a correct answer on a test does not indicate whether students have ownership of a word or whether they are applying it in meaningful and genuine ways.

Review

Learning about words is an important part of language arts. English is a historic language, and both the meaning and the spelling of many words can be explained within a historical context. Few words have only one meaning, and students in the elementary grades learn about multiple meanings as well as about root words and affixes; homonyms, synonyms, and antonyms; and figurative meanings of words, such as idioms. Students learn approximately 3,000 new words each year during the elementary grades, and they learn most of these words incidentally through reading and across-the-curriculum study. In learning a word, students must be able to recognize it as a sight word, understand the concept, and know the specific meaning (if the word has more than one). Teachers teach minilessons and word study activities as part of the responding and exploring stages of the reading process. The best measure of students' learning of words is their ability to use the words in meaningful, functional, and genuine activities.

Extensions

1. Learn more about the history of English by reading one or more of the books listed in Figure 8–1.
2. Identify a literature focus unit or theme cycle for a particular grade level, and choose the vocabulary you would teach. Which words do you think will be sight words, new words, new concepts, or new meanings for students?
3. Observe in an elementary classroom and note how vocabulary is taught both formally and informally. Or, interview an elementary teacher and ask how

he or she teaches vocabulary. Compare the teacher's answers with the information presented in this chapter.
4. Plan and teach a series of minilessons on homonyms, synonyms, or antonyms using the teaching strategy in this chapter.
5. Think back to the discussion on language-rich classrooms in Chapter 2, and describe 10 ways to facilitate students' incidental learning of vocabulary through the classroom environment.

References

Alexander, H. (1962). *The story of our language.* Garden City, NY: Doubleday.

Baugh, A. C., & Cable, T. (1978). *The history of the English language* (3rd ed.). Englewood Cliffs, NJ: Prentice-Hall.

Carr, E., & Wixon, K. K. (1986). Guidelines for evaluating vocabulary instruction. *Journal of Reading, 29,* 588–595.

Dale, E., & O'Rourke, J. (1971). *Techniques of teaching vocabulary.* Palo Alto, CA: Field Educational Publications.

Flexner, S. B. (1987). *The Random House dictionary of the English language* (2nd ed.). New York: Random House.

Graves, M. (1985). *A word is a word . . . or is it?* Portsmouth, NH: Heinemann.

Hook, J. N. (1975). *History of the English language.* New York: Ronald Press.

Klein, M. L. (1988). *Teaching reading comprehension and vocabulary: A guide for teachers.* Englewood Cliffs, NJ: Prentice-Hall.

Nagy, W. E. (1988). *Teaching vocabulary to improve reading comprehension.* Urbana, IL: ERIC Clearinghouse on Reading and Communication Skills and the National Council of Teachers of English and the International Reading Association.

Nagy, W. E., & Herman, P. (1985). Incidental vs. instructional approaches to increasing reading vocabulary. *Educational Perspectives, 23,* 16–21.

Tompkins, G. E. (1994). *Teaching writing: Balancing process and product* (2nd ed.). New York: Merrill/Macmillan.

Tompkins, G. E., & Yaden, D. B., Jr. (1986). *Answering students' questions about words.* Urbana, IL: ERIC Clearinghouse on Reading and Communication Skills and the National Council of Teachers of English.

White, T. G., Sowell, J., & Yanagihara, A. (1989). Teaching elementary students to use word-part clues. *The Reading Teacher, 42,* 302–308.

Children's Book References

Adams, A. (1971). *A woggle of witches.* New York: Scribner.

Barracca, D., & Barracca, S. (1990). *The adventures of taxi dog.* New York: Dial.

Cox, J. A. (1980). *Put your foot in your mouth and other silly sayings.* New York: Random House.

Dahl, R. (1978). *The enormous crocodile.* New York: Knopf.

Gwynne, F. (1970). *The king who rained.* New York: Windmill Books.

Gwynne, F. (1976). *A chocolate moose for dinner.* New York: Windmill Books.

Gwynne, F. (1980). *The sixteen hand horse.* New York: Prentice-Hall.

Gwynne, F. (1988). *A little pigeon toad.* New York: Simon & Schuster.

Hall, R. (1985). *Sniglets for kids.* Yellow Springs, OH: Antioch.

Hanson, J. (1973). *Homographic homophones.* Minneapolis, MN: Lerner.

Horwitz, E. L. (1975). *When the sky is like lace.* Philadelphia: Lippincott.

Howe, D., & Howe, J. (1979). *Bunnicula: A rabbit-tale of mystery.* New York: Atheneum.

Konigsburg, E. L. (1967). *From the mixed-up files of Mrs. Basil E. Frankweiler.* New York: Atheneum.

Lasky, K. (1983). *Sugaring time.* New York: Macmillan.

Lester, H. (1988). *Tacky the penguin.* Boston: Houghton Mifflin.

Maestro, G. (1984). *What's a frank Frank? Tasty homograph riddles.* New York: Clarion Books.

Nevin, A., & Nevin, D. (1977). *From the horse's mouth.* Englewood Cliffs, NJ: Prentice-Hall.

Schwartz, A. (1979). *Chin music: Tall talk and other talk.* Philadelphia: Lippincott.

Terban, M. (1982). *Eight ate: A feast of homonym riddles.* New York: Clarion Books.

Terban, M. (1983). *In a pickle and other funny idioms.* New York: Clarion Books.

Van Allsburg, C. (1979). *The garden of Abdul Gasazi.* Boston: Houghton Mifflin.

Wittels, H., & Greisman, J. (1985). *A first thesaurus.* Racine, WI: Western.

Zalben, J. B. (1977). *Lewis Carroll's Jabberwocky.* New York: Harper & Row.

> *There's so much to do with a chapter book like The Sign of the Beaver. I use it to teach about characters and to connect with our theme cycle on Native Americans.*
>
> **Kathy Brown**
> *Fourth-Grade Teacher*
> *Jackson Elementary School*

PROCEDURE

My class is reading *The Sign of the Beaver* (Speare, 1983). I have copies for each student, and we're reading it together in groups—two or three short chapters each day. Each group has a leader, and when I want to share something about a chapter, I give the information to the leader, who shares it with the group. I move from group to group to keep tabs on their progress, but the groups operate without me.

Students read silently or with a buddy and then write in their reading logs. In the entries, they write reactions and questions to use in the literature conversation. After everyone in the group finishes, the leader starts the conversation by asking a question or by asking a student to read his or her reading log entry. Students take turns talking about the chapter and sharing their ideas, comments, and questions. I take a few minutes at the end of the conversation to bring the class together so that each group can share something

or make a prediction about what will happen in the story.

I'm focusing on one element of story structure—character—in this story. Students are examining how Mrs. Speare develops Matt's character. Before beginning the story, I told the students a bit about Matt, the 12-year-old main character. I asked them to write in their reading logs and predict what they thought this boy living in the Maine wilderness in 1769 would be like and what might happen to him in the story. Every two or three days we talk again about Matt and how Mrs. Speare has unveiled more about this character through appearance, action, dialogue, and monologue. Students add new information to the character cluster chart hanging on the wall. The cluster has Matt's name in the middle and rays for "What he looks like," "What he does," "What he says," and "What he thinks."

After reading 10 chapters, my students were surprised to find that Mrs. Speare tells about Matt primarily through his actions. The only fact students have learned about his appearance is that he wore boots, until his disastrous attempt to get honey from a beehive, and now he wears Indian moccasins.

Afterwards, we will think about the character traits that were revealed through Matt's actions. For example, Matt exhibited carelessness when he didn't close the cabin door, and he lacked common sense when he tried to get some honey from the beehive. Not all Matt's actions suggest negative traits, though. He showed resourcefulness when he learned to trap and determination when he waited for his family. My goal is for the students to understand that Matt, like everyone else, is a combination of character traits, some good and some bad.

Also, each student will do a project related to the book. We've started a list of activities to choose from: read informational books about Maine, write a poem about Matt, make a map of the area in Maine where the story takes place, research Indians of the New England area, read another book by Mrs. Speare, write a sequel about life after Matt's parents arrive, and so on.

ASSESSMENT

I use a checklist of the assignments to monitor the students' work. I pass out the checklist at the beginning of the unit, and students keep the checklist in their unit folders along with their reading log, book, and other materials. Students check off each assignment as it is completed. Later, as I review the work, I assign points and total them for the unit grade. A copy of the checklist is shown in the accompanying figure.

ADAPTATIONS

This year most of my students can read *The Sign of the Beaver* independently or with the assistance of a classmate. Other years, I've had more students who needed help. I've tried several approaches to make the book more accessible for these students. My most successful approach is to have a sixth grader read along with each group. This student can supply words that students don't know or read aloud to the group, if necessary. I've also tape-recorded the book for students to listen to at the listening center.

REFLECTIONS

I'm learning how to make connections between the different areas of the curriculum, and through *The Sign of the Beaver* I'm connecting language arts and social studies. The students learn more and enjoy it more. It makes so much sense—I just wonder why I didn't think of it sooner.

Literature Focus Unit Checklist for *The Sign of the Beaver*

Name _____

	Points	Score
1. Read *The Sign of the Beaver* with your group.	20	_____
2. Work cooperatively with your group.	5	_____
3. Share your ideas in literature conversations.	5	_____
4. Write at least eight entries in your reading log.	20	_____
5. Do a character activity:	10	_____

_____ Open mind poster
_____ Venn diagram of Matt and Attean
_____ Character quilt
_____ Before and after scenes

6. Do a project.	20	_____
7. Share the project.	10	_____
8. Write a letter to me about your learning and work in this unit.	10	_____

9

Reading
and
Writing
Stories

INSIGHT _____

As they read, some students become so immersed in the story they are reading that
they seem to step into another world. These
students have favorite stories that they reread again and again, and they choose to
read as a leisure time activity. For other students, though, reading is a job—something
that they do only when they have to. One
goal of reading instruction is to show all
students how pleasurable reading can be
so that they will become lifelong readers.
Teachers hope that students will sometimes
choose to pick up a book and read a story
rather than to play a video game, for example. As you read this chapter, think
about this question:

How can teachers help students become
lifelong readers?

Stories give meaning to the human experience, and they are a powerful way of knowing and learning. Preschool children listen to family members tell and read stories aloud, and they have developed an understanding or concept about stories by the time they come to school. Students use and refine this knowledge as they read and write stories during the elementary grades. Many educators, including Jerome Bruner (1986), recommend using stories as a way into literacy.

Primary-grade students read and respond to stories such as *The Tale of Peter Rabbit* (Potter, 1902), *Where the Wild Things Are* (Sendak, 1962), and *Ira Sleeps Over* (Waber, 1972), and older students read and respond to *Charlotte's Web* (White, 1952), *Bunnicula: A Rabbit-Tale of Mystery* (Howe & Howe, 1979), and *The Lion, the Witch and the Wardrobe* (Lewis, 1981). These stories are becoming modern "classics" to be cherished by generation after generation of children. Sometimes teachers call all literature that students read and write "stories," but stories are a particular type. They have specific structural elements, including characters and plot.

Students tell and write stories about events in their lives—a birthday party, a fishing trip, or a car accident—retell familiar stories, including "The Gingerbread Man," and write sequels for stories such as *Jumanji* (Van Allsburg, 1981). The stories that students write reflect the stories they have read. De Ford (1981) and Eckhoff (1983) found that when primary-grade students read stories in basal reading textbooks, the stories they write reflect the short, choppy linguistic style of the readers, but when students read stories in trade books, their writing reflects the more sophisticated language structures and literary style of the trade books. Dressel (1990) also found that the quality of fifth graders' writing was dependent on the quality of the stories they read or listened to someone else read aloud, regardless of the students' reading levels.

DEVELOPING STUDENTS' CONCEPT OF STORY

Young children have a rudimentary awareness about what makes a story. Knowledge about stories is called a *concept of story*. Children's concept of story includes information about the elements of story structure, such as characters, plot, and setting, as well as information about the conventions authors use. This knowledge is usually intuitive; that is, children are not conscious of what they know. Golden (1984) describes children's concept of story as "a mental representation of story structure, essentially an outline of the basic story elements and their organization" (p. 578).

Researchers have documented that children's concept of story begins in the preschool years, and that children as young as 2½ years have a rudimentary sense of story (Applebee, 1978, 1980; Pitcher & Prelinger, 1963). Children acquire this concept of story gradually, by listening to stories read to them, by reading stories themselves, and by telling and writing stories. Not surprisingly, older children have a better understanding of story structure than do younger children. Similarly, the stories older children tell and write are increasingly more complex; the plot structures are more tightly organized, and the characters are more fully developed. Yet, Applebee (1980) found that by the time children begin kindergarten, they have already developed a basic concept of what a story is, and these expectations guide them in responding to

One way that students learn about the elements of story structure is by listening as the teacher reads stories aloud.

stories and telling their own stories. He found, for example, that kindergartners could use three story markers: "Once upon a time . . ." to begin a story; the past tense in telling a story; and formal endings such as "The End" or ". . . and they lived happily ever after."

Students' concept of story plays an important role in interpreting stories they read (Mandler & Johnson, 1977; Rumelhart, 1975; Stein & Glenn, 1979), and it is just as important in writing (Golden, 1984). Students continue to grow in their understanding of stories through reading and writing experiences (Golden, Meiners, & Lewis, 1992). As they respond to and explore stories they are reading and writing, students learn about elements of story structure and *genre* or categories of stories. Golden and her colleagues say that story meaning is dynamic, growing continuously in the reader's mind.

Elements of Story Structure

Stories have unique structural elements that distinguish them from other forms of writing. In fact, the structure of stories is quite complex—plot, characters, setting, and other elements interact with each other to produce a story. Authors manipulate the elements to make their stories complex and interesting. We will focus on five elements of story structure—plot, characters, setting, theme, and point of view—and will illustrate each element with familiar and award-winning trade books.

Plot. Plot is the sequence of events involving characters in conflict situations. A story's plot is based on the goals of one or more characters and the processes they go through to attain these goals (Lukens, 1991). The main characters want to achieve a goal, and other characters are introduced to oppose or prevent the main characters from being successful. The story events are put in motion by characters as they attempt to overcome conflict, reach their goals, and solve their problems.

The most basic aspect of plot is the division of the main events of a story into three parts: beginning, middle, and end. Upper-grade students may substitute the terms *introduction, development* or *complication,* and *resolution.* In *The Tale of Peter Rabbit* (Potter, 1902), for instance, one can easily pick out the three story parts: As the story begins, Mrs. Rabbit sends her children out to play after warning them not to go into Mr. McGregor's garden; in the middle, Peter goes to Mr. McGregor's garden and is almost caught; then Peter finds his way out of the garden and gets home safely—the end of the story. Students can cluster the beginning-middle-end of a story as the cluster for *The Tale of Peter Rabbit* in Figure 9–1 shows.

Specific types of information are included in each of the three story parts. In the beginning the author introduces the characters, describes the setting,

Figure 9–1   *A Beginning-Middle-End Cluster for* The Tale of Peter Rabbit

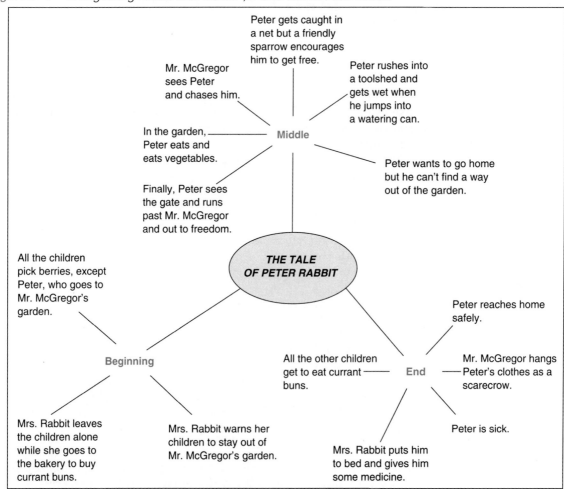

and presents a problem. Together, the characters, setting, and events develop the plot and sustain the theme throughout the story. In the middle the author adds to events presented in the beginning, with each event preparing readers for what will follow. Conflict heightens as the characters face roadblocks that keep them from solving their problems. How the characters tackle these problems adds suspense to keep readers interested. In the end the author reconciles all that has happened in the story, and readers learn whether or not the characters' struggles are successful.

Conflict is the tension or opposition between forces in the plot, and it is what interests readers enough to continue reading the story. Conflict usually occurs (Lukens, 1991):

- Between a character and nature
- Between a character and society
- Between characters
- Within a character

Conflict between a character and nature occurs in stories in which severe weather plays an important role, as in *Julie of the Wolves* (George, 1972), and in stories set in isolated geographic locations, such as *Island of the Blue Dolphins* (O'Dell, 1960), in which the Indian girl Karana struggles to survive alone on a Pacific island. In some stories a character's activities and beliefs differ from those of other members of the society, and the differences cause conflict between that character and the local society. One example of this type of conflict is *The Witch of Blackbird Pond* (Speare, 1958) in which Kit Tyler is accused of being a witch because she continues activities in a New England Puritan community that were acceptable in the Caribbean community where she grew up but which are not acceptable in her new home. Conflict between characters is a common type of conflict in children's literature. In *Tales of a Fourth Grade Nothing* (Blume, 1972), for instance, the never-ending conflict between Peter and his little brother Fudge is what makes the story interesting. The fourth type of conflict is conflict within a character, and stories such as *Ira Sleeps Over* (Waber, 1972) and *The Summer of the Swans* (Byars, 1970) are examples. In *Ira Sleeps Over*, 6-year-old Ira must decide whether to take his teddy bear with him when he goes next door to spend the night with a friend, and in *The Summer of the Swans,* Sara feels guilty when her mentally retarded brother wanders off and is lost. Figure 9–2 lists stories representing the four conflict situations.

The plot is developed through conflict that is introduced in the beginning of a story, expanded in the middle, and finally resolved at the end. Plot development involves four components:

1. *A problem.* A problem that introduces conflict is presented at the beginning of a story.
2. *Roadblocks.* In the middle of the story, characters face roadblocks in attempting to solve the problem.
3. *The high point.* The high point in the action occurs when the problem is about to be solved. This high point separates the middle and end of the story.
4. *Solution.* The problem is solved and the roadblocks are overcome at the end of the story.

The problem is introduced at the beginning of the story, and the main character is faced with trying to solve it. The problem determines the conflict. The problem in *The Ugly Duckling* (Mayer, 1987) is that the big, gray duckling does not fit in with the other ducklings, and conflict develops between the ugly duckling and the other ducks. This is an example of conflict between characters.

After the problem has been introduced, authors use conflict to throw roadblocks in the way of an easy solution. As characters remove one roadblock, the author devises another to further thwart the characters. Postponing the solution by introducing roadblocks is the core of plot development. Stories may contain any number of roadblocks, but many children's stories contain three, four, or five.

The first conflict in *The Ugly Duckling* comes in the yard when the ducks, the other animals, and even the woman who feeds the ducks make fun of him. The conflict is so great that the duckling goes out into the world. Next, conflict comes from the wild ducks and other animals who scorn him, too. Third, the duckling spends a miserable, cold winter in the marsh.

The high point of the action occurs when the solution of the problem hangs in the balance. Tension is high, and readers continue reading to learn whether

Figure 9–2   *Stories That Illustrate the Four Types of Conflict*

Conflict Between a Character and Nature

Ardizzone, E. (1971). *Little Tim and the brave sea captain.* New York: Scholastic. (P)

George, J. C. (1972). *Julie of the wolves.* New York: Harper & Row. (M–U)

O'Dell, S. (1960). *Island of the blue dolphins.* Boston: Houghton Mifflin. (M–U)

Paulsen, G. (1987). *Hatchet.* New York: Bradbury Press. (M–U)

Polacco, P. (1990). *Thundercake.* New York: Philomel. (P–M)

Sperry, A. (1968). *Call it courage.* New York: Macmillan. (U)

Conflict Between a Character and Society

Hickman, J. (1978). *Zoar blue.* New York: Macmillan. (U)

Kellogg, S. (1973). *The island of the skog.* New York: Dial. (P–M)

Lowry, L. (1989). *Number the stars.* New York: Atheneum. (M–U)

Nixon, J. L. (1987). *A family apart.* New York: Bantam. (M–U)

O'Brien, R. C. (1971). *Mrs. Frisby and the rats of NIMH.* New York: Atheneum. (M)

Speare, E. G. (1958). *The witch of Blackbird Pond.* Boston: Houghton Mifflin. (M–U)

Conflict Between Characters

Blume, J. (1972). *Tales of a fourth grade nothing.* New York: Dutton. (M)

Cohen, B. (1983). *Molly's pilgrim.* New York: Lothrop, Lee & Shepard. (M)

Hoban, R. (1970). *A bargain for Frances.* New York: Scholastic. (P)

Naylor, P. R. (1991). *Shiloh.* New York: Atheneum. (M–U)

Raskin, E. (1978). *The westing game.* New York: Dutton. (U)

Zelinsky, P. O. (1986). *Rumpelstiltskin.* New York: Dutton. (P–M)

Conflict Within a Character

Bauer, M. D. (1986). *On my honor.* Boston: Houghton Mifflin. (M–U)

Byars, B. (1970). *The summer of the swans.* New York: Viking. (M)

Fritz, J. (1958). *The cabin faced west.* New York: Coward-McCann. (M)

Henkes, K. (1991). *Chrysanthemum.* New York: Greenwillow. (P)

Taylor, T. (1969). *The cay.* New York: Doubleday. (U)

Waber, B. (1972). *Ira sleeps over.* Boston: Houghton Mifflin. (P)

P = primary grades (K–2); M = middle grades (3–5); U = upper grades (6–8).

the main characters solve the problem. With *The Ugly Duckling,* readers are relieved that the duckling has survived the winter, but tension continues because he is still an outcast. Then the swan flies to a pond and sees three beautiful swans. He flies near to them even though he expects to be scorned.

As the story ends, the problem is solved and the goal is achieved. When the swan joins the other swans at the garden pond, they welcome him. The swan sees his reflection in the water and realizes that he is no longer an ugly duckling. Children come to feed the swans and praise the new swan's beauty. The newly arrived swan is happy at last!

Students can diagram or chart the plot of a story. A plot diagram is shaped somewhat like a mountain, and information about any story's plot can be added to this diagram. Figure 9–3 presents a plot diagram of *The Ugly Duckling* with information about the problem, roadblocks, the high point in the action, and the resolution of the problem at the end of the story.

Another way to examine plot is for students to make a chart called a *plot profile* to track the tension or excitement in a story (Johnson & Louis, 1987). Figure 9–4 presents a plot profile for *Stone Fox* (Gardiner, 1980), a story about a boy who wins a dog sled race to save his grandfather's farm. A class of fourth graders met in small groups to talk about each chapter, and after these discussions the whole class came together to decide how to mark the chart. At

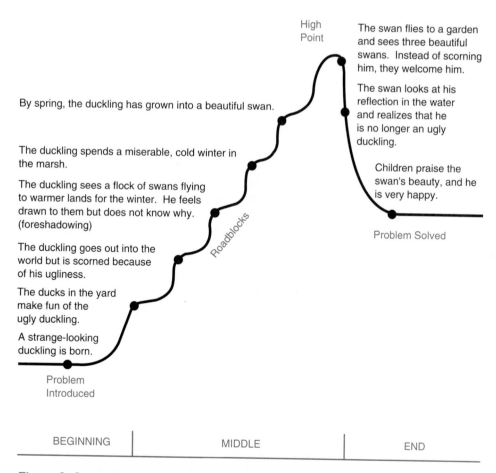

Figure 9–3   A Plot Diagram for The Ugly Duckling

Figure 9–4   *A Plot Profile for* Stone Fox

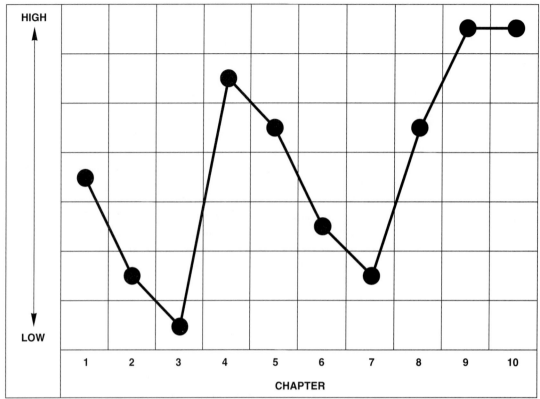

the end of the story, students analyzed the chart and rationalized the tension dips in Chapters 3 and 7. They decided that the story would be too stressful without these dips. Also, students were upset about the abrupt ending to the story and wished the story had continued a chapter or two longer so that their tension would have been reduced.

Characters.   *Characters* are the people or personified animals who are in-volved in the story. Characters are often the most important element of story structure because the story is centered on a character or group of characters. Usually, one or two fully rounded and several supporting characters are involved in a story. Fully developed main characters have many character traits, both good and bad. That is to say, they have all the characteristics of real people. Knowing and inferring a character's traits is an important part of reading. Through character traits we get to know a character well, and the character seems to come alive. A list of stories with fully developed main characters is presented in Figure 9–5.

Supporting characters may be individualized, but they will be portrayed much less vividly than the main character. The extent to which supporting characters are developed depends on the author's purpose and the needs of the story. In *Queenie Peavy* (Burch, 1966), for instance, Queenie is the main character, whom we get to know as a real person. She pretends that she is tough, as when the other children taunt her about her father being in the chain

Figure 9–5   *Stories With Fully Developed Main Characters*

Character	Story
Queenie	Burch, R. (1966). *Queenie Peavy.* New York: Viking. (U)
Ramona	Cleary, B. (1981). *Ramona Quimby, age 8.* New York: Morrow. (M)
Leigh	Cleary, B. (1983). *Dear Mr. Henshaw.* New York: Morrow. (M)
Johnny	Forbes, E. (1974). *Johnny Tremain.* Boston: Houghton Mifflin. (U)
Little Willy	Gardiner, J. R. (1980). *Stone Fox.* New York: Harper & Row. (M–U)
Sam	George, J. C. (1959). *My side of the mountain.* New York: Dutton. (U)
Patty	Greene, B. (1973). *Summer of my German soldier.* New York: Dial. (U)
Beth	Greene, B. (1974). *Philip Hall likes me. I reckon maybe.* New York: Dial. (U)
Chrysanthemum	Henkes, K. (1991). *Chrysanthemum.* New York: Greenwillow. (P)
Alex	Jukes, M. (1984). *Like Jake and me.* New York: Knopf. (P–M)
Frog, Toad	Lobel, A. (1970). *Frog and Toad are friends.* New York: Harper & Row. (P)
Sarah	MacLachlan, P. (1985). *Sarah, plain and tall.* New York: Harper & Row. (M)
Marty	Naylor, P. R. (1991). *Shiloh.* New York: Atheneum. (M–U)
Karana	O'Dell, S. (1960). *Island of the blue dolphins.* Boston: Houghton Mifflin. (M–U)
Gilly	Paterson, K. (1978). *The great Gilly Hopkins.* New York: Crowell. (M–U)
Peter	Potter, B. (1902). *The tale of Peter Rabbit.* New York: Warne. (P)
Billy	Say, A. (1990). *El Chino.* Boston: Houghton Mifflin. (M)
Matt	Speare, E. (1983). *The sign of the beaver.* Boston: Houghton Mifflin. (M–U)
Mafatu	Sperry, A. (1968). *Call it courage.* New York: Macmillan. (U)
Irene	Steig, W. (1986). *Brave Irene.* New York: Farrar, Straus & Giroux. (P–M)
Cassie	Taylor, M. (1976). *Roll of thunder, hear my cry.* New York: Dial. (U)
Moon Shadow	Yep, L. (1975). *Dragonwings.* New York: Harper & Row. (U)

gang, but actually Queenie is a sensitive girl who wants a family to care for her. In contrast, the author tells us little about the supporting characters in the story: Queenie's parents, her neighbors, and her classmates and teachers. The story focuses on Queenie and how this lonely 13-year-old copes with times that have "turned off hard" in the 1930s.

Characters are developed in four ways: appearance, action, dialogue, and monologue. Authors present the characters to involve readers in the story's experiences. Similarly, readers notice these four types of information as they read in order to understand the characters.

Authors generally provide some information about the characters' physical description when they are introduced. Readers learn about characters by the description of their facial features, body shapes, habits of dress, mannerisms, and gestures. Dahl (1961) vividly describes James's two wicked aunts in *James and the Giant Peach:*

> Aunt Sponge was enormously fat and very short. She had small piggy eyes, a sunken mouth, and one of those white flabby faces that looked exactly as though it had been boiled. She was like a great white soggy overboiled cabbage. Aunt Spiker, on the other hand, was lean and tall and bony, and she wore steel-rimmed spectacles that fixed onto the end of her nose with a clip. She had a screeching voice and long wet narrow lips, and whenever she got angry or excited, little flecks of spit would come shooting out of her mouth as she talked. (p. 7)

Dahl has carefully chosen the specific details so that readers can appreciate James's dismay at having to live with these two aunts.

The second way to learn about characters is through their actions, and what a character does is often the best way to know about that character. In Byars's story about three unwanted children, *The Pinballs* (1977), 15-year-old Carlie is described as "as hard to crack as a coconut" (p. 4), and her dialogue is harsh and sarcastic; however, Carlie's actions belie these other ways of knowing about her. She demonstrates through her actions that she cares about her two fellow-pinballs and the foster family who cares for them, for example, when she gets Harvey a puppy and sneaks it into the hospital.

Dialogue is the third way characters are developed. What characters say is important, but so is how they speak. The register of the characters' language is determined by the social situation. A character might speak less formally with friends than with respected elders or characters in positions of authority. The geographic location of the story and the characters' socioeconomic status also determine how characters speak. In *Roll of Thunder, Hear My Cry* (Taylor, 1976), for example, Cassie and her family speak Black English, and in *Ida Early Comes over the Mountain* (Burch, 1980), Ida's speech is characteristic of rural Georgia, and she says, "Howdy-do?" and "Yes, sir-ee."

Authors also provide insight into characters by revealing their thoughts or monologue. In *Anastasia Krupnik* (Lowry, 1979), for example, Lowry shares 10-year-old Anastasia's thinking with us. Anastasia has enjoyed being an only child and is upset that her mother is pregnant. To deal with Anastasia's feelings of sibling rivalry, her parents suggest that she choose a name for the new baby, and Anastasia agrees. Through monologue, readers learn why Anastasia has agreed to choose the name: She plans to pick the most awful name she can think of for the baby. Lowry also has Anastasia keep a journal in which she lists things she likes and hates, another reflection of her thinking.

Students draw character clusters to examine characters, as shown in Figure 9–6. This character cluster describes Rumpelstiltskin from Zelinsky's (1986) retelling of the Grimms' folktale. Rumpelstiltskin, the name of the character, is the nucleus word for the cluster, and the four ways authors develop characters—*appearance, action, dialogue,* and *monologue*—are the main idea rays. Students add details to each main idea, as the cluster illustrates. Drawing this cluster helps students realize the importance of monologue in this story. The Queen's servant overhears Rumpelstiltskin's musings about his name and reports to the Queen so that the Queen can guess the man's name and keep her child.

Setting.   In some stories the setting is barely sketched, and these settings are called *backdrop settings.* The setting in many folktales, for example, is relatively unimportant and may simply use the convention, "Once upon a time . . ." to set the stage. In other stories the setting is elaborated and integral to the story's effectiveness. These settings are called *integral settings* (Lukens, 1991). A list of stories with integral settings is shown in Figure 9–7. The setting

Figure 9–6   *A Character Cluster for Rumpelstiltskin*

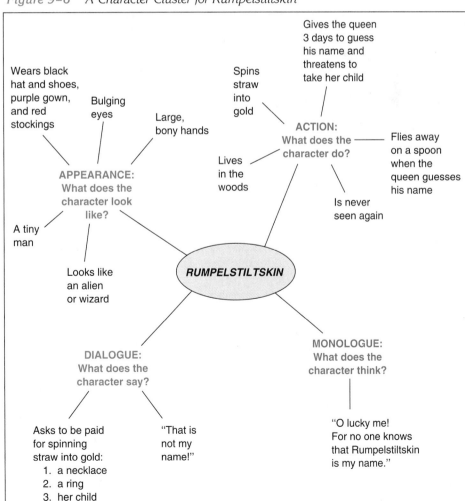

Figure 9–7   Stories With Integral Settings

Babbitt, N. (1975). *Tuck everlasting.* New York: Far-rar, Straus & Giroux. (M–U)

Cauley, L. B. (1984). *The city mouse and the country mouse.* New York: Putnam. (P–M)

Choi, S. N. (1991). *Year of impossible goodbyes.* Boston: Houghton Mifflin. (U)

Fleischman, S. (1963). *By the great horn spoon!* Boston: Little, Brown. (M–U)

Friedman, I. R. (1984). *How my parents learned to eat.* Boston: Houghton Mifflin. (P–M)

Gates, D. (1968). *Blue willow.* New York: Viking. (M–U)

George, J. C. (1972). *Julie of the wolves.* New York: Harper & Row. (M–U)

Harvey, B. (1988). *Cassie's journey: Going west in the 1860s.* New York: Holiday House. (M)

Konigsburg, E. L. (1983). *From the mixed-up files of Mrs. Basil E. Frankweiler.* New York: Atheneum. (M)

L'Engle, M. (1962). *A wrinkle in time.* New York: Farrar, Straus & Giroux. (U)

Lowry, L. (1989). *Number the stars.* Boston: Houghton Mifflin. (M–U)

McCloskey, R. (1969). *Make way for ducklings.* New York: Viking. (P)

Myers, W. D. (1988). *Scorpions.* New York: Harper & Row. (U)

Ness, E. (1966). *Sam, Bangs, and moonshine.* New York: Holt, Rinehart & Winston. (P)

Paterson, K. (1977). *Bridge to Terabithia.* New York: Crowell. (M–U)

Paulsen, G. (1990). *Woodsong.* New York: Bradbury Press. (M–U)

Polacco, P. (1988). *The keeping quilt.* New York: Simon & Schuster. (M)

Ringgold, F. (1991). *Tar beach.* New York: Crown. (P–M)

Roop, P., & Roop, C. (1985). *Keep the lights burning, Abbie.* Minneapolis: Carolrhoda. (P–M)

Say, A. (1990). *El Chino.* Boston: Houghton Mifflin. (M)

Speare, E. G. (1958). *The witch of Blackbird Pond.* Boston: Houghton Mifflin. (M–U)

Speare, E. G. (1983). *The sign of the beaver.* Boston: Houghton Mifflin. (M–U)

Uchida, Y. (1993). *The bracelet.* New York: Philomel. (P–M)

Wilder, L. I. (1971). *The long winter.* New York: Harper & Row. (M)

Yep, L. (1975). *Dragonwings.* New York: Harper & Row. (U)

in these stories is specific, and authors take care to ensure the authenticity of the historical period or geographic location in which the story is set. Four dimensions of setting are location, weather, time period, and time.

Location is an important dimension in many stories. For example, the Boston Commons in *Make Way for Ducklings* (McCloskey, 1969) and the Alaskan North Slope in *Julie of the Wolves* (George, 1972) are integral to the stories' effectiveness. The settings are artfully described and add something unique to the story. In contrast, many stories take place in predictable settings that do not contribute to the story's effectiveness.

Weather is a second dimension of setting and, like location, is crucial in some stories. A rainstorm is essential to the plot development in both *Bridge to Terabithia* (Paterson, 1977) and *Sam, Bangs, and Moonshine* (Ness, 1966). At other times weather is not mentioned because it does not affect the outcome of the story. Many stories take place on warm, sunny days. Think about the impact weather can have on a story; for example, what might have happened if a snowstorm had prevented Little Red Riding Hood from reaching her grandmother's house?

The third dimension of setting is the time period, an important element in stories set in the past or future. If *The Witch of Blackbird Pond* (Speare, 1958) and *Number the Stars* (Lowry, 1989) were set in different eras, for example, they would lose much of their impact. Today, few people would believe that Kit

Tyler is a witch, and Jewish people are not persecuted as they were during the Holocaust. In stories such as *A Wrinkle in Time* (L'Engle, 1962) that take place in the future, things are possible that are not possible today.

The fourth dimension, time, includes both time of day and the passage of time. Most stories ignore time of day, except for scary stories which take place after dark. In stories such as *The Ghost-Eye Tree* (Martin & Archambault, 1985), a story of two children who must walk past a scary tree at night to get a pail of milk, time is a more important dimension than in stories that take place during the day, because night makes things scarier.

Many short stories span a brief period of time, often less than a day, and sometimes less than an hour. In *Jumanji* (Van Allsburg, 1981), Peter and Judy's bizarre adventure, during which their house is overtaken by exotic jungle creatures, lasts only the several hours their parents are at the opera. Other stories, such as *Charlotte's Web* (White, 1952) and *The Ugly Duckling* (Mayer, 1987), span a long enough period for the main character to grow to maturity.

Students can draw maps to show the setting of a story. These maps may show the path a character traveled or the passage of time in a story. Figure 9–8 shows a map for *Number the Stars* (Lowry, 1989). In this chapter book set in Denmark during World War II, a Christian girl and her family help a Jewish family flee to safety in Sweden. The map shows where the families lived in Copenhagen, their trip to a fishing village in northern Denmark, and the ship they hid away on for the trip to Sweden.

Point of View. Stories are written from a particular viewpoint, and this focus determines to a great extent readers' understanding of the characters and the events of the story. The four points of view are first-person viewpoint, omniscient viewpoint, limited omniscient viewpoint, and objective viewpoint (Lukens, 1991). A list of stories written from each viewpoint is presented in Figure 9–9.

The first-person viewpoint is used to tell a story through the eyes of one character using the first-person pronoun "I." In this point of view, the reader experiences the story as the narrator tells it. The narrator, usually the main character, speaks as an eyewitness to and a participant in the events. For example, in *The Slave Dancer* (Fox, 1973), Jessie tells the story of his kidnapping and frightful voyage on a slave ship, and in *Alexander and the Terrible, Horrible, No Good, Very Bad Day* (Viorst, 1977), Alexander tells about a day when everything seemed to go wrong for him. One limitation is that the narrator must remain an eyewitness.

In the omniscient viewpoint the author is godlike, seeing and knowing all. The author tells readers about the thought processes of each character without worrying about how the information is obtained. *Doctor De Soto* (Steig, 1982), a story about a mouse dentist who outwits a fox with a toothache, is told from the omniscient viewpoint. Steig lets readers know that the fox wants to eat the dentist as soon as his toothache is cured and that the mouse dentist is aware of the fox's thoughts and plans a clever trick.

The limited omniscient viewpoint is used so that readers can know the thoughts of one character. The story is told in third person, and the author concentrates on the thoughts, feelings, and significant past experiences of the main character or another important character. Burch used the limited omni-

Figure 9–8   A Story Map for
Number the Stars

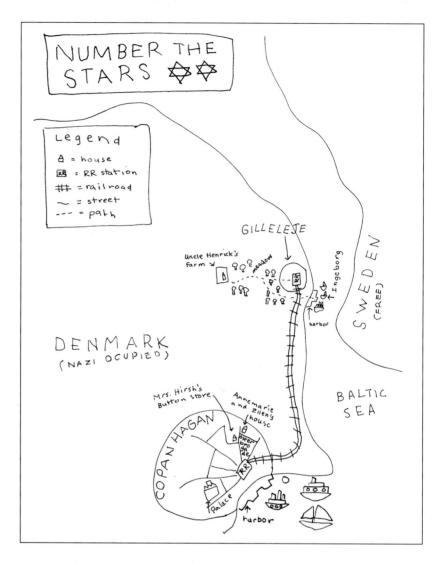

scient viewpoint in *Queenie Peavy* (1966), and Queenie is the character Burch concentrates on, showing why she has a chip on her shoulder and how she overcomes it.

In the objective viewpoint readers are eyewitnesses to the story and are confined to the immediate scene. They learn only what is visible and audible, without knowing what any character thinks. *Cinderella* (Galdone, 1978) and *The Little Red Hen* (Zemach, 1983) are examples of stories told from the objective viewpoint. The focus is on recounting events, not on developing the personalities of the characters.

Most teachers postpone introducing the four viewpoints until the upper grades, but younger children can experiment with point of view to understand how the author's viewpoint affects a story. One way to demonstrate point of view is to contrast *The Three Little Pigs* (Galdone, 1970), the traditional version of the story told from an objective viewpoint, with *The True Story of the Three Little Pigs* (Scieszka, 1989), a self-serving narrative told by Mr. A. Wolf from a first-person viewpoint. In this unusual and satirical retelling, the wolf tries to

Figure 9–9   Stories That Illustrate the Four Points of View

First-Person Viewpoint

Greene, B. (1974). *Philip Hall likes me. I reckon maybe.* New York: Dial. (M–U)

Howe, D., & Howe, J. (1979). *Bunnicula: A Rabbit-Tale of Mystery.* New York: Atheneum. (M)

MacLachlan, P. (1985). *Sarah, plain and tall.* New York: Harper & Row. (M)

Rylant, C. (1992). *Missing May.* New York: Orchard Books. (U)

Viorst, J. (1977). *Alexander and the terrible, horrible, no good, very bad day.* New York: Atheneum. (P)

Omniscient Viewpoint

Babbitt, N. (1975). *Tuck everlasting.* New York: Farrar, Straus & Giroux. (M–U)

Grahame, K. (1961). *The wind in the willows.* New York: Scribner. (M)

Lewis, C. S. (1981). *The lion, the witch and the wardrobe.* New York: Macmillan. (M–U)

Myers, W. D. (1988). *Scorpions.* New York: Harper & Row. (U)

Steig, W. (1982). *Doctor De Soto.* New York: Farrar, Straus & Giroux. (P)

Limited Omniscient Viewpoint

Burch, R. (1966). *Queenie Peavy.* New York: Dell. (U)

Cleary, B. (1981). *Ramona Quimby, age 8.* New York: Morrow. (M)

Gardiner, J. R. (1980). *Stone Fox.* New York: Harper & Row. (M)

Lionni, L. (1969). *Alexander and the wind-up mouse.* New York: Pantheon. (P)

Lowry, L. (1979). *Anastasia Krupnik.* Boston: Houghton Mifflin. (M)

Objective Viewpoint

Brown, M. (1954). *Cinderella.* New York: Scribner. (P)

Cauley, L. B. (1988). *The pancake boy.* New York: Putnam. (P)

Lobel, A. (1972). *Frog and Toad together.* New York: Harper & Row. (P)

Wells, R. (1973). *Benjamin and Tulip.* New York: Dial. (P)

Zemach, M. (1983). *The little red hen.* New York: Farrar, Straus & Giroux. (P)

explain away his bad image. Even first graders are struck by how different the two versions are and how the narrator filters the information.

Another way to demonstrate the impact of different viewpoints is for students to retell or rewrite a familiar story, such as *Little Red Riding Hood* (Hyman, 1983), from specific points of view—through the eyes of Little Red Riding Hood; her sick, old grandmother; the hungry wolf; or the hunter. As they shift the point of view, students learn that they can change some aspects of a story but not others. To help them appreciate how these changes affect a story, have them take a story such as *The Lion, the Witch and the Wardrobe* (Lewis, 1981), which is told from the omniscient viewpoint, and retell short episodes from the viewpoints of different characters. As students shift to other points of view, they must decide what to leave out according to the new perspective.

Theme.   *Theme* is the underlying meaning of a story and embodies general truths about human nature (Lehr, 1991). It usually deals with the characters' emotions and values. Themes can be stated either explicitly or implicitly. Explicit themes are stated openly and clearly in the story. Lukens (1991) uses *Charlotte's Web* to point out how one theme of friendship—the giving of oneself for a friend—is expressed as an explicit theme:

> Charlotte has encouraged, protected, and mothered Wilbur, bargained and sacrificed for him, and Wilbur, the grateful receiver, realizes that "Friendship is one of the most satisfying things in the world." And Charlotte says later, "By helping you perhaps I was trying to lift up my life a little. Anyone's life can stand a little of that."

Because these quoted sentences are exact statements from the text they are called explicit themes. (p. 102)

Implicit themes are implied rather than explicitly stated in the story. They are developed as the characters attempt to overcome the obstacles that prevent them from reaching their goals. The theme emerges through the thoughts, speech, and actions of the characters as they seek to resolve their conflicts. Lukens also uses *Charlotte's Web* to illustrate implicit themes:

Charlotte's selflessness—working late at night to finish a new word, expending her last energies for her friend—is evidence that friendship is giving oneself. Wilbur's protection of Charlotte's egg sac, his sacrifice of first turn at the slops, and his devotion to Charlotte's babies—giving without any need to stay even or to pay back—leads us to another theme: True friendship is naturally reciprocal. As the two become fond of each other, still another theme emerges: One's best friend can do no wrong. In fact, a best friend is sensational! Both Charlotte and Wilbur believe in these ideas; their experiences verify them. (p. 112)

Charlotte's Web has several friendship themes, one explicitly stated and others inferred from the text. Stories usually have more than one theme, and their themes usually cannot be articulated with a single word. Friendship is a multidimensional theme. Teachers can ask questions during grand conversations to guide students' thinking as they work to construct a theme (Au, 1992). Students must go beyond one-word labels in describing the theme and construct their own ideas about a theme.

Teaching Students About Stories

The most important way that students refine their concepts of story is by reading and writing stories, but teachers help students expand their concepts through minilessons that focus on particular story elements. Minilessons are usually taught during the exploring stage of the reading process after students have had an opportunity to read and respond to a story and share their reactions.

Minilessons About Stories.   Teachers use the teaching strategy set out in the first chapter to teach minilessons on the elements of story structure and other procedures, concepts, and strategies and skills related to stories. The steps in teaching a minilesson are:

*Step
by
Step*

1. *Introducing the Element.*   Teachers introduce the element of story structure using a chart to define and list the characteristics of the element. Figure 9–10 shows charts that can be developed for the elements. Next, students think about stories they have read recently that exemplify the element, and they talk about how these stories were organized.

2. *Analyzing the Element in Stories.*   Students read or listen to one or more stories that illustrate the element. After reading and responding to the story, students analyze how the author used the element in the story. As students talk about the stories they have read, they tie their analyses to the information about

Figure 9–10   Charts for the Elements of Story Structure

Chart 1

Stories

Stories have three parts:

1. A beginning
2. A middle
3. An end

Chart 2

Beginnings of Stories

Writers put these things in the beginning of a story:

1. The characters are introduced.
2. The setting is described.
3. A problem is established.
4. Readers get interested in the story.

Chart 3

Middles of Stories

Writers put these things in the middle of a story:

1. The problem gets worse.
2. Roadblocks thwart the main character.
3. More information is provided about the characters.
4. The middle is the longest part.
5. Readers become engaged with the story and empathize with the characters.

Chart 4

Ends of Stories

Writers put these things in the end of a story:

1. The problem is resolved.
2. The loose ends are tied up.
3. Readers feel a release of emotions that were built up in the middle.

Chart 5

Conflict

Conflict is the problem that characters face in the story. There are four kinds of conflict:

1. Conflict between a character and nature
2. Conflict between a character and society
3. Conflict between characters
4. Conflict within a character

---

the element presented in the first step. Students can also write the information from the chart in their reading logs.

3. ***Exploring the Story.***   Students participate in exploring activities to investigate how authors use the element in particular stories. Activities include:

- Retell a story.
- Write a retelling of a story in book format.
- Dramatize a story.

Figure 9–10   continued

Chart 6 **Plot** Plot is the sequence of events in a story. It has four parts: 1. A Problem: The problem introduces conflict at the beginning of the story. 2. Roadblocks: Characters face roadblocks as they try to solve the problem in the middle of the story. 3. The High Point: The high point in the action occurs when the problem is about to be solved. It separates the middle and the end. 4. The Solution: The problem is solved and the roadblocks are overcome at the end of the story.	**Chart 7** **Setting** The setting is where and when the story takes place. 1. Location: Stories can take place anywhere. 2. Weather: Stories take place in different kinds of weather. 3. Time of Day: Stories take place during the day or at night. 4. Time Period: Stories take place in the past, at the current time, or in the future.	**Chart 8** **Characters** Writers develop characters in four ways: 1. Appearance: How characters look 2. Action: What characters do 3. Dialogue: What characters say 4. Monologue: What characters think

Chart 9 **Theme** Theme is the underlying meaning of a story. 1. Explicit Themes: The meaning is stated clearly in the story. 2. Implicit Themes: The meaning is suggested by the characters, action, and monologue.	**Chart 10** **Point of View** Writers tell the story according to one of four viewpoints: 1. First-Person Viewpoint: The writer tells the story through the eyes of one character using "I." 2. Omniscient Viewpoint: The writer sees all and knows all about each character. 3. Limited Omniscient Viewpoint: The writer focuses on one character and tells that character's thoughts and feelings. 4. Objective Viewpoint: The writer focuses on the events of the story without telling what the characters are thinking and feeling.

- Present a puppet show of a story.
- Draw clusters or other diagrams to graphically display the structure of a story.
- Make a class book of the story, with each student contributing one page.

As students participate in these activities, the teacher draws their attention to the element being studied.

4. *Reviewing the Element.*   The teacher reviews the information about the element, using the charts introduced in the first step. Students explain the element in their own words, using one story they have read as an example.

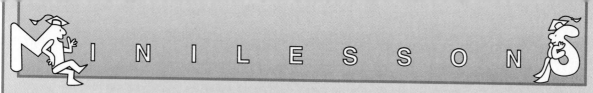

Reading and Writing Stories

Procedures	Concepts	Strategies and Skills
Make a beginning-middle-end cluster	Concept of story	Visualize
Make a story map	Beginning-middle-end	Predict and confirm
Make a plot diagram	Plot	Retrospect
Make a plot profile	Characters	Engage with text
Make a character cluster	Setting	Empathize with characters
Use storyboards	Theme	Identify with characters
Make a chart to compare versions of a folktale or other story	Point of view	Write dialogue for characters
	Genre of story	Elaborate on the plot
	Aesthetic reading	Notice opposites in the story
	Interpretation	Retell the story
Make a class collaboration book	Authors	Monitor understanding
Write a pattern book	Illustrators	Connect to one's own life
Write a sequel	Types of illustrations	Connect to previously read literature
Assess effectiveness of a story	Sequels	Extend the story
Assess use of reading/writing strategies		Value the story
		Evaluate the story
		Analyze the story

A list of topics for minilessons about stories is presented above. These topics include procedures, concepts, and strategies and skills for reading and writing stories.

Adapting to Meet the Needs of Every Student.   Stories are a large part of the elementary language arts program, and teachers must find ways to involve all students in successful reading and writing experiences with stories. A list of suggestions for adapting the information presented in this chapter to meet students' needs is presented on page 000. These suggestions emphasize the importance of allowing students to respond to stories before exploring them and finding ways to support students as they read and write.

Assessing Students' Concept of Stories

Teachers assess students' concept of stories in many ways. They observe students as they read and respond to stories. They can note whether or not students are sensitive to story elements as they talk about stories during grand conversations. Some students talk about the character who is most like them, or they compare two stories they have read. Teachers note whether students use terminology related to story elements. Do they talk about conflict, or the way a story ends? If they are talking about point of view, do they use that term? Teachers also ask questions about story elements during grand conversations and note the responses that students make. Students' reading logs also provide evidence of the same sorts of comments and reactions.

Adapting . . .
Reading and Writing Stories
To Meet the Needs of Every Student

1. Reading Aloud to Students

Teachers can make stories that students cannot read independently accessible by reading them aloud to students. When students listen to a story together in a small group or as a class, they become an interpretive community, and the shared experience of the story develops a strong bond among the students. Students can also listen to stories at a listening center.

2. Encouraging Students to Choose Stories to Read

Teachers should schedule reading workshop on a regular basis so that students can read stories they are interested in reading or reread favorite stories. Classroom libraries should be well stocked with a wide variety of books, and teachers can give book talks to introduce students to stories and authors from which they might choose.

3. Dramatizing Stories

Drama is an effective technique that students can use to understand stories they are reading and to create stories they will write. When students are reading a complex story, they can role-play important scenes in order to better understand the characters and events.

4. Writing Retellings of Stories

Students can write retellings of favorite stories or retell the story from a particular character's viewpoint. Many students are more successful in writing retellings than writing original stories because they are better able to control the familiar storyline.

5. Working in Collaborative Reading and Writing Groups

Students can work together in pairs or in small groups to read and write stories. This way, students support each other as they read and write.

Another way that students demonstrate their understanding of story elements is by making clusters, charts, and diagrams. These activities are a natural outgrowth of students' responses to a story, not the reason why students are reading stories (Urzua, 1992). Teachers also document students' understanding of story elements by examining the stories that they have written to see how they have applied their knowledge about stories.

READING STORIES

Students read stories aesthetically, and their concept of story informs and supports their reading. They read popular and award-winning stories together as a class during literature focus units, they read stories they choose themselves in reading workshop, and they read other stories as part of theme cycles. Students use the reading process to read, respond to, explore, and extend their reading. Reading stories with students is more than simply a pleasurable way to spend an hour; it is how classroom communities are created (Cairney, 1992). Reading, writing, and talking about stories are natural extensions of the relationships that students have built together. Students share stories they are reading with classmates, and they work together on projects to extend their interpretations.

Aesthetic Reading

According to Louise Rosenblatt (1978), reading is a personal experience during which readers connect the story they are reading to their own lives and previous experiences with literature. The goal of aesthetic reading is interpretation, the negotiation of meaning between the reader and the text (Rosenblatt, 1978, 1985). Readers do not search for the author's "correct" meaning; instead, they create a personal meaning for themselves. A story evokes different meanings from different readers or even from the same reader at different times in his or her life.

Students use strategies as they create interpretations. These strategies for reading and responding to stories include the following:*

Imaging. Students create images or pictures of the story in their minds.

Anticipating. Students anticipate or make predictions about what will happen in the story.

Retrospecting. Students think back to what they have read and how it impacts on what they are now reading.

Engaging. Students become involved in the story, so much so that they feel as though they are transported through time and space into the story.

Empathizing. Students respond with their feelings as they read.

Identifying. Students make connections between a character and themselves.

Elaborating. Students make inferences and add information to what they read.

Noticing opposites. Students note opposing tensions or contrasts in the story.

Retelling. Students retell or paraphrase what they have read.

Monitoring. Students make sure that what they are reading makes sense to them.

Connecting to life. Students make connections between events, characters, and other aspects of the story with their own lives.

Connecting to literature. Students make connections between the story they are reading and other stories they have read.

Extending. Students go beyond the story to think about sequels or ways they would adapt the story if they were writing it.

---

*Corcoran, 1987; Cox & Many, 1992; Tompkins & McGee, 1993.

Valuing and evaluating. Students make judgments about why they liked a story or whether it was worth reading.

Analyzing. Students analyze the author's use of the elements of story structure.

Teachers explain these strategies during minilessons, and students learn to use the strategies as they read aesthetically and participate in response activities.

Interpretation develops gradually. As students pick up a book by a favorite author or look at the cover of a book, they call to mind past experiences and make predictions, and the interpretation begins to form. It continues to develop as students read, respond to, and explore the story. As students discuss the story and write responses in reading logs, the interpretation deepens. Students move beyond the actual text as they work on projects, and these projects extend the interpretation further.

Students use the aesthetic stance when reading stories, as opposed to the efferent stance when they read to remember information. The stance readers take indicates the focus of their attention during reading. In her study on the effects of aesthetic and efferent stances on fourth, sixth, and eighth graders' interpretation of stories, Joyce Many (1991) found that students who read aesthetically had higher levels of interpretation.

Teachers encourage aesthetic reading and interpretation in many ways. From the stories they share with students to the minilessons they teach and the types of response and exploring activities they plan for students, teachers set a classroom climate for aesthetic reading. A list of ways teachers can encourage interpretation in their classrooms is presented in the Teacher's Notebook on page 337.

Intertextuality.   As students create interpretations, they make connections to books they have read previously, and these connections are called *intertextuality* (de Beaugrande, 1980). Students use intertextuality as they respond to books they are reading by recognizing similarities between characters, plots, and themes. Students also use intertextuality as they incorporate ideas and structures from the stories they have read into the stories they are writing. Five characteristics of intertextuality are (Cairney, 1990, 1992):

1. *Individual and unique.* Students' literary experiences and the connections they make among them are different.
2. *Dependent on literary experiences.* Intertextuality is dependent on the types of books students have read, their purpose for and interest in reading, and the literary communities to which they belong.
3. *Metacognitive awareness.* Most students are aware of intertextuality and consciously make connections among texts.
4. *Links to concept of story.* Students' connections among stories are linked to their knowledge about literature.
5. *Reading-writing connections.* Students make connections between stories they read and stories they write.

The sum of students' experiences with literature—including the stories parents have read and told to young children, the books students have read or listened to the teacher read aloud, film versions they have viewed, their concepts of story and knowledge about authors and illustrators, and the books

Teacher's Notebook
Ways to Encourage Interpretation

1. Encouraging Aesthetic Reading

Students learn about the aesthetic and efferent stances and the differences between them. Students are encouraged to read stories aesthetically for the lived-through experience of reading.

2. Group Books Into Text Sets

Students read a wide variety of literature, including stories, poems, and informational books. Often, teachers should group the literature into text sets, or students can make their own text sets.

3. Making Initial Responses

Students make initial responses to stories through grand conversations, writing in reading logs, and participating in role-playing activities.

4. Exploring the Story

Students explore the story through activities such as creating word walls, rereading the story, sequencing the events using storyboards, making diagrams, looking for opposites, and noting examples of literary style.

5. Teaching Reading Strategies

Teachers teach minilessons on reading strategies, including imaging, predicting, engaging, connecting to life and literature, valuing, and evaluating.

6. Expanding Concept of Story

Teachers teach minilessons about the elements of story structure, genre, authors and illustrators, and illustration to help students expand their concept of story.

7. Developing Intertextuality

Students make connections from the story to their own lives and to other literature they have read.

8. Creating Projects

Students extend their interpretations through reading, writing, talk, drama, and research projects. It is important that students choose the projects they pursue.

students have written—constitute their intertextual histories (Cairney, 1992). Cairney's research indicates that elementary students are aware of their past experiences with literature and use this knowledge as they read and write.

One way teachers encourage students to make intertextual ties is by grouping literature into *text sets,* collections of three or more books that are related in some way. Possible text sets include:

Stories written by the same author

Stories featuring the same character

Stories illustrating the same theme

Different versions of a folktale

Stories in the same genre

Stories and other books related to a theme cycle

As students read and discuss these books, they make connections among them. As students share the connections they are making, classmates gain insights about literature and build on classmates' ideas. Teachers can prompt students and ask them to describe commonalities among the books. Students can also make charts and other diagrams to compare authors, characters, and other aspects of stories.

Literary Opposites.　Stories are usually built around opposites or contrasts, and these literary opposites help to create excitement in a story (Temple, 1992). *Where the Wild Things Are* (Sendak, 1962), for example, is built around the contrast between Max's bedroom and the land of the wild things. While his bedroom is safe and secure, where the wild things live is thrilling but a little scary, too. Max's mother sends him to his bedroom for misbehaving, and she is clearly in charge; but when Max becomes king of the wild things, he is in charge. In Phyllis Reynolds Naylor's *Shiloh* (1991), the main characters, Marty Preston and Judd Travers, are opposites. Marty is the "good" character who bravely works for mean-spirited Travers to buy a beagle pup that has been mistreated. Through the experience, Marty learns about human nature and about himself.

Opposites can be between settings, characters, or events in the story, and there is more than one opposite in most stories. For example, after reading Steig's *Amos and Boris* (1971), a class of third graders listed these opposites:

big	little
land animal	sea animal
helping	being helped
Amos and Boris	*The Lion and the Mouse*
life	death
forgetting	remembering
hope	hopeless
in the sea	out of the sea
hello	good-bye

Students each picked the opposite that seemed most important to them and drew pictures and wrote about them. This was a valuable way for students to think deeply about stories. One student made the intertextual tie between

Amos and Boris and *The Lion and the Mouse* (Young, 1979), pointing out the same theme.

In Literature Focus Units

Teachers plan literature focus units featuring popular and award-winning stories for children and adolescents. Some literature focus units feature a single book, either a picture book or a chapter book, and others feature a text set of books. During these units students move through the five stages of the reading process as they read and respond to stories. Some of the activities in each stage are:

1. *Preparing to read.* Teachers introduce the story or stories and activate students' background knowledge.
2. *Reading.* Students read the story in one of several ways: They might listen to the teacher read the book aloud, read it independently or with a buddy, or read it through shared reading.
3. *Responding.* Students respond to the story through discussions and by writing in reading logs.
4. *Exploring the text.* Students participate in a variety of exploring activities to dig more deeply into the story. A list of exploring activities is presented in the Teacher's Notebook on page 340. Students also add interesting and important words from the story to a word wall. Teachers often teach minilessons about story elements, aesthetic reading, interpretation, reading strategies, and other topics during this stage.
5. *Extending the interpretation.* Students do projects to extend their interpretations of the story and share their completed projects with classmates.

Second graders might spend a week reading *Tacky the Penguin* (Lester, 1988), a popular story about an oddball penguin who saves all the penguins from some hunters. During the unit students read the story several times, respond to the story, participate in a variety of exploring activities, and do projects to extend their interpretations. A week-long plan for teaching a unit on *Tacky the Penguin* is presented in Figure 9–11.

Several different types of exploring activities are included in this plan. One type focuses on vocabulary. On Monday, students list words from the story on a word wall; the next day they reread the words and sort them according to the character they refer to; and on Thursday the teacher teaches a minilesson about peeling off the *-ly* suffix to learn the "main" word (root word). It's not typical to teach a lesson on derivational suffixes in second grade, but second graders notice that many of the words on the word wall have *-ly* at the end of them and often ask about the suffix.

Another activity examines character. The teacher teaches a minilesson on characters on Tuesday. Then students make a character cluster about Tacky and draw open minds to show what Tacky is thinking. To make an open-mind portrait, students draw a portrait of the penguin, cut around the head so that it will flip open, and draw or write what Tacky is thinking on another sheet of paper that has been attached behind the paper with the portrait.

Genre Studies. Genre units provide an opportunity for students to learn about a particular genre or category of literature. Students read stories

Teacher's Notebook
Activities to Explore Stories

Storyboards

The teacher cuts apart two copies of a picture book, backs each page with a sheet of posterboard, and laminates each page. Storyboards are especially useful when there are only one or two other copies of the story available in the classroom. Students read storyboards and identify important words for the word wall, memorable quotes, and so on. Students can also create storyboards for a chapter book. After reading the book, students each choose a chapter, reread it, draw a picture about it, and write a summary of it. Then the pictures and summaries are backed with posterboard and laminated.

Story Boxes

Students and the teacher collect items related to a story and place them in a box. The box cover is decorated with the title and author, pictures of scenes from the story, pictures of the characters, and memorable quotes. Making the box is a good way to focus students' attention on what is important about the story, and students can examine the items in a box prepared by students in a previous class as they talk about the story and what it means to them.

Open-Mind Portraits

In order to probe a character, students draw portraits of the character and cut around the face so that the head flips up. Next they back the page with another sheet of paper. Then they write words and draw pictures in the "open mind" behind the face that reflect the character's thoughts.

Story Maps

Students draw story maps to illustrate a character's journey in a story. Other types of story maps are beginning-middle-end clusters, Venn diagrams to compare characters, and plot profiles. For more information about story maps, see *Responses to Literature, Grades K–8* (Macon, Bewell, & Vogt, 1991).

Story Quilts

Students and the teacher design a quilt motif, such as a circle, tree, or star, that relates to the story. Then students each make one square using either construction paper or fabric and write a memorable sentence from the story on it. Students can make a larger square (the size of four squares) with information about the title and author of the story to place in the middle in the quilt. Then the squares are taped or sewn together, and the completed quilt is hung in the classroom.

Figure 9–11   A Week-Long Plan for Teaching Tacky the Penguin

Monday

Talk about penguins to introduce the story.

Read the story aloud to students as they follow along in their copies of the story. Stop several times and ask students to make predictions.

Discuss the story in a grand conversation. Ask why Tacky is called an "odd" bird. Ask if students think they are more like Tacky or more like the other penguins.

Add words that students suggest to the word wall.

Have students draw and write about the story in their reading logs.

Tuesday

Have students share their reading log entries in small groups, and have one student from each group share with the class.

Reread the words on the word wall. Pass out word cards for students to sort according to whether they relate to Tacky, to the other penguins, or to the hunters.

Have students reread the story with a buddy.

Teach a minilesson about characters and explain that authors develop characters in four ways.

Make a character cluster about Tacky.

Have students draw portraits of Tacky and add open minds to show what he is thinking.

Wednesday

Make a list of students' questions about penguins.

Real aloud *A Penguin Year* (Bonners, 1981) to answer many of their questions. Research answers to any remaining questions.

Discuss possible projects and begin work on projects.

Thursday

Work on projects.

Reread *Tacky the Penguin* with small groups of students.

Teach minilesson on the suffix *-ly* and how to "peel" the suffix off to find the main word. Use words from the word wall for the lesson.

Friday

Finish work on projects.

Share projects.

Have students add favorite quotes from the story to a large penguin poster.

End the literature focus unit with a discussion to value the story and reflect on the unit.

illustrating the genre and then participate in a variety of activities to deepen their interpretations and knowledge about the genre. In these units students participate in these activities:

Read several stories illustrating a genre.

Learn the characteristics of the genre.

Read other stories illustrating the genre.

Respond to and explore the genre stories.

Write or rewrite stories exemplifying the genre.

Genre studies about traditional literature, including fables, folktales, legends, and myths, are very appropriate for elementary students.

During a genre study of folktales, for example, third-grade students read folktales such as *The Little Red Hen* (Zemach, 1983), *The Mitten* (Brett, 1989), and *Little Red Riding Hood* (Hyman, 1983), and the teacher explains that these stories are folktales and that folktales are relatively short stories that originated as part of the oral tradition. They make a list of these characteristics of folktales:

- The story is often introduced with the words "Once upon a time."
- The setting is usually generalized and could be located anywhere.
- The plot structure is simple and straightforward.
- The problem usually revolves around a journey from home to perform some tasks, a journey that involves a confrontation with a monster, the miraculous change from a harsh home to a secure home, or a confrontation between a wise character and a foolish character.
- Characters are portrayed in one dimension, either good or bad, stupid or clever, or industrious or lazy.
- The end is happy, and everyone "lives happily ever after."

Then students spend several days reading and responding to other folktales from a special display set up in the classroom. The teacher brings the class together, and they share the folktales they have read and find examples of the characteristics in the stories. Then the teacher explains that folktales have motifs, or small, recurring elements, such as three wishes, a magical ring, or a character who is a trickster. Next the teacher presents this list of six common motifs, and students name a folktale illustrating each motif:

- *A long sleep or enchantment. The Sleeping Beauty* (Yolen, 1986) is an example of a story with the long sleep motif.
- *Magical powers.* Characters in folktales often have magical powers, such as the fool's companions in *The Fool of the World and the Flying Ship* (Ransome, 1968).
- *Magical transformations.* In stories such as *Beauty and the Beast* (Mayer, 1978), characters are magically transformed from one form into another.
- *Magical objects.* Magical objects play an important role in some folktales. One example is *Aladdin and the Wonderful Lamp* (Carrick, 1989).
- *Wishes.* Characters are granted wishes but sometimes use them unwisely, as in *The Stonecutter* (Newton, 1990).
- *Trickery.* Animals and people trick each other in many folktales. For example, the wolf tricks the little girl in *Little Red Riding Hood* (Hyman, 1983).

Students spend several more days reading and rereading folktales and finding other examples of motifs.

Next, students read different versions of "Cinderella" in small groups. Then they get back together as a class to talk about their reading and make a chart to compare the versions. Later in the unit students work on projects. Some choose to write their own versions of folktales, some make puppets and produce a play of a folktale, and others read versions of different folktales and

In author study units, students read books written by the featured author and learn about the author.

compare them on a chart. A list of versions of "Cinderella" and other familiar folktales is presented in Figure 9–12.

Author Studies. During author studies, students read and respond to stories written by a particular author. They also learn about the author, his or her writing style, and other interesting information about the person. If possible, students write to the author or arrange to meet him or her.

One way that students learn about authors and illustrators is by reading about them. A number of biographies and autobiographies of well-known authors and illustrators, including Beatrix Potter (Aldis, 1969), Jean Fritz (1992), and Tomie de Paola (1989), are available for elementary students. Filmstrips, videotapes, and other audiovisual materials about authors and illustrators are becoming increasingly available. In addition, upper-grade students can read articles about favorite writers. Many articles profiling authors and illustrators have been published in *Language Arts, Horn Book,* and other journals, which teachers can clip and file. Appendix B lists books, articles, and audiovisual materials about authors.

In Reading Workshop

Reading workshop brings "real-world" reading into the classroom. Students read and respond to stories in authentic ways, more like people do outside of school settings. They choose books they want to read. Sometimes they choose books by favorite authors, books recommended by classmates, or old favorites they want to reread. As they read, students are so engaged in reading that they often lose track of where they are and don't hear when someone calls their

Figure 9–12   *Versions of Folktales and Related Stories*

"Cinderella"

Brown, M. (1954). *Cinderella*. New York: Scribner. (P–M)

Climo, S. (1989). *The Egyptian Cinderella*. New York: Crowell. (M)

Climo, S. (1993). *The Korean Cinderella*. New York: HarperCollins. (M)

Cole, B. (1987). *Prince Cinders*. New York: Putnam. (M)

Ehrlich, A. (1985). *Cinderella*. New York: Dial. (P–M)

Galdone, P. (1978). *Cinderella*. New York: McGraw-Hill. (P–M)

Hogrogian, N. (1981). *Cinderella*. New York: Greenwillow. (P–M)

Hooks, W. H. (1987). *Moss gown*. New York: Clarion. (M–U)

Huck, C. (1989). *Princess Furball*. New York: Greenwillow. (P–M)

Karlin, B. (1989). *Cinderella*. Boston: Little, Brown. (P–M)

Louie, A. L. (1982). *Yeh-Shen: A Cinderella story from China*. New York: Philomel. (M–U)

Munsch, R. N. (1980). *The paper bag princess*. Toronto, Canada: Annick Press. (P–M)

Shorto, R. (1990). *Cinderella: The untold story*. New York: Birch Lane Press. (P–M–U)

Steptoe, J. (1987). *Mufaro's beautiful daughters: An African tale*. New York: Lothrop. (P–M–U)

"The Gingerbread Boy"

Asbjorsen, P. C., & Moe, J. (1980). *The runaway pancake*. New York: Larousse. (P)

Brown, M. (1972). *The bun: A tale from Russia*. New York: Harcourt Brace Jovanovich. (P)

Cauley, L. B. (1988). *The pancake boy: An old Norwegian folk tale*. New York: Putnam. (P)

Galdone, P. (1975). *The gingerbread boy*. New York: Seabury. (P)

Jarrell, R. (1964). *The gingerbread rabbit*. New York: Collier. (P–M)

Lobel, A. (1978). *The pancake*. New York: Greenwillow. (P)

Oppenheim, J. (1986). *You can't catch me!* Boston: Houghton Mifflin. (P)

Sawyer, R. (1953). *Journey cake, ho!* New York: Viking. (P–M)

"Little Red Riding Hood"

de Regniers, B. S. (1972). *Red Riding Hood*. New York: Atheneum. (M–U)

Emberley, M. (1990). *Ruby*. Boston: Little, Brown. (M–U)

Galdone, P. (1974). *Little Red Riding Hood*. New York: McGraw-Hill. (P–M)

Goodall, J. S. (1988). *Little Red Riding Hood*. New York: McElderry Books. (P–M–U)

Grimm, J. (1983). *Little Red Cap*. New York: Morrow. (M–U)

Hyman, T. S. (1983). *Little Red Riding Hood*. New York: Holiday House. (P–M)

Marshall, J. (1987). *Red Riding Hood*. New York: Dial. (P–M)

Young, E. (1989). *Lon po po: A Red-Riding Hood story from China*. New York: Philomel. (M–U)

Zwerger, L. (1983). *Little Red Cap*. New York: Morrow. (M)

"The Princess and the Frog"

Berenzy, A. (1989). *A frog prince*. New York: Henry Holt. (P–M–U)

Gwynne, F. (1990). *Pondlarker*. New York: Simon & Schuster. (M–U)

Isadora, R. (1989). *The princess and the frog*. New York: Crowell. (P–M–U)

Isele, E. (1984). *The frog prince*. New York: Crowell. (P–M–U)

Scieszka, J. (1991). *The frog prince continued*. New York: Viking. (M–U)

Tarcov, E. H. (1974). *The frog prince*. New York: Scholastic. (P–M–U)

"Stone Soup"

Brown, M. (1975). *Stone soup*. New York: Aladdin Books. (M)

McGovern, A. (1968). *Stone soup*. New York: Scholastic. (M)

Ross, T. (1987). *Stone soup*. New York: Dial. (M)

Stewig, J. W. (1991). *Stone soup*. New York: Holiday House. (M)

Van Rynbach, I. (1988). *The stone soup*. New York: Greenwillow. (M)

"The Three Little Pigs"

Bishop, G. (1989). *The three little pigs*. New York: Scholastic. (M)

Galdone, P. (1970). *The three little pigs*. New York: Seabury. (P)

Hooks, W. H. (1989). *The three little pigs and the fox*. New York: Macmillan. (P)

Marshall, J. (1989). *The three little pigs*. New York: Dial. (P–M)

Scieszka, J. (1989). *The true story of the three little pigs*. New York: Viking. (P–M–U)

Zemach, M. (1988). *The three little pigs*. New York: Farrar, Straus & Giroux. (P)

name. Students respond emotionally—by laughing or crying—and make connections to their own lives and other literature they have read.

Teachers encourage students to develop interpretations during all three parts of reading workshop. They teach minilessons about aesthetic reading, interpretation, and reading strategies, and they provide opportunities for students to apply what they are learning as they read and respond to stories. During the independent reading time, students move through all five stages of the reading process. They choose the stories they will read and begin the process of interpretation during the preparing-to-read step. Next, they read the story independently, with a buddy, or in a small group. After reading, they write and draw a response in a reading log and talk about the story with a small group of students or in a conference with the teacher. When students particularly enjoy a story, they extend the reading experience by working on a project. They share the story and their project during sharing time. Sharing is a social time, and when students share the stories they have read, they have the opportunity to celebrate their reading and value the story. Sharing is also important because students often choose a book based on classmates' recommendations.

Teachers often connect reading workshop with literature focus units and author studies. They may begin with a book that all students in the class read, and then move into a reading workshop so that students can read independently. For example, during a literature focus unit, students might read *Bunnicula: A Rabbit-Tale of Mystery* (Howe & Howe, 1979) together as a class and then read other books in the series in a reading workshop. Or, during a unit on folktales, students may read several folktales together as a class and then break into small groups to read other folktales. During an author unit on Tomie de Paola, Eric Carle, or Beverly Cleary, students may read one or more books together as a class and then break into small groups to read others.

In Theme Cycles

Students often read stories as part of theme cycles, and stories are useful because they provide an additional viewpoint to that provided in informational books. Stories personalize history in a way that informational books cannot. Many stories have been written to chronicle events in American history. Here is a sampling:

Life in the Connecticut colony—*The Witch of Blackbird Pond* (Speare, 1958)

The American Revolution—*Johnny Tremain* (Forbes, 1970)

The slave trade—*The Slave Dancer* (Fox, 1973)

Life in a New England mill town—*Lyddie* (Paterson, 1991)

The California gold rush—*Chang's Paper Pony* (Coerr, 1988)

Pioneers traveling west—*Cassie's Journey: Going West in the 1860s* (Harvey, 1988)

The settlement of orphans on prairie farms—*A Family Apart* (Nixon, 1987)

Russian Jews coming to America for religious freedom—*Molly's Pilgrim* (Cohen, 1983)

Discrimination that African Americans faced in Mississippi during the 1930s—*Roll of Thunder, Hear My Cry* (Taylor, 1976)

Japanese Americans' internment in concentration camps during World War II—*Journey to Topaz* (Uchida, 1971)

These books are historical fiction, and the historical settings have been described accurately; moreover, these stories introduce readers to memorable characters and present themes that transcend the historical period in which the book is set.

Students also read books in connection with science themes. For example, during a theme cycle on mice, a multi-age classroom of first, second, and third graders read many of these stories about mice:

Do You Want to Be My Friend? (Carle, 1971)

The Town Mouse and the Country Mouse (Cauley, 1984)

Chrysanthemum (Henkes, 1991)

The Island of the Skog (Kellogg, 1973)

Alexander and the Wind-Up Mouse (Lionni, 1969)

Mouse Soup (Lobel, 1970)

Mouse Tales (Lobel, 1972)

If You Give a Mouse a Cookie (Numeroff, 1985)

Amos and Boris (Steig, 1971)

Doctor De Soto (Steig, 1982)

The Lion and the Mouse (Young, 1979)

Students in this classroom had two mice as classroom pets, and their curiosity about their pets set the stage for the theme. The teacher read some of the books aloud to students, and students read other books independently or with buddies during reading workshop. After reading, students talked about the stories and drew and wrote responses in their mice learning logs. They also did projects to extend their interpretations.

Assessing Students' Interpretation of Stories

Students' interpretations are unique and personal, and having students answer comprehension questions or fill in the blanks on worksheets is not an effective assessment technique. Teachers can better assess students' interpretation in these ways (Cairney, 1990):

- Listen to students as they talk about stories during grand conversations and other literature discussions.
- Read students' entries in reading logs.
- Note students' use of reading strategies.
- Observe students' participation in exploring activities.
- Examine the projects that students do.

Teachers also ask students to reflect on their interpretations during reading conferences or in reading log entries.

WRITING STORIES

As students read and talk about literature, they learn how writers craft stories. They also draw from stories they have read as they create their own stories, intertwining several story ideas and adapting story elements to meet their own needs (Atwell, 1987; Graves, 1989; Hansen, 1987; Harste, Short, & Burke, 1988; Harwayne, 1992). In his research about intertextuality, Cairney (1990) found that elementary students do think about stories they have read as they write, and Blackburn (1985) describes a cycle of intertextuality: Students read and talk about trade books; they weave bits of the stories they have read into the stories they write; they share their compositions; and then bits of these compositions make their way into classmates' compositions. Students make intertextual links in different ways, such as:

- Use specific story ideas without copying the plot.
- Copy the plot from a story, but add new events, characters, and settings.
- Use a specific genre they have studied for a story.
- Use a character borrowed from a story read previously.
- Write a retelling of the story.
- Incorporate content from an informational book into a story.
- Combine several stories into a new story.

The first two strategies were most commonly used in Cairney's study of sixth graders. It is interesting to note that the next to the last strategy was used only by low readers, and the last one only by high readers.

Students incorporate what they have learned about stories when they write stories, and they use the writing process to draft and refine their stories. They write stories as part of literature focus units, during theme cycles, and in writing workshop. Stories are probably the most complex writing form that elementary students use. It is difficult—even for adults—to craft well-formed stories with plot and character development and other elements of story structure incorporated.

In Literature Focus Units

Students often write stories as part of literature focus units. These writing activities are often done as projects during the extending stage of the reading process. Students make intertextual links and write retellings of stories, new stories using patterns from stories they have read, sequels to stories they have read, and original genre stories.

Writing Retellings of Stories. Elementary students often write retellings of stories they have read and enjoyed. As they retell a story, they internalize the structure of the story and play with the language that the author used. Sometimes students work together to write a collaborative retelling, and at other times they write their own individual retellings.

Students can work together as a group to write or dictate the retelling, or they can divide the story into sections or chapters, and each student or pair of students writes a small part. Then the parts are compiled. A class of first graders worked together to dictate this retelling of *Where the Wild Things Are* (Sendak, 1962) which was published as a big book:

Page 1: *Max got in trouble. He scared his dog and got sent to bed.*
Page 2: *This room turned into a jungle. It grew and grew.*
Page 3: *A boat came for Max. It was his private boat.*
Page 4: *He sailed to where the wild things lived.*
Page 5: *They made him king of all the wild things.*
Page 6: *The wild things had a wild rumpus. They danced and hung on trees.*
Page 7: *Max sent them to bed without any supper.*
Page 8: *Then Max wanted to come back home. He waved good-bye and sailed home on his boat.*
Page 9: *And his dinner was waiting for him. It was still hot from the microwave.*

As the first graders dictated the retelling, their teacher wrote it on chart paper. Then they read over the story several times, making revisions. Next, the students divided the text into sections for each page. Then students recopied the text onto each page for the big book, drew pictures to illustrate each page, and added a cover and a title page. Students also wrote their own books, including the major points in the beginning, middle, and end of the story.

Students also write individual retellings of stories, and young children use drawings to retell most of the story. Figure 9–13 presents a first grader's picture retelling of *The Tale of Peter Rabbit* (Potter, 1902). This story has four pages—the title page, the beginning page, the middle page, and the end page—and the basic information about the story is contained in this brief retelling.

Figure 9–13   *A First Grader's Retelling of* The Tale of Peter Rabbit

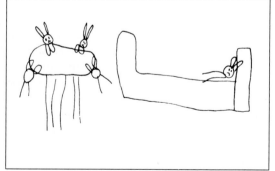

Sometimes students change the point of view in their retellings and tell the story from a particular character's viewpoint. A fourth grader has written this retelling of "Goldilocks and the Three Bears" from Baby Bear's perspective:

One day mom got me up. I had to take a bath. I hate to take baths, but I had to. While I was taking my bath, Mom was making breakfast. When I got out of the tub breakfast was ready. But Dad got mad because his breakfast porridge was too hot to eat. So Mom said, "Let's go for a walk and let it cool." I thought, "Oh boy, we get to go for a walk!" My porridge was just right, but I could eat it later.

When we got back our front door was open. Dad thought it was an animal so he started to growl. I hate it when Dad growls. It really scares me. Anyway, there was no animal anywhere so I rushed to the table. Everybody was sitting down to eat. I said, "Someone ate my porridge." Then Dad noticed someone had tasted his porridge. He got really mad.

Then I went into the living room because I did not want to get yelled at. I noticed my rocking chair was broken. I told Dad and he got even madder.

Then I went into my bedroom. I said, "Someone has been sleeping in my bed and she's still in it." So this little girl with long blond hair raises up and starts to scream. Dad plugged his ears. She jumped up like she was scared of us and ran out of the house. We never saw that little girl again.

Writing Pattern Stories. Many stories have a repetitive pattern or refrain, and students can use this structure to write their own stories. As part of a literature focus unit on mice, a first-grade class read *If You Give a Mouse a Cookie* (Numeroff, 1985) and talked about the circle structure of the story. The story begins with giving a mouse a cookie and ends with the mouse getting a second cookie. Then first graders wrote stories about what they would do if they were given a cookie. One student named Michelle drew the circle diagram shown in Figure 9–14 to organize her story, and then she wrote this story which has been transcribed into conventional English spelling:

If you gave Michelle a cookie she would probably want some pop. Then she would want a napkin to clean her face. That would make her tired and she would go to bed to take a nap. Before you know it, she will be awake and she would like to take a swim in a swimming pool. Then she would watch cartoons on T.V. And she would be getting hungry again so she would probably want another cookie.

Judith Viorst's *Alexander and the Terrible, Horrible, No Good, Very Bad Day* (1972) is a more sophisticated pattern story, and after reading the book, students often write about their own bad days. A fifth grader named Jacob wrote his version entitled "Jacob and the Crummy, Stupid, Very Bad Day":

One day I was riding my bike and I fell off and broke my arm and sprained my foot. I had to go to the hospital in an ambulance and get my arm set in a cast and my foot wrapped up real tight in a bandage. I knew it was going to be a crummy, stupid, very bad day. I think I'll swim to China.

Then I had to go to the dentist with my sister Melissa. My sister had no cavities, but guess who had two cavities. I knew it was going to be a crummy, stupid, very bad day. I think I'll swim to China.

My mom felt bad for me because it was such a bad day so she went and bought me a present—two Nintendo games. But my sister started fighting with me and my mom blamed me for it even though it wasn't my fault. So my mom took the games away. I wonder if there are better sisters in China?

Figure 9–14   A Circle Diagram for A Child's Version of If You Give a Mouse a Cookie

Then I went outside and found out that someone had stolen my bike. It was gone without a trace. It really was a crummy, stupid, very bad day. Now I am going to swim to China for sure.

Writing Sequels.   Students often choose to write sequels as projects during literature focus units. For example, after reading *The Sign of the Beaver* (Speare, 1983), students often write sequels in which Matt and Attean meet again. Students write additional adventures about the boa constrictor after reading *The Day Jimmy's Boa Ate the Wash* (Noble, 1980). Many stories lend themselves to sequels, and students enjoy extending a favorite story.

Writing Genre Stories.   During some literature focus units, students read books and learn about a particular genre, such as folktales, historical fiction, myths, or fables. After learning about the genre, students try their hands at writing stories that incorporate the characteristics of the genre. After reading gingerbread man stories, a class of kindergartners dictated this story which their teacher wrote on chart paper. Interestingly, the students asked their teacher to write the story in two columns. In the left column the teacher wrote the story, and in the right column she wrote the refrain:

The Runaway Horse

Once upon a time	*Run, run,*
there was a horse.	*as fast as you can,*
He jumped over the	*you can't catch me!*
stable gate and ran away.	

He meets a farmer.	Run, run,
The farmer chases him	as fast as you can,
but the horse runs	you can't catch me!
as fast as the wind.	

The horse meets a dog.	Run, run,
The dog chases him.	as fast as you can,
The horse runs	you can't catch me!
as fast as the wind.	

The horse meets the wolf.	Run, run,
The wolf chases him.	as fast as you can,
The horse runs	you can't catch me!
as fast as the wind.	

| Then the horse meets a fox. | Snip, snap, snout, |
| And the fox gobbles him up. | This tale is told out. |

A seventh-grade class read and examined myths and compared myths from various cultures. Then they applied what they had learned about myths in this class collaboration myth, "Suntaria and Lunaria: Rulers of the Earth," about the origin of the sun and the moon:

Long ago when gods still ruled the earth, there lived two brothers, Suntaria and Lunaria. Both brothers were wise and powerful men. People from all over the earth sought their wisdom and counsel. Each man, in his own way, was good and just, yet the two were as different as gold and coal. Suntaria was large and strong with blue eyes and brilliantly golden hair. Lunaria's hair and eyes were the blackest black.

One day Zeus, looking down from Mount Olympus, decided that Earth needed a ruler—someone to watch over his people whenever he became too tired or too busy to do his job. His eyes fell upon Suntaria and Lunaria. Both men were wise and honest. Both men would be good rulers. Which man would be the first ruler of the earth?

Zeus decided there was only one fair way to solve his problem. He sent his messenger, Postlet, down to earth with ballots instructing the mortals to vote for a king. There were only two names on the ballot—Suntaria and Lunaria.

Each mortal voted and after the ballots were placed in a secure box, Postlet returned them to Zeus. For seven years Zeus and Postlet counted and recounted the ballots. Each time they came up with the same results: 50% of the votes were for Suntaria and 50% were for Lunaria. There was only one thing Zeus could do. He declared that both men would rule over the earth.

This is how it was, and this is how it is. Suntaria still spreads his warm golden rays to rule over our days. At night he steps down from his throne, and Lunaria's dark, soft night watches and protects us while we dream.

The students incorporated the characteristics of myths in their story. First, their myth explained a phenomenon that has more recently been explained scientifically. The setting is backdrop and barely sketched. Finally, the characters in their myth are heroes with supernatural powers. It is interesting to compare this myth to the sun and moon myths told by aboriginal Australians, Native Americans, Nigerians, and Polynesians collected in *Legends of the Sun and Moon* (Hadley & Hadley, 1983).

In Theme Cycles

Students also write stories as part of theme cycles. During a theme cycle on weather, students might write stories set in different types of weather, or during an upper-grade theme on medieval life, students might write a story set in a castle. In these stories, students weave the information they are learning into their stories. For example, a multi-age class of middle-grade students were traveling around the world during their year-long social studies theme cycle. As they studied Hawaii, the students wrote stories and incorporated information into their stories, as this student's story shows:

My Trip to Hawaii

Today I reached Hawaii, the fiftieth state. On the way to my hotel I saw fields of sugarcane, coffee and pineapple. Then I stopped my car. There was a coconut laying in the middle of the road. I got out and got it. A coconut is a fruit that contains milk inside. However the milk does not rot.

Finally I got to my hotel. My hotel is by an extinct volcano called Diamond Head. It is the most known volcano on the islands. I was glad to be on the top of a 15 story high hotel. I wanted to go surfing in the Pacific Ocean, but I got to the part of the day that it started raining. It rains every day here. Well, I'm going to go eat a sandwich. The Hawaiian Islands were first discovered by Capt. James Cook in 1778. He named them the Sandwich Islands.

Now I'm going to go to the museum. I heard they have a travel guide today and I'm going to go. When I got there they gave me a map of where we're going to go. We're going to go to the coffee fields. Yuck! I hate coffee but I will go because Hawaii is the only state that grows coffee.

Next we're going to drive by Pearl Harbor. If you are a war lover and you are wondering how the United States got in World War 2, well, it's because the Japanese bombed Pearl Harbor in 1941. There is about 68 people on this bus and about 100 more people waiting back at the museum.

Oh and tonight I'm going to a hula dance. Tomorrow my hotel reservation expires so I better go pack so I'll be ready for the hula dance. Then I'm going to Australia.

Even though the insertion of information about Hawaii into this story is somewhat awkward, the student was proud that he could incorporate more than 10 facts in his story.

In Writing Workshop

Much of the writing that students do during writing workshop is stories. First graders often write single draft stories that feature prominent illustrations and are bound into books, but older students and more experienced writers move through all five stages of the writing process as they write stories. Students apply what they have learned about the elements of story structure in their stories, and teachers often teach minilessons about the elements of story structure during writing workshop.

Many students write stories about their pets and family members. In this example, a first grader writes about her dog Sebastian. Her story is entitled "Sebastian Goes to the Circus," and it was written in a book format with a sentence and a picture on each page:

Page 1: *Sebastian walks to the circus.*
Page 2: *It takes him a long time to get to the circus.*
Page 3: *When he gets there he can't find a man to help him.*
Page 4: *Sebastian tried to do some tricks but he couldn't.*
Page 5: *He found the Dog Trainer and he learned to do many tricks.*
Page 6: *Now he is the most famous circus dog in the world!*

As they write stories during writing workshop, eighth graders apply what they have learned about the elements of story structure.

Older students also write stories about themselves. A sixth grader wrote this story, "The Cave," in which he and his friends are the main characters:

> There were five of us when we started. Now there is just me and my friend Joe. This is what happened.
>
> The five of us, me (Boris Mudlumpus), Joe Marvinson, Ted Vergille, Jerry Marvinson (Joe's brother), and Mike Gorgolo, decided to explore the old cave on the hill before they cemented up the entrance. It has seemed like a great thing to do, then. But slowly, one by one, we started disappearing. Ted Vergille was a kind of fat guy who liked to crack jokes. We were laughing at one of his jokes when he suddenly he wasn't there anymore. We found him a little farther down the cave. His bones had been disjointed and his neck was broken. There were many punctures in his veins but no blood was anywhere. Someone, or something, had drained his blood and his eyes had the look that made you think he had seen horrors untold. We ran to the entrance as fast as we could, but by the time we got there, there was only me and Joe left, and the entrance had already been cemented over! We could never get out!
>
> That's the way it happened. Now we are trapped. Oh, no! It's closing in on us. Augh!!!!
>
> "George, wake up," my mother was calling. "It's time to go to school." I let out a long deep sigh. It was only a dream.

This story can be used to make two important points. Many students include gruesome descriptions and events in their stories, and teachers must decide for themselves where to set the limit on what is acceptable in their classrooms. Also, students often use dreams as a way to escape from a story. When the story gets complicated, the main character escapes by waking up from a dream.

Students also write retellings of stories, sequels, and pattern stories during writing workshop. They get ideas for the stories they write as they listen to classmates share their studies and through minilessons that teachers teach about different types of stories.

Assessing the Stories Students Write

Assessing the stories students write with this approach involves far more than simply judging the quality of the finished stories. Assessment also takes into account students' knowledge of story structure as well as the activities they engage in while writing and refining their stories. Teachers consider four components in assessing students' stories: (1) students' knowledge of the element of story structure, (2) their application of the element in writing, (3) their use of the writing process, and (4) the quality of the finished stories.

Determining whether students learned about the element and applied what they learned in their stories is crucial in assessing students' stories. Consider the following points:

Can the student define or identify the characteristics of the element?

Can the student explain how the element was used in a particular story?

Did the student apply the element in the story he or she has written?

Teachers assess students' use of the writing process by observing them as they write and asking these questions:

Did the student write a rough draft?

Did the student participate in a writing group?

Did the student revise the story according to feedback received from the writing group?

Did the student complete a revision checklist?

Did the student proofread the story and correct as many mechanical errors as possible?

Did the student share the story?

The fourth component, the quality of the story, is difficult to measure. Students who write high-quality and interesting stories use the elements of story structure to their advantage. Their stories are creative and well organized. Ask these questions to assess the quality of children's stories:

Is the story interesting?

Is the story well organized?

The assessment and grading of students' stories reflects more than simply the quality of the finished product. It should reflect all four components of students' involvement with stories.

Review

During the elementary grades students learn about five elements of story structure: plot, characters, setting, theme, and point of view. Students apply this knowledge as they read and write stories. They read stories aesthetically and develop interpretations as they read and respond to stories. Students read stories as part of literature focus units, reading workshop, and theme cycles. Students use the writing process to write retellings of familiar stories, new versions of stories, sequels, and original stories during literature focus units, in theme cycles, and in writing workshop.

Extensions

1. Compile a list of books to use in teaching about story elements at the grade level you teach or plan to teach. Write a brief summary for each book, commenting specifically on the element of story structure or genre that the book exemplifies.
2. Construct a set of charts to use in teaching the elements of story structure, as shown in Figure 9–10.
3. Interview several students about their concept of stories and what they think about as they read and write stories. Ask questions such as these:

   Tell me about a story you have read that is really a good one.

   What things do authors include in stories to make them good?

   Do you like to read stories? Write stories?

   Tell me about some of the stories you have written.

   Tell me some of the things you think about while you are writing a story.

   What do you include in stories you write to make them good?

   What have your teachers taught you about reading and writing stories?

4. Teach a series of minilessons about one of the elements of story structure or reading strategies to a small group of students. Use the teaching strategy presented in this chapter.
5. Plan a literature focus unit on a picture book or a chapter book.
6. Collect samples of children's stories and examine them to see how students use the elements of story structure.
7. Plan an author study unit and collect information about the author and copies of the stories the author has written.

References

Applebee, A. N. (1978). *The child's concept of story: Ages 2 to 17.* Chicago: The University of Chicago Press.

Applebee, A. N. (1980). Children's narratives: New directions. *The Reading Teacher, 34,* 137–142.

Atwell, N. (1987). *In the middle: Writing, reading, and learning with adolescents.* Portsmouth, NH: Heinemann.

Au, K. H. (1992). Constructing the theme of a story. *Language Arts, 69,* 106–111.

Blackburn, E. (1985). Stories never end. In J. Hansen, J. Newkirk, & D. Graves (Eds.), *Breaking ground: Teachers relate reading and writing in the elementary school* (pp. 3–13). Portsmouth, NH: Heinemann.

Bruner, J. (1986). *Actual minds, possible worlds.* Cambridge, MA: Harvard University Press.

Cairney, T. (1990). Intertextuality: Infectious echoes from the past. *The Reading Teacher, 43,* 478–484.

Cairney, T. (1992). Fostering and building students' intertextual histories. *Language Arts, 69,* 502–507.

Corcoran, B. (1987). Teachers creating readers. In B. Corcoran & E. Evans (Eds.), *Readers, texts, teachers* (pp. 41–74). Upper Montclair, NJ: Boynton/Cook.

Cox, C., & Many, J. E. (1992). Toward an understanding of the aesthetic response to literature. *Language Arts, 69,* 28–33.

de Beaugrande, R. (1980). *Text, discourse and process.* Norwood, NJ: Ablex.

De Ford, D. (1981). Literacy: Reading, writing, and other essentials. *Language Arts, 58,* 652–658.

Dressel, J. H. (1990). The effects of listening to and discussing different qualities of children's literature on the narrative writing of fifth graders. *Research in the Teaching of English, 24,* 397–414.

Eckhoff, B. (1983). How reading affects children's writing. *Language Arts, 60,* 607–616.

Golden, J. M. (1984). Children's concept of story in reading and writing. *The Reading Teacher, 37,* 578–584.

Golden, J. M., Meiners, A., & Lewis, S. (1992). The growth of story meaning. *Language Arts, 69,* 22–27.

Graves, D. H. (1987). *Experiment with fiction.* Portsmouth, NH: Heinemann.

Hansen, J. (1987). *When writers read.* Portsmouth, NH: Heinemann.

Harste, J. C., Short, K., & Burke, C. (1988). *Creating classrooms for authors: The reading-writing connection.* Portsmouth, NH: Heinemann.

Harwayne, S. (1992). *Lasting impressions: Weaving literature into writing workshop.* Portsmouth, NH: Heinemann.

Johnson, T. D., & Louis, D. R. (1987). *Literacy through literature.* Portsmouth, NH: Heinemann.

Lehr, S. S. (1991). *The child's developing sense of theme: Responses to literature.* New York: Teachers College Press.

Lukens, R. J. (1991). *A critical handbook of children's literature* (4th ed.). Glenview, IL: Scott, Foresman.

Macon, J. M., Bewell, D., & Vogt, M. E. (1991). *Responses to literature, grades K–8.* Newark, DE: International Reading Association.

Mandler, J. M., & Johnson, N. S. (1977). Remembrance of things parsed: Story structure and recall. *Cognitive Psychology, 9,* 111–115.

Many, J. E. (1991). The effects of stance and age level on children's literary responses. *Journal of Reading Behavior, 23,* 61–85.

Pitcher, E. G., & Prelinger, E. (1963). *Children tell stories: An analysis of fantasy.* New York: International Universities Press.

Rosenblatt, L. M. (1978). *The reader, the text, the poem: The transactional theory of the literary work.* Carbondale: Southern Illinois University Press.

Rosenblatt, L. M. (1985). The transactional theory of the literary work: Implications for research. In C. R. Cooper (Ed.), *Researching response to literature and the teaching of literature* (pp. 33–53). Norwood, NJ: Ablex.

Rumelhart, D. (1975). Notes on a schema for stories. In D. G. Bobrow (Ed.), *Representation and understanding: Studies in cognitive science.* New York: Academic Press.

Stein, N. L., & Glenn, C. G. (1979). An analysis of story comprehension in elementary school children. In R. O. Freedle (Ed.), *New Directions in Discourse Processing.* Norwood, NJ: Ablex.

Temple, C. (1992). Lots of plots: Patterns, meanings, and children's literature. In C. Temple & P. Collins (Eds.), *Stories and readers: New perspectives on literature in the elementary classroom* (pp. 3–13). Norwood, MA: Christopher-Gordon.

Tompkins, G. E., & McGee, L. M. (1993). *Teaching reading with literature: Case studies to action plans.* New York: Merrill/Macmillan.

Urzua, C. (1992). Faith in learners through literature studies. *Language Arts, 69,* 492–501.

Children's Book References

Aldis, D. (1969). *Nothing is impossible: The story of Beatrix Potter.* New York: Atheneum.

Blume, J. (1972). *Tales of a fourth grade nothing.* New York: Dutton.

Bonners, S. (1981). *A penguin year.* New York: Delacorte.

Brett, J. (1989). *The mitten.* New York: Putnam.

Burch, R. (1966). *Queenie Peavy.* New York: Viking.

Burch, R. (1980). *Ida Early comes over the mountain.* New York: Viking.

Byars, B. (1970). *The summer of the swans.* New York: Viking.

Byars, B. (1977). *The pinballs.* New York: Harper & Row.

Carle, E. (1971). *Do you want to be my friend?* New York: Philomel.

Carrick, C. (1989). *Aladdin and the wonderful lamp.* New York: Scholastic.

Cauley, L. B. (1984). *The town mouse and the country mouse.* New York: Putnam.

Coerr, E. (1988). *Chang's paper pony.* New York: Harper & Row.

Cohen, B. (1983). *Molly's pilgrim.* New York: Lothrop.

Dahl, R. (1961). *James and the giant peach.* New York: Knopf.

de Paola, T. (1989). *The art lesson.* New York: Holiday House.

Forbes, E. (1970). *Johnny Tremain.* Boston: Houghton Mifflin.

Fox, P. (1973). *The slave dancer.* New York: Bradbury.

Fritz, J. (1992). *Surprising myself.* Katonah, NY: Richard C. Owen.

Galdone, P. (1970). *The three little pigs.* New York: Seabury.

Galdone, P. (1978). *Cinderella.* New York: McGraw-Hill.

Gardiner, J. R. (1980). *Stone fox.* New York: Harper & Row.

George, J. C. (1972). *Julie of the wolves.* New York: Harper & Row.

Hadley, E., & Hadley, T. (1983). *Legends of the sun and moon*. Cambridge: Cambridge University Press.

Harvey, B. (1988). *Cassie's journey: Going west in the 1860s*. New York: Holiday House.

Henkes, K. (1991). *Chrysanthemum*. New York: Greenwillow.

Howe, D., & Howe, J. (1979). *Bunnicula: A rabbit-tale of mystery*. New York: Atheneum.

Hyman, T. S. (1983). *Little Red Riding Hood*. New York: Holiday House.

Kellogg, S. (1973). *The island of the Skog*. New York: Dial.

L'Engle, M. (1962). *A wrinkle in time*. New York: Farrar, Straus & Giroux.

Lester, H. (1988). *Tacky the penguin*. Boston: Houghton Mifflin.

Lewis, C. S. (1981). *The lion, the witch and the wardrobe*. New York: Macmillan.

Lionni, L. (1969). *Alexander and the wind-up mouse*. New York: Pantheon.

Lobel, A. (1970). *Mouse soup*. New York: Harper & Row.

Lobel, A. (1972). *Mouse tales*. New York: Harper & Row.

Lowry, L. (1979). *Anastasia Krupnik*. Boston: Houghton Mifflin.

Lowry, L. (1989). *Number the stars*. Boston: Houghton Mifflin.

Martin, B., Jr., & Archambault, J. (1985). *The ghost-eye tree*. New York: Holt, Rinehart & Winston.

Mayer, M. (1978). *Beauty and the beast*. New York: Macmillan.

Mayer, M. (1987). *The ugly duckling*. New York: Macmillan.

McCloskey, R. (1969). *Make way for ducklings*. New York: Viking.

Naylor, P. R. (1991). *Shiloh*. New York: Atheneum.

Ness, E. (1966). *Sam, Bangs, and moonshine*. New York: Holt, Rinehart & Winston.

Newton, P. (1990). *The stonecutter*. New York: Putnam.

Nixon, J. L. (1987). *A family apart*. New York: Bantam Books.

Noble, T. H. (1980). *The day Jimmy's boa ate the wash*. New York: Dial.

Numeroff, L. (1985). *If you give a mouse a cookie*. New York: Harper & Row.

O'Dell, S. (1960). *Island of the blue dolphins*. Boston: Houghton Mifflin.

Paterson, K. (1977). *Bridge to Terabithia*. New York: Crowell.

Paterson, K. (1991). *Lyddie*. New York: Viking.

Potter, B. (1902). *The tale of Peter Rabbit*. New York: Warne.

Ransome, A. (1968). *The fool of the world and the flying ship*. New York: Farrar, Straus & Giroux.

Scieszka, J. (1989). *The true story of the three little pigs*. New York: Viking.

Sendak, M. (1962). *Where the wild things are*. New York: Harper & Row.

Speare, E. G. (1958). *The witch of Blackbird Pond*. Boston: Houghton Mifflin.

Speare, E. G. (1983). *The sign of the beaver*. Boston: Houghton Mifflin.

Steig, W. (1971). *Amos and Boris*. New York: Farrar, Straus & Giroux.

Steig, W. (1982). *Doctor De Soto*. New York: Farrar, Straus & Giroux.

Taylor, M. D. (1976). *Roll of thunder, hear my cry*. New York: Dial.

Uchida, Y. (1971). *Journey to Topaz*. Berkeley, CA: Creative Arts.

Van Allsburg, C. (1981). *Jumanji*. Boston: Houghton Mifflin.

Viorst, J. (1977). *Alexander and the terrible, horrible, no good, very bad day*. New York: Atheneum.

Waber, B. (1972). *Ira sleeps over*. Boston: Houghton Mifflin.

White, E. B. (1952). *Charlotte's web*. New York: Harper & Row.

Yolen, J. (1986). *The sleeping beauty*. New York: Knopf.

Young, E. (1979). *The lion and the mouse*. New York: Putnam.

Zelinsky, P. O. (1986). *Rumpelstiltskin*. New York: Dutton.

Zemach, M. (1983). *The little red hen*. New York: Farrar, Straus & Giroux.

> **" "** *I introduce my girls and boys to autobiography by having them make "Me" boxes about themselves. Anything is possible in kindergarten, and an added benefit from this project is forging strong links between home and school.* **" "**
>
> Albena Reinig
> Kindergarten Teacher
> Thomas Oleatas Elementary School

PROCEDURE

We do our "Me" box project at the beginning of the school year. The children make their boxes at home and bring them to school to share. These boxes are great! Not only do I introduce the concept of autobiography, but the children are sharing with classmates and speaking in front of the class. I learn a lot about my children and their families.

I bring my own Me box to share with the class. I used a shoebox, and I've written my name and decorated the outside of the box with rose-colored paper—my favorite color. Inside I have a picture of my family, a small stuffed cat like my Boots, a postcard from our vacation last year in New York City, and a small cross-stitch kit because I like to do needlework. Next, I explain that everyone is going to make a Me box, and I distribute a letter about the project for children to take home to their parents. I ask each child to make a Me box from a shoe-box, a tissue box, or another container, and to decorate the outside of their boxes with their names and favorite colors, pictures cut from magazines, or gift wrap. Sometimes they add glitter, stickers, or other decorations on it. They put three or four objects inside that represent people, pets, events, and other things in their lives.

I give children a week to prepare their boxes, and as they bring their Me boxes to school, they begin sharing them. Several children share each day until everyone has shared. Here is one child's sharing:

This is my Me box. My mom helped me put this Happy Birthday paper on it and you can count these candles [candles are taped on the top of the box]—1–2–3–4–5. That's how old I am. And this is my name—J–E–R–E–D. My mom she cut these name letters for me and I pasted them on my box.

Now look inside. Here's one thing I got inside—my TeeTee. He's a tiger and I got him when I was little. I forgot where. He always sleeps on my bed. See this? He's got one of my little shirts from when I was a baby on. You can touch him but be real careful.

Now . . . this is a picture of me and Santa Claus. My mom put a four on the back. It means I was four when I got the picture made. And here's a picture of my family. It's got my mom and my dad and Josh—he's my baby brother.

And this is my Mickey Mouse. My Gramps and Nana gave it to me for my birthday because they are going to take me to Disneyland when school is out.

I explain that they need to show the outside of the box and then tell about each object or picture they have placed in the box. As they share each item, they show it to the class and tell something about it.

Then I put the boxes away in a safe place, and several times during the year we add things to the boxes. This year I am saving the hand prints and the number books we made to put in the boxes. At the end of the school year we'll write a class poem about kindergarten friends which everyone will sign, and I'll make a copy for each child. Then parents will collect boxes at our spring back-to-school night.

ASSESSMENT

My assessment is simple. I make sure that every child brings a Me box and shares it with the class. I expected to have to help one or two children who did not have assistance at home prepare their boxes at school, but it wasn't necessary. My children's parents take the project very seriously.

ADAPTATIONS

I've started making book boxes, too. In my box for *The Very Busy Spider* by Eric Carle (1984), I have a spider puppet, a spider web made of sticks and yarn, and pictures of the horse, cow, sheep, goat, pig, dog, cat, duck, rooster, and fly that I have colored, cut out, and laminated for my children to use in retelling the story. I also have boxes for informational books. In my box for *Growing Vegetable Soup* (Ehlert, 1987), I have several packages of vegetable seeds, a toy shovel and rake, plastic vegetables, and the recipe for vegetable soup.

I introduce the box when I first read the story or informational book, and then I provide opportunities for my children to look at the book again and explore the objects in the box in small groups. Of course, I remove any dangerous objects or very fragile items before setting the box out.

REFLECTIONS

Me boxes are a wonderful way to get to know my children at the beginning of the kindergarten year. My students are very proud when they share their Me boxes with us. They're sharing themselves and their families. I began using Me boxes to introduce autobiography to my students, but I've accomplished much more.

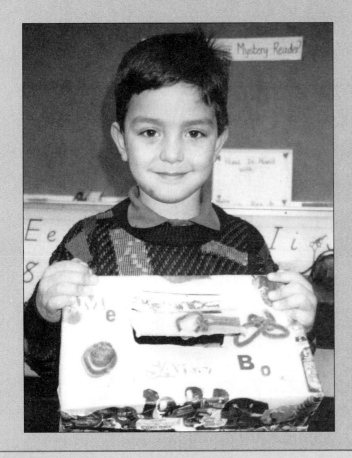

10

Reading and Writing Information

INSIGHT _____

Almost every book that students read and write is called a "story." It's common to hear teachers say, "I have an exciting story *to read to you today about how whales migrate" and "What a wonderful* story *you've written, and I learned a lot about baleen whales!" These books about whales may be stories, but it is more likely that they are nonfiction or informational books, because their primary purpose is to provide information. Often many teachers use the word* story *as a generic term, thinking that* stories *is an easier term for students to understand. Recent research suggests that stories are not more basic for children to understand, or that children should read and write stories before informational texts. One issue about informational books is:*

What is the difference between stories and informational books?

*F*or many years stories have been the primary genre for reading and writing instruction in the elementary grades because it was assumed that constructing stories in the mind was a fundamental way of learning (Wells, 1986). Recent research, however, suggests that children prefer to read informational books and are able to understand them as well as they do stories (Pappas, 1991, 1993). Children are interested in learning about their world, and informational books provide this knowledge. The information might be about baleen whales, how a road is built, threats to the environment of Antarctica, or Helen Keller's courage.

Students often assume the efferent stance as they read informational books to locate facts, but students do not always use efferent reading (Rosenblatt, 1978). Many times they pick up an informational book to check a fact and then continue reading—aesthetically—because they are fascinated by what they are reading. They get carried away in the book, just as they do when reading stories. At other times students read books about topics they are interested in, and they read aesthetically, engaging in the lived-through experience of reading and connecting what they are reading to their own lives and prior reading experiences.

Russell Freedman (1992), who won the 1988 Newbery Medal for *Lincoln: A Photobiography* (1987), talks about the purpose of informational books and explains that it is not enough for an informational book to provide information:

> [An informational book] must animate its subject, infuse it with life. It must create a vivid and believable world that the reader will enter willingly and leave only with reluctance. . . . It should be just as compelling as a good story. (p. 3)

High-quality informational books like Freedman's encourage students to read aesthetically because they engage readers and tap their curiosity.

Primary- and middle-grade students also write books about the information they are learning during theme cycles. The informational books they have read serve as models for their writing, and they organize the information that they present using the same types of patterns or structures used in informational books (Freeman, 1991; Tompkins, Smith, & Hitchcock, 1987).

DEVELOPING STUDENTS' KNOWLEDGE ABOUT INFORMATIONAL BOOKS

As students read informational books, they learn about the world around them and many other things as well. They learn how to vary their reading, depending on their purpose. Sometimes they read informational books from beginning to end like stories, or they may use the index to locate a specific topic and then read the section in the book about that topic. They learn how to use an index and a table of contents, and how to read charts, graphs, maps, and diagrams. They also notice the different ways informational books are organized and how authors develop interrelationships among the pieces of information being presented.

Types of Informational Books

There is a new wave of engaging and artistic informational books being published today, and these books show increased respect for children. Peter

Roop (1992) explains that for years informational books were the "ugly duckling" of children's literature, but now they have grown into a beautiful swan.

Four qualities of informational books are accuracy, organization, design, and style (Vardell, 1991). First and foremost, the facts must be current and complete. They must be well researched, and, when appropriate, varying points of view should be presented. Stereotypes are to be avoided, and the details in both the text and the illustrations must be authentic. Second, information should be presented clearly and logically, using organizational patterns to increase the book's readability. Third, the design of the book should be eye-catching and should enhance its usability. Illustrations should complement the text, and explanations should accompany each illustration. Last, style is becoming an increasingly important criterion. The style should be lively and stimulating so as to engage the reader's curiosity and wonder.

A wide variety of informational books are available today. Topics include the biological sciences, the physical sciences, the social sciences, the arts, and biographies. *Cactus Hotel* (Guiberson, 1991) is a fine informational book that shows the desert ecosystem. The author describes the life cycle of a giant saguaro cactus and its role as a home for other desert creatures. Other books—such as *Whales* (Simon, 1989), illustrated with striking, full-page color photos, and *Antarctica* (Cowcher, 1990), illustrated with dramatic double-page paintings—are socially responsible and emphasize the threats people present to animals and the earth.

Other books present historical and geographic concepts. *New Providence: A Changing Cityscape* (von Tscharner & Fleming, 1987), for instance, traces the evolution of a small, fictional city; and *Surrounded by Sea: Life on a New England Fishing Island* (Gibbons, 1991) describes the social life and customs

Sixth graders read from a text set of books during a theme cycle on the solar system.

of island residents throughout the four seasons. These books are exciting to read, and they provide an engaging and enriching reading experience for elementary students.

Some informational books focus on mathematical concepts (Whitin & Wilde, 1992). Tana Hoban's *26 Letters and 99 Cents* (1987) presents concepts about money; *What Comes in 2's, 3's and 4's?* (Aker, 1990) introduces multiplication; and *If You Made a Million* (Schwartz, 1989) focuses on big numbers. Many stories also involve mathematical concepts, but these books are designed to teach these concepts.

Life-stories are another type of informational books; one type of life-story is a biography and another is an autobiography. Life-stories being written today are more realistic than in the past, and they present well-known personalities, warts and all. Jean Fritz's portraits of Revolutionary War figures, such as *Will You Sign Here, John Hancock?* (1976), are among the best known, but she has also written comprehensive biographies, including *The Great Little Madison* (1989). As mentioned earlier, another fine biography is Russell Freedman's *Lincoln: A Photobiography* (1987), which won the Newbery Medal. Authors often include notes in the back of books to explain how the details were researched and to provide additional information.

Fewer autobiographies are available to elementary students today, but more are being published each year. Autobiographies about authors and illustrators, such as Roald Dahl's *Boy* (1984) and Cynthia Rylant's *Best Wishes* (1992), are popular.

In addition to these main types of informational books, there are other more specialized types. Four types that elementary students read are:

1.   Alphabet and Counting Books.   While many alphabet and counting books with pictures of familiar objects are designed for young children, others provide a wealth of information on various topics. In his alphabet book *Illuminations* (1989), Jonathan Hunt presents detailed information about medieval life, and in *The Underwater Alphabet Book* (1991), Jerry Pallotta provides information about 26 types of fish and other sea creatures. Muriel and Tom Feelings present information about Africa in *Moja Means One: Swahili Counting Book* (1971), and Ann Herbert Scott presents information about cowboys in *One Good Horse: A Cowpuncher's Counting Book* (1990). In some of these books new terms are introduced and illustrated, and in others the term is explained in a sentence or a paragraph.

2.   Books That Present Information Through a Song or Poem.   In these powerful books, songs and poems are illustrated with a word, line, or stanza on each page. Together the text and illustrations provide information. In *America the Beautiful* (Bates, 1993), Neil Waldman's expressionistic illustrations highlight 14 natural and man-made wonders including the Great Smokies and Mesa Verde, and information about each is presented in the back of the book. Jeannette Winter's haunting illustrations underscore the dangers of the underground railroad in *Follow the Drinking Gourd* (1988). Diane Siebert's poem and Wendell Minor's paintings combine to present a powerful portrait in *Sierra* (1991) and Jane Yolen's poem and Laura Regan's illustrations combine to describe the lush rain forest environment in *Welcome to the Green House* (1993).

3.   Books That Present Information Within a Story.   Authors are devising innovative strategies for combining information with a story. Margy Burns

Knight's *Who Belongs Here? An American Story* (1993), a two-part book, is a good example. One part is the story of Nary, a young Cambodian refugee who escapes to the United States after his parents are killed by the Khmer Rouge. This story is told in a picture book format, with the story text accompanying each picture. The second part of the book is information about refugees, immigration laws, and cultural diversity in America. The text for this second part is printed in a different typeface and set apart and under the story text on each page. Additional information about America as a nation of immigrants is presented at the back of the book. The two parts create a very powerful book.

A New Coat for Anna (Ziefert, 1986) is set in a post–World War II Europe, and the story shows how Anna's mother bartered to have a new coat made for her daughter. The steps in making a coat—from procuring wool to having the coat sewn by a tailor—are shown. There is also a powerful message about how difficult life is in the period right after a war ends.

Flashback is another useful technique. In *The House on Maple Street* (Pryor, 1987) a flashback is used to show all the different groups of people who have lived on the same piece of land. The text and the illustrations combine to present information, and the presentation of information is more central to the book than the storyline is.

Some combination informational books–and–stories are imaginative fantasies. The Magic School Bus series, written by Joanne Cole and illustrated by Bruce Degen, is perhaps the best known. In *The Magic School Bus Inside the Earth* (Cole, 1987), for example, Ms. Frizzle and her class study the earth and take a field trip on the magic school bus to the inner core of the earth and out again through a volcano. Charts and reports with factual information are presented throughout the book. Another fantasy story with factual information is Faith Ringgold's *Aunt Harriet's Underground Railroad in the Sky* (1992). Information and a map about the underground railroad and a biographical sketch of Harriet Tubman are included in the back of the book.

Other authors use the story format to tell about experiences in their own lives. Sherley Anne Williams tells her own childhood story of migrant farming in *Working Cotton* (1992), and Junko Morimoto tells of her experiences in the atomic blast in *My Hiroshima* (1987). In both of these books factual information about the topics is woven into the text.

4. *Journals and Letters.* Journals and letters are other types of informational books, and these artifacts provide a glimpse into historical periods and the lives of historical personalities. One example is *Off the Map: The Journals of Lewis and Clark* (Roop & Roop, 1993). Journals of pioneers are increasingly used in picture books. *The Way West: Journal of a Pioneer Woman* (Knight, 1993) describes the hardships of a woman and her family as they travel west on the Oregon Trail.

Some journals and collections of letters are authentic accounts, but others are fictionalized. The Roops' *I, Columbus: My Journal 1492–1493* (1989) is an informational book with excerpts from Columbus's journal, and *Pedro's Journal: A Voyage with Christopher Columbus August 3, 1492–February 14, 1493* (Conrad, 1991) is a fictionalized account. *Marco Polo: His Notebook* (Roth, 1992) is another fictionalized account, even though it looks very authentic. The journal is well researched and based on Marco Polo's autobiography. *Nettie's Trip South* (Turner, 1987) is a fictionalized letter written by a Northern girl about her trip to antebellum Richmond. She tells about the horrors of a slave market. Even the fictionalized accounts can be used in conjunction with informational books, but teachers and students should be aware of the differences between the two types.

Expository Text Structures

Informational books are organized or patterned in particular ways called *expository text structures.* Five of the most common organizational patterns are description, sequence, comparison, cause and effect, and problem and solution (Meyer & Freedle, 1984; Niles, 1974). Figure 10–1 describes these patterns and presents sample passages and cue words that signal use of each pattern.

Description.   In this organizational pattern, the writer describes a topic by listing characteristics, features, and examples. Phrases such as *for example* and *characteristics are* cue this structure. Examples of books using description include *Spiders* (Gibbons, 1992) and *Mercury* (Simon, 1993), and in these books the authors describe many facets of their topic. When students delineate any topic, such as the Mississippi River, eagles, or Alaska, they use description.

Sequence.   The writer lists items or events in numerical or chronological order. Cue words include *first, second, third, next, then,* and *finally.* Caroline Arnold describes the steps in creating a museum display in *Dinosaurs All Around: An Artist's View of the Prehistoric World* (1993), and David Macaulay describes how a castle was constructed in *Castle* (1977). Students use the sequence pattern to write directions for completing a math problem, the stages in an animal's life cycle, or events in a biography.

Comparison.   The writer explains how two or more things are alike or different. *Different, in contrast, alike, same as,* and *on the other hand* are cue words and phrases that signal this structure. In *Horns, Antlers, Fangs, and Tusks* (Rauzon, 1993), for example, the author compares animals with these distinctive types of headgear. When students compare and contrast book and movie versions of a story, reptiles and amphibians, or life in ancient Greece with life in ancient Egypt, they use this organizational pattern.

Cause and Effect.   The writer explains one or more causes and the resulting effect or effects. *Reasons why, if . . . then, as a result, therefore,* and *because* are words and phrases that cue this structure. Explanations of why dinosaurs became extinct, the effects of pollution on the environment, or the causes of the Civil War use the cause-and-effect pattern. Betsy Maestro's *How Do Apples Grow?* (1992) and Paul Showers's *What Happens to a Hamburger?* (1985) are two informational books that exemplify the cause-and-effect structure.

Problem and Solution.   In this expository structure the writer states a problem and offers one or more solutions. In *Man and Mustang* (Ancona, 1992), for example, the author describes the problem of wild mustangs and explains how they are rescued. A variation is the question-and-answer format, in which the writer poses a question and then answers it, and one question-and-answer

Figure 10–1 *The Five Expository Text Structures*

Pattern	Description	Cue Words	Graphic Organizer	Sample Passage
Description	The author describes a topic by listing characteristics, features, and examples.	*for example* *characteristics are*	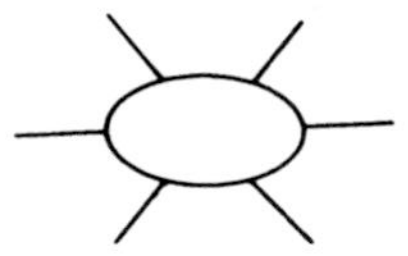	The Olympic symbol consists of five interlocking rings. The rings represent the five continents—Africa, Asia, Europe, North America, and South America—from which athletes come to compete in the games. The rings are colored black, blue, green, red, and yellow. At least one of these colors is found in the flag of every country sending athletes to compete in the Olympic games.
Sequence	The author lists items or events in numerical or chronological order.	*first, second, third* *next* *then* *finally*	1. _____ 2. _____ 3. _____ 4. _____ 5. _____	The Olympic games began as athletic festivals to honor the Greek gods. The most important festival was held in the valley of Olympia to honor Zeus, the king of the gods. It was this festival that became the Olympic games in 776 B.C. These games were ended in A.D. 394 by the Roman Emperor who ruled Greece. No Olympic games were held for more than 1,500 years. Then the modern Olympics began in 1896. Almost 300 male athletes competed in the first modern Olympics. In the games held in 1900, female athletes were allowed to compete. The games have continued every four years since 1896 except during World War II, and they will most likely continue for many years to come.
Comparison	The author explains how two or more things are alike and/or how they are different.	*different* *in contrast* *alike* *same as* *on the other hand*	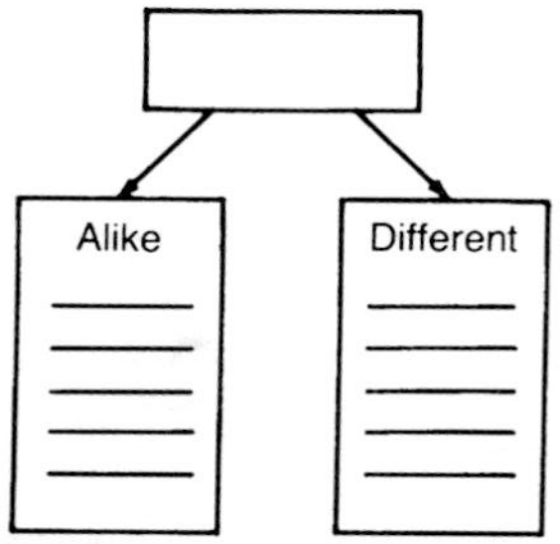	The modern Olympics is very unlike the ancient Olympic games. Individual events are different. While there were no swimming races in the ancient games, for example, there were chariot races. There were no female contestants and all athletes competed in the nude. Of course, the ancient and modern Olympics are also alike in many ways. Some events, such as the javelin and discus throws, are the same. Some people say that cheating, professionalism, and nationalism in the modern games are a disgrace to the Olympic tradition. But according to the ancient Greek writers, there were many cases of cheating, nationalism, and professionalism in their Olympics, too.

Figure 10-1 *continued*

Pattern	Description	Cue Words	Graphic Organizer	Sample Passage
Cause and Effect	The author lists one or more causes and the resulting effect or effects.	*reasons why* *if . . . then* *as a result* *therefore* *because*	Cause → Effect #1, Effect #2, Effect #3	There are several reasons why so many people attend the Olympic games or watch them on television. One reason is tradition. The name *Olympics* and the torch and flame remind people of the ancient games. People can escape the ordinariness of daily life by attending or watching the Olympics. They like to identify with someone else's individual sacrifice and accomplishment. National pride is another reason, and an athlete's or a team's hard earned victory becomes a nation's victory. There are national medal counts and people keep track of how many medals their country's athletes have won.
Problem and Solution	The author states a problems and lists one or more solutions for the problem. A variation of this pattern is the question-and-answer format in which the author poses a question and then answers it.	*problem is* *dilemma is* *puzzle is* *solved* *question . . .* *answer*	Problem → Solution	One problem with the modern Olympics is that it has become very big and expensive to operate. The city or country that hosts the games often loses a lot of money. A stadium, pools, and playing fields must be built for the athletic events and housing is needed for the athletes who come from around the world. And all of these facilities are used for only 2 weeks! In 1984, Los Angeles solved these problems by charging a fee for companies who wanted to be official sponsors of the games. Companies like McDonald's paid a lot of money to be part of the Olympics. Many buildings that were already built in the Los Angeles area were also used. The Coliseum where the 1932 games were held was used again and many colleges and universities in the area became playing and living sites.

book is . . . *If You Traveled West in a Covered Wagon* (Levine, 1986). Cue words and phrases include *the problem is, the puzzle is, solve,* and *question . . . answer.* Students use this structure when they write about why money was invented, saving endangered animals, and building dams to stop flooding. They often use the problem-solution pattern in writing advertisements and other persuasive writing as well.

These organizational patterns correspond to the traditional organization of main ideas and details within paragraphs. The main idea is embodied in the organizational pattern, and the details are the elaboration; for example, in the same passage of the comparison pattern in Figure 10–1, the main idea is that the modern Olympic games are very different from the ancient Olympic games. The details are the specific comparisons and contrasts.

Diagrams called *graphic organizers* can help students organize ideas for the five organizational patterns (Piccolo, 1987; Smith & Tompkins, 1988). Sample diagrams of the graphic organizers also appear in Figure 10–1.

Most of the research on expository text structures has focused on older students' use of these patterns in reading; however, elementary students also use the patterns and cue words in their writing (Langer, 1986; Raphael, Englert, & Kirschner, 1989; Tompkins, 1994). A class of second graders examined the five expository text structures and learned that authors use cue words as a secret code to signal the structures. Then the students read informational books that used each of the expository text structures, and they developed graphic organizers and wrote paragraphs to exemplify each of the five organizational patterns. The graphic organizers and paragraphs are presented in Figure 10–2; the secret code (or cue) words in each paragraph appear in boldface type.

Teaching Students About Expository Text Structures

Students learn to recognize the five organizational patterns and use them to improve their reading as well as to organize their writing (Flood, Lapp, & Farnan, 1986; McGee & Richgels, 1985; Piccolo, 1987). The steps in the teaching strategy are:

Step by Step

1. *Introducing an Organizational Pattern.* Explain the pattern and when writers use it; note cue words that signal the pattern. Then share an example of the pattern and describe the graphic organizer for that pattern.

2. *Analyzing Examples of the Pattern in Informational Books, Not in Stories.* Figure 10–3 lists books that illustrate each of the five expository text structures. Sometimes the pattern is signaled clearly by means of titles, topic sentences, and cue words, and sometimes it is not. Students learn to identify cue words, and they talk about why writers may or may not explicitly signal the structure. They also diagram the structure using a graphic organizer.

3. *Writing Paragraphs Using the Pattern.* The first writing activity may be a whole class activity; later, students can write paragraphs in small groups and individually. Students choose a topic, gather information, and organize it using a graphic organizer. Next they write a rough draft of the paragraph, inserting cue words to signal the structure. They revise, edit, and write a final copy of the

Figure 10–2   *Second Graders' Graphic Organizers and Paragraphs Illustrating the Five Expository Text Structures*

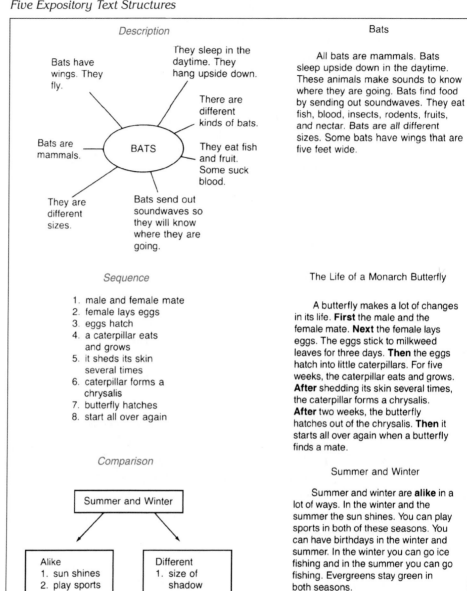

Description

Bats have wings. They fly.

They sleep in the daytime. They hang upside down.

There are different kinds of bats.

BATS

Bats are mammals.

They eat fish and fruit. Some suck blood.

They are different sizes.

Bats send out soundwaves so they will know where they are going.

Bats

All bats are mammals. Bats sleep upside down in the daytime. These animals make sounds to know where they are going. Bats find food by sending out soundwaves. They eat fish, blood, insects, rodents, fruits, and nectar. Bats are all different sizes. Some bats have wings that are five feet wide.

Sequence

1. male and female mate
2. female lays eggs
3. eggs hatch
4. a caterpillar eats and grows
5. it sheds its skin several times
6. caterpillar forms a chrysalis
7. butterfly hatches
8. start all over again

The Life of a Monarch Butterfly

A butterfly makes a lot of changes in its life. **First** the male and the female mate. **Next** the female lays eggs. The eggs stick to milkweed leaves for three days. **Then** the eggs hatch into little caterpillars. For five weeks, the caterpillar eats and grows. **After** shedding its skin several times, the caterpillar forms a chrysalis. **After** two weeks, the butterfly hatches out of the chrysalis. **Then** it starts all over again when a butterfly finds a mate.

Comparison

Summer and Winter

Alike
1. sun shines
2. play sports
3. evergreen trees
4. fishing
5. birthdays

Different
1. size of shadow
2. snow— no snow
3. temperature
4. flowers— no flowers

Summer and Winter

Summer and winter are **alike** in a lot of ways. In the winter and the summer the sun shines. You can play sports in both of these seasons. You can have birthdays in the winter and summer. In the winter you can go ice fishing and in the summer you can go fishing. Evergreens stay green in both seasons.

Summer and winter are **different** in a lot of ways. In the winter it snows and in the summer it doesn't. In the winter we have big shadows and in the summer we have little shadows. Summer is hot and winter is cold.

Figure 10–2   continued

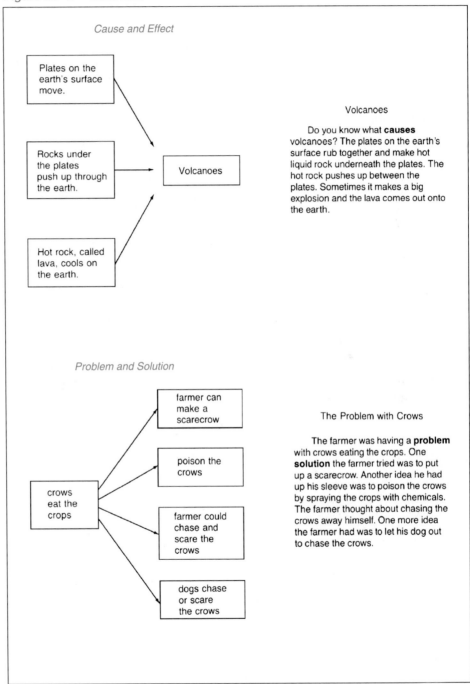

Cause and Effect

Plates on the earth's surface move.

Rocks under the plates push up through the earth.

Hot rock, called lava, cools on the earth.

Volcanoes

Volcanoes

Do you know what **causes** volcanoes? The plates on the earth's surface rub together and make hot liquid rock underneath the plates. The hot rock pushes up between the plates. Sometimes it makes a big explosion and the lava comes out onto the earth.

Problem and Solution

crows eat the crops

farmer can make a scarecrow

poison the crows

farmer could chase and scare the crows

dogs chase or scare the crows

The Problem with Crows

The farmer was having a **problem** with crows eating the crops. One **solution** the farmer tried was to put up a scarecrow. Another idea he had up his sleeve was to poison the crows by spraying the crops with chemicals. The farmer thought about chasing the crows away himself. One more idea the farmer had was to let his dog out to chase the crows.

Description

Balestrino, P. (1971). *The skeleton inside you.* New York: Crowell. (P)

Branley, F. M. (1986). *What the moon is like.* New York: Harper & Row. (M)

Fowler, A. (1990). *It could still be a bird.* Chicago: Childrens Press. (P–M)

Hansen, R., & Bell, R. A. (1985). *My first book of space.* New York: Simon & Schuster. (M)

Horvatic, A. (1989). *Simple machines.* New York: Dutton. (M)

Patent, D. H. (1992). *Feathers.* New York: Cobblehill. (M–U)

Sequence

Aliki. (1992). *Milk from cow to carton.* New York: HarperCollins. (P–M)

Cole, J. (1991). *My puppy is born.* New York: Morrow. (P–M)

Jaspersohn, W. (1988). *Ice cream.* New York: Macmillan. (M–U)

Lasky, K. (1983). *Sugaring time.* New York: Macmillan. (M–U)

Provensen, A. (1990). *The buck stops here.* New York: HarperCollins. (M–U)

Wheatley, N. (1992). *My place.* New York: Kane/Miller. (M–U)

Comparison

Gibbons, G. (1984). *Fire! Fire!* New York: Harper & Row. (P–M)

Lasker, J. (1976). *Merry ever after: The story of two medieval weddings.* New York: Viking. (M–U)

Markle, S. (1993). *Outside and inside trees.* New York: Bradbury Press. (M)

Munro, R. (1987). *The inside-outside book of Washington, D.C.* New York: Dutton. (M–U)

Rauzon, M. J. (1993). *Horns, antlers, fangs, and tusks.* New York: Lothrop, Lee & Shepard. (P–M)

Spier, P. (1987). *We the people.* New York: Doubleday. (M–U)

Cause and Effect

Branley, F. M. (1985). *Flash, crash, rumble, and roll.* New York: Harper & Row. (P–M)

Branley, F. M. (1985). *Volcanoes.* New York: Harper & Row. (P–M)

Branley, F. M. (1986). *What makes day and night?* New York: Harper & Row. (P–M)

Heller, R. (1983). *The reason for a flower.* New York: Grosset & Dunlap. (M)

Selsam, M. E. (1981). *Where do they go? Insects in winter.* New York: Scholastic. (P–M)

Showers, P. (1985). *What happens to a hamburger?* New York: Harper & Row. (P–M)

Problem and Solution

Cole, J. (1983). *Cars and how they go.* New York: Harper & Row. (P–M)

Heller, R. (1986). *How to hide a whippoorwill and other birds.* New York: Grosset & Dunlap. (P–M)

Lauber, P. (1990). *How we learned the Earth is round.* New York: Crowell. (P–M)

Levine, E. (1988). *If you traveled on the underground railroad.* New York: Scholastic. (M–U)

Showers, P. (1980). *No measles, no mumps for me.* New York: Crowell. (P–M)

Simon, S. (1984). *The dinosaur is the biggest animal that ever lived and other wrong ideas you thought were true.* New York: Harper & Row. (M)

Combination

Aliki. (1981). *Digging up dinosaurs.* New York: Harper & Row. (M)

Carrick, C. (1993). *Whaling days.* New York: Clarion. (P–M)

Guiberson, B. Z. (1991). *Cactus hotel.* New York: Henry Holt. (P–M)

Hoyt-Goldsmith, D. (1992). *Hoang Anh: A Vietnamese-American Boy.* New York: Holiday House. (M)

Simon, S. (1985). *Meet the computer.* New York: Harper & Row. (M–U)

Venutra, P., & Ceserani, G. P. (1985). *In search of Tutankhamun.* Morristown, NJ: Silver Burdett. (U)

P = primary grades (K–2); M = middle grades (3–5); U = upper grades (6–8).

paragraph. Then they share the paragraphs they have written and explain how they have used the particular organizational pattern in their writing.

4. *Repeating Steps 1–3 for Each Pattern.* Teachers repeat the first three steps in the teaching strategy to teach each of the five expository text structures.

5. *Choosing the Most Appropriate Pattern.* After students have learned to use the five patterns, they need to learn to choose the most appropriate pattern to communicate effectively. Students can experiment to discover the appropriateness of various patterns by writing paragraphs about one set of information using different organizational patterns. For example, information about igloos might be written as a description, as a comparison to Indian teepees, or as a solution to a housing problem in the Arctic.

Assessing Students' Use of Expository Text Structures

When students write paragraphs using an expository text structure, they:

- Choose the most appropriate structure
- Develop a graphic organizer before writing
- Write a topic sentence that identifies the structure
- Use cue words to signal the structure

These four components can be used to develop a checklist to assess students' use of expository text structures. Also, teachers may want to monitor students' use of the five structures in reports and other across-the-curriculum writing.

REPORTS

Often, students are not exposed to report writing until they are faced with writing a term paper in high school, and they are overwhelmed with learning how to take notes on notecards, how to organize and write the paper, and how to compile a bibliography. There is no reason to postpone report writing until students reach high school. Students in the elementary grades write both class collaboration and individual reports (Krogness, 1987; Queenan, 1986). Early, successful experiences with informative writing teach students about content area topics as well as how to write reports.

Young Children's Reports

Contrary to the popular assumption that young children's first writing is narrative, educators have found that kindergartners and first graders write many nonnarrative compositions in which they provide information about familiar topics, including "Signs of Fall," or directions for familiar activities, such as "How to Feed Your Pet" (Bonin, 1988; Sowers, 1985). Many of these writings might be termed "All About . . ." books, and others are informational pieces that children dictate for the teacher to record. These two types introduce young children to informational writing.

First graders write facts about rabbits and display them on the bulletin board.

In young children's "All About . . ." books, they write an entire booklet on a single topic. Usually one piece of information and an illustration appear on each page. A second grader wrote an "All About . . ." book, *Snowy Thoughts*, shown in Figure 10–4. It was written as part of a theme on the four seasons. Even though the student omitted some capital letters and punctuation marks and used invented spelling for a few words in his book, the information can be easily deciphered.

Young children can dictate reports to their teacher, who serves as scribe to record them. After listening to a guest speaker, viewing a film, or reading several books about a particular topic, kindergartners and first graders can dictate brief reports. A class of kindergartners compiled this book-length report on police officers:

Page 1:   *Police officers help people who are in trouble. They are nice to kids. They are only mean to robbers and bad people. Police officers make people obey the laws. They give tickets to people who drive cars too fast.*

Page 2:   *Men and women can be police officers. They wear blue uniforms like Officer Jerry's. But sometimes police officers wear regular clothes when they work undercover. They wear badges on their uniforms and on their hats. Officer Jerry's badge number is 3407. Police officers have guns, handcuffs, whistles, sticks, and two-way radios. They have to carry all these things.*

Page 3:   *Police officers drive police cars with flashing lights and loud sirens. The cars have radios so the officers can talk to other police officers at the police station. Sometimes they ride on police motorcycles or on police horses or in police helicopters or in police boats.*

Page 4:   *Police officers work at police stations. The jail for the bad people that they catch is right next door. One police officer sits at the radio to talk to the police officers who are driving their cars. The police chief works at the police station, too.*

Page 5:   *Police officers are your friends. They want to help you so you shouldn't be afraid of them. You can ask them if you need some help.*

Figure 10–4   A Second Grader's "All About . . ." Book

John-David

Snowy Thoughts.

the best thing about Snow is a Snonman

When it stats to snow I think about having a snowball fight

When its snowing I like to play with my brother.

My favorite swon-day food is hot sup.

Page 6:   *How We Learned about Police Officers for Our Report*
1. *We read these books:*
Police by Ray Broekel
What Do They Do? Policemen and Firemen by Carla Greene
2. *We interviewed Officer Jerry.*
3. *We visited the police station.*

The teacher read two books aloud to the students, and Officer Jerry visited the classroom and talked to the students about his job. The students also took a field trip to the police station. The teacher took photos of Officer Jerry, his police car, and the police station to illustrate the report. With this background, the students and the teacher together developed a cluster with these five main ideas: what police officers do, what equipment police officers have, how police officers travel, where police officers work, and police officers are your friends. The students added details to each main idea until each main idea developed into one page of the report. The background of experiences and the clustering activity prepared students to compose their report. After students completed the report, included a bibliography called "How We Learned About Police Officers for Our Report," and inserted the photographs, it was ceremoniously presented to the school library to be enjoyed by all students in the school.

Collaborative Reports

A successful first report-writing experience for middle- and upper-grade students is a class collaboration research report. Small groups of students work together to write sections of the report, which are then compiled. Students benefit from writing a group report first because they learn the steps in writing a research report—with the group as a scaffold or support system—before tackling individual reports. Also, working in groups lets them share the laborious parts of the work.

A group of four fourth graders wrote a collaborative report on hermit crabs. The students sat together at one table and watched hermit crabs in a terrarium. They cared for the crustaceans for two weeks and made notes of their observations in learning logs. After this period the students were bursting with questions about the hermit crabs and were eager for answers. They wanted to know about the crabs' natural habitat and what the best habitat was for them in the classroom, how they breathed air, why they lived in "borrowed" shells, why one pincer was bigger than the other, and so on. Their teacher provided some answers and directed them to books that would provide additional information. As they collected information, they created a cluster that they taped to the table next to the terrarium. The cluster became inadequate for reporting information, so they decided to share their knowledge by writing a book titled *The Encyclopedia About Hermit Crabs*. This book and the cluster used in gathering the information appear in Figure 10–5.

The students decided to share the work of writing the book, and they chose four main ideas, one for each to write: what hermit crabs look like, how they act, where they really live, and what they eat. One student wrote each section and returned to the group to share the rough draft. The students gave each other suggestions and made revisions based on the suggestions. Next, they edited their report with the teacher and added an introduction, a conclusion, and a bibliography. Finally, they recopied their report and added illustrations in

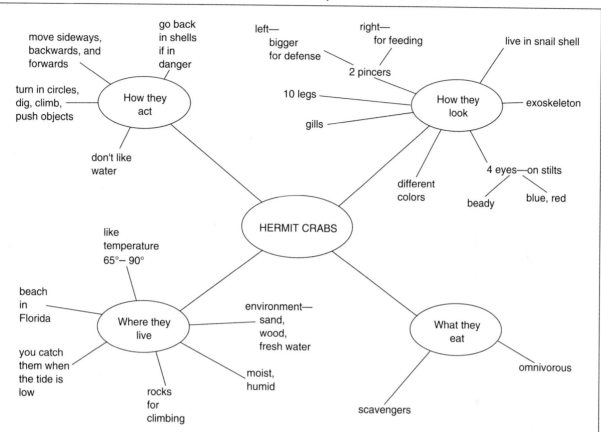

The Encyclopedia About Hermit Crabs

How They Look

Hermit crabs are very much like regular crabs but hermit crabs transfer shells. They have gills. Why? Because they are born in water and when they mature they come to land and kill snails so they can have a shell. They have two beady eyes that look like they are on stilts. Their body is a sight! Their shell looks like a rock. Really it is an exoskeleton which means the skeleton is on the outside. They have two pincers. The left one is bigger so it is used for defense. The right one is for feeding. They also have ten legs.

Where They Live

Hermit crabs live mostly on beaches in Florida where the weather is 65° – 90°. They live in fresh water. They like humid weather and places that have sand, wood, and rocks (for climbing on). The best time to catch hermit crabs is a low tide.

What They Eat

Hermit crabs are omnivorous scavengers which means they eat just about anything. They even eat leftovers.

How They Act

Hermit crabs are very unusual. They go back into their shell if they think there is danger. They are funny because they walk sideways, forwards, and backwards. They can go in circles. They can also get up when they get upside down. And that's how they act.

a cloth-bound book, which they read to each class in the school before adding it to the school library.

Individual Reports

Toby Fulwiler (1985) recommends that students do "authentic" research, in which they explore topics that interest them or hunt for answers to questions that puzzle them. When students become immersed in content area study, questions arise that they want to explore. A fourth-grade class that was studying dinosaurs quickly asked more questions than the teacher could answer. The teacher encouraged them to search for answers in the books they had checked out of the school and community libraries. When they located answers to their questions, the students were eager to share their new knowledge and decided to write reports and publish them as books.

One fourth grader's "The World of the Dinosaurs" report is presented in Figure 10–6. Each chapter focuses on a question he examined. The first chapter, "The Death Star," answered his question about how the dinosaurs died out. The second chapter—to answer his question about whether the dinosaurs all lived at the same time—focuses on the three time periods. In the third chapter he described the pterodactyl, an unusual flying lizard that lived when the dinosaurs did. He chose this topic after locating an interesting book about these flying lizards.

Students can organize reports in a variety of formats—formats they see used in informational books. One possibility is a question-and-answer format; another possibility is an alphabet book. One group of fourth-grade students wrote *The ABC Nintendo Book of Strategies* with one page for each letter of the alphabet. The *G* page appears in Figure 10–7.

Teaching Students to Write Research Reports

To write a report, either as a class collaboration or individually, students use a process approach. They search for answers to questions about a topic, then compose a report to share what they have learned. Designing questions and gathering information comprise the prewriting stage; students complete the stages by drafting, revising, editing, and publishing their reports.

Writing Class Collaboration Reports.   To apply the process approach in writing class collaboration reports, students follow six steps:

*Step
by
Step*

1. *Choosing a Topic.*   The first step is to choose a topic, which should be something students are studying or want to study. Almost any social studies, science, or current events topic that can be subdivided into 4 to 10 parts works well for class collaboration reports. Some possible general topics are oceans, dinosaurs, the solar system, the human body, continents, life in the Middle Ages, and transportation.

    From these general topics, students choose specific topics for small groups or pairs of students to research. For a report on the continents, students choose which continent they will research; for a theme on the solar system, they choose a planet. For a theme such as dinosaurs or the Middle Ages, students may not

Figure 10–6 *A Fourth Grader's Dinosaur Report*

The World of the Dinosaurs

Chapter 1
The Death Star

Over the years, scientists have noticed that almost all stars have a sister star. But what about the sun? Scientists have found out that the sun does have a sister star. It's darker than the sun, and it takes 28 million years to orbit around our solar system. They named it Nemesis after the Greek god of revenge. When Nemesis reaches its closest point to the sun, it makes the asteroid belt go beserk! Asteroids and comets were flying everywhere! The earth was a disaster! Scientists have studied and found out that if a comet or an asteroid hit the earth it would be like dropping an atomic bomb (or a thousand billion tons of dynamite) on the earth. Whenever that happens, almost everything on the face of the earth is destroyed. The next time Nemesis reaches its closest point to the sun will be in about fifteen million years.

Chapter 2
The Three Periods: Triassic, Jurassic, and Cretaceous

There were three periods when the dinosaurs came, and then they were just wiped off the face of the earth. It may have been the Death Star. Whatever the reason, nobody knows. The three periods were the Triassic, Jurassic, and the Cretaceous.
Most of the smaller animals like Orniholestes and Hysilophodon came in the Triassic Period. They were mostly plant eaters.
Most of the flying dinosaurs like Pteradactyl and Pteranadon came in the Jurassic Period. A number of the big plant eaters like Brontosaurus and Brachiosaurus also came in that period. A lot of sea reptiles came in that time, too.
The bigger dinosaurs like Tyrannosaurus Rex and Trachodon came in the Cretaceous Period. Most of these were meat eaters.

Chapter 3
Pterodactyl: The Flying Lizard

The Pterodactyl is a flying lizard that lived millions of years ago when the dinosaurs lived. Pterodactyl means "flying lizard." It was huge animal. It had skin stretched between the hind limb and a long digit of the forelimb. It didn't have any feathers. Some had a wingspan of 20 feet. Some paleontologists think Pterodactyl slept like a bat, upside down, because of the shape of its wings. It had a long beak and very sharp teeth. When it would hunt for food, it would fly close to the water and look for fish. When it saw one, it would dive in and get it. It also had sharp claws that helped it grab things. The Pterodactyl had a strange looking tail. It was long with a ball shape at the end. Some people say it really looked like a flying lizard.

---

be able to identify the specific topic they will research until they have learned more and designed research questions.

2. *Designing Research Questions.*   Research questions emerge as students study a topic. They brainstorm a list of questions on a chart posted in the classroom, and they add to the list as other questions arise. If they are planning a report on the human body, for example, the small groups that are studying each organ may decide to research the same three, four, or five questions: "What does the organ look like? What job does the organ do? Where is the organ located in the human body?" (Elementary students who research the human body

Figure 10–7   The G Page from
The ABC Nintendo Book of
Strategies

G   is   for   Godzilla

In Godzilla you breathe fire to kill other monsters. You can change into Mothra which is a giant butterfly. You try to transport to other planets and defeat the main boss of that planet. To breathe fire you press select.

often want to include a question as to whether a person can live without the organ; this interest probably reflects the current attention in the news media on organ transplants.)

Students studying a theme such as the Middle Ages might brainstorm the following questions about life in that era: "What did the people wear? What did they eat? What were their communities like? What kind of entertainment did people enjoy? What kinds of occupations? How did people protect themselves? What kinds of transportation did people use?" Each small group selects one of the questions as the specific topic for its report and chooses questions related to the specific topic.

To provide a rehearsal before students research and write their section of the report, the teacher and students may work through the procedure using a research question that no one chose. Together as a class, students gather information, organize it, and write the section of the report using the drafting, revising, and editing stages of the writing process.

3. *Gathering and Organizing Information.*   Students work in small groups or in pairs to search for answers to their research questions. The questions provide the structure for data collection, because students are seeking answers to specific questions, not just randomly writing down information. Students can use clusters or data charts to record the information they gather. The research questions are the same for each data collection instrument. On a cluster, students add information as details to each main idea ray; if they are working with data charts, they record information from the first source in the first row under the appropriate question, from the second source in the second row, and so on. These two instruments are effective because they organize the data collection question by question and limit the amount of information that can be gathered from any source. Students list their sources of information for clusters and data charts on the back of the paper.

Students gather information from a variety of reference materials, including trade books, textbooks, encyclopedias, magazines, films, videotapes, filmstrips, field trips, interviews, demonstrations, and observations. Teachers often require that students consult two or three different sources and that no more than one source be an encyclopedia.

Report writing has been equated with copying facts out of an encyclopedia, but even elementary students are not too young to understand what plagiarism is and why it is wrong. Even primary-grade students realize they should not "borrow" items belonging to classmates and pretend the items are theirs. Similarly, students should not "borrow" someone else's words, especially without giving credit in the composition. The format of clusters and data charts makes it easier for students to take notes without plagiarizing.

After students gather information, they read it over to check that they have answered their research questions fully and to delete unnecessary or redundant information. Next, they consider how they will sequence the information in their rough drafts. Some students tentatively number the research questions in the order they plan to use them in their composition. They also identify a piece of information that is especially interesting to use as the lead-in to the section.

4. *Drafting the Sections of the Report.* Students write their report sections using the process approach to writing. They write the rough draft, skipping every other line to allow space for revising and editing. Because students are working in pairs or in small groups, one student can be the scribe to write the draft while the other students in the group dictate the sentences, using information from a cluster or a data chart. Next, they share their draft with students from other small groups and revise it on the basis of feedback they receive. Last, students proofread and correct mechanical errors.

5. *Compiling the Sections.* Students compile their completed sections of the research report and, as a class, write the introduction, conclusion, and bibliography to add to the report. A list at the end of the report should identify the authors of each section. After all the parts are compiled, the entire report is read aloud so that students can catch inconsistencies or redundant passages.

6. *Publishing the Report.* The last step in writing a class collaboration research report is to publish it. A final copy is made with all the parts of the report in the correct sequence. If the report has been written on a microcomputer, it is easy to print out the final copy; otherwise, the report can be typed or recopied by hand. Copies are made for each student, and special bound copies can be constructed for the class or school library.

Writing Individual Reports. Writing an individual report is similar to writing a collaborative report. Students continue to design research questions, gather information to answer the questions, and compile what they have learned in a report. Writing individually demands two significant changes: Students must (1) narrow their topics and (2) assume the entire responsibility for writing the report.

Step by Step

1. *Choosing and Narrowing a Topic.* Students choose topics for research reports from a content area, hobbies, or other interests. After choosing a general topic, such as cats or the human body, they need to narrow the topic so that it is manageable. The broad topic of cats might be narrowed to pet cats or tigers, and the human body to one organ or system.

2. *Designing Research Questions.* Students design research questions by brainstorming a list of questions in a learning log. They review the list, combine some questions, delete others, and finally arrive at four to six questions that are worthy

of answering. When they begin their research, they may add new questions and delete others if they reach a dead end.

3. *Gathering and Organizing Information.*   As in collaborative reports, students use clusters or data charts to gather and organize information. Data charts, with their rectangular spaces for writing information, serve as a transition for upper-grade students between clusters and notecards.

4. *Drafting the Report.*   Students write a rough draft from the information they have gathered. Each research question can become a paragraph, a section, or a chapter in the report.

5. *Revising and Editing the Report.*   Students meet in writing groups to share their rough drafts and make revisions based on the feedback they receive from their classmates. After they revise, students use an editing checklist to proofread their reports and identify and correct mechanical errors.

6. *Publishing the Report.*   Students recopy their reports in books and add bibliographic information. Research reports can also be published in several other ways, for example, as a filmstrip or video presentation, as a series of illustrated charts or dioramas, or as a dramatization.

Assessing Students' Research Reports

Students need to know the requirements for the research project and how they will be assessed or graded. Many teachers distribute a checklist of requirements for the project before students begin working so that the students know what is expected of them and can assume responsibility for completing each step of the assignment. The checklist for an individual research report might include these observation behaviors and products:

Choose a narrow topic.

Identify four or five research questions.

Use a cluster to gather information to answer the questions.

Write a rough draft with a section or a chapter to answer each question.

Meet in writing groups to share your report.

Make at least three changes in your rough draft.

Complete an editing checklist with a partner.

Add a bibliography.

Write the final copy of the report.

Share the report with someone.

The checklist can be simpler or more complex depending on students' ages and experiences. Students staple the checklist to the inside cover of the folder in which they keep all the work for the project, and they check off each requirement as they complete it. A checklist enables students to monitor their own work and learn that writing is a process, not just a final product.

After completing the project, students submit their folders to the teacher for assessment. The teacher considers all the requirements on the checklist in determining a student's grade. If the checklist has 10 requirements, each requirement might be worth 10 points, and the grading can be done objectively on an 100-point scale. Thus, if the student's project is complete with all required materials, the student scores 100, or a grade of A. Points can be subtracted for work that is sloppy or incomplete.

LETTERS

Letters are a way of talking to people who live too far away to visit. Audience and function are important considerations, but form is also important in letter writing. Although letters may be personal, they involve a genuine audience of one or more persons. Students have the opportunity not only to sharpen their writing skills through letter writing but also to increase their awareness of audience. Because letters are written to communicate with a specific and important audience, students take more care to think through what they want to say; to use spelling, capitalization, and punctuation conventions correctly; and to write legibly.

Elementary students' letters are typically classified as friendly or business letters. Formats for friendly and business letters are shown in the Teacher's Notebook on page 384. The choice of format depends on the function of the letter. Friendly letters might be informal, chatty letters to pen pals or thank-you notes to a television newscaster who has visited the classroom. When students write to General Mills requesting information about the nutritional content of breakfast cereals or letters to the President expressing an opinion about current events, they use the more formal, business letter style. Before students write either type of letter, they need to learn how to format them.

Friendly and business letter formats are accepted writing conventions, and most teachers simply explain the formats to students and prepare a set of charts to illustrate them. Attention to format should not suggest, however, that form is more important than content; rather, it should highlight formatting considerations of letter writing that elementary students are typically unfamiliar with.

Friendly Letters

Children write friendly letters to classmates, friends who live out of town, relatives, and pen pals. Students may want to keep a list of addresses of people to write friendly letters to on a special page in their journals or in address booklets. In these casual letters, they share news about events in their lives and ask questions to learn more about the person they are writing to and to encourage that person to write back. Receiving mail is the real reward for letter writing!

After teachers have introduced the friendly letter format, students need to choose a "real" someone to write to. Writing authentic letters that will be delivered is much more valuable than writing practice letters to be graded by the teacher. Students may draw names and write letters to classmates, to pen pals from another class in the same or another school, or to friends and relatives.

Students use the writing process in letter writing. In the prewriting stage they decide what to include in their letters. Brainstorming and clustering are

Teacher's Notebook

Forms for Friendly and Business Letters

Friendly Letter Form

Street
City, State ZIP
Date ← **Return Address**

Greeting → Dear _____,

```
_____
_____
_____
_____
_____
_____
```
Body

Your friend,

Signature ← **Complimentary Closing**

Business Letter Form

Street
City, State ZIP
Date ← **Return Address**

Inside Address →
Person's Name
Company Name
Street
City, State ZIP

Greeting → Dear _____:

```
_____
_____
_____
_____
```
Body

Sincerely,

Signature ← **Complimentary Closing**

effective strategies to help students choose information to include and questions to ask. Figure 10–8 shows a cluster with four rays developed by a third-grade class for pen pal letters. As a class, the students brainstormed a list of possible topics and finally decided on the four main idea rays (me and my family, my school, my hobbies, and questions for my pen pal). Then students completed the clusters by adding details to each main idea.

Students' rough drafts incorporated the information from one ray into the first paragraph, information from a second ray into the second paragraph, and so on, for the body of the letters. After writing their rough drafts, students met in writing groups to revise content and edit to correct mechanical errors, first with a classmate and later with the teacher. Next, they recopied their final drafts, addressed envelopes, and mailed them. A sample letter is also presented in Figure 10–8. Comparing each paragraph of the letter with the cluster reveals that using the cluster helped the student write a well-organized and interesting letter that was packed with information.

Pen Pal Letters.   Teachers can arrange for their students to exchange letters with students in another class by contacting a teacher in a nearby school or local educational associations, or by answering advertisements in educational magazines.

Individual students can also arrange for pen pals by contacting one of the following organizations:

International Friendship League
22 Batterymarch
Boston, MA 02109

League of Friendship
P.O. Box 509
Mt. Vernon, OH 43050

Student Letter Exchange
910 Fourth Street SE
Austin, MN 55912

World Pen Pals
1690 Como Avenue
St. Paul, MN 55108

Students should write to one of the organizations, describing their interests and including their name, address, age, and sex. They should ask if a fee is required and should enclose a self-addressed, stamped envelope (identified by the acronym SASE) for a reply.

Another possible arrangement is to have an elementary class become pen pals with college students in a language arts methods class. Over a semester the elementary students and preservice teachers can write back and forth to each other four, five, or six times, and perhaps can even meet each other at the end of the semester. The children have the opportunity to be pen pals with college students, and the college students have the opportunity to get to know an elementary student and examine the student's writing. In a recent study (Greenlee, Hiebert, Bridge, & Winograd, 1986), a class of second graders became pen pals with a class of college students who were majoring in elementary education. The researchers investigated whether having a genuine audience would influence the quality of the letters the students wrote. They compared the second graders' letters to letters written by a control group who wrote letters to imaginary audiences and received traditional teacher comments on their letters. The researchers found that the students who wrote to pen pals wrote longer and more complex letters once they received responses to their letters. The results of this study emphasize the importance of providing real audiences for student writing.

Figure 10–8   A Third Grader's Cluster and Pen Pal Letter

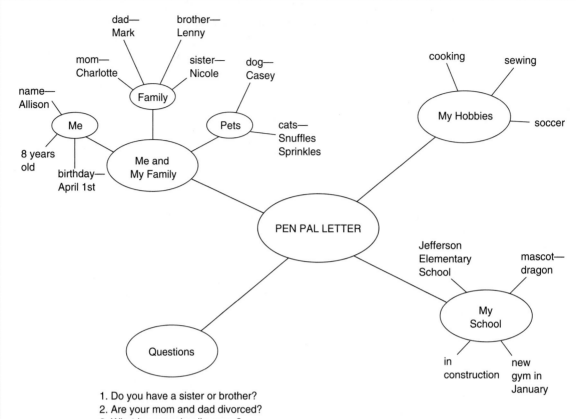

1. Do you have a sister or brother?
2. Are your mom and dad divorced?
3. What is your school's name?
4. What is your mascot?
5. What is your teacher's name?
6. Do you have a pet?
7. How many pets do you have?
8. Will you send a photograph?

December 10

Dear Annie,

I'm your pen pal now. My name is Allison and I'm 8 years old. My birthday is on April 1st.

I go to Jefferson Elementary School. Our mascot is a dragon. We are in construction because we're going to have a new gym in January.

My hobbies are soccer, sewing, and cooking. I play soccer, sewing I do in free time, and I cook dinner sometimes.

My pets are two cats and a dog. The dog's name is Casey and he's a boy. He is two years old. The cat is a girl and her name is Snuffles. She is four years old. The kitten is a girl and her name is Sprinkles. She is two months old.

My dad's name is Mark and my mom's name is Charlotte. Her birthday is the day after Mother's Day. My brother's name is Lenny. He is 13 years old. My sister's name is Nicole. She is 3 years old.

I have some questions for you. Do you have a sister or a brother? Are your mom and dad divorced? Mine aren't. What is your school's name? What is your mascot? What is your teacher's name? Do you have a pet? How many pets do you have? Will you send me a photograph of yourself?

Your friend,
Allison

Figure 10–9   A First Grader's Letter to Dr. Seuss

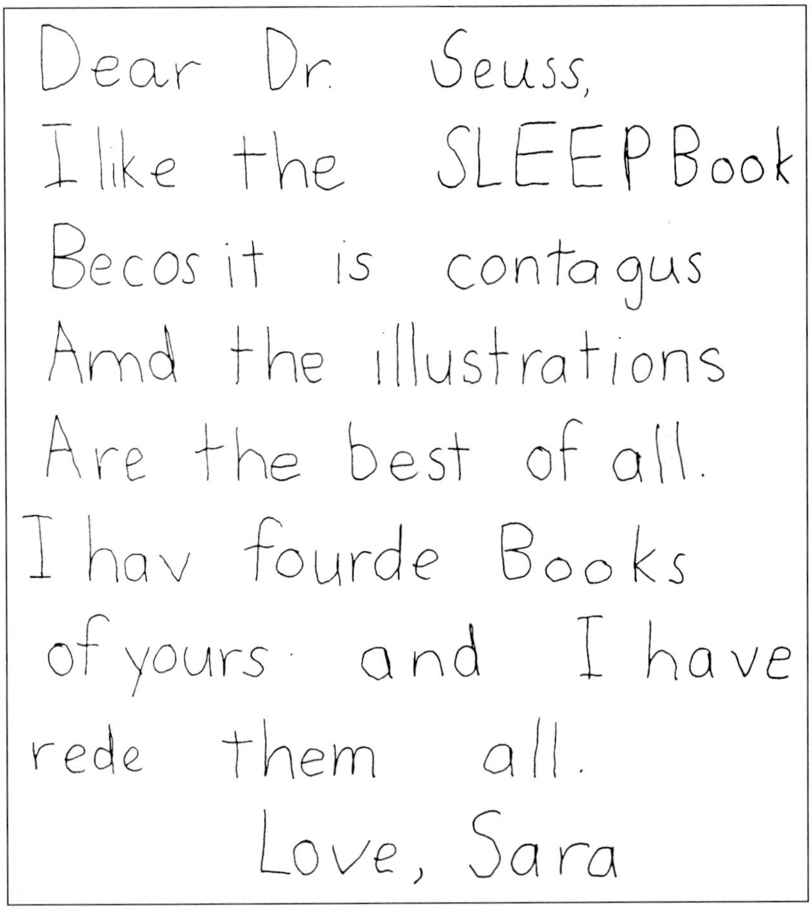

Dear Dr. Seuss,
I like the SLEEP Book
Becos it is contagus
Amd the illustrations
Are the best of all.
I hav fourde Books
of yours· and I have
rede them all.
             Love, Sara

Courtesy Letters. Invitations and thank-you notes are two other types of friendly letters that elementary students write. They may write to parents to invite them to an after-school program, to the class across the hall to invite them to visit a classroom exhibit, or to a community person to invite him or her to be interviewed as part of a content area unit. Similarly, children write letters to thank people who have been helpful.

*Letters to Authors and Illustrators.** Students write letters to favorite authors and illustrators to share their ideas and feelings about the books they have read. They ask questions about how a particular character·was developed or why the illustrator used a certain art medium. Students also describe the books they have written. A first grader's letter to Dr. Seuss is presented in Figure 10–9. Most authors and illustrators reply to children's letters when possible; however, they receive thousands of letters from children every year and cannot be pen pals with students.

Beverly Cleary's award-winning book *Dear Mr. Henshaw* (1983) offers a worthwhile lesson about what students (and their teachers) can realistically

---

*The suggestions in this section are adapted from Cleary (1983, 1985).

expect from authors and illustrators. The following guidelines are suggested when writing to authors and illustrators:

Follow the correct letter format with return address, greeting, body, closing, and signature.

Use the process approach to write, revise, and edit the letter. Be sure to proofread and correct errors.

Recopy the letter so that it will be neat and easy to read.

Write the return address on both envelope and letter.

Include a stamped, self-addressed envelope for a reply.

Be polite in the letter; use the words "please" and "thank you."

Students should write genuine letters to share their thoughts and feelings about the author's writing or the illustrator's artwork, and they should write only to authors and illustrators whose work they are familiar with. In their letters students should avoid asking a long list of questions to be answered or asking personal questions, such as how much money he or she earns. They should not ask for free books, because authors/illustrators do not have copies of their books to give away. Students send their letters to the author/illustrator in care of the publisher. The publisher's name appears on the book's title page, and the address usually appears on the copyright page, the page following the title page. If students cannot find the complete mailing address, they can check *Books in Print* or *Literary Market Place,* reference books that are available in most public libraries.

Young Children's Letters.   Young children can write individual letters, as the first grader's letter to Dr. Seuss in Figure 10–9 illustrates. They prewrite as older students do, by brainstorming or clustering possible ideas before writing. A quick review of how to begin and end letters is also helpful. In contrast with older children's letters, kindergartners and first graders' letters may involve only a single draft, since invented spellings and the artwork may carry much of the message.

Primary-grade students can also compose class collaboration letters. The children brainstorm ideas, which the teacher records on a large chart. After the letter is finished, children add their signatures. They might write collaborative letters to thank community persons who have visited the class, to invite another class to attend a puppet show, or to compliment a favorite author. Class collaboration letters can also serve as pen pal letters to another class.

Two books are useful in introducing young children to letter writing: *The Jolly Postman or Other People's Letters* (Ahlberg & Ahlberg, 1986) is a fantastic, storylike introduction to the reasons people write letters, and *Arthur's Pen Pal* (Hoban, 1982) is a delightful way to explain what it means to be a pen pal.

Business Letters

Students write business letters to seek information, to complain and compliment, and to transact business. They use this more formal letter style to communicate with businesses, local newspapers, and governmental agencies.

Students may write to businesses to order products, to ask questions, and to complain about or compliment specific products; they write letters to the editors of local newspapers and magazines to comment on articles and to express their opinions. It is important that students support their comments and opinions with facts if they hope to have their letters published. Students can also write to local, state, and national government officials to express concerns, make suggestions, or seek information.

Addresses of local elected officials are listed in the telephone directory, and addresses of state officials are available in the reference section of the public library. Here are the addresses of the president and U.S. senators and representatives:

President's name   Representative's name
The White House   House of Representatives Office Building
Washington, DC 20500   Washington, DC 20515

Senator's name
Senate Office Building
Washington, DC 20510

Students may also write other types of business letters to request information and free materials. One source of free materials is *Free Stuff for Kids* (Lansky, 1994), which lists more than 250 free or inexpensive materials that elementary students can write for and which is updated yearly. Children can also write to NASA, the National Wildlife Federation, publishers, state tourism bureaus, and other businesses to request materials.

Simulated Letters

Students can also write simulated letters, in which they assume the identity of a historical or literary figure. They can write letters as though they were Davy Crockett or another of the men defending the Alamo, or Thomas Edison, inventor of the electric light. Students can write from one book character to another; for example, after reading *Sarah, Plain and Tall* (MacLachlan, 1985), students can assume the persona of Sarah and write a letter to her brother William, as this third grader did in this letter:

Dear William,
I'm having fun here. There was a very big storm here. It was so big it looked like the sea. Sometimes I am very lonesome for home but sometimes it is very fun here in Ohio. We swam in the cow pond and I taught Caleb how to swim. They were afraid I would leave. Maggie and Matthew brought some chickens.

Love,
Sarah

Even though these letters are never mailed, they provide an opportunity for students to focus on a specific audience. After they write their original letters, students can exchange letters among classmates and reply to the letters.

Teaching Students to Write Letters

Students use the process approach to write both friendly and business letters. The steps are:

*Step
by
Step*

1. *Gathering and Organizing Information for the Letter.*   Students participate in prewriting activities, such as brainstorming or clustering, to decide what information to include in their letters. If they are writing friendly letters, particularly to pen pals, they also identify several questions to include.

2. *Reviewing the Friendly or Business Letter Form.*   Before writing the rough drafts of their letters, students review the friendly or business letter form.

3. *Writing the Letters Using a Process Approach.*   Students write a rough draft, incorporating the information developed during prewriting and following either the friendly or the business letter style. Next, students meet in a writing group to share their rough drafts, receive compliments, and get feedback. They make changes based on the feedback and edit their letters with a partner, proofreading to identify errors and correcting as many as possible. They also make sure they have used the appropriate letter format. After making all the mechanical corrections, students recopy their letters and address envelopes. The crucial last step is to mail the letters.

Assessing Students' Letters

Traditionally, students wrote letters and turned them in for the teacher to grade. The letters were returned to the students after they were graded, but they were never mailed. Educators now recognize the importance of having an audience for student writing, and research suggests that students write better when they know that their writing will be read by someone other than the teacher. Whereas it is often necessary to assess student writing, it would be inappropriate for the teacher to put a grade on the letter if it is going to be mailed to someone. Teachers can instead develop a checklist for evaluating students' letters without marking on them.

A third-grade teacher developed the checklist in Figure 10–10, which identifies specific behaviors and measurable products. The teacher shares the checklist with students before they begin to write so that they know what is expected of them and how they will be graded. At an evaluation conference before the letters were mailed, the teacher reviewed the checklist with each student. The letters were mailed without evaluative comments or grades written on them, but the completed checklist went into students' writing folders. A grading scale can be developed from the checklist; for example, points can be awarded for each check mark in the *yes* column, or five check marks can be determined to equal a grade of A, four check marks a B, and so on.

LIFE-STORIES

Elementary students enjoy sharing information about their lives and learning about the lives of well-known personalities. As they read life-stories written for young people, students examine their structure and use the books as models for their own writing. Life-stories combine expository writing with some elements of narration.

Figure 10–10   A Checklist for Assessing Students' Pen Pal Letters

Pen Pal Letter Checklist

Name _____

	Yes	No
1. Did you complete the cluster?	☐	☐
2. Did you include questions in your letter?	☐	☐
3. Did you put your letter in the friendly letter form?	☐	☐

_____ return address
_____ greeting
_____ 3 or more paragraphs
_____ closing
_____ salutation and name

	Yes	No
4. Did you write a rough draft of your letter?	☐	☐
5. Did you revise your letter with suggestions from people in your writing group?	☐	☐
6. Did you proofread your letter and correct as many errors as possible?	☐	☐

Authors use several different approaches in writing autobiographies and biographies (Fleming & McGinnis, 1985). The most common approach is historical; the writer focuses on dates and events and presents them chronologically. Many autobiographies and biographies that span the person's entire life follow this pattern.

A second pattern is the sociological approach, wherein the writer describes life during a historical period, providing information about family life, food, clothing, education, economics, transportation, and so on. For instance, *Worlds Apart: The Autobiography of a Dancer From Brooklyn* (Maiorano, 1980) describes the author's childhood in an impoverished New York City neighborhood and how he escapes it through a career with the Metropolitan Opera Company.

A third approach is psychological: The writer focuses on conflicts the central figure faces. Conflicts may be with oneself, others, nature, or society. The psychological approach has many elements in common with stories and is most often used in shorter autobiographies and biographies that revolve around particular events or phases. An example is the single-event biography, *And Then What Happened, Paul Revere?* (Fritz, 1973), in which Paul Revere faces a conflict with the British army.

Autobiographies

When students write autobiographies, they relive and document their lives, usually in chronological order. They describe the memorable events that are necessary to know them. A second grader's autobiography is shown in Figure 10–11. In six chapters Eddie describes himself and his family, his pets, his "favorites" and hobbies, and his vacations to a Texas town. Autobiographical writing grows out of children's personal journal entries and "All About Me" books that they write in kindergarten and first grade. Their primary source of information for writing is their own experiences.

Figure 10–11   A Second Grader's Autobiography

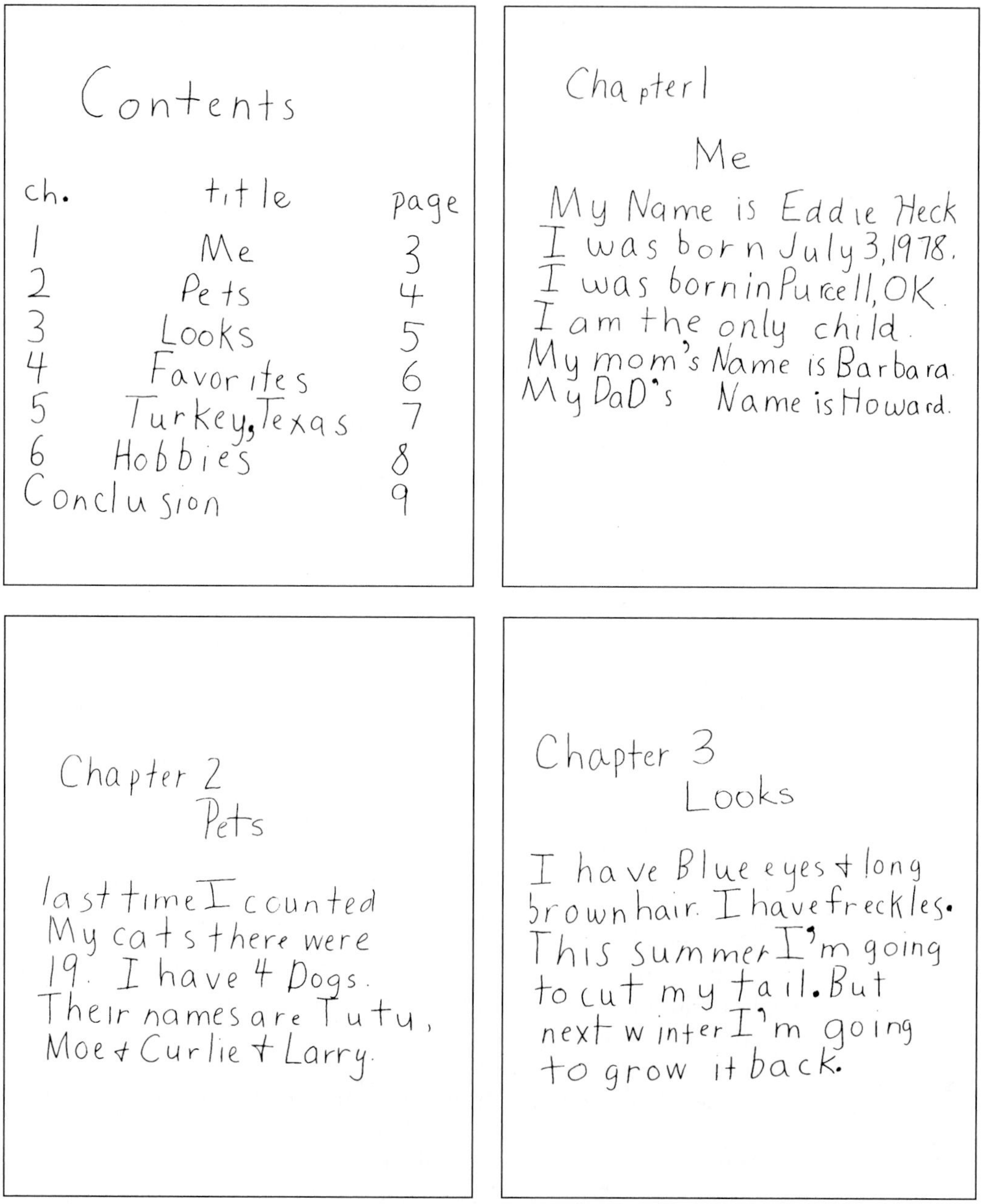

Contents

ch.	title	page
1	Me	3
2	Pets	4
3	Looks	5
4	Favorites	6
5	Turkey, Texas	7
6	Hobbies	8
Conclusion		9

Chapter 1

Me

My Name is Eddie Heck
I was born July 3, 1978.
I was born in Purcell, OK.
I am the only child.
My mom's Name is Barbara.
My DaD's   Name is Howard.

Chapter 2
Pets

last time I counted
My cats there were
19. I have 4 Dogs.
Their names are Tutu,
Moe & Curlie & Larry.

Chapter 3
Looks

I have Blue eyes & long
brown hair. I have freckles.
This summer I'm going
to cut my tail. But
next winter I'm going
to grow it back.

"All About Me" Books.   Children in kindergarten and first grade often compile "All About Me" books. These first autobiographies usually list information such as the child's birthday, family members, friends, and favorite activities, with drawings as well as text. Figure 10–12 shows two pages from a first grader's "All About Me" book. To write these books, the children and the teacher decide on a topic for each page, and, after brainstorming possible ideas for the topic, children draw a picture and write about it. Children may

Figure 10–11 continued

Chapter 4
Favorites

My favorite president is Georrge Washington. My favorite pet is a Dog. My favorite thing is my Bike My favorite toy is GI.LoE. My favorite color is black. My favorite Game is NINJA.

Chapter 5
Turkey, Texas

I went to Turkey, Texas for My first time at 2½ yrs. old I liked it so much we have gone ever since. I went to see BoB Wills and his Texas Play Boys but BoB Wills is dead now.

Chapter 6
Hobbies

My favorite hobbies are inventing games. I've invented these games: NINJA & Goldtar defender of The Universe. These are Games that some times I play by my self and some times I play with my friends.

Conclusion

The day after school is out I'm going to Dog-Patch, Arkansas to see Daisy Mae and Mammy Yoakum. I may go to Six Flags this summer I may also go to Frontier City. I will be looking forward to school starting.

also need to ask their parents for information about their birth and events during their preschool years.

Biographies

Biographies are accounts of a person's life written by someone else, and writers try to make the account as accurate and authentic as possible. Writers consult a variety of sources of information to research a biography. The best

Figure 10–12   Two Pages from a First Grader's "All About Me" Book

I have 3 best friends. they are very nice to do things with me. My friends names are Randy,Kasey,and Kimberly I go to Randy's house every morning. Her mom baby sits me.

This is my Grammy's house. I have my own room in it Sometimes I sleep on the love seat I like to see Papa Sometimes my papa takes me fishing I love to go fishing My Grammy makes me feel Special.

source, of course, is the biography's subject, and writers can learn many things about the person through an interview. Other primary sources include diaries and letters, photographs, mementos, historical records, and recollections of people who know the person. Secondary sources are books, newspapers, and films written by someone other than the biographical subject.

Biographies are categorized as contemporary or historical. Contemporary biographies are written about a living person, especially someone the writer can interview. Historical biographies are about persons who are no longer alive, and the information must come from secondary sources.

Contemporary Biographies.   Students write biographies about living people they know personally as well as about famous personalities. In contrast to the primary sources of information available for gathering information about local people, students may have to depend on secondary sources (e.g., books, newspapers, letters) for information about well-known and geographically more distant persons. Sometimes, however, students can write letters to well-known personalities or perhaps arrange conference telephone calls.

Historical Biographies.   Whereas biographies are based on known facts, some parts of historical biographies must necessarily be fictionalized. Dialogue and other details about daily life, for example, must often be invented after careful research of the period. In *The Double Life of Pocahontas* (Fritz, 1983), for instance, the author had to take what sketchy facts are known about Pocahontas and make some reasonable guesses to fill in the missing links. To give one example, historians know that Pocahontas was a young woman when she died in 1617, but they are unsure how old she was when John Smith and the other English settlers arrived in Virginia in 1607. Fritz chose to make her 11 years old when the settlers arrived.

When children write historical biographies, they will have to make some of the same types of reasonable guesses that Fritz did. In the following biography of Daniel Boone, a third grader added details and dialogue to complete his report:

Daniel Boone was born in 1734 in Omley, Pennsylvania. When Daniel grew up, he hunted a lot. He began his journey to Kentucky to hunt for game. Every day, Daniel tried to hunt for game in Kentucky. In the morning, he would catch two or three deers. At night, he wouldn't hunt because all the animals would be hiding. Daniel wouldn't give up hunting for game in Kentucky.

Finally, he decided to travel through Kentucky. Soon Indians took their meat and furs away. Would Daniel and his family survive?

One day when Daniel was walking to his fellow friend's fort, he looked all around. Indians were surrounding him. One Indian called Chief Blackfish said, "Take me to your men. If you do, I will not hurt you or them. If you don't, I will kill you and your friends." Daniel was trapped. When they were walking to the fort, Daniel ran inside. Just then, gunshots were fired. They were at war. Soon the war was over. Daniel's people had won.

Daniel died in 1820 at the age of 85. Daniel Boone is remembered for opening the land of Kentucky for white men to hunt in and fighting for Kentucky.

When students study someone else's life in preparation for writing a biography, they need to become personally involved in the project (Zarnowski, 1988). There are several ways to engage students in biographical study, that is, to help them walk in the subject's footsteps. For contemporary biographies, meeting and interviewing the person is the best way; for other projects, students read books about the person, view films and videos, dramatize events from the person's life, and write about the persons they are studying. An

These middle-grade students are planning a television interview program during which their classmates will appear as well-known historical persons.

especially valuable activity is writing simulated journals, in which students assume the role of the person they are studying and write journal entries just as that person might have.

Teaching Students to Write Life-Stories

Students learn to write life-stories through a process approach. The teaching strategy is similar for writing autobiographies and biographies, but the two forms are different and should be taught separately.

Step by Step

1. ***Reading to Learn About the Format and Unique Conventions.*** Autobiographies and biographies written for children can serve as models for the life-stories students write. Many autobiographies of scientists, entertainers, sports figures, and others are available for upper-grade students, but, unfortunately, only a few autobiographies have been written for younger children. A list of suggested autobiographies appears in Figure 10–13; some are entire-life and others are shorter-event types. When students read autobiographies, they should note

Figure 10–13   Recommended Life-Stories for Elementary Students

Autobiographies

Aardema, V. (1992). *A bookworm who hatched.* Katonwah, NY: Richard C. Owens. (M)

Begley, K. A. (1977). *Deadline.* New York: Putnam. (U)

Bulla, C. R. (1985). *A grain of wheat: A writer begins.* New York: Godine. (U)

Chukosky, K. (1976). *The silver crest: My Russian boyhood* (B. Stillman, Trans.). New York: Holt, Rinehart & Winston. (U)

Collins, M. (1976). *Flying to the moon and other strange places.* New York: Farrar, Straus & Giroux. (M–U)

de Paola, T. (1989). *The art lesson.* New York: Putnam. (P–M)

Fisher, L. E. (1972). *The death of evening star: Diary of a young New England whaler.* New York: Doubleday. (U)

Fritz, J. (1982). *Homesick: My own story.* New York: Putnam. (M–U)

Fritz, J. (1992). *Surprising myself.* Katonwah, NY: Richard C. Owens. (M)

Gish, L. (1988). *An actor's life for me.* New York: Viking. (U)

Goodall, J. (1988). *My life with the chimpanzees.* New York: Simon & Schuster.

Hamill, D. (with E. Clairmont). (1983). *Dorothy Hamill: On and off the ice.* New York: Knopf. (M)

Hopkins, L. B. (1992). *The writing bug.* Katonwah, NY: Richard C. Owens. (M)

James, N. (1979). *Alone around the world.* New York: Coward-McCann. (U)

Jenner, B. (with R. S. Kiliper). (1980). *The Olympics and me.* New York: Doubleday. (M)

Keller, H. (1980). *The story of my life.* New York: Watermill Press. (M–U)

Maiorano, R. (1980). *Worlds apart: The autobiography of a dancer from Brooklyn.* New York: Coward-McCann. (U)

Nuynh, Q. N. (1982). *The land I lost: Adventures of a boy in Vietnam.* New York: Harper & Row. (M–U)

O'Kelley, M. L. (1983). *From the hills of Georgia: An autobiography in paintings.* Boston: Little, Brown. (P–M–U)

Peet, B. (1989). *An autobiography.* Boston: Houghton Mifflin. (M)

Rudolph, W. (1977). *Wilma: The story of Wilma Rudolph.* New York: New American Library. (U)

Schulz, C. M. (with R. S. Kiliper). (1980). *Charlie Brown, Snoopy and me: And all the other Peanuts characters.* New York: Doubleday. (M–U)

Singer, I. B. (1969). *A day of pleasure: Stories of a boy growing up in Warsaw.* New York: Farrar, Straus & Giroux. (U)

Sullivan, T., & Gill, D. (1975). *If you could see what I hear.* New York: Harper & Row. (U)

Zindel, P. (1992). *The pigman and me.* New York: HarperCollins. (M–U)

Figure 10–13   continued

Biographies

Adler, D. A. (1992). *A picturebook of Anne Frank.* New York: Holiday House. (See other biographies by the same author.) (P–M)

Aliki. (1988). *The many lives of Benjamin Franklin.* New York: Simon & Schuster. (See other biographies by the same author.) (M)

Burleigh, R. (1985). *A man named Thoreau.* New York: Atheneum. (U)

Dobrin, A. (1975). *I am a stranger on Earth: The story of Vincent Van Gogh.* New York: Warne. (M–U)

Faber, D. (1992). *Calamity Jane: Her life and her legend.* Boston: Houghton Mifflin. (M–U)

Fisher, L. E. (1992). *Gutenberg.* New York: Macmillan. (M–U)

Freedman, R. (1987). *Lincoln: A photobiography.* New York: Clarion. (M–U)

Fritz, J. (1973). *And then what happened, Paul Revere?* New York: Coward-McCann. (See other biographies by the same author.) (P–M)

Gherman, B. (1989). *Agnes de Mille: Dancing off the earth.* New York: Atheneum. (U)

Giblin, J. C. (1992). *George Washington: A picturebook biography.* New York: Scholastic. (P–M)

Giff, P. R. (1987). *Laura Ingalls Wilder.* New York: Viking. (M)

Golenbock, P. (1990). *Teammates.* San Diego: Harcourt Brace Jovanovich. (P–M)

Hamilton, V. (1974). *Paul Robeson: The life and times of a free black man.* New York: Harper & Row. (U)

Harrison, B., & Terris, D. (1992). *A twilight struggle: The life of John Fitzgerald Kennedy.* New York: Lothrop, Lee & Shepard. (M–U)

Haskins, J. (1992). *Amazing grace: The story behind the song.* New York: Millbrook (P–M)

Houston, G. (1992). *My great-aunt Arizona.* New York: HarperCollins. (P–M)

Jakes, J. (1986). *Susanna of the Alamo: A true story.* New York: Harcourt Brace Jovanovich. (M)

McKissack, P. C., & McKissack, F. (1992). *Soujourner Truth: Ain't I a woman?* New York: Scholastic. (M–U)

Meltzer, M. (1992). *Thomas Jefferson: The revolutionary aristocrat.* New York: Franklin Watts. (U)

Mitchell, B. (1986). *Click: A story about George Eastman.* Minneapolis: Carolrhoda Books. (M)

Provensen, A., & Provensen, M. (1984). *Leonardo da Vinci.* New York: Viking. (A moveable book) (M–U)

Quackenbush, R. (1981). *Ahoy! Ahoy! are you there? A story of Alexander Graham Bell.* Englewood Cliffs, NJ: Prentice-Hall. (See other biographies by the same author.) (P–M)

St. George, J. (1992). *Dear Dr. Bell . . . your friend Helen Keller.* New York: Putnam. (U)

Stanley, D., & Vennema, P. (1992). *Bard of Avon: The story of William Shakespeare.* New York: Morrow. (M–U)

Stevens, B. (1992). *Frank Thompson: Her Civil War story.* New York: Macmillan. (M–U)

Wisniewski, D. (1992). *Sundiata: Lion king of Mali.* New York: Clarion. (P–M)

---

which events the narrator focuses on, how the narrator presents information and feelings, and what the narrator's viewpoint is.

Biographies of well-known people such as explorers, kings and queens, scientists, sports figures, artists, and movie stars, as well as "common" people who have endured hardship and shown exceptional courage, are available for elementary students to read. Figure 10–13 also lists biographies. Biographers David Adler and Jean Fritz have written many excellent biographies for primary- and middle-grade students, some of which are noted in the list, and numerous authors have written biographies for older students. Students' autobiographies and biographies from previous years are another source of books for your class to read. Students can often be persuaded to bring their prized life-stories back the following year to share with other students.

2. *Gathering Information for the Life-Story.*   Students gather information about themselves or about the person they will write about in several different ways.

Students are the best source of information about their own lives, but they may need to get information from parents and other family members. Parents often share information from baby books and photo albums, and older brothers and sisters can share their remembrances. Another strategy students can use to gather information for an autobiography is to collect objects that symbolize their life and hang them on a "lifeline" clothesline or put them in a life-box made from a shoebox (Fleming, 1985). They can then write briefly about each object, explaining what it is and how it relates to their lives. They can also decorate the box with words and pictures clipped from magazines to create an autobiographical collage.

For biographical writing, students can interview their subject, either in person or by telephone and letter. To write a historical biography, students read books to learn about the person and the time period in which he or she lived. Other sources of information are films, videotapes, and newspaper and magazine articles. Students also need to keep a record of their sources for the bibliography they will include with their biographies.

Students sequence the information they gather, about either their life or someone else's, on a lifeline or timeline. This activity helps students identify and sequence milestones and other events. They can use the information on the lifeline to identify topics for the life-story.

3. *Organizing the Information for the Life-Story.*   Students select from their lifelines the topics they will write about; then they develop a cluster with each topic as a main idea. They add details from the information they have gathered; if they do not have four or five details for each topic, they can search for additional information. When students aren't sure if they have enough information, they can cluster the topic using the "5Ws plus one" questions (who, what, when, where, why, and how) and try to answer the six questions. If they can complete the cluster, they are ready to write; if they cannot, they need to gather additional information. After developing the cluster, students decide on the sequence of topics and add an introduction and a conclusion.

4. *Writing the Life-Story Using the Writing Process.*   Students use their clusters to write their rough drafts. The main ideas become topic sentences for paragraphs, and details are expanded into sentences. After they write the rough draft, students meet in writing groups to get feedback on their writing; then they make revisions. Next, they edit and recopy. They add drawings, photographs, or other memorabilia. Students also add a bibliography to a biography, listing their sources of information. Besides making the final copy of their life-stories, students can share what they have learned in other ways. They might dress up as the subject of their biography and tell the person's story or let classmates interview them.

Minilessons.   Students learn the procedures, concepts, and strategies and skills for reading and writing informational books through minilessons. A list of topics for minilessons is presented on page 399. Teachers adapt the teaching strategy presented in the first chapter for minilessons about informational books.

Teachers choose the topics for minilessons based on the needs of their students and the opportunities provided in the reading materials and writing

MINILESSONS

Reading and Writing Information

	Procedures	Concepts	Strategies and Skills
Expository Text Structures	Identify expository text structures in books Make graphic organizers Write paragraphs using the structures	Informational books Efferent reading Expository text structures Cue words	Vary reading according to purpose Locate information using index Identify expository text structures Note cue words Use graphic organizers
Reports	Read charts, diagrams, and maps Make KWL charts Collect data on clusters Collect data on data charts Write collaborative reports Write individual reports Write tables of contents Write bibliographies Compile ABC books Assess effectiveness of report	Reports versus stories ABC books	Design research questions Narrow topics Gather information Organize information Take a stand Summarize Present information in charts
Letters	Write pen pal letters Write courtesy letters Write letters to authors and illustrators Write business letters Write simulated letters Assess effectiveness of letter	Friendly letter format Business letter format	Use letter format correctly Ask questions to elicit information Respond to correspondent's questions
Life-stories	Make lifelines Make timelines Make "Me" boxes Write "All About Me" books Write autobiographies Write biographies Assess effectiveness of life-story	Life-stories Autobiographies Biographies Phase biographies Contemporary biographies Historical biographies	Choose events to write about Elaborate events Sequence events Add details Add descriptions Include information in illustrations Assume a point of view

projects. When fifth graders are reading biographies as part of a theme cycle on the American Revolution, for example, teachers might plan to teach a series of minilessons about life-stories, including these topics:

- The difference between stories and biographies
- How to make a lifeline
- Author information about Jean Fritz
- The difference between phase and life biographies
- Creating a view of life during a historical period using information in a biography
- Interpreting lessons about life from a biography
- Writing simulated journal entries as a historical personality

In these minilessons students apply the information the teacher presents in the biographies they are reading and the response projects that students are involved in after reading.

Some minilessons are taught as students begin reading, others while students are reading or after they have read. A minilesson on how to make a lifeline, for example, might be taught as students are beginning to read so that they can then make lifelines about the personalities in their biographies. The lesson about creating a view of life during a historical period might be presented while students are reading so that they can begin to note descriptions in the book. Minilessons on interpreting lessons about life and writing simulated journal entries might be taught during the exploring stage of the reading process to help students develop and refine their interpretations of the biography.

Adapting to Meet the Needs of Every Student.   Teachers can make adaptations as students read and write informational books so that every student can be successful. A list of recommendations is presented on page 401. It is important to teach students about the genre of informational books and the unique conventions these books have to help readers—including diagrams, glossaries, and indexes. Students also need to learn about the five expository text patterns because research has shown that less fluent readers are not as conscious of them as better readers are. Informational books are available on a wide variety of topics and at a range of reading levels, so selecting reading materials to meet the needs of every student should not be too difficult.

Assessing Students' Life-Stories

Students need to know the requirements for their autobiography or biography project and how they will be assessed or graded. A checklist for an autobiography might include the following components:

Make a lifeline showing at least one important event for each year of your life.

Draw a cluster showing at least three main-idea topics and at least five details for each topic.

Write a rough draft with an introduction, three or more chapters, and a conclusion.

Meet in a writing group to share your autobiography.

Adapting . . .
Reading and Writing Information
To Meet the Needs of Every Student

1. Examining Informational Books

Informational books are organized differently than stories, and they often have unique conventions. Teachers can help students examine this genre and compare these books with stories so that they can recognize the differences.

2. Comparing Aesthetic and Efferent Reading

Students read informational books efferently to locate specific information, and aesthetically for the lived-through experience of reading. Too often less fluent readers read efferently and assume that they must read the entire book and remember everything, even when they are reading to locate a specific piece of information. These students need to learn how to assume an efferent stance to locate specific information and an aesthetic stance at other times.

3. Examining Expository Text Structures

Because less fluent readers are less aware of expository text structures, it is important to teach the five patterns. Students also use the graphic organizers to help them take notes.

4. Writing "All About . . ." Books

Less experienced writers can write "All About . . ." books. In these books students write information they are learning during theme cycles or information about hobbies. Because students draw a picture and write only a sentence or two on each page, they are able to complete the project before they lose interest or become frustrated.

5. Writing Collaborative Biographies

Students work together to write collaborative biographies, with each student writing one page. They identify important events in the person's life. Each student writes about one event. Then the pages are compiled for the book.

Make at least three changes in your rough draft.

Complete an editing checklist with a partner.

Write a final copy with photos or drawings as illustrations.

Add an "All About the Author" page.

Compile your autobiography as a book.

Decorate the cover.

The checklist for a biography might list the following requirements:

Learn about the person's life from at least three sources (and no more than one encyclopedia).

Make a lifeline listing at least 10 important events.

Write at least 10 simulated journal entries as the person you are studying.

Make a cluster with at least three main-idea topics and at least five details for each topic.

Write a rough draft with at least three chapters and a bibliography.

Meet in a writing group to share your biography.

Make at least three changes in your rough draft.

Complete an editing checklist with a partner.

Recopy the biography.

Add an "All About the Author" page.

Students keep the checklist in their project folders and check off each item as it is completed; at the end of the project, they submit the folders to be assessed or graded. Teachers can award credit for each item on the checklist, as we discussed regarding research reports. This approach helps students assume greater responsibility for their own learning and gives them a better understanding of why they receive a particular grade.

Review

Recent research suggests that reading and writing information may be as primary as reading and writing stories. As they read and write informational books, students learn about the expository text structures. Three types of informational writing are reports, letters, and life-stories. Students read informational books both aesthetically and efferently during theme cycles, and they apply what they have learned in writing reports. Two types of letters that elementary students write are friendly letters to pen pals and to favorite authors, and business letters to request information, to complain and compliment, and to transact business. Autobiographies and biographies are life-stories. Students read life-stories to learn about this writing form; then they write their own. Students use the writing process for all types of informational writing, and after writing, it is crucial to share the compositions with genuine audiences.

Extensions

1. Follow the guidelines in this chapter to write a class collaboration report on a social studies topic, such as modes of transportation, types of houses, or the countries in Europe, or on a science topic, such as the solar system or the human body.

2. Choose a topic related to teaching language arts in the elementary school, such as writing in journals, aesthetic and efferent reading, the writing process, or the uses of drama. Research the topic following the guidelines in this chapter and write an "All About . . ." book or a report that you can share with your elementary students.

3. Have students interview a community leader and then write a collaborative biography.

4. Arrange for a group of students to write friendly letters to pen pals in another school. Review the friendly letter form and how to address an envelope. Use the writing process in which students draft, revise, and edit their letters before mailing them.

5. Have a small group of students develop a lifeline for a historical personality or other famous person, choose several events from the lifeline to write about, and compile the writings to form a biography.

6. Read one of the biographies or autobiographies listed in Figure 10–13. Then develop a lifeline or a cluster about the subject's life.

References

Bonin, S. (1988). Beyond storyland: Young writers can tell it other ways. In T. Newkirk & N. Atwell (Eds.), *Understanding writing* (2nd ed.) (pp. 47–51). Portsmouth, NH: Heinemann.

Cleary, B. (1985). Dear author, answer this letter now . . .. *Instructor, 95,* 22–23, 25.

Fleming, M. (1985). Writing assignments focusing on autobiographical and biographical topics. In M. Fleming & J. McGinnis (Eds.), *Portraits: Biography and autobiography in the secondary school* (pp. 95–97). Urbana, IL: National Council of Teachers of English.

Fleming, M., & McGinnis J. (Eds.). (1985). *Portraits: Biography and autobiography in the secondary school.* Urbana, IL: National Council of Teachers of English.

Flood, J., Lapp, D., & Farnan, N. (1986). A reading-writing procedure that teaches expository paragraph structure. *The Reading Teacher, 39,* 556–562.

Freedman, R. (1992). Fact or fiction? In Freeman, E. B., & Person, D. G. (Eds.), *Using nonfiction tradebooks in the elementary classroom: From ants to zeppelins* (pp. 2–10). Urbana IL: National Council of Teachers of English.

Freeman, E. B. (1991). Informational books: Models for student report writing. *Language Arts, 68,* 470–473.

Fulwiler, T. (1985). Research writing. In M. Schwartz (Ed.), *Writing for many roles* (pp. 207–230). Upper Montclair, NJ: Boynton/Cook.

Greenlee, M. E., Hiebert, E. H., Bridge, C. A., & Winograd, P. N. (1986). The effects of different audiences on young writers' letter writing. In J. A. Niles & R. V. Lalik (Eds.), *Solving problems in literacy: Learners, teachers, and researchers* (pp. 281–289). Rochester, NY: National Reading Conference.

Krogness, M. M. (1987). Folklore: A matter of the heart and the heart of the matter. *Language Arts, 64,* 808–818.

Langer, J. A. (1986). *Children reading and writing: Structures and strategies.* Norwood, NJ: Ablex.

McGee, L. M. & Richgels, D. J. (1985). Teaching expository text structure to elementary students. *The Reading Teacher, 38,* 739–748.

Meyer, B. J., & Freedle, R. O. (1984). Effects of discourse type on recall. *American Educational Research Journal, 21,* 121–143.

Niles, O. S. (1974). Organization perceived. In H. L. Herber (Ed.), *Perspectives in reading: Developing study skills in secondary schools.* Newark, DE: International Reading Association.

Pappas, C. C. (1991). Fostering full access to literacy by including information books. *Language Arts, 68,* 449–462.

Pappas, C. C. (1993). Is narrative "primary"? Some insights from kindergartners' pretend readings of stories and information books. *Journal of Reading Behavior, 25,* 97–129.

Piccolo, J. A. (1987). Expository text structures: Teaching and learning strategies. *The Reading Teacher, 40,* 838–847.

Queenan, M. (1986). Finding grain in the marble. *Language Arts, 63,* 666–673.

Raphael, T. E., Englert, C. S., & Kirschner, B. W. (1989). Acquisition of expository writing skills. In J. M. Mason (Ed.), *Reading and writing connections* (pp. 261–290). Boston: Allyn & Bacon.

Roop, P. (1992). Nonfiction books in the primary classroom: Soaring with the swans. In Freeman, E. B., & Person, D. G. (Eds.), *Using nonfiction tradebooks in the elementary classroom: From ants to zeppelins* (pp. 106–112). Urbana, IL: National Council of Teachers of English.

Rosenblatt, L. M. (1978). *The reader, the text, the poem: The transactional theory of the literary work.* Carbondale: Southern Illinois University Press.

Smith, P. L., & Tompkins, G. E. (1988). Structured notetaking: A new strategy for content area readers. *Journal of Reading, 32,* 46–53.

Sowers, S. (1985). The story and the "all about" book. In J. Hansen, T. Newkirk, & D. Graves (Eds.), *Breaking ground: Teachers relate reading and writing in the elementary school* (pp. 73–82). Portsmouth, NH: Heinemann.

Tompkins, G. E. (1994). *Teaching writing: Balancing process and product* (2nd ed.). New York: Merrill/Macmillan.

Tompkins, G. E., Smith, P. L., & Hitchcock, M. E. (1987). *Elementary students' use of expository text structures in report writing.* Paper presented at the National Reading Conference, St. Petersburg Beach, FL.

Vardell, S. (1991). A new "picture of the world": The NCTE Orbis Pictus Award for outstanding nonfiction for children. *Language Arts, 68,* 474–479.

Wells, G. (1986). *The meaning makers: Children learning language and using language to learn.* Portsmouth, NH: Heinemann.

Whitin, D. J., & Wilde, S. (1992). *Read any good math lately? Children's books for mathematical learning, K–6.* Portsmouth, NH: Heinemann.

Zarnowski, M. (1988, February). The middle school student as biographer. *Middle School Journal, 19,* 25–27.

Children's Book References

Ahlberg, J., & Ahlberg, A. (1986). *The jolly postman or other people's letters.* Boston: Little, Brown.

Aker, S. (1990). *What comes in 2's, 3's, and 4's?* New York: Simon & Schuster.

Ancona, G. (1992). *Man and mustang.* New York: Macmillan.

Arnold, C. (1993). *Dinosaurs all around: An artist's view of the prehistoric world.* New York: Clarion.

Bates, K. L. (1993). *America the beautiful.* New York: Atheneum.

Carle, E. (1984). *The very busy spider.* New York: Philomel.

Cleary, B. (1983). *Dear Mr. Henshaw.* New York: Morrow.

Cole, J. (1987). *The magic school bus inside the earth.* New York: Scholastic.

Conrad, P. (1991). *Pedro's journal: A voyage with Christopher Columbus, August 3, 1492–February 14, 1493.* Honedale, PA: Boyds Mill Press.

Cowcher, H. (1990). *Antarctica.* New York: Farrar, Straus & Giroux.

Dahl, R. (1984). *Boy.* New York: Farrar, Straus & Giroux.

Ehlert, L. (1987). *Growing vegetable soup.* San Diego: Harcourt Brace Jovanovich.

Feelings, M. (1971). *Moja means one: Swahili counting book.* New York: Dial.

Freedman, R. (1987). *Lincoln: A photobiography.* New York: Clarion.

Fritz, J. (1973). *And then what happened, Paul Revere?* New York: Putnam.

Fritz, J. (1976). *Will you sign here, John Hancock?* New York: Coward-McCann.

Fritz, J. (1983). *The double life of Pocahontas.* New York: Putnam.

Fritz, J. (1989). *The great little Madison.* New York: Putnam.

Gibbons, G. (1991). *Surrounded by sea: Life on a New England fishing island.* Boston: Little, Brown.

Gibbons, G. (1992). *Spiders.* New York: Holiday House.

Guiberson, B. Z. (1991). *Cactus hotel.* New York: Henry Holt.

Hoban, L. (1982). *Arthur's pen pal.* New York: Harper & Row.

Hoban, T. (1987). *26 letters and 99 cents.* New York: Greenwillow.

Hunt, J. (1989). *Illuminations.* New York: Bradbury.

Knight, A. S. (1993). *The way west: Journal of a pioneer woman.* New York: Simon & Schuster.

Knight, M. B. (1993). *Who belongs here? An American story.* Gardiner, ME: Tulbury House.

Lansky, B. (1994). *Free stuff for kids.* New York: Simon & Schuster.

Levine, E. (1986). *. . . . If you traveled west in a covered wagon.* New York: Scholastic.

Macaulay, D. (1977). *Castle.* Boston: Houghton Mifflin.

MacLachlan, P. (1985). *Sarah, plain and tall.* New York: Harper & Row.

Maestro, B. (1992). *How do apples grow?* New York: HarperCollins.

Maiorano, R. (1980). *Worlds apart: The autobiography of a dancer from Brooklyn.* New York: Coward-McCann.

Morimoto, J. (1987). *My Hiroshima.* New York: Viking.

Pallotta, J. (1991). *The underwater alphabet book.* Watertown, MA: Charlesbridge.

Pryor, B. (1987). *The house on Maple Street.* New York: Morrow.

Rauzon, M. J. (1993). *Horns, antlers, fangs, and tusks.* New York: Lothrop, Lee & Shepard.

Ringgold, F. (1992). *Aunt Harriet's underground railroad in the sky.* New York: Crown.

Roop, P., & Roop, C. (1990). *I Columbus: My journal 1492–1493.* New York: Walker.

Roop, P., & Roop, C. (1993). *Off the map: The journals of Lewis and Clark.* New York: Walker.

Roth, S. L. (1992). *Marco Polo: His notebook.* New York: Doubleday.

Rylant, C. (1992). *Best wishes.* Katonwah, NY: Richard C. Owens.

Schwartz, D. (1989). *If you made a million.* New York: Lothrop, Lee & Shepard.

Scott, A. H. (1990). *One good horse: A cowpuncher's counting book.* New York: Greenwillow.

Showers, P. (1985). *What happens to a hamburger?* New York: Harper & Row.

Siebert, D. (1991). *Sierra.* New York: HarperCollins.

Simon, S. (1989). *Whales.* New York: Crowell.

Simon, S. (1993). *Mercury.* New York: Morrow.

Turner, A. (1987). *Nettie's trip south.* New York: Macmillan.

von Tscharner, R., & Fleming, R. L. (1987). *New Providence: A changing cityscape.* San Diego: Harcourt Brace Jovanovich.

Williams, S. A. (1992). *Working cotton.* San Diego: Harcourt Brace Jovanovich.

Winter, J. (1988). *Follow the drinking gourd.* New York: Knopf.

Yolen, J. (1993). *Welcome to the green house.* New York: Putnam.

Ziefert, H. (1986). *A new coat for Anna.* New York: Knopf.

66 *My seventh graders think they don't like poetry. Then we read lots of poems by Shel Silverstein, Jack Prelutsky, and others, and the students discover that poetry can be fun!* 99

Sandy Harris
Seventh-Grade Teacher
Anadarko Middle School

PROCEDURE

I bring at least 50 books of poetry into the classroom. I share some of my favorites, and soon the students bring their favorites to read aloud to the class. The seventh graders invite each other to comment on the poetry they read aloud. Some of our favorite poems are listed in the accompanying figure, and I share Karla Kuskin's "Take a Word Like Cat," Mary O'Neill's "Feelings About Words," and other poems in *Inner Chimes: Poems on Poetry* (Goldstein, 1992) during the minilessons that I teach.

I start the school year with a unit on poetry because I can demonstrate the writing process without getting bogged down in extensive revision and editing work, as often happens with longer compositions. The experience my students have reading and sharing poetry and discussing their favorites is reflected in the comments I hear them making in writing groups.

I've taken many of my ideas from Kenneth Koch's *Rose, Where Did You Get That Red?* (1973). One poetry writing activity my students enjoy is creating "model" poems; for example, I read William Blake's "The Tyger," and my students try their hands at writing poems in which they speak directly to an animal. Like Blake, they try to create strong images. One of my students wrote this poem in which he talks to an eagle:

*Eagle, is it the color you see
from the sky, or is it the movement
that catches your eye?*

*Eagle, at what moment do you know
as you dive from the sky,
precisely when something will die?*

*Eagle, do you have fear
while you dive and peal,
or might your nerves be made of steel?*

*Eagle, what are your thoughts,
as your claws and beak
prepare the main course?*

*Eagle, do you know
as you perch majestically on the tree,
that you represent our country's liberty?*

After drafting their poems, students refine them in writing groups; then they meet with me for editing. Finally, students recopy their poems. For this activity, I'm working with the art teacher, and my students will make papier-mâché animals to accompany their poems.

Our Favorite Books of Poetry

Dakos, K. (1990). *If you're not here, please raise your hand: Poems about school.* New York: Macmillan. (Also *Don't read this book, whatever you do! More poems about school* by the same author)

Eliot, T. S. (1967). *Old Possum's book of practical cats.* New York: Harcourt Brace Jovanovich.

Fleischman, P. (1988). *Joyful noise: Poems for two voices.* New York: Harper & Row. (Also *I am phoenix* by the same author)

Frost, R. (1988). *Birches.* New York: Henry Holt.

Janeczko, P. B. (1993). *Looking for your name: A collection of contemporary poems.* New York: Orchard.

Jones, H. (1993). *The trees stand shining: Poetry of the North American Indians.* New York: Dial.

Lobel, A. (1983). *The book of pigericks.* New York: Harper & Row.

Longfellow, H. W. (1990). *Paul Revere's ride.* New York: Dutton.

Noyes, A. (1983). *The highwayman.* New York: Lothrop, Lee & Shepard.

O'Neill, M. (1989). *Hailstones and halibut bones.* New York: Doubleday.

Prelutsky, J. (1984). *The new kid on the block.* New York: Greenwillow.

Sandburg, C. (1982). *Rainbows are made: Poems by Carl Sandburg.* San Diego: Harcourt Brace Jovanovich. (Also Sandburg's *Arithmetic* illustrated by Ted Rand)

Siebert, D. (1989). *Heartland.* New York: Crowell.

Silverstein, S. (1974). *Where the sidewalk ends.* New York: Harper & Row.

Soto, G. (1992). *Neighborhood odes.* San Diego: Harcourt Brace Jovanovich.

- Writing invitation poems following the model of Shakespeare's "Come Unto These Yellow Sands"
- Writing about a common thing from a number of perspectives following the model of Wallace Stevens's "Thirteen Ways of Looking at a Blackbird"
- Writing an apology for something you are secretly glad that you did following the model of William Carlos Williams's "This Is Just to Say"
- Writing a quiet poem following the model of D. H. Lawrence's "The White Horse"
- Writing a shape poem following the model of Guillaume Apolliaire's shape poems

REFLECTIONS

By observing the poems my students choose to share, I get a clearer idea of their preferences. By beginning from a base that is popular with the students, I can extend their appreciation to more sophisticated poetry—even Blake and Shakespeare. I begin with their choices, and before long my students—even the "jocks"—are reading poetry and enjoying it. Then when the students write poems, I use models and other formulas so they can be successful. The formulas provide the skeleton so that students can concentrate on creating images and using interesting words. I de-emphasize rhyme because it often gets in the way when my students write.

ASSESSMENT

Before writing these "Talk to the Animals" poems, the students and I make a checklist of the components they should include. In these poems, they were to (1) speak directly to an animal, (2) ask the animal a question in each stanza, and (3) create a strong visual image in each stanza. Almost every student is successful using this approach. I think identifying the criteria before the students begin and having them meet in writing groups make the difference. In writing groups, students check each poem against the criteria and offer suggestions to authors on how to revise their poems if they don't meet the criteria.

ADAPTATIONS

"Talking to the Animals" is only one type of poem that my students write. Other forms that I've taken from *Rose, Where Did You Get That Red?* and used are:

candle candle candle candle candle

FROSTING

cake cake cake cake cake cake cake cake cake

ants ants ants ants ants ants ants ant

11

Reading and Writing Poetry

INSIGHT _____

Rhyme is an important poetic device, and because of their experiences with nursery rhymes, Dr. Seuss books, and other rhyming songs, many children assume that poetry always rhymes. Children's expectation that poems rhyme influences both the poems they choose to read and their success in writing their own poems. If students read only rhyming poems, they miss out on haiku poems which describe striking natural images, odes written to celebrate common objects, and concrete poems written as a picture. Similarly, if students write only rhyming poems, they create inane verse about fat cats sitting on mats holding baseball bats *rather than experimenting with a variety of poetic forms. Rhyme is a sticking point for many children, and one question about teaching poetry is:*

What other poetic devices are used in poetry written for and by children?

*P*oetry "brings sound and sense together in words and lines," according to Donald Graves (1992), "ordering them on the page in such a way that both the writer and reader get a different view of life" (p. 3). Poetry surrounds us; children chant jump-rope rhymes on the playground, clap out the rhythm of favorite poems, and dance in response to songs and their lyrics. Larrick (1991) believes that we enjoy poetry because of the physical involvement that the words evoke. Also, people play with words as they invent rhymes and ditties, create new words, and craft powerful comparisons.

Today more poets are writing for children, and more books of poems for children are being published than ever before. No longer is poetry confined to rhyming verse about daffodils, clouds, and love. Recently published poems about dinosaurs, Halloween, chocolate, and insects are very popular with children. Children choose to read poetry and share favorite poems with classmates. They read and respond to poems with beautiful language written on topics that are meaningful to them.

Children, too, are writing poems as never before. The current attention on the writing process and publishing students' writing makes poetry a natural choice. Poems are usually short and can easily be revised and edited. They lend themselves to anthologies more readily than stories and other longer forms of writing. Through a variety of poetry writing activities, students paint word pictures, make comparisons, and express themselves in imaginative and poignant ways.

PLAYING WITH WORDS

As students play with words, they laugh with language, create word pictures, experiment with rhyme, and invent new words. These types of activities provide the background of experiences children need for reading and writing poetry. Although these activities are not poetry, students gain confidence and flexibility in using words to write poetry. Figure 11–1 lists wordplay books that elementary students enjoy.

Laughing With Language

As children learn that words have the power to amuse, they enjoy reading, telling, and writing riddles and jokes. Linda Gibson Geller (1985) has researched children's humorous language and has identified two stages of riddle play that elementary students move through. Primary-grade children experiment with the riddle form and its content, and middle- and upper-grade students explore the paradoxical constructions in riddles. Riddles are written in a question-and-answer format, but young children at first may only ask questions, or ask questions and offer unrelated answers. With more experience, students both provide questions and give related answers, and their answers may be either descriptive or nonsensical. An example of a descriptive answer is *Why did the turtle go out of his shell? Because he was getting too big for it;* a nonsensical answer involving an invented word for the riddle *Why did the cat want to catch a snake?* is *Because he wanted to turn into a rattlecat* (Geller, 1981, p. 672). Many primary-grade students' riddles seem foolish by adult standards, but wordplay is an important precursor to creating true riddles.

Figure 11-1   Wordplay Books for Elementary Students

Barcheck, L. (1976). *Snake in, snake out.* New York: Crowell. (M)

Barrett, J. (1983). *A snake is totally tail.* New York: Atheneum. (P–M)

Bayer, J. (1984). *A my name is Alice.* New York: Dial. (P–M)

Bierhorst, J. (Ed.). (1992). *Lightning inside you: And other Native American riddles.* New York: Morrow. (M–U)

Brown, M. (1983). *What do you call a dumb bunny? And other rabbit riddles, games, jokes, and cartoons.* Boston: Little, Brown. (P–M)

Cox, J. A. (1980). *Put your foot in your mouth and other silly sayings.* New York: Random House. (P–M)

Degen, B. (1983). *Jamberry.* New York: Harper & Row. (P)

Eiting, M., & Folsom, M. (1980). *Q is for duck: An alphabet guessing game.* New York: Clarion. (P–M)

Esbensen, B. J. (1986). *Words with wrinkled knees.* New York: Crowell. (M–U)

Funk, C. E. (1948). *A hog on ice and other curious expressions.* New York: Harper & Row. (U)

Gwynne, F. (1970). *The king who rained.* New York: Dutton. (M–U)

Gwynne, F. (1976). *A chocolate moose for dinner.* New York: Dutton. (M–U)

Gwynne, F. (1980). *The sixteen hand horse.* New York: Prentice-Hall. (M–U)

Gwynne, F. (1988). *A little pigeon toad.* New York: Simon & Schuster. (M–U)

Hall, F., & Friends. (1985). *Sniglets for kids.* Yellow Springs, OH: Antioch. (M–U)

Hall, K., & Eisenberg, L. (1992). *Spacey riddles.* New York: Dial. (P)

Hanson, J. (1972). *Homographic homophones.* Fly *and* fly *and other words that look and sound the same but are as different in meaning as* bat *and* bat. Minneapolis: Lerner. (M)

Hanson, J. (1972). *Homographs:* Bow *and* bow *and other words that look the same but sound as different as* sow *and* sow. Minneapolis: Lerner. (M)

Hartman, V. (1992). *Westward ho ho ho! Jokes from the wild west.* New York: Viking. (M–U)

Houget, S. R. (1983). *I unpacked my grandmother's trunk: A picture book game.* New York: Dutton. (P–M)

Juster, N. (1982). *Otter nonsense.* New York: Philomel. (P–M)

Kellogg, S. (1987). *Aster Aardvark's alphabet adventures.* New York: Morrow. (P–M)

Maestro, G. (1984). *What's a frank Frank? Tasty homograph riddles.* New York: Clarion. (P–M)

McMillan, B. (1990). *One sun: A book of terse verse.* New York: Holiday House. (M)

Merriam, E. (1992). *Fighting words.* New York: Morrow. (P–M)

Most, B. (1992). *Zoodles.* San Diego: Harcourt Brace Jovanovich. (M)

Perl, L. (1988). *Don't sing before breakfast, don't sing in the moonlight.* New York: Random House. (M–U)

Schwartz, A. (1973). *Tomfoolery: Trickery and foolery with words.* Philadelphia: Lippincott. (M–U)

Schwartz, A. (1982). *The cat's elbow and other secret languages.* New York: Farrar, Straus & Giroux. (M–U)

Schwartz, A. (1992). *Busy buzzing bumblebees and other tongue twisters.* New York: HarperCollins. (P–M)

Smith, W. J., & Ra, C. (1992). *Behind the king's kitchen: A roster of rhyming riddles.* Honesdale, PA: Wordsong. (M–U)

Steig, J. (1992). *Alpha beta chowder.* New York: HarperCollins. (P–M)

Sterne, N. (1979). *Tyrannosaurus wrecks: A book of dinosaur riddles.* New York: Crowell. (M)

Terban, M. (1982). *Eight ate: A feast of homonym riddles.* New York: Clarion. (P–M)

Terban, M. (1983). *In a pickle and other funny idioms.* New York: Clarion. (M)

Terban, M. (1985). *Too hot to hoot: Funny palindrome riddles.* New York: Clarion. (M–U)

Terban, M. (1992). *Funny you should ask: How to make up jokes and riddles with wordplay.* New York: Clarion. (M–U)

Van Allsburg, C. (1987). *The z was zapped.* Boston: Houghton Mifflin. (M)

Zalben, J. B. (1977). *Lewis Carroll's Jabberwocky.* New York: Warne. (M–U)

P = primary grades (K–2); M = middle grades (3–5); U = upper grades (6–8).

Riddles depend on manipulating words with multiple meanings or similar sounds and using metaphors. The Opies (1959) identified five riddle strategies used by elementary students:

1. Using multiple referents for a noun: What has an eye but cannot see? *(A needle)*
2. Combining literal and figurative interpretations for a single phrase: Why did the kid throw the clock out the window? *(Because he wanted to see time fly)*
3. Shifting word boundaries to suggest another meaning: Why did the cookie cry? *(Because its mother was a wafer/away for/so long)*
4. Separating a word into syllables to suggest another meaning: When is a door not a door? *(When it's ajar/a jar/)*
5. Creating a metaphor: What are polka dots on your face? *(Pimples)*

Children begin riddle play by telling familiar riddles and reading riddles written by others. Several excellent books of riddles to share with elementary students are *Tyrannosaurus Wrecks: A Book of Dinosaur Riddles* (Sterne, 1979), *What Do You Call a Dumb Bunny? And Other Rabbit Riddles, Games, Jokes, and Cartoons* (Brown, 1983), and *Eight Ate: A Feast of Homonym Riddles* (Terban, 1982). Soon children are composing their own by adapting riddles they have read; others turn jokes into riddles. An excellent book for helping children write riddles is *Fiddle with a Riddle: Write Your Own Riddles* (Bernstein, 1979).

A third grader wrote this riddle using two meanings for Milky Way: *Why did the astronaut go to the Milky Way? Because he wanted a Milky Way Bar.* Terry, a fifth grader, wrote this riddle using the homophones *hair* and *hare:* *What is gray and jumpy and on your head? A gray hare!* The juxtaposition of words is important in many jokes and riddles.

Creating Word Pictures

In the primary grades children learn to place words in horizontal lines from left to right and top to bottom across a sheet of paper just as the lines on this page are printed; however, they can break this pattern and create word pictures by placing words as they would draw lines in a drawing. These word pictures can be single-word pictures or a string of words or a sentence arranged in a picture.

Word Pictures.   Students use words instead of lines to draw a picture, as the *rabbit* picture in Figure 11–2 illustrates. Students first draw a picture with lines, then place a second sheet of paper over the drawing and replace all or most of the lines with repeated words.

Descriptive Words.   Students write descriptive words so that the arrangement, size, and intensity of the letters in the word illustrate the meaning. The word *nervous* is written concretely in Figure 11–2. Students can also write the names of objects and animals, such as *bird,* concretely, illustrating features of the named item through the style of the letters.

Sentence Pictures.   Students can compose a descriptive phrase or sentence and write it in the shape of an object, as the ice-cream cone in Figure 11–2 illustrates. An asterisk indicates where to start reading the sentence picture.

Figure 11–2   Students' Word Pictures

Experimenting With Rhyme

Because of their experience with Dr. Seuss stories, finger plays, and nursery rhymes, kindergartners and first graders enjoy creating rhymes. When it comes naturally, rhyme adds a delightful quality to children's writing, but when it is equated with poetry, it can get in the way of wordplay and vivid images. The following three-line poem shows a fifth grader's effective use of rhyme:

Fifth graders work together to write a new version of a rhyming book.

Thoughts After a 40-Mile Bike Ride

My feet
And seat
Are beat.

A small group of first graders created their own version of *Oh, A-Hunting We Will Go* (Langstaff, 1974). After reading the book, they identified the refrain (lines 1, 2, and 5) and added their own rhyming couplets:

Oh, a-hunting we will go,
a-hunting we will go.
We'll catch a little bear
and curl his hair,
and never let him go.
Oh, a-hunting we will go,
a-hunting we will go.
We'll catch a little mole
and put him in a hole,
and never let him go.
Oh, a-hunting we will go,
a-hunting we will go.
We'll catch a little snake
and hit him with a rake,
and never let him go.
Oh, a-hunting we will go,
a-hunting we will go.
We'll catch a little bug
and give him a big hug
and never let him go.
Oh, a-hunting we will go,
a-hunting we will go.

We'll catch a little bunny
and fill her full of honey,
and never let her go.
Oh, we'll put them in a ring
and listen to them sing
and then we'll let them go.

The first graders wrote this collaboration with the teacher taking dictation on a large chart. After the rough draft was written, students reread it, checking the rhymes and changing a word here or there. Then each student chose one stanza to copy and illustrate. The pages were collected and compiled to make a book. Students shared the book with their classmates, with each student reading his or her "own" page.

Hink-pinks are short rhymes that either take the form of an answer to a riddle or describe something. Hink-pinks are composed with 2 one-syllable rhyming words; they are called *hinky-pinkies* when 2 two-syllable words are used, and *hinkity-pinkities* with 2 three-syllable words (Geller, 1981). Two examples of these rhymes are:

Ghost   *What do you call an astronaut?*
White   *A sky guy.*
Fright

Other Poetic Devices

Poets choose words carefully (Kennedy & Kennedy, 1982). They create powerful images when they use unexpected comparisons, repeat sounds within a line or stanza, imitate sounds, and repeat words and phrases. These techniques are *poetic devices,* and students need to learn about the devices so that they can use them in their writing. The terminology is also helpful in writing groups, so that students can compliment classmates on the use of a device or suggest that they try a particular device when they revise their writing.

Comparison.   One way to describe something is to compare it to something else. Students can compare images, feelings, and actions to other things using two types of comparisons—similes and metaphors. A *simile* is an explicit comparison of one thing to another—a statement that one thing is like something else. Similes are signaled by the use of *like* or *as . . . as.* In contrast, a *metaphor* compares two things by implying that one is something else, without using *like* or *as.* Differentiating between the two terms is less important than using comparisons to make writing more vivid; for example, children can compare anger to a thunderstorm. Using a simile, they might say, "Anger is like a thunderstorm, screaming with thunder-feelings and lightning-words." Or, as a metaphor, they might say, "Anger is a volcano, erupting with poisonous words and hot-lava actions."

Students begin by learning traditional comparisons and idioms, and they learn to avoid stale comparisons, such as "high as a kite," "butterflies in your stomach," and "soft as a feather." Then they invent fresh, unexpected comparisons. A sixth grader uses a combination of expected and unexpected comparisons in this poem:

People

People are like birds
who are constantly getting their feathers ruffled.
People are like alligators
who find pleasure in evil cleverness.
People are like bees
who are always busy.
People are like penguins
who want to have fun.
People are like platypuses—
unexplainable!

Alliteration.   *Alliteration* is the repetition of the same initial consonant sound in consecutive words or in words in close proximity to one another. Repeating the same initial sound makes poetry fun to read, and children enjoy reading and reciting alliterative verses like *A My Name is Alice* (Bayer, 1984) and *The Z Was Zapped* (Van Allsburg, 1987). After reading one of these books, children can create their own versions. A fourth-grade class created its own version of Van Allsburg's book, which they called *The Z Was Zipped*. Students divided into pairs, and each pair composed two pages for the class book. Students illustrated their letter on the front of the paper and wrote a sentence on the back to describe their illustration, following Van Allsburg's pattern. Two pages from the book are shown in Figure 11–3. Before reading the sentences, examine the illustrations and try to guess the sentences. These are the students' alliterative sentences:

The D got dunked by the duck.
The T was totally terrified.

Tongue twisters are an exaggerated type of alliteration in which every word (or almost every word) in the twister begins with the same letter. Dr. Seuss has compiled an easy-to-read collection of tongue twisters in *Oh Say Can You Say?* (1979) for primary-grade students. Schwartz's *A Twister of Twists, a Tangler of Tongues* (1972) and Kellogg's *Aster Ardvark's Alphabet Adventures* (1987) are two good books of tongue twisters for middle- and upper-

Figure 11–3   *Two Pages From* The Z Was Zipped, *a Book of Alliterations*

grade students. Practice with tongue twisters and alliterative books increases children's awareness of the poetic device in poems they read and write. Few students consciously think about adding alliteration to a poem they are writing, but they get high praise in writing groups when classmates notice an alliteration and compliment the writer on it.

Onomatopoeia.   *Onomatopoeia* is a device in which poets use sound words to make their writing more sensory and more vivid. Sound words (e.g., *crash, slurp, varoom, me-e-e-ow*) sound like their meanings. Students can compile a list of sound words they find in stories and poems and display the list on a classroom chart or in their writer's notebooks to refer to when they write their own poems.

Spier has compiled two books of sound words; *Gobble Growl Grunt* (1971) is about animal sounds, and *Crash! Bang! Boom!* (1972) is about the sounds people and machines make. Students can use these books to select sound words for their writing. Comic strips are another good source of sound words; children collect frames from comic strips with sound words to add to a classroom chart.

In *Wishes, Lies, and Dreams* (1970), Koch recommends having children write noise poems that include a noise or sound word in each line. These first poems often sound contrived (e.g., "A dog barks bow-wow"), but the experience helps children learn to use onomatopoeia, as this poem dictated by a kindergartner illustrates:

Elephant Noses

Elephant noses
Elephant noses
Elephants have big noses
Big noses
Big noses
Elephants have big noses
through which they drink
SCHLURRP

Repetition.   Repetition of words and phrases is another device writers use to structure their writing as well as to add interest. Poe's use of the word *nevermore* in "The Raven" is one example, as is the gingerbread boy's boastful refrain in "The Gingerbread Boy." In this riddle a fourth grader uses a refrain effectively:

A Man

I am a little man standing all alone
In the deep, dark wood.
I am standing on one foot
In the deep, dark wood.
Tell me quickly, if you can,
What to call this little man
Standing all alone
In the deep, dark wood.
Who am I?

(Answer: a mushroom)

READING POEMS

Children grow rather naturally into poetry. The Opies (1959) have verified what we know from observing children: Children have a natural affinity to verse, songs, riddles, jokes, chants, and puns. Preschoolers are introduced to poetry when their parents repeat Mother Goose rhymes, read *The House at Pooh Corner* (Milne, 1956) and the Dr. Seuss stories, and sing little songs to them. During the elementary grades, youngsters often create jump-rope rhymes and other ditties on the playground.

Types of Poems Children Read

Poems for children assume many different forms. The most common type of poetry is *rhymed verse,* such as Robert Louis Stevenson's "Where Go the Boats?," Vachel Lindsay's "The Little Turtle," and "Mummy Slept Late and Daddy Fixed Breakfast" by John Ciardi. Poems that tell a story are *narrative poems;* examples are Clement Moore's "The Night Before Christmas," "The Pied Piper of Hamelin" by Robert Browning, and Henry Wadsworth Longfellow's "The Song of Hiawatha." A Japanese form, haiku, is popular in anthologies of poetry for children. *Haiku* is a three-line poem that contains just 17 syllables. Because of its brevity, it has been considered an appropriate form of poetry for children to read and write. *Free verse* has lines that do not rhyme, and rhythm is less important than in other types of poetry. Images take on greater importance in free-form verse. Langston Hughes's "Subway Rush Hour" and "This Is Just to Say" by William Carlos Williams are two examples of free verse. Other forms of poetry include *limericks,* a short, five-line rhymed verse form popularized by Edward Lear, and *concrete poems,* poems arranged on the page to create a picture or an image.

Three types of poetry books are published for children. A number of picture book versions of single poems in which each line or stanza is illustrated on a page are available, such as *Paul Revere's Ride* (Longfellow, 1990). Other books are specialized collections of poems, either written by a single poet or related to a single theme, such as dinosaurs or Halloween. Comprehensive anthologies are the third type of poetry books for children, and they feature 50 to 500 poems or more arranged by category. One of the best anthologies is *The Random House Book of Poetry for Children* (Prelutsky, 1983). A list of poetry books including examples of each of the three types is presented in Figure 11–4.

In addition to poetry written specifically for children, some poetry written for adults can be used effectively with elementary students, especially at upper-grade levels. Apseloff (1979) explains that poems written for adults use more sophisticated language and imagery and provide children with an early introduction to poems and poets they will undoubtedly study later. For instance, elementary students will enjoy Shakespeare's "The Witches' Song" from *Macbeth* and Carl Sandburg's "Fog." A list of poems written for adults that may be appropriate with some elementary students is shown in Figure 11–5.

Children's Favorite Poems

Children have definite preferences about which poems they like best, just as adults do. Fisher and Natarella (1982) surveyed the poetry preferences of first,

Figure 11–4   *Collections of Poetry Written for Children*

Picture Book Versions of Single Poems

Carroll, L. (1977). (Ill. by J. B. Zalben). *Lewis Carroll's Jabberwocky.* New York: Warne. (M–U)

Frost, R. (1988). (Ill. by E. Young). *Birches.* New York: Henry Holt. (U)

Lear, E. (1986). (Ill. by L. B. Cauley). *The owl and the pussycat.* New York: Putnam. (P–M)

Longfellow, H. W. (1990). (Ill. by T. Rand). *Paul Revere's ride.* New York: Dutton. (M–U)

Mahy, M. (1987). *17 kings and 42 elephants.* New York: Dial. (M)

Moore, C. (1980). *The night before Christmas.* New York: Holiday House. (P–M)

Noyes, A. (1981). (Ill. by C. Keeping). *The highwayman.* Oxford, England: Oxford University Press. (U)

Sandburg, C. (1993). *Arithmetic.* New York: Harcourt Brace. (P–M)

Thayer, E. L. (1988). (Ill. by P. Polacco). *Casey at the bat: A ballad of the republic, sung in the year 1888.* New York: Putnam. (M–U)

Westcott, N. B. (1988). *The lady with the alligator purse.* Boston: Little, Brown. (P–M)

Specialized Collections

Carle, E. (1989). *Animals, animals.* New York: Philomel. (P–M)

Dickinson, E. (1978). *I'm nobody! Who are you? Poems of Emily Dickinson for children.* Owing Mills, MD: Stemmer House. (M–U)

Fleischman, P. (1985). *I am phoenix: Poems for two voices.* New York: Harper & Row. (M–U)

Fleischman, P. (1988). *Joyful noise: Poems for two voices.* New York: Harper & Row. (M–U)

Froman, R. (1974). *Seeing things: A book of poems.* New York: Crowell. (M)

Frost, R. (1982). *A swinger of birches: Poems of Robert Frost for young people.* Owing Mills, MD: Stemmer House. (U)

Greenfield, E. (1988). *Under the Sunday tree.* New York: Harper & Row. (M)

Hopkins, L. B. (1984). *Surprises* (An I Can Read Book). New York: Harper & Row. (P)

Hopkins, L. B. (1987). *Click, rumble, roar: Poems about machines.* New York: Crowell. (M)

Janeczko, P. B. (Sel.). (1993). *Looking for your name: A collection of contemporary poems.* New York: Orchard Books. (U)

Jones, H. (Ed.). (1993). *The trees stand shining: Poetry of the North American Indians.* New York: Dial. (M–U)

Kuskin, K. (1980). *Dogs and dragons, trees and dreams.* New York: Harper & Row. (P–M)

Lewis, R. (1965). *In a spring garden.* New York: Dial. (haiku) (M–U)

Livingston, M. C. (1985). *Celebrations.* New York: Holiday House. (M)

Lobel, A. (1983). *The book of pigericks.* New York: Harper & Row. (limericks) (P–M)

Livingston, M. C. (1986). *Earth songs.* New York: Holiday House. (See also *Sea songs* and *Space songs*.) (M–U)

McCord, D. (1974). *One at a time.* Boston: Little, Brown. (M–U)

Pomerantz, C. (1982). *If I had a paka: Poems in 11 languages.* New York: Greenwillow. (M–U)

Prelutsky, J. (1981). *It's Christmas.* New York: Scholastic. (Collections for other holidays, too.) (P–M)

Prelutsky, J. (1984). *The new kid on the block.* New York: Greenwillow. (P–M)

Prelutsky, J. (1989). *Poems of A. Nonny Mouse.* New York: Knopf. (P–M)

Prelutsky, J. (1990). *Something big has been here.* New York: Greenwillow. (P–M)

Prelutsky, J. (1993). *A. Nonny Mouse writes again!* New York: Knopf. (M–U)

Siebert, D. (1984). *Truck song.* New York: Harper & Row. (P–M)

Siebert, D. (1989). *Heartland.* New York: Crowell. (M–U)

Silverstein, S. (1974). *Where the sidewalk ends.* New York: Harper & Row. (P–M–U)

Yolen, J. (1990). *Bird watch: A book of poetry.* New York: Philomel. (M–U)

Comprehensive Anthologies

de Paola, T. (Compiler). (1988). *Tomie de Paola's book of poems.* New York: Putnam. (P–M)

de Regniers, B. S., Moore, E., White, M. M., & Carr, J. (Compilers). (1988). *Sing a song of popcorn: Every child's book of poems.* New York: Scholastic. (P–M–U)

Dunning, S., Leuders, E., & Smith, H. (Compilers). (1967). *Reflections on a gift of watermelon pickle, and other modern verse.* New York: Lothrop, Lee & Shepard. (U)

Kennedy, X. J. (Compiler). (1985). *The forgetful wishing well: Poems for young people.* New York: McElderry Books. (U)

Kennedy, X. J., & Kennedy, D. M. (Compilers). (1982). *Knock at a star: A child's introduction to poetry.* Boston: Little, Brown. (P–M–U)

Prelutsky, J. (Compiler). (1983). *The Random House book of poetry for children.* New York: Random House. (P–M–U)

Figure 11–5 *Adult Poems Appropriate for Elementary Students*

Poet	Poems and/or Books of Poetry
William Blake	"The Lamb," "The Tyger," "The Piper," and other selections from *Songs of Experience* and *Songs of Innocence.* Compare with Nancy Willard's *A Visit to William Blake's Inn: Poems for Innocent and Experienced Travelers* (1981).
e. e. cummings	Deborah Kogan Ray has created a picture book version of *hist whist* (1989).
Emily Dickinson	"I'm Nobody! Who Are You?," "There Is No Frigate Like a Book," and other favorite poems from *I'm Nobody! Who Are You? Poems of Emily Dickinson for Children* (1978) and *A Brighter Garden* (1990).
T. S. Eliot	Poems about cats from *Old Possum's Book of Practical Cats* (1967).
Robert Frost	"The Pasture," "Birches," "Fire and Ice," "Stopping by Woods on a Snowy Evening," and other favorites are included in *A Swinger of Birches: Poems of Robert Frost for Young People* (1982). *Stopping by Woods on a Snowy Evening,* illustrated by Susan Jeffers (1978), and *Birches* (1988) are picture book versions of individual poems.
Langston Hughes	"Dreams," "City," "April Rain Song," and other selections are included in *The Dream Keeper and Other Poems* (1960). Also, Lee Bennett Hopkins has compiled a collection of Hughes's poetry for young people: *Don't You Turn Back: Poems by Langston Hughes* (1969).
D. H. Lawrence	William Cole has prepared a selection of Lawrence's poetry suitable for upper-grade students: *D. H. Lawrence: Poems Selected for Young People* (1967). Also, Alice and Martin Provensen have illustrated a collection of D. H. Lawrence's poems for students, *Birds, Beasts and the Third Thing: Poems by D. H. Lawrence* (1982).
Henry Wadsworth Longfellow	Ted Rand's illustrations evoke the historical moment in a picture book version of Longfellow's poem, *Paul Revere's Ride* (1990).
Carl Sandburg	"Fog," "Daybreak," "Buffalo Dusk," and other poems for elementary students are included in *Wind Song* (1960), *Chicago Poems* (1944), and other books of Sandburg's poetry. Ted Rand has illustrated a stunning picture book version of *Arithmetic* (1993). Also see Lee Bennett Hopkins's collection of Sandburg's poems, *Rainbows Are Made: Poems by Carl Sandburg* (1982).
Walt Whitman	Lee Bennett Hopkins has compiled *Voyages: Poems of Walt Whitman* (1988), and Robert Sabuda has illustrated a picture book version of *I Hear America Singing* (1991).
John Greenleaf Whittier	Nancy Winslow Parker has created a picture book of Whittier's Civil War poem, *Barbara Frietchie* (1992).

second, and third graders; Terry (1974) investigated fourth, fifth, and sixth graders' preferences; and Kutiper (1985) researched seventh, eighth, and ninth graders' preferences. The results of the three studies are important for teachers to consider when they select poems. The most popular forms of poetry were limericks and narrative poems; least popular were haiku and free verse. In addition, children preferred funny poems, poems about animals, and poems about familiar experiences; they disliked poems with visual imagery and figurative language. The most important elements were rhyme, rhythm, and sound. Primary-grade students preferred traditional poetry, middle graders preferred modern poetry, and upper-grade students preferred rhyming verse. The 10 best-liked poems for each grade group are ranked in Figure 11–6. The researchers found that children in all three studies liked poetry, enjoyed listening to poetry read aloud, and could give reasons why they liked or disliked particular poems.

Researchers have also used school library circulation figures to examine children's poetry preferences. In a recent study Kutiper and Wilson (1993) found that the humorous poetry of Shel Silverstein and Jack Prelutsky was the most popular. The three most widely circulated books were *The New Kid on the Block* (Prelutsky, 1984), *Where the Sidewalk Ends* (Silverstein, 1974), and *A Light in the Attic* (Silverstein, 1981). In fact, 14 of the 30 most popular books used in the study were written by these two poets. Both Silverstein and Prelutsky use rhyme and rhythm effectively in their poems and write humorous, narrative poems about familiar, everyday occurrences; these are the same qualities that children liked in the earlier poetry preference studies.

Poets Who Write for Children. Many poets are writing for children today, among them Arnold Adoff, Byrd Baylor, Gwendolyn Brooks, Aileen Fisher, Lee Bennett Hopkins, Karla Kuskin, Myra Cohn Livingston, Lilian Moore, Mary O'Neill, Jack Prelutsky, and Shel Silverstein. Thumbnail sketches of six contemporary children's poets are presented in Figure 11–7. Children are just as interested in learning about favorite poets as they are in learning about authors who write stories and informational books. When children view poets and other writers as real people, people whom they can relate to and who enjoy the same things they do, they begin to see themselves as poets—a necessary criterion for successful writing. Information about poets is available in *Speaking of Poets: Interviews With Poets Who Write for Children and Young Adults* (Copeland, 1993) and from many of the sources about authors listed in Appendix B.

Inviting poets to visit the classroom to share their poetry is one of the most valuable poetry experiences for children. For example, Chapman (1985) shares what happened when poet Arnold Adoff visited her classroom, and Parker (1981) relates a visit by Karla Kuskin.

Teaching Students to Read Poems

The focus in teaching students to read poems is on enjoyment. Students should have many, many opportunities to read and listen to poems read aloud, and they should learn a variety of approaches for sharing poems. Also, teachers should share poems that they especially like with students. Students are not expected to analyze poems; instead they read poems they like and share

Figure 11–6   Children's Poetry Preferences

First, Second, and Third Graders' Favorite Poems		
Rank	Title	Author
1	"The Young Lady of Lynn"	Unknown
2	"The Little Turtle"	Vachel Lindsay
3	"Bad Boy"	Lois Lenski
4	"Little Miss Muffet"	Paul Dehn
5	"Cat"	Eleanor Farjeon
6	"Adventures of Isabel"	Ogden Nash
7	"Mummy Slept Late and Daddy Fixed Breakfast"	John Ciardi
8	"The Lurpp Is on the Loose"	Jack Prelutsky
9	"A Bookworm of Curious Breed"	Ann Hoberman
10	"The Owl and the Pussy-cat"	Edward Lear

Fourth, Fifth, and Sixth Graders' Favorite Poems		
Rank	Title	Author
1	"Mummy Slept Late and Daddy Fixed Breakfast"	John Ciardi
2	"Fire! Fire!"	Unknown
3	"There was an old man of Blackheath"	Unknown
4	"Little Miss Muffet"	Paul Dehn
5	"There once was an old kangaroo"	Edward S. Mullins
6	"There was a young lady of Niger"	Unknown
7	"Hughbert and the Glue"	Karla Kuskin
8	"Betty Barter"	Unknown
9	"Lone Dog"	Irene Rutherford McLeod
10	"Eletelephony"	Laura E. Richards

Seventh, Eighth, and Ninth Graders' Favorite Poems		
Rank	Title	Author
1	"Sick"	Shel Silverstein
2	"Oh, Teddy Bear"	Jack Prelutsky
3	"Mother Doesn't Want a Dog"	Judith Viorst
4	"Mummy Slept Late and Daddy Fixed Breakfast"	John Ciardi
5	"The Unicorn"	Shel Silverstein
6	"Why Nobody Pets the Lion at the Zoo"	John Ciardi
7	"Homework"	Jane Yolen
8	"Dreams"	Langston Hughes
9	"Questions"	Marci Ridlon
10	"Willie Ate a Worm Today"	Jack Prelutsky

Fisher & Natarella, 1982, p. 344; Kutiper, 1985, p. 51; Terry, 1974, p. 15.

their favorite poems with classmates. Students use the reading process as they read and respond to poems, and they often read poems in connection with literature focus units and theme cycles and during reading workshop.

Introducing Students to Poetry.   In her poem "How to Eat a Poem" (1966), Eve Merriam provides useful advice for students who are reading poems: She

Figure 11–7   Thumbnail Sketches of Six Contemporary Children's Poets

Arnold Adoff

Black Is Brown Is Tan (1973)
Make a Circle Keep Us in: Poems for a Good Day (1975)
Eats Poems (1979)
Sports Pages (1986)
Chocolate Dreams (1989)
In for Winter, Out for Spring (1991)

Arnold Adoff grew up in New York City, and he taught at a public school in Harlem for 12 years. During his teaching Adoff was frustrated by the lack of materials about African American culture and began to collect the work of African American writers to use with his students. Adoff's poems are arranged on the page to pull the eye and to reflect the rhythm and rhyme. Some of his poems have no capital letters or punctuation marks. Much of his writing focuses on African American and interracial family life; however, Adoff says he sees himself as a student of rather than an expert on the African American culture. Today he lives in Yellow Springs, Ohio.

Eloise Greenfield

Africa Dream (1977)
Honey, I Love and Other Love Poems (1978)
Daydreamers (1981)
Under the Sunday Tree (1988)
Nathaniel Talking (1989)
Night on Neighborhood Street (1991)

Eloise Greenfield has written more than 20 books for children, including poetry, stories, and biographies. Many of her poems focus on family life, present vivid characters, and introduce the theme of developing the inner strength necessary to succeed in life. Greenfield depicts the everyday lives of African American children that she says they know they lead, not the negative ones that are often presented in the media. In *Nathaniel Talking,* for example, there are 17 inspiring poems, including a rap, told from Nathaniel's viewpoint about being 9 years old, gaining knowledge, misbehaving, missing his mama, and shaping his future. Greenfield was born in North Carolina but has lived in Washington, DC, for many years.

Karla Kuskin

The Rose on My Cake (1964)
Any Me I Want to Be (1972)
Near the Window Tree (1975)
Dogs and Dragons, Trees and Dreams (1980)
Soap Soup and Other Verses (1992)

Karla Kuskin is a native New Yorker who wrote and published her first book, *Roar and More* (1956), as a class assignment while a student at Yale University. Kuskin writes both humorous picture books for preschoolers and books of poetry for older children. Her poems are often short, with a gentle rhythm and whimsical tone; "Knitted Things" is a good example. She says she writes from her memories of childhood, and she is especially successful in capturing the essence of childhood experiences in poems such as "I Woke Up This Morning." Kuskin discusses how she writes poetry on "Poetry Explained by Karla Kuskin," a sound filmstrip available from Weston Woods.

Figure 11–7   *continued*

Myra Cohn Livingston

A Circle of Seasons (1982)
New Year's Poems (1987)
Dog Poems (1990)
If You Ever Meet a Whale (1992)
Light and Shadow (1992)
Roll Along: Poems on Wheels (1993)

Myra Cohn Livingston was born in Omaha, Nebraska, and began writing poems and stories as soon as she could read. She had a special interest in both writing and music. As a teenager she played the French horn in the California Junior Symphony and wrote for her high school newspaper. Livingston wrote her first book of poems, *Whispers and Other Poems* (1958), while she was in college, but it was not published until 12 years later. Since then she has written nearly 50 books of poetry. Today Livingston lives in Beverly Hills, California. She has written a book for elementary students on how to write poetry, *Poem-Making: Ways to Begin Writing Poetry* (1991).

Jack Prelutsky

Nightmares: Poems to Trouble Your Sleep (1976)
It's Halloween (1977)
The Random House Book of Poetry for Children (1983)
The New Kid on the Block (1984)
Poems of A. Nonny Mouse (1989)
Something BIG Has Been Here (1990)

Jack Prelutsky was born in New York City. His career has included singing and acting jobs as well as writing poetry. He has sung with opera companies in Boston and Seattle and has written more than 30 books of poetry. His poetry is delightful nonsense in rhymed, rhythmic verse, and his poems are often about imaginary animals, as in *The Baby Uggs Are Hatching* (1982). Prelutsky now makes his home in Olympia, Washington, and he travels around the country to visit libraries and schools. He says that by talking to children and sharing his poems with them, he is better able to craft his writing to appeal to children.

Shel Silverstein

The Giving Tree (1964)
Where the Sidewalk Ends (1974)
The Missing Piece (1976)
The Light in the Attic (1981)

Shel Silverstein was born in Chicago but now divides his time among homes in Greenwich Village, Key West, and a houseboat in Sausalito, California. Silverstein began to write and draw when he was a teenager and, when he served in the U.S. armed forces in the 1950s, was a cartoonist for the military newspaper *Stars and Stripes*. Silverstein never planned to write or draw for children, but friends convinced him that his work had appeal for children as well as for adults. He says he hopes that readers will experience a "personal sense of discovery" when they read his poems. Silverstein has other interests in addition to writing poetry: He is a folksinger, a lyricist, and a playwright.

says that reading a poem is like eating a piece of fruit, and she advises to bite right in and let the juice run down your chin. Poetry sharing does not need to be scheduled for a particular time of day. First thing in the morning or right after lunch are good times, but because poems can be shared quickly, they can be tied in with almost any activity. Often poems are coordinated with literature focus units and theme cycles.

When teachers and students read poems aloud, they enhance their reading using these four elements (Stewig, 1981):

- *Tempo*—how fast or slowly to read the lines
- *Rhythm*—which words to stress or say loudest
- *Pitch*—when to raise or lower the voice
- *Juncture*—when and how long to pause

Students experiment with these elements during minilessons and learn how to vary them to make their reading of poetry more interpretive. Students also learn that in some poems one element may be more important than another. Knowing about these elements reinforces the importance of rehearsing a poem several times before reading it aloud. During rehearsal students experiment with tempo, rhythm, pitch, and juncture in order to read the poem effectively.

Teachers begin by reading favorite poems aloud to students and hanging charts with the poems written on them in the classroom. After doing this for several days, teachers point out a collection of poetry books in the classroom library and invite students to prepare a poem to share with the class the next day. Before long students will be eagerly volunteering to read poems to the class. A list of guidelines for reading poems with children is presented in the Teacher's Notebook on page 426.

In Reading Workshop.   Students sometimes choose collections of poetry to read during reading workshop, or teachers can plan a special poetry workshop. Some teachers devote one day a week for poetry workshop or plan a period of several weeks when all students read and respond to poems. Poetry workshops have the same components as regular reading workshop, and a poetry workshop can combine both reading workshop and writing workshop (Tompkins & McGee, 1993).

During a poetry workshop the reading time is often divided into two parts. During the first part students spend time browsing in collections of poetry and selecting poems that they want to share with classmates. Then during the second part of reading time, students read poems aloud to partners or small groups of classmates. Because poetry is intended to be shared orally, students need to have the opportunity to read poems aloud. Students also write responses about poems they have read in reading logs and do projects to extend their poetry experience.

In Literature Focus Units.   Teachers often share poems with students in conjunction with stories and other books they read aloud. For example, they might read Langston Hughes's poem "Dreams" (Prelutsky, 1983) together with *Number the Stars* (Lowry, 1989) or "Night Bear" by Lee Bennett Hopkins (1984) before or after reading *Ira Sleeps Over* (Waber, 1972). Sometimes teachers read a poem as a preparing-to-read activity, and at other times they read it as an exploring activity. Whether a poem is used before or after reading depends on the particular story or poem and how the teacher plans to use it.

Teacher's Notebook
Guidelines for Reading Poems

1. Children and teachers read poetry aloud, not silently. Even if students are reading independently they should speak each word, albeit softly or in an undertone.
2. Children become the primary readers and sharers of poetry as quickly as possible. Try group poetry reading or reciting and choral reading activities.
3. Children and teachers read or recite poems that they like. The goal is for every student to have favorite poems, books of poetry, and poets.
4. Teach students how to read a poem with expression, how to emphasize the rhythm and feel of the words, and where to pause.
5. Readers rehearse poems several times before reading aloud so that they can read fluently and with expression. Encourage students to read "poetically."
6. A collection of poetry books should be included in the classroom library for children to read during reading workshop and other independent reading times.
7. A listening center with audiocassettes of poems should also be available. Students may want to record their favorite poems for the listening center.
8. Children should not be assigned to memorize a particular poem; rather, children who are interested in learning a favorite poem should be encouraged to do so and share it with class members.
9. Children do not analyze the meaning of a poem or its rhyme scheme; instead, they talk about poems they like and why they like them. Many students stop enjoying poetry when teachers require them to analyze poems.
10. Teachers coordinate poems to share during social studies and science theme cycles and with literature focus units.

Students may also locate a poem related to a story or other book and share it with the class as a project during the extending stage.

Teachers can teach a unit on poetry, and during the unit students read and respond to a collection of poems. In this unit, poetry is at the center, rather than an introduction or extension for other types of literature. Teachers choose some poems that all students will read and respond to, and students themselves select other poems.

Teachers read many poems to students, and students read other poems themselves. One way for students to read poems is using *choral reading,* in which students take turns reading a poem together. Students need multiple copies of the poem for choral reading, or the poem must be displayed on a chart or an overhead projector so that everyone can read it. Then students and

During an author unit, these sixth graders read many of Jack Prelutsky's poems, including "Mean Maxine," "I'm Thankful," and "The New Kid on the Block."

the teacher decide how to arrange the poem for choral reading. Students may read the poem aloud together or in small groups, or individual students can read particular lines or stanzas. Four possible arrangements are (Stewig, 1981):

1. *Echo reading.* The leader reads each line, and the group repeats it.
2. *Leader and chorus reading.* The leader reads the main part of the poem, and the group reads the refrain or chorus in unison.
3. *Small group reading.* The class divides into two or more groups, and each group reads one part of the poem.
4. *Cumulative reading.* One student or one group reads the first line or stanza, and another student or group joins in as each line or stanza is read so that a cumulative effect is created.

Choral reading makes students active participants in the poetry experience, and it helps students learn to appreciate the sounds, feelings, and magic of poetry. Two books of award-winning poems written specifically for choral reading are *I Am Phoenix* (Fleischman, 1985), a collection of poems about birds, and *Joyful Noise* (Fleischman, 1988), a collection of poems about insects. Many other poems can be used for choral reading; try, for example, Shel Silverstein's "Boa Constrictor," "Full of the Moon" by Karla Kuskin, Laura E. Richards's "Eletelephony," and "Catch a Little Rhyme" by Eve Merriam.

After reading, students respond to the poem they have read or listened to someone else read aloud. Sometimes the response is brief, and students talk informally about the poem, sharing connections to their own lives or expressing

Teacher's Notebook

Ways to Respond to a Poem

1. Students read the poem aloud to classmates.
2. Students write a reading log entry, discussing what the poem brings to mind or why they like it.
3. Students arrange the poem for choral reading and with classmates present it to the class.
4. Students identify a favorite line in a poem and explain why they like it, either by talking to a classmate or in a reading log entry.
5. Students draw or paint a picture of an image the poem brings to mind and write a favorite line or two from the poem on the picture.
6. Students make a picture book with lines or a stanza of the poem written on each page and illustrated.
7. Students make a mobile with stanzas cut apart and hung together with pictures.
8. Students "can" or "box" a poem by decorating a container and inserting a copy of the poem and two items related to the poem.
9. Students read other poems written by the same author.
10. Students investigate the poet and, perhaps, write a letter to the poet.
11. Students make a cluster on a topic related to the poem.
12. Students write a poem on the same topic or following the format of the poem they have read.
13. Students dramatize the poem with a group of classmates.
14. Students make a filmstrip of the poem.
15. Students make a poster to illustrate the poem and attach a copy of the poem to it.

whether they liked it. They also might write responses in reading logs or quickwrites. At other times students' responses are more elaborate. They may explore the poem, rereading it, choosing favorite lines, or illustrating it. A list of additional ways students respond to poems is presented in the Teacher's Notebook above.

During poetry units students often create projects. They use drama, art, and music activities to extend their interpretations of favorite poems. For instance, students can role-play Kuskin's "I Woke Up This Morning" or construct monster puppets for the Lurpp creature in Prelutsky's "The Lurpp Is on the Loose." Students may also compile picture book versions of narrative poems, such as Ciardi's "Mummy Slept Late and Daddy Cooked Breakfast," or they may make filmstrip versions of a poem using a filmstrip kit. Several frames from a filmstrip illustrating "Mummy Slept Late . . ." are presented in Figure 11–8.

Some students enjoy compiling anthologies of their favorite poems. This activity often begins quite naturally when students read poems. They copy favorite poems to keep, and soon they are stapling their collections together to make books. Copying poems can also be a worthwhile handwriting activity because students are copying something meaningful to them, not just words and sentences in a workbook. Poet and anthologist Lee Bennett Hopkins (1987) suggests setting up a dead tree branch or an artificial Christmas tree in the classroom as a "poetree" on which students can hang copies of their favorite poems for classmates to read and enjoy.

Students may also compile a book of poems and illustrate them with photographs. In *A Song in Stone: City Poems* (1983), Lee Bennett Hopkins compiled a collection of city poems, and Anna Held Audette selected black-and-white photographs to illustrate each one. Students can create a similar

Figure 11–8   Excerpt from a Child's Filmstrip Illustrating "Mummy Slept Late and Daddy Fixed Breakfast"

Daddy fixed the breakfast.
He made us each a waffle.
It looked like gravel pudding.
It tasted something awful.

"Ha, ha," he said, "I'll try again.
This time I'll get it right."

But what *I* got was in between
Bituminous and anthracite.

"A little too well done? Oh well,
I'll have to start all over."
That time what landed on my plate
Looked like a manhole cover.

I tried to cut it with a fork:
The fork gave off a spark.

I tried a knife and twisted it

Into a question mark.

I tried it with a hack-saw.

I tried it with a torch.

It didn't even make a dent.
It didn't even scorch.

The next time Dad gets breakfast
When Mummy's sleeping late,
I think I'll skip the waffles.
I'd sooner eat the plate.

type of book, and photocopies can be made so that each child will have a personal copy.

In Theme Cycles.   Teachers often share poems in connection with theme cycles. They read poems from *Dinosaurs* (Hopkins, 1987) and *Tyrannosaurus Was a Beast* (Prelutsky, 1988) during a theme on dinosaurs and from *Mojave* (Siebert, 1988) and *Desert Voices* (Baylor & Parnall, 1981) during a theme cycle on the desert. Text sets of books for theme cycles should include books of poetry or copies of poems written on charts whenever possible. A list of poetry collections that can be coordinated with theme cycles and holiday celebrations is presented in Figure 11–9. Including poems in theme cycles is important because poetry gives students a different perspective about social studies and science concepts.

Both teachers and students can share poems during theme cycles. Teachers read poems aloud to students, or they can duplicate copies of a poem for students to read, perhaps using choral reading. Then students can add these poems to their learning logs. Also, teachers can display poems related to a theme on a bulletin board or in a display. Students also can select poems to share as projects or write a favorite poem related to a theme on a poster or in a book.

Assessing Students' Experiences With Poems

Teachers assess students' experiences with poetry in several ways. They observe students as they are involved in poetry reading activities and keep anecdotal notes of students as they read and respond to poems and share poems they like with classmates. They read students' reading logs and monitor the projects they create. Teachers can also conference with students and ask them about favorite poems and poets and assess students' interest in poetry. They also notice students' attention to how poets use wordplay and poetic devices. Students can also write reflections about their learning and work habits during the poetry activities, and these reflections provide valuable assessment information.

During poetry units teachers prepare assessment checklists and keep track of students' reading and response activities. For example, during a 2-week poetry unit, fourth graders might be assessed on these activities:

- Read 20 poems.
- Keep a list of the 20 poems read.
- Write in a reading log about five favorite poems.
- Participate in choral reading activities.
- Participate in minilessons about choral reading techniques, poet Jack Prelutsky, rhyme, and word pictures.
- Make a page for a class book on a favorite poem.
- Do a project about a poem.

Some people might argue that it is difficult to grade students on reading poetry, but students can earn points for these activities, and the points can be added together for a grade.

Figure 11–9   Books of Poetry for Theme Cycles

Adoff, A. (1979). *Eats poems*. New York: Lothrop. (P–M)

Amon, A. (Sel.). (1981). *The earth is sore: Native Americans on nature*. New York: Atheneum. (M–U)

Bauer, C. F. (Sel.). (1986). *Snowy day: Stories and poems*. New York: Lippincott. (See other books of weather stories and poems by the same selector.) (P–M)

Baylor, B. (1981). *Desert voices*. New York: Scribner. (P–M)

Benet, R., & Benet, S. V. (1961). *A book of Americans*. New York: Holt. (M–U)

Carle, E. (Sel.). (1989). *Eric Carle's animals, animals*. New York: Philomel. (P–M)

Esbensen, B. J. (1984). *Cold stars and fireflies: Poems of the four seasons*. New York: Crowell. (U)

Fisher, A. (1983). *Rabbits, rabbits*. New York: Harper & Row. (P)

Fisher, A. (1988). *The house of a mouse*. New York: Harper & Row. (Poems about mice) (P–M)

Fleischman, P. (1985). *I am phoenix: Poems for two voices*. New York: Harper & Row. (Poems about birds) (M–U)

Fleischman, P. (1988). *Joyful noise: Poems for two voices*. New York: Harper & Row. (Poems about insects) (M–U)

Goldstein, B. S. (Sel.). (1989). *Bear in mind: A book of bear poems*. New York: Puffin. (P–M)

Goldstein, B. S. (Sel.). (1992). *What's on the menu?* New York: Viking. (Poems about food) (P–M)

Harvey, A. (Sel.). (1992). *Shades of green*. New York: Greenwillow. (Poems about ecology) (U)

Hopkins, L. (Sel.). (1985). *Munching: Poems about eating*. Boston: Little, Brown. (M–U)

Hopkins, L. B. (Sel.). (1976). *Good morning to you, valentine*. New York: Harcourt Brace Jovanovich. (See other collections of holiday poems by the same selector.) (P–M)

Hopkins, L. B. (Sel.). (1983). *A song in stone: City poems*. New York: Crowell. (M)

Hopkins, L. B. (Sel.). (1983). *The sky is full of song*. New York: Harper & Row. (Poems about the seasons) (P–M)

Hopkins, L. B. (Sel.). (1987). *Dinosaurs*. San Diego: Harcourt Brace Jovanovich. (M–U)

Hopkins, L. B. (Sel.). (1987). *Click, rumble, roar: Poems about machines*. New York: Crowell. (M)

Hopkins, L. B. (Sel.). (1991). *On the farm*. Boston: Little, Brown. (P–M)

Hopkins, L. B. (Sel.). (1992). *To the zoo: Animal poems*. Boston: Little, Brown. (P–M)

Janeczko, P. B. (Sel.). (1984). *Strings: A gathering of family poems*. New York: Bradbury Press. (U)

Larrick, N. (Sel.). (1988). *Cats are cats*. New York: Philomel. (M–U)

Larrick, N. (Sel.). (1990). *Mice are nice*. New York: Philomel. (M)

Livingston, M. C. (1982). *Circle of seasons*. New York: Holiday House. (M–U)

Livingston, M. C. (1985). *Celebrations*. New York: Holiday House. (Poems about holidays) (P–M)

Livingston, M. C. (Sel.). (1984). *Sky songs*. New York: Holiday House. (M–U)

Livingston, M. C. (Sel.). (1986). *Earth songs*. New York: Holiday House. (M–U)

Livingston, M. C. (Sel.). (1986). *Sea songs*. New York: Holiday House. (M–U)

Livingston, M. C. (Sel.). (1987). *Cat poems*. New York: Holiday House. (P–M–U)

Livingston, M. C. (Sel.). (1987). *New year's poems*. New York: Holiday House. (See other collections of holiday poems by the same selector.) (P–M–U)

Livingston, M. C. (Sel.). (1988). *Space songs*. New York: Holiday House. (M–U)

Livingston, M. C. (Sel.). (1990). *If the owl calls again: A collection of owl poems*. New York: McElderry Books. (U)

Livingston, M. C. (Sel.). (1990). *Dog poems*. New York: Holiday House. (M–U)

Livingston, M. C. (Sel.). (1992). *If you ever meet a whale*. New York: Holiday House. (P–M)

Morrison, L. (1985). *The break dance kids: Poems of sport, motion, and locomotion*. New York: Lothrop, Lee & Shepard. (U)

Prelutsky, J. (1984). *It's snowing! It's snowing!* New York: Greenwillow. (P–M)

Prelutsky, J. (1977). *It's Halloween*. New York: Greenwillow. (See other books of holiday poems by the same author.) (P–M)

Prelutsky, J. (1983). *Zoo doings: Animal poems*. New York: Greenwillow. (P–M)

Prelutsky, J. (1988). *Tyrannosaurus was a beast: Dinosaur poems*. New York: Greenwillow. (P–M)

Russo, S. (Sel.). (1984). *The ice cream ocean and other delectable poems of the sea*. New York: Lothrop, Lee & Shepard. (P–M)

Turner, A. (1986). *Street talk*. Boston: Houghton Mifflin. (Poems about city life) (M–U)

Yolen, J. (1990). *Bird watch: A book of poetry*. New York: Philomel. (M–U)

Yolen, J. (1990). *Dinosaur dances*. New York: Putnam. (M)

WRITING POEMS

Elementary students can have successful experiences writing poetry if they use poetic formulas. They can write formula poems by beginning each line with particular words, as is the case with color poems; count syllables for haiku; or create word pictures in concrete poems. Writing quickly and using guidelines, students can use the writing process to revise, edit, and share their writing without a time-consuming process of making changes, correcting errors, and recopying. Poetry also allows students more freedom in punctuation, capitalization, and page arrangement.

Many types of poetry do not use rhyme, and rhyme is the sticking-point for many would-be poets. In searching for a rhyming word, children often create inane verse; for example:

> I see a funny little goat
> Wearing a blue sailor's coat
> Sitting in an old motorboat.

Whereas children should not be forbidden to write rhyming poetry, rhyme should never be imposed as a criterion for acceptable poetry. Children may use rhyme when it fits naturally into their writing. When children write poetry during the elementary grades, they are searching for their own voices, and they need freedom to do that. Freed from the pressure to create rhyming poetry or from other constraints, children create sensitive word pictures, vivid images, and unique comparisons, as we see in the poems throughout this chapter.

Five types of poetic forms are formula poems, free-form poems, syllable- and word-count poems, rhymed poems, and model poems. Elementary students' poems illustrate each poetic form. Kindergartners' and first graders' poems may seem little more than lists of sentences compared to the more sophisticated poems of older students, but the range of poems effectively shows how elementary and middle-grade students grow in their ability to write poetry through these writing activities.

Formula Poems

The poetic forms may seem like recipes, but they are not intended to be followed rigidly. Rather, they provide a scaffold, organization, or skeleton for students' poems. After collecting words, images, and comparisons through brainstorming, clustering, quickwriting, or another prewriting strategy, students craft their poems, choosing words and arranging them to create a message. Meaning is always most important, and form follows the search for meaning. Perhaps a better description is that children "dig for poems" (Valentine, 1986) through words, ideas, poetic forms, rhyme, rhythm, and conventions. Poet Kenneth Koch (1970), working with students in the elementary grades, developed some simple formulas that make it easy for nearly every child to become a successful poet. These formulas call for students to begin every line the same way or to insert a particular kind of word in every line. The formulas use repetition, a stylistic device that is more effective for young poets than rhyme. Some forms may seem more like sentences than poems, but the dividing line between poetry and prose is a blurry one, and these poetry experiences help children move toward poetic expression.

"I Wish . . ." Poems.   Children begin each line of their poems with the words "I wish" and complete the line with a wish (Koch, 1970). In a second-grade class collaboration, children simply listed their wishes:

Our Wishes

I wish I had all the money in the world.
I wish I was a star fallen down from Mars.
I wish I were a butterfly.
I wish I were a teddy bear.
I wish I had a cat.
I wish I were a pink rose.
I wish it wouldn't rain today.
I wish I didn't have to wash a dish.
I wish I had a flying carpet.
I wish I could go to Disney World.
I wish school was out.
I wish I could go outside and play.

After this experience students choose one of their wishes and expand on the idea in another poem. Brandi expanded her wish this way:

I Wish

I wish I were a teddy bear
Who sat on a beautiful bed
Who got a hug every night
By a little girl or boy
Maybe tonight I'll get my wish
And wake up on a little girl's bed
And then I'll be as happy as can be.

Color Poems.   Students begin each line of their poems with a color. They can repeat the same color in each line or choose a different color (Koch, 1970). For example, a class of seventh graders writes about yellow:

Yellow

Yellow is shiny galoshes
splashing through mud puddles.
Yellow is a street lamp
beaming through a dark, black night.
Yellow is the egg yolk
bubbling in a frying pan.
Yellow is the lemon cake
that makes you pucker your lips.
Yellow is the sunset
and the warm summer breeze.
Yellow is the tingling in your mouth
after a lemon drop melts.

Students can also write more complex poems by expanding each idea into a stanza, as this poem about black illustrates:

Black

Black is a deep hole
sitting in the ground
waiting for animals
that live inside.

Black is a beautiful horse
standing on a high hill
with the wind
swirling its mane.

Black is a winter night sky
without stars
to keep it
company.

Black is a panther
creeping around a jungle
searching for
its prey.

Hailstones and Halibut Bones (O'Neill, 1961) is another source of color poems; however, O'Neill uses rhyme as a poetic device, and it is important to emphasize that students' poems need not rhyme.

Writing color poems can be coordinated with teaching young children to read and write color words. Instead of having kindergartners and first graders read worksheets and color pictures the designated colors, students can create color poems in booklets of paper stapled together. They write and illustrate one line of the poem on each page.

Five-Senses Poems.   Students write about a topic using each of the five senses. Sense poems are usually five lines long, with one line for each sense, as this poem written by a sixth grader demonstrates:

Being Heartbroken

Sounds like thunder and lightning
Looks like a carrot going through a blender
Tastes like sour milk
Feels like a splinter in your finger
Smells like a dead fish
It must be horrible!

It is often helpful to have students develop a five-senses cluster and collect ideas for each sense. Students select from the cluster the strongest or most vivid idea for each sense to use in a line of the poem.

"If I Were . . ." Poems.   Children write about how they would feel and what they would do if they were something else—a tyrannosaurus rex, a hamburger, or the sunshine (Koch, 1970). They begin each poem with "If I were" and tell what it would be like to be that thing; for example, 7-year-old Robbie writes about what he would do if he were a dinosaur:

If I were a tyrannosaurus rex
I would terrorize other dinosaurs
And eat them up for supper.

Students use personification in composing "If I were . . ." poems, explore ideas and feelings, and consider the world from a different vantage point.

"I Used to . . ./But Now . . ." Poems.   In these contrast poems, students begin the first line (and every odd-numbered line) with "I used to" and the second line (and every even-numbered line) with "But now" (Koch, 1970). Students can use this formula to explore ways they have changed as well as how things change. Two third-grade students wrote:

> *I used to be a kernel*
> *but now I am a crunchy,*
> *tasty, buttery cloud*
> *popped by Orville Redenbacher.*

". . . Is" Poems.   In these description or definition poems, students describe what something is or what something or someone means to them. To begin, the teacher or students identify a topic to fill in the blank, such as *anger, a friend, liberty,* or *fear;* then students start each line with ". . . is" and describe or define that thing. A group of second graders wrote the following poem as a part of their weather unit. Before discussing what causes thunder, they brainstormed a list of possible explanations for this phenomenon:

> *Thunder Is . . .*
>
> *Thunder is someone bowling.*
> *Thunder is a hot cloud bumping against a cold cloud.*
> *Thunder is someone playing basketball.*
> *Thunder is dynamite blasting.*
> *Thunder is a brontosaurus sneezing.*
> *Thunder is people moving their furniture.*
> *Thunder is a giant laughing.*
> *Thunder is elephants playing.*
> *Thunder is an army tank.*
> *Thunder is Bugs Bunny chewing his carrots.*

Students often write powerful poems using this formula, when they move beyond the cute "Happiness is . . ." and "Love is . . ." patterns.

Preposition Poems.   Students begin each line of preposition poems with a preposition, and this pattern often produces a delightful poetic effect. Seventh grader Mike wrote this preposition poem about a movie superhero:

> *Superman*
>
> *Within the city*
> *In a phone booth*
> *Into his clothes*
> *Like a bird*
> *In the sky*
> *Through the walls*
> *Until the crime*
> *Among us*
> *is defeated!*

It is helpful for children to brainstorm a list of prepositions to refer to when they write preposition poems. Students may find that they need to ignore the formula for a line or two to give the content of their poems top priority, or they may mistakenly begin a line with an infinitive verb (e.g., *to say*) rather than a preposition. These forms provide a structure or skeleton for students' writing that should be adapted as necessary.

Free-Form Poems

In free-form poems children choose words to describe something and put the words together to express a thought or tell a story, without concern for rhyme or other arrangements. The number of words per line and the use of punctuation vary. In the following poem, an eighth grader poignantly describes his topic concisely, using only 15 well-chosen words:

Loneliness

A lifetime
Of broken dreams
And promises
Lost love
Hurt
My heart
Cries
In silence

Students can use one of several methods for writing free-form poems. They can select words and phrases from brainstormed lists and clusters, or they can write a paragraph and then "unwrite" it to create the poem by deleting unnecessary words. They arrange the remaining words to look like a poem.

Concrete Poems. Students create concrete poems through art and the careful arrangement of words on a page. Words, phrases, and sentences can be written in the shape of an object, or word pictures can be inserted within poems written left to right and top to bottom. Concrete poems are extensions of the word pictures discussed earlier. Two concrete poems are shown in Figure 11–10. In "Ants," the words *ants, cake,* and *frosting* create the image

Figure 11–10   Students' Concrete Poems

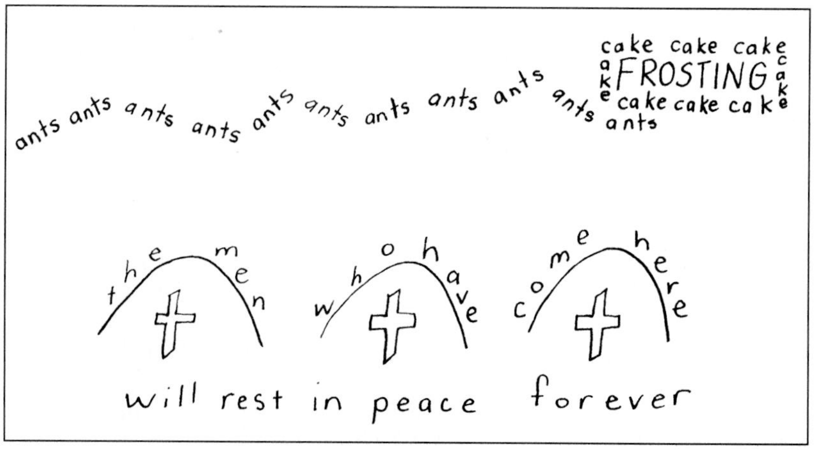

of a familiar picnic scene, and in "Cemetery," repetition and form create a reflection of peace. Three books of concrete poems for students are *Concrete Is Not Always Hard* (Pilon, 1972), *Seeing Things* (Froman, 1974), and *Walking Talking Words* (Sherman, 1980).

Found Poems. Students create poems by culling words from other sources, such as newspaper articles, songs, and stories. A seventh grader "found" this poem in an article about race-car driver Richard Petty:

Fast Moving

Moving down the track,
faster than fast, is Richard Petty
seven-time winner of
the crowned jewel
Daytona 500.
At 210 mph—dangerous—
pushing his engine to the limit.
Other NASCARs running fast
but Richard Petty takes the lead
at last.
Running across the line
with good time.

The student developed this poem by circling powerful words and phrases in the 33-line newspaper article and rearranging the words in a poetic form. After reading over the draft, he deleted two words and added three others that were not in the newspaper article but that he needed for transitions. Found poems give students the opportunity to manipulate words and sentence structures they don't write themselves.

Syllable- and Word-Count Poems

Haiku and other syllable- and word-count poems provide a structure that helps students succeed in writing; however, the need to adhere to these poems' formulas may restrict freedom of expression. In other words, the poetic structure may both help and hinder. The exact syllable counts force students to search for just the right words to express their ideas and feelings and provide a valuable opportunity for students to use thesauruses and dictionaries.

Haiku. The most familiar syllable-counting poem is *haiku* (high-KOO), a Japanese poetic form consisting of 17 syllables arranged in three lines of 5, 7, and 5 syllables. Haiku poems deal with nature and present a single clear image. Haiku is a concise form, much like a telegram. A fourth grader wrote this haiku poem about a spider web she saw one morning:

Spider web shining
Tangled on the grass with dew
Waiting quietly.

Books of haiku to share with students include *My Own Rhythm: An Approach to Haiku* (Atwood, 1973), *Haiku: The Mood of the Earth* (Atwood, 1971), *In a Spring Garden* (Lewis, 1965), *Cricket Songs* (Behn, 1964), and *More Cricket Songs* (Behn, 1971). The photographs and artwork in these trade books may give students ideas for illustrating their haiku poems. Lewis (1968, 1970) has written about the lives of two of the greatest Japanese haiku poets, Issa and Basho; he provides biographical information as well as a collection of poems.

Tanka.   *Tanka* (TANK-ah) is a Japanese verse form containing 31 syllables arranged in five lines, 5–7–5–7–7. This form is similar to haiku, with two additional lines of 7 syllables each. Amy wrote this tanka poem about stars that was published in her middle school anthology:

> *The summer dancers*
> *Dancing in the midnight sky,*
> *Waltzing and dreaming.*
> *Stars glistening in the night sky.*
> *Wish upon a shooting star.*

Even though one line is a syllable short and another is a syllable long in this poem, it illustrates the beauty of this syllable-counting form.

Cinquain.   A *cinquain* (SIN-cane) is a five-line poem containing 22 syllables in a 2–4–6–8–2 syllable pattern. Cinquain poems often describe something, but they may also tell a story. Have students ask themselves what their subject looks like, smells like, sounds like, and tastes like, and record their ideas using a five-senses cluster. The formula is as follows:

Line 1: a one-word subject with two syllables

Line 2: four syllables describing the subject

Line 3: six syllables showing action

Line 4: eight syllables expressing a feeling or an observation about the subject

Line 5: two syllables describing or renaming the subject

Here is a cinquain poem written by an upper-grade student:

> *Wrestling*
> *skinny, fat*
> *coaching, arguing, pinning*
> *trying hard to win*
> *tournament*

If you compare this poem to the cinquain formula, you'll notice that some lines are short a syllable or two. The student bent some of the guidelines in choosing words to create a powerful image of wrestling; however, the message of the poem is always more important than adhering to the formula.

An alternate cinquain form contains five lines, but instead of following a syllable count, each line has a specified number of words. The first line contains a one-word title; the second line has two words that describe the title; the third line has three words that express action; the fourth line has four words that express feelings; and the fifth line contains a two-word synonym for the title.

Diamante. Tiedt (1970) invented the diamante (dee-ah-MAHN-tay), a seven-line contrast poem written in the shape of a diamond. This poetic form helps students apply their knowledge of opposites and parts of speech. The formula is as follows:

Line 1: one noun as the subject

Line 2: two adjectives describing the subject

Line 3: three participles (ending in *-ing*) telling about the subject

Line 4: four nouns (the first two related to the subject and the second two related to the opposite)

Line 5: three participles telling about the opposite

Line 6: two adjectives describing the opposite

Line 7: one noun that is the opposite of the subject

A third-grade class wrote this diamante poem about the stages of life:

BABY
wrinkled tiny
crying wetting sleeping
rattles diapers money house
caring working loving
smart helpful
ADULT

Notice that the students created a contrast between *baby,* the subject represented by the noun in the first line, and *adult,* the opposite in the last line. This contrast gives students the opportunity to play with words and apply their understanding of opposites. The third word, *money,* in the fourth line begins the transition from *baby* to its opposite, *adult.*

Rhymed Verse Forms

Several rhymed verse forms such as limericks and clerihews can be used effectively with middle- and upper-grade students. It is important that teachers try to prevent the forms and rhyme schemes from restricting students' creative and imaginative expression.

Limericks. The *limerick* is a form of light verse that uses both rhyme and rhythm. The poem consists of five lines; the first, second, and fifth lines rhyme, while the third and fourth lines rhyme with each other and are shorter than the other three. The rhyme scheme is a-a-b-b-a, and a limerick is arranged this way:

Line		Rhyme
1	_____	a
2	_____	a
3	_____	b
4	_____	b
5	_____	a

The last line often contains a funny or surprise ending, as in this limerick written by an eighth grader:

> There once was a frog named Pete
> Who did nothing but sit and eat.
> He examined each fly
> With so careful an eye
> And then said, "You're dead meat."

Writing limericks can be a challenging assignment for many upper-grade students, but middle-grade students can also be successful with this poetic form, especially if they write a class collaboration.

Limericks are believed to have originated in the city of Limerick, Ireland, and were first popularized over a century ago by Edward Lear (1812–88). Poet X. J. Kennedy (1982) described limericks as the most popular type of poem in the English language today. Introduce students to limericks by reading aloud some of Lear's verses so that students can appreciate the rhythm of the verse. One fine edition of Lear's limericks is *How Pleasant to Know Mr. Lear!* (Livingston, 1982). Another popular book is *They've Discovered a Head in the Box of Bread and Other Laughable Limericks* (Brewton & Blackburn, 1978). Arnold Lobel has also written a book of unique pig limericks, *Pigericks* (1983). After reading Lobel's pigericks, students will want to write "birdericks" or "fishericks."

Clerihews. Clerihews (KLER-i-hyoos), four-line rhymed verses that describe a person, are named for Edmund Clerihew Bentley (1875–1956), a British detective writer who invented the form. The formula is as follows:

Line 1:	The person's name.
Line 2:	The last word rhymes with the last word in the first line.
Lines 3 and 4:	The last words in these lines rhyme with each other.

Clerihews can be written about anyone—historical figures, characters in stories, and even the students themselves. A sixth grader named Heather wrote this clerihew about Albert Einstein:

> Albert Einstein
> His genius did shine.
> Of relativity and energy did he dream
> And scientists today hold him in high esteem.

Model Poems

Students can model their poems on poems composed by adult poets. Koch suggested this approach in *Rose, Where Did You Get That Red?* (1973); students read a poem and write their own, using the theme expressed in the model poem.

Apologies. Using William Carlos Williams's "This Is Just to Say" as the model, children write a poem in which they apologize for something they are secretly glad they did (Koch, 1973). Middle- and upper-grade students are familiar with offering apologies and enjoy writing humorous apologies. A seventh grader named Jeff, for example, wrote this apology to his dad:

The Truck

Dad,
I'm sorry
that I took
the truck
out for
a spin.
I knew it
was wrong.
But . . .
the exhilarating
motion was
AWESOME!

Apology poems don't have to be humorous; they may be sensitive, genuine apologies, as a seventh grader's poem demonstrates:

Open Up

I didn't
open my
immature eyes
to see
the pain
within you
a death
had caused.
Forgive me,
I misunderstood
your anguished
broken heart.

Invitations.   Students write poems in which they invite someone to a magical, beautiful place full of sounds and colors and where all kinds of marvelous things happen. The model is Shakespeare's "Come Unto These Yellow Sands" (Koch, 1973). Guidelines for writing an invitation poem are that it must be an invitation to a magical place and it must include sound or color words. The following example of an invitation poem written by seventh grader Nikki follows these two guidelines:

The Golden Shore

Come unto the golden shore
Where days are filled with laughter,
And nights filled with whispering winds.
Where sunflowers and sun
Are filled with love.
Come take my hand
As we walk into the sun.

Prayers From the Ark.   Students write a poem or prayer from the viewpoint of an animal, following the model poems in Carmen Bernos de Gasztold's

Prayers From the Ark (1992). Gasztold was a French nun during World War II, and in her poems she assumed the persona of the animals on Noah's ark as they prayed to God, questioning their existence and thanking Him for His mercies. Children can write similar poems in which they assume the persona of an animal. Sixth grader Davis assumes the persona of a monkey for his prayer:

> *Dear Lord,*
> *I forgive you for making my face so ugly.*
> *I thank you for giving me hands.*
> *Thank you for placing the trees so high away*
> *from my enemies.*
> *I almost forgot,*
> *Bless you for last month's big crop of bananas.*

If I Were in Charge of the World.   Students write poems in which they describe what they would do if they were in charge of the world. Judith Viorst's "If I Were in Charge of the World" (1981) is the model for this poetic form. Children are eager to share ideas about how they would change the world, as this fourth grade's collaborative poem illustrates:

> **If I Were in Charge of the World**
>
> *If I were in charge of the world*
> *School would be for one month,*
> *Movies and videogames would be free, and*
> *Foods would be McCalorieless at McDonalds.*
> *Poor people would have a home,*
> *Bubble gum would cost a penny, and*
> *Kids would have cars to drive.*
> *Parents wouldn't argue,*
> *Christmas would be in July and December, and*
> *We would never have bedtimes.*
> *A kid would be president,*
> *I'd meet my long lost cousin, and*
> *Candybars would be vegetables.*
> *I would own the mall,*
> *People would have as much money as they wanted, and*
> *There would be no drugs.*

Teaching Students to Write Poems

As they write poetry, students use what they have learned about poetry through reading poems and the information presented in minilessons on the poetic forms. They often have misconceptions that interfere with their ability to write poems. Many students think poems must rhyme, and in their search for rhymes they create inane verse. It is important that teachers help students develop a concept of poetry before writing poems.

One way to introduce students to writing poetry is to read excerpts from the first chapter of *Anastasia Krupnik* (Lowry, 1979), in which 10-year-old Anastasia, the main character, is excited when her teacher, Mrs. Westvessel, announces that the class will write poems. Anastasia works at home for eight nights to write a poem. Lowry does an excellent job of describing how writers search long and hard for words to express meaning and the delight that comes when they realize their poems are finished. Then Anastasia and her classmates bring their poems to class to read aloud; one student reads his four-line rhymed verse:

I have a dog whose name is Spot.
He likes to eat and drink a lot.
When I put water in his dish,
He laps it up just like a fish. (p. 10)

Anastasia is not impressed. She knows the child who wrote the poem has a dog named Sputnik, not Spot! But Mrs. Westvessel gives it an A and hangs it on the bulletin board. Soon it is Anastasia's turn, and she is nervous because her poem is very different. She reads her poem about tiny creatures that move about in tidepools at night:

hush   hush   the sea-soft night is aswim
    with wrinklesquirm creatures
                                listen(!)
    to them   move   smooth   in the moistly dark
    here in the   whisperwarm wet. (pp. 11–12)

In this free-form poem without rhyme or capital letters, Anastasia has created a marvelous picture with invented words. Regrettably, Mrs. Westvessel has an antiquated view that poems should be about only serious subjects, be composed of rhyming sentences, and use conventional capitalization and punctuation. She doesn't understand Anastasia's poem, and gives Anastasia an F because she didn't follow directions.

Although this first chapter presents a depressing picture of elementary teachers and their lack of knowledge about poetry, it is a dramatic introduction about what poetry is and what it is not. After reading excerpts from the chapter, develop a chart with your students comparing what poetry is in Mrs. Westvessel's class and what poetry is in your class. A class of upper-grade students developed the chart in Figure 11–11.

Figure 11–11   A Comparison Chart Created After Reading Anastasia Krupnik

Rules About Writing Poetry

Mrs. Westvessel's Rules	*Our Rules*
1. Poems must rhyme.	1. Poems do not have to rhyme.
2. The first letter in each line must be capitalized.	2. The first letter in each line does not have to be capitalized.
3. Each line must start at the left margin.	3. Poems can take different shapes and be anywhere on a page.
4. Poems must have a certain rhythm.	4. You hear the writer's voice in a poem—with or without rhythm.
5. Poems should be written about serious things.	5. Poems can be about anything—serious or silly things.
6. Poems should be punctuated like other types of writing.	6. Poems can be punctuated in different ways or not be punctuated at all.
7. Poems are failures if they don't follow these rules.	7. There are no real rules for poems, and no poem is a failure.

After this introduction to writing poetry, teachers teach minilessons about the poetic formulas and writing poems, and they provide opportunities for students to write poems. Students write poems during writing workshop and as part of literature focus units and theme cycles. A list of guidelines for writing poetry is shown in the Teacher's Notebook on page 445.

Poetry Minilessons.   Teachers use minilessons to teach students about the procedures, concepts, and strategies and skills for reading and writing poetry. As part of poetry writing activities, teachers teach minilessons to introduce students to particular poetic forms or to review the forms. Steps in teaching a minilesson about a poetic form are:

*Step
by
Step*

1. *Explaining the Poetic Form.*   Describe the poetic form to students and explain what is included in each line or stanza. Then display a chart that describes the form, or have students write a brief description of the poetic form in their poetry notebooks.

2. *Sharing Sample Poems.*   Read aloud poems that are written by children and adults and that adhere to the form. Then share sample poems from this chapter and poems written by students in previous years, or share poems from poetry collections written for children by adult poets. After reading and responding to each poem, students point out how the writer of each poem used the form.

3. *Writing Class Collaboration Poems.*   Students write a class collaboration poem or poems in small groups before writing individual poems. Each student contributes a line for a class collaboration "I wish . . ." poem or a couplet for an "I used to . . ./But now . . ." poem.
   To write other types of poems, such as concrete poems, students can work together by suggesting ideas and words. They dictate the poem to the teacher, who records it on the chalkboard or on chart paper. Older students work in small groups to create poems. Through collaborative poems, students review the form and gather ideas to use later in writing their own poems. The teacher should compliment students when they play with words or use poetic devices. Students also need information about how to arrange the poem on the page, how to decide about capital letters and punctuation marks, and why it may be necessary to "unwrite" and delete some words.

4. *Writing Individual Poems Using the Writing Process.*   Students use the writing process to write poems. They write rough drafts, meet in writing groups to receive feedback, make revisions based on this feedback, and then edit their poems with a classmate or the teacher. Students then share their poems.

Teachers often simply explain several poetic forms and then allow students to choose a form and write a poem. This approach ignores the teaching component; it's back to the "assign and do" syndrome. Instead, students need to experiment with each poetic form. After these preliminary experiences, they can apply what they have learned and write poems that adhere to any of the forms they have learned during writing workshop or as part of literature focus

Teacher's Notebook
Guidelines for Writing Poetry

1. Explain what poetry is and what makes a good poem. Too often students assume that all poems must rhyme, are written on topics such as love and flowers, must be punctuated in a particular way, or have other restrictions.

2. Set out books of poetry for students to read in a special section of the classroom library. Students learn about poetry through reading, and some poems can serve as models for the poems students write.

3. Teach students 5 to 10 formulas to use when they write poems so that they have a range of formulas from which to choose. At the same time, it is important that students know that they can break the formulas in order to express themselves more effectively.

4. Teach students about comparison, alliteration, onomatopoeia, and repetition, and encourage them to use poetic devices other than rhyme as they write.

5. Encourage students to play with words, invent new words, and create word pictures as they write poems.

6. Teach students strategies to use as they write poems:

   - Adapting poetic formulas to meet their needs
   - Brainstorming lists of words and phrases
   - Reading drafts aloud to hear how they sound
   - Using wordplay and poetic devices
   - Unwriting, or deleting unnecessary words
   - Choosing how to arrange words on the page
   - Choosing how to capitalize words and punctuate the poem

7. Have students use the writing process to craft poems, and have them save their rough drafts so that they can document their use of the writing process.

8. Invite students to write poems during writing workshop, and provide time for them to share the poems they have written with classmates.

9. Encourage students to write poetry as part of literature focus units and social studies and science theme cycles. Students can write found poems using excerpts from books, write poems about characters in stories, and write poems about topics related to themes.

10. Create a class anthology of students' poems, and duplicate copies of the anthology for each student. Students can operate as a publishing company with writers, editors, artists, computer experts, a business manager, and other roles.

11. Plan and teach units about Jack Prelutsky and other poets who write for children. Set out books of poetry written by the poet being studied, present biographical information about the poet, and encourage students to experiment with the techniques this poet uses.

units and theme studies. Class collaborations are crucial because they are a practice run for children who are not sure what to do. The 5 minutes it takes to write a class collaboration poem can be the difference between success and failure for would-be poets.

Teachers teach many other poetry minilessons in addition to lessons on the poetic forms. They teach minilessons on a concept of poetry, on wordplay, and on how to read poems. A list of topics for minilessons related to reading and writing poetry is presented on page 447.

In Writing Workshop.   After students learn about various poetic forms, they often choose to write poems during writing workshop. They write poems about favorite topics or to express their feeling. They also experiment with forms that have been introduced during recent minilessons. Students who especially like to write poems publish collections of their poems during writing workshop and share them with their classmates. This sharing often stimulates other students to write poetry.

Teachers also plan poetry workshops that incorporate both reading workshop and writing workshop components. Students read and respond to poems during the reading workshop component, and then they write poems during the writing workshop component. One possible schedule for a 2-hour poetry workshop is:

15 minutes	The teacher leads a whole class meeting to:
	• give a book talk on a new poetry book
	• talk about a poet
	• read several favorite poems using choral reading
	• talk about a "difficult" or "confusing" poem
30 minutes	Students read poems independently.
15 minutes	Students share poems with classmates.
15 minutes	The teacher teaches a poetry minilesson.
30 minutes	Students write poems using the writing process.
15 minutes	Students share poems they have written.

In Literature Focus Units.   Students often write poems as part of literature focus units. Sometimes they write poems together as a class during the exploring stage, and at other times they write poems individually or in small groups as projects during the extending stage. To explore the language of a book, students might write found poetry using a paragraph from a favorite book. Or students might write acrostic poems about a book title or a character's name. This acrostic poem about *Jumanji* (Van Allsburg, 1981) was written by a fourth grader:

> *Jungle adventure game and*
> *fUn for a while.*
> *Monkeys ransacking kitchens*
> *And boa constrictors slithering past.*
> *No way out until the game is done—*
> *Just reach the city of Jumanji,*
> *I don't want to play!*

MINI LESSON

Reading and Writing Poetry

	Procedures	Concepts	Strategies and Skills
Wordplay	Craft riddles Create word pictures Invent words Craft tongue twisters	Wordplay Word pictures Hink-pinks Sniglets Metaphors Similes Alliteration Tongue twisters Onomatopoeia Repetition Rhyme	Rhyme Compare Use alliteration Use onomatopoeia Use repetition

Reading Poetry	Read a poem
	   interpretively
	Do choral reading
	Share poems
	Respond to poems in
	   quickwrites
	Discuss poems
	Do a project
	Compile an anthology
		Poetry
		Rhymed verse
		Narrative poems
		Free verse
		Concrete poems
		Information about poets
		Arrangements for choral
		   reading
			Vary tempo
			Emphasize rhythm
			Vary pitch
			Stress juncture

Writing Poetry	Write formula poems
	Write "I wish . . ." poems
	Write color poems
	Write five-senses poems
	Write "If I were . . ."
	   poems
	Write "I used to . . ./But
	   now . . ." poems
	Write ". . . is" poems
	Write preposition poems
	Write free-form poems
	Design concrete poems
	Craft found poems
	Write haiku poems
	Write cinquain poems
	Write diamante poems
	Write limericks
	Write clerihews
	Write model poems
	Craft found poems
		Poetic forms	Use poetic forms
			Create sensory images
			Paint word pictures
			Unwrite
			Use model poems
			Write rhymes
			Punctuate poems
			Capitalize poems
			Arrange poems on the
			   page

447

During regularly scheduled sharing times, students share with their classmates the poems they write during writing workshop.

Sometimes poetry writing activities are planned, and at other times they happen spontaneously. During a unit on Patricia MacLachlan's *Sarah, Plain and Tall* (1985), a third-grade class was discussing the two kinds of dunes in the story and they wrote this free-form poem:

Dunes

Dunes of sand
on the beach.
Sarah walks on them
and watches the ocean.

Dunes of hay
beside the barn.
Papa makes them for Sarah
because she misses Maine.

As part of a unit on *Where the Wild Things Are* (Sendak, 1963), first graders made wild thing costumes out of large grocery paper bags and then wrote color poems about the wild things they created. This is one boy's poem:

My Wild Thing

Purple hair
it's like spaghetti.
Black eyes
they stare inside you.
Yellow teeth
they're sharp and long.

> *Green scales*
> *he's just like a fish.*
> *Red feet*
> *and he's got fifty toes.*
> *Orange face*
> *he's my wild thing.*

In these response-to-literature activities, students extend their interpretations, learn about literary language, and experiment with poetry.

In Theme Cycles.   Students also write poems as projects during theme cycles. A small group of third graders composed the following found poem after reading *Sarah Morton's Day: A Day in the Life of a Pilgrim Girl* (Waters, 1989):

This Is My Day*

> *Good day.*
> *I must get up and be about my chores.*
> *The fire is mine to tend.*
> *I lay the table.*
> *I muck the garden.*
> *I pound the spices.*
> *I draw vinegar to polish the brass.*
> *I practice my lessons.*
> *I feed the fire again.*
> *I milk the goats.*
> *I eat dinner.*
> *I say the verses I am learning.*
> *My father is pleased with my learning.*
> *I fetch the water for tomorrow.*
> *I bid my parents good night.*
> *I say my prayers.*
> *Fare thee well.*
> *God be with thee.*

To compose the found poem, the students collected their favorite words and sentences from the book and organized them sequentially to describe the pilgrim girl's day.

In a fourth-grade class, students often wrote cinquains as part of a theme cycle on westward movement. One student wrote this cinquain about the transcontinental railroad:

> *Railroads*
> *One crazy guy's*
> *Transcontinental dream . . .*
> *With a golden spike it came true.*
> *Iron horse*

Other students wrote about California's gold rush. One student wrote:

> *Gold rush*
> *Forty-niners*
> *were sure to strike it rich.*
> *Homesickness, pork and beans, so tired.*
> *Panning*

---

*Tompkins & McGee, 1993, pp. 200–201.

And another wrote about the Donner party's fateful journey to California in 1846–1847. The Donner brothers led a group of 82 pioneers west, but the group became snowbound in the Sierra Nevada mountains and were forced to spend the winter there. Only 47 people survived:

Donner
Treacherous trip
Trapped in the Sierras
Eating shoe leather and tree bark
Party

A fifth-grade teacher adapted the "I used to . . ./But now . . ." formula for a writing activity at the end of a theme cycle on the American Revolution. Her students wrote this class collaboration "I used to think . . ./But now I know . . ." poem using the information they had learned during the theme:

On the American Revolution

I USED TO THINK that Florida was one of the thirteen colonies,
BUT NOW I KNOW it belonged to Spain.
I USED TO THINK the War for Independence was one big battle,
BUT NOW I KNOW it was made up of many battles.
I USED TO THINK that Americans and British fought the same way,
BUT NOW I KNOW they had different military styles.
I USED TO THINK when the War for Independence ended, our troubles were over,
BUT NOW I KNOW we still had trouble with Britain.
I USED TO THINK that the Constitution was our first set of rules,
BUT NOW I KNOW that the Articles of Confederation were.
I USED TO THINK that the United States was founded all at once,
BUT NOW I KNOW it grew little by little.
I USED TO THINK that war was exciting and glamorous,
BUT NOW I KNOW that it was not that way at all.

Adapting to Meet the Needs of Every Student.   Poetry should be an important part of reading and writing, and teachers must find ways to involve all students in poetry activities. Poetry that has been written for children is available today that will evoke strong feelings and powerful images in students, and poetry writing is a valuable way for students to play with language and express themselves. As teachers plan poetry workshops and connect reading and writing poetry activities to literature focus units and theme cycles, they must find ways to adapt the activities to meet the needs of every student. A list of suggestions for adapting poetry activities to meet the needs of all students is presented on page 450.

Assessing Poems That Students Write

As teachers read, respond to, and assess the poems that students write, they need to recognize the nuggets of promise in the poems and support and build on them, instead of noticing children's lack of adult conventions (Tway, 1980). Donald Graves (1992) recommends that teachers focus on the passion and wonder in students' writing and on students' unique ability to make the common seem uncommon. Teachers can also notice the specific details, strong

Adapting . . .
Reading and Writing Poetry
To Meet the Needs of Every Student

1. Working in Groups

Have students read and write poems in small groups so that less capable readers and writers have classmates with whom to work. Students can use choral reading techniques and write collaborative poems.

2. Using Choral Reading

Use choral reading to share poems with students. As students read in groups, more capable readers support less capable readers.

3. Playing With Poems

Encourage students to play or experiment with poems as they are read aloud. Students clap the rhythm or add sound effects to poems as they are read aloud. They create a refrain for a poem that does not have one, using a favorite line, the title, or a line they invent.

4. Using Songs

Songs are poems, and teacher can use songs that students are familiar with for poetry reading activities. Songs can be transcribed into stanzas and then read or sung.

5. Using Easy-to-Read Poems

Many poems are short and easy to read. Teachers who work with emergent readers and less fluent readers can collect these poems and write them on charts. Two collections of easy-to-read poems that are available as paperback books are Lee Bennett Hopkins's *Surprises* (1984) and *More Surprises* (1987). These readers can also read some collections of riddles and jokes. The lines are short and easily remembered, and the structure is predictable.

images, wordplay, comparisons, onomatopoeia, alliteration, and repetitions of words and lines that students incorporate in their poems.

The poetic formulas discussed in this chapter provide options for students as they experiment with ways to express their thoughts. Although children experiment with a variety of forms during the elementary grades, it is not necessary to test their knowledge of particular forms. Knowing that haiku is a Japanese poetic form composed of 17 syllables arranged in three lines will not make a child a poet. Descriptions of the forms should instead be posted in the classroom or added to writing notebooks for students to refer to as they write.

Assessing the quality of students' poems is especially difficult, because poems are creative combinations of wordplay, poetic forms, and poetic devices.

Instead of trying to give a grade for quality, teachers can assess students on other criteria:

Has the student experimented with the poetic form presented in a mini-lesson?

Has the student used the process approach in writing, revising, and editing the poem?

Has the student used wordplay or another poetic device in the poem?

Teachers also ask students to assess their own progress in writing poems. They choose their best efforts and poems that show promise. They can explain which writing strategies they used in particular poems and which poetic forms they used.

Students keep copies of their poems in their writing folders or poetry booklets so that they can review and assess their own work. They may also place copies of some poems in their language arts portfolios. If a grade for quality is absolutely necessary, students should choose several of the poems in their writing folders for the teacher to evaluate.

Review

During the elementary grades, students read and write poetry as part of literature focus units, poetry workshop, and theme cycles. Wordplay provides an excellent introduction to poetry as students laugh with language, create word pictures, experiment with rhyme, and experiment with poetic devices. Five types of poems that elementary students can learn to write successfully are formula, free-form, syllable- and word-count, rhymed, and model poems. Teachers teach minilessons about the procedures, concepts, and strategies and skills related to reading and writing poetry.

Extensions

1. Invite a small group of students to study a favorite poet. Students read the poet's work and learn about his or her life. They may also want to arrange a conference telephone call or write letters to the poet. (*Note:* You can arrange for a conference call by contacting the poet's publisher and renting a special telephone from the telephone company.)
2. Plan and teach a poetry workshop for 2 weeks. During the workshop involve students with reading and writing poetry activities, and teach minilessons on topics from the list on page 447.
3. Compile a collection of poems related to literature focus units or theme cycles that are appropriate for the grade level you teach or plan to teach.
4. Collect a group of poems for choral reading and teach a group of students to do choral reading using the four arrangements listed on page 427.
5. Plan and teach a unit on wordplay to a group of elementary students.
6. Prepare a set of charts listing the formulas for poetic forms to use in teaching students to write poetry.
7. Teach a small group of students to write several types of poems, and have students compile their poems in a class anthology or in hardbound books.

References

Apseloff, M. (1979). Old wine in new bottles: Adult poetry for children. *Children's Literature in Education, 10,* 194–202.

Chapman, D. L. (1985). Poet to poet: An author responds to child writers. *Language Arts, 62,* 235–242.

Copeland, J. S. (1993). *Speaking of poets: Interviews with poets who write for children and young adults.* Urbana, IL: National Council of Teachers of English.

Fisher, C. J., & Natarella, M. A. (1982). Young children's preferences in poetry: A national survey of first, second, and third graders. *Research in the Teaching of English, 16,* 339–354.

Geller, L. G. (1981). Riddling: A playful way to explore language. *Language Arts, 58,* 669–674.

Geller, L. G. (1985). *Word play and language learning for children.* Urbana, IL: National Council of Teachers of English.

Graves, D. H. (1992). *Explore poetry.* Portsmouth, NH: Heinemann.

Hopkins, L. B. (1987). *Pass the poetry, please!* New York: Harper & Row.

Koch, K. (1970). *Wishes, lies, and dreams.* New York: Vintage.

Koch, K. (1973). *Rose, where did you get that red?* New York: Vintage.

Kutiper, K. (1985). *A survey of the poetry preferences of seventh, eighth, and ninth graders.* Unpublished doctoral dissertation, University of Houston.

Kutiper, K., & Wilson, P. (1993). Updating poetry preferences: A look at the poetry children really like. *The Reading Teacher, 47,* 28–35.

Larrick, N. (1991). *Let's do a poem! Introducing poetry to children.* New York: Delacorte.

Opie, I., & Opie, P. (1959). *The lore and language of school children.* Oxford: Oxford University Press.

Parker, M. K. (1981). A visit from a poet. *Language Arts, 58,* 448–451.

Stewig, J. W. (1981). Choral speaking: Who has the time? Why take the time? *Childhood Education, 57,* 25–29.

Terry, A. (1974). *Children's poetry preferences: A national survey of upper elementary grades* (NCTE Research Report No. 16). Urbana, IL: National Council of Teachers of English.

Tiedt, I. (1970). Exploring poetry patterns. *Elementary English, 45,* 1082–1084.

Tompkins, G. E., & McGee, L. M. (1993). *Teaching reading with literature: From case studies to action plans.* New York: Merrill/Macmillan.

Tway, E. (1980). How to find and encourage the nuggets in children's writing. *Language Arts, 57,* 299–304.

Valentine, S. L. (1986). Beginning poets dig for poems. *Language Arts, 63,* 246–252.

Children's Book References

Atwood, S. (1971). *Haiku: The mood of the Earth.* New York: Scribner.

Atwood, S. (1973). *My own rhythm: An approach to haiku.* New York: Scribner.

Bayer, J. (1984). *A my name is Alice.* New York: Dial.

Baylor, B., & Parnall, P. (1981). *Desert voices.* New York: Scribner.

Behn, H. (1964). *Cricket songs.* New York: Harcourt Brace Jovanovich.

Behn, H. (1971). *More cricket songs.* New York: Harcourt Brace Jovanovich.

Bernstein, J. E. (1979). *Fiddle with a riddle: Write your own riddles.* New York: Dutton.

Brewton, J. E., & Blackburn, L. A. (1978). *They've discovered a head in the box of bread and other laughable limericks.* New York: Crowell.

Brown, M. (1983). *What do you call a dumb bunny? And other rabbit riddles, games, jokes, and cartoons.* Boston: Little, Brown.

de Gasztold, C. B. (1992). *Prayers from the ark.* New York: Viking.

Fleischman, P. (1985). *I am phoenix: Poems for two voices.* New York: Harper & Row.

Fleischman, P. (1988). *Joyful noise: Poems for two voices.* New York: Harper & Row.

Froman, R. (1974). *Seeing things: A book of poems.* New York: Crowell.

Goldstein, B. S. (Ed.). (1992). *Inner chimes: Poems on poetry.* Honesdale, PA: Wordsong.

Hopkins, L. B. (1983). *A song in stone: City poems.* New York: Crowell.

Hopkins, L. B. (1984). *Surprises.* New York: Harper & Row.

Hopkins, L. B. (1987). *Dinosaurs*. San Diego: Harcourt Brace Jovanovich.

Hopkins, L. B. (1987). *More surprises*. New York: Harper & Row.

Kellogg, S. (1987). *Aster Aardvark's alphabet adventures*. New York: Morrow.

Kennedy, X. J., & Kennedy, D. M. (1982). *Knock at a star: A child's introduction to poetry*. Boston: Little, Brown.

Langstaff, J. (1974). *Oh, a-hunting we will go*. New York: Atheneum.

Lewis, R. (Ed.). (1965). *In a spring garden*. New York: Dial.

Lewis, R. (1968). *Of this world: A poet's life in poetry*. New York: Dial.

Lewis, R. (1970). *The way of silence: The prose and poetry of Basho*. New York: Dial.

Livingston, M. C. (Ed.). (1982). *How pleasant to know Mr. Lear!* New York: Holiday House.

Lobel, A. (1983). *Pigericks: A book of pig limericks*. New York: Harper & Row.

Longfellow, H. W. (1990). *Paul Revere's ride*. New York: Dutton.

Lowry, L. (1979). *Anastasia Krupnik*. Boston: Houghton Mifflin.

Lowry, L. (1989). *Number the stars*. Boston: Houghton Mifflin.

MacLachlan, P. (1985). *Sarah, plain and tall*. New York: Harper & Row.

Merriam, E. (1966). *It doesn't always have to rhyme*. New York: Atheneum.

Milne, A. A. (1956). *The house at Pooh Corner*. New York: Dutton.

O'Neill, M. (1961). *Hailstones and halibut bones: Adventures in color*. Garden City, NJ: Doubleday.

Pilon, B. (1972). *Concrete is not always hard*. Middletown, CT: Xerox Educational Publications.

Prelutsky, J. (Sel.). (1983). *The Random House book of poetry for children*. New York: Random House.

Prelutsky, J. (1988). *Tyrannosaurus was a beast*. New York: Greenwillow.

Prelutsky, J. (1984). *The new kid on the block*. New York: Greenwillow.

Schwartz, A. (1972). *A twister of twists, a tangler of tongues*. New York: Harper & Row.

Sendak, M. (1963). *Where the wild things are*. New York: Harper & Row.

Seuss, Dr. (1979). *Oh say can you say?* New York: Beginner Books.

Sherman, I. (1980). *Walking talking words*. New York: Harcourt Brace Jovanovich.

Siebert, D. (1988). *Mojave*. New York: Harper & Row.

Silverstein, S. (1974). *Where the sidewalk ends*. New York: Harper & Row.

Silverstein, S. (1981). *A light in the attic*. New York: Harper & Row.

Spier, P. (1971). *Gobble growl grunt*. New York: Doubleday.

Spier, P. (1972). *Crash! Bang! Boom!* New York: Doubleday.

Sterne, N. (1979). *Tyrannosaurus wrecks: A book of dinosaur riddles*. New York: Crowell.

Terban, M. (1982). *Eight ate: A feast of homonym riddles*. New York: Clarion.

Van Allsburg, C. (1987). *The Z was zapped*. Boston: Houghton Mifflin.

Viorst, J. (1981). *If I were in charge of the world and other worries*. New York: Atheneum.

Waber, B. (1972). *Ira sleeps over*. Boston: Houghton Mifflin.

Waters, K. (1989). *Sarah Morton's day: A day in the life of a pilgrim girl*. New York: Scholastic.

PRO-File
Assessing Handwriting as Part of the Writing Process

> **"** I'd like to say that my second graders' handwriting doesn't concern me. I'd like to, but I can't. My students print well, but I have to plan time to review skills and constantly stress the importance of legible handwriting. **"**
>
> *Gordon Martindale*
> *Second-Grade Teacher*
> *Columbia Elementary School*

PROCEDURE

I teach handwriting as part of the writing process, and I tell my students that they must be able to write both quickly and legibly so that others can read it. Before we write the final copy of a writing project, I take 10 to 15 minutes for a handwriting minilesson on a skill that my students need, such as forming letters, spacing between letters and words, or touching the baseline consistently. This week my students are writing reports on the planets in the solar system that they will copy into hard-bound books. Because grades often speak louder than I do, I use these published books to critique students' handwriting and assign handwriting grades.

The steps I use in teaching a minilesson are:

1. I introduce the handwriting skill, explain two or three key points, and demonstrate how to perform it.

2. I show examples of the skill done correctly and other examples done incorrectly. I try to point out how the incorrect examples made the handwriting less fluent to write or less legible to read.

3. I ask students to practice the skill on their own paper, on the chalkboard, or on slates, and I supervise while they practice the skill several times.

4. I review the skill and ask students to identify the key points and to tell me how they will use the skill as they write.

Sometimes I teach a minilesson for the whole class and sometimes with a small group. It depends on which skill I am teaching and which students need the skill.

Afterwards, I remind the students about the importance of legible and fluent handwriting, and they begin writing the final copies of their reports. I circulate among them, observing as they apply the handwriting skill that I've reviewed. I offer positive comments to students and provide additional instruction to students who need it. Through this observation, I also note other handwriting skills that individual students need help with or skills for future handwriting minilessons. I use those little yellow notes with the sticky back to take notes about particular students' handwriting. Later, I add these notes to students' language arts portfolios so that I can refer to them during conferences that I hold with each student.

After their books are published and shared with classmates and with their sixth-grade reading buddies, I ask them to review their handwriting according to the elements of legibility that I've taught. This is a good time for thinking about handwriting because my students can see that the quality of their handwriting affects how well the sixth-grade readers understand and enjoy their books. Legible handwriting becomes part of the overall goal of successful communication with an audience, not just an exercise.

Then I hold brief conferences with each student to talk about his or her handwriting. Through our discussion, we make a list of two or three good points and two or three things they need to work on which we add to the student's writing folder. We also decide on a handwriting grade which I record in my grade book.

ASSESSMENT

Handwriting isn't the most exciting part of the language arts curriculum in second grade. It's just one of those things that has to be done, and I teach handwriting as a means to an end—as a tool for writers. In order to adequately assess my students' progress, I like to collect three or four differ-

ent kinds of assessment information, including:

1. Handwriting samples
2. Anecdotal notes
3. Conference notes
4. Grades

I think that the samples are the most important kind of information because they demonstrate whether or not legible handwriting matters to my students.

ADAPTATIONS

I also teach minilessons on spelling, capitalization, punctuation, and sentence structure during the editing stage of the writing process. Here's a list of some of the topics we cover during the year:

Spelling

Sounding out consonant and vowel digraphs

Using spelling patterns

Adding inflectional endings

Writing abbreviations

Differentiating between homophones

Using a dictionary

Thinking out the spelling of a word

Capitalization

Capitalizing proper nouns

Capitalizing titles

Punctuation

Marking the end of a sentence

Using quotation marks

Using commas

Punctuating abbreviations

Using apostrophes

Sentence Structure

Writing simple and compound sentences

Combining sentences

Slotting sentences

Expanding sentences

REFLECTIONS

In this school we don't introduce cursive handwriting until third grade, and I support this decision. Because my students don't have to learn a whole new handwriting form, I'm able to stress fluency, and during second grade my students finally come to see handwriting as a tool for writers. This happens as they become more fluent writers and as they write real books that their classmates are eager to read.

I've found that this approach works, and it works better than using a handwriting workbook or dittos. This way, students' handwriting on their book projects and other writing assignments is easier to read because I teach at that teachable moment. I'm able to individualize instruction and show my students why they need to learn these skills. My students are learning to analyze their handwriting and identify their own strengths and weaknesses even though they are only 8 years old! Teaching handwriting through the writing process makes a difference in my classroom.

12

Language Tools: Spelling, Handwriting, and Grammar

INSIGHT

Conventional spelling, neat handwriting, and standard English grammar have been considered the hallmarks of an educated person. These components have been important parts of language arts instruction since the beginning of public education. Today, however, more and more people are viewing spelling, handwriting, and grammar as tools that readers and writers use. They are the means to the end, rather than the goal of education. Now many teachers focus far more attention on the writing process and teaching students how to develop and refine their meaning, even though they still expect students to use conventional spelling and legible handwriting when they write. An issue for you to think about is:

What is the role of spelling, handwriting, and grammar instruction during the elementary grades?

S pelling, handwriting, and grammar are tools for communicating through language. Spelling and handwriting are tools that writers use in order to communicate conventionally and legibly with readers. Students use their knowledge of grammar—how English is structured into sentences—in order to understand what they read and to write so that readers will understand their meaning. This chapter is divided into three parts, and each part focuses on one of the language arts tools.

SPELLING

arctic	consciousness	embarrass	grammar	ingenious
liquefy	marshmallow	occasion	professor	souvenir

Which of these words are spelled correctly? If you are like most people, you may be confused about the spelling of one or more of these words. All words are spelled correctly, but it's easy to question the spelling of one or two words, especially if you expect pronunciation to determine spelling. English is not a purely phonetic language, and many words, such as *souvenir,* reflect their origins in other languages.

Spelling is a tool for writers that allows them to communicate convention-ally with readers. As Graves (1983) explains:

> Spelling is for writing. Children may achieve high scores on phonic inventories, or weekly spelling tests. But the ultimate test is what the child does under "game conditions," within the process of moving toward meaning. (pp. 193–194)

Rather than equating spelling instruction with weekly spelling tests, students need to learn to spell words conventionally so that they can communicate effectively through writing. English spelling is complex, and attempts to teach spelling through weekly lists have not been very successful. Many students spell the words correctly on the weekly test, but they continue to misspell them in their writing.

CHILDREN'S SPELLING DEVELOPMENT

The alphabetic principle suggests a one-to-one correspondence between phonemes and graphemes, but English spelling is phonetic only about half the time. Other spellings reflect the language from which a word was borrowed. For example, like most words beginning with *al-, alcohol* is an Arabic word, and *energy* is a Greek word. Other words are spelled to reflect semantic relationships, not phonological ones. The spelling of *national* and *nation* and of *grade* and *gradual* indicates related meanings even though there are vowel or consonant changes in the pronunciations of the word pairs. If English were a purely phonetic language, it would be easier to spell, but, at the same time, it would lose much of its sophistication.

Elementary students learn to spell the phonetic elements of English as they learn about phoneme-grapheme correspondences, and they continue to refine their spelling knowledge through reading and writing. Children's spelling that reflects their growing awareness of English orthography is known as *invented spelling,* and during the elementary grades children move from using scribbles and single letters to represent words through a series of stages until they adopt conventional spellings.

Invented Spelling

As young children begin to write, they create unique spellings, called invented spellings, based on their knowledge of English orthography. Other names for *invented spelling* include *temporary spelling* and *kid spelling*. Charles Read (1971, 1975, 1986), one of the first researchers to study preschoolers' efforts to spell words, discovered that they used their knowledge of phonology to invent spellings. These children used letter names to spell words such as U (*you*) and R (*are*), and they used consonant sounds rather consistently: GRL, (*girl*), TIGR (*tiger*), and NIT (*night*). The preschoolers used several unusual but phonetically based spelling patterns to represent affricates. They spelled *tr* with *chr* (e.g., CHRIBLES for *troubles*) and *dr* with *jr* (e.g., JRAGIN for *dragon*), and they substituted *d* for *t* (e.g., PREDE for *pretty*). Words with long vowels were spelled using letter names: MI (*my*), LADE (*lady*), and FEL (*feel*). The children used several ingenious strategies to spell words with short vowels. The 3-, 4-, and 5-year-olds rather consistently selected letters to represent short vowels on the basis of place of articulation in the mouth. Short *i* was represented with *e* as in FES (*fish*), short *e* with *a* as in LAFFT (*left*), and short *o* with *i* as in CLIK (*clock*). These spellings may seem odd to adults, but they are based on phonetic relationships. The children often omitted nasals within words (e.g., ED for *end*) and substituted -*eg* or -*ig* for -*ing* (e.g., CUMIG for *coming* and GOWEG for *going*). Also, they often ignored the vowel in unaccented syllables, as in AFTR (*after*) and MUTHR (*mother*).

These children developed strategies for their spellings based on their knowledge of the phonological system and of letter names, their judgments of phonetic similarities and differences, and their ability to abstract phonetic information from letter names. Read suggested that from among the many phonetic properties in the phonological system, children abstract away certain phonetic details and preserve others in their invented spellings.

Based on Read's seminal work, other researchers began to systematically study the development of children's spelling abilities. Henderson and his colleagues (Beers & Henderson, 1977; Gentry, 1978, 1981; Templeton, 1979; Zutell, 1979) have studied the manner in which children proceed developmentally from invented spelling to conventional spelling.

Based on observations of children's spellings, researchers have identified five stages that children move through on their way to becoming conventional spellers, and at each stage they use different types of strategies. The stages are precommunicative spelling, semiphonetic spelling, phonetic spelling, transitional spelling, and conventional spelling (Gentry, 1978, 1981, 1982a, 1982b, 1987; Gentry & Gillet, 1993). The characteristics of each of the five stages of invented spelling are summarized in Figure 12–1.

1. Precommunicative Spelling. In this stage children string scribbles, letters, and letterlike forms together, but they do not associate the marks they make with any specific phonemes. Precommunicative spelling represents a natural, early expression of the alphabet and other concepts about writing. Children may write from left to right, right to left, top to bottom, or randomly across the page. Some precommunicative spellers have a large repertoire of

Figure 12–1   Characteristics of the Stages of Invented Spelling

Stage 1: Precommunicative Spelling

Child uses scribbles, letterlike forms, letters, and sometimes numbers to represent a message.

Child may write from left to right, right to left, top to bottom, or randomly on the page.

Child shows no understanding of phoneme-grapheme correspondences.

Child may repeat a few letters again and again or use most of the letters of the alphabet.

Child frequently mixes upper- and lowercase letters but shows a preference for uppercase letters.

Stage 2: Semiphonetic Spelling

Child becomes aware of the alphabetic principle that letters are used to represent sounds.

Child uses abbreviated one-, two-, or three-letter spelling to represent an entire word.

Child uses letter-name strategy to spell words.

Stage 3: Phonetic Spelling

Child represents all essential sound features of a word in spelling.

Child develops particular spellings for long and short vowels, plural and past-tense markers, and other aspects of spelling.

Child chooses letters on the basis of sound without regard for English letter sequences or other conventions.

Stage 4: Transitional Spelling

Child adheres to basic conventions of English orthography.

Child begins to use morphological and visual information in addition to phonetic information.

Child may include all appropriate letters in a word but reverse some of them.

Child uses alternate spellings for the same sound in different words, but only partially understands the conditions governing their use.

Child uses a high percentage of correctly spelled words.

Stage 5: Conventional Spelling

Child applies the basic rules of the English orthographic system.

Child extends knowledge of word structure including the spelling of affixes, contractions, compound words, and homonyms.

Child demonstrates growing accuracy in using silent consonants and doubling consonants before adding suffixes.

Child recognizes when a word doesn't "look right" and can consider alternate spellings for the same sound.

Child learns irregular spelling patterns.

Child learns consonant and vowel alternations and other morphological structures.

Child knows how to spell a large number of words conventionally.

Adapted from Gentry, 1982a, 1982b; Gentry & Gillet, 1993.

letter forms to use in writing, and others repeat a small number of letters over and over. Children use both upper- and lowercase letters, but they show a distinct preference for uppercase letters. At this stage children have not discovered how spelling works or that letters represent sounds in words. This stage is typical of preschoolers, ages 3 to 5.

2. Semiphonetic Spelling. At this stage children begin to represent phonemes in words with letters, indicating that they have a rudimentary understanding of the alphabetic principle—that a link exists between letters and sounds. Spellings are quite abbreviated, and children use only one, two, or three letters to represent an entire word. Examples of stage 2 spelling are DA (*day*), KLZ (*closed*), and SM (*swimming*). As these examples illustrate, semiphonetic spellers use a letter-name strategy to determine which letters to use to spell a word, and their spellings represent some sound features of words while ignoring other equally important features. Spellers at this stage include 5- and 6-year-old children.

3. Phonetic Spelling. Children's understanding of the alphabetic principle is further refined in this stage. They continue to use letter names to represent sounds, but they also use consonant and vowel sounds at this stage. Examples of stage 3 spelling are LIV (*live*), DRAS (*dress*), and PEKT (*peeked*). As these examples show, children choose letters on the basis of sound alone, without considering acceptable English letter sequences (e.g., using -*t* rather than -*ed* as a past-tense marker in *peeked*). These spellings do not resemble English words, but they can be deciphered. The major achievement of this stage is that for the first time children represent *all* essential sound features in the words. Henderson (1980) explains that words are "bewilderingly homographic" at this stage because children spell on the basis of sound alone; for example, *bat, bet,* and *bait* might all be spelled BAT (Read, 1971). Phonetic spellers are typically about 6 years old.

4. Transitional Spelling. Transitional spellers come close to the conventional spellings of English words. They spell many words correctly but continue to misspell words with irregular spellings. Examples of stage 4 spelling are HUOSE (*house*), TRUBAL (*trouble*), EAGUL (*eagle*), and AFTERNEWN (*afternoon*). This stage is characterized by children's growing ability to represent the features of English orthography. They include a vowel in every syllable and demonstrate knowledge of vowel patterns even though they might make a faulty decision about which marker to use. For example, *toad* is often spelled TODE when children choose the wrong vowel marker, or TAOD when the two vowels are reversed. Also, transitional spellers use common letter patterns in their spelling, such as YOUNIGHTED for *united* and HIGHCKED for *hiked*. In this stage children use conventional alternatives for representing sounds, and although they continue to misspell words according to adult standards, transitional spelling resembles English orthography and can easily be read. As the examples show, children stop relying entirely on phonological information and begin to use visual clues and morphological information. Spellers in this stage are generally 7, 8, and 9 years old.

5. Conventional Spelling. As the name implies, children spell most words (90% or more) conventionally (as they are spelled in the dictionary) at this stage. They have mastered the basic principles of English orthography.

Children typically reach stage 5 by the age of 8 or 9. During the next 4 or 5 years, children learn to control homonyms (e.g., *road–rode*), contractions, affixes (e.g., *running*), and vowel and consonant alternations. They also learn to spell common irregularly spelled words (e.g., *school* and *they*). If the curriculum expects students to study lists of spelling words and take weekly spelling tests, they should not begin these tests until they reach the conventional stage (Gentry, 1981, 1982a; Gentry & Gillet, 1993).

In a short period of 4 or 5 years, children move from precommunicative spelling to conventional spelling. This learning happens through reading and writing experiences rather than through weekly spelling tests; when too much attention is placed on conventional or correct spelling before children have reached the fifth stage, their natural development is interrupted.

Too often, children are advised to "sound out" spellings for unfamiliar words or to limit the words they use in their writing to words they are sure they already know how to spell, but these practices thwart children's spelling development. Sounding out the spellings of words reinforces children's emphasis on the phoneme-grapheme correspondences rather than supporting students as they experiment with nonphonetic components of spelling as they move through the developmental sequence.

Older Students' Spelling Development

Researchers are continuing to study children's spelling development beyond age 8. Hitchcock (1989) studied children's spellings in grades 2 through 6 and classified the errors that these older, conventional stage spellers continue to make as semiphonetic, phonetic, and transitional stage spellings. Very few errors were categorized as semiphonetic, and these spellings seemed to serve as placeholders (Wilde, 1993), in which students used one, two, or three letters to stand for a longer word (e.g., using A to stand for *America*). More than half of their errors were classified as phonetic spellings, in which students spell words according to the way they sound or as they pronounce them (e.g., *wat* for *want, to* for *two, babes* for *babies*). That students continue to misspell words by spelling them phonetically is not surprising because teachers and parents often encourage students to sound out the spelling when children ask how to spell an unknown word. The other errors were categorized as transitional stage spellings. Students misapplied rules about vowels, plurals, verb tenses, possessives, contractions, compound words, and affixes (e.g., *ca'nt* for *can't, alot* for *a lot, acter* for *actor,* and *huose* for *house*). Words with reversed letters and extra letters were also included in this category.

Other research has focused on the relationship between reading and spelling (Anderson, 1985). Researchers have examined the spelling strategies of poor readers in fourth through sixth grade and found that these students were likely to use a sounding-out strategy. Good readers, on the other hand, used a variety of spelling strategies, including visual information, knowledge about root words and affixes, and analogy to known words (Barron, 1980; Marsh, Friedman, Desberg, & Welsh, 1980). Frith (1980) concluded that older students who are good readers and spellers make spelling errors characteristic of the transitional stage, whereas students who are poor readers and spellers make spelling errors characteristic of the semiphonetic and phonetic stages.

The press and concerned parent groups periodically raise concerns about invented spelling and the importance of weekly spelling tests. There seems to be a public misperception that today's children cannot spell. Researchers who are examining the types of errors students make have noted that the *number* of misspellings increases in grades 1 through 4, as students write longer compositions, but that the *percentage* of errors decreases. The percentage continues to decline in the upper grades, although some students continue to make errors (Taylor & Kidder, 1988). The Educational Testing Service (Applebee, Langer, & Mullis, 1987) reported on the frequency of spelling errors in formal writing assessments. Nine-year-olds averaged 92% correct spelling; 13-year-olds spelled 97% of words correctly; and 17-year-olds scored 98%. Stewig (1987) reported that the fourth graders in his study spelled 98%–99% of words correctly. These data suggest that by third or fourth grade most students are conventional spellers, making fewer than 10% errors.

Analyzing Children's Spelling Development

Teachers can analyze spelling errors in children's compositions by classifying the errors according to the five stages of spelling development. This analysis will provide information about the child's current level of spelling development and the kinds of errors the child makes. Knowing the stage of a student's spelling development suggests the appropriate type of instruction. Children who are not yet at the conventional stage of spelling development—that is, who do not spell at least 90% of words correctly and whose errors are not mostly at the transitional level—do not benefit from formal spelling instruction. Instead, early instruction should support students' spelling development. Minilessons that are appropriate to a student's stage of development, such as learning visual and morphological strategies for a transitional speller, are much more beneficial.

A composition written by Marc, a first grader, is presented in Figure 12–2.

Figure 12–2   A First Grader's Composition Using Invented Spelling

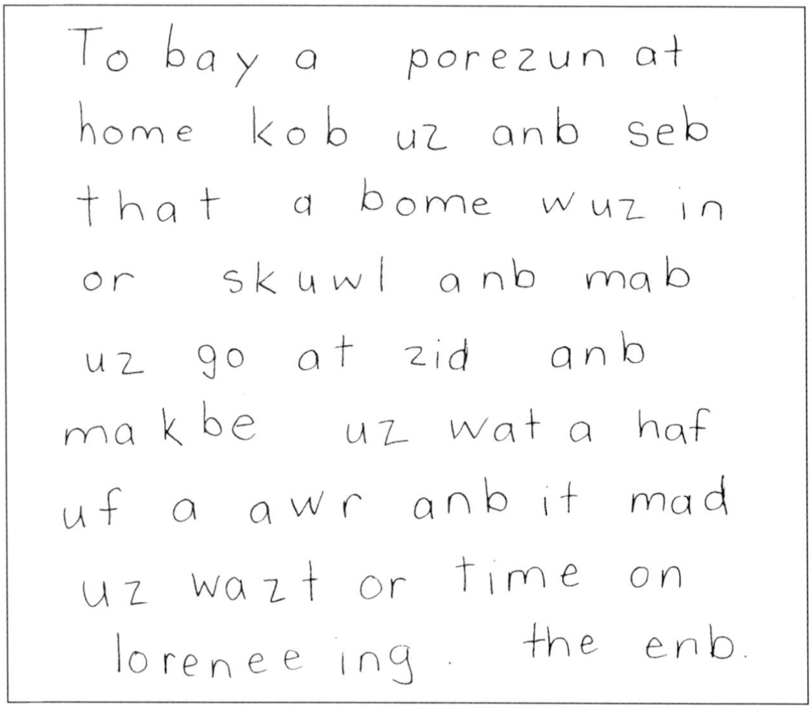

To bay a porezun at home kob uz anb seb that a bome wuz in or skuwl anb mab uz go at zid anb makbe uz wat a haf uf a awr anb it mad uz wazt or time on lorenee ing. the enb.

He reverses *b* and *s*, and these two reversals make his writing more difficult to decipher. Here is a translation of Marc's composition:

✏️ *Today a person at home called us and said that a bomb was in our school and made us go outside and made us wait a half of an hour and it made us waste our time on learning. The end.*

Marc was writing about a traumatic event, and it was appropriate for him to use invented spelling in his composition. Primary-grade students should write using invented spelling, and correct spelling is appropriate only if the composition will "go public." Prematurely differentiating between "kid" and "adult" spelling interferes with children's natural spelling development and makes them dependent on adults to supply the "adult" spelling.

Spelling can be categorized by a chart, such as that illustrated in Figure 12–3, to gauge students' stages of spelling development and to anticipate upcoming changes in their spelling strategies. Teachers write the stages of spelling development across the top of the chart and list each word in the student's composition under one of the categories, ignoring proper nouns, capitalization errors, and poorly formed or reversed letters.

Perhaps the most interesting thing about Marc's writing is that he spelled 56% of the words correctly. Only one word, *kod* (*called*), is categorized as semiphonetic, and it is classified this way because the spelling is extremely

Figure 12–3   An Analysis of Marc's Invented Spellings

Precommunicative	Semiphonetic	Phonetic	Transitional	Conventional
	kod	sed	poresun	today
		wus	bome	a
		or	skuwl	at
		mad	uf	home
		at sid	makde	us
		wat	loreneeing	and
		haf		that
		awr		a
		mad		in
		wast		and
		or		us
				go
				and
				us
				a
				a
				and
				it
				us
				time
				on
				the
				end
Total 0	1	11	6	23
Percent 0	2	27	15	56

abbreviated, with only the first and last sounds represented. The 12 words categorized as phonetic are words in which it appears that his spelling represents only the sounds heard; unpronounced letters, such as the final *e* in *made* and the *i* in *wait,* are not represented. Marc pronounces *our* as though it were a homophone for *or,* so *or* is a reasonable phonetic spelling. Homophone errors are phonological, because the child focuses on sound, not on meaning.

The words categorized as transitional exemplify a spelling strategy other than sound. In *bome* (*bomb*), for example, Marc applied the final *e* rule he recently learned, even though it isn't appropriate in this word. In time he will learn to spell the word with an unpronounced *b* and will learn that this *b* is needed because *bomb* is a newer, shortened form of *bombard,* in which the *b* in the middle of the word is pronounced. The *b* remains in *bomb* because of the etymology of the word. The word *makde* is especially interesting. Marc pronounced the word ''maked,'' and the *de* is a reversal of letters, a common characteristic of transitional spelling. Transitional spellers often spell *girl* as *gril* and *friend* as *freind.* Marc's use of *maked,* not *made,* for the past tense of *make* is a grammatical error and unimportant in determining the stage of spelling development. *Loreneeing* (*learning*) is categorized as transitional because Marc added long vowel markers (an *e* after *lor* and *ee* after *n*). Because the spelling is based on his pronunciation of *learning,* the long vowel markers and the conventional spelling of the suffix *-ing* signal a transitional spelling. Categorizing spelling errors in a child's composition and computing the percentage of errors in each category is a useful tool for diagnosing the level of spelling development and deciding whether or not to begin weekly spelling tests.

From the spelling in Marc's composition, he might be classified as a phonetic speller who is moving toward the transitional stage. Marc's paper in Figure 12–2 was written in January of his first-grade year, and he is making expected progress in spelling. During the next few months he will begin to notice that his spelling doesn't look right (e.g., *sed* for *said*), and he will note visual features of words. He will apply the vowel rules he is learning more effectively, particularly the final *e* (*mad* will become *made, sid* will become *side,* and *wast* will become *waste*).

Marc is not ready for weekly spelling tests, in which he would memorize correct spellings of words, because he has not yet internalized the visual and morphological spelling strategies of the transitional stage. Also, Marc will probably self-correct the two letter reversals through daily writing experiences, as long as he is not placed under great pressure to form the letters correctly.

TEACHING SPELLING IN THE ELEMENTARY GRADES

Spelling instruction is more than weekly spelling tests. It is involving students in genuine reading and writing opportunities and teaching minilessons about English orthography and spelling procedures and strategies as well as spelling tests.

Components of Spelling Instruction

Students learn about spelling through reading and writing and related activities. In this section we discuss eight components of spelling instruction.

Daily Writing Opportunities.   Providing opportunities for students to write every day is prerequisite to any spelling program. Spelling is a writer's tool, and it is best learned through the experience of writing. Students who write daily and invent spellings for unfamiliar words move naturally toward conventional spelling. When they write, children guess at spellings using their developing knowledge of sound-symbol correspondences and spelling patterns. Most of the informal writing that students do each day does not need to be graded, and spelling errors should not be marked. Learning to spell is a lot like learning to play the piano. These daily writing opportunities are the practice sessions, not the lesson with the teacher.

When students use the writing process to develop and polish their writings, emphasis on conventional spelling belongs in the editing stage. Through the process approach, children learn to recognize spelling for what it is—a courtesy to readers. As they write, revise, edit, and share their writing with genuine audiences, students understand that they need to spell conventionally so that their audience can read their compositions.

Daily Reading Opportunities.   Reading also plays an enormous role in learning to spell. During reading, students store the visual shapes of words. The ability to recall how words look helps students decide when a spelling they are writing is correct. When students decide that a word does not look right, they can rewrite the word several different ways until it does look right, ask the teacher or a classmate who knows the spelling, or check the spelling in a dictionary.

Word Walls.   One way to highlight students' attention to words in books they are reading or in social studies and science theme cycles is through the use of word walls. Students and the teacher choose words to write on word walls, large sheets of paper hanging in the classroom. Then students refer to these word walls for word study activities and when they are writing. Seeing the words posted on word walls, clusters, and other charts in the classroom and using them in their writing help students to learn to spell the words.

Teachers also hang word walls with high-frequency words. Researchers have identified the most commonly used words and recommend that elementary students learn to spell 100 to 500 of these words because of their usefulness. The 100 most frequently used words represent more than 50% of all the words children and adults write (Horn, 1926)! The Teacher's Notebook on page 469 lists the 100 most frequently used words. Some teachers type the alphabetized word list on small cards—personal word walls—that students keep at their desks.

Proofreading.   Proofreading is a special kind of reading that students use to locate misspelled words and other mechanical errors in their rough drafts. As students learn about the writing process, they are introduced to proofreading. In the editing stage, they receive more in-depth instruction about how to use proofreading to locate spelling errors and then correct these misspelled words. Through a series of minilessons, students can proofread sample student papers and mark misspelled words. Then, working in pairs, students can correct the misspelled words.

Proofreading should be introduced in the primary grades. Young children and their teachers proofread class collaboration and dictated stories together,

Teacher's Notebook

The 100 Most Frequently Used Words

a	for	mother	there
about	from	my	they
after	get	no	things
all	got	not	think
am	had	now	this
an	have	of	time
and	he	on	to
are	her	one	too
around	him	or	two
as	his	our	up
at	home	out	us
back	house	over	very
be	how	people	was
because	I	put	we
but	if	said	well
by	in	saw	went
came	into	school	were
can	is	see	what
could	it	she	when
day	just	so	who
did	know	some	will
didn't	like	that	with
do	little	the	would
don't	man	them	you
down	me	then	your

and students can be encouraged to read over their own compositions and make necessary corrections soon after they begin writing. This way students accept proofreading as a natural part of both spelling and writing. Proofreading activities are more valuable for teaching spelling than dictation activities, in which teachers dictate sentences for students to write and correctly capitalize and punctuate. Few people use dictation in their daily lives, but students use proofreading skills every time they polish a piece of writing.

Dictionary Procedure.   Students need to learn how to locate the spelling of unknown words in the dictionary. Of the approximately 450,000 entry words in an unabridged dictionary, students typically learn to spell 3,000 by the end of

469

eighth grade—leaving 447,000 words unaccounted for! Obviously, students must learn how to locate the spellings of some additional words. While it is relatively easy to find a "known" word in the dictionary, it is hard to locate an unfamiliar word, and students need to learn what to do when they do not know how to spell a word. One approach is to predict possible spellings for unknown words, then check the the most probable spellings in a dictionary. This procedure involves six steps:

1. Identify root words and affixes.
2. Consider related words (e.g., *medicine–medical*).
3. Determine the sounds in the word.
4. Generate a list of possible spellings.
5. Select the most probable alternatives.
6. Consult a dictionary to check the correct spelling.

The fourth step is undoubtedly the most difficult. Using knowledge of both phonology and morphology, students develop a list of possible spellings. Phoneme-grapheme relationships may rate primary consideration in generating spelling options for some words; root words and affixes or related words may be more important in determining how other words are spelled.

Spelling Options.   In English there are alternate spellings for many sounds because so many words have been borrowed from other languages and they retain their native spellings. There are many more options for vowel sounds than for consonants. Even so, there are four spelling options for /f/ (*f, ff, ph, gh*). Spelling options sometimes vary according to position in the word. For example, *ff* and *gh* are used to represent /f/ only at the end of a word, as in *cuff* and *laugh*. Common spelling options for phonemes are listed in Appendix D.

Teachers point out spelling options as they write words on word walls and when students ask about the spelling of a word. They can also use a series of minilessons to teach upper-grade students about these options. During each minilesson students can focus on one phoneme, such as /f/ or /ar/, and as a class or small group develop a list of the various ways the sound is spelled in English with examples of each spelling. A sixth-grade chart on long *o* is presented in Figure 12–4.

Strategies for Spelling Unfamiliar Words.   Students need to develop a repertoire of strategies in order to spell unfamiliar words. Some of these spelling strategies are:

- Invent spellings for words based on phonological, semantic, and historical knowledge of words.
- Proofread to locate and correct spelling errors.
- Locate words on word walls and other charts.
- Predict the spelling of a word by generating possible spellings and choose the best alternative.
- Apply affixes to root words.
- Spell unknown words by analogy to known words.
- Locate the spelling of unfamiliar words in a dictionary or other resource book.
- Write a string of letters as a placeholder to stand for an unfamiliar word in a rough draft.

Figure 12–4   *A Sixth-Grade Class Chart on Spelling Options: Ways to Spell Long* o

Spelling	Word	Location		
		Initial	**Medial**	**Final**
o	oh, obedient	x		
	go, no, so			x
o-e	home, pole		x	
ow	own	x		
	known		x	
	blow, elbow, yellow			x
oa	oaf, oak, oat	x		
	boat, groan		x	
ew	sew			x
ol	yolk, folk		x	
oe	toe			x
ough	though			x
eau	beau			x
ou	bouquet		x	

- Ask the teacher or a classmate how to spell a word.
- Have ownership of a word or know when the spelling of a word has been internalized.

The last three strategies are adapted from Wilde's (1993) study of children's spelling development.

Instead of the traditional "sound it out" advice when students ask how to spell an unfamiliar word, teachers should help them use a strategic approach. We suggest that teachers encourage students to "think it out." This advice reminds students that spelling involves more than phonological information and suggests a more strategic approach.

Teachers teach students about spelling procedures, concepts, and strategies and skills during minilessons. A list of topics for spelling minilessons is presented on page 473. Some of the topics are more appropriate for primary-grade students, and others are for older students.

A Spelling Conscience. The goal of spelling instruction is to help students develop what Hillerich (1977) calls a *spelling conscience*—a positive attitude toward spelling and a concern for using standard spelling. Two dimensions of a spelling conscience are understanding that standard spelling is a courtesy to readers and developing the ability to proofread to spot and correct misspellings.

Students in the middle and upper grades need to learn that it is unrealistic to expect readers to try to decipher numerous misspelled words. This dimension of a spelling conscience develops as students write frequently and for varied audiences. As students move from writing for self to writing to communicate

A teacher teaches a minilesson on spelling options for long a.

with others, they internalize this concept. Teachers help students recognize the purpose of conventional spelling by providing meaningful writing activities directed to a variety of genuine audiences.

Weekly Spelling Tests

Many teachers question the use of spelling tests to teach spelling since research on invented spelling suggests that spelling is best learned through reading and writing (Gentry & Gillet, 1993; Wilde, 1993). In addition, teachers complain that spelling word lists are unrelated to the words students are reading and writing, and the 30 minutes of valuable instructional time spent each day in completing spelling textbook activities is excessive. We recommend that weekly spelling tests, when they are used, be individualized so that children learn to spell the words they need for their writing.

In the individualized approach to spelling instruction, students choose the words they will study, and many of the words they choose are words they use in their writing projects. Students study five to eight specific words during the week using a specific study strategy. This approach places more responsibility on students for their own learning, and when students have responsibility, they tend to perform better.

The Master Word List.   Teachers develop a weekly word list of 25 to 50 words of varying levels of difficulty from which students select words to study. Words for the master list are drawn from words students needed for their writing projects during the previous week, high-frequency words, and words related to

M I N I L E S S O N S

Language Tools

	Procedures	Concepts	Strategies and Skills
Spelling	Invent spellings Locate words on a word wall Locate words in a dictionary Proofread Form contractions Form plurals Use other inflectional endings Use a thesaurus Study a spelling word Assess use of spelling strategies Analyze spelling errors	Alphabetic principle "Kid" or invented spelling Homophones Root words and affixes Spelling options High-frequency words Dictionary Thesaurus Spelling conscience Phoneme-grapheme correspondences Contractions Compound words Possessives	Use placeholders Sound it out Think it out Visualize words Use analogy Apply affixes Generate possible spellings Choose probable alternatives Proofread Apply capitalization rules
Handwriting	Grip a pencil Form letters Space between letters Size letters Make letters parallel Write manuscript letters Write cursive letters Make letters touch the baseline Keep letters uniform in size Make lines steady and of even thickness Assess handwriting problems	Legible Fluent Manuscript handwriting Cursive handwriting D'Nealian handwriting Uppercase letters Lowercase letters Public and private handwriting Elements of legibility	Determine purpose of handwriting Choose manuscript or cursive Apply elements of legibility Personalize handwriting
Grammar	Identify parts of speech Classify sentence types Slot sentences Manipulate sentences Combine sentences Make concept books Assess appropriateness of usage Assess use of strategies	Grammar Usage Register Parts of speech Simple sentences Compound sentences Complex sentences Declarative sentences Interrogative sentences Imperative sentences Exclamatory sentences	Use complete sentences Expand sentences Combine sentences Consider register Proofread to locate usage errors

473

literature focus units and theme cycles ongoing in the classroom. Words from spelling textbooks can also be added to the list, but they should never be the entire list. The master word list can be used for minilessons during the week. Students can look for phoneme-grapheme correspondences, add words to charts of spelling options, and note root words and affixes.

The Monday Pretest.   On Monday the teacher administers the pretest using the master list of words, and students try to spell as many of the words as they can. Students correct their own pretests, and from the words that they misspell, they each choose five to eight words to study. They make two copies of their study list. Students number their spelling words using the numbers on the master list to make it easier to take the final test on Friday. Students keep one copy of the list to study, and the teacher keeps the second copy.

Researchers have found that the pretest is a critical component in learning to spell. The pretest eliminates words that students already know how to spell so that they can direct their study toward words that they don't know yet. According to Horn (1947), the best way to improve students' spelling is for them to get immediate feedback by correcting their own pretests.

Word Study During the Week.   Students spend approximately 5 to 10 minutes studying the words on their study lists each day during the week. Instead of "busy-work" activities, such as using their spelling words in sentences or gluing yarn in the shape of the words, research shows that it is more effective for students to use this strategy for practicing spelling words:

1. Look at the word and say it to yourself.
2. Say each letter in the word to yourself.
3. Close your eyes and spell the word to yourself.
4. Write the word, and check that you spelled it correctly.
5. Write the word again, and check that you spelled it correctly.

This strategy focuses on the whole word rather than breaking it apart into sounds or syllables. During a minilesson at the beginning of the school year, teachers explain how to use the strategy, and then they post a copy of the strategy in the classroom. In addition to this word study strategy, sometimes students trade word lists on Wednesday or Thursday and give each other a practice test.

The Friday Test.   A final test is administered on Friday. The teacher reads the master list, and students write only those words they have practiced during the week. To make it easier to administer the test, students first list the numbers of the words they have practiced from their study lists on their test papers. Any words that students misspell should be included on their lists the following week.

This individualized approach is recommended instead of a textbook approach. Typically, textbooks are arranged in week-long units, with lists of 10 to 20 words and practice activities that often require at least 30 minutes per day to complete. Research indicates that only 60 to 75 minutes per week should be spent on spelling instruction, however, and greater periods of time do not result in increased spelling ability (Johnson, Langford, & Quorn, 1981). Moreover, many textbook activities focus on language arts skills that are not directly related to learning to spell (Graves, 1977).

The words in each unit are often grouped according to spelling patterns or phonetic generalizations even though researchers question this approach; Johnson, Langford, and Quorn (1981) found that "the effectiveness of teaching spelling via phonic generalizations is highly questionable" (p. 586). Students often memorize the rule or spelling pattern and score perfectly on the spelling test but later are unable to choose among spelling options in their writing. For example, after learning the *i-e* vowel rule and the *-igh* spelling pattern in isolation, students are often stumped about how to spell a word such as *light*. They have learned two spelling options for /ay/, *ie* and *-igh*, and *lite* is an option, one they often see in their environment. Instead of organizing words according to phonetic generalizations and spelling rules, we recommend that teachers teach minilessons and point out the rules as they occur when writing words on word walls.

Adapting to Meet the Needs of Every Student

Spelling and the other language tools can be adapted to meet the needs of all students, and the single most important adaptation teachers can make is to understand the relative importance of language tools in the language arts program. Communicative competence is the goal of language arts instruction, and language tools support communication, but they do not equal it. For spelling instruction, that means encouraging students to use invented spelling so that they can communicate with others before they reach conventional stage spelling. Students who are learning English as a second language or have special needs may take longer to move through the five stages of invented spelling, and their invented spelling will reflect their pronunciation of words and use of inflectional endings. For example, a child who says "I have two *cat*" or "Yesterday I *play* with my friend" usually spells words the same way. Suggestions for adapting the spelling program to meet the needs of all students are presented on page 476.

Assessing Students' Progress in Spelling

Grades on weekly spelling tests are the traditional measure of progress in spelling, and the individualized approach to spelling instruction provides this convenient way to assess students. This method of assessing student progress is somewhat deceptive, however, because the goal of spelling instruction is not simply to spell words correctly on weekly tests but to use the words, spelled conventionally, in writing. Samples of student writing should be collected periodically to determine whether words that were spelled correctly on tests are being spelled correctly in writing projects. If students are not applying in their writing what they have learned through the weekly spelling instruction, they may not have learned to spell the words after all.

When students perform poorly on spelling tests, consider whether faulty pronunciation or poor handwriting is to blame. Ask students to pronounce words they habitually misspell to see if their pronunciation or dialect differences may be contributing to spelling problems. Students need to recognize that pronunciation does not always predict spelling. For example, in some parts of the United States, people pronounce the words *pin* and *pen* as though they were spelled with the same vowel. Sometimes we pronounce *better* as though it were spelled *bedder* and *going* as though it were spelled *goin'*. Also,

Adapting . . .
Spelling Instruction
To Meet the Needs of Every Student

1. Encouraging Invented Spelling

Too often poor spellers don't want to write because there are so many words they don't know how to spell. Teachers should encourage students to use invented spelling, no matter how old they are, because it allows them to write independently. Their invented spellings provide valuable insights to what students know about English orthography and what kind of instruction they need.

2. Teaching High-Frequency Words

Poor spellers should learn to spell the 100 most frequently used words because of their usefulness. Knowing the 100 most frequently used words allows students to spell approximately half of all words they write correctly!

3. Teaching the Think-It-Out Strategy

Poor spellers typically rely on a sound-it-out strategy to spell words while better spellers understand that sound is only a rough guide to spelling. Teachers use minilessons to teach students how to think out and predict the spelling of unfamiliar words.

4. Reading and Writing Every Day

Students who are poor spellers often don't read or write very much, but they need to read and write every day in order to become better spellers.

5. Recognizing That Errors Are Part of Learning

Primary-grade students who use invented spelling and older students who are poor spellers do not benefit by having teachers circle spelling errors on their papers. Instead, the teacher and student should work together to identify and correct errors on writing projects that will be published. Too much emphasis on what students misspell does not help them to spell; it teaches them that they cannot spell.

ask students to spell orally the words they spell incorrectly in their writing to see whether handwriting difficulties are contributing to spelling problems. Sometimes a minilesson on how to connect two cursive letters (e.g., *br*) or a reminder about the importance of legible handwriting will solve the problem.

It is essential that teachers keep anecdotal information and samples of children's writing to monitor their overall progress in spelling. Teachers can examine error patterns and spelling strategies in these samples. Checking to see if students have spelled their spelling words correctly in writing samples provides one type of information, and examining writing samples for error patterns and spelling strategies provides additional information. Fewer misspellings do not necessarily indicate progress, because to learn to spell, students must experiment with spellings of unfamiliar words, which will result in errors from time to time. Students often misspell a word by misapplying a newly learned spelling pattern. The word *extension* is a good example. Middle-grade students spell the word *extenshun,* then change their spelling to *extention* after they learn the suffix -*tion.* Although they are still misspelling the word, they have moved from using sound-symbol correspondences to using a spelling pattern—from a less sophisticated to a more sophisticated spelling strategy.

Students' behavior as they proofread and edit their compositions also provides evidence of spelling development. They should become increasingly able to spot misspelled words in their compositions and locate the spelling of unknown words in a dictionary. It is easy for teachers to calculate the number of spelling errors students have identified in proofreading their compositions and to chart students' progress in learning to spot errors. Locating errors is the first step in proofreading; correcting the errors is the second step. It is fairly easy for students to correct the spelling of known words, but to correct unknown words, they must consider spelling options and predict possible spellings before they can locate the words in a dictionary. Teachers can also document students' growth in locating unfamiliar words in a dictionary by observing their behavior when they edit their compositions.

Teachers can collect writing samples to document children's spelling development. They can note primary-grade students' progression through the stages of invented spelling by analyzing writing samples against a checklist such as in Figure 12–3 to determine a general stage of development. Teachers can adapt the checklist for students in the middle and upper grades, and students can use this checklist to analyze their own spelling errors.

HANDWRITING

Like spelling, handwriting is a tool for writers. Graves (1983) explains further:

> Children win prizes for fine script, parents and teachers nod approval for a crisp, well-crafted page, a good impression is made on a job application blank . . . all important elements, but they pale next to the *substance* they carry. (p. 171)

It is important to distinguish between *writing* and *handwriting.* Writing is the substance of a composition; handwriting is the formation of alphabetic symbols on paper. Students need to develop a legible and fluent style of handwriting so that they will be able to fully participate in all written language activities.

The goal in handwriting instruction is to help students develop legible forms to communicate effectively through writing. The two most important criteria in determining quality in handwriting are *legibility* (the writing can be easily and quickly read) and *fluency* (the writing can be easily and quickly written). Even though a few students take great pleasure in developing flawless handwriting skills, most students feel that handwriting instruction is boring and unnecessary. It is imperative, therefore, to recognize the functional purpose of handwriting and convey the importance of developing legible handwriting to students. Writing for genuine audiences is the best way to convey the importance of legibility. A letter sent to a favorite author that is returned by the post office because the address is not decipherable or a child's published, hard-cover book that sits unread on the library shelf because the handwriting is illegible makes clear the importance of legibility. Illegible writing means a failure to communicate, a harsh lesson for a writer!

HANDWRITING FORMS

Two forms of handwriting are currently used in elementary schools: *manuscript,* or printing, and *cursive,* or connected writing, illustrated in Figure 12–5. Typically, students in the primary grades learn and use the manuscript form and switch to cursive handwriting in the middle grades, usually in second or third grade. In the middle and upper grades, students use both handwriting forms.

Manuscript Handwriting

Until the 1920s, students learned only cursive handwriting. Marjorie Wise is credited with introducing the manuscript form for primary-grade students in 1921 (Hildreth, 1960). Manuscript handwriting is considered better for young children because they seem to lack the necessary fine motor control and eye-hand coordination for cursive handwriting. In addition, manuscript handwriting is similar to the type style in primary-level reading textbooks. Only two lowercase letters, *a* and *g,* are different in typed and handwritten forms. The similarity is assumed to facilitate young children's introduction to reading and writing.

Barbe and Milone (1980) suggest several additional reasons that students in the primary grades should learn manuscript before cursive handwriting. First, manuscript handwriting is easier to learn. Studies show that young children can copy letters and words written in the manuscript form more easily than those written in the cursive form. Also, young children can form the vertical and horizontal lines and circles of manuscript handwriting more easily than the cursive strokes. Furthermore, manuscript handwriting is more legible than cursive handwriting. Because it is easier to read, signs and advertisements are printed in letter forms closely approximating manuscript handwriting. Finally, people are often requested to print when completing applications and other forms. For these reasons, manuscript handwriting has become the preferred handwriting form for young children as well as a necessary handwriting skill for older children and adults.

Students' use of the manuscript form often disappears in the middle grades after they have learned cursive handwriting. It is essential that middle- and upper-grade teachers learn and use the manuscript form with their students so that it remains an option. Second and third graders learn cursive handwriting, a new form, just when they are becoming proficient in the manuscript form, so it is not surprising that some students want to switch back and forth between the two. The need to develop greater writing speed is often given as the reason for the quick transfer to cursive handwriting, but research does not show that one form is necessarily written more quickly than the other.

There have also been criticisms of the manuscript form. A major complaint is the reversal problem caused by some similar lowercase letters; *b* and *d* are particularly confusing. Other detractors argue that using both the manuscript

Figure 12-5   Manuscript and Cursive Handwriting Forms

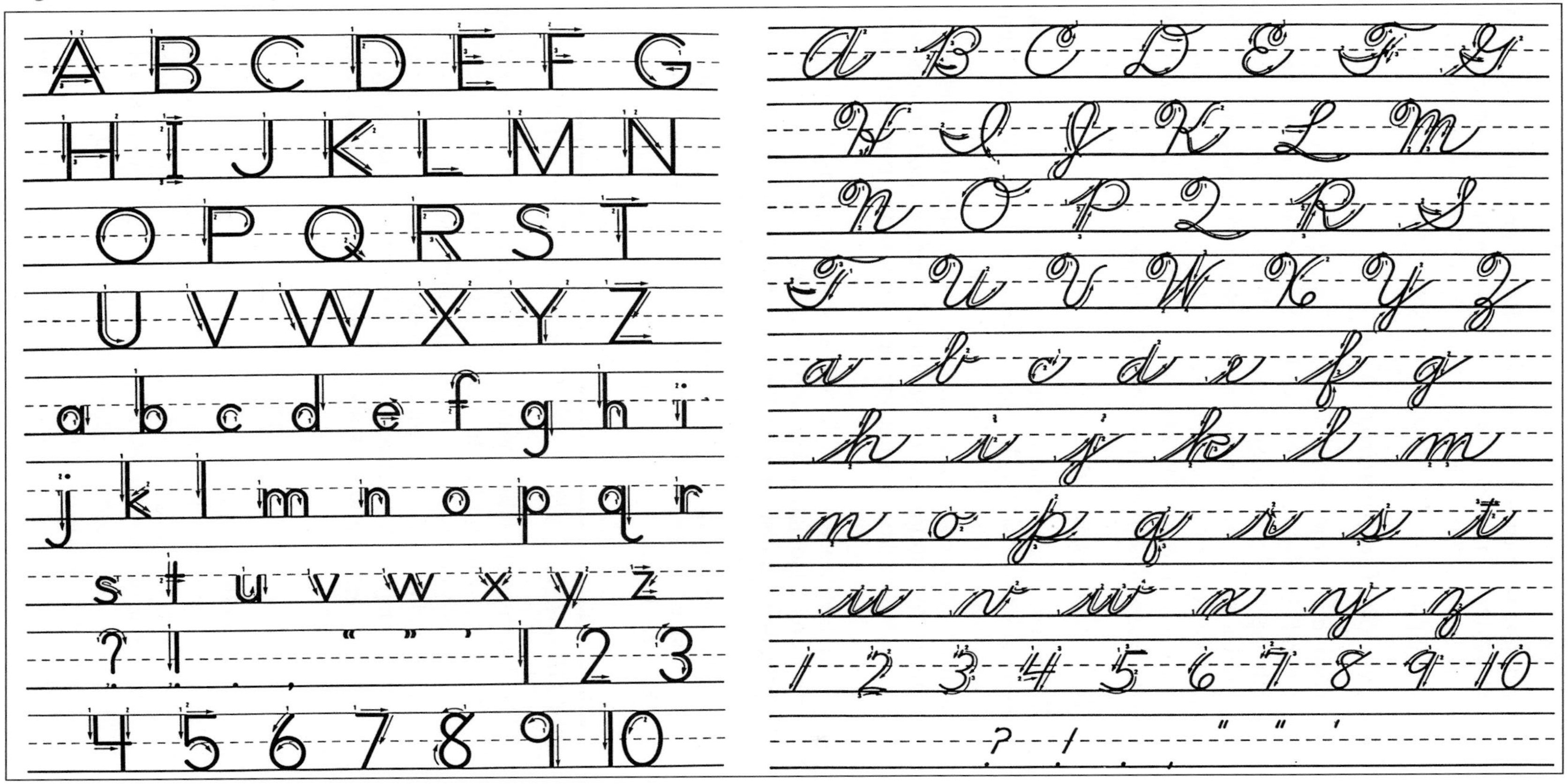

Used with permission of the publisher, Zaner-Bloser, Inc., Columbus, OH, copyright 1993.
From *Handwriting: A Way to Self-Expression*, by Clinton Hackney.

and cursive forms in the elementary grades requires teaching students two totally different kinds of handwriting within the span of several years. They also complain that the "circle and sticks" style of manuscript handwriting requires frequent stops and starts, thus inhibiting a smooth and rhythmic flow of writing.

Cursive Handwriting

When most people think of handwriting, the cursive or connected form comes to mind. The letters in cursive handwriting are joined together to form a word with one continuous movement. Children often view cursive handwriting as the "grown-up" type. Primary-grade students often attempt to imitate this form by connecting the manuscript letters in their names and other words before they are taught how to form and join the letters. Awareness of cursive handwriting and interest in imitating it are indicators that students are ready for instruction.

D'Nealian Handwriting

D'Nealian handwriting is an innovative manuscript and cursive handwriting program developed by a teacher in Michigan. The D'Nealian handwriting forms are shown in Figure 12–6. In the manuscript form, letters are slanted and formed with a continuous stroke; in the cursive form, the letters are simplified, without the flourishes of traditional cursive. Both forms were designed to increase legibility and fluency and to ease the transition from manuscript to cursive handwriting.

The purpose of the D'Nealian program was to ameliorate some of the problems associated with the traditional manuscript form (Thurber, 1987). D'Nealian manuscript uses the same basic letter forms that students will need for cursive handwriting as well as the slant and rhythm required for cursive. Another advantage of the D'Nealian style is that the transition from manuscript to cursive involves adding only connective strokes to most manuscript letters. Only five letters—*f, r, s, v,* and *z*—are shaped differently in the cursive form.

CHILDREN'S HANDWRITING DEVELOPMENT

During the elementary grades children grow from using scribbles and letterlike forms in kindergarten to learning the manuscript handwriting form in the primary grades and the cursive form beginning in the middle grades. Students in the middle and upper grades use both forms interchangeably for a variety of handwriting tasks. Examples of children's handwriting from kindergarten through eighth grade are shown in Figure 12–7. The excerpts were selected from letters.

Handwriting Before First Grade

Children's handwriting grows out of their drawing activities. Young children observe words all around them in their environment: *McDonald's, Coke, STOP.* They also observe parents and teachers writing messages. From this early interest in written words and communicating through writing, preschoolers begin to write letterlike forms and scribbles. In kindergarten, children watch the teacher transcribe experience stories, and they begin to copy their names and familiar words. Once they are familiar with some of the letters, they use

Figure 12–6 D'Nealian Manuscript and Cursive Handwriting Forms

D'Nealian is a registered trademark of Donald Neal Thurber. Copyright © 1987 by Scott, Foresman and Company.

invented spelling to express themselves in writing. Through this drawing-reading-writing-handwriting connection, youngsters discover that they can experiment with letters and words and communicate through written language. Handwriting becomes the tool for this written communication.

Young children enter kindergarten with different backgrounds of handwriting experience. Some 5-year-olds have never held a pencil, and many others have written cursivelike scribbles or manuscript letterlike forms. Some preschoolers have learned to print their names and some other letters. Handwrit-

Figure 12–7   Examples of Children's Handwriting

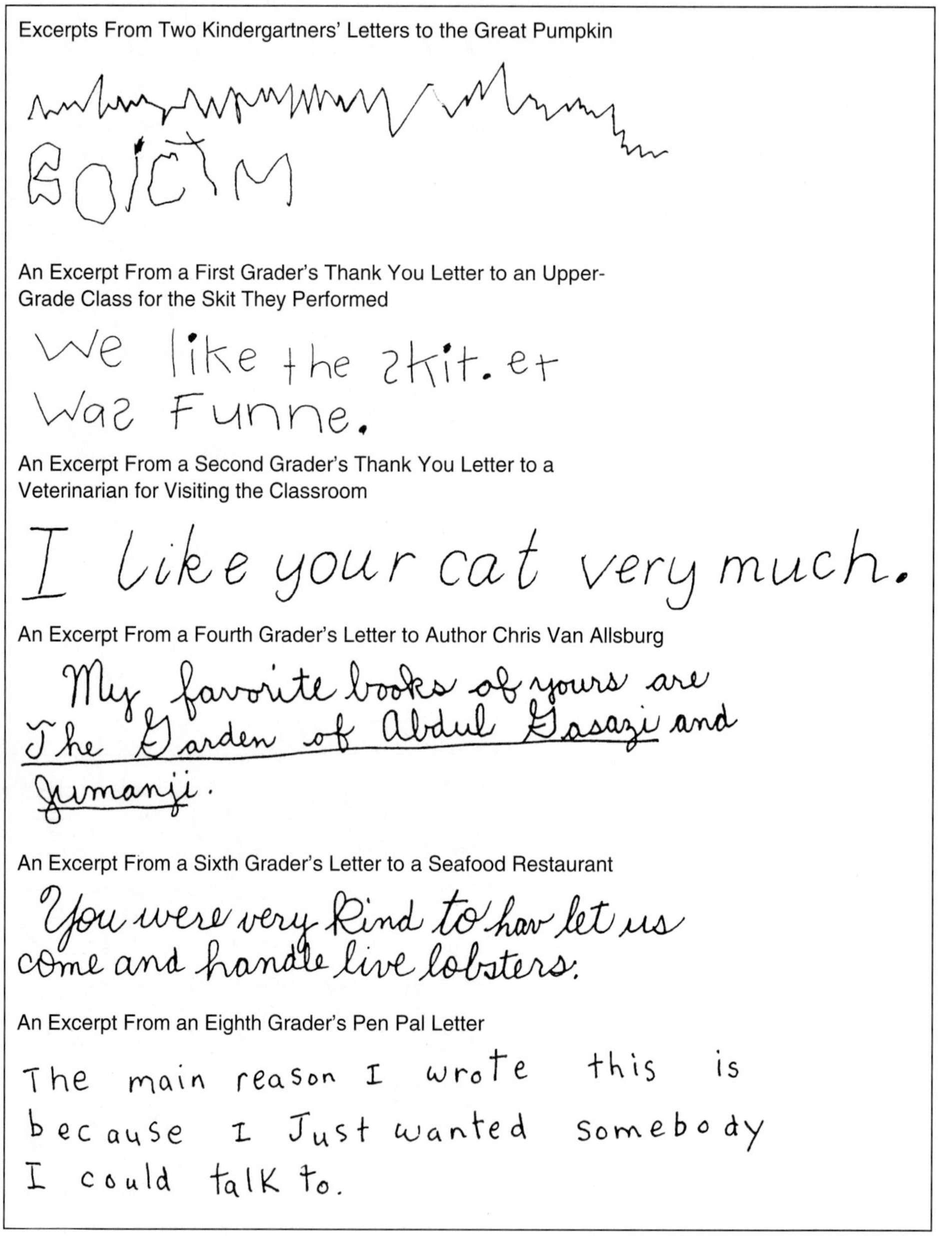

Excerpts From Two Kindergartners' Letters to the Great Pumpkin

BOICTM

An Excerpt From a First Grader's Thank You Letter to an Upper-Grade Class for the Skit They Performed

We like the zkit. et Waz Funne.

An Excerpt From a Second Grader's Thank You Letter to a Veterinarian for Visiting the Classroom

I like your cat very much.

An Excerpt From a Fourth Grader's Letter to Author Chris Van Allsburg

My favorite books of yours are The Garden of Abdul Gasazi and Jumanji.

An Excerpt From a Sixth Grader's Letter to a Seafood Restaurant

You were very kind to hav let us come and handle live lobsters.

An Excerpt From an Eighth Grader's Pen Pal Letter

The main reason I wrote this is because I Just wanted somebody I could talk to.

ing in kindergarten typically includes three types of activities: stimulating children's interest in writing, developing their ability to hold writing instruments, and refining their fine motor control. Adults are influential role models in stimulating children's interest in writing. They record children's talk and write labels on signs. They can also provide paper, pencils, and pens so that children can experiment with writing. Students develop the ability to hold a pencil or other writing instrument by modeling and through numerous opportunities to experiment with pencils, pens, paintbrushes, crayons, and other writing instruments. Young children develop fine motor skills through experiences with manipulative materials, including building with blocks, stringing beads, completing puzzles, and art activities.

Handwriting instruction in kindergarten usually focuses on teaching children to form upper- and lowercase letters and to print their names. Many kindergarten teachers use a multisensory approach: Students trace letters in shaving cream, sand, and fingerpaint; glue popcorn in the shape of letters; and arrange blocks or pipe cleaners to form letters. Children learn to print their names through similar multisensory activities and through daily practice in writing their names on attendance sheets, experience stories, paintings, and other papers.

Handwriting must be linked with writing at all grade levels, even in kindergarten. Young children write labels, draw and write stories, keep journals, and write other messages (Klein & Schickedanz, 1980). The more they write, the greater their need becomes for instruction in handwriting. Writers need to know how to grip a pencil, how to form letters, and how to space between letters and words. Instruction is necessary so that students do not learn bad habits that later must be broken. Students often devise rather bizarre ways to form a letter, and these bad habits can cause problems when they need to develop greater writing speed.

Handwriting in the Primary Grades

Formal handwriting instruction begins in first grade. Students learn how to form manuscript letters and space between them, and they develop skills related to the six elements of legibility. Researchers have found that primary-grade students have more difficulty forming the lowercase than the uppercase letters, and by third grade some students still have difficulty forming *r, u, h,* and *t* (Stennett, Smithe, & Hardy, 1972).

A common handwriting activity requires students to copy short writing samples from the chalkboard, but this type of activity is not recommended. For one thing, young children have great difficulty with far-to-near copying (Lamme, 1979); a piece of writing should be placed close to the child for copying. Children can recopy their own compositions, language experience stories, and self-selected writing samples; other types of copying should be avoided. It is far better for children to create their own writing than to copy words and sentences they may not even be able to read!

Special pencils and handwriting paper are often provided for handwriting instruction. Kindergartners and first graders commonly use "fat" beginner pencils, because it has been assumed that these pencils are easier for young children to hold; however, most children prefer to use regular-sized pencils that older students and adults use. Moreover, regular pencils have erasers! Research now indicates that beginner pencils are not better than regular-sized pencils for young children (Lamme & Ayris, 1983). Likewise, there is no evidence that specially shaped pencils and little writing aids that slip onto pencils to improve children's grip are effective.

Many types of paper, both lined and unlined, are used in elementary classrooms. Paper companies manufacture paper lined in a range of sizes. Typically, paper is lined at 2-inch intervals for kindergartners and at 7/8- to 3/8-inch intervals for older students. Lined paper for first and second graders

Forming letters in shaving cream is a good way for young children to practice fine motor skills.

has an added midline, often dotted, to guide students in forming lowercase letters. Sometimes a line appears below the baseline to guide placement of letters such as lowercase *g, p, q,* and *y* that have "tails" that drop below the baseline. The few research studies that have examined the value of lined paper in general and paper lined at specific intervals offer conflicting results. One study suggests that younger children's handwriting is more legible when they use unlined paper, and older children's is better when they use lined paper (Lindsay & McLennan, 1983). Most teachers seem to prefer that students use lined paper for handwriting activities, but students easily adjust to whichever type of writing paper is available. Children often use rulers to line their paper when they are given unlined paper, and, likewise, they ignore the lines on lined paper if they interfere with their drawing or writing.

Transition to Cursive Handwriting

Students' introduction to cursive handwriting typically occurs in the second semester of second grade or the first semester of third grade. Parents and students often attach great importance to the transition from manuscript to cursive, thus adding unnecessary pressure for the students. Beverly Cleary's *Muggie Maggie* (1990) describes the pressure one child feels. The time of transition is usually dictated by tradition rather than by sound educational theory. All students in a school or school district are usually introduced to cursive handwriting at the same time, regardless of their interest in making the change.

Some students indicate an early interest in cursive handwriting by trying to connect manuscript letters or by asking their parents to demonstrate how to write their names. Because of individual differences in motor skills and levels of interest in cursive writing, it is better to introduce some students to cursive handwriting in first or second grade while providing other students with additional time to refine their manuscript skills. These students then learn cursive handwriting in third or fourth grade.

Before students learn to form the cursive letters, they first learn to recognize the upper- and lowercase cursive letters. Flash cards and lotto games are useful for teaching cursive letter recognition. Next, students learn to read words and sentences written in the cursive form.

The practice of changing to cursive handwriting only a year or two after children learn the manuscript form is receiving increasing criticism. The argument has been that students need to learn cursive handwriting as early as possible because of their increasing need for handwriting speed. Because of its continuous flow, cursive handwriting was thought to be faster to write than manuscript; however, research suggests that manuscript handwriting can be written as quickly as cursive handwriting (Jackson, 1971). The controversy over the benefits of the two forms and the best time to introduce cursive handwriting is likely to continue.

Handwriting in the Middle and Upper Grades

Students are introduced to the cursive handwriting form in second and third grades. Usually, the basic strokes that make up the letters (e.g., slant stroke, undercurve, downcurve) are taught first. Next, the lowercase letters are taught in isolation, and then the connecting strokes are introduced. Uppercase letters are taught later because they are used far less often and are more difficult to form. Which cursive letters are most difficult? According to the results of a study that examined sixth graders' handwriting, the lowercase *r* is the most troublesome letter. The other lowercase letters students frequently form incorrectly are *h, k, p,* and *z* (Horton, 1970).

After students have learned both manuscript and cursive handwriting, they need to review both forms periodically. By this time, too, they have firmly established handwriting habits, both good and bad. At the middle- and upper-grade levels, emphasis is on helping students diagnose and correct their handwriting trouble spots so that they can develop a legible and fluent handwriting style. Older students both simplify their letter forms as well as add unique flourishes to their handwriting to develop their own "trademark" styles.

Teachers often insist that students demonstrate their best handwriting every time they pick up a pencil or pen. This requirement is unrealistic; certainly there are times when handwriting is important, but at other times speed or other considerations outweigh neatness. Children need to learn to recognize two types of writing occasions—*private* and *public.* Legibility counts in public writing, but when students make notes for themselves or write a rough draft of a composition, they are doing private writing and should decide for themselves whether neatness is important.

Left-Handed Writers

Approximately 10% of the American population is left-handed, and there may be two or three left-handed students in most classrooms. Until recently teachers insisted that left-handed students use their right hands for handwriting because left-handed writers were thought to have inferior handwriting skills. Parents and teachers are more realistic now and accept children's natural tendencies for left- or right-handedness. In fact, research has shown that there is no significant difference in the quality or speed of left- or right-handed students' writing (Groff, 1963).

Most young children develop *handedness,* the preference for using either the right or the left hand for fine motor activities, before entering kindergarten or first grade. Teachers must help those few students who have not already developed handedness to choose and consistently use one hand for handwriting and other fine motor activities. Your role consists of observing the student's behavior and hand preference in play, art, writing, and playground activities. Over a period of days or weeks, observe and note which hand the child uses in activities such as building with blocks, catching balls, cutting with scissors, holding a paintbrush, manipulating clay, pouring water or sand, and throwing balls.

During the observation period, teachers may find that a child who has not established hand preference uses both hands interchangeably; for example, a child may first reach for several blocks with one hand and then reach for the next block with the alternate hand. During drawing activities the child will sometimes switch hands every few minutes. Consult the child's parents and ask them to observe and monitor the child's behavior at home, noting hand preferences when the child eats, brushes his or her teeth, turns on the television, opens doors, and so on. The teacher, the child, and the child's parents should then confer, and, based on the results of joint observations, the handedness of family members, and the child's wishes, a tentative decision about hand preference can be made. At school, teacher and child will work closely together so that the child will use only the chosen hand. As long as the child continues to use both hands interchangeably, neither hand will develop the prerequisite fine motor control for handwriting, and teachers should postpone handwriting instruction until the child develops a dominant hand.

Teaching handwriting to left-handed students is not simply the reverse of teaching handwriting to right-handed students (Howell, 1978). Left-handed students have unique handwriting problems, and special adaptations of the procedures for teaching right-handed students are necessary. In fact, many of the problems that left-handed students have can be made worse by using the procedures designed for right-handed writers (Harrison, 1981). The special adjustments are necessary to allow left-handed students to write legibly, fluently, and with less fatigue. A list of suggested adjustments is presented in the Teacher's Notebook on page 487.

The basic difference between right- and left-handed writers is physical orientation. Right-handed students pull their arms toward their bodies as they write, whereas left-handed writers push away. As left-handed students write, they move their left hands across what they have just written, often covering it. Many children adopt a "hook" position to avoid covering and smudging what they have written. Because of their different physical orientation, left-handed writers need to make three major types of adjustments: how they grip their pens or pencils, how they position the writing paper on their desks, and how they slant their writing (Howell, 1978).

First, left-handed writers should hold pencils or pens an inch or more farther back from the tip than right-handed writers do. This change helps them

Teacher's Notebook
Guidelines for Teaching Left-Handed Students

1. Group left-handed students together for handwriting instruction.
2. Provide a left-handed person to serve as the model if you are not left-handed. Perhaps another teacher, a parent, or an older student could come to the class-room to assist left-handed students.
3. Direct students to hold their pencils farther back from the point than right-handed students do.
4. Encourage students to practice handwriting skills at the chalkboard.
5. Have students tilt their papers to the right, rather than to the left, as right-handed students do.
6. Encourage students to slant their cursive letters slightly to the right, but allow them to form them vertically or even with a slight backhand slant.
7. Encourage students to eliminate excessive loops and flourishes from their writing to increase handwriting speed.

see what they have just written and avoid smearing their writing. Left-handed writers need to work to avoid "hooking" their wrists. Have them keep their wrists straight and elbows close to their bodies to avoid the awkward hooked position. Practicing handwriting on the chalkboard is one way to help them develop a more natural style.

Next, left-handed students should tilt their writing papers slightly to the right, in contrast to right-handed students, who tilt their papers to the left. Sometimes it is helpful to place a piece of masking tape on the student's desk to indicate the proper amount of tilt.

Third, whereas right-handed students are encouraged to slant their cursive letters to the right, left-handed writers often write vertically or even slant their letters slightly backward. Some handwriting programs recommend that left-handed writers slant their cursive letters slightly to the right as right-handed students do, but others advise teachers to permit any slant between vertical and 45 degrees to the left of vertical.

Left-handed writers need special support, and one way to provide support is by grouping left-handed students together for handwriting instruction. Right-handed teachers should consider asking a left-handed teacher, parent, or older student to come into the classroom to work with left-handed writers. It is important to carefully monitor left-handed students while they are develop-ing handwriting skills, because bad habits such as "hooking" are difficult to break.

TEACHING HANDWRITING IN THE ELEMENTARY GRADES

Handwriting is best taught in separate periods of direct instruction and teacher-supervised practice. As soon as skills are taught, they should be applied in real-life writing activities. "Busy-work" assignments, such as copying sentences from the chalkboard, lack educational significance. Moreover, students may develop poor handwriting habits or learn to form letters incorrectly if they practice without direct supervision. It is much more difficult to correct bad habits and errors in letter formation than to teach handwriting correctly in the first place.

Handwriting instruction and practice periods should be brief; 15-minute periods of instruction several times a week are more effective than a single lengthy period weekly or monthly. Regular periods of handwriting instruction are necessary when teaching the manuscript form in kindergarten and first grade and the cursive form in second or third grade. In the middle and upper grades, instruction depends on specific handwriting problems that students demonstrate and periodic reviews of both handwriting forms.

The Teaching Strategy

The teaching strategy presented in Chapter 1 can be adapted to teach mini-lessons on handwriting. The strategy is multisensory, with visual, auditory, and kinesthetic components, and is based on research in the field of handwriting (Askov & Greff, 1975; Furner, 1969; Hirsch & Niedermeyer, 1973). The five steps are:

Step by Step

1. *Introducing the Topic.*   The teacher demonstrates a specific handwriting procedure, strategy, or skill while students observe. During the demonstration, the teacher describes the steps involved in executing it.

2. *Describing the Steps.*   Students describe the procedure, strategy, or skill and the steps for executing it as the teacher or a classmate demonstrates it again.

3. *Reviewing the Topic.*   The teacher reviews the specific handwriting procedure, strategy, or skill, summarizing the steps involved.

4. *Practicing Handwriting as the Teacher Circulates.*   Students practice the procedure, strategy, or skill using pencils, pens, or other writing instruments. As they practice, students softly repeat the steps, and the teacher circulates, providing assistance as needed.

5. *Applying Handwriting in Writing Activities.*   Students apply the procedure, strategy, or skill they have learned in their writing. To check that they have learned it, students can review their writing over a period of several days and mark examples of correct use.

An example of applying this strategy in teaching manuscript letter formation is shown in Figure 12–8. The teacher introduces the handwriting skill and then supervises as students practice it. Research has shown the importance of

Figure 12–8   *Using the Teaching Strategy to Teach Letter Formation*

---

1. **Initiating**

   Demonstrate the formation of a single letter or family of letters (e.g., the manu-script circle letters—*O, o, C, c, a, e, Q*) on the chalkboard while explaining how the letter is formed.

2. **Structuring and Conceptualizing**

   Have students describe how the letter is formed while you or a student forms the letter on the chalkboard. At first you may need to ask questions to direct students' descriptions. Possible questions include:

   How many strokes are used in making the letter?

   Which stroke comes first?

   Where do you begin the stroke?

   In which direction do you go?

   What size will the letter be?

   Where does the stroke stop?

   Which stroke comes next?

   Students will quickly learn the appropriate terminology, such as *baseline, left-right, slant line, counterclockwise,* and so on, to describe how the letters are formed.

3. **Summarizing**

   Review the formation of the letter or letter family with students while demon-strating how to form the letter on the chalkboard.

4. **Generalizing**

   Have the students print the letter at the chalkboard, in sand, and with a variety of other materials such as clay, shaving cream, fingerpaint, pudding, and pipe-cleaners. As students form the letter, they should softly describe the formation process to themselves.

   Have students practice writing the letter on paper with the accompanying verbal descriptions.

   Circulate among students providing assistance and encouragement. Demon-strate and describe the correct formation of the letter as the students observe.

5. **Applying**

   After the students have practiced the letter or family of letters, have them apply what they have learned in authentic writing activities. This is the crucial step!

---

the teacher's active involvement in handwriting instruction and practice. Teachers often print or write handwriting samples in advance on practice sheets. Then they distribute the sheets and ask students to practice a hand-writing skill by copying the model they have written. Researchers have found, however, that "moving" models, that is, having students observe the teacher write the handwriting sample, are of far greater value than copying models that have already been written (Wright & Wright, 1980). Moving models are possible when the teacher circulates around the classroom, stopping to demonstrate a procedure, strategy, or skill for one student and moving to assist another; circling incorrectly formed letters and marking other errors with a red pen on completed handwriting sheets is of little value. As in the writing process, the teacher's assistance is far more worthwhile while the students are writing, not after they have completed writing.

As Graves (1983) said, "Handwriting is for writing" (p. 171), and for the most meaningful transfer of skills, students should be involved in writing for various purposes and for genuine audiences. Students apply their handwriting procedures, strategies, and skills whenever they write, and the best way to practice handwriting is through writing.

In addition to the writing activities discussed in previous chapters, students at all grade levels can use copybooks to compile a collection of favorite poems, quotes, and excerpts from stories. Students choose poems, quotations, paragraphs from stories, riddles, or other short pieces of writing they would like to write and save in their copybooks (spiral-bound notebooks or bound blank books). Usually students make one or two entries each week in either manuscript or cursive handwriting. Students can concentrate on their handwriting when they make entries in their books, because they do not have to worry about creating content at the same time. Examples of students' copybook entries are shown in Figure 12–9. Copybooks are especially beneficial because they provide a meaningful context for handwriting practice. Instead of writing rows of letters and isolated words, students are immersed in language and literature. For many students, copybooks become valued, personal anthologies of favorite literary selections.

Adapting to Meet the Needs of Every Student

The goal of handwriting instruction is for every student to develop legible and fluent handwriting. Students' handwriting does not need to match textbook

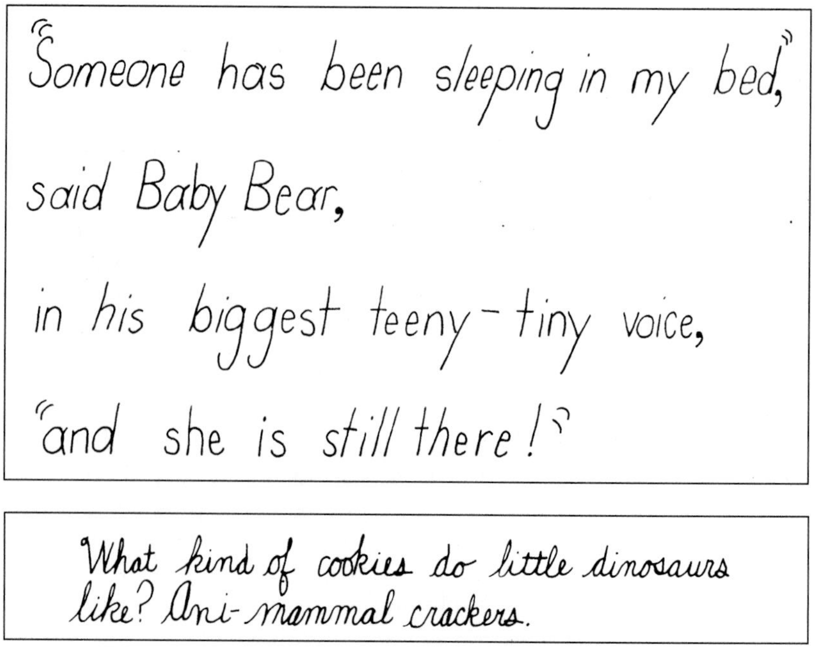

Figure 12–9   Entries from Students' Copybooks (excerpts from Galdone's The Three Bears and Sterne's Tyrannosaurus Wrecks: A Book of Dinosaur Riddles)

"Someone has been sleeping in my bed,"

said Baby Bear,

in his biggest teeny-tiny voice,

"and she is still there!"

What kind of cookies do little dinosaurs like? Ani-mammal crackers.

samples, but it does need to be easy to read and quickly produced. When students are writing for genuine audiences, their handwriting is likely to be better than when they are writing for themselves. It is important that students understand and differentiate between public and private occasions for writing. For students who have difficulty doing handwriting, the D'Nealian handwriting program may be more effective because the letter forms are simplified. Students with severe handwriting problems can use microcomputers with word-processing programs to produce most of their written work. Teachers also need to adapt handwriting instruction for left-handed students, and the suggestions offered in the Teacher's Notebook on page 487 may be useful.

Elements of Legibility

The goal of handwriting instruction is for students to develop legible handwriting. To reach this goal, students need to know what qualities or elements determine legibility and then analyze their own handwriting according to these elements (Hackney, 1993). The six elements of legible and fluent handwriting are:

1. Letter Formation. Letters are formed with specific strokes. Letters in manuscript handwriting are composed of vertical, horizontal, and slanted lines plus circles or parts of circles. The letter *b,* for example, is composed of a vertical line and a circle, and *M* is composed of vertical and slanted lines. Cursive letters are composed of slanted lines, loops, and curved lines. The lowercase cursive letters *m* and *n*, for instance, are composed of a slant stroke, a loop, and an undercurve stroke. An additional component in cursive handwriting is the connecting stroke used to join letters.

2. Size and Proportion. During the elementary grades, students' handwriting becomes smaller, and the proportional size of uppercase to lowercase letters increases. First graders' uppercase manuscript letters are twice the size of lowercase letters. When second- and third-grade students first begin cursive handwriting, the proportional size of letters remains 2:1; later, the proportion increases to 3:1 for middle- and upper-grade students.

3. Spacing. Students should leave adequate space between letters in words and between words in sentences. Spacing between words in manuscript handwriting should equal one lowercase letter *o,* and spacing between sentences should equal two lowercase. The most important aspect of spacing within words in cursive handwriting is consistency. To correctly space between words, the writer should make the beginning stroke of the new word directly below the end stroke of the preceding word. Spacing between sentences should equal one uppercase letter, and spacing between paragraphs should equal two uppercase letter *O*'s.

4. Slant. Letters should be consistently parallel. Letters in manuscript handwriting are vertical, and in the cursive form letters slant slightly to the right. To ensure the correct slant, right-handed students tilt their papers to the left, and left-handed students tilt their papers to the right.

5. Alignment. For proper alignment in both manuscript and cursive handwriting, all letters should be uniform in size and consistently touch the baseline.

Figure 12–10   A Checklist for Assessing Manuscript Handwriting

---

Handwriting Checklist

Name _____

Writing Project _____

Date _____

_____ 1. Did I form my letters correctly?

             Did I start my line letters at the top?

             Did I start my circle letters at 1:00?

             Did I join the round parts of the letters neatly?

             Did I join the slanted strokes in sharp points?

_____ 2. Did my lines touch the midline or top line neatly?

_____ 3. Did I space evenly between letters?

_____ 4. Did I leave enough space between words?

_____ 5. Did I make my letters straight up and down?

_____ 6. Did I make all my letters sit on the baseline?

---

6. *Line Quality.* Students should write at a consistent speed and hold their writing instruments correctly and in a relaxed manner to make steady, unwavering lines of even thickness.

Correct letter formation and spacing receive the major focus in handwriting instruction during the elementary grades. Although the other four elements usually receive less attention, they, too, are important in developing legible and fluent handwriting.

Diagnosing and Correcting Handwriting Problems

Students use the six elements of legibility to diagnose their handwriting problems. Primary-grade students, for example, can check to see if they have formed a particular letter correctly, if the round parts of letters are joined neatly, and if slanted letters are joined in sharp points. Older students can examine a piece of handwriting to see if their letters are consistently parallel and if the letters touch the baseline consistently. A sample checklist for evaluating manuscript handwriting is shown in Figure 12–10. Checklists can also be developed for cursive handwriting. It is important to involve students in developing the checklists so that they appreciate the need to make their handwriting more legible.

Another reason students need to diagnose and correct their handwriting problems is that handwriting quality influences teacher evaluation and grading. Markham (1976) found that teachers consistently graded papers with better handwriting higher than papers with poor handwriting, regardless of the quality of the content. Students in the elementary grades are not too young to learn that poor quality or illegible handwriting may lead to lower grades.

GRAMMAR

Grammar is probably the most controversial area of language arts. Suhor (1987) calls it one of the "orthodoxies" that divides language arts educators.

Teachers, parents, and the community disagree about the content of grammar instruction, how to teach it, and when to begin teaching it. Some people believe that formal instruction in grammar is unnecessary—if not harmful— during the elementary grades; others believe that grammar instruction should be the central emphasis of language arts instruction. Before getting into the controversy, let's clarify terms. *Grammar* is the description of the structure of a language. It involves principles of word and sentence formation. In contrast, *usage* is "correctness," or using the appropriate word in a sentence—the socially preferred way of using language within a dialect. *My friend, she; the man brung;* and *hisself* are examples of standard English usage errors that elementary students sometimes make. Fraser and Hodson (1978) explain the distinction between grammar and usage this way: "Grammar is the rationale of a language; usage is its etiquette" (p. 52).

Children learn the structure of the English language—its grammar— intuitively as they learn to talk; the process is an unconscious one. They have almost completed it by the time they enter kindergarten. The purpose of grammar instruction, then, is to make this intuitive knowledge about the English language explicit and to provide labels for words within sentences, parts of sentences, and types of sentences. Children speak the dialect their parents and community members speak. Dialect, whether standard or non-standard English, is informal and differs to some degree from the written standard English or "book language" that students will read and write in elementary school (Edelsky, 1989; Pooley, 1974). Figure 12–11 shows the cover and a page from a second-grade ABC book that students developed while combining their study of adjectives and animals.

Applebee and his colleagues (1987) examined compositions written by 9-, 13-, and 17-year-olds as a part of the National Assessment of Educational

Figure 12–11   *An Excerpt From a Second-Grade Class Book on Adjectives*

 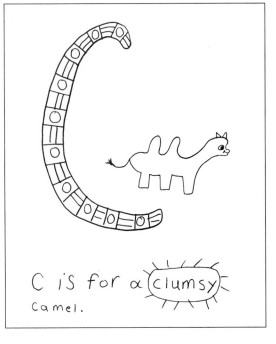

Progress testing and were encouraged by the results. They concluded that most students made only a few grammatical errors in the compositions they wrote. They examined students' sentences and categorized them as simple, compound, complex, run-on, or fragment. They found that approximately a quarter of the sentences that 9-year-olds wrote were complex, and the proportion increased to 43% for 17-year-olds. The researchers also found that the proportion of sentence fragments and run-on sentences decreased with age, particularly between the ages of 9 and 13. Moreover, even at age 9, many students had no run-on sentences (50%) or fragments (75%) in their writing. A major conclusion of this research was that "instructional procedures that encourage students to edit their work for grammar, punctuation, and spelling as a last stage in the writing experience would seem to reflect what the best writers do" (p. 7). They also noted that everyone makes some errors, and because patterns of error differed from student to student, small group instruction may be more effective than whole class instruction.

Teachers, parents, and the community at large cite many reasons for teaching grammar. First, using standard English is the mark of an educated person, and students should be given a choice to use standard English. Many teachers feel that teaching grammar will help students understand sentence structure and form sentences to express their thoughts. Another reason is that parents expect that grammar will be taught, and teachers must meet these expectations. Other teachers explain that they teach grammar to prepare students for the next grade or for instruction in a foreign language. Others pragmatically rationalize grammar instruction because it is a part of norm-referenced achievement tests mandated by state departments of education.

Language arts textbooks have traditionally emphasized grammar; often, more than half of the pages have been devoted to drills on parts of speech, parts of sentences, and sentence types. Many teachers and parents assume that the content of a language arts textbook indicates what the curriculum should be, but it is important to separate the two so that the textbook is only one of many resources for implementing the curriculum.

Conventional wisdom is that knowledge about grammar and usage should improve students' writing, but research since the beginning of the century has not confirmed this assumption. Based on their review of research conducted before 1963, Braddock, Lloyd-Jones, and Schoer (1963) concluded:

> The teaching of formal grammar has a negligible or, because it usually displaces some instruction and practice in actual composition, even a harmful effect on the improvement of writing. (pp. 37–38)

Since then, other studies have reached the same conclusion (cf. Elley, Barham, Lamb, & Wyllie, 1976; Hillocks, 1987).

Despite the controversy about teaching grammar and its value for elementary students, grammar is a part of the elementary language arts curriculum and will undoubtedly remain so for some time. Given this fact, it is only reasonable that grammar should be taught in the most beneficial manner possible. Researchers suggest that integrating grammar study with reading and writing produces the best results (Noyce & Christie, 1983). Elbow (1973) and Haley-James (1981) view grammar as a tool for writers and recommend integrating grammar instruction with the revising and editing stages of the writing process.

TYPES OF GRAMMAR

Grammarians describe the structure of English in three ways, and the three perspectives influence how grammar is taught in elementary schools. The three types are traditional grammar, structural grammar, and transformational grammar.

Traditional Grammar

Traditional grammar is *prescriptive,* providing rules for socially correct usage. This perspective dates back to medieval times and has its roots in the study of Latin. The major contribution of traditional grammar is its terminology—parts of speech, parts of sentences, and types of sentences—that teachers and students can use in talking about language. The shortcoming of traditional grammar is that the terms and rules are inadequate for English and cannot adequately explain how language works.

Even though researchers have repeatedly concluded that the formal teaching of grammar is not effective, traditional concepts about grammar continue to be taught in the elementary grades. The three most common types of information taught are the parts of speech, parts of sentences, and types of sentences.

Grammarians have sorted English words into eight groups, called *parts of speech:* nouns, pronouns, verbs, adjectives, adverbs, prepositions, conjunctions, and interjections. Words in each group are used in essentially the same way in all sentences. Nouns and verbs are the basic building blocks of sentences, and pronouns substitute for nouns. Adjectives, adverbs, and prepositions build upon and modify the nouns and verbs. Conjunctions connect individual words or groups of words, and interjections express strong emotion or surprise.

According to the traditional viewpoint, a sentence is made up of one or more words to express a complete thought and, to express the thought, must have a subject and a predicate. Sentences are classified in two ways. First, they are classified according to structure, or how they are put together. The structure of a sentence may be simple, compound, complex, or compound-complex. A *simple* sentence contains only one independent clause, and a *compound* sentence is made up of two or more simple sentences. A *complex* sentence contains one independent clause and one or more dependent clauses. A *compound-complex* sentence contains two or more independent clauses and one or more dependent clauses.

Second, sentences are classified according to the type of message they contain. Sentences that make statements are *declarative,* those that ask questions are *interrogative,* those that make commands are *imperative,* and those that communicate strong emotion or surprise are *exclamatory.*

Structural Grammar

The second approach is structural grammar, which attempts to describe how language is really used. Proponents of the structural approach have distinguished between spoken and written language and have analyzed the patterns of sentences unique to English, taking into account differences among language users. The study of structural linguistics has provided detailed information about both standard and nonstandard forms of English, but this approach focuses on form and does not explain how meaning relates to use.

Seven basic sentence patterns are described in structural grammar. The basic sentence parts consist of nouns, verbs, and complements. The noun by itself serves as the subject of the sentence; the verb by itself or with complements serves as the predicate of the sentence. Modifiers are added to the nouns, verbs, and complements. Connectives are used to join words, phrases, and clauses. The following paragraphs describe each of the seven basic sentence patterns:

1. Noun-Verb. This pattern consists of a subject and a predicate with no complements. The verb is intransitive, so it does not take any complements. Both the noun and the verb may take modifiers that will expand the possible sentences and make them more interesting. This N-V sentence pattern (and all the succeeding sentence patterns) may be expanded by adding adjectives, adverbs, prepositional phrases, participial phrases, and absolute phrases. We will illustrate each basic sentence pattern and show one expanded sentence in the pattern:

Lions roared.

Hungry *lions,* searching for food, their mouths open wide, *roared* angrily in frustration.

2. Noun-Verb-Noun. The N-V-N pattern consists of subject, transitive verb, and direct object complement. The direct object receives the action initiated by the subject and specified by the verb. The verb carries the action from the subject to the object, as the following sentences illustrate:

The lion stalked the jungle.

The hungry *lion,* swaying from side to side, his skin stretched taut, *stalked the jungle* menacingly.

3. Noun–Linking Verb–Noun. In this pattern the complement is a subjective complement because it completes the meaning of the subject. The linking verb links a description to the subject. The subjective complement further identifies the subject:

Lions are animals.

Lions, penned in cages, their freedom taken from them, *are* very unhappy *animals.*

4. Noun–Linking Verb–Adjective. The N–LV–Adj pattern consists of a subject, a linking verb, and a predicate adjective. The predicate adjective is a subjective complement that points out a quality of the subject. The linking verb links the description of the adjective to the subject:

Lions are cautious.

The young *lions,* stalking their prey in the African grasslands, their tails twitching nervously, *are* extremely *cautious.*

5. Noun-Verb-Noun-Noun. The fifth pattern, N-V-N-N, consists of subject, transitive verb, and two complements—an indirect object and a direct object. The verb specifies an action that is passed from the subject to the object, but another person or thing is also involved in the action. The subject passes the object on to someone or something else, the indirect object:

> Lions give cubs meat.
>
> Moving away from the kill, the *lions,* their paws red with blood, *give* their hungry *cubs meat.*

6. *Noun-Verb-Noun-Noun.* This pattern consists of subject, transitive verb, and two complements—a direct object and an objective complement. The objective complement completes the meaning of the object by identifying what the verb has passed on to the object. The objective complement refers to the same person or thing as the object:

> Lions make cubs hunters.
>
> *Lions,* living at the edge of the jungle, painstakingly *make* their young *cubs hunters* of small game.

7. *Noun-Verb-Noun-Adjective.* This pattern consists of subject, transitive verb, and two complements—a direct object and an objective complement. The objective complement in this pattern is an adjective; it still, however, completes the meaning of the action passed on from the subject to the object. The adjective points out a quality of the object. If the objective complement is a noun, as in pattern 6, it renames the object rather than pointing out a quality of the object:

> Lions make cubs happy.
>
> The old *lions,* pacing back and forth, their heads swinging from side to side, *make* the *cubs* very *happy.*

Variations and combinations of the seven basic sentence patterns are used to produce almost all sentences that we speak and write. Sentences can be changed from positive to negative, for example, by adding a form of *not* and an auxiliary verb; questions are formed by transposing the subject and an auxiliary verb or by adding *how* or *who, what,* or other *wh-* words. Sentences are made more complex by joining two sentences or embedding one sentence within another. Linguists have identified a number of transformations that change sentences from one form to another; a list of the most common transformations appears in Figure 12–12. Although the transformations are presented separately, several transformations can be applied to a sentence simultaneously. Elementary students already know and use most of the simple transformations, but the more complex joining and embedding transformations are often taught through sentence-combining activities.

Transformational Grammar

Transformational grammar is the third and most recent approach. Transformational linguists attempt to describe both the way language works and the cognitive processes we use to produce language. They refer to two levels or structures, called *surface* and *deep levels,* to explain how meaning in the brain (deep level) is transformed into the sentences we speak and write (surface level). This approach also explains how standard and nonstandard surface-level

Figure 12–12   *The Most Common Transformations*

Transformation	Description	Sample Sentence
Simple Transformations		
1. Negative	*Not* or *n't* and auxiliary verb inserted	Lions roar. Lions don't roar.
2. Yes-No Question	Subject and auxiliary verb switched.	The lion stalked the jungle? Did the lion stalk the jungle?
3. *Wh-* Question	*Wh-* word (*who, what, which, when, where, why*) or *how,* and auxiliary verb inserted	Lions roar. Why do lions roar?
4. Imperative	*You* becomes the subject	Lions give cubs meat. Give cubs meat.
5. There	*There* and auxiliary verb inserted	Lions are cautious. There are cautious lions.
6. Passive	Subject and direct object switched and the main verb changed to past-participle form	Lions make cubs hunters. Cubs are made hunters by lions.
Complex Transformations		
1. Joining	Two sentences joined using conjunctions such as *and, but, or*	Lions roar. Tigers roar. Lions and tigers roar.
2. Embedding	Two (or more) sentences combined by embedding one into the other	Lions are animals. Lions are cautious. Lions are cautious animals.

Adapted from Malmstrom, 1977.

sentences (e.g., *I don't have any money* and *I ain't got no money*) can be generated from the same thought.

The rise of transformational grammar has led many educators to seek ways to make it operational for classroom use. The method that seems most promising is sentence combining, wherein students focus on sentence construction as they analyze, combine, select, rearrange, elaborate on, organize, refocus, and edit their writing (Strong, 1986). The term *sentence combining* obviously suggests that one combines sentences to make them longer or conceptually more dense, but Strong argues that it should be thought of more broadly to include both "tightening" and "decombining" (p. 6). Making sentences longer does not always promote better writing, but it is a good way to help students manipulate sentences.

Mellon (1969) suggested that sentence-combining activities might be an effective way to increase students' syntactic development. Work by Hunt and O'Donnell (1970) and O'Hare (1973) showed that students' writing was improved when sentence-combining exercises were taught. Since these studies, many teachers have introduced sentence-combining activities to their students.

Students use complex transformations in sentence-combining activities. Sentences can be joined or embedded in a variety of ways. Two sentences (S) are transformed to create a matrix (or combined) sentence (M) in these examples:

(S) Tom found a wallet.

(S) The wallet was brown.

(M1) Tom found a wallet that was brown.

(M2) Tom found a brown wallet.

The two possible matrix sentences (M1 and M2) show embedding of the adjective *brown*. Matrix sentence M1 uses a relative clause transformation; M2 uses an adjective transformation. Neither matrix sentence is right or wrong; rather, they provide two options. The goal of sentence combining is for students to experiment with different combinations. Examples of other sentence-combining exercises are shown in Figure 12–13.

Sentence-combining activities give students opportunities to manipulate sentence structures; however, they are rather artificial. They are most effective when combined with other writing assignments. Weaver (1979) cautions that "sentence combining activities are only an adjunct to the writing program and the writing process and should never be used as substitutes for actual writing" (pp. 83–84). The drawback of the transformational approach is that it is

Figure 12–13   Examples of Sentence Combining

Sentence Joining

1. (S)   Joe is tall.
   (S)   Bill is tall.
   (M)   Joe and Bill are tall.

2. (S)   John fell off his bike.
   (S)   Mary screamed.
   (M)   When John fell off his bike, Mary screamed.

3. (S)   Tom hit the ball over the wall.
   (S)   Tom ran around the bases.
   (M)   Tom hit the ball over the wall and ran around the bases.

Sentence Embedding

1. (S)   The boy is fat.
   (S)   The boy is eating cake.
   (M)   The boy who is eating cake is fat.
   (M)   The fat boy is eating cake.

2. (S)   John fights fires.
   (S)   John is a fireman.
   (M)   John who is a fireman fights fires.
   (M)   John, a fireman, fights fires.

3. (S)   The bird is beautiful.
   (S)   The bird is flying over the tree.
   (M)   The bird which is flying over the tree is beautiful.
   (M)   The bird flying over the tree is beautiful.

S = sentence to be combined; M = matrix or combined sentence.

difficult to apply the phrase structure rules, which explain how sentences are created, in grammar instruction for elementary students.

TEACHING GRAMMAR TO ELEMENTARY STUDENTS

The traditional way to teach grammar is to use language arts textbooks. Students read rules and definitions, copy words and sentences, and mark them to apply the concepts presented in the text. This type of activity often seems meaningless to students. Instead, teachers should use literature and the students' own writing; the study of words and their arrangement into sentences allows students to manipulate language (Cullinan, Jaggar, & Strickland, 1974; Tompkins & McGee, 1983).

Teachers identify concepts they need to teach by assessing students' writing and noting what types of grammar and usage errors they are making. The concepts can be taught to the whole class or to small groups of students, but they should be taught only to students who don't already know them. Atwell (1987) suggests using minilessons because of their immediate connections to reading and writing.

Grammar Minilessons

Teachers can teach minilessons on various procedures, concepts, and strategies and skills related to traditional, structural, or transformational grammar. No worksheets are recommended; instead, excerpts from books students are

During editing conferences, teachers help students locate and correct grammatical errors in their compositions.

reading or from students' own writing are used. Five topics for minilessons are identifying parts of speech, creating concept books, slotting sentences, expanding sentences, and manipulating sentences; other topics for minilessons are suggested on page 473.

Identifying Parts of Speech.   Students work in small groups to identify words representing one part of speech or all eight parts of speech from books they are reading or from their own writing. A group of fifth graders identified the following words representing each part of speech from Van Allsburg's *The Polar Express* (1985):

Nouns	train, children, Santa Claus, elves, pajamas, roller coaster, conductor, sleigh, hug, clock, Sarah
Pronouns	we, they, he, it, us, you, his, I, me
Verbs	filled, ate, flickered, raced, were, cheered, marched, asked, pranced, stood, shouted
Adjectives	melted, white-tailed, quiet, no, first, magical, cold, dark, polar, Santa's
Adverbs	soon, faster, wildly, apart, closer, alone
Prepositions	in, through, over, with, of, in front of, behind, at, for, across, into
Conjunctions	and, but
Interjections	oh, well, now

Similarly, students can hunt for parts of sentences or sentence types in books of children's literature.

Creating Concept Books.   Students examine concept books that focus on one part of speech or another grammatical concept. For example, Barrett describes the essential characteristics of a variety of animals in *A Snake Is Totally Tail* (1983), and most of the descriptions include an adverb. After students read the book and identify the adverbs, they can write their own sentences, following the same pattern, and illustrate the sentences using posters, mobiles, a mural, or a class book. (Useful books for teaching traditional grammar concepts are listed in Figure 12–14.

Slotting Sentences.   Students experiment with words and phrases to see how they function in sentences by filling in sentences that have slots, or blanks. Sentence slotting teaches students about several different grammatical concepts. They can experiment with parts of speech using a sentence like this:

The snake slithered _____ the rock.
> over
> around
> under
> to

Students brainstorm a number of words to fill in the slot, all of which will be prepositions; adjectives, nouns, verbs, and adverbs will not make sense. This activity can be repeated to introduce or review any part of speech.

Figure 12–14   Books That Illustrate Traditional Grammar Concepts

Nouns

Heller, R. (1987). *A cache of jewels and other collective nouns.* New York: Grosset & Dunlap.

Heller, R. (1990). *Merry-go-round: A book about nouns.* New York: Grosset & Dunlap.

Hoban, T. (1981). *More than one.* New York: Greenwillow.

MacCarthy, P. (1991). *Herds of words.* New York: Dial.

Terban, M. (1986). *Your foot's on my feet! and other tricky nouns.* New York: Clarion.

Wildsmith, B. (1968). *Fishes.* New York: F Watts.

Verbs

Beller, J. (1984). *A-B-Cing: An action alp   ew York: Crown.

Burningham, J. (1986). *Cluck baa, jangle t   g, slam bang, skip trip, sniff shout, wobble   . New York: Viking.

Heller, R. (1988). *Kites sail high: A book about verbs.* New York: Grosset & Dunlap.

Hoban, T. (1975). *Dig, drill, dump, fill.* New York: Greenwillow.

McMillan, B. (1984). *Kitten can . . . A concept book.* New York: Lothrop, Lee & Shepard.

Maestro, B., & Maestro, G. (1985). *Camping out.* New York: Crown.

Neumeier, M., & Glasser, B. (1985). *Action alphabet.* New York: Greenwillow.

Shiefman, V. (1981). *M is for move.* New York: Dutton.

Terban, M. (1984). *I think I thought and other tricky verbs.* New York: Clarion.

Adjectives

Boynton, S. (1983). *A is for angry: An animal and adjective alphabet.* New York: Workman.

Duke, K. (1983). *Guinea pig ABC.* New York: Dutton.

Heller, R. (1989). *Many luscious lollipops: A book about adjectives.* New York: Grosset & Dunlap.

Hoban, T. (1981). *A children's zoo.* New York: Greenwillow.

Hubbard, W. (1990). *C is for curious: An ABC book of feelings.* San Francisco: Chronicle Books.

Maestro, B., & Maestro, G. (1979). *On the go: A book of adjectives.* New York: Crown.

McMillan, B. (1989). *Super, super, superwords.* New York: Lothrop, Lee & Shepard.

Adverbs

Barrett, J. (1983). *A snake is totally tail.* New York: Atheneum.

Heller, R. (1991). *Up, up and away: A book about adverbs.* New York: Grosset & Dunlap.

Prepositions

Bancheck, L. (1978). *Snake in, snake out.* New York: Crowell.

Berenstain, S., & Berenstain, J. (1968). *Inside, outside, upside, down.* New York: Random House.

Berenstain, S., & Berenstain, J. (1971). *Bears in the night.* New York: Random House.

Hoban, T. (1973). *Over, under, and through and other spatial concepts.* New York: Macmillan.

Hoban, T. (1991). *All about where.* New York: Greenwillow.

Sentence slotting also demonstrates to students that parts of speech can substitute for each other. In the following sentence common and proper nouns as well as pronouns can be used in the slot:

_____ asked his secretary to get him a cup of coffee.
The man
Mr. Jones
He

A similar sentence-slotting example demonstrates how phrases can function as an adverb:

The dog gro   d _____ .
ferociously
with his teeth bared
daring us to reach for his bone

In this example the adverb *ferociously* can be used in the slot, as well as prepositional and participial phrases.

Sentences with an adjective slot can be used to demonstrate that phrases function as adjectives. The goal of this activity is to demonstrate the function of words in sentences. Many sentence-slotting activities, such as the last example, also illustrate that sentences become more specific with the addition of a word or phrase. The purpose of these activities is to experiment with language; they should be done with small groups of students or the whole class, not as worksheets.

Expanding Sentences. Students expand simple, or kernel, sentences, such as *A frog leaps* or *The car raced,* by adding modifiers. The words and phrases with which they expand the basic sentence can add qualities and attributes, details, and comparisons. The "5 Ws plus one" help students focus on expanding particular aspects of the sentence; for example:

Basic sentence	A frog leaps.
What kind?	green, speckled
How?	high into the air
Where?	from a half-submerged log and lands in the water with a splash
Why?	to avoid the noisy boys playing nearby
Expanded sentence	To avoid the noisy boys playing nearby, *a* green, speckled *frog leaps* high into the air from a half-submerged log and lands in the water with a splash.

Depending on what questions one asks and the answers students give, many other expanded sentences are possible from the same basic sentence. Students enjoy working in small groups to expand a basic sentence so that they can compare their expanded versions with those of the other groups. Instead of the "5 Ws plus one" questions to expand sentences, the teacher can ask older students to supply a specific part of speech or modifier at each step of expansion.

Students or the teacher can create basic sentences for expansion or take them from children's literature. Very few basic sentences appear in stories, but a basic sentence within an expanded sentence can be identified. Students enjoy comparing their expanded versions of the basic sentence with the author's. When students are familiar with the story the sentence was taken from, they can try to approximate the author's meaning. Even so, it is likely that they will go in a variety of directions, and because students' expanded sentences may vary greatly from the author's, they come to realize the power of modifiers to transform a sentence.

Manipulating Sentences. Hudson (1980) suggests "moving language around" to help students learn about the structure of English and how to manipulate sentences. Students begin with a sentence and then apply four operations to it: They add, delete, substitute, and rearrange. With the sentence *Children play games,* these manipulations are possible:

Add	Children play games at home.
	Children like to play games.
Delete	Children play.
Substitute	Adults play games.
	Children like games.
	Children play Nintendo.
Rearrange	Games are played by children.
	Games play children.

The last sentence is nonsensical, but thought-provoking, nonetheless.

Students apply the newly learned grammatical concept in their writing. In writing groups students can focus on how the writer used the grammatical concept. They can compliment the writer for using the concept or make suggestions as to how the writer can revise the writing to incorporate the concept. As teachers grade students' writing, they can award points to students who have used the grammatical concept in their writing.

Learning Grammar Through Writing

Because children's knowledge of grammar and usage is dependent on the language spoken in their homes and neighborhoods, some primary- and middle-grade students do not recognize a difference between *me and him* and *he and I.* When the error is brought to their attention, they do not understand, because semantically—at a meaning level—the two versions are identical. Moreover, *me and him* sounds "right" to these students because they hear this construction at home. When other corrections are pointed out to middle- and upper-grade students, they repeat the correct form, shake their heads, and say that it doesn't sound right. *Real* sounds better to some than *really* because it is more familiar. An explanation that adverbs rather than adjectives modify adjectives is not useful either, even if students have had traditional grammar instruction. Correction of nonstandard English errors is perceived as a repudiation of the language spoken in children's homes rather than an explanation that written language requires a more formal language register or dialect. Jaggar (1980) recommends that teachers allow for language differences, acknowledging that everyone speaks a dialect and one is not better or more correct than another.

A better way to deal with grammar and usage errors is to use a problem-solving approach during the editing stage of the writing process. Locating and correcting errors in students' writing is not as threatening as correcting their talk, because it is not as personal. Also, students can more easily accept that "book language" is a different kind of English. During editing, students are error-hunting, trying to make their papers "optimally readable" (Smith, 1982). They recognize that it is a courtesy to readers to make their papers as correct as possible. Through revising and editing, classmates note errors and correct each other, and teachers point out other errors. Sometimes teachers explain the correction (e.g., the past tense of bring is *brought,* not *brung*), and at other times they simply mark the correction, saying that "we usually write it this way." Some errors should be ignored, especially young children's errors;

correcting too many errors teaches students only that their language is inferior or inadequate. The goal in dealing with nonstandard English speakers is not to replace their dialects but to add standard English to their language options.

Adapting to Meet the Needs of Every Student

The goal of grammar instruction is to increase students' ability to structure and manipulate sentences, not to improve their ability to identify parts of speech or, worse yet, to teach them that their language does not meet the teacher's standards. Teaching grammar is a controversial issue, and it is especially so for students whose native language is not English or for students who speak a nonstandard form of English. The best way to encourage students' language development and the acquisition of standard English is to encourage students to talk without fear of embarrassment for being corrected. Teachers and classmates model standard English through their talk, and students also learn standard English syntactic patterns in the books they read.

We offer two suggestions for teaching grammar. First, teachers can teach minilessons about manipulating sentences and provide opportunities for students to build sentences and experiment with new ways of expressing themselves. Second, teachers can deal with nonstandard English in older students' compositions during the editing stage of the writing process.

Assessing Students' Knowledge About Grammar

The traditional way to assess knowledge about grammar is by giving students a written test that asks them to identify parts of speech or to write sentences that are simple, compound, or complex. As we discussed regarding spelling and handwriting, however, a better gauge of students' understanding of language tools is to observe how they use them in genuine communication projects.

Teachers can develop checklists of grammar and usage skills to teach at a particular grade level, or they can list errors they observe in students' writing. Then teachers observe students as they write and examine their compositions to note errors, plan and teach minilessons based on students' needs, note further errors, plan and teach other minilessons, and so on. As teachers identify grammar and usage problems, they should plan minilessons to call students' attention to the problems that make a bigger difference in writing (Pooley, 1974). For example, in the sentences *Mom leave me go outside* and *I fell off of my bike,* the use of *leave* for *let* is a more important problem than the redundant use of *of.*

Review

Spelling, handwriting, and grammar are tools that students use to communicate more effectively. To learn to spell conventionally, students need daily opportunities for reading and writing, and they need to learn proofreading strategies, dictionary procedures, and strategies for predicting the spelling of words. The goal of handwriting instruction is for students develop legible and fluent handwriting. First they learn the manuscript form, and in second or third grade they are introduced to cursive handwriting. During the upper grades students continue to use both forms. Grammar is the structure of language, while usage is the socially accepted way of using words in sentences. Controversy exists today about teaching grammar. Our position is that grammar is best taught as part of the editing stage of the writing process. The three types of grammar are traditional, structural, and transformational, and each has a contribution to make to grammar instruction.

Extensions

1. Observe how spelling is taught in an elementary classroom. How is the spelling program organized? Which components described in this chapter are being used in this classroom?
2. Collect samples of a student's writing and analyze the spelling errors as shown in Figure 12–3 to determine the student's stage of spelling development.
3. Interview a middle- or upper-grade student about spelling. Ask questions such as these:

   Are you a good speller? Why? Why not?

   What do you do when you do not know how to spell a word?

   What else do you do?

   How would you help a classmate who did not know how to spell a word?

   Are some words harder for you to spell than other words? Which words?

   What rules about how to spell words have you learned?

   Do you think that "sound it out" is a good way to try to figure out the spelling of a word you do not know? Why or why not?

   Do you use a dictionary to look up the spelling of words you do not know how to spell?

4. Help students proofread their writing and identify possible misspelled words. Watch what strategies students use to identify and correct misspelled words.
5. Practice forming the manuscript and cursive letters shown in Figures 12–5 and 12–6 until your hand-writing approximates the models. Practicing these handwriting forms will prepare you for working with elementary students. Be sure to take note of the handwriting charts displayed in the classroom before beginning to work with students because several different handwriting programs are available today. The programs are similar, but students are quick to point out when you are not forming a letter correctly!

6. Observe in a primary-grade classroom where the D'Nealian handwriting program is used. Talk with teachers and students about this innovative form. How do the students like it? Do the teachers believe that it ameliorates some of the problems with manuscript handwriting and the transition to cursive, as the developer claims?
7. Observe a left-handed writer and compare this student to right-handed writers in the same classroom. How does the left-handed student's handwriting differ from right-handed students'? What types of special adaptations has the teacher made for teaching the left-handed student?
8. Examine your feelings about whether grammar should be taught in elementary schools. If you decide that it should be, how should it be taught? Compare your opinions with the arguments you find for and against teaching grammar in Davis's "In Defense of Grammar" (1984) and Small's "Why I'll Never Teach Grammar Again" (1985) or in "Grammar Should Be Taught and Learned in Our Schools" (Goba & Brown, 1982).

References

Anderson, K. F. (1985). The development of spelling ability and linguistic strategies. *The Reading Teacher, 39,* 140–147.

Applebee, A. N., Langer, J. A., & Mullis, I. V. S. (1987). *Grammar, punctuation, and spelling: Controlling the conventions of written English at ages 9, 13, and 17* (Report No. 15–W–03). Princeton, NJ: Educational Testing Service.

Askov, E., & Greff, K. N. (1975). Handwriting: Copying versus tracing as the most effective type of practice. *Journal of Educational Research, 69,* 96–98.

Atwell, N. (1987). *In the middle: Writing, reading, and learning with adolescents.* Upper Montclair, NJ: Boynton/Cook.

Barbe, W. B., & Milone, M. N., Jr. (1980). *Why manuscript writing should come before cursive writing* (Zaner-Bloser Professional Pamphlet No. 11). Columbus, OH: Zaner-Bloser.

Barron, R. W. (1980). Visual and phonological strategies in reading and spelling. In U. Frith (Ed.), *Cognitive processes in learning to spell.* London: Academic Press.

Beers, J. W., & Henderson, E. H. (1977). A study of developing orthographic concepts among first graders. *Research in the Teaching of English, 11,* 133–148.

Braddock, R., Lloyd-Jones, R., & Schoer, L. (1963). *Research in written composition.* Champaign, IL: National Council of Teachers of English.

Cullinan, B., Jaggar, A., & Strickland, D. (1974). Oral language expansion in the primary grades. In B. Cullinan (Ed.), *Black dialects and reading.* Urbana, IL: National Council of Teachers of English.

Davis, F. (1984). In defense of grammar. *English Education, 16,* 151–164.

Edelsky, C. (1989). Putting language variation to work for you. In P. Rigg & V. G. Allen (Eds.), *When they don't all speak English: Integrating the ESL student into the regular classroom* (pp. 96–107). Urbana, IL: National Council of Teachers of English.

Elbow, P. (1973). *Writing without teachers.* New York: Oxford University Press.

Elley, W. B., Barham, I. H., Lamb, H., & Wyllie, M. (1976). The role of grammar in a secondary school English curriculum. *Research in the Teaching of English, 10,* 5–21.

Fraser, I. S., & Hodson, L. M. (1978). Twenty-one kicks at the grammar horse. *English Journal, 67,* 49–53.

Frith, U. (1980). Unexpected spelling problems. In U. Frith (Ed.), *Cognitive processes in learning to spell.* London: Academic Press.

Furner, B. A. (1969). Recommended instructional procedures in a method emphasizing the perceptual-motor nature of learning in handwriting. *Elementary English, 46,* 1021–1030.

Gentry, J. R. (1978). Early spelling strategies. *Elementary School Journal, 79,* 88–92.

Gentry, J. R. (1981). Learning to spell developmentally. *The Reading Teacher, 34,* 378–381.

Gentry, J. R. (1982a). An analysis of developmental spellings in *Gnys at wrk. The Reading Teacher, 36,* 192–200.

Gentry, J. R. (1982b). Developmental spelling: Assessment. *Diagnostique, 8,* 52–61.

Gentry, J. R. (1987). *Spel . . . is a four-letter word.* Portsmouth, NH: Heinemann.

Gentry, J. R., & Gillet, J. W. (1993). *Teaching kids to spell.* Portsmouth, NH: Heinemann.

Goba, R. I., & Brown, P. A. (1982). Grammar should be taught and learned in our schools. *English Journal, 73,* 20–23.

Graves, D. H. (1977). Research update: Spelling texts and structural analysis methods. *Language Arts, 54,* 86–90.

Graves, D. H. (1983). *Writing: Teachers and children at work.* Exeter, NH: Heinemann.

Graves, D. H. (1983). *Writing: Teachers and students at work.* Portsmouth, NH: Heinemann.

Groff, P. J. (1963). Who writes faster? *Education, 83,* 367–369.

Hackney, C. (1993). *Handwriting: A way to self-expression.* Columbus, OH: Zaner-Bloser.

Haley-James, S. (Ed.). (1981). *Perspectives on writing in grades 1–8.* Urbana, IL: National Council of Teachers of English.

Harrison, S. (1981). Open letter from a left-handed teacher: Some sinistral ideas on the teaching of handwriting. *Teaching Exceptional Children, 13,* 116–120.

Henderson, E. H. (1980). Word knowledge and reading disability. In E. H. Henderson & J. W. Beers (Eds.), *Developmental and cognitive aspects of learning to spell: A reflection of word knowledge* (pp. 138–148). Newark, DE: International Reading Association.

Hildreth, G. (1960). Manuscript writing after sixty years. *Elementary English, 37,* 3–13.

Hillerich, R. L. (1977). Let's teach spelling—not phonetic misspelling. *Language Arts, 54,* 301–307.

Hillocks, G., Jr. (1987). *Research on written composition: New directions for teaching.* Urbana, IL: National Conference on Research in English and the ERIC Clearinghouse on Reading and Communication Skills.

Hirsch, E., & Niedermeyer, F. C. (1973). The effects of tracing prompts and discrimination training on kindergarten handwriting performance. *Journal of Educational Research, 67,* 81–83.

Hitchcock, M. E. (1989). *Elementary students' invented spellings at the correct stage of spelling development.* Unpublished doctoral dissertation, Norman, University of Oklahoma.

Hodges, R. E. (1982). Research update: On the development of spelling ability. *Language Arts, 59,* 284–290.

Horn, E. (1926). *A basic writing vocabulary.* Iowa City: University of Iowa Press.

Horn, E. (1957). Phonetics and spelling. *Elementary School Journal, 57,* 233–235, 246.

Horn, E. (1960). Spelling. In C. W. Harris (Ed.), *Encyclopedia of educational research* (3rd ed.), pp. 1337–1354. New York: Macmillan.

Horn, T. D. (1947). The effect of the corrected test on learning to spell. *Elementary School Journal, 47,* 277–285.

Horn, T. D. (1969). Spelling. In R. L. Ebel (Ed.), *Encyclopedia of educational research* (4th ed.) (pp. 1282–1299). New York: Macmillan.

Horton, L. W. (1970). Illegibilities in the cursive handwriting of sixth graders. *Elementary School Journal, 70,* 446–450.

Howell, H. (1978). Write on, you sinistrals! *Language Arts, 55,* 852–856.

Hudson, B. A. (1980). Moving language around: Helping students become aware of language structure. *Language Arts, 57,* 614–620.

Hunt, K. W., & O'Donnell, R. C. (1970). *An elementary school curriculum to develop better writing skills.* Washington, DC: U.S. Government Printing Office.

Jackson, A. D. (1971). A comparison of speed of legibility of manuscript and cursive handwriting of intermediate grade pupils. Unpublished doctoral dissertation, University of Arizona. *Dissertation Abstracts, 31,* 4384A.

Jaggar, A. (1980). Allowing for language differences. In G. S. Pinnell (Ed.), *Discovering language with children* (pp. 25–28). Urbana, IL: National Council of Teachers of English.

Johnson, T. D., Langford, K. G., & Quorn, K. C. (1981). Characteristics of an effective spelling program. *Language Arts, 58,* 581–588.

Klein, A., & Schickedanz, J. (1980). Preschoolers write messages and receive their favorite books. *Language Arts, 57,* 742–749.

Lamme, L. L. (1979). Handwriting in an early childhood curriculum. *Young Children, 35,* 20–27.

Lamme, L. L., & Ayris, B. M. (1983). Is the handwriting of beginning writers influenced by writing tools? *Journal of Research and Development in Education, 17,* 32–38.

Lindsay, G. A., & McLennan, D. (1983). Lined paper: Its effects on the legibility and creativity of young children's writing. *British Journal of Educational Psychology, 53,* 364–368.

Malmstrom, J. (1977). *Understanding language: A primer for the language arts teacher.* New York: St. Martin's Press.

Markham, L. R. (1976). Influences of handwriting quality on teacher evaluation of written work. *American Educational Research Journal, 13,* 277–283.

Marsh, G., Friedman, M., Desberg, P., & Welsh, V. (1981). The development of strategies in spelling. In U. Frith (Ed.), *Cognitive processes in learning to spell.* London: Academic Press.

Mellon, J. C. (1969). *Transformational sentence combining: A method for enhancing the development of syntactic fluency in English composition* (NCTE Research Report No. 10). Urbana, IL: National Council of Teachers of English.

Noyce, R. M., & Christie, J. F. (1983). Effects of an integrated approach to grammar instruction on third graders' reading and writing. *Elementary School Journal, 84,* 63–69.

O'Hare, F. (1973). *Sentence combining: Improving student writing without formal grammar instruction* (NCTE Research Report No. 15). Urbana, IL: National Council of Teachers of English.

Pooley, R. C. (1974). *The teaching of English usage.* Urbana, IL: National Council of Teachers of English.

Read, C. (1971). Pre-school children's knowledge of English phonology. *Harvard Educational Review, 41,* 1–34.

Read, C. (1975). *Children's categorization of speech sounds in English* (NCTE Research Report No. 17). Urbana, IL: National Council of Teachers of English.

Read, C. (1986). *Children's creative spelling.* London: Routledge & Kegan Paul.

Small, R. (1985). Why I'll never teach grammar again. *English Education, 17,* 174–178.

Smith, F. (1982). *Writing and the writer.* New York: Holt, Rinehart & Winston.

Stennett, R. G., Smithe, P. C., & Hardy, M. (1972). Developmental trends in letter-printing skill. *Perceptual and Motor Skills, 34,* 183–186.

Stewig, J. W. (1987). Students' spelling errors. *Clearing House, 61,* 34–37.

Strong, W. (1986). *Creative approaches to sentence combining.* Urbana, IL: ERIC Clearinghouse on Reading and Communication Skills and the National Council of Teachers of English.

Suhor, C. (1987). Orthodoxies in language arts education. *Language Arts, 64,* 416–419.

Taylor, K. K., & Kidder, E. B. (1988). The development of spelling skills: From first grade through eighth grade. *Written Communication, 5,* 222–244.

Templeton, S. (1979). Spelling first, sound later: The relationship between orthography and higher order phonological knowledge in older students. *Research in the Teaching of English, 13,* 255–265.

Thurber, D. N. (1987). *D'Nealian handwriting* (Grades K–8). Glenview, IL: Scott, Foresman.

Tompkins, G. E., & McGee, L. M. (1983). Launching nonstandard speakers into standard English. *Language Arts, 60,* 463–469.

Weaver, C. (1979). *Grammar for teachers: Perspectives and definitions.* Urbana, IL: National Council of Teachers of English.

Wilde, S. (1993). *You kan red this! Spelling and punctuation for whole language classrooms, K–6.* Portsmouth, NH: Heinemann.

Wright, C. D., & Wright, J. P. (1980). Handwriting: The effectiveness of copying from moving versus still models. *Journal of Educational Research, 74,* 95–98.

Zutell, J. (1979). Spelling strategies of primary school children and their relationship to Piaget's concept of decentration. *Research in the Teaching of English, 13,* 69–79.

Children's Book References

Barrett, J. (1983). *A snake is totally tail.* New York: Atheneum.

Cleary, B. (1990). *Muggie Maggie.* New York: Morrow.

Galdone, P. (1972). *The three bears.* New York: Houghton Mifflin.

Sterne, N. (1979). *Tyrannosaurus wrecks: A book of dinosaur riddles.* New York: Crowell.

Van Allsburg, C. (1985). *The polar express.* Boston: Houghton Mifflin.

PROCEDURE

Two-thirds of my first graders are Spanish speakers, and the other one-third are English speakers. I speak both languages, and it's natural for me to use them both in my classroom. I have signs and messages written in both languages. Our calendar is labeled in both English and Spanish, and our bulletin board displays are labeled in both languages.

I have both Spanish and English books in the class library. I used to have trouble finding Spanish versions of the books, but now more books are available in Spanish. I try to have Spanish and English versions of the same book. For example, I have *Doctor De Soto* (Steig, 1982), *Frog and Toad Are Friends* (Lobel, 1970), *Corduroy* (Freeman, 1968), *Where the Wild Things Are* (Sendak, 1963), and *The True Story of the Three Little Pigs* (Scieszka, 1989) in both languages. My first graders really like the Robert Munsch books,

including *Mortimer* (1985), and I'm glad that these books are available in both languages.

I have only one or two copies of most books, but I have sets (10 in Spanish and 5 in English) of our focus books. I spend approximately one week on each book, and my students read these books, talk and write about them, and work on art projects and other related activities.

Each week I teach students to read a new poem and hang the English and Spanish versions in the Poetry Center. I have two racks with pocket charts. I write each line of the poem on sentence strips using one color marking pen for the English version and a different color for the Spanish version. Groups of students sort and sequence the strips in the pocket charts, and they reread the poem using choral reading techniques.

My students also write in journals every day. They write about events in their own lives, books we are reading, or things we are studying. My aide works with students at the Writing Center. She encourages them to use invented spelling and helps them sound out words as they write. I also write back to students. If the student writes in Spanish, she responds in Spanish, and if the student writes in English, she

> *My goal is for every student to learn to read and write. Some students use Spanish; others use English. Both languages are valued in my classroom, and the processes of reading and writing are the same in Spanish and English.*

Paula Schiefer
First-Grade Bilingual Teacher
Washington School

uses English. One of Jessica's journal entries is shown in the accompanying figure. Jessica is learning to read and write in Spanish. At the top of the entry she writes "Today is Tuesday." Along the left side of the paper she has written "I like the stars in the sky." Jessica's spelling is almost entirely conventional, but she began the word *cielo* (sky) with an *s* instead of a *c* because she concentrated on the /s/ sound at the beginning of the word. My aide did not correct Jessica; instead, she complimented her on how easy her writing was to read and encouraged her to write more. Later my aide responded in Spanish on the right side of the entry, "Jessica, I also really like the stars."

My students spend two hours each morning involved in reading, writing, listening, and talking activities. My schedule is:

8:30–9:00—*Class Meeting*
I introduce students to the focus book of the week. Later they will reread the book with me. I also present the poems for the poetry center and teach minilessons.

9:00–10:00—*Students Work at Centers*
They reread the focus book with me at the Reading Center, write in journals at the Writing Center, and also work on projects, listen to books at the Listening Center, read independently at the Library Center, and read the poem at the Poetry Center.

10:00–10:15—*Recess*

10:15–10:45—*Read Aloud*

I read aloud books related to the literature focus unit, and we talk about the book in grand conversations or do quickdraws.

ASSESSMENT

I think it's my job to listen and watch students as they work. I track my students' development in writing, for example, by noting the topics they choose, their invented spellings, and the length and complexity of their writing. For reading, I listen to my students read orally, examine their responses to books, and watch them read independently at the Library Center.

ADAPTATIONS

I think that children learn to read and write by reading and writing—

in a safe, supportive environment, so I don't change my program very much for individual students. I do provide more individual attention and support for any student who is not off to a smooth start. My aide and I read and write more often with this student. I encourage students who are off to a strong start to select challenging books to read, and I involve them in writing books and other projects.

REFLECTIONS

Teaching a bilingual class isn't any more difficult than teaching a monolingual class. I teach my students to respect each other and to value their own language and culture. Both my Spanish and English speakers learn to read and write. That's success!

13

Expecting Diversity: The Multicultural Classroom

INSIGHT _____

Given the ever-changing demographics of American society, teachers can expect diversity in their classrooms. Almost every teacher will work with students representing a variety of cultures during their teaching careers, and nurturing sensitivity to and respect for all ethnic and linguistic groups is every teacher's responsibility. Multicultural language arts activities such as creating a readers theatre presentation from a book about Martin Luther King, Jr., and keeping a simulated journal from the viewpoint of a Japanese American during a study of World War II are important first steps, but beyond isolated activities, multicultural themes should be infused throughout the curriculum. As you read this chapter, an issue for you to think about is:

How can teachers use language arts to teach cultural diversity?

*A*merica is a culturally pluralistic society, and our ethnic, racial, and socioeconomic diversity is increasingly being reflected in elementary classrooms. According to the 1990 Census, 25% of the population in the United States classified themselves as non–European Americans. The percentage of culturally diverse children is even higher. In California 51% of school-aged children belong to ethnic minority groups, and in New York state 40% do. Given current birth rates of minority groups and immigration patterns, it has been estimated that by the year 2000, both Hispanic American and Asian American populations will have grown by more than 20%. The African American population is estimated to grow by 12%. In fact, demographers predict that by the year 2000, one in three Americans will be nonwhite (American Council on Education and the Education Commission of the States, 1988). These changing demographic statistics will have a significant impact on elementary classrooms, as more and more students come from linguistically and culturally diverse backgrounds. More than ever before, all of today's students will live in a global society, and they need the skills and knowledge to live harmoniously with other cultural groups.

America is a nation of immigrants, and dealing with cultural diversity is not a new responsibility for public schools; however, the magnitude of diversity is much greater now. In the past, America was viewed as a melting pot in which language and cultural differences would be assimilated or combined to form a new, truly American culture. What actually happened, though, was that the European American culture rose to the top because it was the dominant immigrant group, and the cultures of other groups sank (Banks, 1994). The concept of cultural pluralism has replaced assimilation. According to cultural pluralism, people have the right to retain their cultural identity within American society, and each culture contributes to and enriches the total society. This concept is an outgrowth of the civil rights movement of the 1960s. Other ethnic cultures were inspired by the civil rights movement and the pride that African Americans showed for their culture, and they have been empowered, too.

Children of diverse cultures come to school with a broad range of language and literacy experiences, even if they are not the same as those of mainstream or European American children. Minority children have already learned to communicate in at least one language, and, if they don't speak English, they want to learn English in order to make friends, learn, and communicate just like their classmates. Teachers who teach culturally and linguistically diverse students must implement a language arts program that is sensitive to and reflective of these students' backgrounds and needs. In fact, all teachers must be prepared to work with this ever-growing population, and teachers who have no minority students in their classrooms still need to incorporate a multicultural perspective in their curriculum in order to prepare their students to interact effectively in the increasingly multicultural American society.

We take the perspective that cultural and linguistic diversity is not a problem for teachers to overcome; instead, it provides an opportunity to enhance and enrich the learning of all students. Teachers need to provide literacy experiences that reflect the multitude of backgrounds from which the students come, and multicultural literature plays an important role in filling that need (Yokota, 1993).

514

LINGUISTICALLY AND CULTURALLY DIVERSE STUDENTS

We focus on four diverse cultural groups in this chapter: African Americans, Asian Americans, Hispanic Americans, and Native Americans. These umbrella labels are deceiving, as there are substantial differences among the cultures within a label. For example, there are no composite Native Americans; instead, Eskimos and the more than 100 Indian tribes in North America are grouped together under the Native American umbrella label.

The people within a cultural group share common ancestry, language, cultural history, traditions, and interests. Some groups have been in America for hundreds of years, while others are new immigrants who have been in America for only months or a few years. Some are native speakers of English, and others are learning English as a second language. Even though umbrella labels are used for convenience, teachers must be careful to distinguish among cultural groups within a label.

1. African Americans. African Americans are the ancestors of the slaves brought from Africa in chains to work on plantations in the United States between 1650 and 1850. Many African Americans speak a dialect of English known as Black English.

2. Asian Americans. Asian Americans are a very diverse group, including Chinese, Japanese, Koreans, Taiwanese, Vietnamese, Hmong, Fillipinos, and Thai. Some Asian Americans immigrated to the United States more than 100 years ago, including the Chinese who worked in the California gold fields and laid track for the first transcontinental railroad. People from other Asian American groups, such as Vietnamese and Hmong, have immigrated more recently as war and political upheaval have caused them to flee their homelands.

3. Hispanic Americans. Hispanic Americans are not one culture but a collection of cultures originating in Central and South America. The three most populous groups are Puerto Rican Americans, Cuban Americans, and Mexican Americans. Most Hispanics have immigrated to the United States during this century. Many Cubans arrived when Castro assumed power in Cuba, and stories of Haitians' and Mexicans' desperate attempts to reach America are shown on television news programs almost every week.

4. Native Americans. Eskimos and American Indians are called Native Americans. These people were the original inhabitants of the United States, and they had developed complex societies hundreds of years before the European explorers and colonists arrived.

Of course, there are other groups, too, including Arabic Americans, Indian Americans, and Polish Americans. Also, there are regional groups and religious groups within the United States.

Impact of Culture on Learning Language Arts

Culture affects the way people think and the way they use language. In her study of three culturally different American communities, Shirley Brice Heath (1983) found that because of different lifestyles and child-rearing practices, children come to school with radically different literacy experiences and expectations about learning. Since the American families in the Heath study had dramatically different experiences with written language in their English-speaking homes, the diversity of experiences of children from other than English-speaking homes is so much greater.

Children from each cultural group bring their own unique backgrounds of experience to the process of learning, and they have difficulty reading concepts outside their backgrounds of experience. This difficulty is worse for students who are learning English as a second language. Think, for example, of the different experiences and language knowledge that children of the Vietnamese refugees, Native American children, and the children of Russian Jewish immigrants bring to school. No matter what ethnic group they belong to or what language they speak, all students use the same cognitive and linguistic processes to learn.

Children of diverse ethnic groups have met with varying degrees of success in schools, depending on their previous cultural experiences, the expectations that students and their parents have, and the expectations that teachers have for them. Often a discrepancy exists between the way classrooms operate and the ways students from various ethnic groups behave (Law & Eckes, 1990). Four common cultural behaviors that differ from mainstream behaviors are:

- *No eye contact.* In some Asian and Hispanic cultures, avoiding eye contact is polite and respectful behavior. Mainstream teachers sometimes mistakenly assume that when students avoid eye contact, they are not paying attention or are sullen and uncooperative.

- *Cooperation.* Students from many Southeast Asian, Polynesian, and Native American cultures are taught to cooperate and help each other, and in school they often assist classmates with their work. In contrast, many mainstream students are more competitive than cooperative, and sometimes mainstream teachers view cooperating on assignments as cheating.

- *Fear of making mistakes.* Mainstream teachers encourage students to take risks and view making mistakes as a natural part of the learning process. In some cultures, especially the Japanese culture, correctness is valued above all else, and students are taught not to guess or take risks.

- *Informal classroom environment.* In some cultures, including European and Asian cultures, the school environment is much more formal than it is in American schools. Students from these cultures view American schools as chaotic, and they interpret the informality as permission to misbehave.

Many Asian American students have been taught to keep a social distance between the teacher and themselves. For example, out of respect to the teacher, they look down when they are spoken to and feel more comfortable remaining in their assigned seats. Grand conversations and other informal activities can make these students feel uncomfortable because the lack of structure appears to indicate disrespect for the teacher. Asian American parents typically equate learning and knowledge with factual information, and they expect a great deal of homework (Cheng, 1987).

Hakuta and Garcia (1989) found that the most effective classrooms for Mexican American students have a discourse style similar to the one they know at home. Many Mexican American students are familiar with the give-and-take of cooperative learning, and they value working together and learning in a warm, responsive environment. These students work well in a child-centered, integrated program that is responsive to children's needs. When it is possible, children in the primary grades should have the opportunity to develop literacy in their home language first.

African American and Native American students have special needs, too. For too long schools have neglected and failed these students. Teachers understand and build on these students' abilities, appreciate their varied backgrounds, and their potential for learning (Brooks, 1985). Teachers must also take into account historical, economic, psychological, and linguistic barriers that have led to oppression and low expectations. One way to help raise children's self-esteem and build pride in their cultural groups is by incorporating literature about African Americans and Native Americans into their instructional programs. Teachers' acceptance of students' nonstandard English dialects is also important.

Bilingual Students and Students Who Speak English as a Second Language

Students whose native languages are not English are referred to as English as a Second Language (ESL) students, and students who are not yet sufficiently fluent in English to perform academic tasks successfully are sometimes called Limited English Proficient (LEP) students. Some educators have argued that the term LEP promotes negative attitudes toward linguistically diverse students, and they recommend using a more positive term such as Potentially English Proficient (PEP) (Freeman & Freeman, 1992) or Readers and Writers of English as Another Language (REAL) (Rigg & Allen, 1989). Children who speak their native language at home and speak English fluently at school are *bilingual speakers.*

Students learning English as a second language are a diverse group. Some are fluent in both English and their native language, and others know little or no English. Some learn to speak English quickly, and others learn more slowly. It often takes 4 to 7 years to become a proficient speaker of English, and the more similar the first language is to English, the easier it will be to learn English (Allen, 1991).

One conflict for bilingual students is that learning and speaking standard English are often perceived by family and community members as a rejection of family and culture. Cultural pluralism has replaced the "melting pot" point of view, and people in minority ethnic groups are no longer as willing to give up their culture and language to join the mainstream culture. Often they choose to live and function in both cultures, with free access to their cultural patterns, and switch from one culture to the other as the situation demands.

Valuing Students' Native Languages. Until recently, most non-English-speaking students were submerged into English-speaking classrooms and left to "sink or swim." Unfortunately, many students sank and dropped out of school before graduating from high school. To better meet the needs of linguistically diverse students, teachers now value students' native language and help their students develop a high level of proficiency in their native language as well as in English as a second language. Instruction in students' native language is effective and equitable for large groups of language-minority students (Faltis, 1993). Freeman and Freeman (1993) recommend the following guidelines for supporting and valuing students' native languages. Teachers can accomplish most of these guidelines using a foreign language dictionary, even if they do not speak or write the language themselves.

1. *Environmental Print.*   Teachers post signs and other environmental print written in students' native language in the classroom. In a primary-grade classroom posters with color words, numbers, and the days of the week should be written both in English and in students' native language. Bulletin board titles and captions on posters can also be translated in students' native language.

2. *Reading Materials.*   Teachers add books, magazines, and other reading materials written in the students' native language in the library center. Quality books for children written in a variety of languages are becoming increasingly available in the United States. Also, award-winning books of children's literature are being translated into other languages, especially Spanish and Chinese. Books such as *Where the Wild Things Are* (Sendak, 1963) have been translated for younger children, and *Tuck Everlasting* (Babbitt, 1975) for older children. Sometimes parents and other members of the community are willing to lend books written in a child's native language for the child to use in school. Or, sometimes parents can translate a book being used in class for their child.

These bilingual students take turns pointing to the words as they use choral reading to reread a favorite poem.

3. Writing Books. Language-minority students can write and publish books in their native language. They use the writing process just as English-speaking students do, and they can share their published books with classmates and place them in the classroom library.

4. Bilingual Tutors. Language-minority students can read and write with tutors, older students, classmates, and parents who speak their native language. Some classrooms have native language aides who read and write with students in the native language. Other times parents or older native-speaking students come into the classroom to work with students.

5. Native Language Videotapes. Teachers can use videotapes of students reading and dramatizing stories in their native language. In addition, they can dramatize events in history or demonstrate how to do something in their native language. Creating and viewing these videotapes are useful for building students' proficiency in their native language.

Through these activities teachers value language-minority students' native languages. The activities also help students expand their native language proficiency, develop greater self-confidence, and value their own language.

Learning a Second Language.   Learning a second language is a constructive process just as learning a native language is, and children develop language in a predictable way through interactions with children and adults. Research suggests that second-language acquisition is similar to first-language acquisition. Urzua (1980) lists three principles culled from the research:

- *Learning strategies.* People use many similar language-learning strategies whether they are small children learning their native language or older children or adults learning a second language.
- *Stages of acquisition.* Just as children learning to speak their native language move through a series of developmental stages, second-language learners move through several stages as they learn a new language.
- *Meaningful, functional, and genuine opportunities to use language.* First- or second-language learning takes place only when learners have the opportunity to use language for meaningful, functional, and genuine purposes.

When children and adults first arrive in the United States, they go through a silent period (Krashen, 1982) of several months in which they observe others communicating prior to talking or writing in English themselves. Then they begin tentatively to use language to communicate, and through listening, talking, reading, and writing, their language use becomes more cognitively and linguistically complex. The stages of second-language acquisition are listed in Figure 13–1.

The English spoken by newcomers is syntactically less complex. In addition, idiomatic expressions are avoided, words are enunciated clearly, and the rate of speech is slower. Sentences are very short, often with two or three key words, much like the telegraphic speech of young children. For example, a newcomer might say "No pencil" for "I don't have a pencil" or "Book table" for "The book is on the table." They also overgeneralize and call all adults in the school "teachers." As second-language learners acquire labels for more concepts and more sophisticated syntactic structures, they progressively use

Figure 13–1   Stages in Second-Language Acquisition

Stage 1

Yes-no answers
Positive statements
Subject pronouns (e.g., he, she)
Present tense/present habitual verb tense
Possessive pronouns (e.g., my, your)

Stage 2

Simple plurals of nouns
Affirmative sentences
Subject and object pronouns (all)
Possessive ('s)
Negation
Possessive pronouns (e.g., mine)

Stage 3

Present progressive tense (-ing)
Conjunctions (e.g., and, but, or, because, so, as)

Stage 4

Questions (who? what? which? where?)
Irregular plurals of nouns
Simple future tense (going to)
Prepositions

Stage 5

Future tense (will)
Questions (when? how?)
Conjunctions (e.g., either, nor, neither, that, since)

Stage 6

Regular past-tense verbs
Questions (why?)
Contractions (e.g., isn't)
Modal verbs (e.g., can, must, do)

Stage 7

Irregular past-tense verbs
Past-tense questions
Auxilliary verbs (has, is)
Passive voice

Stage 8

Conditional verbs
Imperfect verb tense
Conjunctions (e.g., though, if, therefore)
Subjunctive verb mood

Gonzales, 1981a, pp. 156–157.

longer and more complex sentences. They move out of the here-and-now, present-tense verb constructions to past and future constructions; however, many students learning English as a second language have difficulty adding the -ed past-tense marker to verbs, as in "Yesterday I play ball."

When parents talk with preschool children learning to speak their native language, they support and extend the children's language. Parents also understand their children's special words for things. These adaptations are called "motherese." There are striking parallels between the adaptations made by people who interact effectively with ESL students and those described for caretaker speech.

Students learning English as a second language often mix English with their native language, shifting back and forth even within sentences. This often-misunderstood phenomenon is called code-switching (Troika, 1981; Lara, 1989). Sometimes students read the text in English but mentally translate it into their native language in order to understand it. This takes a little more time than native speakers need, so teachers must allow more time for ESL students to translate teachers' and classmates' questions and comments from English into their native language and translate their ideas from their native language into English. Too often teachers assume that students have not understood or do not know the answer when they do not respond immediately. Code-switching is a special linguistic and social skill; it is not a confusion between languages or a corruption of students' native language.

After approximately 2 years, many second-language learners are fluent enough in English to carry on everyday conversations, but it can take students learning English as a second language up to 5, 6, or 7 years to achieve the same level of fluency in English as their classmates (Cummins, 1989). Interestingly, Wong-Fillmore (1985) has found that students learn English in class from teachers and classmates who speak fluent English rather than from their cultural peer group. Moreover, school may be the only place where students speak English!

Instructional Programs for ESL Students.   Three programs are being used with students who are learning English as a second language. One type is submersion in which students are thrown into the regular classroom with no special help. A second type is immersion. The language of the classroom is English, but a teacher's aide or other classmates speak the student's native language and translate for the language-minority student in the classroom. A third type of program is bilingual. In this program instruction is conducted in both English and the student's native language. Of these three programs, researchers have found that bilingual programs are the most effective.

The preferred approach to bilingual education is preview/teach/review. In this approach the content of the lesson is previewed in one language, the body of the lesson is taught in the second language, and then the lesson is reviewed in the first language (Scarcella, 1990). This approach is often used when two teachers—one English-speaking teacher and one fluent in Spanish or another language—team teach. Alternative approaches for bilingual education are alternating English and another language day by day or using direct translation in which the teacher provides instant translation in the second language for everything that is said in English. These two approaches are not as effective because students learn to tune out when the unfamiliar language is being spoken.

Students are moved out of bilingual programs into English-only programs as soon as they reach a level where they can communicate in English. These programs are known as early exit programs. In other programs students remain in bilingual programs longer, and they receive instruction to further develop their native language proficiency. These programs are late exit or bilingual maintenance programs, and they are preferred (Scarcella, 1990). There is strong evidence that language-minority children do better in bilingual than English-only programs because bilingual students do not fall as far behind in content area courses, have better self-esteem, and reach higher levels of proficiency in both languages (Scarcella, 1990).

Bilingual programs, however, are not possible when students in a school speak too many different languages or when there are not enough qualified bilingual teachers. In classrooms, for example, with one Punjabi speaker, one Portugese speaker, and one Arabic speaker, the teacher will not be able to help these three students learn to read and write in their native languages first. However, teachers can convey an interest in and appreciation for the students' home languages and cultures. Students can bring a native language book from home to display or read during reading workshop. Teachers can find out about the students' home cultures and languages from parents or other sources; and by finding out which aspects of the classroom environment are most alien to students' home cultures and languages, teachers can help make students and parents more at ease by modifying expectations and by working on areas of special need.

The English-Only Movement.   In 1986, voters in California approved Proposition 63, which declared English as the official language in the state; since then, more than a dozen other states have enacted similar laws. Some interpret this English-only movement to mean that bilingual programs and the use of languages other than English in elementary classrooms are not permissible. Many educators are concerned about the initiative, because they believe bilingual education offers non-English-speaking children their greatest opportunity for success.

At its convention in 1987, the National Council of Teachers of English responded to the English-only movement by passing a resolution to condemn "any attempts to render invisible the native languages of any Americans or to deprive English of the rich influences of the languages and cultures of any of the peoples of America" and to actively oppose "any actions intended to mandate or declare English as an official language or to 'preserve,' 'purify,' or 'enhance' the language [because] any such action will not only stunt the vitality of the language, but also ensure its erosion and in effect create hostility toward English, making it more difficult to teach and learn" (NCTE, 1988).

This is a controversial issue. Federal legislation is pending that would make English the official language in America. Harvey Daniels (1990) suggests several things teachers can do to nuture linguistic pluralism and tolerance for ethnic minorities. First of all, teachers can become more informed about multicultural education. Three professional organizations for teachers who work with culturally and linguistically diverse students are:

National Association for Bilingual Education (NABE)
1220 L Street NW, Suite 605
Washington, DC 20005

Teachers of English to Speakers of Other Languages (TESOL)
1600 Cameron Street, Suite 300
Alexandria, VA 22314

National Association for Multicultural Education (NAME)
James B. Boyer, Executive Director
261 Bluemont Hall
Kansas State University
Manhattan, KS 66505

Second, in their own classrooms teachers can model tolerance and open-minded attitudes about linguistic and cultural diversity. This is especially important when teachers have minority group students in their own classrooms. Teachers teach concepts about multiculturalism and language diversity in literature focus units and theme cycles. As students read folktales from around the world, they learn about the universality of stories, and as they read stories such as *Hello, My Name Is Scrambled Eggs* (Gilson, 1985), a story about a Vietnamese refugee becoming acculturated in the United States, students become more sympathetic to the challenges facing newly arrived immigrants. Or, students can research and share their own family histories during a theme cycle about pilgrims or immigrants.

Third, teachers can support bilingual instruction for minority group students in their own schools and work to reform the school's curriculum to make it more multilingual and multicultural. Beyond the school level committed teachers can become active in local and national professional organizations and work for proactive legislation that respects linguistic diversity and cultural pluralism.

Nonstandard English Speakers

A single "pure" form of English does not exist; all English speakers speak one dialect or another. Dialects vary across geographic regions, ethnic backgrounds, and socioeconomic levels. Speakers of particular dialects are distinguished by their pronunciations, word choices, and grammatical forms. Consider the different pronunciations of Bostonians, New Yorkers, and Texans; the different words—*pop, soda, soft drink, soda pop,* and *tonic*—used to describe the same carbonated beverage; and the double negatives of some dialects as in "I ain't got no bread." This diversity reflects America's cultural pluralism.

Some dialects, however, command more respect than others. The dialect of television reporters and commentators, of authors of books and newspaper and magazine articles, and of school is known as standard English (SE). The other dialects are collectively termed nonstandard English (NSE). Students who use nonstandard speech patterns in 20% to 30% of their conversation are generally referred to as nonstandard-English speakers. Research suggests that before adolescence children are not even aware that standard English is the prestige dialect (Labov, 1970).

In the past, African American students, Appalachian students, and others who spoke a dialect different from standard English were considered to have little language ability. Myths about nonstandard dialects that were perpetuated for generations have been disproved. Nonstandard English dialects are not inferior language systems; rather, they are different, rule-governed systems that have patterns of their own (Labov, 1969). Children and adults who speak these dialects are neither cognitively nor linguistically deficient.

Children who speak NSE dialects develop language competency in the same way and at a rate parallel to standard English development. Distinctive phonological and syntactic features of Black English and other nonstandard dialects are listed in Figure 13–2. Researchers have found that NSE speakers gradually incorporate some features of standard English into their speech and writing during the elementary grades. The increasing use of SE features may be due to peer interaction, exposure to standard English on television, or instruction in standard English at school.

Labov (1966) has identified seven areas of language arts instruction necessary for NSE students; they are, in order of priority:

1. Understanding spoken standard English
2. Reading books written in standard English
3. Communicating effectively through talk
4. Communicating effectively through writing
5. Using standard English forms in writing: spelling words correctly
6. Using standard English forms in talk
7. Using standard English pronunciation

Figure 13–2   Contrasts Between Standard and Nonstandard English

Contrast	Standard English	Nonstandard English
Phonological Contrasts		
1. *r*-lessness	guard, fort	god, fought
2. *l*-lessness	help, you'll	hep, you
3. Final consonant cluster simplified	past, desk, meant	pass, des, men
4. Substitutions for /th/	then, mouth	den, mouf
5. Substitution of /n/ for /ing/	coming	comin'
Syntactic Contrasts		
1. Plural marker	two girls	two girl
2. Possessive marker	a dog's bone	a dog bone
3. Double negatives	don't have any, doesn't have	don't got none, ain't got no
4. Preposition	at his friend's house, lives on 3rd Street	to his friend's house, live 3rd Street
5. Indefinite article	an apple	a apple
6. Pronoun form	we have, his ball	us got, he ball
7. Double subjects	John runs	John he run
8. Person-number agreement	she walks, Bill has	she walk, Bill have
9. Present participle	he is coming	he comin'
10. Past marker	Mother asked	Mother ask
11. Verb form	I said	I say
12. Verb "to be" (present tense)	she is busy	she busy, she be busy
13. Verb "to be" (past tense)	we were happy	we was happy
14. Future form	I will go	I'ma go, I gonna go
15. "If" construction	I asked if	I ask did

Notice that the sequence moves from competency in basic oral and written communication to the acquisition of standard English syntactic and phonological features. Using standard English in writing precedes oral language proficiency.

The teacher's role is threefold: to become sensitive to the needs of NSE speakers; to learn about the distinctive features of NSE so as to understand the difficulties and frustrations that NSE students face in learning to read, write, and spell in standard English; and to accept and show respect for students' language. Teachers' rejection of nonstandard dialects as well as confusion about nonstandard English interferes with students' learning (Goodman & Buck, 1983). Teachers should establish a climate in their classrooms where students will feel that their language is accepted. Students' language reflects their culture, and it is essential to respect it. Teachers should also demonstrate that they truly believe their students capable of handling two or more dialects. Teachers usually assume that non-English speakers who have recently arrived in the United States will learn to speak standard English, but this same confidence is rarely shown to NSE speakers.

Students naturally use their NSE dialect in reading aloud. Even though students comprehend the standard English they are reading, they often "translate" the language of the textbook into their dialect. This phenomenon can be explained using transformational grammar terminology: Whereas the surface structures of NSE and SE are different, the deep, meaning levels are the same, and the dialectal errors do not interfere with meaning (Goodman & Buck, 1983).

Accepting students' linguistic differences, however, is not synonymous with not teaching standard English. Students who speak an NSE dialect need to participate in oral language activities to be able to use the forms of standard English. Many of the oral language activities can be used to help these students expand their use of sentence patterns and grammatical structures. Interrupting students while they are speaking or reading aloud to correct their NSE "errors," however, is not an effective practice. In fact, students may choose not to talk or read aloud if they do not feel that their language will be accepted. Activities to teach standard English are as follows.

Use children's literature that involves SE patterns in teaching standard English. Programs using children's literature as a model have been found to be successful in expanding students' language repertoire (Cullinan, Jaggar, & Strickland, 1974; Strickland, 1973). A three-step approach has been developed to introduce NSE speakers to SE syntactic patterns (Tompkins & McGee, 1983):

1. Introduce an SE pattern by reading a predictable book that repeats the syntactic pattern.
2. Provide extensive practice with the pattern through reading, role-playing, puppetry, and dictating or writing the story.
3. Have students manipulate the pattern by inventing new text for the pattern they are practicing.

Emphasis in this approach is on imitating and repeating the pattern. At first, students will use their own dialect in repeating the pattern, but as they feel more comfortable with it, they should be encouraged to substitute the SE form. Emphasize the specific contrast between the dialect and the standard form. A list of predictable books with patterns and sample activities to teach some NSE/SE contrasts is presented in Figure 13–3. Teachers can locate additional predictable books to use in introducing other NSE/SE syntactic and phonological contrasts.

Teaching Linguistically and Culturally Diverse Students

To help bilingual and non-English-speaking students learn English as a second language, teachers need to develop an understanding and appreciation of the culture and language the students bring with them. A teacher's attitude toward students' language and culture is one key to success or failure in teaching language-different students.

Welcoming "Newcomers" and New Students. "Newcomers" are recently arrived immigrants who speak little or no English and who are unfamiliar with

Figure 13–3   Pattern Books and Sample Activities to Teach Some SE/NSE Contrasts

SE/NSE Contrast	Sample Book	Book's Pattern	Steps 2 and 3 Sample Activities
Plural	Carle, E. (1969). *The Very Hungry Caterpillar.* Cleveland: Collins World.	The very hungry caterpillar eats through: 1 apple 2 pears 3 plums, etc.	Have children draw pictures of more foods and punch holes in them. Have children use the food pictures to tell and write new stories.
Possessive	Flack, M. (1932). *Ask Mr. Bear.* New York: Macmillan.	Danny asks Mr. Bear and other animals, "Can you give me something for my mother's birthday?"	Have children make labels using possessives for pencils and other belongings. Then children read the labels aloud.

Person-Number Agreement	Zemach, M. (1969). *The Judge.* New York: Farrar, Straus & Giroux.	Each prisoner describes the horrible thing in more detail:
		    It growls, it groans
		    It chews up stones
		    It spreads its wings
		    And does bad things
			Have children use collage materials to construct their own horrible things. Then children write descriptions of their horrible things.

Past Tense	Westcott, N. (1980). *I Know an Old Lady Who Swallowed a Fly.* Boston: Little, Brown.	This is a cumulative tale about an old lady who swallowed a fly and a series of other animals to catch the fly.	Have children make an old lady puppet and draw pictures of the animals she eats. Then children use the puppet to retell the story.
Present Participle	Galdone, P. (1968). *Henny Penny.* New York: Clarion.	Henny Penny warns everyone, "The sky is falling!"	Have the children act out the story and repeat the refrain.
Negative	Guarino, D. (1989). *Is Your Mama a Llama?* New York: Scholastic.	A llama asks other young animals, "Is your mama a llama?" They respond, "No she is not."	Have children compose new episodes and record them in individual booklets.
Verb "to be" (Present tense)	Wood, A. (1982). *Quick as a Cricket.* London: Child's Play.	A child compares himself to a variety of animals using similes, for example: I'm as mean as a shark.	Have children choose their favorite comparisons and create new ones using the format: I'm as _____ as a _____ .
Verb "to be" (Past tense)	Mack, S. (1974). *10 Bears in My Bed.* New York: Pantheon.	A little boy tries to get 10 bears out of his bed. Each page begins: There were (number) in his bed and the little one said, "Roll over!"	Tape-record the story, leaving space on the tape for children to repeat the sentence pattern.

Adapted from Tompkins & McGee, 1983.

American life and the mainstream culture. These students are usually apprehensive as they try to cope in an unfamiliar and confusing school environment. In addition, they may have very recently survived a life-threatening escape from their homeland. Other students who are learning English as a second language are new to the school, but they have lived in the United States for a longer time, or perhaps all of their lives. Both groups of students have special needs, and teachers must take care to welcome the students and help them adjust to the classroom. Law and Eckes (1990) and Gibbons (1991) suggest the following steps:

1. Prepare the Class. Tell students about the new student and the country he or she comes from. Also talk with students about how to make the student feel welcome.

2. Welcome the Student. Both the teacher and classmates can welcome the new student even if no one speaks the new student's language. Everyone can smile and through gestures and body language make the new student feel welcome.

3. Learn How to Pronounce and Spell the New Student's Name. Teachers learn how to pronounce the new student's name by asking the student's parents or the student himself or herself. Our feelings of self-worth are linked with our names, so it is important that the new student's name be treated with respect. Teachers should not try to shorten or Anglicize the student's name to make it easier to pronounce or spell.

4. Introduce the New Student. Teachers introduce the new student to the class and tell a little about the country the student is from. Also, if possible, introduce a few words and phrases in the student's native language.

5. Show Respect for the New Student. Teachers model appropriate behavior and how to show respect for the new student, his or her culture, and ways of dressing. Children can be cruel, but when teachers model how to show respect for the new student, classmates are more likely to, as well.

6. Allow the Student to be Silent. New students can take weeks to develop enough confidence to begin speaking English. At first the talk they hear in the classroom may be meaningless noise, and students need time to listen to the talk going on around them and watch how their classmates use language.

The next step is to orient the student to the school and classroom routines and to teach newcomers survival vocabulary. English-speaking students can serve as peer-tutors and "buddies" for the new students. Wagner (1982) reports that her students took turns teaching the language-minority students in her class. The program was terminated after one semester because the non-English-speaking students had learned to speak English! Suggestions for orienting new students include (Gonzales, 1981b):

- Teach survival vocabulary, including courtesy words and phrases such as "hello," "thank you," and "I need to go to the bathroom."
- Try to locate an adult or older student who speaks both the child's native language and English to teach English-speaking students a few survival

words and phrases in the child's native language and to serve as a volunteer aide to ease the new student's transition to the classroom.

• Orient the new student to the school setting and the classroom. Take the child on a "survival tour" of the school, pointing out the cafeteria, library, bathroom, principal's office, and other essential locations, as well as how to return to the classroom from these locations. Continue with a classroom "survival tour," and add labels for classroom objects. If possible, write the labels in both the child's native language and English. Draw maps of the classroom and school with the student.

• Ask students to volunteer to serve as "buddies" or peer-tutors for the non-English-speaking student. Buddies involve the new student in hands-on and natural-language activities, such as playing basketball, erasing the chalkboard, delivering messages to other classrooms, or working on a jigsaw puzzle.

From the first day, teachers should involve new students in activities, often working with a buddy or a small group of classmates. They should also seat the new students so that they can watch what classmates do and the teacher can easily monitor the new students' progress. If other students in the class speak the same language, they should be seated close to each other in order to explain assignments and work together.

Strategies for Teaching Language- and Cultural-Minority Students. The single most important strategy for teaching diverse learners is to provide *comprehensible input* (Krashan, 1985), or messages that students understand. Students understand better when they have background knowledge about the topic being presented and when pictures, models, demonstrations, and other contextually rich information is provided.

Cummins (1981) has developed a model to explain why students who are learning English may have success or difficulty learning in various instructional settings. This model has two components: cognitive activity and contextual assistance. Cognitive activity refers to the knowledge or thinking involved in the activity, and any activity may range from cognitively undemanding to demanding. If students are familiar with the topic being presented, know the specialized vocabulary, or have experienced this type of thinking, the activity is less demanding.

The contextual assistance component refers to the amount of contextual assistance that is provided for an activity. Contextual assistance includes concrete materials, diagrams, charts, illustrations, demonstrations, and dramatic activities. When contextual information is presented, the activity is contextually embedded, and when there is no contextual information, the activity is contextually reduced. When students have contextual assistance, they are able to understand concepts that otherwise might be too difficult for them.

Cummins's model is presented in Figure 13–4; the two components are drawn to create four quadrants to show how instruction in the classroom impacts on second-language learners. Activities that are cognitively undemanding and context-embedded (category 1) are the least difficult for students, and activities that are cognitively demanding and context-reduced (category 4) are the most difficult.

Figure 13–4   Comprehensible Input

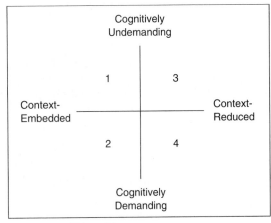

Cummins, 1981, p. 21.

As teachers plan instruction for students learning English, it is crucial that they find ways to make the input comprehensible. Providing background knowledge and increasing the amount of contextual information are the two most important ways. Sometimes teachers try to speak in shorter, simpler sentences and use less complex vocabulary, but these strategies are not particularly useful; students don't grow in their understanding of the topic or in their ability to use English. Instead, researchers recommend that teachers adjust the language they use slightly beyond the students' levels because students need to hear models of language beyond what they can produce themselves (Gibbons, 1991). Their understanding is always ahead of what they can produce.

Researchers recommend using linguistically heterogeneous cooperative learning groups for second-language learners (Cummins, 1980; Dulay & Burt, 1977). When students work in small groups, they use all four language arts for meaningful purposes and learn language more quickly. They are relieved of the pressure of having to work independently. There are social benefits, too. As they work together in small groups, students become better acquainted, learn that all classmates have contributions to share with the group, and forge friendships.

Teachers help students reach their potential English proficiency by shifting the focus of their instruction from direct teaching of language to a literature focus unit, a theme cycle, and reading and writing workshop activities in which language is naturally and functionally learned. This happens when students are engaged with literature, reading and writing books, and involved in compelling and intellectually stimulating study during theme cycles (Lim & Watson, 1993). Other guidelines for teaching language-minority students are presented in the Teacher's Notebook on page 530.

Many of the language arts activities presented in earlier chapters are effective with culturally and linguistically diverse students. Assisted reading, language experience, buddy-reading, and choral reading are recommended reading activities. Choral reading, for example, is useful because students read and reread with a group of classmates, not independently. Students are familiar with the text, and there's plenty of reading practice in a low-risk environment.

Teacher's Notebook
Guidelines for Teaching Language-Minority Students

1. Provide Comprehensible Input
- Use language that is neither too hard nor too easy for students.
- Embed language in context-rich activities.
- Speak more slowly, and rarely use idioms.
- Highlight key words.
- Expand the two- and three-word sentences that students produce.

2. Create a Stress-Free Environment
- Show genuine interest in students, their language, and their culture.
- Allow students to speak and write their own language.
- Avoid forcing students to speak.
- Encourage risk-taking.
- Don't correct grammatical errors.
- Understand that diverse students are caught between two cultures.

3. Provide Opportunities to Use English
- Provide many opportunities for students to listen to and speak English and to read and write English in low-risk situations.
- Have students work together with buddies and in cooperative groups.
- Promote friendships among students.

4. Examine Your Prejudice
- Avoid stereotyping any linguistic or cultural group.
- Do not lower your expectations for certain groups of students.
- Encourage bilingualism.
- Consider your tolerance for non-standard English and code-switching.

5. Alleviate Home-School Mismatches
- Consider whether there is a mismatch between the way children use language in child-adult interactions in minority-culture communities and at school.
- Smooth the transition between home and school.
- Expect students to be uncomfortable in unfamiliar activities.

6. Involve Language-Minority Parents
- Make home visits.
- Encourage parents to participate in school activities.
- Translate letters, information sheets, and memos into native languages.
- Have translators available for school meetings and conferences.
- Plan parent-child and home-school activities.

Gibbons, 1991; Faltis, 1993; Law & Eckes, 1990; Scarcella, 1990.

A first grader who is learning English teams up with a native English-speaking classmate to write a big book.

As they read with English-speaking classmates, students learn to use the intonation patterns that native English speakers use (McCauley & McCauley, 1992).

Studies have shown that students learning English begin to write in English before they become fluent speakers; in fact, writing aids the development of oral language (Hudelson, 1984; Rigg, 1981; Urzua, 1987). They use invented spelling, and the way they spell words reflects their knowledge of English orthography as well as their pronunciation of English words. As in reading, second-language learners sometimes inject words, spellings, and sentence structures from their first language, especially if they are having difficulty communicating. It is important to focus on content rather than on the form of the writing when students are using writing as a learning tool or as a way to develop fluency. Writing activities that are particularly beneficial for students who are learning English include dialogue journals and "All About . . ." books.

A list of language arts activities for linguistically and culturally diverse students is presented in Figure 13–5. All of these activities have been described in previous chapters. Students who are literate in their first language should be encouraged to read and write in that language as well as in English. Many of the activities listed in Figure 13–5 can be used with elementary students whether they are using English or another language.

MULTICULTURAL EDUCATION

The cultural pluralism movement has led to multicultural education. The goal of multicultural education is to create a school environment that fosters

Figure 13–5 Language Arts Activities Recommended for Culturally and Linguistically Diverse Students

Activity	Why It Is Recommended
Assisted Reading	The teacher, an aide, or an older student reads with an individual student using the assisted reading strategy. The teacher or other person assisting the student does most of the reading until the student knows some of the words and can join in.
Language Experience	Students cut pictures out of magazines and glue them in a scrapbook. Then the teacher or an aide takes the student's dictation using the language experience approach. Students later reread what they dictated.
Listening Center	Students listen to stories and informational books read aloud in English. They can listen to them again and again.
Role-Playing	Students can dramatize events and stories without having to talk.
Choral Reading	Students read together as a group and support one another. Linguistically diverse students practice reading using the phrasing and expression used by English-speaking classmates.
Read With a Buddy	Students read with a buddy, and the buddy assists the language-minority student by providing background information and identifying unfamiliar words.
Read and Retell Predictable Books	Students read predictable books with repetitive or cumulative language, such as *The Little Red Hen* (Zemach, 1983) and *The Very Hungry Caterpillar* (Carle, 1969) more easily than other types of books. Similarly, students retell orally or in writing predictable books more easily than other types of books because the repetitive language makes the retelling less demanding.
Quickdraws	Students often express their ideas and information they have learned through drawing more easily than through writing.
Dialogue Journals	Students practice reading and writing in a safe environment for genuine communication purposes. Also, teachers get better acquainted with students through this activity.
Invented Spelling	Students write sooner using invented spelling, and their invented spellings provide evidence of their knowledge of English orthography.
"All About . . . " Books	Students write "All About . . . " books on a topic they are learning about in a theme cycle. Books with factual information are often easier for students to write than stories and poems.
Word Walls	Teachers highlight key words on word walls, and students draw pictures to illustrate these words. Students may also want to make personal word walls with these key words and add illustrations.

cultural pluralism. In multicultural classrooms, students from all cultural and linguistic groups have equal educational opportunities. Instruction reflects the cultures, experiences, and perspectives of linguistic and cultural groups, and students' cultural differences and similarities are valued (Banks, 1988; Gollnick & Chinn, 1986; Kendall, 1983).

Multicultural education includes studying different cultures, providing equal educational opportunities for all students, introducing cultural alternatives, and promoting tolerance and appreciation of ethnic diversity. Multiculturalism should permeate the curriculum, not simply be tacked on through reading about historical personalities and celebrating holidays. Advocates hope that it will help reduce the racial conflict and tension. If multicultural education is to make a difference, a reassessment of educational philosophy, curriculum content, and teaching methods is needed. As long as a significant achievement gap remains between African Americans, Hispanic Americans, and other ethnic minorities and European Americans, ethnic conflicts and tensions will continue.

Components of Multicultural Classrooms

In multicultural classrooms, teachers and students appreciate linguistic and cultural diversity (Edwards, Beasley, & Thompson, 1991). Teachers often begin by talking about differences openly and in a positive way. As students draw self-portraits, for example, teachers can share a variety of crayons in skin-tone colors so that students can accurately portray their own skin colors in their pictures. Teachers are aware of cultural differences and adapt their instructional programs to facilitate students' learning. They also use multicultural literature to help students appreciate diversity and become more tolerant of members of minority groups. Reading multicultural literature presents students with the opportunity to "walk a mile" in an African American's shoes in books like *Roll of Thunder, Hear My Cry* (Taylor, 1976) or in a recent immigrant's shoes through *How Many Days to America? A Thanksgiving Story* (Bunting, 1988) or *Angel Child, Dragon Child* (Surat, 1983).

In multicultural classrooms, students' languages and cultures are respected and fostered. Teachers recognize that the school's function is to increase students' options, not to restrict them, and difference is not equated with deficiency (May, 1993). Students work cooperatively, without competition.

1. The Classroom Environment. The classroom environment is safe, and students feel comfortable taking risks and experimenting with language (Law & Eckes, 1990). They know that errors are a normal part of learning and that they will not be ridiculed for language errors they might make.

2. Respect for Students' Languages and Cultures. Children's languages and cultures are respected and fostered in multicultural schools (May, 1993). Children are encouraged to continue speaking their native languages, and English is viewed as an alternative way of communicating, not a better way. Schools with students learning English as a second language have English, bilingual, and native language classrooms available. Parents choose the type of language classrooms for their children.

3. Grouping Patterns. Students work in multi-age groups and stay with the same teachers for extended periods (May, 1993). Multi-age groupings allow students to experience a variety of roles and develop a range of social skills, and teachers get to know students' families well, fostering interaction and trust.

4. Multicultural Curriculum. Teachers incorporate multicultural components in the literature focus units and theme cycles they develop. In particular, these multicultural components focus on the ethnic groups represented in the school.

5. Language Arts Instruction. Students use the approaches to listening, talking, reading, and writing instruction presented in this book. The activities they are involved in are meaningful, functional, and genuine.

6. Assessment Procedures. Teachers monitor students' learning using "kid watching." They document students' use of the reading and writing processes, and they encourage students to collect samples of their work in portfolios.

Culturally Conscious Literature

Multicultural literature is "literature that represents any distinct cultural group through accurate portrayal and rich detail" (Yokota, 1993, p. 157); it has generally been described as stories and books by and about people of color. We expand this classification to include literature about the experiences of all peoples who have immigrated to America and some religious and regional groups within the United States, such as Jewish and Appalachian cultures.

Multicultural literature is a vehicle for fostering cultural awareness and appreciation. It affirms the cultural identity of students of diverse backgrounds and develops all students' understanding of and appreciation for other cultures. Students explore and expand their cultural values and beliefs as they read multicultural literature (Rasinski & Padak, 1990). Students vicariously experience other cultures, and these experiences influence the way they interact with people in this culturally pluralistic world (Yokota, 1993).

Multicultural literature includes six types of literature, and each type offers a different perspective on the lives and contributions of each cultural group. The six types of multicultural literature are described in the following paragraphs.

1. Folktales and Other Traditional Stories. Traditional stories— including folktales, legends, and myths—are a part of every culture, and a wide variety of these stories are available for children. Cinderella stories, for example, come from many different cultures and include *Mufaro's Beautiful Daughters: An African Tale* (Steptoe, 1987), *Yeh-Shen: A Cinderella Story From China* (Louie, 1982), *The Egyptian Cinderella* (Climo, 1989), and *The Rough Face Girl* (Martin, 1992), an Algonquin Indian version.

2. Historical Fiction. These books describe the immigration of different cultural groups to the United States and their assimilation into American life. Two stories about the struggles of Jewish immigrants from Russia set in the late 1880s are *Immigrant Girl: Becky of Eldridge Street* (Harvey, 1987) and *Molly's Pilgrim* (Cohen, 1983).

3. Contemporary Realistic Fiction. These contemporary stories focus on the experiences of culturally diverse people, and they take place in America. Two stories that show the difficulties in adjusting to life in the United States are *I Hate English!* (Levine, 1989) about Mei Mei who moves to New York from Hong Kong and has difficulty learning to speak English, and *Hello, My Name is Scrambled Eggs* (Gilson, 1985) about a Vietnamese refugee who is overwhelmed by iced tea, hair dryers, escalators, and other unfamiliar aspects of American life.

4. Biographies. These books detail the contributions of people from various cultural groups. Some biographies—such as *Escape From Slavery: The Boyhood of Frederick Douglass in His Own Words* (McCurdy, 1994)—detail the lives of historical figures; others—such as *Connie Chung: Broadcast Journalist* (Malone, 1992)—highlight contemporary persons.

5. Poetry. There are a few collections of poems, songs, and chants written by people of various cultural groups that are available for children. John Bierhorst, for example, has collected Native American poetry for *A Cry From the Earth: Music of the North American Indians* (1979) and *The Sacred Path: Spells, Prayers, and Power Songs of the American Indians* (1983).

6. Informational Books. Other books provide information about various cultures, including information about holidays and rituals, language, cooking, and the arts, as well as information about the country in which the culture originated. Two informational books about Mexican Americans are *Hector Lives in the United States Now: The Story of a Mexican American Child* (Hewett, 1990) and *The Mexicans in America* (Pinchot, 1989).

Educators recommend selecting multicultural literature that is culturally conscious (Sims, 1982), that is to say, literature that accurately reflects a group's culture, language, history, and values without perpetuating stereotypes. It often deals with issues of prejudice, discrimination, and human dignity. According to Yokota (1993), these books should be rich in cultural details with authentic dialogue and should present cultural issues in enough depth that readers can think and talk about them. Inclusion of cultural group members should be purposeful. They should be distinct individuals whose lives are rooted in the culture; they should never be included simply to fulfill a quota.

In addition, multicultural literature must meet the criteria for good literature as well as for cultural consciousness. One example is *The Gold Cadillac* (Taylor, 1987), a story about the harsh realities of racial discrimination that an African American family encounter as they travel from Ohio to Mississippi in their new Cadillac during World War II. The story is well written, and the details are both historically and culturally accurate (Yokota, 1993).

Until recently, most books about Native Americans, Hispanic Americans, and other cultural groups have been written by European American authors who, because of their own ethnicity, represent an "outside" viewpoint (Bishop, 1992). An inside perspective is more likely to give an authentic view of what members of the cultural group believe to be true about themselves, while an outside perspective describes how others see that group's beliefs and behaviors. The difference in perspective means that there is a difference in what the authors say and how they say it, as well as a difference in their purpose for writing (Reimer, 1992). Some authors, however, do successfully write about another culture. Byrd Baylor and Paul Goble are notable examples. They have a sensitivity learned through research about and participation in different cultural groups. Today more people within each cultural group are writing about their own cultures and are providing more authentic "inside" viewpoints in multicultural literature.

There are many reasons to use multicultural literature in elementary classrooms, whether students represent diverse cultures or not. First, multicultural literature is good literature. Students enjoy reading stories, informational books, and poems; through reading they learn more about what it means to be human, and they discover that people of all cultural groups are real people with similar emotions, needs, and dreams. Allen Say's *El Chino* (1990), for example, tells about a Chinese American who achieves his dream of becoming a great athlete, and the book provides a model for children and adults of all ethnic groups.

Second, students learn about the wealth of diversity in the United States through multicultural books, and they develop sensitivity to and appreciation for people of other cultural groups (Walker-Dalhouse, 1992). *Teammates* (Golenbock, 1990), for example, tells about the friendship of baseball greats Jackie Robinson and Pee Wee Reese, and it teaches a valuable lesson in tolerance and respect for fellow human beings. Multicultural literature also challenges racial and ethnic stereotypes by providing an inside view of a culture.

Next, students broaden their knowledge of geography and learn different views of history through multicultural literature. They read about the countries that minority groups left as they immigrated to America, and they gain non-mainstream perspectives about historical events. For example, Yoshiko Uchida tells of her experiences in Japanese American internment camps in the United States during World War II in *The Bracelet* (1993) and *Journey to Topaz* (1971). Through reading and responding to multicultural books, students challenge traditional assumptions about the history of America and gain a more balanced view of historical events and the contributions of people from various cultural groups. They learn that traditional historical accounts have emphasized the contributions of European Americans, and particularly those made by men.

Fourth, multicultural literature raises issues of social injustice—prejudice, racism, discrimination, segregation, colonization, anti-Semitism, and geno- cide. Two books that describe the discrimination and mistreatment of Chinese Americans during the 1800s as well as their contributions to the settlement of the Western United States are *Chang's Paper Pony* (Coerr, 1988), a story set during the California gold rush, and *Ten Mile Day and the Building of the Transcontinental Railroad* (Fraser, 1993), a factual account of the race to complete the construction of the first railroad across North America.

Using multicultural literature has additional benefits for non-mainstream students. When students read books about their own cultural group, they develop pride in their cultural heritage and learn that their culture has made important contributions to the United States and to the rest of the world (Harris, 1992a, 1992b). In addition, students often become more interested in reading because they identify with the characters and events.

Literature About African Americans.   More books are available about Afri- can Americans than about other cultural groups, and books published after 1970 do not seem to perpetuate stereotypes as much as those written earlier. Some books—such as *Follow the Drinking Gourd* (Winter, 1988) about the underground railroad and *Roll of Thunder, Hear My Cry* (Taylor, 1976) about discrimination in the South during the 1930s—document events in the history of African Americans. Other books focus on contemporary events, such as *Tar Beach* (Ringgold, 1991) about a family who spends hot summer nights on the roof of their city apartment building and *Ben's Trumpet* (Isadora, 1979) about a boy who wants to become a jazz musician. African American authors have written collections of poems such as *Some of the Days of Everett Anderson* (Clifton, 1970) and book-length poems, such as *Africa Dream* (Greenfield, 1977). Also, many biographies of African American personalities—athletes and political figures in particular—have been published.

Some of the best-known African American authors are Lucille Clifton, Eloise Greenfield, Virginia Hamilton, Walter Dean Myers, John Steptoe, Mildred

Taylor, and Patricia McKissack; books by these authors and others who write about the African American experience are presented in Figure 13–6. Themes of these books include survival through love and help of extended families, factors that mold a person's character, and the value of cultural traditions. Some books about African Americans use nonstandard language forms.

Literature About Asian Americans. Literature about Asian Americans should deal with a specific Asian American group. The characters in the books should go beyond common stereotypes and should correct historical errors and omissions. Asian American authors who write books for children and adolescents include Allen Say, Yoshiko Uchida, Taro Yashima, Paul Yee, Laurence Yep, and Ed Young.

A list of books about the Asian experience in America is presented in Figure 13–7. Many of the books have been written by Asian Americans and are about their own assimilation experiences or remembrances as children in the United States. For example, *Angel Child, Dragon Child* (Surat, 1983) is the story of a Vietnamese American child who adjusts to life in the United States, and *Journey to Topaz* (Uchida, 1971) tells of a Japanese American girl's experiences in a concentration camp in the United States during World War II.

Literature About Hispanic Americans. Very few Hispanic American writers are writing stories, informational books, or poetry for children. Fewer books about Hispanic Americans are available than for other cultural groups, despite the fact that Hispanic Americans are one of the largest minority groups in the United States. Two authors who are making a significant contribution are Nicholasa Mohr, who writes short stories and novels about life in the Puerto Rican American community in New York, and Gary Soto who writes poems and short stories about life in the Mexican American community in California. Both writers bring first-hand knowledge of life in a barrio to make their writing authentic (Soto, 1992; Zarnowski, 1991). A list of books about Hispanic Americans is presented in Figure 13–8. The themes in these books emphasize the richness of life in the barrio, as well as the importance of maintaining cultural identity, the struggles and triumphs of everyday life, and surviving oppression (Harris, 1992a).

Literature About Native Americans. Many books are available about Native Americans, but very few were written by Native American authors. Authors who have written sensitively about Native American topics are Byrd Baylor, Jamake Highwater, and Paul Goble.

Most books about Native Americans are retellings of traditional folktales, myths, and legends, such as *The Legend of the Indian Paintbrush* (de Paola, 1988) and *Iktomi and the Boulder* (Goble, 1988). A number of biographies about Indian chiefs are also available. Other books describe Indian rituals and ceremonies, such as *Totem Pole* (Hoyt-Goldsmith, 1990) in which a contemporary Indian boy describes how his father carved a totem pole. A list of books about Native Americans is presented in Figure 13–9. The themes in these books include passing on rituals and stories to the next generation, mistreatment and injustice that Native Americans have suffered at the hands of Europeans and European Americans, and a reverence for living things and the earth.

Figure 13–6   Literature About African Americans

Adoff, A. (1973). *Black is brown is tan.* New York: Harper & Row. (P–M)

Collier, J., & Collier, C. (1981). *Jump ship to freedom.* New York: Delacorte. (U)

Crews, D. (1991). *Bigmama's.* New York: Greenwillow. (P–M)

Ferris, J. (1988). *Go free or die: A story of Harriet Tubman.* Minneapolis: Carolrhoda. (M–U)

Flournoy, C. (1985). *The patchwork quilt.* New York: Dial. (M)

Fox, P. (1973). *Slave dancer.* New York: Bradbury. (U)

Freedman, F. B. (1990). *Two tickets to freedom: The true story of Ellen and William Craft, fugitive slaves.* New York: Bedrick. (M–U)

Greene, B. (1974). *Philip Hall likes me. I reckon maybe.* New York: Dial. (M–U)

Greenfield, E. (1974). *Sister.* New York: Crowell. (U)

Greenfield, E. (1975). *Paul Robeson.* New York: Crowell. (M–U)

Greenfield, E. (1989). *Nathaniel talking.* New York: Black Butterfly Children's Books. (P–M)

Greenfield, E. (1991). *First pink light.* New York: Black Butterfly Children's Books. (P–M)

Greenfield, E. (1991). *Night on Neighborhood Street.* New York: Dial. (P–M)

Hamilton, V. (1967). *Zeely.* New York: Macmillan. (U)

Hamilton, V. (1968). *The house of Dies Drear.* New York: Macmillan. (U)

Hamilton, V. (1974). *M. C. Higgins, the Great.* New York: Macmillan. (M–U)

Hamilton, V. (1974). *Paul Robeson: The life and times of a free black man.* New York: Harper & Row. (U)

Hamilton, V. (1985). *The people could fly: American black folktales.* New York: Knopf. (M–U)

Hamilton, V. (1987). *The mystery of Drear house.* New York: Greenwillow. (U)

Hamilton, V. (1988). *Anthony Burns: The defeat and triumph of a fugitive slave.* New York: Knopf. (U)

Hamilton, V. (1992). *Drylongso.* San Diego: Harcourt Brace Jovanovich. (M)

Hoffman, M. (1991). *Amazing Grace.* New York: Dial. (P–M)

Howard, E. F. (1991). *Aunt Flossie's hats (and crab cakes later).* New York: Clarion. (P–M)

Keats, E. J. (1965). *John Henry: An American legend.* New York: Pantheon. (M)

Lester, J. (1987). *The tales of Uncle Remus: The adventures of Brer Rabbit.* New York: Dial. (M)

Mathis, S. B. (1975). *The hundred penny box.* New York: Viking. (M)

McKissack, P. (1986). *Flossie and the fox.* New York: Dial. (P–M)

McKissack, P. (1988). *Mirandy and brother wind.* New York: Knopf. (M)

McKissack, P., & McKissack, F. (1989). *A long hard journey: The story of the Pullman Porter Walker.* New York: Walker. (U)

Meltzer, M. (1984). *The black Americans: A history in their own words, 1619–1983.* New York: Crowell. (U)

Monjo, N. (1970). *The drinking gourd.* New York: Harper & Row. (P)

Myers, W. D. (1988). *Scorpions.* New York: Harper & Row. (U)

Parks, R., with J. Haskins. (1992). *Rosa Parks, my story.* New York: Dial. (M)

Rappaport, D. (1991). *Escape from slavery.* New York: HarperCollins. (M–U)

Ringgold, F. (1991). *Tar beach.* New York: Crown. (P–M)

Ringgold, F. (1992). *Aunt Harriet's underground railroad in the sky.* New York: Crown. (M)

Slote, A. (1991). *Finding Buck McHenry.* New York: HarperCollins. (U)

Stolz, M. (1991). *Go fish.* New York: HarperCollins. (M–U)

Taylor, M. (1976). *Roll of thunder, hear my cry.* New York: Dial. (U)

Taylor, M. (1981). *Let the circle be unbroken.* New York: Dial. (U)

Taylor, M. (1987). *The gold cadillac.* New York: Dial. (M)

Taylor, M. (1990). *Mississippi bridge.* New York: Dial. (M–U)

Williams, S. A. (1992). *Working cotton.* San Diego: Harcourt Brace Jovanovich. (P–M)

Williams, V. B. (1986). *Cherries and cherry pits.* New York: Mulberry. (P)

Yarbrough, C. (1979). *Cornrows.* New York: Coward-McCann. (M)

P = primary grades (K–2); M = middle grades (3–5); U = upper grades (6–8).

Figure 13-7 *Literature About Asian Americans*

Ashley, B. (1991). *Cleversticks.* New York: Crown. (P) (Chinese American)

Bang, M. (1985). *The paper crane.* New York: Greenwillow. (P–M)

Chiemroum, S. (1992). *Dara's Cambodian new year.* New York: Scholastic. (P–M)

Choi, S. N. (1991). *The year of impossible goodbyes.* Boston: Houghton Mifflin. (U) (Korean American)

Coerr, E. (1985). *Chang's paper pony.* New York: Harper & Row. (M) (Chinese American)

Crew, L. (1989). *Children of the river.* New York: Dell. (U) (Cambodian American)

Crofford, E. (1992). *Born in the year of courage.* Minneapolis: Carolrhoda. (U) (Japanese American)

Feeney, S. (1985). *A is for aloha.* Honolulu: University of Hawaii Press. (Hawaiian American)

Fraser, M. A. (1993). *Ten mile day and the building of the transcontinental railroad.* New York: Henry Holt. (M–U) (Chinese American)

Friedman, I. R. (1984). *How my parents learned to eat.* Boston: Houghton Mifflin. (M) (Japanese American)

Gilson, J. (1985). *Hello, my name is scrambled eggs.* New York: Morrow. (U) (Vietnamese American)

Graff, N. P. (1993). *Where the river runs: A portrait of a refugee family.* Boston: Little, Brown. (M–U) (Cambodian American)

Hamanaka, S. (1990). *The journey: Japanese Americans, racism, and renewal.* New York: Orchard. (U)

Ho, M. (1992). *The clay marble.* New York: Farrar, Straus & Giroux. (U)

Houston, J. (1974). *Farewell to Manzanar.* New York: Harper & Row. (U) (Japanese American)

Hoyt-Goldsmith, D. (1992). *Hoang Anh: A Vietnamese American boy.* New York: Holiday House. (M)

Kitano, H. (1987). *The Japanese Americans.* New York: Chelsea House. (M–U)

Kraus, J. (1992). *Tall boy's journey.* Minneapolis: Carolrhoda. (M–U) (Korean American)

Leathers, N. L. (1991). *The Japanese in America.* Minneapolis: Lerner. (M–U)

Lee, M. G. (1993). *If it hadn't been for Yoon Jun.* Boston: Houghton Mifflin. (M–U) (Korean American)

Lehrer, B. (1988). *The Korean Americans.* New York: Chelsea House. (M–U)

Levine, E. (1989). *I hate English!* New York: Scholastic. (M) (Chinese American)

Lord, B. (1984). *In the year of the boar and Jackie Robinson.* New York: Harper & Row. (M–U) (Chinese American)

Malone, M. (1992). *Connie Chung: Broadcast journalist.* Hillside, NJ: Enslow. (M–U) (Chinese American)

Martin, A. M. (1988). *Yours turly* [sic], *Shirley.* New York: Harper & Row. (U) (Vietnamese American)

Nhuong H. Q. (1982). *The land I lost: Adventures of a boy in Vietnam.* New York: Harper & Row. (M–U)

O'Connor, K. (1992). *Dan Thuy's new life in America.* Minneapolis: Lerner. (U) (Vietnamese American)

Pettit, J. (1992). *My name is San Ho.* New York: Scholastic. (U) (Vietnamese American)

Say, A. (1990). *El Chino.* Boston: Houghton Mifflin. (M) (Chinese American)

Say, A. (1991). *Tree of cranes.* Boston: Houghton Mifflin. (M) (Japanese American)

Say, A. (1993). *Grandfather's journey.* Boston: Houghton Mifflin. (M) (Japanese American)

Surat, M. M. (1983). *Angel child, dragon child.* Milwaukee: Raintree. (P–M) (Vietnamese American)

Toff, N. (1990). *The Filipino Americans.* New York: Chelsea House. (M–U)

Uchida, Y. (1971). *Journey to Topaz.* Berkeley, CA: Creative Arts. (U) (Japanese American)

Uchida, Y. (1972). *Samurai of Gold Hill.* New York: Scribner. (M–U) (Japanese American)

Uchida, Y. (1978). *Journey home.* New York: Atheneum. (U) (Japanese American)

Uchida, Y. (1981). *A jar of dreams.* New York: Atheneum. (M–U). (Japanese American)

Uchida, Y. (1983). *The best bad thing.* New York: Atheneum. (Japanese American)

Uchida, Y. (1985). *The happiest ending.* New York: McElderry Books. (Japanese American)

Uchida, Y. (1991). *The invisible thread.* New York: Messner. (U) (Japanese American)

Uchida, Y. (1993). *The bracelet.* New York: Philomel. (P-M) (Japanese American)

Waters, K. (1990). *Lion dancer: Ernie Wan's Chinese new year.* New York: Scholastic. (M)

Winter, F. H. (1988). *The Filipinos in America.* Minneapolis: Lerner. (M–U)

Yee, P. (1989). *Tales from Gold Mountain.* New York: Macmillan. (M–U) (Chinese American)

Yep, L. (1975). *Dragonwings.* New York: Harper & Row. (U) (Chinese American)

Yep, L. (1977). *Child of the owl.* New York: Harper & Row. (M–U) (Chinese American)

Yep, L. (1985). *Mountain light.* New York: Harper & Row. (U) (Chinese American)

Yep, L. (1991). *The lost garden: A memoir.* New York: Messner. (U) (Chinese American)

Yep, L. (1991). *The star fisher.* New York: Morrow. (U) (Chinese American)

Yep, L. (Ed.). (1993). *American dragons: 25 Asian American voices.* New York: HarperCollins. (U)

Figure 13–8   *Literature About Hispanic Americans*

Anzaldua, G. (1993). *Friends from the other side/ Amigos del otro lado.* San Francisco: Children's Book Press. (P–M) (Mexican American)

Behrens, J. (1978). *Fiesta!* Chicago: Childrens Press. (M)

Brimmer, L. D. (1992). *Migrant family.* Minneapolis: Lerner. (M–U) (Mexican American)

Cazet, D. (1993). *Born in the gravy.* New York: Orchard. (P)

Cisneros, S. (1983). *The house on Mango Street.* Houston: Arte Publico. (U)

Concord, B. W. (1992). *Cesar Chavez.* New York: Chelsea House. (M–U)

Delacre, L. (1989). *Arroz con leche.* New York: Scholastic. (P)

Dorros, A. (1991). *Abuela.* New York: Dutton. (P)

Garza, C. L. (1990). *Family pictures.* San Francisco: Children's Book Press. (P) (Mexican American)

Hewett, J. (1990). *Hector lives in the United States now: The story of a Mexican-American child.* New York: Lippincott. (M–U)

Krumgold, J. (1953). *. . . And now, Miguel.* New York: Crowell. (M–U)

Larsen, R. J. (1989). *The Puerto Ricans in America.* Minneapolis: Lerner. (M–U)

Lattimore, D. (1987). *The flame of peace: A tale of the Aztecs.* New York: Harper & Row. (M)

Lomas, G. C. (1990). *Family pictures.* San Francisco: Children's Book Press. (P–M)

Metzer, M. (1982). *The Hispanic Americans.* New York: Crowell. (M–U)

Mohr, N. (1979). *Felita.* New York: Dial. (M) (Puerto Rican American)

Mohr, N. (1986). *El Bronx remembered.* Houston: Arte Publico. (U) (Puerto Rican American)

Mohr, N. (1986). *Going home.* New York: Dial. (U) (Puerto Rican American)

Mohr, N. (1986). *Nilda.* Houston: Arte Publico. (U) (Puerto Rican American)

Mohr, N. (1988). *In Nueva York.* Houston: Arte Publico. (U) (Puerto Rican American)

Mora, P. (1992). *A birthday present for Tia.* New York: Macmillan. (P) (Mexican American)

O'Dell, S. (1979). *The captive.* Boston: Houghton Mifflin. (Mexican American)

O'Dell, S. (1981). *Carlota.* Boston: Houghton Mifflin. (U) (Mexican American)

O'Dell, S. (1981). *The feathered serpent.* Boston: Houghton Mifflin. (U) (Mexican American)

O'Dell, S. (1983). *The amethyst ring.* Boston: Houghton Mifflin. (U) (Mexican American)

Pinchot, J. (1989). *The Mexicans in America.* Minneapolis: Lerner. (M–U)

Politi, L. (1949). *Song of the swallows.* New York: Scribner. (P–M) (Mexican American)

Politi, L. (1973). *The nicest gift.* New York: Scribner. (P–M) (Mexican American)

Politi, L. (1976). *Three stalks of corn.* New York: Scribner. (P–M) (Mexican American)

Prago, A. (1973). *Strangers in their own land: A history of Mexican-Americans.* New York: Four Winds Press. (U)

Roberts, M. (1986). *Henry Cisneros: Mexican American mayor.* Chicago: Childrens Press. (M–U)

Soto, G. (1986). *Small faces.* New York: Dell. (U) (Mexican American)

Soto, G. (1990). *Baseball in April and other stories.* Orlando: Harcourt Brace Jovanovich. (M–U) (Mexican American)

Soto, G. (1990). *A fire in my hands.* New York: Scholastic. (U) (Mexican American)

Soto, G. (1990). *A summer life.* New York: Dell. (U) (Mexican American)

Soto, G. (1992). *Neighborhood odes.* Orlando: Harcourt Brace Jovanovich. (U) (Mexican American)

Soto, G. (1992). *Pacific crossing.* Orlando: Harcourt Brace Jovanovich. (U) (Mexican American)

Soto, G. (1992). *Taking sides.* Orlando: Harcourt Brace Jovanovich. (U) (Mexican American)

Soto, G. (1993). *Too many tamales.* Orlando: Harcourt Brace Jovanovich. (P–M) (Mexican American)

Soto, G. (1994). *Crazy weekend.* New York: Scholastic. (U) (Mexican American)

Stanek, M. (1989). *I speak English for my mom.* New York: Whitman. (M)

Williams, V. B. (1982). *A chair for my mother.* New York: Mulberry. (P)

Williams, V. B. (1983). *Something special for me.* New York: Greenwillow. (P)

Figure 13–9   *Literature About Native Americans*

Aliki. (1976). *Corn is maize: The gift of the Indians.* New York: Crowell. (P–M)

Ancona, G. (1993). *Powwow.* Orlando: Harcourt Brace. (M–U)

Ashabranner, B. (1984). *To live in two worlds: American Indian youth today.* New York: Dodd, Mead. (U)

Baylor, B. (1975). *The desert is theirs.* New York: Scribner. (P–M)

Baylor, B. (1978). *The other way to listen.* New York: Scribner. (P–M)

Bierhorst, J. (1979). *A cry from the earth: Music of the North American Indians.* New York: Four Winds Press. (P–M–U)

Bierhorst, J. (1983). *The sacred path: Spells, prayers, and power songs of the American Indians.* New York: Morrow. (P–M–U)

Bruchac, J., & London, J. (1991). *Thirteen moons on turtle's back.* New York: Philomel. (M)

Cohen, C. L. (1988). *The mud pony.* New York: Scholastic. (M)

Freedman, R. (1987). *Indian chiefs.* New York: Holiday House. (U)

Freedman, R. (1988). *Buffalo hunt.* New York: Holiday House. (U)

Freedman, R. (1992). *An Indian winter.* New York: Holiday House. (M–U)

Fritz, J. (1983). *The double life of Pocahontas.* New York: Putnam. (M–U)

George, J. C. (1972). *Julie of the wolves.* New York: Harper & Row. (U) (Eskimo)

George, J. C. (1983). *The talking earth.* New York: Harper & Row. (U)

Highwater, J. (1977). Anpao: An American Indian odyssey. New York: Lippincott. (U)

Hoyt-Goldsmith, D. (1990). *Totem pole.* New York: Holiday House. (M)

Hoyt-Goldsmith, D. (1991). *Pueblo storyteller.* New York: Holiday House. (M–U)

Hoyt-Goldsmith, D. (1992). *Arctic hunter.* New York: Holiday House. (M)

Jones, H. (1993). *The trees stand shining: Poetry of the North American Indians.* New York: Dial. (P–M–U)

Jones, J. C. (1991). *The American Indians in America.* Minneapolis: Lerner. (M–U)

Keegan, M. (1991). *Pueblo boy: Growing up in two worlds.* New York: Cobblehill Books. (P–M)

Krensky, S. (1992). *Children of the earth and sky: Five stories about Native American children.* New York: Scholastic. (P)

Locker, T. (1991). *The land of gray wolf.* New York: Dial. (M–U)

Luenn, N. (1990). *Nessa's fish.* New York: Atheneum. (P–M) (Eskimo)

Martin, R. (1992). *The rough-face girl.* New York: Putnam. (P–M)

Martin, B., & Archambault, J. (1987). *Knots on a counting rope.* New York: Holt, Rinehart & Winston. (P–M)

McDermott, G. (1993). *Raven: A trickster tale from the Pacific northwest.* Orlando: Harcourt Brace. (P–M)

Medearis, A. S. (1991). *Dancing with the Indians.* New York: Holiday House. (M)

Miles, M. (1971). *Annie and the old one.* Boston: Little, Brown. (P–M)

Nashone. (1989). *Where Indians live: American Indian houses.* Sacramento, CA: Sierra Oaks. (M)

O'Dell, S. (1970). *Sing down the moon.* Boston: Houghton Mifflin. (U)

O'Dell, S. (1988). *Black star, bright dawn.* Boston: Houghton Mifflin. (U)

O'Dell, S., & Hall, E. (1992). *Thunder rolling in the mountains.* Boston: Houghton Mifflin. (U)

Paulsen, G. (1988). *Dogsong.* New York: Bradbury Press. (U)

Red Hawk, R. (1991). *A, B, C's: The American Indian way.* Sacramento, CA: Sierra Oaks. (P–M)

Regguinti, G. (1992). *The sacred harvest: Ojibway wild rice gathering.* Minneapolis: Lerner. (M)

Seattle, C. (1991). *Brother eagle, sister sky.* New York: Dial. (P–M–U)

Sneve, V. D. H. (1972). *High elk's treasure.* New York: Holiday House. (M)

Sneve, V. D. H. (1972). *Jimmy yellow hawk.* New York: Holiday House. (M)

Sneve, V. D. H. (1974). *When thunder spoke.* New York: Holiday House. (M–U)

Sneve, V. D. H. (1989). *Dancing teepees: Poems of American Indian youth.* New York: Holiday House. (P–M–U)

Speare, E. G. (1983). *The sign of the beaver.* Boston: Houghton Mifflin. (M–U)

Yolen, J. (1990). *Sky dogs.* San Diego: Harcourt Brace Jovanovich. (M)

Literature About Other American Cultural Groups. In addition to the four cultural groups we have already discussed, there are distinct regional and religious cultures in the United States, including Jewish, Amish, Cajun, and Appalachian groups. As the majority culture, European Americans are sometimes ignored in discussions of cultural groups, but to ignore them denies the distinct cultures of many Americans (Yokoto, 1993). Within the European American umbrella category are a variety of groups, including German Americans, Italian Americans, Swedish Americans, and Russian Americans. A list of books featuring European American cultures and American regional and religious cultures is presented in Figure 13–10.

Figure 13–10   Literature About Other American Cultural Groups

Ammon, R. (1989). *Growing up Amish.* New York: Atheneum. (M–U)

Ancona, G. (1989). *The American family farm: A photo essay by George Ancona.* San Diego: Harcourt Brace Jovanovich. (M)

Angell, J. (1985). *One-way to Ansonia.* New York: Bradbury Press. (M–U) (Russian American)

Ashabranner, B. (1989). *Born to the land: An American portrait.* New York: Putnam. (M–U)

Ashabranner, B. (1991). *An ancient heritage: The Arab-American minority.* New York: HarperCollins. (M–U)

Barbour, K. (1987). *Little Nino's pizzeria.* Orlando: Harcourt Brace Jovanovich. (P) (Italian American)

Baylor, B. (1982). *The best town in the world.* New York: Aladdin. (M)

Bolick, N. O., & Randolph, S. G. (1990). *Shaker inventions.* New York: Walker. (U)

Bonner, S. (1991). *The wooden doll.* New York: Lothrop, Lee & Shepard. (P) (Polish American)

Clifford, E. (1985). *The remembering box.* Boston: Houghton Mifflin. (M–U) (Jewish American)

Cohen, B. (1983). *Molly's pilgrim.* New York: Lothrop, Lee & Shepard. (M) (Jewish American)

Cooney, B. (1990). *Hattie and the wild waves.* New York: Viking. (P–M) (German American)

Dooley, N. (1991). *Everybody cooks rice.* Minneapolis: Carolrhoda. (P–M)

Faber, D. (1991). *The Amish.* New York: Doubleday. (P)

Gibbons, G. (1991). *Surrounded by sea: Life on a New England fishing island.* Boston: Little, Brown. (P–M)

Graff, N. P. (1992). *The call of the running tide: A portrait of an island family.* Boston: Little, Brown. (M)

Harvey, B. (1987). *Immigrant girl: Becky of Eldridge Street.* New York: Holiday House. (M) (Jewish American)

Heide, F. P., & Gilliland, J. H. (1992). *Sami and the time of the troubles.* New York: Clarion. (P–M) (Lebanese American)

Hiser, B. T. (1986). *The adventure of Charlie and his wheat-straw hat: A memorat.* New York: Dodd, Mead. (P) (Appalachian)

Houston, G. (1992). *My great-aunt Arizona.* New York: HarperCollins. (P–M) (Appalachian)

Kendall, R. (1992). *Eskimo boy: Life in an Inupiaq Eskimo village.* New York: Scholastic. (P–M)

Khalsa, D. K. (1986). *Tales of a gambling grandma.* New York: Potter. (P–M) (Russian American)

Kuklin, S. (1992). *How my family lives in America.* New York: Bradbury Press. (P–M)

Lasky, K. (1983). *Sugaring time.* New York: Macmillan. (M)

Lowry, L. (1987). *Rabble Starkey.* Boston: Houghton Mifflin. (M–U) (Appalachian)

McKissack, P. (1992). *A million fish . . . More or less.* New York: Knopf. (M) (Creole)

Naylor, P. R. (1991). *Shiloh.* New York: Atheneum. (M–U) (Appalachian)

Paterson, K. (1985). *Come sing, Jimmy Jo.* New York: Dutton. (M–U) (Appalachian)

Polacco, P. (1990). *Babushka's doll.* New York: Simon & Schuster. (P) (Russian American)

Polacco, P. (1990). *Just plain fancy.* New York: Bantam. (P–M) (Amish)

Polacco, P. (1990). *Thunder cake.* New York: Philomel. (P–M) (Russian American)

Rylant, C. (1985). *The relatives came.* New York: Bradbury. (P–M) (Appalachian)

Rylant, C. (1991). *Appalachia: The voices of sleeping birds.* San Diego: Harcourt Brace Jovanovich. (M–U)

Rylant, C. (1992). *Missing May.* New York: Orchard. (M–U) (Appalachian)

Classroom Multicultural Library.   Too often the books used for instruction in elementary classrooms and displayed in classroom libraries reflect the majority culture and were written predominately by white male authors. Researchers who have examined the books that teachers select for classroom use have found that their choices suggest an unconscious cultural bias because few books feature experiences of minority groups and even fewer were written by members of these groups (Jipson & Paley, 1991; Shannon, 1986; Traxel, 1983). These researchers call this pattern the selective tradition, and it is a serious concern because books reflect and convey sociocultural values, beliefs, and attitudes to readers. It is important that teachers be aware of the ideas conveyed by their selection patterns and become more reflective about the books they choose for classroom use.

Teachers' choices of books for instruction and in the classroom library influence students in other ways, too. Students tend to choose familiar books and those that reflect their own cultures for reading workshop and other independent reading activities (Rudman, 1976). If teachers read aloud culturally conscious books, include these books in literature focus units and theme cycles, and display them in the classroom library, they become familiar, and students are more likely to pick them up and read them independently.

Teaching About Cultural Diversity

Some teachers periodically share books of multicultural literature with their students while other teachers include multicultural components in lessons they teach and teach literature focus units and theme cycles to raise students' awareness of equality and other social issues. We encourage teachers to develop units and theme cycles using multicultural literature. According to Zarillo (1994), the characteristics of multicultural literature focus units and theme cycles are that they:

1. Celebrate cultural diversity in the United States
2. Increase cultural understanding and respect
3. Provide opportunities for listening, talking, reading, and writing
4. Provide opportunities for students who are learning English to use language in meaningful ways
5. Incorporate aesthetic reading and response-to-literature activities
6. Use books that accurately portray cultural groups

Rasinski and Padak (1990) have identified four approaches for teaching students about cultural diversity and integrating concepts about cultural pluralism into literature focus units and theme cycles. These approaches are based on Banks's (1989) multicultural curriculum model and differ in the extent to which multicultural issues become a central part of the curriculum.

The Contributions Approach.   This approach focuses on lessons taught in connection with a holiday or other special occasions (Rasinski & Padak, 1990). The purpose of activities is to familiarize students with the contributions of important people, holidays, or specific customs, but these activities do not teach cultural values or challenge students to re-examine their beliefs. Single lessons might focus on reading *Seven Candles for Kwanzaa* (Pinkney, 1993), a story about Kwanzaa, an African American holiday celebrated from Decem-

As part of a year-long introduction to cultures around the world, these first graders read books about China and examine Chinese artifacts.

ber 16 to January 1, or reading *How My Parents Learned to Eat* (Friedman, 1984), a story about an American sailor who courts a young Japanese woman after World War II. The young woman learns to eat with a knife and fork to surprise the sailor, and the sailor learns to eat with chopsticks to surprise the woman. Or, teachers might read *A Picture Book of Martin Luther King, Jr.* (Adler, 1989), to celebrate the civil rights leader's birthday. This approach is an easy way to include a multicultural component in the curriculum, but students gain only a superficial understanding of cultural diversity.

The Additive Approach.   In this second approach, lessons using multicultural literature are added to the existing curriculum (Rasinski & Padak, 1990). In a genre unit on folktales, for example, *Mufaro's Beautiful Daughters: An African Tale* (Steptoe, 1987), *Yeh-Shen: A Cinderella Story from China* (Louie, 1982), and *The Egyptian Cinderella* (Climo, 1989) might be added as international versions of the Cinderella story. Or, for a literature focus unit, an upper-grade teacher might choose a multicultural chapter book such as *Year of Impossible Goodbyes* (Choi, 1991), the story of a Korean girl who is forced to immigrate to America after enduring the cruelties of the Japanese military force occupying her country at the end of World War II. The teacher would choose to read this book because it is a powerful, well-written book and one that the students would enjoy. This approach is similar to the contributions approach because

Figure 13–11   Books About Immigration

Anderson, J. (1989). *Spanish pioneers of the Southwest.* New York: Lodestar. (M–U)

Ashabranner, B. (1991). *An ancient heritage: The Arab-American minority.* New York: HarperCollins. (M–U)

Ashabranner, B. (1993). *Still a nation of immigrants.* New York: Cobblehill. (M–U)

Ashabranner, B., & Ashabranner, M. (1987). *Into a strange land: Unaccompanied refugee youth in America.* New York: Putnam. (U)

Bode, J. (1989). *New kids in town: Oral histories of immigrant teens.* New York: Franklin Watts. (U)

Bresnick-Perry, R. (1992). *Leaving for America.* San Francisco: Children's Book Press. (P–M)

Bunting, E. (1988). *How many days to America? A Thanksgiving story.* New York: Clarion. (M)

Buss, F. L. (1991). *Journey of the sparrow.* New York: Lodestar. (U)

Caroli, B. B. (1990). *Immigrants who returned home.* New York: Chelsea House. (U)

Cech, J. (1991). *My grandmother's journey.* New York: Bradbury Press (P–M)

Chetin, H. (1982). *Angel Island prisoner 1922.* (M)

Clapp, P. (1968). *Constance.* New York: Morrow. (U)

Cowing, S. (1989). *Searches in the American desert.* New York: Macmillan. (U)

Dixon, E. H., & Galan, M. A. (1990). *The Immigration and Naturalization Service.* New York: Chelsea House. (U)

Fassler, D. (1993). *Coming to America: The kids' book about immigration.* New York: Henry Holt. (P–M)

Fleming, A. (1988). *The king of Prussia and a peanut butter sandwich.* New York: Scribner. (M–U)

Fox, P. (1973). *Slave dancer.* New York: Bradbury Press. (U)

Freedman, R. (1980). *Immigrant kids.* New York: Dutton. (M–U)

Garland, S. (1993). *The lotus seed.* Orlando: Harcourt Brace. (M)

Girard, L. W. (1989). *We adopted you, Benjamin Koo.* New York: Albert Whitman. (P–M)

Goldfarb, M. (1982). *Fighters, refugees, immigrants: A story of the Hmong.* Minneapolis: Carolrhoda. (U)

Hartman, E. G. (1991). *American immigration.* Minneapolis: Lerner. (M–U)

Harvey, B. (1987). *Immigrant girl: Becky of Eldridge Street.* New York: Holiday House. (M)

Haskins, J. (1986). *The Statue of Liberty: America's proud lady.* Minneapolis: Lerner. (M–U)

Hauser, P. N. (1990). *Illegal aliens.* New York: Chelsea House. (U)

Hesse, K. (1992). *Letters from Rifka.* New York: Henry Holt. (M–U)

Jacobs, W. J. (1990). *Ellis Island: New hope in a new land.* New York: Scribner. (M–U)

Knight, M. B. (1993). *Who belongs here? An American story.* Gardiner, ME: Tilbury House. (M)

Leighto, M. R. (1992). *An Ellis Island Christmas.* New York: Viking. (P–M)

Levine, E. (1993). *. . . If your name was changed at Ellis Island.* Scholastic. (M).

Levinson, R. (1985). *Watch the stars come out.* New York: Dutton. (P)

Maestro, B., & Maestro, G. (1991). *The discovery of the Americas.* New York: Lothrop, Lee & Shepard. (P–M)

Mayerson, E. (1990). *The cat who escaped from steerage.* New York: Scribner. (M–U)

Murphy, J. (1993). *Across America on an emigrant train.* New York: Clarion. (M–U)

Nixon, J. L. (1992). *Land of hope.* New York: Bantam. (M–U)

Paterson, K. (1988). *Park's quest.* New York: Lodestar. (M–U)

Poynter, M. (1992). *The uncertain journey: Stories of illegal aliens in El Norte.* New York: Atheneum. (U)

Sandin, J. (1981). *The long way to a new land.* New York: HarperCollins. (P–M)

Say, A. (1993). *Grandfather's journey.* Boston: Houghton Mifflin. (M)

Shefelman, J. (1992). *A peddler's dream.* Boston: Houghton Mifflin. (P–M)

Shiefman, V. (1993). *Good-bye to the trees.* New York: Atheneum. (U)

Stanek, M. (1985). *We came from Vietnam.* New York: Albert Whitman. (M–U)

Winter, J. (1992). *Klara's new world.* New York: Knopf. (P–M)

the curriculum is based in the European American perspective. Information about cultural diversity is added to the curriculum, but not woven through it.

The Transformation Approach.   Literature focus units and theme cycles are modified in this approach to promote the study of historical events and contemporary issues from the viewpoint of culturally diverse groups (Rasinski & Padak, 1990). Primary-grade students, for instance, might read *A Chair for My Mother* (Williams, 1982), *Everybody Cooks Rice* (Dooley, 1991) and *Bigmama's* (Crews, 1991) as part of a unit on families and then talk about the common features of families from diverse cultural groups. Or, during a theme cycle on World War II, upper-grade students might read *Journey to Topaz* (Uchida, 1971) to learn about the Japanese American viewpoint about the war and their unfair internment. These literature experiences and response activities allow students to see the interconnectedness of various ethnic groups within American society and the ways that diverse cultural groups have shaped American history.

The Social Action Approach.   In this fourth approach, students study important social issues and take action to solve problems through theme cycles (Rasinski & Padak, 1990). Students read culturally conscious literature in order to gain an "inside" view on social issues. For example, students might study immigration; a list of books about immigration and immigrants coming to the United States is presented in Figure 13–11. They might begin by reading *How Many Days to America? A Thanksgiving Story* (Bunting, 1988) to learn about modern-day refugees who risk their lives coming to America. Afterwards they can talk about their own attitudes toward immigrant groups and research how and when their families came to America. Another book they might read is *Who Belongs Here? An American Story* (Knight, 1993). The question "Who belongs here?" might direct their study and lead them to find ways to encourage tolerance and assist with refugee programs in their community. In this approach, students read and do research, think deeply about social issues, and apply what they are learning in their own communities.

Review

The United States is increasingly becoming a pluralistic society, and teachers must learn ways to teach culturally and linguistically diverse students in their classrooms and teach all students to value members of ethnic groups and appreciate the contributions that each cultural group makes to American society. Cultural pluralism has led to multicultural education, and its goal is to help students better understand themselves by looking at their culture and behavior through the perspectives of other cultures. Socially conscious, multicultural literature can be used to help students learn about African Americans, Asian Americans, Hispanic Americans, Native Americans, and other cultural groups in the United States. Stories, informational books, and poems about these cultures help students to understand the viewpoints of minority groups and encourage greater appreciation for other cultures. Teachers begin by integrating multicultural literature in their curriculum and then encourage students toward social action.

Extensions

1. Observe in a multicultural classroom and document the ways instruction is modified to meet the needs of particular students and the ways cultural pluralism is fostered.
2. Interview several culturally or linguistically diverse students to learn about their educational experiences. If possible, also talk to their parents and teachers to learn their viewpoints about educational equity and cultural pluralism.
3. Investigate the number of ESL students in your community, their native languages, and the educational programs available for ESL students in your community.
4. Read a collection of multicultural books and create an annotated reading list or cardfile.
5. Plan and teach a literature focus unit or theme cycle using the transformation or social action approach. Include literature about diverse cultural groups and ways to help students respond to these books and extend their interpretations.
6. Plan and teach a genre unit about folktales and other traditional literature, and include multicultural literature in the unit.

References

Allen, V. A. (1991). Teaching bilingual and ESL children. In J. Flood, J. M. Jensen, D. Lapp, & J. R. Squire (Eds.), *Handbook of research on teaching the English language arts.* New York: Macmillan.

American Council on Education and the Education Commission of the States. (1988). *One-third of a nation: A report of the Commission on minority participation in education and American life.* Washington, DC: American Council on Education.

Banks, J. A. (1988). *Multiethnic education: Theory and practice.* Boston: Allyn & Bacon.

Banks, J. A. (1989). Integrating the curriculum with ethnic content: Approaches and guidelines. In J. A. Banks & C. A. McGee Banks (Eds.), *Multicultural education: Issues and perspectives* (pp. 189–207). Boston: Allyn & Bacon.

Banks, J. A. (1994). *An introduction to multicultural education.* Boston: Allyn & Bacon.

Bishop, R. S. (1992). Multicultural literature for children: Making informed choices. In V. J. Harris (Ed.), *Teaching multicultural literature in grades K–8* (pp. 37–54). Norwood, MA: Christopher-Gordon.

Brooks, C. K. (Ed.). (1985). *Tapping potential: English and language arts for the black learner.* Urbana, IL: National Council of Teachers of English.

Cheng, L. R. (1987). *Assessing Asian language performance.* Rockville, MD: Aspen.

Cullinan, B. E., Jaggar, A. M., & Strickland, D. (1974). Language expansion for black children in the primary grades: A research report. *Young Children, 39,* 98–112.

Cummins, J. (1980). The cross-lingual dimensions of language proficiency: Implications for bilingual education and the optimal age issue. *TESOL Quarterly, 14,* 175–187.

Cummins, J. (1981). *Schooling and minority students: A theoretical framework.* Sacramento: California State Department of Education.

Cummins, J. (1989). *Empowering minority students.* Sacramento, CA: California Association for Bilingual Education.

Daniels, H. A. (Ed.). (1990). *Not only English: Affirming America's multilingual heritage.* Urbana, IL: National Council of Teachers of English.

Dulay, H., & Burt, M. (1977). Remarks on creativity in language acquisition. In M. Burt & M. Finocciaro (Eds.), *Viewpoints on English as a second language.* New York: Newbury House.

Edwards, P. A., Beasley, K., & Thompson, J. (1991). Teachers in transition: Accommodating reading curriculum to cultural diversity. *The Reading Teacher, 44,* 436–437.

Faltis, C. J. (1993). *Joinfostering: Adapting teaching strategies for the multilingual classroom.* New York: Merrill/Macmillan.

Freeman, D. E., & Freeman, Y. S. (1993). Strategies for promoting the primary languages of all students. *The Reading Teacher, 46,* 552–558.

Gibbons, P. (1991). *Learning to learn in a second language.* Portsmouth, NH: Heinemann.

Gonzales, P. C. (1981a). Beginning English reading for ESL students. *The Reading Teacher, 35,* 154–162.

Gonzales, P. C. (1981b). How to begin language instruction for non-English-speaking students. *Language Arts, 58,* 175–180.

Gollnick, D. M., & Chinn, P. C. (1986). *Multicultural education in a pluralistic society.* New York: Merrill/Macmillan.

Goodman, K. S., & Buck, C. (1983). Dialect barriers to reading comprehension revisited. *The Reading Teacher, 27,* 6–12.

Hakuta, K., & Garcia, E. (1989). Bilingualism and education. *American Psychologist, 44,* 374–379.

Harris, V. J. (1992a). Multiethnic children's literature. In K. D. Wood & A. Moss (Eds.), *Exploring literature in the classroom: Content and methods.* Norwood, MA: Christopher-Gordon.

Harris, V. J. (Ed.). (1992b). *Teaching multicultural literature in grades K–8.* Norwood, MA: Christopher-Gordon.

Heath, S. B. (1983). *Ways with words: Language, life, and work in communities and classrooms.* Cambridge: Cambridge University Press.

Hudelson, S. (1984). Kan yu ret and rayt en Ingles: Children become literate in English as a second language. *TESOL Quarterly, 18,* 221–238.

Jipson, J., & Paley, N. (1991). The selective tradition in teachers' choice of children's literature: Does it exist in the elementary classroom? *English Education, 23,* 148–159.

Kendall, F. E. (1983). *Diversity in the classroom.* New York: Teachers College Press.

Krashen, S. (1982). *Principles and practices of second language acquisition.* Oxford: Pergamon Press.

Krashen, S. (1985). *The input hypothesis: Issues and implications.* London: Longman.

Labov, W. (1966). *The social stratification of English in New York City.* Washington, DC: Center for Applied Linguistics.

Labov, W. (1969). The logic of nonstandard English. *The Florida FL Reporter, 7,* 60–74.

Labov, W. (1970). *The study of nonstandard English.* Urbana, IL: National Council of Teachers of English.

Lara, S. G. M. (1989). Reading placement for code-switchers. *The Reading Teacher, 42,* 278–282.

Law, B., & Eckes, M. (1990). *The more than just surviving handbook: ESL for every classroom teacher.* Winnipeg, Canada: Peguis.

Lim, H. J. L., & Watson, D. J. (1993). Whole language content classes for second-language learners. *The Reading Teacher, 46,* 384–393.

May, S. A. (1993). Redeeming multicultural education. *Language Arts, 70,* 364–372.

McCauley, J. K., & McCauley, D. S. (1992). Using choral reading to promote language learning for ESL students. *The Reading Teacher, 45,* 526–533.

Rasinski, T. V., & Padak, N. D. (1990). Multicultural learning through children's literature. *Language Arts, 67,* 576–580.

Reimer, K. M. (1992). Multiethnic literature: Holding fast to dreams. *Language Arts, 69,* 14–21.

Rigg, P. S. (1981). Beginning to read in English the LEA way. In C. W. Twyford, W. Diehl, & K. Feathers (Eds.), *Reading English as a second language:*

Moving from theory. Bloomington, IN: Indiana University.

Rigg, P. S., & Allen, V. A. (1989). *When they don't all speak English: Integrating the ESL student into the regular classroom.* Urbana, IL: National Council of Teachers of English.

Rudman, M. (1976). *Children's literature: An issues approach (2nd ed.).* New York: Longman.

Scarcella, R. (1990). *Teaching language minority students in the multicultural classroom.* Englewood Cliffs, NJ: Prentice-Hall.

Shannon, P. (1986). Hidden within the pages: A study of social perspective in young children's favorite books. *The Reading Teacher, 39,* 656–661.

Sims, R. B. (1982). *Shadow and substance.* Urbana, IL: National Council of Teachers of English.

Soto, G. (1992). Author for a day: Glitter and rainbows. *The Reading Teacher, 46,* 200–202.

Strickland, D. S. (1973). A program for linguistically different black children. *Research in the Teaching of English, 7,* 79–86.

Tompkins, G. E., & McGee, L. M. (1983). Launching nonstandard speakers into standard English. *Language Arts, 60,* 463–469.

Traxel, J. (1983). The American Revolution in children's fiction. *Research in the Teaching of English, 17,* 61–83.

Troika, R. C. (1981). Synthesis of research on bilingual education. *Educational Leadership, 38,* 498–504.

Urzua, C. (1980). Doing what comes naturally: Recent research in second language acquisition. In G. S. Pinnel (Ed.), *Discovering language with children* (pp. 33–38). Urbana, IL: National Council of Teachers of English.

Urzua, C. (1987). "You stopped too soon": Second language children composing and revising. *TESOL Quarterly, 21,* 279–304.

Wagner, H. S. (1982). Kids can be ESL teachers. In C. Carter (Ed.), *Non-native and nonstandard dialect students: Classroom practices in teaching English, 1982–1983* (pp. 62–65). Urbana, IL: National Council of Teachers of English.

Walker-Dalhouse, D. 1992). Using African-American literature to increase ethnic understanding. *The Reading Teacher, 45,* 416–422.

Wong-Fillmore, L. (1985). When does teacher talk work as input? In S. M. Gass & C. G. Madden (Eds.), *Input in second language acquisition* (pp. 17–50). Rowley, MA: Newbury House.

Yokota, J. (1993). Issues in selecting multicultural children's literature. *Language Arts, 70,* 156–167.

Zarnoski, M. (1991). An interview with author Nicholasa Mohr. *The Reading Teacher, 45,* 100–106.

Zarrillo, J. (1994). *Multicultural literature, multicultural teaching: Units for the elementary grades.* Fort Worth, TX: Harcourt Brace.

Children's Book References

Adler, D. A. (1989). *A picture book of Martin Luther King, Jr.* New York: Holiday House.

Babbitt, N. (1975). *Tuck everlasting.* New York: Farrar, Straus & Giroux.

Bierhorst, J. (1979). *A cry from the earth: Music of the North American Indians.* New York: Four Winds Press.

Bierhorst, J. (1983). *The sacred path: Spells, prayers, and power songs of the American Indians.* New York: Morrow.

Bunting, E. (1988). *How many days to America? A Thanksgiving story.* New York: Clarion.

Carle, E. (1969). *The very hungry caterpillar.* New York: Philomel.

Choi, S. N. (1991). *Year of impossible goodbyes.* Boston: Houghton Mifflin.

Clifton, L. (1970). *Some of the days of Everett Anderson.* New York: Henry Holt.

Climo, S. (1989). *The Egyptian Cinderella.* New York: Crowell.

Coerr, E. (1988). *Chang's paper pony.* New York: Harper & Row.

Cohen, B. (1983). *Molly's pilgrim.* New York: Lothrop, Lee & Shepard.

Crews, D. (1991). *Bigmama's.* New York: Greenwillow.

de Paola, T. (1988). *The legend of the Indian paintbrush.* New York: Putnam.

Dooley, N. (1991). *Everybody cooks rice.* Minneapolis: Carolrhoda.

Fraser, M. A. (1993). *Ten mile day and the building of the transcontinental railroad.* New York: Henry Holt.

Freeman, D. (1968). *Corduroy.* New York: Viking.

Friedman, I. R. (1984). *How my parents learned to eat.* Boston: Houghton Mifflin.

Gilson, J. (1985). *Hello, my name is scrambled eggs.* New York: Morrow.

Goble, P. (1988). *Iktomi and the boulder.* New York: Orchard.

Golenbock, P. (1990). *Teammates.* San Diego: Harcourt Brace Jovanovich.

Greenfield, E. (1977). *Africa dream.* New York: HarperCollins.

Harvey, B. (1987). *Immigrant girl: Becky of Eldridge Street.* New York: Holiday House.

Hewett, J. (1990). *Hector lives in the United States now: The story of a Mexican American child.* New York: Lippincott.

Hoyt-Goldsmith, D. (1990). *Totem pole.* New York: Holiday House.

Isadora, R. (1979). *Ben's trumpet.* New York: Morrow.

Knight, M. B. (1993). *Who belongs here? An American story.* Gardiner, ME: Tilbury House.

Levine, E. (1989). *I hate English!* New York: Scholastic.

Lobel, A. (1970). *Frog and Toad are friends.* New York: Harper & Row.

Louie, A. (1982). *Yeh-Shen: A Cinderella story from China.* New York: Philomel.

Malone, M. (1992). *Connie Chung: Broadcast journalist.* Hillside, NJ: Enslow.

Martin, F. (1992). *The rough face girl.* New York: Putnam.

McCurdy, M. (Ed.). (1994). *Escape from slavery: The boyhood of Frederick Douglass in his own words.* New York: Knopf.

Munsch, R. (1985). *Mortimer.* Toronto: Annick Press.

Pinchot, J. (1989). *The Mexicans in America.* Minneapolis: Lerner.

Pinkney, A. (1993). *Seven candles for Kwanzaa.* New York: Dial.

Ringgold, F. (1991). *Tar beach.* New York: Crown.

Say, A. (1990). *El Chino.* Boston: Houghton Mifflin.

Scieszka, J. (1989). *The true story of the three little pigs.* New York: Viking.

Sendak, M. (1963). *Where the wild things are.* New York: Harper & Row.

Steig, W. (1982). *Doctor De Soto.* New York: Farrar, Straus & Giroux.

Steptoe, J. (1987). *Mufaro's beautiful daughters: An African tale.* New York: Lothrop, Lee & Shepard.

Surat, M. M. (1983). *Angel child, dragon child.* Milwaukee: Raintree.

Taylor, M. D. (1976). *Roll of thunder, hear my cry.* New York: Dial.

Taylor, M. D. (1987). *The gold Cadillac.* New York: Dial.

Uchida, Y. (1971). *Journey to Topaz.* Berkeley: Creative Arts Book Company.

Uchida, Y. (1993). *The bracelet.* New York: Philomel.

Williams, V. B. (1982). *A chair for my mother.* New York: Mulberry.

Winter, J. (1988). *Follow the drinking gourd.* New York: Knopf.

Zemach, M. (1983). *The little red hen.* New York: Farrar, Straus & Giroux.

> **My students use the four language arts to find answers to the questions they pose at the beginning of theme cycles.**
>
> *Loretta Toews*
> *Second-Grade Teacher*
> *Bellevue Elementary School*

PROCEDURE

At the beginning of each school year, we make a list of topics the students want to study, and this year they want to learn about whales, dinosaurs, Native Americans, the solar system, President Clinton and the other presidents, rivers, Africa, and China. During the year I try to incorporate all of these topics in theme cycles that span 2, 3, or 4 weeks.

I involve my second graders in the planning. I collect the books and other materials I have available so that I know the perimeters I'm working within. Then we make more concrete plans. We do a KWL chart (Ogle, 1986) to find out what they already know about the topic and what questions they have. I also ask them what types of activities they are interested in pursuing. Now, that's not to say that we do only what the students suggest. I include other necessary activities like map reading, but as much as possible I follow their lead. We also decide what our goals will be for the theme cycle.

Our theme cycle on whales will last three weeks. During the first week, we read informational books about whales, wrote key words on a word wall, and took notes in our learning logs. A list of our text set of whale books is shown in the accompanying figure. I also taught five minilessons: identifying the parts of a whale, contrasting fish and whales, locating where whales live on a world map, comparing baleen and toothed whales, and reviewing the history of whales and whaling.

This week my students chose five whales to study: killer whales, narwhal whales, blue whales, beluga whales, and sperm whales. They research their whale and write a whale book with at least five facts about the whale. Students are also beginning to work on the papier-mâché model of the whale they are studying.

Next week, the students will finish their books and whale models. We will also finish our KWL chart, and I'll read other books from the text set. I have a surprise planned, too. A friend who has been on a whale watch will show a videotape of the whale watch.

ASSESSMENT

I use three techniques for assessing students' learning during the whale theme. I keep track of the activities they are involved in, using a checklist that students keep in their whale theme cycle folders. They also have learning logs in their folders, and I read some of their entries several times during the theme. Together, the students and I decide what they will learn in the theme, and for our whale theme cycle, each student agreed to learn at least five facts about one type of whale. Of course, they'll learn a lot more than that, but this is one goal my second graders can understand and accomplish. They demonstrate what they have learned in the whale books they are writing. That will be my "proof" that they have accomplished the goal.

ADAPTATIONS

I use basically the same procedure for every theme cycle. I always begin with the students helping me plan. I provide background information during the first part of the theme, and then students explore topics and find answers to their questions. I use language arts activities during theme cycles:

Listening and Talking

- Listening aesthetically to stories and poems
- Listening efferently to informational books
- Taking notes from books and oral presentations
- Participating in conversations

- Making KWL charts
- Giving oral reports
- Interviewing community persons
- Presenting puppet shows
- Role-playing

Reading and Writing

- Reading and responding to stories, informational books, and poems
- Using choral reading
- Reading maps, diagrams, and charts
- Making clusters, maps, graphs, and other charts
- Writing in learning logs

- Writing stories and scripts
- Writing poems
- Writing, "All About . . ." books, ABC books, and reports
- Writing advertisements

REFLECTIONS

I used to think that I had to do all the work—identify the goals, plan the activities, and test my students' learning. Now I see my job quite differently. My students help me identify goals and make plans for our theme cycles. They are genuinely involved in learning and demonstrating their learning.

Text Set on Whales

Stories

McFarlane, S. (1991). *Waiting for the whales.* New York: Philomel.
Sheldon, D. (1990). *The whales' song.* New York: Dial.
Siberell, A. (1982). *Whale in the sky.* New York: Viking.
Steig, W. (1971). *Amos and Boris.* New York: Farrar, Straus & Giroux.

Informational Books

Carrick, C. (1993). *Whaling days.* New York: Clarion.
Gibbons, G. (1991). *Whales.* New York: Holiday House.
Mallory, K., & Conley, A. (1989). *Rescue of the stranded whales.* New York: Simon & Schuster.
McMillan, B. (1992). *Going on a whale watch.* New York: Scholastic.
Patent, D. H. (1993). *Killer whales.* New York: Holiday House.
Ryder, J. (1991). *Winter whale.* New York: Morrow.
Simon, S. (1989). *Whales.* New York: Crowell.
Sis, P. (1992). *An ocean world.* New York: Greenwillow.
Stidworthy, J., & Colville, J. (1987). *A year in the life of a whale.* Morristown, NJ: Silver Burdett.
Waters, J. F. (1991). *Watching whales.* Bergenfield, NJ: Cobblehill Books.

Poems and Songs

Livingston, M. C. (1992). *If you ever meet a whale.* New York: Holiday House.
Raffi. (1990). *Baby beluga.* New York: Crown.

14

Extending Language Arts Across the Curriculum

INSIGHT _____

Not only are the language arts a central component of the elementary school curriculum, but listening, talking, reading, and writing are also used as tools for learning in math, social studies, science, and other content areas. For example, students listen to classmates explain how they solved math problems, they read books and dramatize events in connection with a social studies theme, and they write notes and label diagrams as they conduct science experiments. An added benefit of using language arts as learning tools is that students enhance their language arts competencies at the same time. One issue to reflect on about extending language arts across the curriculum is:

How do elementary students use listening, talking, reading, and writing as learning tools?

Students use listening, talking, reading, and writing throughout the school day and across the curriculum, not just during the small part of the day known as language arts. Language is a learning tool, and whenever students are learning social studies, science, math, and other curricular areas, they are most likely using language.

Theme cycles are a new way of developing curriculum in which students use language to learn (Altwerger & Flores, 1994). Social studies and science topics are often integrated for theme cycles. For example, students might study ways people and animals communicate, life in the oceans, or World War II. In theme cycles, students work with the teacher to plan for the theme by asking questions and suggesting topics they want to learn about. They also identify the ways they want to research the topics and find answers to their questions. During the theme, students use listening, talking, reading, and writing as they learn, and they share what they have learned through books they write, presentations they give, and displays they create.

Gamberg and her colleagues (1988) describe theme study as "the core of what children do in school" (p. 10). At their elementary school in Halifax, Nova Scotia, students participate in large-scale themes; one focuses on houses. Students at different grade levels studied different aspects, but all students focused on houses. One class of primary students, for example, studied homes around the world; a class of middle-grade students investigated how homes have changed throughout history; and a class of upper-grade students learned about building a house.

Theme studies are successful with all students because the students are involved in the planning of the theme, are responsible for their own learning, and cooperate with classmates on projects that they select. They discipline themselves because they want to be a part of the learning community in the classroom. One of the most important outcomes is that students gain self-confidence and self-esteem as they become successful and motivated to learn and apply what they are learning.

Language is a powerful learning tool, and reading, writing, listening, and talk activities are valuable ways to learn in all content areas. When students use language in meaningful ways in theme cycles, they learn information better and refine their language competencies. Through listening, talking, reading, and writing activities, students develop their own knowledge of the subject. Thaiss (1986) identifies three benefits students gain from studying across the curriculum:

1. Students understand and remember better when they use listening, talking, reading, and writing to explore what they are learning.
2. Students' language learning is reinforced when they listen, talk, read, and write about what they are learning.
3. Students learn best through active involvement, collaborative projects, and interaction with classmates, the teacher, and the world.

LEARNING THROUGH LANGUAGE

Halliday (1980) described three components of the language arts curriculum: learning language, learning through language, and learning about language. The first component, learning language, might seem to be the primary responsibility of language arts teachers. Certainly, students do need to develop communicative competence in listening, talking, reading, and writing, and instruction in each of the four language modes is essential. The third component, learning about language, involves "coming to understand the nature and function of language itself" (Halliday, 1980, p. 16). Students develop intuitive knowledge about language and its forms and purposes while they use the four language modes; and through vocabulary, spelling, and grammar instruction, their knowledge is made more explicit. But language learning does not occur in isolation, and the second component is just as important.

Learning through language is described as "how we use language to build up a picture of the world in which we live" (Halliday, 1980, p. 13). It involves using language to learn in content areas across the curriculum. Students learn content area material through language at the same time they are learning, applying, and refining language through content area study. The language arts activities that we have discussed throughout this text are applied through literature and content area study. Rather than learn about listening for the sake of listening, students learn about it so that they can listen more effectively to learn math or science. Similarly, they learn to read and write for content area study.

Learning Science Through Language

In learning about science, students participate in a wide variety of language activities (Hansen, Newkirk, & Graves, 1985). They listen to information presented in filmstrips and videotapes, information presented by the teacher, and information read aloud. They use informal writing strategies to take notes and organize information. Clusters, note-taking/note-making sheets, learning logs, and lab reports are four forms that recording may take. Students read picture books, informational books, reference books, and magazine articles as part of research projects, and they share what they are learning through oral reports, debates, written reports, "All About . . ." books, posters, charts, and diagrams. Interviewing can also be used in science; students can interview a scientist or other knowledgeable person and then share what they have learned by writing a newspaper article or other report.

In a theme cycle about plants, for example, students might be involved in the following types of activities. Listening activities might involve these:

Listen to the teacher share poems about plants with the class.

Listen to the teacher read informational books about plants.

View and listen to films, videotapes, and filmstrips about plants.

Listen to a botanist or gardener talk about plants.

Talk activities include these possibilities:

Participate in discussions about plants.

Talk about the plant experiments they are conducting.

Ask a botanist or gardener questions about plants.

Give oral reports about plants.

Retell or dramatize a plant story, such as *The Giving Tree* (Silverstein, 1964).

Reading activities would include these:

Read informational books about plants.

Read seed packets and planting guides.

Read maps showing where different kinds of plants live.

Do choral readings of poems about plants.

Read a classmate's hardbound book about plants.

Share learning log entries and quickwrites about plants.

These are writing activities that might be part of a science theme on plants:

Brainstorm a list of plant-related words.

Make a cluster about plants, flowers, trees, or some other topic.

Quickwrite or write in a learning log about plants.

Make a poster comparing deciduous and evergreen trees.

Write a letter inviting a botanist to be interviewed.

Record a seed's growth in a learning log.

Make plant or ecology posters.

Write invitations to a tree-planting ceremony.

Write an "All About . . ." book.

Write an ABC book about plants.

Conduct a science experiment about plants and write a lab report.

Research and write a report about plants.

Write poems about plants.

Figure 14–1 shows two writing samples fourth graders wrote as part of a theme on plants. One sample is a lab report about a science experiment; the other is a cluster about nonflowering plants based on *Plants That Never Ever Bloom* (Heller, 1984). It would not be possible to list all the listening, talking, reading, and writing activities that can be related to a theme cycle on plants, but these examples suggest the range of activities teachers should consider when planning instruction. Most importantly, our listing illustrates that the language modes are the vehicles through which students learn about plants.

Learning Social Studies Through Language

Like science, social studies lends itself to language activities. To study history, geography, political science, or another of the social studies, children read picture books, informational books, reference books, magazines, and newspapers. They talk and write informally about their learning, and they talk and write to organize their learning and to share it through reports, poems, stories, and other activities. Upper-grade students who are studying the American Revolution, for instance, might be involved in these language–social studies activities. For listening:

Listen to the teacher read aloud books about the American Revolution.

Listen to songs of the period.

View and listen to films, filmstrips, and videotapes.

Listen to classmates share their writing.

Figure 14–1   Two Writing Activities From a Fourth-Grade Plants Theme

My Experiment on Plants

My Question

Will plants grow without light?

My Prediction

No, plants cannot grow without light because if plants didn't have light the water wouldn't soak in and they wouldn't live because too much water would be on top of the plant.

My Log

April 9

I planted my seeds in a row and watered them after it. My seeds' color is brown. They are about half an inch long. Their texture is very smooth. They are an oval shape. They are bean seeds.

April 11

Mine has been in the dark for 2 days and nothing has changed.

April 14

My plants have grown half an inch tall in the dark. It really surprises me.

April 15

My plants are 4 inches tall (20 cm) according to what I can see.

April 21

Mine have grown 5 more inches and are now 12 inches tall.

April 22

Mine have grown half an inch. I planted another one and can't water it.

April 23

Mine have grown one inch taller. The other is growing too, even without water.

April 24

Mine are now 15 inches tall. My unwatered plant is 4 inches tall.

April 29

My plants are dying out after they've grown a lot.

May 1

My plants are dying and they smell terrible.

May 2

My plants have died and they look terrible.

May 6

My plants have been dying since a while ago. I have taken good care of them.

May 7

My plants have died and we will talk about them on Monday.

May 8

My plants have died and there's not even a root left.

My Conclusion

Now I know that the plants grew so tall because they were reaching for sunlight. They died because they were in the dark.

Figure 14–1   *continued*

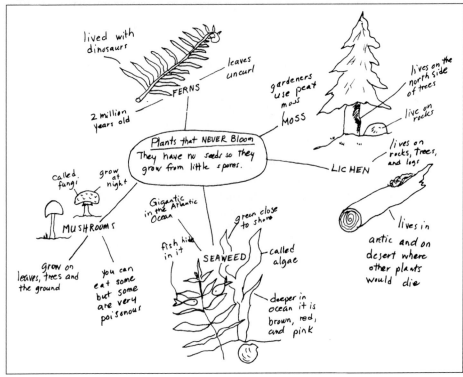

Students might participate in these talk activities:

> Discuss issues of the American Revolution.
>
> Dramatize events from the period.
>
> Give oral reports.
>
> Debate in the role of a Tory or a Patriot.
>
> Pretend to be someone from the period and be interviewed by classmates.

They might read from among these possibilities:

> Fritz's biographies of Revolutionary personalities, such as *Why Don't You Get a Horse, Sam Adams?* (1974)
>
> Informational books about the American Revolution
>
> Chapter books set in Revolutionary War days
>
> Poems such as "Paul Revere's Ride"
>
> Maps, charts, and diagrams about the Revolutionary War
>
> Classmates' stories, reports, and other writings

Writing activities might include these:

> Keep a simulated journal as Paul Revere, Betsy Ross, or another personality from the period.
>
> Keep a learning log with lists of words, clusters, and note-taking/note-making pages.

Make a KWL chart listing what they know about the American Revolution, what they want to learn, and finally, what they have learned.

Write poems about the American Revolution.

Research and write a report about life in the 1700s.

Write a simulated newspaper that might have been published during the American Revolution.

Write a biography of an American Revolutionary War personality.

An excerpt from a fifth grader's biography of Benjamin Franklin is presented in Figure 14–2. In this biography, entitled *The Life of the Great Inventor,* Matthew writes four chapters focusing on Ben's childhood, his experiments with electricity, his *Poor Richard's Almanack,* and his role in the Revolutionary War period. Matthew read Aliki's *The Many Lives of Benjamin Franklin* (1988),

Figure 14–2   An Excerpt From a Fifth Grader's Biography of Ben Franklin

Chapter 1: In Which a Genius Is Born

In 1706 a young genius was born. His name was Benjamin Franklin. At the time the streets of Boston, Massachusetts were still being named. Luckily, the street Ben lived on had already been named Milk Street. Ben had 17 brothers and sisters. When Ben was 9 or 10, he bought a whistle with all his money. That was the last time he spent his money unwisely. That whistle drove his family crazy.

When Ben was 12, he made a swimming machine. He got two boards and cut a hole in the middle of them. When he tested out his invention, he raced his friend Tom. Ben beat him by 10 yards.

At the age of 12, Ben's father wanted him to become a candle maker, but Ben wanted to be a sailor. Ben's father talked him into being an apprentice for his brother James. James was a printer. Back then you had to work until you were 21 if you were an apprentice.

Ben got tired of reading the same old thing from the newspaper every single day. So he wrote letters to James about things so James would put them in the newspaper. He didn't want James to know it was him so he signed it Widow Dogood. Everytime a letter came, everybody got excited. His letters made newspapers sell faster. When James found out what Ben did, he got angry and didn't let Ben give him things to put in the newspaper.

Chapter 2: Ben Discovers Electricity

On a day in 1748 it was on the front cover of the newspaper that a man had died trying to prove electricity was in lightning. The man died instantly when lightning hit the tower the man was in. The newspaper said there was machinery in the tower. So Ben figured that there was electricity in lightning. He wanted to know for sure so he got a handkerchief, 6 sticks, wire, string, and a key. He made a kite. He took the 6 sticks and used 4 of them to made a diamond. He took 2 sticks and used them for a cross for the center of the diamond. Then he used the handkerchief to wrap around the diamond. After that he tied a wire to the end of it. The he tied some string to the end of the wire. After that he slid a key to about the center of the wire. He waited until a storm came with lightning. Then he flew the kite and lightning hit the top of the kite. A streak of electricity zoomed down the wire, but then it hit the string. When it hit Ben it was not so great but it still gave him a great shock. After he found out that electricity was in lightning he made up the lightning rod. Then he got a lot of people to become witnesses. Then he did it again and that's how we have electricity now.

the d'Aulaires' *Benjamin Franklin* (1950), and Jean Fritz's *What's the Big Idea, Benjamin Franklin?* (1976) to gather information about Franklin. He then developed a lifeline showing key events and accomplishments. With this background of information, Matthew chose topics for each chapter and used the writing process to cluster his ideas, write rough drafts of each chapter, revise the chapters in writing groups, edit to identify and correct mechanical errors, and, finally, publish his biography in a hardbound book. His finished book included a title page, a table of contents, four chapters, a bibliography, and an "All About the Author" page. A theme on the American Revolution with activities such as these can be extended to include the times allocated for both language arts and social studies.

Learning Literature Through Language

Literature focus units that focus on a single book, an author, a collection of books by the same author, a theme, or a genre can be developed the same way. Rather than just read and discuss the books, students can participate in a variety of reading, writing, talking, and listening activities (Hancock & Hill, 1987; Moss, 1984; Somers & Worthington, 1979). For a unit on Van Allsburg's fantasy picture books, middle-grade students might be involved in these listening activities:

Listen to the teacher read aloud some of Van Allsburg's books.

Listen to other books at the listening center.

View and listen to a videotape version of *Jumanji* (1981) and compare it to the book.

Listen to classmates share ideas about the books.

Listen to classmates share their writings in response to the books.

Talk activities might include these:

Discuss the books.

Tell stories based on the illustrations in *The Mysteries of Harris Burdick* (1984).

Retell a familiar story from an unusual viewpoint, as Van Allsburg did in *Two Bad Ants* (1988).

Dramatize one of Van Allsburg's stories.

Students might do these reading activities:

Read Van Allsburg's books independently.

Read *Jumanji* (1981) as guided or shared reading.

Read other fantasies, such as *The Lion, the Witch and the Wardrobe* (Lewis, 1950) to compare to Van Allsburg's books.

Examine a collection of ABC books to compare to *The Z Was Zapped* (1987).

After reading *The Garden of Abdul Gasazi* (1979), read books about magic.

Share students' writing about Van Allsburg's books.

Students may participate in these writing activities:

Keep a reading log.

Cluster the beginning-middle-end of one of Van Allsburg's books.

Write a letter to Van Allsburg.

Write a sequel to *Jumanji* (1981).

Write an ABC book similar to *The Z Was Zapped* (1987).

After reading *Ben's Dream* (1982), write plans for a trip around the world.

After reading *Jumanji* (1981), write directions for playing a game or researching a favorite game.

After reading *The Stranger* (1986), make posters about the four seasons.

Write stories to accompany the illustrations in *The Mysteries of Harris Burdick* (1984).

After reading *The Polar Express* (1985), write in response to the question, "Is there a Santa Claus?"

Make posters, charts, or murals about the books.

These listening, talking, reading, and writing activities illustrate some of the possible ways literature can be extended. Students in a fourth-grade class studied Chris Van Allsburg during an author study. They wrote letters to Van Allsburg, and one student's letter appears in Figure 14–3. After the fourth graders read Van Allsburg's books, one student chose to learn more about

During a unit on Chris Van Allsburg, middle-grade students participate in listening, talking, reading, and writing activities.

Figure 14–3   Two Fourth Graders' Projects From an Author Unit on Chris Van Allsburg

Pioneer Intermediate School
P.O. Box 127
Noble, OK 73068
February 22

Mr. Chris Van Allsburg
114 Lorimer Avenue
Providence, RI 02906

Dear Chris,

I really like all of your books. But I wanted to know why there is a dog like Spuds MacKenzie in every book. Also, I'd like to know why almost every woman in your books looks the same.

Are you Harris Burdick or is the story true about him? I kind of believe you. But if it was true, it would probably be on Unsolved Mysteries. By the way, I think you ought to be the host. All right, I guess that's enough of Unsolved Mysteries.

Now let's get back to your books. I've been studying your writing. I have a folder full about you and your books. So does my class. My friend and I are doing a sequel to your book *Jumanji*. We're also tracing Ben's trip in *Ben's Dream* around the world on a big map in our classroom. My favorite book is *Two Bad Ants*.

My name is Annie. I'm ten years old. I've got two bratty sisters and one dog. It's the pits. I wanted to write to you to tell you all of this. Please write back.

Your friend,

Annie Picek

magic, several students read ABC books and made their own, and others wrote sequels to *Jumanji*. One student's sequel is also presented in Figure 14–3.

Learning Other Content Areas Through Language

Listening, talking, reading, and writing can be connected to math and other content areas as well. Two writing activities for use in math class, for example, are keeping learning logs and writing story problems. Students can keep learning logs in which they write about what they are learning during the last 5 minutes of class (Salem, 1982; Schubert, 1987). They can write about what they have learned during that class, list the steps in solving a problem, write definitions of mathematical terms, and describe things that confuse them. Writing in learning logs has several advantages over class discussion. All students participate simultaneously in writing, and teachers can review written responses more carefully than oral ones. Also, students use mathematical vocabulary and become more precise and complete in their answers.

Students can write story problems in which they apply the mathematical concepts they have been learning. In the process of writing the problems, students consider what information to include and how to phrase the question. Audience is especially important in writing story problems, because if students do not write clearly and completely, classmates may not be able to solve the problem. In a sixth-grade class, students clipped advertisements from the local

Figure 14–3 continued

Return to Jumanji

The next day on the way home from school Walter asked Peter if he would like to play a game that he had found in the park. Peter started to act weird and said, "Ah, well, ah . . . I got homework. Ah . . . I'm really tired . . . maybe, another time . . ." and he ran home as fast as he could.

At Walter and Daniel's house, Daniel opened the big long box and saw the directions and said, "Oh, how stupid—directions. Don't they have a game without directions?" "I don't know," said Walter.

Daniel rolled the dice and started to play. Move 10 spaces. Volcano eruption. Suddenly there was the loudest noise and then all of a sudden lava started filling the room. Daniel said, "Ah . . . Walter, I don't think, ah . . . I want to play this game, ah . . . any more."

"Oh, come on ya big baby. This is exciting!" said Walter. "Let's keep on playing and see what happens next."

Daniel agreed and Walter rolled the dice and moved two spaces. Laughing season. Move one space back. Suddenly Walter started laughing. He was laughing so hard his face turned red and fell out of his chair and landed in the lava. Daniel's chair fell over too and he was in it. They just could not stop laughing.

Daniel could hardly roll the dice. He rolled an 8. Dog and cat thunderstorm. Move 2 spaces back. All of a sudden dogs and cats started falling from the sky. A dog fell on Walter's head and a cat fell on Daniel's head. They stopped laughing. There were the strangest noises of meows and bow-wows. A dog got caught on the ceiling and his ears were dangling in Walter's face. The room sounded like a circus with all the meows and bow-wows-of course.

Walter rolled the dice. He rolled a 9. Earthquake attack. Move 8 spaces back. The walls started shaking. Pictures fell from the mantle. Pans and pots fell from the kitchen cupboard. The table started shaking. The game fell but then Walter got it in his hands and put it back on the table.

Daniel rolled the dice. He rolled a 7. Music season. Move 5 spaces back. All of a sudden music started playing really loud. It was so loud they couldn't hear themselves think.

Walter rolled the dice. He rolled a 3. Flowers attack. Move 1 space back. Suddenly flowers started growing everywhere. A flower grew under Walter's chair. He went up to the sky. A flower grew under Daniel's chair and he went up to the sky too. Walter jumped out of his chair and landed in the lava. He said, "Im leaving." Daniel followed him. They walked out the door and closed it. Walter said, "I don't want to play this game anymore."

At 5:00 when Walter and Daniel's mom and dad got home they nearly fainted. The family moved far away from that house. But when Walter got old he got married and had two sons named Bradley and Ben. One day when Bradley and Ben were walking home from school, Bradley saw a house and tried the door. It was open. They walked in and music was blaring in their ears and dogs fell from the sky. They tried to run out but they slipped in the lava and fell down. The door closed and they never came out.

---

newspaper to use in writing story problems. One student used an ad for aspirin: The 72-count package was on sale for $2.99 and the 125-count package for $4.66. From this information she composed the following problem:

Sarah went to the drugstore to buy some aspirin. She found a bottle of 125 aspirin for $4.66 and a bottle of 72 aspirin for $2.99. Which one should she buy to get the most for her money? (Answer: *the bottle of 125*)

Children's books provide another bridge between mathematics and written language. In books such as *The Grouchy Ladybug* (Carle, 1977) and *How Much Is a Million?* (Schwartz, 1985), mathematics is portrayed in a meaningful context and is celebrated as a language (Whitin & Wilde, 1992). Children's books demonstrate that mathematics develops out of human experience; they also integrate math across the curriculum. Students can read and respond to books incorporating math concepts, and they can listen to teachers read these books aloud. Sometimes the books are read as part of theme cycles, and sometimes the books are chosen to teach a mathematical concept. A list of books that incorporate mathematical concepts about counting, addition and subtraction, multiplication and division, geometry, and measurement are presented in Figure 14–4.

To learn more about incorporating language in math class, see Richards's (1990) article in *Language Arts,* in which she describes how she uses language activities to introduce math themes, investigate math concepts, and conclude the theme. Some of the writing activities her students use are

Figure 14–4   Books About Mathematical Concepts

Aker, S. (1990). *What comes in 2's, 3's, and 4's?* New York: Simon & Schuster. (P–M)

Anno, M. (1983). *Anno's mysterious multiplying jar.* New York: Philomel. (M)

Anno, M. (1986). *All in a day.* New York: Philomel. (M)

Ashabranner, M., & Ashabranner, B. (1989). *Counting America: The study of the United States Census.* New York: Putnam. (M–U)

Bang, M. (1983). *Ten, nine, eight.* New York: Greenwillow. (P)

Carle, E. (1969). *The very hungry caterpillar.* New York: Putnam. (P)

Carle, E. (1977). *The grouchy ladybug.* New York: Crowell. (P)

Coerr, E. (1977). *Sadako and the thousand paper cranes.* New York: Putnam. (M)

Ehlert, L. (1989). *Color zoo.* New York: Lippincott. (P)

Ehlert, L. (1990). *Fish eyes: A book you can count on.* San Diego: Harcourt Brace Jovanovich. (P)

Feelings, M. (1971). *Moja means one: A Swahili counting book.* New York: Dial. (M)

Fisher, L. E. (1987). *Calendar art: Thirteen days, weeks, months, and years from around the world.* New York: Four Winds. (M–U)

Gibbons, G. (1979). *Clocks and how they go.* New York: Crowell. (M–U)

Haskins, J. (1987). *Count your way through Japan.* Minneapolis: Carolrhoda. (See other books in the series.) (M)

Hoban, T. (1973). *Over, under and through, and other spatial concepts.* New York: Macmillan. (P–M)

Hoban, T. (1974). *Circles, triangles, and squares.* New York: Macmillan. (P)

Hoban, T. (1981). *More than one.* New York: Greenwillow. (P)

Hopper, M. (1985). *Seven eggs.* New York: Harper & Row. (P)

Hutchins, P. (1986). *The doorbell rang.* New York: Greenwillow. (P)

Macaulay, D. (1975). *Pyramid.* Boston: Houghton Mifflin. (U)

Macaulay, D. (1980). *Unbuilding.* Boston: Houghton Mifflin. (U)

McMillan, B. (1989). *Super super superwords.* New York: Lothrop, Lee & Shepard. (P–M)

Peek, M. (1981). *Roll over!* New York: Clarion. (P)

Schwartz, D. (1985). *How much is a million?* New York: Lothrop, Lee & Shepard. (P–M)

Schwartz, D. (1989). *If you made a million.* New York: Lothrop, Lee & Shepard. (P–M)

Scott, A. H. (1990). *One good horse: A cowpuncher's counting book.* New York: Greenwillow. (P–M).

Tombert, A. (1990). *Grandfather Tang's story.* New York: Crown. (M–U)

Williams, V. B. (1982). *A chair for my mother.* New York: Mulberry. (P)

Wood, A. (1984). *The napping house.* San Diego: Harcourt Brace Jovanovich. (P)

P = primary grades (K–2); M = middle grades (3–5); U = upper grades (6–8).

summaries, definitions, reports, quickwrites, notes, lists, evaluations, predictions, arguments, and explanations. One of Richards's students sums up the value of language in math class this way: "Language helps our maths [*sic*] by being able to write, use words, use symbols, being able to read and listen. . . . It helps explain things" (p. 14).

Students use many of the same listening, talking, reading, and writing activities in other content areas. They use informal writing strategies to take notes and organize what they are learning, and they share their learning through oral and written reports, role-playing, and other activities.

THEME CYCLES

Theme cycles are similar to thematic units in some ways. Like thematic units, theme cycles are built around social studies and science topics, and students are involved in a variety of activities to facilitate learning and higher-level, critical thinking. What makes theme cycles different is that students are involved in the planning and in identifying some of the activities. Students are involved in authentic and meaningful learning activities, not reading chapters in a social studies or science textbook in order to answer the questions at the end of the chapter. Textbooks might be used as a resource, but only as one of many available resources. Students explore topics that interest them and research answers to questions they have posed and are genuinely interested in answering. Students share their learning at the end of the theme cycle and are assessed on what they have learned as well as the processes they used in learning and working in the classroom.

Even though theme cycles are designed for across-the-curriculum learning, we have also included several literature focus units in this chapter to show that they are developed in a similar way.

Planning Theme Cycles

To begin planning a theme cycle, teachers delineate the topic for the theme cycle and think about possible materials and activities to incorporate in the theme. The cluster in Figure 14–5 illustrates 12 possible resources for developing a theme cycle, whether it focuses on social studies (e.g., California gold rush, explorers, American Revolution), science (hibernation, machines, weather), health (parts of the body, drugs, nutrition), geography (continents, the Mississippi River), literature (mystery stories, fables, myths, Halloween stories), or an author (Beverly Cleary, Tomie de Paola, Katharine Paterson). After this initial planning, teachers meet with students to talk about the upcoming theme and possible ways it might develop.

Content Area Information. Teachers consider what they want students to learn and what students want to learn during the theme. Then they develop goals and objectives. They also think about how students will explore the information, using reading, writing, listening, talking, and audiovisual materials. For literature focus units and author studies, information about books, authors, and illustrators is included as well.

Figure 14–5   Possible Resources for Developing a Theme Cycle

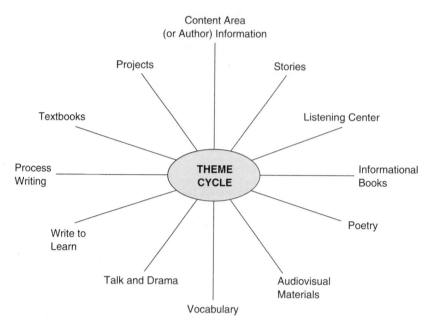

Stories.   Teachers and students locate a text set of picture books and chapter books to use in connection with the theme. Some stories will be read aloud to students (or tape-recorded for the listening center), some will be read independently, and others will be read as shared or guided reading. Investigating the topic in a library card catalog will suggest picture books and chapter books as well as other books by the same author. The stories might be shared using a variety of strategies, including these:

To read aloud to students

For students to read independently

To use for shared or guided reading

To use in teaching elements of story structure

To use as models or patterns for writing stories

The text set will be placed in a special area in the classroom library.

Listening Center.   Teachers select tapes to accompany stories or informational books, or they create their own tapes so that absent students can catch up on a book being read aloud day by day. The tapes can also be used to provide additional reading experiences for students who listen to them when they read or reread a story or an informational book.

Informational Books, Magazines, and Reference Books.   Teachers and students collect informational books, magazines, newspaper articles, and reference books and add these to the text set. These materials can also be used for minilessons to teach students about expository text structure patterns, how to use an index and table of contents, as models or patterns for student writing, and to provide information for reports or other writing projects.

During a literature focus unit on Leo the Late Bloomer, *these bilingual students read the Spanish version of the story.*

Poetry.   Teachers and students locate books of poetry or individual poems that are appropriate to the theme. Teachers write some poems on charts to share with students, or students might arrange a bulletin board display of the poems. Poetry writing activities might be developed using a variety of poetic forms described in Chapter 11.

Audiovisual Materials.   Teachers locate films, videotapes, filmstrips, charts, timelines, maps, models, posters, and other displays to be used during the theme cycle. These materials can be displayed in the classroom, and students can make other materials during the theme. Four excellent resources for locating audiovisual materials (cassette tapes, filmstrips, films, and video-tapes) of children's books and authors who write for children are:

Listening Library, Inc.
One Park Avenue
Old Greenwich, CT 06870

Random House Media
Department 520
400 Hahn Road
Westminster, MD 21157

Spoken Arts
Department B
310 North Avenue
New Rochelle, NY 10801

Weston Woods
Weston, CT 06883

Vocabulary. Teachers think about key theme-related words that students need to know in order to explore topics during the theme. They also hang a word wall chart in the classroom and invite students to add new words as they encounter them. Then these words can be used for a variety of word study activities.

Talk and Drama. Teachers and students consider ways to use talk and drama for learning and to demonstrate learning (Erickson, 1988; Nelson, 1988; San Jose, 1988). Possible activities are:

Share learning by giving an oral report.

Have someone with special expertise on the theme talk to the class.

Participate in a debate related to the theme.

Role-play an event or a personality.

Participate in a readers theatre presentation of a story or poem.

Tell or retell a story, biography, or event.

Use a puppet show to tell a story, biography, or event.

Write and perform a skit or play.

Learning Logs. Teachers and students plan how they will use learning logs. Students can take notes, write questions, make observations, clarify their thinking, and write reactions to what they are learning in learning logs (Tompkins, 1994). They also write quickwrites and make clusters to explore what they are learning. Teachers plan for students to keep learning logs, simulated journals, or reading logs during theme cycles.

The Writing Process. Teachers and students consider how to use the writing process for projects students will pursue during the theme cycle. Students use the writing process to develop and polish these types of writing projects:

ABC books	Individual reports
Advertisements	Letters
"All About . . ." books	Myths and legends
Biographies	Poems
Cartoons	Posters
Collaborative reports	Scripts
Essays	Stories

Textbooks. Theme cycles can be taught without textbooks; however, when information is available in a content area textbook, it can be used. Upper-grade students, in particular, read and discuss concepts presented in textbooks or use them as a reference for further study.

Projects. Students think about projects they can develop to extend their learning during the theme cycle. They work on the project independently or in small groups and then share the project with the class at the end of the theme. Projects involve listening, talking, reading, and writing, as well as art, music, drama, cooking, or other activities. The Teacher's Notebook on page 569 lists some possible projects that can be adapted for various theme cycles.

Teacher's Notebook

Projects to Extend Learning in Theme Cycles

Give an oral report.
Compose a rap or song.
Create a photo display.
Write and perform a readers theatre presentation, skit, or play.
Write a poem.
Construct a mobile.
Make puppets and present a puppet show.
Present an advertisement.
Create a mobile.
Make a map.
Box a theme.
Make a diorama.
Write a simulated journal.
Create a cluster.
Make a chart or poster.
Read a book and keep a reading log.
Write an "All About . . ." or concept book.
Write a simulated newspaper.
Write a simulated letter.
Write an essay arguing one viewpoint.
Write an ABC book.
Create a word search.
Write a report.
Write to a business or other organization to request information.
Write to an author.
Make a lifeline or timeline.
Design a book jacket.
Plan and present a debate.
Create a collage on the theme.
Build a model using modeling clay, blocks, or other materials.
Interview someone knowledgeable about the theme.
Dress up as a personality related to the theme.
Create a filmstrip, handroll movie, or videotape.
Draw or paint a mural.

The goal in developing plans for a theme cycle is for teachers and students to consider a wide variety of resources that integrate listening, talking, reading, and writing with the content of the theme (Pappas, Kiefer, & Levstik, 1990). We will discuss three sample theme cycles for primary-grade students, three for middle-grade students, and three for upper-grade students. These themes integrate the four language modes with literature, social studies, and science, and they utilize many of the resources outlined in Figure 14–5.

Primary-Grade Theme Cycles

Clusters for three primary-grade themes, designed for students in kindergarten, first, or second grade, are presented in Figure 14–6. One theme focuses on "The Gingerbread Boy" (a literature focus unit), the second on Sending and Receiving Mail (a social studies theme), and the third on Arnold Lobel's Frog

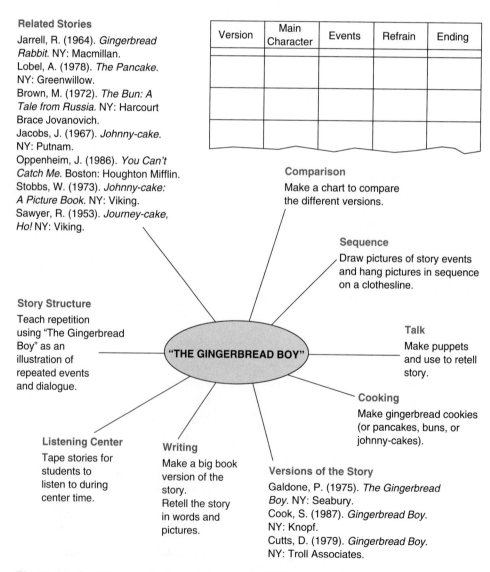

Related Stories

Jarrell, R. (1964). *Gingerbread Rabbit*. NY: Macmillan.
Lobel, A. (1978). *The Pancake*. NY: Greenwillow.
Brown, M. (1972). *The Bun: A Tale from Russia*. NY: Harcourt Brace Jovanovich.
Jacobs, J. (1967). *Johnny-cake*. NY: Putnam.
Oppenheim, J. (1986). *You Can't Catch Me*. Boston: Houghton Mifflin.
Stobbs, W. (1973). *Johnny-cake: A Picture Book*. NY: Viking.
Sawyer, R. (1953). *Journey-cake, Ho!* NY: Viking.

Version	Main Character	Events	Refrain	Ending

Comparison

Make a chart to compare the different versions.

Sequence

Draw pictures of story events and hang pictures in sequence on a clothesline.

Story Structure

Teach repetition using "The Gingerbread Boy" as an illustration of repeated events and dialogue.

"THE GINGERBREAD BOY"

Talk

Make puppets and use to retell story.

Cooking

Make gingerbread cookies (or pancakes, buns, or johnny-cakes).

Listening Center

Tape stories for students to listen to during center time.

Writing

Make a big book version of the story.
Retell the story in words and pictures.

Versions of the Story

Galdone, P. (1975). *The Gingerbread Boy*. NY: Seabury.
Cook, S. (1987). *Gingerbread Boy*. NY: Knopf.
Cutts, D. (1979). *Gingerbread Boy*. NY: Troll Associates.

Figure 14–6   Clusters for Three Primary-Grade Theme Cycles

and Toad stories (an author unit). The clusters suggest eight or more types of activities and resources that can be used in developing lesson plans.

Literature Focus Unit: "The Gingerbread Boy." This folktale can be the basis for a unit for kindergarten and first-grade students. The story, available in many versions (several are listed in the cluster), can be used to teach students about repetition and its use in developing a story. The different stories follow the same general plot but vary as to the characters the gingerbread boy runs past. Even young children can identify the variations from story to story. For additional experiences, students can listen to the stories at the listening center. Students enjoy listening to other journey stories, such as *You Can't Catch Me!* (Oppenheim, 1986), *Johnny-Cake* (Jacobs, 1967), and *Gingerbread Rabbit* (Jarrell, 1964) because of their similarity to "The Gingerbread Boy." The repetitious form of the stories makes them easier to remember, and children enjoy pointing out differences among the stories.

After reading several versions of "The Gingerbread Boy" or related stories, students and the teacher might make a chart to compare the different versions,

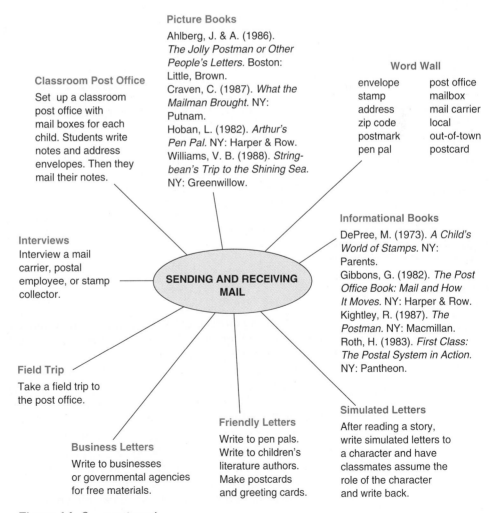

Picture Books

Ahlberg, J. & A. (1986). *The Jolly Postman or Other People's Letters.* Boston: Little, Brown.
Craven, C. (1987). *What the Mailman Brought.* NY: Putnam.
Hoban, L. (1982). *Arthur's Pen Pal.* NY: Harper & Row.
Williams, V. B. (1988). *Stringbean's Trip to the Shining Sea.* NY: Greenwillow.

Classroom Post Office

Set up a classroom post office with mail boxes for each child. Students write notes and address envelopes. Then they mail their notes.

Word Wall

envelope	post office
stamp	mailbox
address	mail carrier
zip code	local
postmark	out-of-town
pen pal	postcard

Interviews
Interview a mail carrier, postal employee, or stamp collector.

SENDING AND RECEIVING MAIL

Informational Books

DePree, M. (1973). *A Child's World of Stamps.* NY: Parents.
Gibbons, G. (1982). *The Post Office Book: Mail and How It Moves.* NY: Harper & Row.
Kightley, R. (1987). *The Postman.* NY: Macmillan.
Roth, H. (1983). *First Class: The Postal System in Action.* NY: Pantheon.

Field Trip
Take a field trip to the post office.

Business Letters
Write to businesses or governmental agencies for free materials.

Friendly Letters
Write to pen pals.
Write to children's literature authors.
Make postcards and greeting cards.

Simulated Letters
After reading a story, write simulated letters to a character and have classmates assume the role of the character and write back.

Figure 14–6   continued

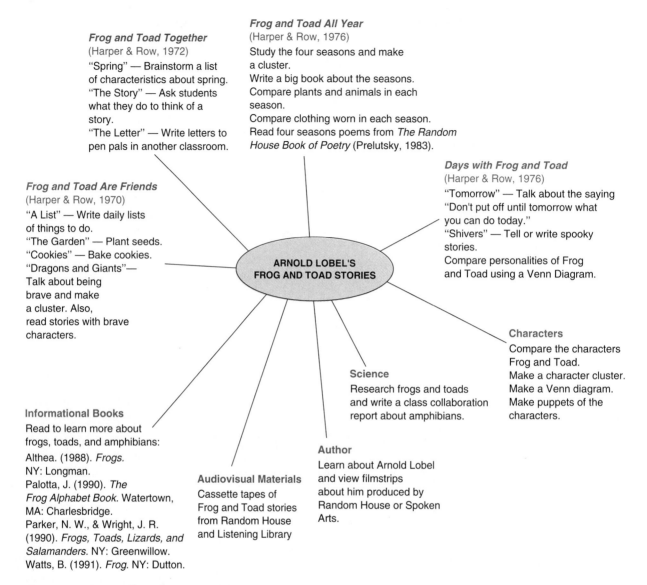

Frog and Toad Together
(Harper & Row, 1972)
"Spring" — Brainstorm a list
of characteristics about spring.
"The Story" — Ask students
what they do to think of a
story.
"The Letter" — Write letters to
pen pals in another classroom.

Frog and Toad All Year
(Harper & Row, 1976)
Study the four seasons and make
a cluster.
Write a big book about the seasons.
Compare plants and animals in each
season.
Compare clothing worn in each season.
Read four seasons poems from *The Random
House Book of Poetry* (Prelutsky, 1983).

Days with Frog and Toad
(Harper & Row, 1976)
"Tomorrow" — Talk about the saying
"Don't put off until tomorrow what
you can do today."
"Shivers" — Tell or write spooky
stories.
Compare personalities of Frog
and Toad using a Venn Diagram.

Frog and Toad Are Friends
(Harper & Row, 1970)
"A List" — Write daily lists
of things to do.
"The Garden" — Plant seeds.
"Cookies" — Bake cookies.
"Dragons and Giants"—
Talk about being
brave and make
a cluster. Also,
read stories with brave
characters.

**ARNOLD LOBEL'S
FROG AND TOAD STORIES**

Characters
Compare the characters
Frog and Toad.
Make a character cluster.
Make a Venn diagram.
Make puppets of the
characters.

Science
Research frogs and toads
and write a class collaboration
report about amphibians.

Informational Books
Read to learn more about
frogs, toads, and amphibians:
Althea. (1988). *Frogs*.
NY: Longman.
Palotta, J. (1990). *The
Frog Alphabet Book*. Watertown,
MA: Charlesbridge.
Parker, N. W., & Wright, J. R.
(1990). *Frogs, Toads, Lizards, and
Salamanders*. NY: Greenwillow.
Watts, B. (1991). *Frog*. NY: Dutton.

Audiovisual Materials
Cassette tapes of
Frog and Toad stories
from Random House
and Listening Library

Author
Learn about Arnold Lobel
and view filmstrips
about him produced by
Random House or Spoken
Arts.

Figure 14–6   continued

as shown on the cluster. Students compare the main character, the events, the refrain, and the ending. In some stories the gingerbread boy (or similar character) doesn't get eaten.

Other exploring activities are possible. Students can draw pictures of the story events and hang the pictures in sequence on a clothesline as they retell the story (Tompkins & McGee, 1989). Similarly, students can make puppets to use in retelling the story or creating a new version of the story. They can bake gingerbread cookies or cook pancakes, buns, johnny-cakes, or other foods and act out the story before eating the main characters.

Students also write in response to the story. They can work together to make a big book version, drawing the illustrations and dictating the text for the teacher to print in the book. Students can also make individual story booklets, by drawing pictures and dictating their stories to the teacher or writing by themselves.

Social Studies Theme: Sending and Receiving Mail.   This theme connects letter writing with social studies, as shown in the cluster in Figure 14–6. Students write friendly and business letters and learn how mail is collected, sorted, and delivered. Students write friendly letters to pen pals and children's authors and notes to classmates that are "mailed" through a classroom post office. Students can also write to businesses and governmental agencies for free materials. Simulated letters are another possibility. After reading a story, students assume the role of a character and write letters to another character in the story; then they exchange letters, change roles, and answer the letters as the other story character.

Picture books and informational books about letters, mail, and the post office are available for primary-grade students; some books are listed in the theme cluster. *The Jolly Postman or Other People's Letters* (Ahlberg & Ahlberg, 1986) is a delightful book in which the Jolly Postman delivers letters to characters from well-known folktales and fairy tales. Each letter or card is tucked into an envelope bound into the book. Informational books such as *The Post Office Book* (Gibbons, 1982) tell what happens to letters after they are mailed. Other activities include taking a field trip to the post office and interviewing a mail carrier, a postal employee, or a stamp collector.

Author Unit: Arnold Lobel's Frog and Toad Stories.   Primary students enjoy reading Lobel's easy-to-read Frog and Toad books: *Frog and Toad Are Friends* (1970), *Frog and Toad Together* (1972), *Frog and Toad All Year* (1976), and *Days With Frog and Toad* (1979). This author unit, also shown in Figure 14–6, includes possible activities to accompany the four books, plus additional author activities. The activities relate to stories in each book; for example, *Frog and Toad All Year* is about the two amphibians' activities throughout the year, so a good extension is to build on the idea of seasons—by studying the seasons, making a cluster, writing a big book, comparing animals and people in each season, comparing clothing worn in each season, and reading poems about the seasons. One of the activities could be used before beginning the book, another between episodes, and others after reading.

Additional literature activities involve reading other of Lobel's stories, other stories about frogs and toads, and viewing the Frog and Toad stories on filmstrips and videotapes and listening to the stories on cassette tapes.

Author activities include learning about Arnold Lobel by viewing filmstrips about him, examining promotional materials from the publisher, and reading other books he has written (or illustrated).

Science activities focus on frogs and toads. Students can read informational books, take a walking field trip to a nearby pond to see live frogs and toads, and write an "All About . . ." book about amphibians.

Middle-Grade Theme Cycles

Clusters for three middle-grade themes appear in Figure 14–7. One cluster focuses on fables, one on insects, and the third on children's author Beverly

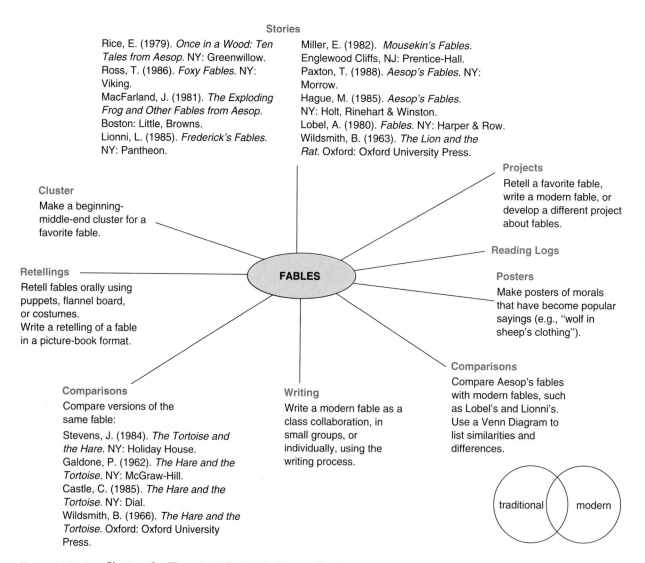

Stories

Rice, E. (1979). *Once in a Wood: Ten Tales from Aesop.* NY: Greenwillow.
Ross, T. (1986). *Foxy Fables.* NY: Viking.
MacFarland, J. (1981). *The Exploding Frog and Other Fables from Aesop.* Boston: Little, Browns.
Lionni, L. (1985). *Frederick's Fables.* NY: Pantheon.

Miller, E. (1982). *Mousekin's Fables.* Englewood Cliffs, NJ: Prentice-Hall.
Paxton, T. (1988). *Aesop's Fables.* NY: Morrow.
Hague, M. (1985). *Aesop's Fables.* NY: Holt, Rinehart & Winston.
Lobel, A. (1980). *Fables.* NY: Harper & Row.
Wildsmith, B. (1963). *The Lion and the Rat.* Oxford: Oxford University Press.

Cluster

Make a beginning-middle-end cluster for a favorite fable.

Retellings

Retell fables orally using puppets, flannel board, or costumes.
Write a retelling of a fable in a picture-book format.

FABLES

Projects

Retell a favorite fable, write a modern fable, or develop a different project about fables.

Reading Logs

Posters

Make posters of morals that have become popular sayings (e.g., "wolf in sheep's clothing").

Comparisons

Compare versions of the same fable:

Stevens, J. (1984). *The Tortoise and the Hare.* NY: Holiday House.
Galdone, P. (1962). *The Hare and the Tortoise.* NY: McGraw-Hill.
Castle, C. (1985). *The Hare and the Tortoise.* NY: Dial.
Wildsmith, B. (1966). *The Hare and the Tortoise.* Oxford: Oxford University Press.

Writing

Write a modern fable as a class collaboration, in small groups, or individually, using the writing process.

Comparisons

Compare Aesop's fables with modern fables, such as Lobel's and Lionni's. Use a Venn Diagram to list similarities and differences.

traditional   modern

Figure 14–7   Clusters for Three Middle-Grade Theme Cycles

Cleary. These plans suggest eight or more types of activities and resources that teachers and students might pursue.

Literature Focus Unit: Fables.   Fables are short stories that teach a lesson, and a number of collections of Aesop's fables as well as contemporary fables have been written for children. As shown in Figure 14–7, this unit provides reading, writing, and talking activities while students learn about this traditional form of literature. Picture book versions of fables can be used for shared reading, guided reading, or independent reading activities. Several of the books are available in paperback, so class sets can be purchased. After students read fables, they write their reactions in reading logs or make clusters of the beginning, middle, and ends of the fables. Or, students can make posters of the morals that have become popular sayings. Students also retell fables orally, using puppets, or in writing.

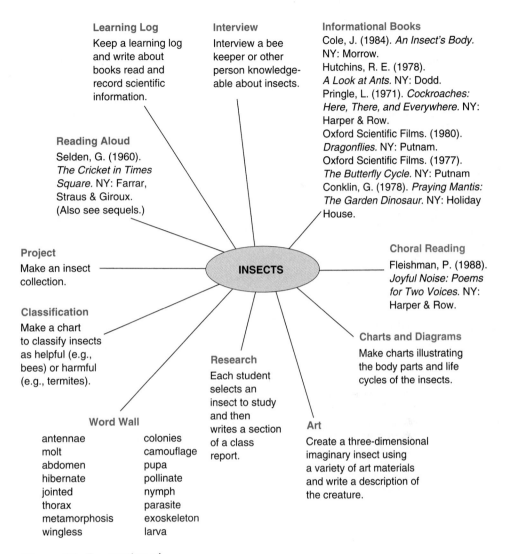

Learning Log

Keep a learning log and write about books read and record scientific information.

Interview

Interview a bee keeper or other person knowledgeable about insects.

Informational Books

Cole, J. (1984). *An Insect's Body.* NY: Morrow.
Hutchins, R. E. (1978). *A Look at Ants.* NY: Dodd.
Pringle, L. (1971). *Cockroaches: Here, There, and Everywhere.* NY: Harper & Row.
Oxford Scientific Films. (1980). *Dragonflies.* NY: Putnam.
Oxford Scientific Films. (1977). *The Butterfly Cycle.* NY: Putnam
Conklin, G. (1978). *Praying Mantis: The Garden Dinosaur.* NY: Holiday House.

Reading Aloud

Selden, G. (1960). *The Cricket in Times Square.* NY: Farrar, Straus & Giroux. (Also see sequels.)

Project

Make an insect collection.

Classification

Make a chart to classify insects as helpful (e.g., bees) or harmful (e.g., termites).

INSECTS

Choral Reading

Fleishman, P. (1988). *Joyful Noise: Poems for Two Voices.* NY: Harper & Row.

Charts and Diagrams

Make charts illustrating the body parts and life cycles of the insects.

Research

Each student selects an insect to study and then writes a section of a class report.

Art

Create a three-dimensional imaginary insect using a variety of art materials and write a description of the creature.

Word Wall

antennae	colonies
molt	camouflage
abdomen	pupa
hibernate	pollinate
jointed	nymph
thorax	parasite
metamorphosis	exoskeleton
wingless	larva

Figure 14–7   continued

Students can compare versions of the same fable. For instance, a number of versions of "The Tortoise and the Hare" are currently available as picture books. Students divide into small groups to read the stories and compare how authors elaborated the beginning, middle, or end in the different versions. Students might also compare the traditional fables to modern ones, such as those of Lobel, and report their findings on a Venn diagram.

After reading and retelling fables, students might choose to write their own fables; their first fables might be written as a class or in small groups. After this experience students choose a moral and write their own fables using the writing process. Some students may write traditional fables using animals as characters, and others may use well-known people, classmates, or family members as characters.

Students who become interested in these traditional stories might research Aesop or de La Fontaine, two great authors of fables. Other projects are also possible: Students might make mobiles of a favorite fable, paint a mural,

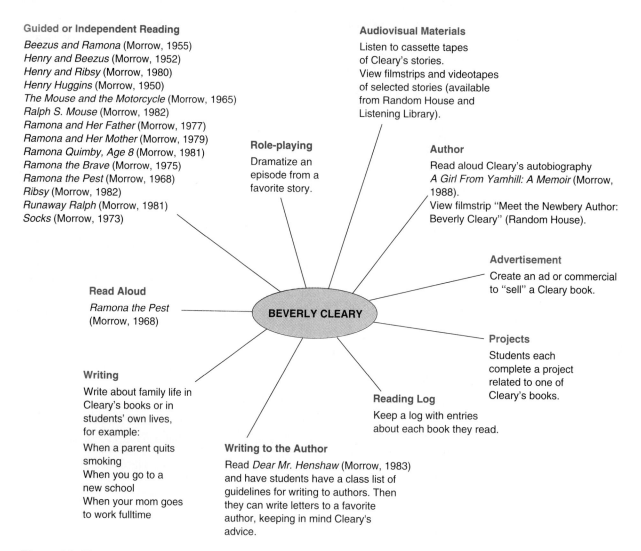

Guided or Independent Reading

Beezus and Ramona (Morrow, 1955)
Henry and Beezus (Morrow, 1952)
Henry and Ribsy (Morrow, 1980)
Henry Huggins (Morrow, 1950)
The Mouse and the Motorcycle (Morrow, 1965)
Ralph S. Mouse (Morrow, 1982)
Ramona and Her Father (Morrow, 1977)
Ramona and Her Mother (Morrow, 1979)
Ramona Quimby, Age 8 (Morrow, 1981)
Ramona the Brave (Morrow, 1975)
Ramona the Pest (Morrow, 1968)
Ribsy (Morrow, 1982)
Runaway Ralph (Morrow, 1981)
Socks (Morrow, 1973)

Audiovisual Materials

Listen to cassette tapes
of Cleary's stories.
View filmstrips and videotapes
of selected stories (available
from Random House and
Listening Library).

Role-playing

Dramatize an
episode from a
favorite story.

Author

Read aloud Cleary's autobiography
A Girl From Yamhill: A Memoir (Morrow,
1988).
View filmstrip "Meet the Newbery Author:
Beverly Cleary" (Random House).

Advertisement

Create an ad or commercial
to "sell" a Cleary book.

Read Aloud

Ramona the Pest
(Morrow, 1968)

BEVERLY CLEARY

Projects

Students each
complete a project
related to one of
Cleary's books.

Writing

Write about family life in
Cleary's books or in
students' own lives,
for example:
When a parent quits
smoking
When you go to a
new school
When your mom goes
to work fulltime

Writing to the Author

Read *Dear Mr. Henshaw* (Morrow, 1983)
and have students have a class list of
guidelines for writing to authors. Then
they can write letters to a favorite
author, keeping in mind Cleary's
advice.

Reading Log

Keep a log with entries
about each book they read.

Figure 14–7   continued

update and rewrite a fable with modern characters, or any of the other project possibilities listed in the Teacher's Notebook on page 569.

Science Theme: Insects.   In this theme cycle listening, talking, reading, and writing activities extend students' learning about insects, as shown in Figure 14–7. Students read informational books about insects, use choral reading to read *Joyful Noise: Poems for Two Voices* (Fleischman, 1988), and listen to a chapter book, *The Cricket in Times Square* (Selden, 1960), read aloud. Reading is a valuable way for middle-grade students to learn about science. They connect reading and writing by keeping a learning log in which they reflect on the book being read aloud and record scientific information from informational books and teacher presentations.

Each student might choose an insect to study in depth, and then students contribute to a class report, with each one reporting on the insect he or she studied. Students can also make charts to illustrate the life cycles or body parts of insects. As individual projects, students might make insect collections

For his project, this third grader rewrote the front page of his hometown newspaper to spread the word that Beverly Cleary's Ramona *is now a movie.*

or choose one of the activities listed in the Teacher's Notebook on page 569. Other possible activities include making a chart to classify insects as helpful or harmful, or creating imaginary insects and writing about them.

Author Unit: Beverly Cleary. Beverly Cleary is a popular children's author and a good choice for a unit because she has written many books, most of which are available in paperback. This cluster also appears in Figure 14–7. Teachers may want to begin the author unit by reading one of Cleary's Ramona books aloud. *Ramona the Pest* (1968) is a favorite of middle-grade students; this book introduces students to the Quimby family. Then students choose one or more of Cleary's books to read independently or as guided reading with the teacher. Students may also listen to Cleary's stories at a listening center or view filmstrips or videotapes of some books. They keep a reading log and respond to each Cleary book that they read. After reading, students can prepare a project related to the book they read, role-play a favorite episode from a story, or create an advertisement or commercial to "sell" their book.

Other ideas for projects include reading *Dear Mr. Henshaw* (1983) and inviting students to write to a favorite author (after making a class list of things to remember when writing to authors). Or, students can write about family life in Cleary's books or about their own lives. They might compare events in their own lives to events in Ramona's life; possible parallels are her father's quitting smoking, her mother's going to work full-time, and her moving to a new school. If students want to learn more about this author, teachers may read aloud Cleary's autobiography, *A Girl from Yamhill: A Memoir* (1988), or show a filmstrip about her.

Upper-Grade Theme Cycles

Clusters for three themes designed for students in grades 6, 7, and 8 are presented in Figure 14–8. The first is a literature focus unit on *Anne Frank: The Diary of a Young Girl*. Connected to this modern classic is a study of the Holocaust. The second cluster is a social studies theme on the Middle Ages, and the third is a biography unit featuring Martin Luther King, Jr., and other famous African Americans.

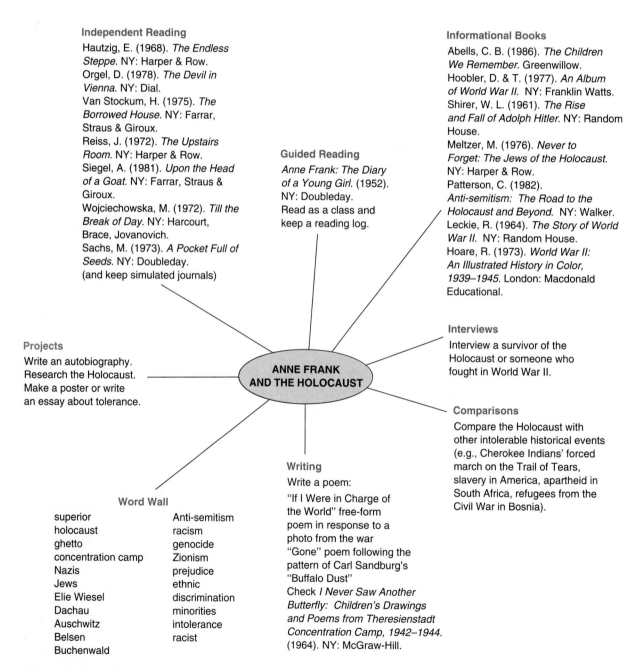

Independent Reading

Hautzig, E. (1968). *The Endless Steppe*. NY: Harper & Row.
Orgel, D. (1978). *The Devil in Vienna*. NY: Dial.
Van Stockum, H. (1975). *The Borrowed House*. NY: Farrar, Straus & Giroux.
Reiss, J. (1972). *The Upstairs Room*. NY: Harper & Row.
Siegel, A. (1981). *Upon the Head of a Goat*. NY: Farrar, Straus & Giroux.
Wojciechowska, M. (1972). *Till the Break of Day*. NY: Harcourt, Brace, Jovanovich.
Sachs, M. (1973). *A Pocket Full of Seeds*. NY: Doubleday.
(and keep simulated journals)

Guided Reading

Anne Frank: The Diary of a Young Girl. (1952). NY: Doubleday.
Read as a class and keep a reading log.

Informational Books

Abells, C. B. (1986). *The Children We Remember*. Greenwillow.
Hoobler, D. & T. (1977). *An Album of World War II*. NY: Franklin Watts.
Shirer, W. L. (1961). *The Rise and Fall of Adolph Hitler*. NY: Random House.
Meltzer, M. (1976). *Never to Forget: The Jews of the Holocaust*. NY: Harper & Row.
Patterson, C. (1982). *Anti-semitism: The Road to the Holocaust and Beyond*. NY: Walker.
Leckie, R. (1964). *The Story of World War II*. NY: Random House.
Hoare, R. (1973). *World War II: An Illustrated History in Color, 1939–1945*. London: Macdonald Educational.

Projects

Write an autobiography.
Research the Holocaust.
Make a poster or write an essay about tolerance.

ANNE FRANK AND THE HOLOCAUST

Interviews

Interview a survivor of the Holocaust or someone who fought in World War II.

Comparisons

Compare the Holocaust with other intolerable historical events (e.g., Cherokee Indians' forced march on the Trail of Tears, slavery in America, apartheid in South Africa, refugees from the Civil War in Bosnia).

Word Wall

superior	Anti-semitism
holocaust	racism
ghetto	genocide
concentration camp	Zionism
Nazis	prejudice
Jews	ethnic
Elie Wiesel	discrimination
Dachau	minorities
Auschwitz	intolerance
Belsen	racist
Buchenwald	

Writing

Write a poem:
"If I Were in Charge of the World" free-form poem in response to a photo from the war
"Gone" poem following the pattern of Carl Sandburg's "Buffalo Dust"
Check *I Never Saw Another Butterfly: Children's Drawings and Poems from Theresienstadt Concentration Camp, 1942–1944*. (1964). NY: McGraw-Hill.

Figure 14–8   Clusters for Three Upper-Grade Theme Cycles

Literature Focus Unit: Anne Frank: The Diary of a Young Girl.   Anne Frank's autobiographical diary is a modern classic that many eighth graders read, and a cluster of ideas for developing the unit is presented in Figure 14–8. For young adults to understand the book's complex historical and psychological implications, they need a background of experiences related to World War II. At the center of the unit is *Anne Frank: The Diary of a Young Girl* (Frank, 1952) which students might read together as a class. Students keep a reading log to reflect on and respond to their reading. Students can also read informational

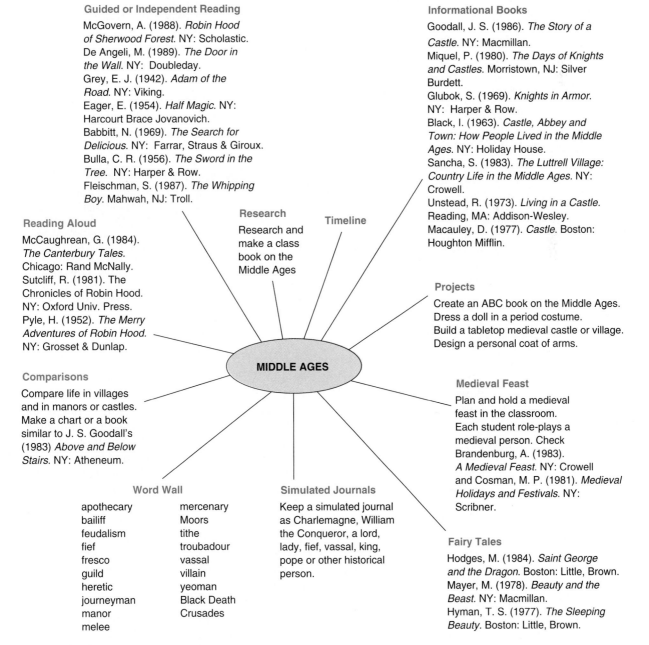

Guided or Independent Reading

McGovern, A. (1988). *Robin Hood of Sherwood Forest.* NY: Scholastic.
De Angeli, M. (1989). *The Door in the Wall.* NY: Doubleday.
Grey, E. J. (1942). *Adam of the Road.* NY: Viking.
Eager, E. (1954). *Half Magic.* NY: Harcourt Brace Jovanovich.
Babbitt, N. (1969). *The Search for Delicious.* NY: Farrar, Straus & Giroux.
Bulla, C. R. (1956). *The Sword in the Tree.* NY: Harper & Row.
Fleischman, S. (1987). *The Whipping Boy.* Mahwah, NJ: Troll.

Reading Aloud

McCaughrean, G. (1984). *The Canterbury Tales.* Chicago: Rand McNally.
Sutcliff, R. (1981). The Chronicles of Robin Hood. NY: Oxford Univ. Press.
Pyle, H. (1952). *The Merry Adventures of Robin Hood.* NY: Grosset & Dunlap.

Comparisons

Compare life in villages and in manors or castles. Make a chart or a book similar to J. S. Goodall's (1983) *Above and Below Stairs.* NY: Atheneum.

Research

Research and make a class book on the Middle Ages

Timeline

Informational Books

Goodall, J. S. (1986). *The Story of a Castle.* NY: Macmillan.
Miquel, P. (1980). *The Days of Knights and Castles.* Morristown, NJ: Silver Burdett.
Glubok, S. (1969). *Knights in Armor.* NY: Harper & Row.
Black, I. (1963). *Castle, Abbey and Town: How People Lived in the Middle Ages.* NY: Holiday House.
Sancha, S. (1983). *The Luttrell Village: Country Life in the Middle Ages.* NY: Crowell.
Unstead, R. (1973). *Living in a Castle.* Reading, MA: Addison-Wesley.
Macauley, D. (1977). *Castle.* Boston: Houghton Mifflin.

Projects

Create an ABC book on the Middle Ages.
Dress a doll in a period costume.
Build a tabletop medieval castle or village.
Design a personal coat of arms.

MIDDLE AGES

Medieval Feast

Plan and hold a medieval feast in the classroom.
Each student role-plays a medieval person. Check Brandenburg, A. (1983). *A Medieval Feast.* NY: Crowell and Cosman, M. P. (1981). *Medieval Holidays and Festivals.* NY: Scribner.

Word Wall

apothecary	mercenary
bailiff	Moors
feudalism	tithe
fief	troubadour
fresco	vassal
guild	villain
heretic	yeoman
journeyman	Black Death
manor	Crusades
melee	

Simulated Journals

Keep a simulated journal as Charlemagne, William the Conqueror, a lord, lady, fief, vassal, king, pope or other historical person.

Fairy Tales

Hodges, M. (1984). *Saint George and the Dragon.* Boston: Little, Brown.
Mayer, M. (1978). *Beauty and the Beast.* NY: Macmillan.
Hyman, T. S. (1977). *The Sleeping Beauty.* Boston: Little, Brown.

Figure 14–8   continued

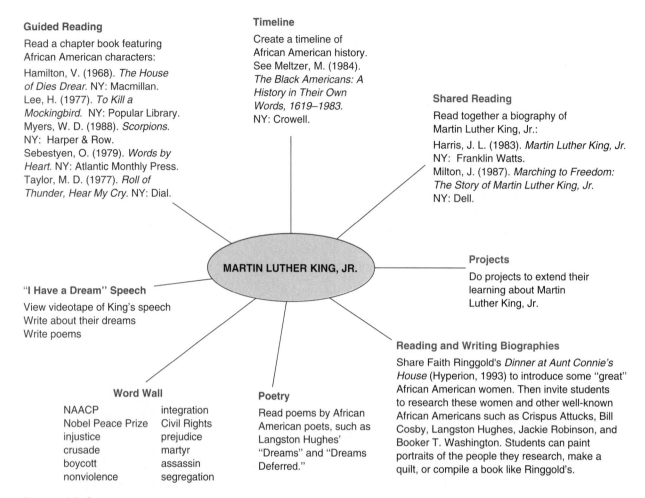

Guided Reading

Read a chapter book featuring African American characters:

Hamilton, V. (1968). *The House of Dies Drear*. NY: Macmillan.
Lee, H. (1977). *To Kill a Mockingbird*. NY: Popular Library.
Myers, W. D. (1988). *Scorpions*. NY: Harper & Row.
Sebestyen, O. (1979). *Words by Heart*. NY: Atlantic Monthly Press.
Taylor, M. D. (1977). *Roll of Thunder, Hear My Cry*. NY: Dial.

Timeline

Create a timeline of African American history. See Meltzer, M. (1984). *The Black Americans: A History in Their Own Words, 1619–1983.* NY: Crowell.

Shared Reading

Read together a biography of Martin Luther King, Jr.:

Harris, J. L. (1983). *Martin Luther King, Jr.* NY: Franklin Watts.
Milton, J. (1987). *Marching to Freedom: The Story of Martin Luther King, Jr.* NY: Dell.

MARTIN LUTHER KING, JR.

Projects

Do projects to extend their learning about Martin Luther King, Jr.

"I Have a Dream" Speech

View videotape of King's speech
Write about their dreams
Write poems

Reading and Writing Biographies

Share Faith Ringgold's *Dinner at Aunt Connie's House* (Hyperion, 1993) to introduce some "great" African American women. Then invite students to research these women and other well-known African Americans such as Crispus Attucks, Bill Cosby, Langston Hughes, Jackie Robinson, and Booker T. Washington. Students can paint portraits of the people they research, make a quilt, or compile a book like Ringgold's.

Word Wall

NAACP	integration
Nobel Peace Prize	Civil Rights
injustice	prejudice
crusade	martyr
boycott	assassin
nonviolence	segregation

Poetry

Read poems by African American poets, such as Langston Hughes' "Dreams" and "Dreams Deferred."

Figure 14–8   continued

books to gain more understanding of World War II and the Holocaust and read other stories with Jewish characters set during the war. Two highly recommended books are *Upon the Head of a Goat* (Siegal, 1981), the story of the Davidowitz family of Hungary, who are sent to the Auschwitz concentration camp; and *The Borrowed House* (Van Stockum, 1975), the story of 12-year-old Janna, who lives with her family in a rented Dutch house and finds a Jewish Dutch boy hiding in the attic. Students might want to keep a simulated journal as they read these stories independently so that they can more fully walk in these people's footsteps.

Students learn a variety of words through their reading, including *ghetto, concentration camp, intolerance, genocide,* and *anti-Semitism*. These words are added to a word wall hanging in the classroom, and students write them in their unit folders. The words can be used for various activities, and students are encouraged to use the words in their reading logs and simulated journals.

Poetry provides a good outlet for students' emotions during this unit; they might write "If I Were in Charge of the World" poems and "I Am" poems as if they were Anne Frank, Adolf Hitler, or other personalities from the war. They can also model the form of Sandburg's poem "Buffalo Dust" and write about the concentration camps or about life after the Nazis have gone and what people remember. They can write a free-form poem in response to a stark black-and-white photo of the war. Students will also be interested in examining *I Never Saw Another Butterfly* (1964), a collection of poems and drawings made by children in the Theresienstadt concentration camp.

Other possible activities related to this unit include inviting a concentration camp survivor to visit the classroom to be interviewed or interviewing other persons who remember the war. Students can also investigate other intolerant events in history (e.g., the Cherokee Indians' forced march on the Trail of Tears, slavery in America, apartheid in South Africa, the Civil War in Bosnia) and compare them to the Holocaust.

Students also develop a project related to the unit; they may choose from the list of projects in the Teacher's Notebook on page 569, or they may write an autobiography (perhaps in diary format), research the Holocaust and prepare an oral or written report, or make a poster or write an essay about tolerance.

Reading *Anne Frank: The Diary of a Young Girl* in isolation is difficult because the students are unfamiliar with the events of World War II and the Holocaust. Connecting history with literature in this unit makes the literature more meaningful, and students have a variety of opportunities to respond to what they are learning through listening, talking, reading, and writing.

Social Studies Theme: The Middle Ages. In a theme cycle on the Middle Ages, reading, writing, listening, and speaking are integrated with history, as shown in Figure 14–8. Students use informational books to learn about the historical era; then they use what they are learning for a variety of purposes. They can keep a simulated journal as a well-known person of the period, such as Charlemagne or William the Conqueror, or they may become an unrecorded personality—lord, lady, knight, vassal, pope, or troubadour.

Students add information to a class timeline that circles around the classroom, or they can make their own timeline using several sheets of computer paper. At the beginning of the theme, the teacher sets the limits of the time period (i.e., 1066–1485) and other key dates; then students add other dates as they read and learn more about the period.

Individual students or small groups can draw maps of the countries during the Middle Ages with an overlay of the modern countries, and they can make maps of the Crusades. They can make other types of charts, such as diagrams of castles, cathedrals, and villages, and they can also make drawings of costumes, modes of transportation, weapons, and other items related to the era. Students can also compare life in villages and in manors and castles and report the differences they find on a chart or by making a book similar to Goodall's *Above and Below Stairs* (1983).

As students research the Middle Ages, they each choose a topic for in-depth study and then write a report to share what they have learned. These reports are collected to form a larger class book on the Middle Ages.

Some novels written for older students are set in the Middle Ages, and students can read these stories independently, or class sets can be purchased, for example, *Robin Hood of Sherwood Forest* (McGovern, 1968). There are also some traditional tales set in the period, such as *Saint George and the Dragon* (Hodges, 1984) and *The Pied Piper of Hamelin* (Mayer, 1987), that students can read to retell or rewrite. Some stories set in the Middle Ages can be shared when read aloud by the teacher.

Word study activities can also be related to the theme. Words should be chosen from the informational books and stories students are reading; possible words are listed in the cluster in Figure 14–8. Another related activity is to study the history of English, particularly the Middle English period, and learn what French words were added to English during that time. Many of the words show the impact the Norman kings had on English.

Students independently read the chapters and take notes using a cluster. Students each prepare a project to extend what they are learning in the theme. They choose projects, which may come from the list in the Teacher's Notebook on page 569, in consultation with the teacher. Other possible projects are creating a castle or village, making a small tapestry, creating a coat of arms, dressing a doll in a medieval costume, or painting a mural.

As the culminating activity for the theme cycle, students might choose to plan and hold a medieval feast. Each student assumes the role of a medieval person, dresses in clothing of the era, and shares something (e.g., a poem, a simulated journal entry, a song, a reading, a piece of art, a skit) as that person. Students plan food that might have been served and use music and activities typical of the time. Students share their projects during the feast. For more information about medieval feasts and festivals, check *A Medieval Feast* (Aliki, 1983) and *Medieval Holidays and Festivals* (Cosman, 1981).

Biography Unit: Martin Luther King, Jr.   In this unit students learn about a great African American, Martin Luther King, Jr., at the same time that they learn about African American history in general and about biographies. The cluster for the unit appears in Figure 14–8. The unit begins with shared reading (or reading aloud) of a book about Martin Luther King, Jr., and learning about his life. Students view a videotape of King's "I Have a Dream" speech and write about their own dreams; they share Hughes's poems "Dreams" and "Dreams Deferred" along with poems by other African American poets. Students apply words that are introduced in their own reading.

Teachers might read Faith Ringgold's *Dinner at Aunt Connie's House* (1993) or do a book talk about biographies of African Americans available in the classroom. Then students choose a prominent African American, historical or modern—such as Harriet Tubman, Mary McLeod Bethune, or Jesse Jackson—to research and read about. They write a report or create a poster to highlight that person's contribution to America. Together students might develop a timeline of African American history and share it with an elementary school as part of Martin Luther King, Jr.'s birthday celebration or during Black History Month (in February).

Students might read chapter books written by African American authors or with African American main characters, or the teacher might read one aloud. Two books listed in the cluster are *Roll of Thunder, Hear My Cry* (Taylor, 1977) and *Words by Heart* (Sebestyen, 1979). Students keep a reading log to reflect on their reading.

Instructional Activities

From these plans and from students' questions and suggestions, teachers develop lesson plans. They include special activities that students suggested to initiate and conclude the theme. The plans may be part of content area classes or language arts class, or they may extend throughout the school day. There are always difficult choices to make in selecting and sequencing activities for the theme. Rarely can teachers include all the activities outlined in a theme cluster; instead, they must choose activities that are most appropriate for their students within the time and material constraints imposed on them. Teachers and students often identify so many possible activities and projects that students could spend 6, 9, or even twelve weeks on a theme cycle, which is simply not possible, given the great number of topics that must be taught during the school year. Limited supplies of trade books, models, films, and other materials also have an impact on teachers' planning.

During theme cycles, students are involved in whole class, small group, and individual activities. Whole group activities often include:

- Making a KWL chart
- Viewing a presentation by the teacher
- Listening to the teacher read a book aloud
- Adding words to the word wall
- Interviewing a person with special expertise on a topic related to the theme cycle
- Viewing a film, filmstrip, video, or demonstration
- Participating in a literature discussion
- Sharing projects with classmates
- Writing a class book

Small group activities may include:

- Creating a chart, diagram, or map
- Conducting a science experiment
- Reading a book from the text set
- Participating in a literature discussion
- Listening at the listening center
- Researching the answer to a question
- Performing a puppet show or play
- Doing a choral reading
- Working on a project

Individual activities often include:

- Reading or rereading a book from the text set
- Writing in a learning log
- Researching the answer to a question
- Writing a report
- Giving an oral report
- Making a poster
- Doing a project

Students use listening, talking, reading, and writing as they learn about the topic of the theme cycle and research answers to their questions. Students also use the four language modes as they present the answers to their questions and extend their learning through projects.

Assessing Students' Learning

As they plan the theme cycle with students and develop the lesson plans, teachers need to decide how to assess students' work during the theme.

Figure 14–9   An Assessment Checklist for a Middle-Grade Theme Cycle

Insect Theme Checklist

Name _____

_____ 1. Keep a learning log.
_____ 2. Read five informational books about insects and write about them in your learning log.
_____ 3. Help your group make an insect life-cycle chart.
_____ 4. Construct an imaginary insect and write a description of it. (Make sure your insect has the characteristics of an insect.)
_____ 5. Listen to *The Cricket in Times Square* and write or draw a reading log about each chapter.
_____ 6. Do a choral reading with a friend from *Joyful Noise*.
_____ 7. Make a page for our class ABC book. What is your page? _____
_____ 8. Do a word cluster on a word from the word wall on insects.
_____ 9. Learn more about insects and do a project to share your learning. What is your project?_____
_____ 10. Write a letter to Mr. R. about your learning and work habits during this theme.

Together students and the teacher can identify particular activities and projects that will be assessed. Some activities will be assessed simply as completed or not completed; others might be assessed according to the level of quality displayed. Some activities require individual work, and others involve small group and class work. Activities should represent all four language modes: listening, talking, reading, and writing. Both informal writing activities, such as learning logs or quickwrites, and writing process activities should be included.

One way to assess students' learning in theme cycles is using checklists. Checklists identify the activities that will be assessed or graded and are distributed to students at the beginning of the theme so that they will understand what is expected of them. Teachers who use checklists have found that their students become more responsible in completing assignments. An assessment checklist for a middle-grade theme on insects is shown in Figure 14–9. Students receive this checklist at the beginning of the theme and keep it in their unit notebooks or file folders. Students check off each of the nine activities after completing it. At the end of the theme cycle the teacher collects and assesses students' work on each activity.

Review

Language arts can be integrated into theme cycles for across-the-curriculum study. Integration of listening, talking, reading, and writing into science, social studies, literature, and other areas of the curriculum enhances students' learning of the content area information and their language competencies. Teachers and students plan theme cycles together. First, teachers consider their available resources, and students identify questions and the types of activities they are interested in pursuing. Second, teachers develop clusters, outlining possible resources and activities. Next, teachers write lesson plans from the clusters, incorporating whole class, small group, and individual activities. The final step is to develop an assessment checklist to use in assessing students' learning.

Extensions

1. Plan a theme cycle using a cluster. Choose a grade level and develop a social studies or science theme cycle. Also develop a checklist for assessing students' work.
2. Plan an author unit at the grade level you teach or hope to teach. Choose a variety of books written by the author and create a cluster. Then develop the unit and an assessment checklist.
3. Read 10 trade books listed in Figure 14–4 and explain how they can be used in teaching mathematics.
4. Choose a grade level that you teach or hope to teach and identify the theme cycles you might teach throughout the school year. Also, interview several students at that level to learn what topics they are interested in learning more about.
5. Make a collection of poems you could use for teaching three theme cycles.

References

Altwerger, B., & Flores, B. (1994). Theme cycles: Creating communities of learners. *Primary Voices K–6, 2,* 2–6.

Erickson, K. L. (1988). Building castles in the classroom. *Language Arts, 65,* 14–19.

Gamberg, R., Kwak, W., Hutchings, M., Altheim, J., & Edwards, G. (1988). *Learning and loving it: Theme studies in the classroom.* Portsmouth, NH: Heinemann.

Halliday, M. A. K. (1980). Three aspects of children's language development: Learning language, learning through language, learning about language. In Y. M. Goodman, M. M. Haussler, & D. S. Strickland (Eds.), *Oral and written language development research: Impact on the schools* 7–19. (Proceedings from the 1979 and 1980 IMPACT Conferences sponsored by the International Reading Association and the National Council of Teachers of English.) Urbana, IL: National Council of Teachers of English.

Hancock, J., & Hill, S. (1987). *Literature-based reading programs at work.* Portsmouth, NH: Heinemann.

Hansen, J., Newkirk, T., & Graves, D. (Eds.). (1985). *Breaking ground: Teachers relate reading and writing in the elementary school.* Portsmouth, NH: Heinemann.

Moss, J. F. (1984). *Focus units in literature: A handbook for elementary school teachers.* Urbana, IL: National Council of Teachers of English.

Nelson, P. A. (1988). Drama, doorway to the past. *Language Arts, 65,* 20–25.

Ogle, D. M. (1986). K-W-L: A teaching model that develops active reading of expository text. *The Reading Teacher, 39,* 564–570.

Pappas, C. C., Kiefer, B. Z., & Levstik, L. S. (1990). *An integrated language perspective in the elementary school: Theory into action.* New York: Longman.

Richards, L. (1990). "Measuring things in words": Language for learning mathematics. *Language Arts, 67,* 14–25.

Salem, J. (1982). Using writing in teaching mathematics. In M. Barr, P. D'Arcy, & M. K. Healy (Eds.), *What's going on? Language/learning episodes in British and American classrooms, grades 4–13* (pp. 123–134). Montclair, NJ: Boynton/Cook.

San Jose, C. (1988). Story drama in the content areas. *Language Arts, 65,* 26–33.

Schubert, B. (1987). Mathematics journals: Fourth grade. In T. Fulwiler (Ed.), *The journal book* (pp. 348–358). Portsmouth, NH: Boynton/Cook.

Somers, A. B., & Worthington, J. E. (1979). *Response guides for teaching children's books.* Urbana, IL: National Council of Teachers of English.

Thaiss, C. (1986). *Language across the curriculum in the elementary grades.* Urbana, IL: ERIC Clearinghouse on Reading and Communication Skills and the National Council of Teachers of English.

Tompkins, G. E. (1994). *Teaching writing: Balancing process and product* (2nd ed.). New York: Merrill/Macmillan.

Tompkins, G. E., & McGee, L. M. (1989). Teaching repetition as a story structure. In K. D. Muth (Ed.), *Children's comprehension of text: Research into practice* (pp. 59–78). Newark, DE: International Reading Association.

Whitin, D. J., & Wilde, S. (1992). *Read any good math lately? Children's books for mathematical learning, K–6*. Portsmouth, NH: Heinemann.

Children's Book References

Ahlberg, J., & Ahlberg, A. (1986). *The jolly postman or other people's letters*. Boston: Little, Brown.

Aliki. (1983). *A medieval feast*. New York: Crowell.

Aliki. (1988). *The many lives of Benjamin Franklin*. New York: Simon & Schuster.

Carle, E. (1977). *The grouchy ladybug*. New York: Crowell.

Cleary, B. (1968). *Ramona the pest*. New York: Morrow.

Cleary, B. (1983). *Dear Mr. Henshaw*. New York: Morrow.

Cleary, B. (1988). *A girl from Yamhill: A memoir*. New York: Morrow.

Cosman, M. P. (1981). *Medieval holidays and festivals*. New York: Scribner.

d'Aulaire, I., & d'Aulaire, E. P. (1950). *Benjamin Franklin*. New York: Doubleday.

Fleischman, P. (1988). *Joyful noise: Poems for two voices*. New York: Harper & Row.

Frank, A. (1952). *Anne Frank: The diary of a young girl*. New York: Doubleday.

Fritz, J. (1974). *Why don't you get a horse, Sam Adams?* New York: Coward-McCann.

Fritz, J. (1976). *What's the big idea, Ben Franklin?* New York: Coward-McCann.

Gibbons, G. (1982). *The post office book*. New York: Harper & Row.

Goodall, J. S. (1983). *Above and below stairs*. New York: Atheneum.

Heller, R. (1984). *Plants that never ever bloom*. New York: Grosset & Dunlap.

Hodges, M. (1984). *Saint George and the dragon*. Boston: Little, Brown.

I never saw another butterfly: Children's drawings and poems from Theresienstadt concentration camp, 1942–1944. (1964). New York: McGraw-Hill.

Jacobs, J. (1967). *Johnny-cake*. New York: Putnam.

Jarrell, R. (1964). *Gingerbread rabbit*. New York: Macmillan.

Lewis, C. S. (1950). *The lion, the witch and the wardrobe*. New York: Macmillan.

Lobel, A. (1970). *Frog and Toad are friends*. New York: Harper & Row.

Lobel, A. (1972). *Frog and Toad together*. New York: Harper & Row.

Lobel, A. (1976). *Frog and Toad all year*. New York: Harper & Row.

Lobel, A. (1979). *Days with Frog and Toad*. New York: Harper & Row.

Mayer, M. (1987). *The pied piper of Hamelin*. New York: Macmillan.

McGovern, A. (1968). *Robin Hood of Sherwood Forest*. New York: Scholastic Books.

Oppenheim, J. (1986). *You can't catch me!* Boston: Houghton Mifflin.

Ringgold, F. (1993). *Dinner at Aunt Connie's house*. New York: Hyperion.

Schwartz, D. (1985). *How much is a million?* New York: Lothrop, Lee & Shepard.

Sebestyen, O. (1979). *Words by heart*. New York: Atlantic Monthly Press.

Selden, G. (1960). *The Cricket in Times Square*. New York: Farrar, Straus & Giroux.

Siegal, A. (1981). *Upon the head of a goat: A childhood in Hungary, 1939–1944*. New York: Farrar, Straus & Giroux.

Silverstein, S. (1964). *The giving tree*. New York: Harper & Row.

Taylor, M. D. (1977). *Roll of thunder, hear my cry*. New York: Dial.

Van Allsburg, C. (1979). *The garden of Abdul Gasazi*. Boston: Houghton Mifflin.

Van Allsburg, C. (1981). *Jumanji*. Boston: Houghton Mifflin.

Van Allsburg, C. (1982). *Ben's dream*. Boston: Houghton Mifflin.

Van Allsburg, C. (1984). *The mysteries of Harris Burdick*. Boston: Houghton Mifflin.

Van Allsburg, C. (1985). *The polar express*. Boston: Houghton Mifflin.

Van Allsburg, C. (1986). *The stranger*. Boston: Houghton Mifflin.

Van Allsburg, C. (1987). *The Z was zapped*. Boston: Houghton Mifflin.

Van Allsburg, C. (1988). *Two bad ants*. Boston: Houghton Mifflin.

Van Stockum, H. (1975). *The borrowed house*. New York: Farrar, Strauss & Giroux.

APPENDIX A

Award-Winning Books
for Children

Caldecott Medal Books

The Caldecott Medal is named in honor of Randolph Caldecott (1846–1886), a British illustrator of children's books. The award is presented by the American Library Association each year to "the artist of the most distinguished American picture book for children" published during the preceding year. The award was first given in 1938 and is awarded annually. The winning book receives the Caldecott Medal, and one or more runners-up are also recognized as "Honor" books.

1994 *Grandfather's journey,* Allen Say (Houghton Mifflin). **Honor books:** *Peppe the lamplighter,* Elisa Bartone (Lothrop); *In the small, small pond,* Denis Fleming (Holt); *Owen,* Kevin Henkes (Greenwillow); *Raven: A trickster tale from the Pacific northwest,* Gerald McDermott (Harcourt Brace Jovanovich); *Yo! Yes?* Chris Raschak (Orchard).

1993 *Mirette on the high wire,* Emily McCully (Putnam). **Honor books:** *Seven blind mice,* Ed Young (Philomel); *The stinky cheese man and other fairly stupid tales,* Jon Scieszka, illustrated by Lane Smith (Viking); *Working cotton,* Sherley Anne Williams, illustrated by Carole Byard (Harcourt Brace Jovanovich).

1992 *Tuesday,* David Wiesner (Clarion). **Honor book:** *Tar beach,* Faith Ringgold (Crown).

1991 *Black and white,* David Macaulay (Houghton Mifflin). **Honor books:** *Puss in boots,* Charles Perrault, illustrated by Fred Marcellino (Farrar, Straus & Giroux); *"More, more, more" said the baby,* Vera B. Williams (Morrow).

1990 *Lon Po Po, A Red Riding Hood story from China,* Ed Young (Philomel). **Honor books:** *Bill Peet: An autobiography,* William Peet (Houghton Mifflin); *Color zoo,* Lois Ehlert (Lippincott); *Herschel and the Hanukkah goblins,* Eric A. Kimmel, illustrated by Trina Schart Hyman (Holiday House); *The talking eggs,* Robert D. San Souci, illustrated by Jerry Pickney (Dial).

1989 *Song and dance man,* Jane Ackerman, illustrated by Stephen Gammell (Knopf). **Honor books:** *Goldilocks,* James Marshall (Dial); *The boy of the three-year nap,* Diane Snyder, illustrated by Allen Say (Houghton Mifflin); *Mirandy and Brother Wind,* Patricia McKissack, illustrated by Jerry Pickney (Knopf); *Free fall,* David Wiesner (Lothrop).

1988 *Owl moon,* Jane Yolen, illustrated by John Schoenherr (Philomel). **Honor book:** *Mufaro's beautiful daughters: An African tale,* John Steptoe (Morrow).

1987 *Hey, Al,* Arthur Yorinks, illustrated by Richard Egielski (Farrah, Straus & Giroux). **Honor books:** *Alphabatics,* Suse MacDonald (Bradbury); *Rumplestiltskin,* Paul O. Zelinsky (E. P. Dutton); *The village of round and square houses,* Ann Grifalconi (Little, Brown).

1986 *The polar express,* Chris Van Allsburg (Houghton Mifflin). **Honor books:** *King Bidgood's in the bathtub,* Audrey Wood (Harcourt Brace Jovanovich); *The relatives came,* Cynthia Rylant (Bradbury).

1985 *Saint George and the dragon,* Margaret Hodges, illustrated by Trina Schart Hyman (Little, Brown). **Honor books:** *Hansel and Gretel,* Rika Lesser, illustrated by Paul O. Zelinsky (Dodd, Mead); *Have you seen my duckling?* Nancy Tafuri (Greenwillow); *The story of jumping mouse,* John Steptoe (Lothrop, Lee & Shepard).

1984 *The glorious flight: Across the channel with Louis Bleriot,* Alice and Martin Provensen (Viking). **Honor books:** *Little red riding hood,* Trina Schart Hyman (Holiday); *Ten, nine, eight,* Molly Bang (Greenwillow).

1983 *Shadow,* Blaise Cendrars, translated and illustrated by Marcia Brown (Scribner). **Honor books:** *A chair for my mother,* Vera B. Williams (Greenwillow);

When I was young in the mountains, Cynthia Rylant, illustrated by Diane Goode (E. P. Dutton).

1982 *Jumanji,* Chris Van Allsburg (Houghton Mifflin). **Honor books:** *On Market Street,* Arnold Lobel, illustrated by Anita Lobel (Greenwillow); *Outside over there,* Maurice Sendak (Harper & Row); *A visit to William Blake's inn: Poems for innocent and experienced travelers,* Nancy Willard, illustrated by Alice and Martin Provensen (Harcourt Brace Jovanovich); *Where the buffaloes begin,* Olaf Baker, illustrated by Stephen Gammell (Warne).

1981 *Fables,* Arnold Lobel (Harper & Row). **Honor Books:** *The Bremen-Town musicians,* Ilse Plume (Doubleday); *The grey lady and the strawberry snatcher,* Molly Bang (Four Winds); *Mice twice,* Joseph Low (Atheneum); *Truck,* Donald Crews (Greenwillow).

1980 *Ox-cart man,* Donald Hall, illustrated by Barbara Cooney (Viking); **Honor books:** *Ben's trumpet,* Rachel Isadora (Greenwillow); *The garden of Abdul Gasazi,* Chris Van Allsburg (Houghton Mifflin); *The treasure,* Uri Shulevitz (Farrar, Straus & Giroux).

1979 *The girl who loved wild horses,* Paul Goble (Bradbury). **Honor books:** *Freight train,* Donald Crews (Greenwillow); *The way to start a day,* Byrd Baylor, illustrated by Peter Parnall (Scribner).

1978 *Noah's ark: The story of the flood,* Peter Spier (Doubleday). **Honor books:** *Castle,* David Macaulay (Houghton Mifflin); *It could always be worse,* Margot Zemach (Farrar, Straus & Giroux).

1977 *Ashanti to Zulu,* Margaret Musgrove, illustrated by Leo and Diane Dillon (Dial). **Honor books:** *The amazing bone,* William Steig (Farrar, Straus & Giroux); *The contest,* Nonny Hogrogian (Greenwillow); *Fish for supper,* M. B. Goffstein (Dial); *The Golem: A Jewish legend,* Beverly Brodsky McDermott (J. B. Lippincott); *Hawk, I'm your brother,* Byrd Baylor, illustrated by Peter Parnall (Scribner).

1976 *Why mosquitoes buzz in people's ears,* Verna Aardema, illustrated by Leo and Diane Dillon (Dial). **Honor books:** *The desert is theirs,* Byrd Baylor (Scribner), illustrated by Peter Parnall; *Strega Nona,* Tomie de Paola (Prentice-Hall).

1975 *Arrow to the sun,* Gerald McDermott (Viking). **Honor book:** *Jambo means hello: A Swahili alphabet book,* Muriel Feelings, illustrated by Tom Feelings (Dial).

1974 *Duffy and the devil,* Harve and Margot Zemach (Farrar, Straus & Giroux). **Honor books:** *Cathedral: The story of its construction,* David Macaulay (Houghton Mifflin); *The three jovial huntsmen,* Susan Jeffers (Bradbury).

1973 *The funny little woman,* Arlen Mosel, illustrated by Blair Lent (E. P. Dutton). **Honor books:** *Hosie's Alphabet,* Hosea, Tobias, and Lisa Baskin, illustrated by Leonard Baskin (Viking); *Snow-White and the seven dwarfs,* translated by Randall Jarrell from the Brothers Grimm, illustrated by Nancy Ekholm Burkert (Farrar, Straus & Giroux); *When clay sings,* Byrd Baylor, illustrated by Tom Bahti (Scribner).

1972 *One fine day,* Nonny A. Hogrogian (Macmillan). **Honor books:** *Hildilid's night,* Cheli Duran Ryan, illustrated by Arnold Lobel (Macmillan); *If all the seas were one sea,* Janina Domanska (Macmillan); *Moja means one: Swahili counting book,* Muriel Feelings, illustrated by Tom Feelings (Dial).

1971 *A story, a story,* Gail E. Haley (Atheneum). **Honor books:** *The angry moon,* William Sleator, illustrated by Blair Lent (Atlantic-Little); *Frog and Toad are friends,* Arnold Lobel (Harper & Row); *In the night kitchen,* Maurice Sendak (Harper & Row).

1970 *Sylvester and the magic pebble,* William Steig (Windmill/Simon & Schuster). **Honor books:** *Alexander and the wind-up mouse,* Leo Lionni (Pantheon); *Goggles!* Ezra Jack Keats (Macmillan); *The judge: An untrue tale,* Harve Zemach, illustrated by Margot Zemach (Farrar, Straus & Giroux); *Pop Corn and Ma Goodness,* Edna Mitchell Preston, illustrated by Robert Andrew Parker (Viking); *Thy friend, Obadiah,* Brinton Turkle (Viking).

1969 *The fool of the world and the flying ship,* Arthur Ransome, illustrated by Uri Shulevitz (Farrar, Straus & Giroux). **Honor book:** *Why the sun and the moon live in the sky: An African folktale,* Elphinstone Dayrell, illustrated by Blair Lent (Houghton Mifflin).

1968 *Drummer Hoff,* Barbara Emberley, illustrated by Ed Emberley (Prentice-Hall). **Honor books:** *Frederick,* Leo Lionni (Pantheon); *Seashore story,* Taro Yashima (Viking); *The emperor and the kite,* Jane Yolen, illustrated by Ed Young (Harcourt Brace Jovanovich).

1967 *Sam, Bangs & Moonshine,* Evaline Ness (Holt, Rinehart & Winston). **Honor book:** *One wide river to cross,* Barbara Emberley, illustrated by Ed Emberley (Prentice-Hall).

1966 *Always room for one more,* Sorche Nic Leodhas, illustrated by Nonny Hogrogian (Holt). **Honor books:** *Hide and seek fog,* Alvin Tresselt, illustrated by Roger Duvoisin (Lothrop); *Just me,* Marie Hall Ets (Viking); *Tom tit tot,* Evaline Ness (Scribner).

1965 *May I bring a friend?,* Beatrice Schenk de Regniers, illustrated by Beni Montresor (Atheneum). **Honor books:** *Rain makes applesauce,* Julian Scheer, illustrated by Marvin Bileck (Holiday

House); *The wave,* Margaret Hodges, illustrated by Blair Lent (Houghton Mifflin); *A pocketful of cricket,* Rebecca Caudill, illustrated by Evaline Ness (Holt).

1964 *Where the wild things are,* Maurice Sendak (Harper & Row). **Honor books:** *Swimmy,* Leo Lionni (Pantheon); *All in the morning early,* Sorche Nic Leodhas, illustrated by Evaline Ness (Holt); *Mother Goose and nursery rhymes,* illustrated by Philip Reed (Atheneum).

1963 *The snowy day,* Ezra Jack Keats (Viking). **Honor books:** *The sun is a golden earring,* Natalia M. Belting, illustrated by Bernarda Bryson (Holt); *Mr. Rabbit and the lovely present,* Charlotte Zolotow, illustrated by Maurice Sendak (Harper & Row).

1962 *Once a mouse . . . ,* Marcia Brown (Scribner). **Honor books:** *The fox went out on a chilly night: An old song,* Peter Spier (Doubleday); *Little bear's visit,* Else Holmelund Minarik, illustrated by Maurice Sendak (Harper & Row); *The day we saw the sun come up,* Alice E. Goudey, illustrated by Adrienne Adams (Scribner).

1961 *Baboushka and the three kings,* Ruth Robbins, illustrated by Nicolas Sidjakov (Parnassus). **Honor book:** *Inch by inch,* Leo Lionni (Obolensky).

1960 *Nine days to Christmas,* Marie Hall Ets & Aurora Labastida, illustrated by Marie Hall Ets (Viking). **Honor books:** *Houses from the sea,* Alice E. Goudey, illustrated by Adrienne Adams (Scribner); *The moon jumpers,* Janice May Udry, illustrated by Maurice Sendak (Harper & Row).

Newbery Medal Books

The Newbery Medal is named in honor of John Newbery (1713–1767), a British publisher and bookseller in the 1700s. Newbery is known as the "father of children's literature" because he was the first to propose publishing books specifically for children. The award is presented each year by the American Library Association to "the author of the most distinguished contribution to American literature for children" published during the preceding year. The award was first given in 1922 and is awarded annually. The winning book receives the Newbery Medal, and one or more runners-up are also recognized as "Honor" books.

1994 *The giver,* Lois Lowry (Houghton Mifflin). **Honor books:** *Crazy lady!,* Jane Leslie Conly (HarperCollins); *Dragon's gate,* Laurence Yep (HarperCollins); *Eleanor Roosevelt: A life of discovery,* Russell Freedman (Clarion).

1993 *Missing May,* Cynthia Rylant (Orchard). **Honor books:** *The dark-thirty: Southern tales of the supernatural,* Patricia McKissack (Knopf); *Some-*

where in the darkness, Walter Dean Myers (Scholastic); *What hearts,* Bruce Brooks (HarperCollins).

1992 *Shiloh,* Phyllis Reynolds Naylor (Atheneum). **Honor books:** *Nothing but the truth,* Avi (Orchard); *The Wright brothers: How they invented the airplane,* Russell Freedman (Holiday).

1991 *Maniac Magee,* Jerry Spinelli (Little, Brown). **Honor book:** *The true confessions of Charlotte Doyle,* Avi (Orchard).

1990 *Number the stars,* Lois Lowry (Houghton Mifflin). **Honor books:** *Afternoon of the elves,* Janet Taylor Lisel (Orchard); *Shabanu, daughter of the wind,* Susan Fisher Staples (Knopf); *The winter room,* Gary Paulsen (Orchard).

1989 *Joyful noise: Poems for two voices,* Paul Fleishman (Harper & Row). **Honor books:** *In the beginning,* Virginia Hamilton (Harcourt Brace Jovanovich); *Scorpions,* Walter Dean Myers (Harper & Row).

1988 *Lincoln: A photobiography,* Russell Freedman (Clarion). **Honor books:** *After the rain,* Norma Fox Mazer (Morrow); *Hatchet,* Gary Paulsen (Bradbury).

1987 *The whipping boy,* Sid Fleischman (Greenwillow). **Honor books:** *A fine white dust,* Cynthia Rylant (Bradbury); *On my honor,* Marion Dane Bauer (Clarion); *Volcano: The eruption and healing of Mount St. Helen's,* Patricia Lauber (Bradbury).

1986 *Sarah, plain and tall,* Patricia MacLachlan (Harper & Row). **Honor books:** *Commodore Perry in the land of the Shogun,* Rhoda Blumberg (Lothrop, Lee & Shepard); *Dog song,* Gary Paulsen (Bradbury).

1985 *The hero and the crown,* Robin McKinley (Greenwillow). **Honor books:** *Like Jake and me,* Mavis Jukes (Alfred A. Knopf); *The moves make the man,* Bruce Brooks (Harper & Row); *One-eyed cat,* Paula Fox (Bradbury).

1984 *Dear Mr. Henshaw,* Beverly Clearly (Morrow). **Honor books:** *The sign of the beaver,* Elizabeth George Speare (Houghton Mifflin); *A solitary blue,* Cynthia Voigt (Atheneum); *Sugaring time,* Kathryn Lasky (Macmillan); *The wish giver,* Bill Brittain (Harper & Row).

1983 *Dicey's song,* Cynthia Voigt (Atheneum). **Honor books:** *The blue sword,* Robin McKinley (Greenwillow); *Doctor DeSoto,* William Steig (Farrar, Straus & Giroux); *Graven images,* Paul Fleischman (Harper & Row); *Homesick: My own story,* Jean Fritz (Putnam); *Sweet Whispers, Brother Rush,* Virginia Hamilton (Philomel).

1982 *A visit to William Blake's inn: Poems for innocent and experienced travelers,* Nancy Willard (Harcourt Brace Jovanovich). **Honor books:** *Ramona Quimby, age 8,* Beverly Clearly (Morrow); *Upon the head of the goat: A childhood in Hungary, 1939–1944,* Aranka Siegal (Farrar, Straus & Giroux).

1981 *Jacob have I loved*, Katherine Paterson (Crowell). **Honor books:** *The fledgling*, Jane Langton (Harper & Row); *A ring of endless light*, Madeleine L'Engle (Farrar, Straus & Giroux).

1980 *A gathering of days: A New England girl's journal, 1830–1832*, Joan W. Blos (Scribner). **Honor book:** *The road from home: The story of an Armenian girl*, David Kerdian (Greenwillow).

1979 *The westing game*, Ellen Raskin (Dutton). **Honor book:** *The great Gilly Hopkins*, Katherine Paterson (Crowell).

1978 *Bridge to Terabithia*, Katherine Paterson (Crowell). **Honor books:** *Anpao: An American Indian odyssey*, Jamake Highwater (Lippincott); *Ramona and her father*, Beverly Clearly (Morrow).

1977 *Roll of thunder, hear my cry*, Mildred Taylor (Dial). **Honor books:** *Abel's Island*, William Steig (Farrar, Straus & Giroux); *A string in the harp*, Nancy Bond (Atheneum).

1976 *The grey king*, Susan Cooper (Atheneum). **Honor books:** *Dragonwings*, Laurence Yep (Harper & Row); *The hundred penny box*, Sharon Bell Mathis (Viking).

1975 *M. C. Higgins, the great*, Virginia Hamilton (Macmillan). **Honor books:** *Figgs and phantoms*, Ellen Raskin (E. P. Dutton); *My brother Sam is dead*, James Lincoln Collier and Christopher Collier (Four Winds); *The perilous gard*, Elizabeth Marie Pope (Houghton Mifflin); *Philip Hall likes me, I reckon maybe*, Bette Green (Dial).

1974 *The slave dancer*, Paula Fox (Bradbury). **Honor book:** *The dark is rising*, Susan Cooper (Atheneum).

1973 *Julie of the wolves*, Jean C. George (Harper & Row). **Honor books:** *Frog and Toad together*, Arnold Lobel (Harper & Row); *The upstairs room*, Johanna Reiss (Crowell); *The witches of worm*, Zilpha Keatley Snyder (Atheneum).

1972 *Mrs. Frisby and the rats of NIMH*, Robert C. O'Brien (Atheneum). **Honor books:** *Annie and the old one*, Miska Miles (Atlantic-Little); *The headless cupid*, Zilpha Keatley Snyder (Atheneum); *Incident at Hawk's Hill*, Allan W. Eckert (Little, Brown); *The planet of Junior Brown*, Virginia Hamilton (Macmillan); *The tombs of Atuan*, Ursula K. LeGuin (Atheneum).

1971 *The summer of the swans*, Betsy Byars (Viking). **Honor books:** *Enchantress from the stars*, Sylvia Louise Engdahl (Atheneum); *Kneeknock rise*, Natalie Babbitt (Farrar, Straus & Giroux); *Sing down the moon*, Scott O'Dell (Houghton Mifflin).

1970 *Sounder*, William Armstrong (Harper & Row). **Honor books:** *Journey outside*, Mary Q. Steele (Viking); *Our Eddie*, Sulamith Ish-Kishor (Pantheon);

The many ways of seeing: An introduction to the pleasures of art, Janet Gaylord Moore (Harcourt Brace Jovanovich).

1969 *The high king*, Lloyd Alexander (Holt, Rinehart & Winston). **Honor books:** *To be a slave*, Julius Lester (Dial); *When Shlemiel went to Warsaw and other stories*, Isaac Bashevis Singer (Farrar, Straus & Giroux).

1968 *From the mixed-up files of Mrs. Basil E. Frankweiler*, E. L. Konigsburg (Atheneum). **Honor books:** *The black pearl*, Scott O'Dell (Houghton Mifflin); *The Egypt game*, Zilpha Keatley Snyder (Atheneum); *The fearsome inn*, Isaac Bashevis Singer (Scribner); *Jennifer, Hecate, Macbeth, William McKinley, and Me, Elizabeth*, E. L. Konigsburg (Atheneum).

1967 *Up a road slowly*, Irene Hunt (Follett). **Honor books:** *The jazz man*, Mary Hays Weik (Atheneum); *The King's Fifth*, Scott O'Dell (Houghton Mifflin); *Zlateh the goat and other stories*, Isaac Bashevis Singer (Harper & Row).

1966 *I, Juan de Pareja*, Elizabeth Borton de Trevino (Farrar, Straus & Giroux). **Honor books:** *The animal family*, Randall Jarrell (Pantheon); *The black cauldron*, Lloyd Alexander (Holt, Rinehart & Winston); *The noonday friends*, Mary Stolz (Harper & Row).

1965 *Shadow of a bull*, Maia Wojciechowska (Atheneum). **Honor book:** *Across five Aprils*, Irene Hunt (Follett).

1964 *It's like this, cat*, Emily Neville (Harper & Row). **Honor books:** *The loner*, Ester Wier (McKay); *Rascal*, Sterling North (E. P. Dutton).

1963 *A wrinkle in time*, Madeleine L'Engle (Farrar, Straus & Giroux). **Honor books:** *Thistle and thyme: Tales and legends from Scotland*, Sorche Nic Leodhas (Holt); *Men of Athens*, Olivia Coolidge (Houghton Mifflin).

1962 *The bronze bow*, Elizabeth George Speare (Houghton Mifflin). **Honor books:** *Frontier living*, Edwin Tunis (World); *The golden goblet*, Eloise McCraw (Coward); *Belling the tiger*, Mary Stolz (Harper & Row).

1961 *Island of the blue dolphins*, Scott O'Dell (Houghton Mifflin). **Honor books:** *America moves forward*, Gerald W. Johnson (Morrow); *Old Ramon*, Jack Schaefer (Houghton Mifflin); *The cricket in Times Square*, George Selden (Farrar, Straus & Giroux).

1960 *Onion John*, Joseph Krumgold (Crowell). **Honor books:** *My side of the mountain*, Jean Craighead George (Dutton); *America is born*, Gerald W. Johnson (Morrow); *The gammage cup*, Carol Kendall (Harcourt Brace Jovanovich).

Resources About Authors and Illustrators

Books About Authors and Illustrators

Aardema, Verna   Aardema, V. (1992). *A bookworm who hatched.* Katonah, NY: Richard C. Owen. (P–M)

Andersen, Hans Christian   Greene, C. (1991). *Hans Christian Andersen: Prince of storytellers.* Chicago: Childrens Press. (P–M)*

Blegvad, Erik   Blegvad, E. (1979). *Self-portrait: Erik Blegvad.* Reading, MA: Addison-Wesley. (P–M–U)

Boston, Lucy   Boston, L. M. (1979). *Perverse and foolish: A memoir of childhood and youth.* New York: Atheneum. (U)

Bulla, Clyde   Bulla, C. R. (1985). *A grain of wheat: A writer begins.* Boston: David R. Godine. (M)

Burnett, Frances Hodgson   Carpenter, A. S., & Shirley, J. (1990). *Frances Hodgson Burnett: Beyond the secret garden.* Minneapolis: Lerner Books. (U)

Byars, Betsy   Byars, B. (1991). *The moon and I.* New York: Messner. (M–U)

Carson, Rachel   Wadsworth, G. (1991). *Rachel Carson: Voice for the earth.* Minneapolis: Lerner Books. (U)

Cleary, Beverly   Cleary, B. (1988). *A girl from Yamhill: A memoir.* New York: Morrow. (M–U)

Cowley, Joy   Cowley, J. (1988). *Seventy kilometres from ice cream: A letter from Joy Cowley.* Katonah, NY: Richard C. Owen. (P)

Dahl, Roald   Dahl, R. (1984). *Boy: Tales of childhood.* New York: Farrar, Straus & Giroux. (M–U)

de Paola, Tomie   de Paola, T. (1989). *The art lesson.* New York: Putnam. (P)

Dillon, Leo and Diane   Preiss, B. (1981). *The art of Leo and Diane Dillon.* New York: Ballantine. (M–U)

Duncan, Lois   Duncan, L. (1982). *Chapters: My growth as a writer.* Boston: Little, Brown. (U)

Fritz, Jean   Fritz, J. (1982). *Homesick: My own story.* New York: Putnam (M–U); Fritz, J. (1992). *Surprising myself.* Katonah, NY: Richard C. Owen. (M)

Goble, Paul   Goble, P. (1994). *Hau cola, hello friends.* Katonah, NY.: Richard C. Owen. (M)

Goodall, John   Goodall, J. S. (1981). *Before the war, 1908–1939. An autobiography in pictures.* New York: Atheneum. (M–U)

Henry, Marguerite   Henry, M. (1980). *The illustrated Marguerite Henry.* Chicago: Rand McNally. (M–U)

Hinton, S. E.   Daly, J. (1989). *Presenting S. E. Hinton.* Boston: Twayne. (U)

Hopkins, Lee Bennett   Hopkins, L. B. (1992). *The writing bug.* Katonah, NY: Richard C. Owen. (M)

Howe, James   Howe, J. (1994). *Playing with words.* Katonah, NY: Richard C. Owen. (M)

Hughes, Langston   Walker, A. (1974). *Langston Hughes, American poet.* New York: Crowell. (M–U)

Hyman, Trina Schart   Hyman, T. S. (1981). *Self-portrait: Trina Schart Hyman.* Reading, MA: Addison-Wesley. (P–M–U)

Lewis, C. S.   Lewis, C. S. (1985). *Letters to children.* New York: Macmillan. (M–U)

Meltzer, Milton   Meltzer, M. (1988). *Starting from home: A writer's beginnings.* NY: Viking. (U)

Naylor, Phyllis   Naylor, P. R. (1978). *How I came to be a writer.* New York: Atheneum. (U)

Peck, Richard   Peck, R. (1991). *Anonymously yours.* New York: Messner. (U)

Peet, Bill   Peet, B. (1989). *Bill Peet: An autobiography.* Boston: Houghton Mifflin. (M–U)

Polacco, Patricia   Polacco, P. (1994). *Fire talking.* Katonah, NY: Richard C. Owen. (M)

Potter, Beatrix   Aldis, D. (1969). *Nothing is impossible: The story of Beatrix Potter.* New York: Atheneum. (M); Collins, D. R. (1989). *The country artist: A story about Beatrix Potter.* Minneapolis: Carolrhoda. (M)

---

*P = Primary grades (K–2); M = Middle grades (3–5); U = Upper grades (6–8).

Rylant, Cynthia Rylant, C. (1992). *Best wishes*. Katonah, NY: Richard C. Owen. (P–M)

Singer, Isaac Bashevis Singer, I. B. (1969). *A day of pleasure: Stories of a boy growing up in Warsaw*. New York: Farrar, Straus & Giroux. (U)

Uchida, Yoshiko Uchida, U. (1991). *The invisible thread*. New York: Messner. (U)

Wilder, Laura Ingalls Blair, G. (1981). *Laura Ingalls Wilder*. New York: Putnam. (P–M); Greene, C. (1990). *Laura Ingalls Wilder: Author of the Little House books*. Chicago: Childrens Press. (P–M)

Yep, Laurence Yep, L. (1991). *The lost garden: A memoir*. New York: Messner. (U)

Yolen, Jane Yolen, J. (1992). *A letter from Phoenix Farm*. Katonah, NY: Richard C. Owen. (P–M–U)

Zemach, Margot Zemach, M. (1978). *Self-portrait: Margot Zemach*. Reading, MA: Addison-Wesley. (P–M–U)

Individual Articles Profiling Authors and Illustrators

Adoff, Arnold White, M. L. (1988). Profile: Arnold Adoff. *Language Arts, 65*, 584–591.

Alexander, Lloyd Greenlaw, M. J. (1984). Profile: Lloyd Alexander. *Language Arts, 61*, 406–413; Tunnell, M. O. (1989). An interview with Lloyd Alexander. *The New Advocate, 2*, 83–96.

Anno, Mitsumasa Aoki, H. (1983). A conversation with Mitsumasa Anno. *Horn Book Magazine, 59*, 132–145; Swinger, A. K. (1987). Profile: Mitsumasa Anno's journey. *Language Arts, 64*, 762–766.

Baker, Keith Baker, K. (1993). "Have you ever been dead?" Questions and letters from children. *The Reading Teacher, 46*, 372–375.

Baylor, Byrd Bosma, B. (1987). Profile: Byrd Baylor. *Language Arts, 64*, 315–318.

Behn, Harry Roop, P. (1985). Profile: Harry Behn. *Language Arts, 62*, 92–94.

Brett, Jan Raymond, A. (April, 1992). Jan Brett: Making it look easy. *Teaching PreK–8, 22*, 38–40.

Brown, Marcia Brown, M. (1983). Caldecott Medal Acceptance. *Horn Book Magazine, 59*, 414–422.

Brown, Margaret Wise Hurd, C. (1983). Remembering Margaret Wise Brown. *Horn Book Magazine, 59*, 553–560.

Browne, Anthony Marantz, S., & Marantz, K. (1985). An interview with Anthony Browne. *Horn Book Magazine, 61*, 696–704.

Bryan, Ashley Marantz, S., & Marantz, K. (1988). Interview with Ashley Bryan. *Horn Book Magazine, 64*, 173–179; Swinger, A. K. (1984). Profile: Ashley Bryan. *Language Arts, 61*, 305–311.

Bunting, Eve Raymond, A. (October, 1986). Eve Bunting: From Ireland with love. *Teaching PreK–8, 17*, 38–40.

Byars, Betsy Robertson, I. (1980). Profile: Betsy Byars—writer for today's child. *Language Arts, 57*, 328–334.

Carle, Eric Yolen, J. (1988). In the artist's studio: Eric Carle. *The New Advocate, 1*, 148–154.

Ciardi, John Odland, N. (1982). Profile: John Ciardi. *Language Arts, 59*, 872–876.

Cleary, Beverly Cleary, B. (1984). Newbery Medal acceptance. *Horn Book Magazine, 50*, 429–438; Reuter, D. (1984). Beverly Cleary. *Horn Book Magazine, 50*, 439–443.

Clifton, Lucille Sims, R. (1982). Profile: Lucille Clifton. *Language Arts, 59*, 160–167.

Collier, James and Christopher Raymond, A. (January, 1988). Meet James and Christopher Collier. *Teaching PreK–8, 18*, 35–38.

Conrad, Pam Raymond, A. (November/December, 1990). Pam Conrad: She said to herself, 'Now what?' *Teaching PreK–8, 21*, 38–40.

Degan, Bruce Elliot, I. (October, 1991). Bruce Degan: Doing what he likes best. *Teaching PreK–8, 21*, 44–47.

DeJong, Meindert Hearne, B. (1984). Meindert DeJong. *Horn Book Magazine, 60*, 566–568.

Dr. Seuss Roth, R. (1989). On beyond zebra with Dr. Seuss. *The New Advocate, 2*, 213–226.

Egielski, Richard Egielski, R. (1987). Caldecott Medal acceptance. *Horn Book Magazine, 63*, 433–435; Yorinks, A. (1987). Richard Egielski. *Horn Book Magazine, 63*, 436–438.

Enright, Elizabeth Cameron, E. (1984). A second look: Gone-Away Lake. *Horn Book Magazine, 60*, 622–626.

Feelings, Tom Feelings, T. (1985). The artist at work: Technique and the artist's vision. *Horn Book Magazine, 61*, 685–695.

Fleischman, Sid Fleischman, P. (1987). Sid Fleischman. *Horn Book Magazine, 63*, 429–432; Fleischman, S. (1987). Newbery Medal acceptance. *Horn Book Magazine, 63*, 423–428; Johnson, E. R. (1982). Profile: Sid Fleischman. *Language Arts, 59*, 754–759.

Fox, Mem Manning, M., & Manning, G. (March, 1990). Mem Fox: Mem's the word in down under? *Teaching PreK–8, 20*, 29–31; Phelan, C. (1993, May). Talking with Mem Fox. *Book Links, 29–32*.

Freedman, Russell Dempsey, F. J. (1988). Russell Freedman. *Horn Book Magazine, 64*, 452–456; Freedman, R. (1988). Newbery Medal acceptance. *Horn Book Magazine, 64*, 444–451.

Fritz, Jean Ammon, R. (1983). Profile: Jean Fritz. *Language Arts, 60*, 365–369; Fritz, J. (1985). Turning history inside out. *Horn Book Magazine, 61*, 29–34; Heins, E. L. (1986). Presentation of the Laura Ingalls Wilder Medal. *Horn Book Magazine, 62*, 430–431.

Gerstein, Mordicai Yolen, J. (1990). In the artist's studio: Mordicai Gerstein. *The New Advocate, 3,* 25–28.

Giff, Patricia Reilly Raymond, A. (April, 1987). Patricia Reilly Giff: A writer who believes in reading. *Teaching PreK–8, 17,* 34–37.

Gilson, Jamie Johnson, R. (1983). Profile: Jamie Gilson. *Language Arts, 60,* 661–667.

Goble, Paul Stott, J. C. (1984). Profile: Paul Goble. *Language Arts, 61,* 867–873.

Goffstein, M. B. Marantz, S., & Martantz, K. (1986). M. B. Goffstein: An interview. *Horn Book Magazine, 62,* 688–694; Shannon, G. (1983). Goffstein and friends. *Horn Book Magazine, 59,* 88–95.

Greenfield, Eloise Kiah, R. B. (1980). Profile: Eloise Greenfield. *Language Arts, 57,* 653–659.

Haley, Gail E. Haley, G. E. (1990). Of mermaids, myths, and meaning: A sea tale. *The New Advocate, 3,* 1–12.

Hamilton, Virginia Hamilton, V. (1986). Coretta Scott King Award acceptance. *Horn Book Magazine, 62,* 683–687; Garrett, J. (1993, January). Virginia Hamilton: 1992 Andersen winner, *Book Links,* 22–25.

Henkes, Kevin Elliot, I. (January, 1989). Meet Kevin Henkes: Young man on a roll. *Teaching PreK–8, 19,* 43–45.

Hoover, H. M. Porter, E. J. (1982). Profile: H. M. Hoover. *Language Arts, 59,* 609–613.

Howe, James Raymond, A. (February, 1987). James Howe: Corn, ham and punster cheese. *Teaching PreK–8, 17,* 32–34.

Hyman, Trina Schart Hyman, K. (1985). Trina Schart Hyman. *Horn Book Magazine, 61,* 422–425; Hyman, T. S. (1985). Caldecott Medal acceptance. *Horn Book Magazine, 61,* 410–421; Saul, W. (1988). Once-upon-a-time artist in the land of now: An interview with Trina Schart Hyman. *The New Advocate, 1,* 8–17; White, D. E. (1983). Profile: Trina Schart Hyman. *Language Arts, 60,* 782–792.

Jonas, Ann Marantz, S., & Marantz, K. (1987). Interview with Ann Jonas. *Horn Book Magazine, 63,* 308–313; Raymond, A. (December, 1987). Ann Jonas: Reflections 1987. *Teaching PreK–8, 18,* 44–46.

Keats, Ezra Jack Lanes, S. G. (1984). Ezra Jack Keats: In memoriam. *Horn Book Magazine, 60,* 551–558; Pope, M., & Pope, L. (1990). Ezra Jack Keats: A childhood revisited. *The New Advocate, 3,* 13–24.

Konigsburg, E. L. Jones, L. T. (1986). Profile: Elaine Konigsburg. *Language Arts, 63,* 177–184.

Lasky, Kathryn Lasky, K. (1990). The fiction of history: Or, what did Miss Kitty really do? *The New Advocate, 3,* 157–166.

L'Engle, Madeleine Raymond, A. (May, 1991). Madeleine L'Engle: Getting the last laugh. *Teaching PreK–8, 21,* 34–36; Samuels, L. A. (1981). Profile: Madeleine L'Engle. *Language Arts, 58,* 704–712.

Lester, Julius Lester, J. (1988). The storyteller's voice: Reflections on the rewriting of Uncle Remus. *The New Advocate, 1,* 137–142.

Livingston, Myra Cohn Porter, E. J. (1980). Profile: Myra Cohn Livingston. *Language Arts, 57,* 901–905.

Lobel, Anita Raymond, A. (November/December, 1989). Anita Lobel: Up from the crossroad. *Teaching PreK–8, 20,* 52–55.

Lobel, Arnold Lobel, A. (1981). Caldecott Medal acceptance. *Horn Book Magazine, 57,* 400–404; Lobel, A. (1981). Arnold at home. *Horn Book Magazine, 57,* 405–410; White, D. E. (1988). Profile: Arnold Lobel. *Language Arts, 65,* 489–494.

Lowry, Lois Lowry, L. (1988). Rabble Starkey. *Horn Book Magazine, 64,* 29–31; Lowry, L. (1990). *Number the stars:* Lois Lowry's journey to the Newbery Award. *The Reading Teacher, 44,* 98–101; Raymond, A. (October, 1987). "Anastasia," and then some. *Teaching PreK–8, 18,* 44–46.

Macaulay, David Ammon, R. (1982). Profile: David Macaulay. *Language Arts, 59,* 374–378.

MacLachlan, Patricia Babbitt, N. (1986). Patricia MacLachlan: The biography. *Horn Book Magazine, 62,* 414–416; Courtney, A. (1985). Profile: Patricia MacLachlan. *Language Arts, 62,* 783–787; MacLachlan, P. (1986). Newbery Medal acceptance. *Horn Book Magazine, 62,* 407–413; MacLachlan, R. (1986). A hypothetical dilemma. *Horn Book Magazine, 62,* 416–419; Raymond, A. (May, 1989). Patricia MacLachlan: An advocate of "Bare boning." *Teaching PreK–8, 19,* 46–48.

Martin, Bill, Jr. Larrick, N. (1982). Profile: Bill Martin, Jr. *Language Arts, 59,* 490–494.

Mayer, Marianna Raymond, A. (January, 1991). Marianna Mayer: Myths, legends, and folklore. *Teaching PreK–8, 21,* 42–44.

McCloskey, Robert Mandel, E. (1991, May). *Make way for ducklings* by Robert McCloskey. *Book Links,* 38–42.

McDermott, Gerald McDermott, G. (1988). Sky father, earth mother: An artist interprets myth. *The New Advocate, 1,* 1–7; White, D. E. (1982). Profile: Gerald McDermott. *Language Arts, 59,* 273–279.

McKinley, Robin McKinley, R. (1985). Newbery Medal acceptance. *Horn Book Magazine, 61,* 395–405; Windling, T. (1985). Robin McKinley. *Horn Book Magazine, 61,* 406–409.

McKissack, Patricia Bishop, R. S. (1992). A conversation with Patricia McKissack. *Language Arts, 69,* 69–74.

Merriam, Eve   Cox, S. T. (1989). A word or two with Eve Merriam: Talking about poetry. *The New Advocate, 2,* 139–150; Sloan, G. (1981). Profile: Eve Merriam. *Language Arts, 58,* 957–964.

Mikolaycak, Charles   White, D. E. (1981). Profile: Charles Mikolaycak. *Language Arts, 58,* 850–857.

Mohr, Nicholasa   Zarnowski, M. (1991). An interview with author Nicholasa Mohr. *The Reading Teacher, 45,* 100–107.

Montresor, Beni   Raymond, A. (April, 1990). Beni Montresor: Carmen, Cannes and Caldecott. *Teaching PreK–8, 20,* 31–33.

Moore, Lilian   Glazer, J. I. (1985). Profile: Lilian Moore. *Language Arts, 62,* 647–652.

Moser, Barry   Moser, B. (1987). Artist at work: Illustrating the classics. *Horn Book Magazine, 63,* 703–709; Moser, B. (1991). Family photographs, gathered fragments. *The New Advocate, 4,* 1–10.

Munsch, Robert   Jenkinson, D. (1989). Profile: Robert Munsch, *Language Arts, 66,* 665–675.

Myers, Walter Dean   Bishop, R. S. (1990). Profile: Walter Dean Myers. *Language Arts, 67,* 862–866.

Naylor, Phyllis Reynolds   Naylor, P. R. (1992). The writing of *Shiloh. The Reading Teacher, 46,* 10–13.

O'Dell, Scott   Roop, P. (1984). Profile: Scott O'Dell. *Language Arts, 61,* 750–752.

Parker, Nancy Winslow   Raymond, A. (May, 1990). Nancy Winslow Parker: "I knew it would happen." *Teaching PreK–8, 20,* 34–36.

Paterson, Katherine   Jones, L. T. (1981). Profile: Katherine Paterson. *Language Arts, 58,* 189–196; Namovic, G. I. (1981). Katherine Paterson. *Horn Book Magazine, 57,* 394–399; Paterson, K. (1981). Newbery Medal acceptance. *Horn Book Magazine, 57,* 385–393.

Prelutsky, Jack   Raymond, A. (November/December, 1986). Jack Prelutsky . . . Man of many talents. *Teaching PreK–8, 17,* 38–42; Vardell, S. (1991). An interview with Jack Prelutsky. *The New Advocate, 4,* 101–112.

Provensen, Alice and Martin   Provensen, A., & Provensen, M. (1984). Caldecott Medal acceptance. *Horn Book Magazine, 50,* 444–448; Willard, N. (1984). Alice and Martin Provensen. *Horn Book Magazine, 50,* 449–452.

Raskin, Ellen   Bach, A. (1985). Ellen Raskin: Some clues about her life. *Horn Book Magazine, 61,* 62–67.

Rice, Eve   Raymond, A. (April, 1989). Meet Eve Rice: Author/artist/doctor (doctor?). *Teaching PreK–8, 19,* 40–42.

Rylant, Cynthia   Silvey, A. (1987). An interview with Cynthia Rylant. *Horn Book Magazine, 63,* 695–702.

Schoenherr, John   Gauch, P. L. (1988). John Schoenherr. *Horn Book Magazine, 64,* 460–463; Schoenherr, J. (1988). Caldecott Medal acceptance. *Horn Book Magazine, 64,* 457–459.

Schwartz, Alvin   Vardell, S. M. (1987). Profile: Alvin Schwartz. *Language Arts, 64,* 426–432.

Scieszka, Jon   Raymond, A. (1992, May). Jon Scieszka: Telling the *true story. Teaching PreK–8, 22,* 38–40.

Sendak, Maurice   Sendak, M. (1983). Laura Ingalls Wilder Award acceptance. *Horn Book Magazine, 59,* 474–477.

Sewall, Marcia   Sewall, M. (1988). *The pilgrims of Plimoth. Horn Book Magazine, 64,* 32–34.

Shulevitz, Uri   Raymond, A. (January, 1992). Uri Shulevitz: For children of all ages. *Teaching PreK–8, 21,* 38–40.

Soto, Gary   Soto, G. (1992). Author for a day: Glitter and rainbows. *The Reading Teacher, 46,* 200–203.

Speare, Elizabeth George   Hassler, P. J. (1993, May). The books of Elizabeth George Speare. *Book Links,* 14–20.

Spinelli, Jerry   Spinelli, J. (1991). Capturing Maniac Magee. *The Reading Teacher, 45,* 174–177.

Steig, Bill   Raymond, A. (August/September, 1991). Jeanne and Bill Steig: It adds up to magic. *Teaching PreK–8, 21,* 52–54.

Steptoe, John   Bradley, D. H. (1991). John Steptoe: Retrospective of an imagemaker. *The New Advocate, 4,* 11–24.

Tafuri, Nancy   Raymond, A. (January, 1987). Nancy Tafuri . . . Nature, picturebooks, and joy. *Teaching PreK–8, 17,* 34–36.

Taylor, Mildred D.   Dussel, S. L. (1981). Profile: Mildred D. Taylor. *Language Arts, 58,* 599–604.

Taylor, Theodore   Bagnall, N. (1980). Profile: Theodore Taylor: His models of self-reliance. *Language Arts, 57,* 86–91.

Uchida, Yoshiko   Chang, C. E. S. (1984). Profile: Yoshiko Uchida. *Language Arts, 61,* 189–194.

Van Allsburg, Chris   Keifer, B. (1987). Profile: Chris Van Allsburg in three dimensions. *Language Arts, 64,* 664–671; Macaulay, D. (1986). Chris Van Allsburg. *Horn Book Magazine, 62,* 424–426; McKee, B. (1986). Van Allsburg: From a different perspective. *Horn Book Magazine, 62,* 566–571; Van Allsburg, C. (1982). Caldecott Medal acceptance. *Horn Book Magazine, 58,* 380–383; Van Allsburg, C. (1986). Caldecott Medal acceptance. *Horn Book Magazine, 62,* 420–424.

Voigt, Cynthia   Kauffman, D. (1985). Profile: Cynthia Voigt. *Language Arts, 62,* 876–880; Voigt, C. (1983). Newbery Medal acceptance. *Horn Book Magazine, 59,* 401–409.

White, E. B.   Hopkins, L. B. (1986). Profile: In memoriam: E. B. White. *Language Arts, 63,* 491–494; Newmeyer, P. F. (1985). The creation of E. B.

White's *The Trumpet of the Swans:* The manuscripts. *Horn Book Magazine, 61,* 17–28; Newmeyer, P. F. (1987). E. B. White: Aspects of style. *Horn Book Magazine, 63,* 586–591.

Wiesner, David Caroff, S. F., & Moje, E. B. (1992/1993). A conversation with David Wiesner: 1992 Caldecott Medal winner. *The Reading Teacher, 46,* 284–289.

Willard, Nancy Lucas, B. (1982). Nancy Willard. *Horn Book Magazine, 58,* 374–379; Willard, N. (1982). Newbery Medal acceptance. *Horn Book Magazine, 58,* 369–373.

Williams, Vera B. Raymond, A. (October, 1988). Vera B. Williams: Postcards and peace vigils. *Teaching PreK–8, 19,* 40–42.

Worth, Valerie Hopkins, L. B. (1991). Profile: Valerie Worth. *Language Arts, 68,* 499–501.

Yolen, Jane White, D. E. (1983). Profile: Jane Yolen. *Language Arts, 60,* 652–660; Yolen, J. (1989). On silent wings: The making of *Owl moon. The New Advocate, 2,* 199–212; Yolen, J. (1991). The route to story. *The New Advocate, 4,* 143–149; Yolen, J. (1992). Past time: The writing of the picture book *Encounter. The New Advocate, 5,* 235–239.

Yorinks, Arthur Raymond, A. (November/December, 1991). Arthur Yorinks: Talent in abundance. *Teaching PreK–8, 21,* 51–53.

Zalben, Jane Breskin Yolen, J. (1990). In the artist's studio: Jane Breskin Zalben. *The New Advocate, 3,* 175–178.

Audiovisual Materials Profiling Authors and Illustrators

Alexander, Lloyd "Meet the Newbery author: Lloyd Alexander," American School Publishers (sound filmstrip). (U)

Andersen, Hans Christian "Meet the author: Hans Christian Andersen," American School Publishers (sound filmstrip or video). (M)

Armstrong, William H. "Meet the Newbery author: William H. Armstrong," American School Publishers (sound filmstrip). (M–U)

Babbitt, Natalie "Meet the Newbery author: Natalie Babbitt," American School Publishers (sound filmstrip). (U)

Berenstain, Stan and Jan "Meet Stan and Jan Berenstain," American School Publishers (sound filmstrip). (P)

Blume, Judy "First choice: Authors and books— Judy Blume," Pied Piper (sound filmstrip). (M–U)

Brown, Marc "Meet Marc Brown," American School Publishers (video). (P–M)

Bulla, Clyde "First choice: Authors and books— Clyde Bulla," Pied Piper (sound filmstrip). (M)

Byars, Betsy "Meet the Newbery author: Betsy Byars," American School Publishers (sound filmstrip). (M–U)

Carle, Eric "Eric Carle: Picture writer," Philomel (video). (P–M)

Cherry, Lynne "Get to know Lynne Cherry," Harcourt Brace (video). (M)

Cleary, Beverly "First choice: Authors and books— Beverly Cleary," Pied Piper (sound filmstrip). (M); "Meet the Newbery author: Beverly Cleary," American School Publishers (sound filmstrip). (M)

Collier, James Lincoln and Christopher "Meet the Newbery authors: James Lincoln Collier and Christopher Collier," American School Publishers (sound filmstrip). (U)

Cooper, Susan "Meet the Newbery author: Susan Cooper," American School Publishers (sound filmstrip). (U)

Dahl, Roald "The author's eye: Roald Dahl," American School Publishers (kit with video). (M–U)

Fleischman, Sid "First choice: Authors and books— Sid Fleischman," Pied Piper (sound filmstrip). (M–U)

Fritz, Jean "Homesick: My own story," American School Publishers (sound filmstrip). (M–U)

George, Jean Craighead "Meet the Newbery author: Jean Craighead George," American School Publishers (sound filmstrip). (U)

Giovanni, Nikki "First choice: Poets and poetry— Nikki Giovanni," Pied Piper (sound filmstrip). (M–U)

Greene, Bette "Meet the Newbery author: Bette Greene," American School Publishers (sound filmstrip). (M–U)

Haley, Gail E. "Tracing a legend: The story of the green man by Gail E. Haley," Weston Woods (sound filmstrip). (M); "Creating Jack and the bean tree: Tradition and technique," Weston Woods (sound filmstrip). (M)

Hamilton, Virginia "First choice: Authors and books—Virginia Hamilton," Pied Piper (sound filmstrip). (U); "Meet the Newbery author: Virginia Hamilton," American School Publishers (sound filmstrip). (U)

Henry, Marguerite "First choice: Authors and books—Marguerite Henry," Pied Piper (sound filmstrip). (M–U); "Meet the Newbery author: Marguerite Henry," American School Publishers (sound filmstrip). (M)

Highwater, Jamake "Meet the Newbery author: Jamake Highwater," American School Publishers (sound filmstrip). (M–U)

Keats, Ezra Jack "Ezra Jack Keats," Weston Woods (film). (P)

Kellogg, Steven "How a picture book is made," Weston Woods (video). (P–M); "Trumpet video visits Steven Kellogg," Trumpet Books (video). (P–M)

Konigsburg, E. L.   "First choice: Authors and books—E. L. Konigsburg," Pied Piper (sound filmstrip). (M–U)

Kuskin, Karla   "First choice: Poets and poetry—Karla Kuskin," Pied Piper (sound filmstrip). (M–U); "Poetry explained by Karla Kuskin," Weston Woods (sound filmstrip). (M–U)

L'Engle, Madeleine   "Meet the Newbery author: Madeleine L'Engle," American School Publishers (sound filmstrip). (U)

Livingston, Myra Cohn   "First choice: Poets and poetry—Myra Cohn Livingston," Pied Piper (sound filmstrip). (M–U)

Lobel, Arnold   "Meet the Newbery author: Arnold Lobel," American School Publishers (sound filmstrip). (P–M)

Macaulay, David   "David Macaulay in his studio," Houghton Mifflin (video). (M–U)

McCloskey, Robert   "Robert McCloskey," Weston Woods (film). (P–M)

McCord, David   "First choice: Poets and poetry—David McCord," Pied Piper (sound filmstrip). (M–U)

McDermott, Gerald   "Evolution of a graphic concept: The stonecutter," Weston Woods (sound filmstrip). (P–M)

Merriam, Eve   "First choice: Poets and poetry—Eve Merriam," Pied Piper (sound filmstrip). (M–U)

Milne, A. A.   "Meet the author: A. A. Milne (and Pooh)," American School Publishers (sound filmstrip or video). (P)

Most, B.   "Get to know Bernard Most," Harcourt Brace (video). (P–M)

O'Dell, Scott   "Meet the Newbery author: Scott O'Dell," American School Publishers (sound filmstrip). (U); "A visit with Scott O'Dell," Houghton Mifflin (video). (U)

Paterson, Katherine   "The author's eye: Katherine Paterson," American School Publishers (kit with video). (M–U); "Meet the Newbery author: Katherine Paterson," American School Publishers (sound filmstrip). (M–U)

Paulsen, Gary   "Trumpet video visits Gary Paulsen," Trumpet Books (video). (U)

Peet, Bill   "Bill Peet in his studio," Houghton Mifflin (video). (M)

Pinkney, Jerry   "Meet the Caldecott illustrator: Jerry Pinkney," American School Publishers (video). (P–M)

Potter, Beatrix   "Beatrix Potter had a pet named Peter," American School Publishers (sound filmstrip or video). (P)

Rylant, Cynthia   "Meet the Newbery author: Cynthia Rylant," American School Publishers (sound filmstrip or video). (M–U); "Meet the picture book author: Cynthia Rylant," American School Publishers (video). (P–M)

Sendak, Maurice   "Sendak," Weston Woods (film). (P–M)

Seuss, Dr.   "Who's Dr. Seuss?: Meet Ted Geisel," American School Publishers (sound filmstrip). (P–M)

Singer, Isaac Bashevis   "Meet the Newbery author: Isaac Bashevis Singer," American School Publishers (sound filmstrip). (U)

Sobol, Donald J.   "The case of the Model-A Ford and the man in the snorkel under the hood: Donald J. Sobol," American School Publishers (sound filmstrip). (M)

White, E. B.   "Meet the Newbery author: E. B. White," American School Publishers (sound filmstrip). (M–U)

Wilder, Laura Ingalls   "Meet the Newbery author: Laura Ingalls Wilder," American School Publishers (sound filmstrip). (M–U)

Willard, Nancy   "Meet the Newbery author: Nancy Willard," American School Publishers (sound filmstrip). (M–U)

Yep, Laurence   "Meet the Newbery author: Laurence Yep," American School Publishers (sound filmstrip). (U)

Zolotow, Charlotte   "Charlotte Zolotow: The grower," American School Publishers (sound filmstrip). (P–M)

Addresses for Audiovisual Manufacturers

American School
  Publishers
P.O. Box 408
Hightstown, NJ 08520

Houghton Mifflin
2 Park Street
Boston, MA 02108

Pied Piper
P.O. Box 320
Verdugo City, CA 91046

Weston Woods
Weston, CT 06883

Joint Statement on Literacy Development and Pre-First Grade

A Joint Statement of Concerns About Present Practices in Pre-First Grade Reading Instruction and Recommendations for Improvement • Association for Supervision and Curriculum Development • International Reading Association • National Association for the Education of Young Children • National Association of Elementary School Principals • National Council of Teachers of English

Prepared by the Early Childhood and Literacy Development Committee of the International Reading Association*

Objectives for a Pre-First Grade Reading Program

Literacy learning begins in infancy. Reading and writing experiences at school should permit children to build upon their already existing knowledge of oral and written language. Learning should take place in a supportive environment where children can build a positive attitude toward themselves and toward language and literacy. For optimal learning, teachers should involve children actively in many meaningful, functional language experiences, including *speaking, listening, writing,* and *reading.* Teachers of young children should be prepared in ways that acknowledge differences in language and cultural backgrounds and emphasize reading as an integral part of the language arts as well as of the total curriculum.

What Young Children Know About Oral and Written Language Before They Come to School

1. Children have had many experiences from which they are building their ideas about the functions and uses of oral language and written language.
2. Children have a command of language, have internalized many of its rules, and have conceptualized processes for learning and using language.
3. Many children can differentiate between drawing and writing.
4. Many children are reading environmental print, such as road signs, grocery labels, and fast good signs.
5. Many children associate books with reading.

---

*From *The Reading Teacher,* April 1986, v. 39, no. 8, pp. 819–820.

6. Children's knowledge about language and communication systems is influenced by their social and cultural backgrounds.
7. Many children expect that reading and writing will be sense-making activities.

Concerns

1. Many pre-first grade children are subjected to rigid, formal pre-reading programs with inappropriate expectations and experiences for their levels of development.
2. Little attention is given to individual development or individual learning styles.
3. The pressures of accelerated programs do not allow children to be risk-takers as they experiment with language and internalize concepts about how language operates.
4. Too much attention is focused upon isolated skill development or abstract parts of the reading process, rather than upon the integration of oral language, writing and listening with reading.
5. Too little attention is placed upon reading for pleasure; therefore, children often do not associate reading with enjoyment.
6. Decisions related to reading programs are often based on political and economic considerations rather than on knowledge of how young children learn.
7. The pressure to achieve high scores on standardized tests that frequently are not appropriate for the kindergarten child has resulted in changes in the content of programs. Program content often does not attend to the child's social, emotional and intellectual development. Consequently, inappropriate activities that deny curiosity, critical thinking and creative expression occur all too frequently. Such activities foster negative attitudes toward communication skill activities.
8. As a result of declining enrollment and reduction in staff, individuals who have little or no knowledge of early childhood education are sometimes assigned to teach young children. Such teachers often select inappropriate methodologies.
9. Teachers of pre-first graders who are conducting individualized programs without depending upon commercial readers and workbooks need to articulate for parents and other members of the public what they are doing and why.

Recommendations

1. Build instruction on what the child already knows about oral language, reading and writing. Focus on meaningful experiences and meaningful language rather than merely on isolated skill development.
2. Respect the language the child brings to school, and use it as a base for language and literacy activities.
3. Ensure feelings of success for all children, helping them see themselves as people who can enjoy exploring oral and written language.
4. Provide reading experiences as an integrated part of the broader communication process, which includes speaking, listening and writing, as well as other communication systems such as art, math and music.

5. Encourage children's first attempts at writing without concern for the proper formation of letters or correct conventional spelling.

6. Encourage risk-taking in first attempts at reading and writing and accept what appear to be errors as part of children's natural patterns of growth and development.

7. Use materials for instruction that are familiar, such as well-known stories, because they provide the child with a sense of control and confidence.

8. Present a model for students to emulate. In the classroom, teachers should use language appropriately, listen and respond to children's talk, and engage in their own reading and writing.

9. Take time regularly to read to children from a wide variety of poetry, fiction and non-fiction.

10. Provide time regularly for children's independent reading and writing.

11. Foster children's affective and cognitive development by providing opportunities to communicate what they know, think and feel.

12. Use evaluative procedures that are developmentally and culturally appropriate for the children being assessed. The selection of evaluative measures should be based on the objectives of the instructional program and should consider each child's total development and its effect on reading performance.

13. Make parents aware of the reasons for a total language program at school and provide them with ideas for activities to carry out at home.

14. Alert parents to the limitations of formal assessments and standardized tests of pre-first graders' reading and writing skills.

15. Encourage children to be active participants in the learning process rather than passive recipients of knowledge, by using activities that allow for experimentation with talking, listening, writing and reading.

Common Spelling Options for Phonemes

Sound	Spellings	Examples	Sound	Spellings	Examples
ā	a-e	date	l	l	last
	a	angel		ll	allow
	ai	aid		le	automobile
	ay	day	m	m	man
ch	ch	church		me	come
	t(u)	picture		mm	comment
	tch	watch	n	n	no
	ti	question		ne	done
ē	ea	each	ng	ng	thing
	ee	feel		n	bank, anger
	e	evil	ō	o	go
	e-e	these		o-e	note
	ea-e	breathe		ow	own
ĕ	e	end		oa	load
	ea	head	ô	o	office
f	f	feel		a	all
	ff	sheriff		au	author
	ph	photograph		aw	saw
j	ge	strange	oi	oi	oil
	g	general		oy	boy
	j	job	o͞o	oo	book
	dge	bridge		u	put
k	c	call		ou	could
	k	keep		o	woman
	x	expect, luxury			
	ck	black			
	qu	quite, bouquet			

continued

Sound	Spellings	Examples	Sound	Spellings	Examples
o͞o	u	cruel	y	u	union
	oo	noon		u-e	use
	u-e	rule		y	yes
	o-e	lose		i	onion
	ue	blue		ue	value
	o	to		ew	few
	ou	group	z	s	present
ou	ou	out		se	applause
	ow	cow		ze	gauze
s	s	sick	syllabic *l*	le	able
	ce	office		al	animal
	c	city		el	cancel
	ss	class		il	civil
	se	else	syllabic *n*	en	written
	x(ks)	box		on	lesson
sh	ti	attention		an	important
	sh	she		in	cousin
	ci	ancient		contractions	didn't
	ssi	admission		ain	certain
t	t	teacher	stressed	er	her
	te	definite	syllabic *r*	ur	church
	ed	furnished		ir	first
	tt	attend		or	world
ŭ	u	ugly		ear	heard
	o	company		our	courage
	ou	country	unstressed	er	better
ū	u	union	syllabic *r*	or	favor
	u-e	use		ure	picture
	ue	value		ar	dollar
	ew	few			

Title and Author Index

Abbott, R. D., 234
Above and Below Stairs, 581
Across Five Aprils, 178
Adams, A., 298
Adams, M. J., 247
Adler, D. A., 47, 397, 544
The Adventures of Taxi Dog, 300
Africa Dream, 536
Ahlberg, A., 181, 388, 573
Ahlberg, J., 181, 388, 573
Aker, S., 364
Aladdin and the Wonderful Lamp, 342
Aldis, D., 343
Alesandrini, K., 121
Alexander, H., 285
Alexander, L., 149
Alexander and the Terrible, Horrible, No Good, Very Bad Day, 327, 349
Alexander and the Wind-Up Mouse, 346
Alice in Wonderland, 297
Aliki, 559, 582
Allen, R. V., 259
Allen, V. A., 517
Allen, V. G., 111
Altheim, J., 51
Altwerger, B., 16, 22, 51, 554
Amelia Bedelia, 251
America the Beautiful, 364
Amos and Boris, 338, 339, 346
A My Name is Alice, 416
Anastasia Krupnik, 324, 442–443
Ancona, G., 366
Anderson, H., 82
Anderson, K. F., 464
Anderson, P., 85
And Then What Happened, Paul Revere?, 391
Angel Child, Dragon Child, 533, 537
Animals, Animals, 47
Anne Frank: The Diary of a Young Girl, 578, 579, 581
Anno, M., 43
Anno's U.S.A., 43
Antarctica, 363
Anthony, R. J., 26
Applebee, A. L., 217

Applebee, A. N., 5, 57, 316–317, 465, 493–494
Apseloff, M., 418
Archambault, J., 327
Arnold, C., 366
Arthur's Pen Pal, 388
Ashton-Warner, S., 259
Askov, E., 488
Aster Ardvark's Alphabet Adventures, 416
As the Crow Flies, 174
Atwell, N., 36, 50, 51, 55, 173, 347, 500
Atwood, S., 437
Au, K. H., 330
Aunt Harriet's Underground Railroad in the Sky, 365
Ayris, B. M., 483

Babbitt, N., 44, 117, 518
Baghban, M. J. M., 20, 246
Banks, J. A., 514, 532, 543
Bank Street Writer III, 47
Barbe, W. B., 478
Barber, B., 49
Barham, I. H., 220, 494
Barone, D., 172, 173, 174
Barracca, D., 300
Barracca, S., 300
Barrett, J., 501
Barron, R. W., 464
Baskwill, J., 62
Bates, K. L., 364
Baugh, A. C., 284
Bayer, J., 416
Baylor, B., 430, 535
Beasley, K., 533
Beatty, P., 178
Beauty and the Beast, 342
Beaver, J. M., 90
Beers, J. W., 461
Behn, H., 437
Benjamin Franklin, 560
Ben's Dream, 561
Ben's Trumpet, 536
Bentley, E. C., 440

Beowulf, 283
Bernstein, J. E., 412
Berthoff, A. E., 99, 174
Best Wishes, 364
Bewell, D., 175
Bierhorst, J., 535
Bigmama's, 546
The Big Sneeze, 79
Bishop, R. S., 535
Bissex, G. L., 20, 220
Blackburn, E., 347
Blackburn, L. A., 440
Blos, J., 183
Blume, J., 93, 319
"Boa Constrictor," 427
Bode, B. A., 168
Bonin, S., 373
Books in Print, 388
Booth, D., 148, 149
The Borrowed House, 580
Bowser, J., 146
Boy, 47, 364
The Bracelet, 536
Braddock, R., 494
Brady, 178
Brent, R., 85
Brett, J., 79, 342
Brewton, J. E., 440
Bridge, C. A., 255, 385
Bridge to Terabithia, 186, 326
Britton, J., 164, 213
Brooks, C. K., 517
Brown, M., 412
Brown, P. A., 506
Brown, R., 17
Brown Bear, Brown Bear, What Do You See?, 16, 79
Bruner, J. S., 2, 4, 57, 316
Buck, C., 524, 525
"Buffalo Dust," 580
Buffalo Hunt, 44
Bunnicula: A Rabbit-Tale of Mystery, 44, 172, 207, 298, 316, 345
Bunting, E., 533, 546
Burch, R., 322, 324, 327–328
Burke, C. L., 62, 198, 245, 264, 269, 347

Burningham, J., 44
Burris, N., 264
Burt, M., 529
Busching, B. A., 132
Butler, A., 22, 230
Byars, B., 117, 319, 324

Cable, T., 284
Cactus Hotel, 363
Cairney, T., 335, 336, 338, 346, 347
Calkins, L. M., 55, 217, 219–220
Camp, D. J., 16, 138, 139
Caps for Sale, 131
Carle, E., 47, 79, 207, 257, 346, 359, 564
Carousel, 47
Carr, E., 302, 304
Carrick, C., 44, 342
Carroll, L., 297
Caselli, G., 44
Cassie's Journey: Going West in the 1860s, 345
Castle, 44, 366
"Catch a Little Rhyme," 427
Cats Are Cats, 43
Cauley, L. B., 247, 346
Cazden, C. B., 12, 57, 120, 138
A Chair for My Mother, 546
Chang's Paper Pony, 345, 536
Chapman, D. L., 421
Charley Skedaddle, 178
Charlie and the Chocolate Factory, 132, 153
Charlotte's Web, 44, 316, 327, 329–330
Cheng, L. R., 516
Children's Plays from Beatrix Potter, 132
Chin Music: Tall Talk and Other Talk, 295
Chinn, P. C., 532
A Chocolate Moose for Dinner, 292
Choi, S. N., 544
Chomsky, C., 13, 20, 49
Christiansen, J., 61
Christiansen, J. L., 61
Christie, J. F., 494
Chrysanthemum, 346
Cinderella, 328
Cintorino, M. A., 122
The City Mouse and the Country Mouse, 247
Clark, E. V., 13
Clay, M. M., 242, 244, 245
Cleary, B., 44, 183, 387, 484, 577
Clifton, L., 536
Climo, S., 534, 544
Coakley, C. G., 82, 83, 84, 85
Coerr, E., 251, 345, 536
Cohen, B., 345, 534
Cohen, P., 251
Cole, J., 44, 174, 365
Color Zoo, 238
"Come Unto These Yellow Sands," 441
Concrete Is Not Always Hard, 437
Connie Chung: Broadcast Journalist, 534
Conrad, P., 365

The Conversation Club, 123, 157
Cooper, K., 145
Copeland, J. S., 421
Corcoran, B., 335n
Corduroy, 160, 227, 510
Cosman, M. P., 582
Cowcher, H., 363
Cox, C., 154, 335n
Cox, J. A., 294, 295
Crafton, L. K., 50
Crash! Bang! Boom!, 417
Crews, D., 47, 546
The Cricket in Times Square, 576
Cricket Songs, 437, 438
A Cry From the Earth: Music of the North American Indians, 535
Cullinan, B. E., 87, 500, 525
Cummins, J., 521, 528, 529
Cutting, B., 248

Dahl, K. L., 247
Dahl, R., 47, 132, 153, 298, 324, 364
Dale, E., 290
Daniels, H. A., 522
D'Aoust, C., 69
D'Arcy, P., 229
A Dark Dark Tale, 79
D'Aulaires, E. P., 560
D'Aulaires, L., 560
The Day Jimmy's Boa Ate the Wash, 350
Days With Frog and Toad, 573
Dear Mr. Henshaw, 183, 387–388, 577
De Beaugrande, R., 336
De Fina, A. A., 64
Defoe, D., 96
De Ford, D., 316
De Gasztold, C. B., 441–442
DeGroff, L., 47
Dekker, M. M., 172, 173
De Paola, T., 93, 130, 239, 343, 537
Desberg, P., 464
Desert Voices, 430
DeStefano, J. S., 12
Devine, T. G., 82, 85, 99, 108
Dickinson, D. K., 47
Dinner at Aunt Connie's House, 582
Dinosaurs, 430
Dinosaurs All Around: An Artist's View of the Prehistoric World, 366
Do Bananas Chew Gum?, 129
Doctor De Soto, 327, 346, 510
Donnelly, J., 174
Dooley, N., 546
Dorsey-Gaines, C., 243
The Double Life of Pocahontas, 394
Downing, J., 244
Do You Want to Be My Friend?, 346
Dressel, J. H., 316
Dudley-Marling, C., 61
Dulay, H., 529
Durkin, D., 242
Durrell, D. D., 248
Dyson, A. H., 215, 225, 245, 247

Eckes, M., 516, 527, 533
Eckhoff, B., 316
Edelsky, C., 16, 22, 493

Edwards, G., 51
Edwards, P. A., 533
Eeds, M., 127, 129, 205
The Egyptian Cinderella, 534, 544
Ehlert, L., 238, 359
Eight Ate: A Feast of Homonym Riddles, 293, 412
Elbow, P., 185, 494
El Chino, 128, 535
"Eletelephony," 427
Elkin, B., 44
Elley, W. B., 220, 494
Elliott, S., 180
The Encyclopedia About Hermit Crabs, 376
Englert, C. S., 369
The Enormous Crocodile, 298
Erickson, A., 82
Erickson, K. L., 568
Escape From Slavery: The Boyhood of Frederick Douglass in His Own Words, 534
Everybody Cooks Rice, 546

Faigley, L., 219
Faltis, C. J., 518
A Family Apart, 345
Farnan, N., 369
Farnan, S., 264
Farris, P. J., 172
Fawson, P. C., 253
Feelings, M., 364
Feelings, T., 364
Ferruggia, A., 257
Fiddle with a Riddle: Write Your Own Riddles, 412
Fiderer, A., 129
Fielding, L., 85
Fine, E. S., 226
A First Thesaurus, 292
FirstWriter, 49
Fisher, B., 269–270
Fisher, C. J., 418
Fitzgerald, J., 233
Fitzhugh, L., 183
Five, C. L., 172
Fleischman, P., 47, 427, 576
Fleischman, S., 44
Fleming, M., 391, 398
Fleming, R. L., 363
Flexner, S. B., 13, 286
Flood, J., 369
Flores, B., 16, 22, 51, 554
Flossie and the Fox, 253
Flower, L. S., 228
"Fog," 418
Follow the Drinking Gourd, 364, 536
The Fool of the World and the Flying Ship, 342
Forbes, E., 148, 345
Foulke, E., 84
Fowler, A., 207, 251
Fox, M., 79, 253
Fox, P., 327, 345
Fox, S. E., 111
Frager, A., 229
Frank, A., 579
Fraser, I. S., 493

Fraser, M. A., 536
Freedle, R. D., 366
Freedman, R., 44, 362, 364
Freeman, D., 160, 227, 510
Freeman, D. E., 517, 518
Freeman, E. B., 362
Freeman, Y. S., 517, 518
Free Stuff for Kids, 389
Freppon, P. A., 247
Friedman, I. R., 544
Friedman, M., 464
Friend, M., 84, 103, 217n
Frith, U., 464
Fritz, J., 47, 178, 364, 391, 394, 395, 397, 558, 560
Frog and Toad All Year, 573
Frog and Toad Are Friends, 151, 510, 573
Frog and Toad Together, 151, 573
Frog Goes to Dinner, 43
Frogs, Toads, Lizards, and Salamanders, 43
Froman, R., 437
From the Horse's Mouth, 295
"Full of the Moon," 427
Fulwiler, M., 166
Fulwiler, T., 166, 176, 378
Furner, B. A., 488

Gackenback, D., 132
Galdone, P., 79, 148, 253, 257, 328
Gamberg, R., 51, 554
Gambrell, L. B., 168
Garcia, E., 516–517
The Garden of Abdul Gasazi, 278, 560, 561
Gardiner, J. R., 321
A Gathering of Days, 183
Geller, L. G., 410, 415
Genishi, C., 47
Gentry, J. R., 461, 464, 472
George, J. C., 319, 326
George, R. E., 132, 153
Gere, A. R., 234
The Ghost-Eye Tree, 327
Gibbons, G., 44, 363, 366, 573
Gibbons, P., 527, 529
Giblin, J. C., 44
Giff, P. R., 44
Gillet, J. W., 461, 464, 472
Gilson, J., 129, 522, 534
The Gingerbread Boy, 79, 148–149, 253, 257
"The Gingerbread Boy," 417, 570, 571
"The Gingerbread Man," 316
Gingerbread Rabbit, 571
A Girl from Yamhill: A Memoir, 577
The Giving Tree, 555
Glass, R. M., 61
Glenn, C. G., 317
Goba, R. I., 506
Gobble Growl Grunt, 417
Goble, P., 535, 537
The Gold Cadillac, 535
Golden, J. M., 316, 317
"Goldilocks and the Three Bears," 349
Goldstein, B. S., 406
Golenbock, P., 536

Gollnick, D. M., 532
Golub, J., 120
Gonzales, P. C., 527
Goodall, J. S., 43, 581
Goodman, K. S., 2, 26, 36, 62, 524, 525
Goodman, Y. M., 26, 62
Good Morning to You, Valentine, 47
Grahame, K., 149
"Grammar Should Be Taught and Learned in Our Schools," 506
Graves, D. H., 26, 36, 43, 55, 64, 70, 211, 215, 220, 272, 273, 347, 410, 450, 460, 474, 477, 490, 555
Graves, M., 299
The Great Little Madison, 364
Green Eggs and Ham, 238
Greenfield, E., 536
Greenlee, M. E., 385
Greff, K. N., 488
Greisman, J., 292
Groff, P. J., 486
The Grouchy Ladybug, 207, 564
Growing Vegetable Soup, 359
Guarino, D., 79
Guiberson, B. Z., 363
Gwynne, F., 292

Hackney, C., 491
Hadley, E., 351
Hadley, T., 351
Haiku: The Mood of the Earth, 437
Hailstones and Halibut Bones, 434
Hakuta, K., 516–517
Haley-James, S. M., 144, 494
Hall, N., 37
Hall, R., 298
Halliday, M. A. K., 7, 14, 213, 554–555
Hamilton, V., 47
Hancock, J., 560
Hancock, M. R., 172
Hanna, J. S., 246
Hanna, P. R., 246
Hannan, E., 49
Hansen, J., 82, 272, 273, 347, 555
Hanson, J., 293
Hardy, M., 483
Harriet the Spy, 183
Harris, V. J., 536, 537
Harrison, S., 486
Harste, J. C., 198, 245, 264, 269, 347
Hartman, G., 174
Harvey, B., 345, 534
Harwayne, S., 36, 347
Hatti, Tom and the Chicken Witch, 132
Hattie and the Fox, 253
Hayes, J. R., 228
Heald-Taylor, G., 61, 255, 257
Heath, S. B., 2, 120, 243
Hector Lives in the United States Now: The Story of a Mexican American Child, 535
Heller, R., 556
Hello, My Name Is Scrambled Eggs, 522, 534
Henderson, E. H., 461, 463
Henkes, K., 346

Henry, M., 200
Hepler, S., 36
Herman, P., 286
Hewett, J., 535
Hickman, J., 91
Hidi, S., 213
Hiebert, E. H., 385
Hildreth, G., 478
Hildyard, A., 213
Hill, S., 560
Hillerich, R. L., 471
Hillocks, G., Jr., 494
Hipple, M. L., 180
Hirsch, E., 488
Hitchcock, M. E., 362, 464
Hoban, T., 364, 388
Hoberman, M. A., 33, 255
Hobson, C. D., 144
Hodges, M., 581
Hodges, R. E., 246
Hodson, L. M., 493
Holdaway, D., 242, 253, 257
Homographic Homophones, 293
Hood, W. J., 26, 62
Hook, J. N., 285
Hopkins, L. B., 47, 425, 429, 430
Hop on Pop, 257
Horn, E., 246, 468, 474
Horns, Antlers, Fangs, and Tusks, 366
Hornsby, D., 51, 55
Horton, L. W., 485
Horwitz, E. L., 298
Hose, J., 316
Hoskisson, K., 250
The House at Pooh Corner, 418
A House Is a House for Me, 33, 255
The House on Maple Street, 365
How Do Apples Grow?, 366
Howe, D., 44, 172, 207, 298, 316, 345
Howe, J., 44, 172, 207, 298, 316, 345
Howell, H., 486
How Many Days to America? A Thanksgiving Story, 533, 546
How Much Is a Million?, 564
How My Parents Learned to Eat, 544
How Pleasant to Know Mr. Lear!, 440
"How to Eat a Poem," 422, 425
Hoyt-Goldsmith, D., 537
Hudelson, S., 531
Hudson, B. A., 503
The Human Body, 44
Hunt, I., 178
Hunt, J., 364
Hunt, K. W., 498
Hutchings, M., 51
Hutchins, P., 253
Hyman, T. S., 43, 329, 342
Hymes, D., 17

I, Columbus: My Journal 1492–1493, 365
I Am Phoenix, 427
Ida Early Comes over the Mountain, 324
"If I Were in Charge of the World," 442
If You Give a Mouse a Cookie, 346, 349
If You Made a Million, 364
If You Traveled West in a Covered Wagon, 369

I Hate English!, 534
Iktomi and the Boulder, 537
Illuminations, 364
Immigrant Girl: Becky of Eldridge Street, 534
In a Pickle and Other Funny Idioms, 295
In a Spring Garden, 437
"In Defense of Grammar," 506
I Never Saw Another Butterfly, 581
Ingram, D., 13
Inner Chimes: Poems on Poetry, 406
Ira Sleeps Over, 316, 319, 425
Isadora, R., 536
Island of the Blue Dolphins, 319
The Island of the Skog, 346
Is Your Mama a Llama?, 79
It Could Still Be Water, 251
It's a Good Thing There Are Insects, 207
"I Woke Up This Morning," 428

Jabberwocky, 297
Jackson, A. D., 485
Jackson, L. A., 229
Jacobs, J., 571
Jaggar, A. M., 9, 500, 504, 525
Jalongo, M. R., 85
James, J. H., 82
James and the Giant Peach, 153, 324
Jarrell, R., 571
Jepsen, M., 200
Jipson, J., 543
Johnny Appleseed, 128
Johnny-Cake, 571
Johnny Tremain, 148, 345
Johnson, N. S., 317
Johnson, T. D., 26, 321
Johnson, T. E., 474, 475
The Jolly Postman or Other People's Letters, 181, 388, 573
The Josefina Story Quilt, 251
Journey to Topaz, 346, 536, 537, 546
Joyful Noise: Poems for Two Voices, 47, 427, 576
Julie of the Wolves, 319, 326
Jumanji, 43, 51, 316, 327, 446, 560, 561, 562

Kardash, C. A. M., 148
Karnowski, L., 263
Kawakami-Arakaki, A., 264
Kellogg, S., 128, 346, 416
Kendall, F. E., 532
Kennedy, D. M., 47, 415
Kennedy, X. J., 47, 415, 440
Kidder, E. B., 465
Kiefer, B. Z., 570
Kimmel, M. M., 88
King, M., 220
Kingore, B. W., 131
The King's Fountain, 149
The King Who Rained, 292
Kirschner, B. W., 369
Kitagawa, M. M., 74
Klein, A., 483
Klein, M. L., 282

Knight, A. S., 365
Knight, M. B., 365, 546
Knock at a Star: A Child's Introduction to Poetry, 47
Koch, K., 406, 417, 432, 433, 434, 435, 440, 441
Korty, C., 132
Kowalczyk, C., 33
Krashen, S., 519
Kreeft, J., 170
Krogness, M. M., 373
Krohm, B., 250
Krushan, S., 528
Kukla, K., 148, 149
Kulik, C., 251
Kulik, J. A., 251
Kuskin, K., 427
Kutiper, K., 421
Kwak, W., 51

Labbo, L. D., 251
Labov, W., 523
Ladybug, 207
Lamb, H., 220, 494
Lamme, L. L., 483
Landry, D., 82
Langer, J. A., 5, 57, 213, 217, 233, 369, 465
Langford, K. G., 474, 475
Langstaff, J., 414
Lansky, B., 389
Lapp, D., 369
Lara, S. G. M., 520
Larrick, N., 43, 410
Lasky, K., 44, 300
Latrobe, K. H., 132
Lauber, P., 199
Laughlin, M. K., 132
Laurie, R., 132
Law, B., 516, 527, 533
Lear, E., 440
Lee, D. M., 259
Lefevre, C. A., 36, 73
The Legend of the Indian Paintbrush, 537
Legends of the Sun and Moon, 351
Lehr, S. S., 329
L'Engle, M., 327
Lester, H., 305, 339
Levine, E., 369, 534
Levstik, L. S., 570
Lewis, C. S., 44, 174, 316, 329, 560
Lewis, R., 437, 438
Lewis, S., 317
A Light in the Attic, 421
Lim, H. L., 529
Lincoln: A Photobiography, 44, 362, 364
Lindfors, J. W., 9, 13, 36
Lindsay, G. A., 484
The Lion, the Witch and the Wardrobe, 44, 174, 316, 329, 560
The Lion and the Mouse, 339, 346
Lionni, L., 91, 346
Literary Market Place, 388
A Little Pigeon Toad, 293
The Little Red Hen, 257, 328, 342

Little Red Riding Hood, 43, 329, 342
"The Little Turtle," 418
Livingston, M. C., 440
Lloyd-Jones, R., 494
Loban, W., 13, 20–21, 22, 82
Lobel, A., 25, 44, 151, 346, 440, 510, 570–571, 573
Longfellow, H. W., 43, 418
Louie, A., 534, 544
Louis, D. R., 321
Lowry, L., 22, 71, 324, 326, 327, 425, 442
Lukens, R. J., 318, 319, 325, 327, 329, 330
Lundsteen, S. W., 82, 83, 85
"The Lurpp Is on the Loose," 428
Lutz, W., 106
Lyddie, 345

Macaulay, D., 44, 366
MacLachlan, P., 44, 215, 389, 448
Macon, J. M., 175
Maestro, B., 366
Maestro, G., 293
The Magic School Bus Inside the Earth, 365
The Magic School Bus Inside the Human Body, 174
Magic Slate, 49
Maiorano, R., 391
Make Way for Ducklings, 326
Mallon, T., 164
Malone, M., 534
Man and Mustang, 366
Mandler, J. M., 317
Manna, A. L., 132
Many, J. E., 335n, 336
The Many Lives of Benjamin Franklin, 559
Marco Polo: His Notebook, 365
Markham, L. R., 492
Marsh, G., 464
Martin, B., Jr., 16, 79, 327
Martin, F., 534
Martin, N., 229
Martinez, M., 90
Mary Wore Her Red Dress, 238
May, S. A., 533
Mayer, M., 43, 320, 327, 342, 581
Mayers, F. C., 47
McCauley, D. S., 531
McCauley, J. K., 531
McCloskey, R., 326
McCully, E. A., 239
McCurdy, M., 534
McGee, L. M., 246, 335n, 369, 425, 449n, 500, 525, 572
McGinnis, J., 391
McGonegal, P., 176
McGovern, A., 581
McKenzie, G. R., 141
McKenzie, L., 230
McKissack, P. C., 253
McLennan, D., 484
A Medieval Feast, 582
Medieval Holidays and Festivals, 582
Meiners, A., 317

Mellon, J. C., 498
Mercury, 366
Merriam, E., 422, 425, 427
The Mexicans in America, 535
Meyer, B. J., 366
Mickelson, N. I., 26
The Midnight Fox, 117
Milne, A. A., 418
Milone, M. N., 478
Misty of Chincoteague, 200
The Mitten, 79, 342
Mohr, M. M., 217
Mohr, N., 537
*Moja Means One: Swahili Counting
Book,* 364
Mojave, 430
Molly's Pilgrim, 345, 534
Money, 44
More Cricket Songs, 437, 438
Morgan, P., 79
Morimoto, J., 365
Morrice, C., 251
Morrow, L. M., 9, 39, 129
Mortimer, 510
Moss, J. F., 560
Mouse Soup, 346
Mouse Tales, 346
Mrs. Frisby and the Rats of NIMH, 149
*Mufaro's Beautiful Daughters: An
African Tale,* 534, 544
Muggie Maggie, 484
Mullis, I. V. S., 465
"Mummy Slept Late and Daddy Fixed
Breakfast," 418, 428, 429
Munsch, R., 510
Murray, D. H., 211
My Backyard History Book, 145
My Hiroshima, 365
*My Own Rhythm: An Approach
to Haiku,* 437
My Puppy Is Born, 44
The Mysteries of Harris Burdick, 227,
560, 561

Nagy, W. E., 286, 298, 302
The Napping House, 79
Natarella, M. A., 418
Nathan, R., 180, 264
*The National Air and Space Museum
ABC,* 47
Naylor, P. R., 117, 338
Nelson, P. A., 149, 568
Ness, E., 189, 326
Nettie's Trip South, 365–366
Nevin, A., 295
Nevin, D., 295
A New Coat for Anna, 365
The New Kid on the Block, 421
Newkirk, T., 555
*New Providence: A Changing
Cityscape,* 363
Newton, B., 229
Newton, P., 342
Niedermeyer, F. C., 488
"Night Bear," 425
"The Night Before Christmas," 418
Night Noises, 79

Niles, O. S., 366
Nixon, J. L., 345
Noble, T. H., 350
Nodset, J. L., 78
Nothing But the Truth, 117
Nowosad, J., 180
Noyce, R. M., 494
Number the Stars, 22, 71, 326, 327, 425
Numeroff, L., 346, 349
Nystrand, M., 120

O'Brien, R. C., 149
Octopus, 44
O'Dell, S., 178, 319
O'Donnell, R. C., 498
*Off the Map: The Journals of Lewis
and Clark,* 365
Ogle, D. M., 135, 550
Oh, A-Hunting We Will Go, 414
O'Hare, F., 498
Ohlhausen, M. M., 200
Oh Say Can You Say?, 416
Oliver, P., 244
*One Good Horse: A Cowpuncher's
Counting Book,* 364
O'Neill, M., 434
Opie, I., 412, 418
Opie, P., 412, 418
Oppenheim, J., 571
Opposites, 44, 47
O'Rourke, J., 290
Oshiro, M., 264

Padak, N. D., 534, 543, 544, 545
Paley, N., 543
Pallotta, J., 364
Pancakes for Breakfast, 130–131, 239
Papandropoulou, I., 244–245
Pappas, C. C., 362, 570
Parish, P., 251
Parker, M. K., 421
Parker, N. W., 43
Parker, R., 229
Parnall, P., 430
Parry, J., 51, 55
Paterson, K., 186, 326, 345
Paul Revere's Ride, 43, 418
*Paul Robeson: The Life and Times
of a Free Black Man,* 47
Pearson, P. D., 85, 233
*Pedro's Journal: A Voyage with
Christopher Columbus August 3,
1492–February 14, 1493,* 365
Peek, M., 238
Peterson, R., 205
Peyton, J. K., 170
Pezzettino, 91
Phenix, J., 49
Piaget, J., 2, 3, 4, 6, 22–23
Piccolo, J. A., 369
Picnic, 239
A Picture Book of Abraham Lincoln, 47
A Picture Book of Helen Keller, 47
*A Picture Book of Martin Luther King,
Jr.,* 544
The Pied Piper of Hamelin, 581
Pigericks, 440

Pilon, B., 437
The Pinballs, 324
Pinchot, J., 535
Pinkney, A., 543
Pinnell, G. S., 16
Pitcher, E. G., 316
Plants That Never Ever Bloom, 556
Plays from African Folktales, 132
A Pocket for Corduroy, 160
The Polar Express, 501, 561
Pooley, R. C., 493, 505
*The Post Office Book: Mail and How It
Moves,* 44, 573
Potter, B., 69, 316, 318, 343, 348
Prayers From the Ark, 441–442
Preece, A., 26
Prelinger, E., 316
Prelutsky, J., 47, 418, 421, 425, 430
Pressley, M., 121
Progoff, I., 180
Pryor, B., 365
Purple Is Part of a Rainbow, 33
*Put Your Foot in Your Mouth and Other
Silly Sayings,* 295

Queenan, M., 373
Queenie Peavy, 322, 324, 328
Quill, 49
Quorn, K. C., 474, 475

Ramona Quimby, Age 8, 44
Ramona the Pest, 577
Rand, T., 43
*The Random House Book of Poetry
for Children,* 47, 418
*The Random House Dictionary of the
English Language,* 13, 286
Rankin, P. R., 82
Ransome, A., 342
Raphael, T. E., 369
Rasinski, T. V., 534, 543, 544, 545
Rauzon, M. J., 366
Read, C., 461, 463
"The Reading-Writing Relationship:
Seven Instructional Principles," 235
Reardon, S. J., 129
Reimer, K. M., 535
The Relatives Came, 199
Reutzel, D. R., 253
Reyes, M. de la Luz, 170
Rhodes, L. K., 61, 255
Richards, L. E., 427, 564
Richgels, D. J., 246, 369
Rico, G. L., 186
The Riddle of the Rosetta Stone, 44
Rigg, P. S., 517, 531
Ringgold, F., 365, 536, 582
Robin Hood of Sherwood Forest, 581
Robinson Crusoe, 96
Roll of Thunder, Hear My Cry, 324,
346, 533, 536, 582
Roop, C., 365
Roop, P., 362–363, 365
Rose, Where Did You Get That Red?,
406, 407, 440
Rosenblatt, L. M., 84, 86, 97, 198, 199,
205, 335, 362

Roser, N., 90
Rosie's Walk, 253
Roth, S. L., 365
The Rough Face Girl, 534
Rudasill, L., 105
Rudman, M., 543
Rudorf, E. H., 246
Rumelhart, D., 317
Rumpelstiltskin, 325
Rylant, C., 199, 364

The Sacred Path: Spells, Prayers, and Power Songs of the American Indians, 535
Saint George and the Dragon, 581
Salem, J., 176, 562
Sam, Bangs, and Moonshine, 189, 326
Samuels, P., 180
San Jose, C., 568
Sarah, Plain and Tall, 44, 215, 389, 448
Sarah Morton's Day: A Day in the Life of a Pilgrim Girl, 449
Say, A., 128, 535, 537
Scarcella, R., 521
Schickedanz, J. A., 245, 483
Schoer, L., 494
Schubert, B., 176, 562
Schwartz, A., 295, 416
Schwartz, D., 364, 564
Scieszka, J., 227, 328, 510
Scott, A. H., 364
Sebestyen, O., 582
Seeing Earth From Space, 199
Seeing Things, 437
Segel, E., 88
Selden, G., 576
Sendak, M., 43, 247, 316, 338, 348, 448, 510, 518
Seuss, Dr., 200, 207, 238, 257, 416
Seven Candles for Kwanzaa, 543–544
Seyoum, M., 170
Shanahan, T., 234, 235
Shannon, P., 543
Sherman, I., 437
Sherman, T., 250
Shiloh, 117, 338
Short, K., 347
The Show-and-Tell War, 139
Showers, P., 366
Shuy, R. W., 120
Siebert, D., 199, 364, 430
Siegal, A., 580
Sierra, 199, 364
The Sign of the Beaver, 94, 96, 312, 313, 350
Silverstein, S., 421, 427, 555
Simmons, M., 251
Simon, S., 363, 366
Sims, R. B., 88, 535
Sinclair, H., 244–245
The Sixteen Hand Horse, 292–293
Slaughter, J. P., 257
The Slave Dancer, 327, 345
The Sleeping Beauty, 43, 342
Slobodkina, E., 131
Small, R., 506

Smith, F., 2, 3, 6, 14, 19, 33, 219, 233, 504
Smith, J., 139
Smith, L., 250
Smith, L. B., 113
Smith, N. J., 49
Smith, P. L., 84, 98, 103, 362, 369
Smithe, P. C., 483
A Snake Is Totally Tail, 501
A Snake's Body, 174
Sniglets for Kids, 298
Some of the Days of Everett Anderson, 536
Somers, A. B., 560
Sommers, N., 216, 219
A Song in Stone: City Poems, 429
"The Song of Hiawatha," 418
Sorenson, M., 122, 123, 129
Soto, G., 537
Sowell, J., 290
Sowers, S., 373
Speaking of Poets: Interviews With Poets Who Write for Children and Young Adults, 421
Speare, E. G., 94, 312, 319, 326, 345, 350
Spiders, 366
Spier, P., 417
Spivey, E., 243
Stanford, B., 176
Stanley, D., 123, 157
Staton, J., 168, 170
Stauffer, R. G., 259
Steig, W., 44, 51, 327, 338, 346, 510
Stein, N. L., 317
Stennett, R. G., 483
Steptoe, J., 534, 544
Sterne, N., 412
Stevens, J., 181
Stewig, J. W., 120, 148, 425, 427, 465
Sticht, T. G., 82
The Stonecutter, 342
Stone Fox, 321
The Story of a Castle, 43
The Stranger, 561
Strickland, D., 500, 525
Strong, W., 498
"Subway Rush Hour," 418
Sugaring Time, 44, 300
Sukarna, D., 51
Sulzby, E., 242, 245
The Summer of the Swans, 319
Sunstein, B. S., 26
Surat, M. M., 533, 537
Surrounded by Sea: Life on a New England Fishing Island, 363–364
Sylvester and the Magic Pebble, 44, 51

Tacky the Penguin, 305, 339
The Tale of Peter Rabbit, 69, 312, 316, 318, 348
Tales of a Fourth Grade Nothing, 93, 94, 319
"Talking About Writing: The Language of Writing Groups," 234
Tar Beach, 536
Taylor, D., 242, 243

Taylor, K. K., 465
Taylor, M. D., 324, 346, 533, 535, 536, 582
Taylor, R., 47
Teale, W. H., 90, 242, 251
Teammates, 536
Temple, C., 264, 338
Temple, F., 264
Templeton, S., 243, 244, 461
Ten Mile Day and the Building of the Transcontinental Railroad, 536
Terban, M., 293, 295, 412
Terkel, S., 146
Terry, A., 421
Thaiss, C., 554
They've Discovered a Head in the Box of Bread and Other Laughable Limericks, 440
"This Is Just to Say," 418, 440
Thompson, J., 533
The Three Billy Goats Gruff, 181
The Three Little Pigs, 148–149, 328
Through the Looking Glass, 297
Thurber, D. N., 480
Thurber's Many Moons, 131
Tiedt, I., 439
Tierney, R. J., 233
Tompkins, G. E., 84, 98, 103, 138, 139, 217n, 230, 246, 255, 282n, 286, 296, 335n, 362, 369, 425, 449n, 500, 525, 568, 572
"The Tortoise and the Hare," 575
Totem Pole, 537
The Town Mouse and the Country Mouse, 346
Trachtenburg, R., 257
Traxel, J., 543
Treiman, R., 248
Trelease, J., 88–89
Troika, R. C., 520
The True Story of the Three Little Pigs!, 227, 328–329, 510
Tuck Everlasting, 44, 117, 518
Turbill, J., 22, 230
Turner, A., 365
The Turnip, 79
Tutolo, D., 105
Tway, E., 183, 188, 229, 230, 450
26 Letters and 99 Cents, 364
A Twister of Twists, a Tangler of Tongues, 416
Two Bad Ants, 560
The 290, 178
Tyrannosaurus Was a Beast, 47, 430
Tyrannosaurus Wrecks: A Book of Dinosaur Riddles, 412

Uchida, Y., 346, 536, 537, 546
The Ugly Duckling, 320, 321, 327
The Underwater Alphabet Book, 364
Upon the Head of a Goat, 580
Urzua, C., 334, 519, 531

Valentine, S. L., 432
Van Allsburg, C., 43, 51, 128, 227, 278, 316, 327, 416, 446, 501, 560, 561

Van Stockum, H., 580
Vardell, S., 363
Venezky, R. L., 246
The Very Busy Spider, 359
The Very Hungry Caterpillar, 79, 257
Viorst, J., 327, 349, 442
Vogt, M. E., 175
Von Tscharner, R., 363
Vygotsky, L. S., 2, 4, 5, 22, 23, 299

Waber, B., 316, 319, 425
Wagner, B. J., 147, 148, 149, 215
Wagner, H. S., 527
Walker-Dalhouse, D., 536
Walking Talking Words, 437
A Wall of Names, 174
Waters, K., 449
Watson, D. J., 529
Watts, B., 207
The Way West: Journal of a Pioneer Woman, 365
Weaver, C., 198, 499
Webeler, M. B., 255
Weitzman, D., 145
Welcome to the Green House, 364
Wells, D., 127, 129
Wells, G., 362
Welsh, V., 464
Werner, E. K., 82
Whales, 363
What Comes in 2's, 3's and 4's?, 364
What Do You Call a Dumb Bunny? And Other Rabbit Riddles, Games, Jokes, and Cartoons, 412
What Happens to a Hamburger?, 366
What's a Frank Frank?, 293
What's the Big Idea, Benjamin Franklin?, 560
When the Sky Is Like Lace, 298
"Where Go the Boats?," 418
Where the Sidewalk Ends, 421
Where the Wild Things Are, 43, 247, 316, 338, 348, 448, 510, 518

The Whipping Boy, 44
White, E. B., 44, 316, 327
White, T. G., 290
Whitin, D. J., 364, 564
Whitman, P., 62
Who Belongs Here? An American Story, 365, 546
Who Put the Cannon in the Courthouse Square? A Guide to Uncovering the Past, 145
Who Took the Farmer's Hat?, 78, 79
Why Don't You Get a Horse, Sam Adams?, 558
"Why I'll Never Teach Grammar Again," 506
Wilde, S., 364, 464, 471, 472, 564
Wilen, W. W., 135
Wilkinson, L. C., 120, 125
Williams, S. A., 365
Williams, V. B., 546
Williams, W. C., 440
Will You Sign Here, John Hancock?, 47, 364
Wilson, P., 421
Wilt, M. E., 82
The Wind in the Willows, 149
Winograd, P. N., 385
Winter, J., 364, 536
Wishes, Lies, and Dreams, 417
"The Witches' Song," 418
The Witch of Blackbird Pond, 319, 326, 345
Witte, S., 219
Wittels, H., 292
Wittrock, M. C., 120
Wixon, K. K., 302, 304
A Woggle of Witches, 298
Wollman-Bonilla, J. E., 172
Wolvin, A. D., 82, 83, 84, 85
Wong-Fillmore, L., 521
Wood, A., 79
Wood, J. W., 58

Woodward, V. A., 198, 245, 264, 269
"Word Processing in the Grade One Classroom," 49
Words by Heart, 582
Working, 146
Working Cotton, 365
Worlds Apart: The Autobiography of a Dancer From Brooklyn, 391
Worthington, J. E., 560
Wright, C. D., 489
Wright, J. P., 489
Wright, J. R., 43
Wright, L., 148
A Wrinkle in Time, 327
Writing Workshop, 47
Wylie, R. E., 248
Wyllie, M., 220, 494

Yaden, D. B., Jr., 90, 243, 246, 282*n*, 296
Yanagihara, A., 290
Yashima, T., 537
Year of Impossible Goodbyes, 544
Yee, P., 537
Yeh-Shen: A Cinderella Story From China, 534, 544
Yep, L., 537
Yokota, J., 514, 534, 535, 542
Yolen, J., 342, 364
Yopp, H. K., 248
You Can't Catch Me!, 571
Young, E., 339, 346, 537

Zaharias, J. A., 49–50
Zalben, J. B., 297
Zarillo, J., 543
Zarnowski, M., 395, 537
Zelinsky, P. O., 325
Zemach, M., 328, 342
Ziefert, H., 365
Zutell, J., 461
The Z Was Zapped, 416, 560, 561

Subject Index

ABC books, 47, 364, 378, 380, 493
Accommodation, 3–4
Acronyms, 297
Across the curriculum
  literature, 560–563
  math, 562–565
  science, 555–556, 557
  social studies, 556–560
Acrostic poems, 446
Adapting to meet the needs of students
  grammar, 505
  handwriting, 490–491
  journals, 186–187, 189
  language arts, 58–61
  letters, 390
  life-stories, 400
  listening, 111, 112
  poetry, 450, 451
  reading and writing stories, 333–334
  reading process, 210–211
  reports, 400
  spelling, 475, 476
  talk, 125, 126
  words, 307–308
  writing process, 228–229
Advertisements, 104–112, 369,
  562–565
Aesthetic listening
  assessing, 96
  minilessons, 93–96
  strategies, 86–88
  teaching, 91–96
Aesthetic reading, 86, 198–200,
  335–336, 362, 401
Aesthetic talk, 127
Affixes, 8, 10, 289–290, 291, 339
African Americans, literature about,
  536–537, 538
"All about . . ." books, 532, 373–376,
  401
"All about me" books, 391, 392
"All about the author" pages, 222, 224
Alliteration, 416–417
Alphabet, 245–248
Alphabetic principle, 245–246, 460
American cultural groups, literature
  about, 536–542
Anecdotal notes, 62–64, 161

Antonyms, 292
Apology poems, 440–441
Asian Americans, literature about, 537,
  539
Assessment
  aesthetic listening, 96
  anecdotal notes, 62–64
  autobiographies, 400–402
  biographies, 400–402
  checklists, 64, 66, 67, 68, 71, 72, 313
  concept of story, 333–334
  conferences, 64, 65
  critical listening, 112
  efferent listening, 104
  expository text structures, 373
  grading, 70–73
  grammar, 505
  handwriting, 492
  interpretation of stories, 346
  interviews, 146
  invented spelling, 465–467
  journals, 188–190
  letters, 390
  monitoring student progress, 62–64
  observations, 62
  as part of learning, 62
  portfolios, 26–28, 64, 66–70
  readers theatre, 133–134
  reading and responding to poems,
    430
  reports, 382–383
  responding to student writing,
    228–230
  show-and-tell, 140
  spelling, 475–477
  stories students write, 354
  storytelling, 131–132
  talk, 125–127
  tests, 27–28, 61–62
  theme cycles, 583–584
  words, 307–309
  writing poems, 450–452
  writing process, 227, 230, 231
Assimilation, 3–4
Assisted reading, 250–251, 253, 532
Audience for writing, 213
Audiovisual materials, 39, 90, 567,
  595–596

Authors, letters to, 387–388
Authors and illustrators, 591–596
Author's chair, 38, 160, 272–274
Author's corner, 32–33
Author studies, 343
Author units
  Cleary, Beverly, 576, 577
  components of, 32–33
  Lobel, Arnold, 572, 573
  Van Allsburg, Chris, 278–279,
    560–562
Autobiographies, 47, 358–359,
  391–396

Beginning-middle-end, 318–319, 331
Big books, 253, 257, 258–259,
  260–261, 347–348
Bilingual instructional programs,
  517–523
Bilingual students, 510–511, 517–523
Biographies, 47, 394–395, 534
Biography unit, Martin Luther King, Jr.,
  580, 582
Book boxes, 359
Book making, big books, 257,
  258–259, 260–261
Book orientation concepts, 244
Books
  autobiographies, 364, 396
  biographies, 364, 397
  Caldecott Medal winners, 587–589
  grammar concepts, 502
  immigration, 545
  informational, 362–366, 372
  math concepts, 564
  Newbery Medal winners, 589–590
  poems, 418, 419, 420
  student-made, 32–33, 222–224
  word play, 411
Book talks, 143–144
Bound morphemes, 8, 10
Buddy reading, 203, 204, 251, 253, 532
Business letters, 388–389

Caldecott Medal, 44, 89, 587
Centers
  message center, 271–272, 274
  writing center, 271

Chapter books, 43–44
Characters, 322–325
Checklists, 64, 66, 67, 68, 71, 72, 221, 231, 391, 492, 584
Children's Choices, 89
Choosing books to read, 200
Choral reading, 425, 426–428
Cinquain, 438, 449–450
Circle structure of a story, 349–350
Class collaborations, 32, 226–227, 444
Classroom library, 38–40, 543
Clerihews, 440
Clusters, 186–187, 215, 279, 289, 301, 318, 325, 380, 382, 558
Code-switching, 520
Cognitive learning theories, 2
Cognitive structure, 3
Coining words, 297
Color poems, 433–434, 448–449
Commercials, 104–112
Communicative competence, 17
Comparison, 415–416
Compound words, 297
Comprehensible input, 528–529
Computer-assisted instruction, 49
Computers, 47, 49–50
Concept of story, 316–317
Concepts about print, 244
Concrete poems, 418, 436–437
Conferences, 64, 65
Conflict in stories, 319–322, 391
Connecting to literature, 87
Connecting to personal experiences, 87
Contemporary realistic fiction, 46, 534
Context clues, 302, 306
Constructivist learning theories, 2–4
Conventional spelling, 462, 463–464
Conversations
    characteristics of, 120–121
    guidelines for conducting, 122
    about literature, 127–129
    roles of speakers and listeners, 122
    teaching strategy, 123–125
    during theme cycles, 134–136
    types of, 123
Copy books, 490
Counting books, 364
Courtesy letters, 387
Critical listening
    assessing, 112
    minilessons, 95, 112
    teaching, 108–112
Cross-age reading buddies, 251, 253
Cultural diversity, teaching about, 513, 543–546
Culturally conscious literature, 534–543
Culturally diverse students, 514–515
Cultural pluralism, 514–517
Culture, 2, 8–9, 514–517
Cursive handwriting, 480

Data charts, 380, 382
Debates, 146–147
Descriptive words, 412, 413
Dialects, 9, 493, 523

Dialogue journals, 165, 168–170, 173–174, 511
Diamante, 439
Dictionary, 281, 302, 469–470
Directed Listening-Thinking Approach (DLTA), 92
Direction concepts, 244
Discriminative listening, 84
Disequilibrium, 3–4
D'Nealian handwriting, 480
Double-entry journals, 174–176
Doublespeak, 106
Drafting, 215–216
Dramatic activities, dramatizations of words, 300
Dramatic play centers, 39, 271, 272–273

Easy-to-read books, 251, 252
Editing, 219–222
Efferent listening
    assessing, 104
    minilessons, 95
    strategies for, 97–102
    teaching, 102–104
Efferent reading, 198–200, 362, 401
Efferent talk, 134
Elements of legibility, 491–492
Elements of story structure
    beginning-middle-end, 318–319, 331
    characters, 322–325, 332
    diagrams and charts, 318, 321, 322, 325, 331–332, 350
    plot, 317–322, 331–332
    point of view, 327–329, 332
    setting, 325–327, 332
    theme, 329–330, 332
Emergent literacy
    assisted reading, 250–251, 253
    author's chair, 272–274
    book orientation concepts, 244
    characteristics of, 242
    compared with learning to talk, 242
    compared with readiness, 240–241, 242
    concepts about the alphabet, 245–248
    concepts about words, 244–245
    easy-to-read books, 251–252
    environmental print, 245
    guidelines, 597–599
    kid writing, 265, 267
    language experience approach, 259, 262–264
    letter names, 246–247
    morning message, 264
    opportunities for writing, 268–274
    phonics, 247–248, 249
    predictable books, 255, 257, 258–259
    reading buddies, 251, 253
    stages of reading development, 248
    writing in journals, 180–181, 182
    written language concepts, 243–248
Emergent reading, 248–264
Emergent writing, 264–274
English-only movement, 522–523

Environmental print, 245
Equilibration, 3–4
Equilibrium, 3–4
ESL instructional programs, 525–531, 532
ESL students, 517–523
Etymologies, 285–286
Expository text structures, 98, 100, 366–369, 401

Fables, 45
Fantasies, 45–46
Fantastic stories, 45–46
Figurative meanings, 415–416
Film scripts, 154–157
Filmstrips, 428–429
Five-senses poems, 434
Folktales and fairy tales, 45–46, 342–343, 344, 534
Forms for writing, 213–214
Found poems, 437, 449
Free morphemes, 8, 10
Free verse, 418, 436, 448
Friendly letters, 383, 385

Genre, 43
Genre units, 339, 340–343, 350–351
Goldilocks strategy, 200, 202
Grades, 70–73, 190
Grammar
    compared with usage, 493
    concept books, 501
    influence on writing, 504–505
    instruction, 494, 499, 500–505
    minilessons, 500–501
    parts of sentences, 495
    parts of speech, 495, 501
    sentence combining, 498–499
    sentence types, 495
    structural grammar, 495–497
    traditional grammar, 495
    transformational grammar, 497–500
    types of, 495–500
    values for teaching, 494
Grand conversations, 205
Graphemes, 7, 10, 245–248
Graphic organizers, 98, 100, 367–368, 369, 370–371
Grouping for instruction, 583
Guided reading, 203, 204
Guides for choosing literature, 89

Haiku, 418, 437–438
Handedness, 486
Handwriting
    before first grade, 480–481, 483
    children's development, 480–487
    compared with writing, 477
    cursive form, 480
    D'Nealian form, 480
    elements of legibility, 491–492
    fluency, 477
    forms, 478–480
    goals of, 477
    instruction, 483, 488–490
    left-handed writers, 485–487
    legibility, 477

manuscript form, 478–480
  in the middle and upper grades, 485
  in the primary grades, 483–484
  public versus private, 485
  transition to cursive, 484–485
  types of paper, 483–484
  writing instruments, 483
High fantasy, 45–46
Hink-pinks, 415
Hispanic Americans, literature about, 537, 540
Historical fiction, 46, 345–346, 534
History of the English language, 246, 283–287
Homonyms, 292–293

Idioms, 294–295, 308
"If I were . . ." poems, 434–435
"If I were in charge of the world . . ." poems, 442
Independent reading, 203–205
Informational books, 43, 44, 361–366, 372, 535
Instructional approaches
  benefits and drawbacks, 35
  literature focus units, 50–51
  reading and writing workshops, 51–52, 55–57
  theme cycles, 51
Instructional materials, 36–37
International Reading Association, 28–29
Interpretation, 198, 335–339
Intertextuality, 336–338, 347
Interviews, 144–146
Invented spelling, 245–248, 465–467, 511, 532
Invitation poems, 441
". . . is" poems, 435
"I used to . . ./But now . . ." poems, 435, 450
"I wish . . ." poems, 433

Jokes, 410
Journals
  buddy journals, 173–174
  dialogue journals, 165, 168–170, 173–174
  diaries versus journals, 164
  double-entry journals, 174–176
  examples from literature, 183, 184
  historical personalities, 164
  learning logs, 165, 176–178
  with Limited English Proficient students, 170
  personal journals, 165, 166–168
  public versus private writing, 166
  purposes of, 163
  reading logs, 160–161, 165
  sharing, 160–161
  simulated journals, 165, 178, 180
  types of, 164–166
  writing notebooks, 165, 170–171

Kid spelling, 461
Kid writing, 62, 78, 161, 265, 267
KWL charts, 135–136, 137

Lab reports, 176–177, 178, 557
Language
  development in the elementary grades, 12–14, 20–21
  functions of, 14, 15, 16, 243–244
  preschool stages of development, 9, 11–12
  second language acquisition, 519
Language arts
  definition of, 17
  impact of culture on, 515–517
  as learning tools, 554–555
  magazines and journals about, 28–29
  modes of, 17–21
  teaching paradigm, 21–25
Language experience approach (LEA), 259, 262–264, 532
Language functions, 243–244
Language-rich classroom, 36–42
Language systems, 7–9
Learning, 1, 2–7
Learning logs
  math, 176
  science, 176–177
  social studies, 177–178
Learning modes, 5–7
Left-handed writers, 485–487
Legends, 45
Letter concepts, 245–248
Letter names, 246–247
Letters
  assessment, 390
  to authors and illustrators, 387–388
  business letters, 388–389
  courtesy letters, 387
  formats for, 383, 384
  friendly letters, 383, 385
  guidelines for writing to authors, 387–388
  pen pal letters, 385–386
  simulated letters, 389
Library center, 38–40
Life-long readers, 315
Life-stories
  autobiographies, 391–393
  biographies, 393–396
  books of, 396–397
Limericks, 418, 439–440
Limited English Proficient (LEP) students, 60–61, 79, 170, 510–511, 517–523
Linguistically diverse students, 517–522, 525–532
Listening
  across the curriculum, 97–112
  paying attention, 83
  process of, 82–84
  purposes for, 84–85
  strategies, 85, 86–88
  teaching versus practice, 85
Listening center, 38, 40–41, 203, 532, 566
Literacy club, 33
Literal meanings, 415–416
Literary opposites, 338–339
Literature conversations
  benefits of, 129

grand conversations, 127
  open-ended questions, 128–129
  steps in, 127–128
Literature focus units
  Anne Frank: Diary of a Young Girl, 578, 579–581
  Bunnicula: A Rabbit-Tale of Mystery, 207, 209, 343
  components of, 50–51
  Corduroy, 160–161
  fables, 574–576
  folktales, 342–343, 344
  "The Gingerbread Boy," 570–571
  A House Is a House for Me, 255–256
  using multicultural literature, 543–546
  Number the Stars, 22, 23, 71, 72
  using poetry, 425–430, 446, 448–449
  the reading process, 207, 209
  reading stories during, 339–343
  role-playing, 148–149
  The Sign of the Beaver, 94, 96, 312–313
  Tacky the Penguin, 305–307, 339, 341
  Tales of a Fourth Grade Nothing, 93–94
  teaching words in, 299, 305–307
  Van Allsburg, Chris, 278–279, 560–562
  the writing process, 227
  writing stories during, 347–351

Mailboxes, 271–272, 274
Manuscript handwriting, 478, 480
"Me" boxes, 358–359
Mechanical errors, 219–220
Message center, 38, 271–272, 274
Metalinguistics, 243
Metaphor, 415
Middle English, 284
Minilessons
  aesthetic listening, 93–96
  critical listening, 95, 112
  drama, 124
  efferent listening, 95, 102–103
  grammar, 473, 500–501
  handwriting, 473, 488
  informational books, 398–400
  journals, 174, 184, 185
  language arts, 52
  letter writing, 398–400
  life-stories, 398–400
  poetry, 445–447
  reading process, 205, 207, 208
  spelling, 471, 473
  stories, 330–333
  talk, 123–125
  teaching strategy, 50–51
  words, 302, 304
  writing process, 227
Minimal distance principle, 13
Modern English, 284–285
Modern literary tales, 45
Monitoring, 98
Morning message, 264

Morphemes, 8, 10, 286–290
Multicultural classrooms, 533–534
Multicultural literature, 534, 535–536
Myths, 45, 351

Narrative poems, 418
National Council of Teachers of
    English, 28–29
National Writing Project, 28–29
Native Americans, literature about,
    537, 541
Newbery Medal, 44, 89, 589
Nonstandard English, 9, 10, 523–525
Note-taking and note-making, 99, 101

Old English, 283–284
Onomatopoeia, 417
Onsets, 248, 249
Open-mind portraits, 339, 340
Oral reports, 140–144
Outlining, 99

Parts of speech, 435–436, 495, 501
Pen pal letters, 385–386
Personal journals, 165, 166–168
Persuasion, 105–108, 369
Phoneme-grapheme correspondences,
    247–248, 460
Phonemes, 7, 10, 245–248
Phonemic awareness, 247–248
Phonetic spelling, 462, 463
Phonics
    the alphabetic principle, 245–246
    instruction, 245–248, 249
    onsets and rimes, 248, 249
    phonemic awareness, 247–248
    word identification, role in, 302
Phonological system, 7, 10
Physical arrangement of the classroom,
    37–42
Picture books, 43
Plagiarism, 229–230, 380–381
Play scripts, 153–154, 155–156
Plot, 317–322
Plot diagram, 321
Plot profile, 321, 322
Poetic devices, 415–417
Poetry
    adult poems suitable for children,
        418, 420
    assessment, 430
    children's favorite poems, 421, 422,
        425
    choral reading, 425, 426–428
    formula poems, 432–436
    free-form poems, 436–437
    guidelines for reading poems, 425,
        426
    guidelines for writing poetry, 445
    in literature focus units, 425–430,
        446, 448–449
    model poems, 407, 440–442
    multicultural books of, 535
    poems children read, 47, 418–422
    poets who write for children, 421,
        423–424
    projects, 428–430
    reading poems aloud, 425, 426

in reading workshop, 425
    rhymed verse forms, 439–440
    syllable- and word-count poems, 437
    in theme cycles, 430, 431
    types of poetry books, 418–420
    ways to respond to poems, 428
    writing workshop, 446
Poets, 421, 423–424
Point of view, 327–329
Portfolios, 26–28, 64, 66–70
Portmanteau words, 297
Pragmatic system, 7, 8–9, 10
Prayers from the ark poems, 441–442
Precommunicative spelling, 461–463
Predictable books, 255, 257, 258–259
Prediction, 4
Prefixes, 8, 10, 289–290, 291
Preposition poems, 435–436
Prewriting, 211, 213–215
Prior knowledge for reading, 200
Projects, 51, 53–54, 227–228, 337,
    428–430, 568–569
Proofreading, 220–222, 468–469,
    477
Propaganda devices, 106, 107
Propaganda, 105–108
Props in dramatic play centers, 271,
    272–273
Psycholinguistic learning theories, 2, 4,
    198
Publishing, 222–226
Punctuation marks, 219–220
Puppets, 151–153

Questions, 128–129, 134–135
Quickdraws, 532
Quickwriting, 184–186, 215
Quiet classrooms, 119

Readers theatre, 132–134
Readiness, 241–242
Reading aloud to students, 88–89,
    203, 204
Reading logs, 171–174, 205, 279
Reading poems, 418–431
Reading process
    compared with writing process, 197,
        198, 230–234
    features of, 201
    stages of, 200–206
    teaching strategy, 206–209
    types of reading, 203–205
Reading stories, 334–346
Reading workshop
    components of, 51–52, 55, 343,
        345
    schedules for, 55
    using poetry, 425
    using the reading process, 208–209
Realistic stories, 46
Reference books, 302, 566
Reference center, 39
Registers, 17
Rehearsal activities, 215
Repeated readings, 90
Repetition, 257, 258–259, 417
Repetitive books, 78–79, 257,
    258–259

Reports
    "All about . . ." books, 373–376
    assessment, 382–383
    book talks, 143–144
    collaborative reports, 376–378
    individual reports, 378
    interviews, 144–146
    oral reports, 140–144
    question-and-answer books, 378
    young children's reports, 373–376
Rereading, 205
Research questions, 379–380,
    381–382
Resources for teachers, 28–29
Retelling stories, 532
Revising, 216–219
Rhyme, 257, 258–259, 409, 410,
    413–415, 432
Riddles, 410, 412, 415
Rimes, 248, 249
Role-playing, 148–151, 215, 532
Root words, 278–279, 282–283,
    286–289
Rough drafts, 216

Scaffold, 4, 57
Schemata, 3
Science fiction, 46
Scriptwriting, 153–154, 157
Selective tradition, 543
Semantic feature analysis, 302, 303
Semantic system, 7, 8, 10
Semiphonetic spelling, 462, 463
Sentence combining, 498–499
Setting, 325–327
Shared reading, 203, 204, 253–255,
    257
Show-and-tell, 136–140
Sign-in sheets, 269–271
Simile, 415
Simulated journals, 165, 178, 180
Simulated letters, 389
Skills, 1, 22
Sniglets, 289
Social interaction, 4, 8–9
Sociolinguistic learning theories, 2, 4,
    198
Sounding out words, 246–247
Spelling
    comparison of good-poor spellers,
        464–465
    invented spelling, 460–467
    reading-spelling connection, 468
    strategies, 470–471, 476
    tool for writers, 460
Spelling conscience, 471–472
Spelling development, older students',
    460–465
Spelling instruction
    components of, 467–472
    dictionary procedure, 469–470
    individualized approach, 464–465,
        467
    minilessons, 471, 473
    most frequently used words, 469
    proofreading, 468–469, 477
    reading, 468
    spelling options, 470–471

strategies, 470–471, 476
tests, 464–465, 467
weekly tests, 472, 473–475
word study procedures, 474
word walls, 278, 299–300, 308, 468, 532
writing, 468
Spelling options, 470–471, 601–602
Spelling strategies, 470–471, 476
Standard English, 9, 10
Stories
    chapter books, 43–44
    compared with informational books, 361, 362
    fantasies, 45–46
    picture books, 43
    predictable books, 255, 257, 258–259
    for readers theatre, 133
    realistic stories, 46
    for storytelling, 130
    traditional literature, 45
    types of, 43, 45–46
    using the four language modes, 20, 21
Storyboards, 109, 110, 154, 157, 279, 340
Story boxes, 340, 359
Story map, 327, 328, 340
Story quilts, 340
Story structure, 87–88
Storytelling, 129–132
Structural analysis of words, 302
Structural grammar, 495–497
Suffixes, 8, 10, 289–290, 291
Synonyms, 290
Syntactic system, 7, 8, 10

Talk, 18–19, 120–121
Talk to the animals poems, 406–407
Tanka poems, 438
Teaching strategy
    aesthetic listening strategies, 93–94
    assisted reading, 250–251, 253
    book talks, 143–144
    commercials and advertisements, 108–112
    efferent listening, 103–104
    expository text structures, 369, 373
    fables, 24, 26–27
    handwriting, 488
    interviews, 144
    introducing students to poetry, 421–422
    journals, 181, 183–186
    language experience approach, 262–263
    letter formation, 489
    literature conversations, 127–128
    minilessons, 50–51
    oral reports, 141–142
    paradigm, 23–24
    quotation marks, 25, 26–27
    readers theatre, 132–133
    reading aloud, 91–93
    revising writing, 218–219
    shared reading, 255
    story elements, 330–333

storytelling, 129–131
vocabulary, 299, 304–305
writing biographies and autobiographies, 396–398
writing class collaboration reports, 378–381
writing individual reports, 381–382
writing letters, 389–390
writing poetry, 442–446
Temporary spelling, 461
Tests, 27–28, 71–73, 309, 464–465, 467
Text, 198
Textbooks, 42–43, 474, 494, 568
Text sets, 32, 47, 48, 253, 254, 337–338
Theatrical productions, 148, 153–157
Theme, 329–330
Theme cycles
    American Revolution, 48, 63, 400, 450
    assessing students' learning, 583–584
    bears, 299
    benefits of, 554
    birds, 186, 187
    characteristics of, 554
    city and country life, 78–79
    Civil War, 178
    compared with thematic units, 554
    components of, 51
    conversations, 134–136
    desert, 22, 25
    dinosaurs, 378, 379
    hermit crabs, 71, 72, 376–379
    human body, 71–73, 378–381
    insects, 207–208, 575, 576–577
    instructional activities, 582–583
    interviews, 144
    KWL charts, 135–136, 137
    learning logs, 176–178
    Martin Luther King, Jr., 299
    mice, 346
    Middle Ages, 378–381, 579, 581–582
    multicultural literature, using, 543–546
    Native Americans, 312–313
    Pilgrims, 150
    projects, 568–569
    questioning strategies, 134–135
    reading poetry, 430, 431
    the reading process, 207–208
    reading stories, 345–346
    resources for developing, 565–570
    rivers, 103–104
    role-playing, 149–151
    sending and receiving mail, 571, 573
    solar system, 185
    teaching words during, 299
    using textbooks, 568
    whales, 550–551
    writing poetry, 449–450
    the writing process, 227–228
    writing stories, 351–352
Therapeutic listening, 84, 85
Thesaurus, 302
Tongue twisters, 416–417

Topics for writing, 211, 213
Trade books, 43–47
Trademarks, 297
Traditional grammar, 495
Traditional literature, 45
Transactive processes, 198
Transformational grammar, 497–500
Transitional spelling, 462, 463
Traveling bags of books, 239–240, 253, 254
Triangulation, 73

Usage, 493

Video scripts, 154, 157
Vocabulary, 8, 13–14, 205. *See also* Words

Word, as unit of language, 244–245
Word chains, 302
Word clusters, 300, 301
Word histories, 285–286
Wordless picture books, 43
Word pictures, 412–413
Word play, 297–298, 410–413
Word posters, 300
Word-processing, 47, 49
Words
    antonyms, 292
    borrowed words, 285, 295–297
    clipping, 297–298
    coining, 297
    compound words, 297
    deceptive language, 106
    doublespeak, 106
    etymologies, 285–286
    euphemisms, 106
    guidelines for instruction, 299, 302, 304
    homographic homophones, 292–293
    homographs, 292
    homophones, 292
    idioms, 294–295, 308
    inflated language, 106
    loaded words, 105
    locating in a dictionary, 469–470
    minilessons on, 302, 304
    most frequently used, 469
    multiple meanings, 13–14, 293–294, 308
    overused, 171
    ownership dictionary, 282, 298
    root words and affixes, 278–279, 282–283, 286–291
    semantic feature analysis, 302, 303
    synonyms, 290
    word chains, 302
    word sorts, 300, 308
    word study activities, 279, 299–305
    word walls, 278, 299–300, 308
    young children's concepts about, 244–245
Word sorts, 300, 302
Word study activities, 279, 299–305
Word walls, 278, 299–300, 308, 468, 532
Workbooks and worksheets, 22, 50–51
Worksheets, 346

Writing, functions of, 213
Writing centers, 38–42, 271
Writing groups, 217–219
Writing notebooks, 170–171
Writing poetry, 432–452
Writing process
  adapting for emergent writers, 268,
    270
  compared with language experience
    approach, 263–264
  compared with reading process, 197,
    198, 230–234
  features of, 212
  to make books, 32–33
  stages of, 211–226
Writing stories, 316, 347–354
  genre stories, 350–351
  making big books, 347–348

  myths, 351
  pattern stories, 349
  point of view stories, 349
  retellings of stories, 347–350
  sequels, 350
Writing welfare, 211
Writing workshop
  components of, 55–57, 194–195,
    228
  on poetry, 446
  schedules for, 55
  writing stories during, 352–354
Written language concepts, 243–248

Young children
  author's chair, 272–274
  concepts about written language,
    243–248

  dramatic play centers, 271, 272–273
  drawing for writing, 161
  message center, 271–272, 274
  personal journals, 180–181, 182
  phonics, 245–248
  reading, 248–264
  reading logs, 160–161, 180–181
  sign-in sheets, 269–271
  writing, 264–274
  writing autobiographies, 391–393
  writing center, 271
  writing in journals, 160–161,
    180–181, 182
  writing letters, 387, 388
  writing reports, 373–376

Zone of proximal development, 4

C H A P T E R 1

Learning and the Language Arts

How Children Learn

The Cognitive Structure
The Process of Learning
Social Contexts for Learning
Implications for Learning Language Arts

How Children Learn Language

The Four Language Systems
Stages of Language Development
Development in the Elementary Grades
Implications for Learning Language Arts

How Children Learn Language Arts

Communicative Competence
The Four Language Modes
A Paradigm for Language Arts Instruction
A Teaching Strategy
Assessing Students' Learning
Resources for Teachers

Terms

constructivist learning theories

psycholinguistic learning theories

sociolinguistic learning theories

schemata

assimilation

accommodation

equilibration

zone of proximal development

scaffold

phonological system

phoneme

grapheme

syntactic system

grammar

morpheme

semantic system

dialect

standard English

nonstandard English

language functions

communicative competence

registers

language modes

Key Concepts

1. Language arts instruction should be based on how children learn and how they learn language.

2. Students learn through immersion in listening, talking, reading, and writing activities.

3. Students need opportunities to participate in language arts activities that are meaningful, functional, and genuine.

4. Two ways to make language arts instruction meaningful are to connect it with literature focus units and social studies and science theme cycles.

5. Students learn through demonstrations—with modeling and scaffolding—that teachers provide.

6. Students become more self-reliant when they make choices about the language arts activities in which they are involved.

7. Students learn more confidently when they understand that teachers do not expect correctness but improvement by trial and error.

8. Students are more likely to be successful when teachers expect them to be successful.

9. A teaching strategy should include initiating, structuring, conceptualizing, summarizing, generalizing, and applying components.

10. Portfolios with a collection of students' language arts samples are an effective way to assess learning.

Teaching Language Arts

Language-Rich Classrooms

The Physical Arrangement

Textbooks

Trade Books

Computers

Instructional Approaches

Literature Focus Units

Theme Cycles

Reading-Writing Workshops

Adapting to Meet the Needs of Every Student

Assessing Students' Learning

Monitoring Students' Progress

Collecting Students' Work in Portfolios

Assigning Grades

Terms

language-rich classrooms

picture books

chapter books

stories

traditional literature

fantasies

realistic fiction

informational books

biographies

ABC books

poems

text sets

literature focus units

minilessons

projects

theme cycles

reading workshop

writing workshop

kid watchers

anecdotal notes

conferences

portfolios

triangulation

Key Concepts

1. Elementary classrooms should be authentic learning environments that encourage students to listen, talk, read, and write.

2. Textbooks should never be equivalent to the total language arts program.

3. Teachers collect three types of trade books—stories, informational books, and poems—for text sets related to literature focus units and theme cycles.

4. Literature focus units include four components: reading books, responding, teaching minilessons, and creating projects.

5. Theme cycles are interdisciplinary units that integrate language arts with social studies, science, math, and other curricular areas.

6. Language arts activities during theme cycles include keeping learning logs, reading books, and creating projects.

7. Reading workshop components are teaching minilessons, reading and responding, and sharing; writing workshop components are teaching minilessons, writing, and sharing.

8. Teachers play many roles during language arts activities, including scaffolds, models, and instructors.

9. Students with special learning needs benefit from the same language arts content and teaching strategies that other students do, given some adaptations.

10. Assessment is an integral part of teaching, and teachers assess students' learning using observations and anecdotal notes, conferences, checklists, portfolios, and tests.

C H A P T E R 3

Listening to Learn

The Listening Process
Steps in the Listening Process
Purposes for Listening
Teaching Listening Strategies

Listening to Literature
Aesthetic Listening
Teaching Aesthetic Listening
Assessing Students' Aesthetic Listening

Listening Across the Curriculum
Efferent Listening
Teaching Efferent Listening
Assessing Students' Efferent Listening
Critical Listening
Teaching Critical Listening
Assessing Students' Critical Listening

Terms

hearing

listening

listening process

discriminative listening

aesthetic listening

efferent listening

critical listening

therapeutic listening

Directed Listening-Thinking Approach
(DLTA)

graphic organizers

note-taking

note-taking and note-making

outlining

persuasion

propaganda

loaded words

doublespeak

euphemisms

inflated language

commercials

advertisements

Key Concepts

1. Listening is the neglected language art because it is rarely taught; instead, teachers admonish students to listen or merely provide practice activities.

2. Listening is a three-step process: receiving, attending, and assigning meaning.

3. Five purposes for listening are: discriminative, aesthetic, efferent, critical, and therapeutic listening.

4. Students listen aesthetically as teachers read stories aloud, view puppet shows and plays, and watch film versions of stories.

5. The Directed Listening-Thinking Approach (DLTA) is one way to actively involve students in aesthetic listening.

6. During theme cycles, students use efferent listening to remember information and critical listening to evaluate a message.

7. Students need to learn to use listening strategies to enhance their listening abilities.

8. Teachers introduce listening strategies during minilessons and then provide opportunities for students to use the strategies during literature focus units and theme cycles.

9. Students need to learn to listen critically because they are exposed to many types of persuasion and propaganda.

10. Students apply what they learning about persuasion and propaganda as they create commercials and advertisements.

C H A P T E R 4

Sustaining Talk in the Classroom

Conversations

Guidelines for Conducting Conversations

Types of Conversations

Teaching Students to Talk in Small Groups

Teaching Minilessons on Talk

Adapting to Meet the Needs of Every Student

Assessing Students' Talk

Aesthetic Talk

Conversations About Literature

Storytelling

Readers Theatre

Efferent Talk

Conversations During Theme Cycles

Show-and-Tell

Oral Reports

Interviews

Debates

Dramatic Activities

Role-playing

Puppets and Other Props

Scriptwriting and Theatrical Productions

Terms

conversations
aesthetic talk
grand conversations
literature conversations
open-ended questions
storytelling
props
readers theatre
efferent talk
KWL chart
show-and-tell
oral reports
cluster
data chart
book talks
interviews
impromptu debate
formal debate
drama
role-playing
stick puppets
paper bag puppets
cylinder puppets
sock puppets
cup puppets
paper plate puppets
cloth puppets
play scripts
storyboards

Key Concepts

1. Talk is a necessary ingredient for learning.

2. Students talk in informal conversations as part of literature focus units and theme cycles.

3. Students participate in many types of small group conversations, and they use talk for both aesthetic and efferent purposes.

4. In literature discussions, or grand conversations, students use aesthetic talk to respond to a book and develop interpretations.

5. In storytelling and readers theatre activities, students use aesthetic talk to present stories.

6. KWL charts are a good way to help students talk about what they are learning in a theme cycle.

7. In show-and-tell, oral reports, interviews, and debates, students use efferent talk to inform and persuade listeners.

8. Drama is not only a powerful form of communication but also a valuable way of knowing.

9. Students use role-playing and puppets to learn and share their learning in literature focus units and in theme cycles.

10. In connection with literature focus units and theme cycles, students can write scripts that they present as a play or on videotape.

C H A P T E R 5

Writing in Journals

Types of Journals

Personal Journals

Dialogue Journals

Writing Notebooks

Reading Logs

Learning Logs

Simulated Journals

Young Children's Journals

Teaching Students to Write in Journals

Introducing Students to Journal Writing

Sustaining Journal Writing

Adapting to Meet the Needs of Every Student

Assessing Students' Journal Entries

Terms

journals

personal journals

dialogue journals

writing notebooks

reading logs

double-entry journals

learning logs

simulated journals

quickwriting

clusters

Key Concepts

1. Students write in six kinds of journals: personal journals, dialogue journals, writing notebooks, reading logs, learning logs, and simulated journals.

2. Dialogue journals are especially useful for students learning English as a second language.

3. Reading logs and simulated journals are used when reading literature.

4. Learning logs and simulated journals are used across the curriculum.

5. Even young children can draw and write in personal journals and reading logs.

6. Teachers teach minilessons about how to write in journals.

7. Students often share entries with classmates, although personal journal entries are often private.

8. Two strategies that students use as they write in journals are quickwriting and clustering.

9. Teachers monitor students' writing in journals by reading selected entries, not by correcting misspelled words and other mechanical errors.

10. The focus in journal writing is on developing writing fluency and using writing as a tool for learning.

C H A P T E R 6

The Reading and Writing Processes

The Reading Process

Aesthetic and Efferent Reading

Stage 1: Preparing to Read

Stage 2: Reading

Stage 3: Responding

Stage 4: Exploring the Text

Stage 5: Extending the Interpretation

Teaching the Reading Process

The Writing Process

Stage 1: Prewriting

Stage 2: Drafting

Stage 3: Revising

Stage 4: Editing

Stage 5: Publishing

Teaching the Writing Process

Connections Between Reading and Writing

Comparing the Two Processes

Classroom Connections

Terms

text

meaning

interpretation

the reading process

aesthetic reading

efferent reading

Goldilocks strategy

previewing

reading aloud

shared reading

buddy reading

guided reading

independent reading

writing process

prewriting

audience

functions of writing

forms of writing

drafting

revising

writing groups

editing

proofreading

mechanics of writing

publishing

Key Concepts

1. Students use aesthetic reading when they read for enjoyment and efferent reading when they read for information.

2. The five stages of the reading process are: preparing to read, reading, responding, exploring the text, and extending the interpretation.

3. Five ways to read a text are: listening as it is read aloud, shared reading, buddy reading, guided reading, and independent reading.

4. During the exploring stage, students reread, examine the author's craft, learn new words, and participate in minilessons.

5. Students use the reading process during literature focus units, theme cycles, and reading workshop.

6. The five stages of the writing process are: prewriting, drafting, revising, editing, and publishing.

7. Function, form, and audience are three considerations that influence students' compositions.

8. Students use the writing process as they write during literature focus units, theme cycles, and writing workshop.

9. Teachers do not always grade students' finished compositions; instead, they can assess students' use of the writing process.

10. The goal of both reading and writing is to construct meaning, and both processes have comparable activities at each stage.

CHAPTER 7

Emergent Literacy

Concepts About Written Language
Concepts About the Functions of Language
Concepts About Print
Concepts About Words
Concepts About the Alphabet

Young Children Emerge Into Reading
Assisted Reading
Shared Reading
Language Experience Approach

Young Children Emerge Into Writing
Introducing Young Children to Writing
Opportunities for Writing

Key Concepts

1. English is a historic language, and its diverse origins account for word meanings and some spelling inconsistencies.

2. Students' vocabularies grow at a rate of about 3,000 words a year.

3. Students use their knowledge of root words and affixes to unlock the meaning of unfamiliar words.

4. Many words have more than one meaning, and students learn additional word meanings through literature focus units and theme cycles.

5. Idioms can be confusing to students because they must be interpreted figuratively rather than literally.

6. Reading and writing are the most important ways students learn vocabulary.

7. Students need to use a word many times before it becomes part of their ownership dictionary.

8. All words are not equally hard or easy to learn; the degree of difficulty depends on what the student already knows about the word.

9. Students use phonics, structural analysis, context clues, and reference books to learn the meanings of words.

10. Word study activities include word walls, word posters, word clusters, word sorts, word chains, and semantic feature analysis.

Terms

Old English
Middle English
Modern English
etymology
extrapolation
root word
affix
prefix
suffix
synonym
antonym
homonym
homophone
homograph
homographic homophone
multiple meanings
idiom
borrowed words
compounding
coining
clipping
trademark
acronym
Sniglet
word wall
word sort
word chain
semantic feature analysis
context clues

C H A P T E R 9

Reading and Writing Stories

Developing Students' Concept of Story
Elements of Story Structure
Teaching Students About Stories

Reading Stories
Aesthetic Reading
In Literature Focus Units
In Reading Workshop
In Theme Cycles
Assessing Students' Interpretation of Stories

Writing Stories
In Literature Focus Units
In Theme Cycles
In Writing Workshop
Assessing the Stories Students Write

Terms

concept of story

genre

elements of story structure

plot

beginning-middle-end

conflict

plot profile

characters

backdrop setting

integral setting

point of view

first person viewpoint

omniscient viewpoint

limited omniscient viewpoint

objective viewpoint

explicit theme

implicit theme

aesthetic reading

interpretation

intertextuality

text sets

literary opposites

storyboards

story boxes

open-mind portraits

story maps

story quilts

Key Concepts

1. Students' acquire a concept of story by reading and writing stories and learning about the elements of story structure.

2. Stories have unique structural elements that distinguish them from other forms of writing: plot, characters, setting, point of view, and theme.

3. Teachers present minilessons about the elements of story structure, and students apply what they learn as they read and write stories.

4. Students read stories aesthetically, and their concept of story informs and supports their reading.

5. The goal of aesthetic reading is interpretation, the negotiation of meaning between the reader and the text.

6. Students use strategies such as imaging, anticipating, empathizing, retelling, and connecting to personal experiences and literature as they create interpretations.

7. Students read stories as part of literature focus units, reading workshop, and theme cycles.

8. Storyboards, story boxes, open-mind portraits, story maps, and story quilts are five ways to explore stories.

9. Students use intertextuality as they incorporate ideas from the stories they have read into the stories they write.

10. Students write stories as part of literature focus units, writing workshop, and theme cycles.

Reading and Writing Information

Developing Students' Knowledge About Informational Books

Types of Informational Books

Expository Text Structures

Teaching Students About Expository
Text Structures

Assessing Students' Use of Expository
Text Structures

Reports

Young Children's Reports

Collaborative Reports

Individual Reports

Teaching Students to Write Research Reports

Assessing Students' Research Reports

Letters

Friendly Letters

Business Letters

Simulated Letters

Teaching Students to Write Letters

Assessing Students' Letters

Life-Stories

Autobiographies

Biographies

Teaching Students to Write Life-Stories

Assessing Students' Life-Stories

Terms

informational books
expository text structures
cue words
graphic organizers
description
sequence
comparison
cause and effect
problem and solution
"All About . . ." books
collaborative reports
individual reports
friendly letters
courtesy letters
business letters
simulated letters
autobiographies
"All About Me" books
biographies
contemporary biographies
historical biographies

Key Concepts

1. Students read informational books to learn information and write informational books to share information with others.

2. Students may use either efferent or aesthetic reading when reading informational books, depending on their purpose for reading.

3. Informational writing is organized using expository text structures: description, sequence, comparison, cause and effect, and problem and solution.

4. Students use their knowledge of expository text structures when reading informational books and writing about information.

5. Elementary students write both class collaboration and individual reports.

6. Students can organize reports in a variety of formats, including ABC books and question-and-answer books.

7. The friendly and business letters that students write should be mailed to authentic audiences.

8. Students write simulated letters in connection with literature focus units and social studies and science theme cycles.

9. Students write autobiographies about events in their own lives and biographies about both historical and contemporary personalities.

10. Students use the writing process to write reports, letters, autobiographies, and biographies.

Reading and Writing Poetry

Reading Poems

Types of Poems Children Read

Children's Favorite Poems

Teaching Students to Read Poems

Assessing Students' Experiences With Poems

Playing With Words

Laughing With Language

Creating Word Pictures

Experimenting With Rhyme

Other Poetic Devices

Writing Poems

Formula Poems

Free-Form Poems

Syllable- and Word-Count Poems

Rhymed Verse Forms

Model Poems

Teaching Students to Write Poems

Assessing Poems That Students Write

Terms

hink-pinks
simile
metaphor
alliteration
onomatopoeia
repetition
narrative poems
haiku
free verse
limericks
concrete poems
choral reading
"I wish . . ." poems
color poems
five-senses poems
"If I were . . ." poems
"I used to/But now . . ." poems
". . . is" poems
preposition poems
found poems
tanka poems
cinquain poems
diamante poems
clerihew poems
apology poems
invitation poems
prayers from the ark
"If I were in charge of the world" poems
acrostic poems

Key Concepts

1. Word play activities with riddles, comparisons, rhyme, and other poetic devices provide the background of experiences students need for reading and writing poetry.

2. Three types of poetry books published for children are picture book versions of single poems, specialized collections of poems, and comprehensive anthologies of poems.

3. Elementary students have definite opinions about the types of poems they like best.

4. The focus in teaching students to read and respond to poems is enjoyment.

5. Tempo, rhythm, pitch, and juncture are four elements to consider when reading poetry aloud.

6. Choral reading is an effective way for students to read poetry.

7. Students read poems during reading workshop and in connection with literature focus units and theme cycles.

8. Students can write poems successfully using poetic formulas in which they begin each line with particular words, count syllables, or create word pictures.

9. Because rhyme is a sticking point for many students, they should be encouraged to experiment with other poetic devices in their writing.

10. Students write poetry during writing workshop and as part of literature focus units and theme cycles.

C H A P T E R 1 2

Language Tools: Spelling, Handwriting, and Grammar

Spelling

Children's Spelling Development
Invented Spelling
Older Students' Spelling Development
Analyzing Children's Spelling Development

Teaching Spelling in the Elementary Grades
Components of Spelling Instruction
Weekly Spelling Tests
Adapting to Meet the Needs of Every Student
Assessing Students' Progress in Spelling

Handwriting

Handwriting Forms
Manuscript Handwriting
Cursive Handwriting
D'Nealian Handwriting

Children's Handwriting Development
Handwriting Before First Grade
Handwriting in the Primary Grades
Transition to Cursive Handwriting
Handwriting in the Middle and Upper Grades
Left-Handed Writers

Teaching Handwriting in the Elementary Grades
The Teaching Strategy
Adapting to Meet the Needs of Every Student
Elements of Legibility
Diagnosing and Correcting Handwriting Problems

Grammar

Types of Grammar
Traditional Grammar
Structural Grammar
Transformational Grammar

Teaching Grammar to Elementary Students
Grammar Minilessons
Learning Grammar Through Writing
Adapting to Meet the Needs of Every Student
Assessing Students' Knowledge About Grammar

Terms

alphabetic principle
phonemes
graphemes
invented spelling
sound-it-out strategy
think-it-out strategy
spelling options
spelling conscience
writing versus handwriting
legibility
fluency
manuscript handwriting
cursive handwriting
D'Nealian handwriting
private versus public handwriting
handedness
grammar
usage
dialect
traditional grammar
parts of speech
types of sentences
structural grammar
types of sentences
transformational grammar
surface and deep levels
sentence combining

Key Concepts

1. Spelling, handwriting, and grammar are tools for communicating through language.

2. Students move from using scribbles and single letters to represent words through a series of stages that lead to conventional spelling.

3. The five stages of invented spelling are precommunicative, semiphonetic, phonetic, transitional, and conventional.

4. Spelling instruction includes opportunities to read and write and minilessons about spelling procedures, concepts, and strategies and skills.

5. Weekly spelling tests, when they are used, should be individualized so that students learn to spell the words they need for writing.

6. The goal of handwriting instruction is to help students develop legible and fluent handwriting forms.

7. Handwriting instruction must be linked with writing at all grade levels, even in kindergarten.

8. The six elements of handwriting are letter formation, size and proportion, spacing, slant, alignment, and line quality.

9. The purpose of grammar instruction is to make students' intuitive knowledge about the English language more explicit.

10. One way to teach students about grammar and usage is through the editing stage of the writing process.

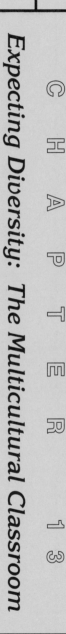

C H A P T E R 1 3

Expecting Diversity: The Multicultural Classroom

Linguistically and Culturally Diverse Students

Impact of Culture on Learning Language Arts

Bilingual Students and Students Who Speak English as a Second Language

Nonstandard English Speakers

Teaching Linguistically and Culturally Diverse Students

Multicultural Education

Components of Multicultural Classrooms

Culturally Conscious Literature

Teaching About Cultural Diversity

Terms

cultural diversity

linguistic diversity

English as a second language (ESL) students

limited English proficient (LEP) students

bilingual students

cultural pluralism

code-switching

dialect

standard English (SE)

nonstandard English (NSE)

comprehensible input

multicultural classroom

multicultural literature

culturally conscious literature

selective tradition

contributions approach

additive approach

transformation approach

social action approach

Key Concepts

1. Culturally diverse children have a broad range of language and literacy experiences, even if they are not the same as those of mainstream children.

2. Cultural and linguistic diversity is not a problem for teachers to overcome; instead, it is an opportunity to enhance the learning of all students.

3. Culture affects the way students think and the way they use language.

4. Learning a second language is a constructive process just like learning a native language.

5. Many students speak nonstandard English dialects, and teachers must respect students' own language as they extend students' awareness of standard English.

6. Three instructional programs that are used with students who are learning English are submersion, immersion, and bilingual programs.

7. The single most important strategy for teaching culturally diverse students is to provide comprehensible input.

8. In multicultural classrooms, students' languages and cultures are respected and fostered.

9. Multicultural literature is an important vehicle for fostering cultural awareness and appreciation.

10. Teachers should choose culturally conscious literature for literature focus units and theme cycles.

C H A P T E R   1 4

Extending Language Arts Across the Curriculum

Learning Through Language

Learning Science Through Language

Learning Social Studies Through Language

Learning Literature Through Language

Learning Other Content Areas Through Language

Theme Cycles

Planning Theme Cycles

Primary-Grade Theme Cycles

Middle-Grade Theme Cycles

Upper-Grade Theme Cycles

Instructional Activities

Assessing Students' Learning

Terms

theme cycle

KWL chart

text set

learning tool

across the curriculum

learning language

learning through language

learning about language

math concept books

projects

literature focus unit

genre unit

author unit

whole group activities

small group activities

individual activities

checklists

Key Concepts

1. Theme cycles are a way of developing curriculum in which students use language to learn about social studies, science, math, and other content areas.

2. When students use language in meaningful ways in theme cycles, they learn information better and refine their language competencies.

3. Students use all four language arts—listening, talking, reading, and writing—as they learn during theme cycles.

4. Many books about math concepts are available for children, and these books provide a bridge between mathematics and written language.

5. As teachers plan theme cycles, they consider resources such as trade books, textbooks, and audiovisual materials, and applications such as vocabulary activities, informal and process writing activities, and projects.

6. Students create projects to extend their learning in theme cycles.

7. Teachers often begin a theme by making a KWL chart to find out what students already know and what they want to learn about a topic.

8. Theme cycles can be used at all grade levels.

9. Teachers plan whole group, small group, and individual activities for theme cycles.

10. Teachers use checklists to assess students' learning during theme cycles.